Intelligent Analysis of Multimedia Information

Siddhartha Bhattacharyya
RCC Institute of Information Technology, India

Hrishikesh Bhaumik
RCC Institute of Information Technology, India

Sourav De
The University of Burdwan, India

Goran Klepac
*University College for Applied Computer Engineering Algebra, Croatia &
Raiffeisenbank Austria, Croatia*

A volume in the Advances in Multimedia and
Interactive Technologies (AMIT) Book Series

Published in the United States of America by
Information Science Reference (an imprint of IGI Global)
701 E. Chocolate Avenue
Hershey PA, USA 17033
Tel: 717-533-8845
Fax: 717-533-8661
E-mail: cust@igi-global.com
Web site: http://www.igi-global.com

Library of Congress Cataloging-in-Publication Data

Names: Bhattacharyya, Siddhartha, 1975- editor. | Bhaumik, Hrishikesh, 1974-
  editor. | De, Sourav, 1979- editor. | Klepac, Goran, 1972- editor.
Title: Intelligent analysis of multimedia information / Siddhartha
  Bhattacharyya, Hrishikesh Bhaumik, Sourav De, and Goran Klepac, editors.
Description: Hershey, PA : Information Science Reference, [2017] | Includes
  bibliographical references and index.
Identifiers: LCCN 2016012756| ISBN 9781522504986 (hardcover) | ISBN
  9781522504993 (ebook)
Subjects: LCSH: Multimedia systems--Databases. | Image analysis. |
  Content-based image retrieval. | Image processing--Digital techniques. |
  Intelligent agents (Computer software).
Classification: LCC QA76.575 .I247 2017 | DDC 006.7--dc23 LC record available at https://lccn.loc.gov/2016012756

This book is published in the IGI Global book series Advances in Multimedia and Interactive Technologies (AMIT) (ISSN: 2327-929X; eISSN: 2327-9303)

British Cataloguing in Publication Data
A Cataloguing in Publication record for this book is available from the British Library.

For electronic access to this publication, please contact: eresources@igi-global.com.

Advances in Multimedia and Interactive Technologies (AMIT) Book Series

Joel J.P.C. Rodrigues
Instituto de Telecomunicações, University of Beira Interior, Portugal

ISSN: 2327-929X
EISSN: 2327-9303

MISSION

Traditional forms of media communications are continuously being challenged. The emergence of user-friendly web-based applications such as social media and Web 2.0 has expanded into everyday society, providing an interactive structure to media content such as images, audio, video, and text.

The **Advances in Multimedia and Interactive Technologies (AMIT) Book Series** investigates the relationship between multimedia technology and the usability of web applications. This series aims to highlight evolving research on interactive communication systems, tools, applications, and techniques to provide researchers, practitioners, and students of information technology, communication science, media studies, and many more with a comprehensive examination of these multimedia technology trends.

COVERAGE

- Digital Communications
- Gaming Media
- Digital Watermarking
- Multimedia Streaming
- Digital Games
- Multimedia technology
- Digital Images
- Mobile Learning
- Social Networking
- Internet Technologies

IGI Global is currently accepting manuscripts for publication within this series. To submit a proposal for a volume in this series, please contact our Acquisition Editors at Acquisitions@igi-global.com or visit: http://www.igi-global.com/publish/.

Titles in this Series

For a list of additional titles in this series, please visit: www.igi-global.com

Digital Tools for Computer Music Production and Distribution
Dionysios Politis (Aristotle University of Thessaloniki, Greece) Miltiadis Tsalighopoulos (Aristotle University of Thessaloniki, Greece) and Ioannis Iglezakis (Aristotle University of Thessaloniki, Greece)
Information Science Reference • copyright 2016 • 291pp • H/C (ISBN: 9781522502647) • US $180.00 (our price)

Contemporary Research on Intertextuality in Video Games
Christophe Duret (Université de Sherbrooke, Canada) and Christian-Marie Pons (Université de Sherbrooke, Canada)
Information Science Reference • copyright 2016 • 363pp • H/C (ISBN: 9781522504771) • US $185.00 (our price)

Trends in Music Information Seeking, Behavior, and Retrieval for Creativity
Petros Kostagiolas (Ionian University, Greece) Konstantina Martzoukou (Robert Gordon University, UK) and Charilaos Lavranos (Ionian University, Greece)
Information Science Reference • copyright 2016 • 388pp • H/C (ISBN: 9781522502708) • US $195.00 (our price)

Emerging Perspectives on the Mobile Content Evolution
Juan Miguel Aguado (University of Murcia, Spain) Claudio Feijóo (Technical University of Madrid, Spain & Tongji University, China) and Inmaculada J. Martínez (University of Murcia, Spain)
Information Science Reference • copyright 2016 • 438pp • H/C (ISBN: 9781466688384) • US $210.00 (our price)

Emerging Research on Networked Multimedia Communication Systems
Dimitris Kanellopoulos (University of Patras, Greece)
Information Science Reference • copyright 2016 • 448pp • H/C (ISBN: 9781466688506) • US $200.00 (our price)

Emerging Research and Trends in Gamification
Harsha Gangadharbatla (University of Colorado Boulder, USA) and Donna Z. Davis (University of Oregon, USA)
Information Science Reference • copyright 2016 • 455pp • H/C (ISBN: 9781466686519) • US $215.00 (our price)

Experimental Multimedia Systems for Interactivity and Strategic Innovation
Ioannis Deliyannis (Ionian University, Greece) Petros Kostagiolas (Ionian University, Greece) and Christina Banou (Ionian University, Greece)
Information Science Reference • copyright 2016 • 378pp • H/C (ISBN: 9781466686595) • US $195.00 (our price)

Design Strategies and Innovations in Multimedia Presentations
Shalin Hai-Jew (Kansas State University, USA)
Information Science Reference • copyright 2015 • 589pp • H/C (ISBN: 9781466686960) • US $225.00 (our price)

www.igi-global.com

701 E. Chocolate Ave., Hershey, PA 17033
Order online at www.igi-global.com or call 717-533-8845 x100
To place a standing order for titles released in this series, contact: cust@igi-global.com
Mon-Fri 8:00 am - 5:00 pm (est) or fax 24 hours a day 717-533-8661

Prof. (Dr.) Siddhartha Bhattacharyya would like to dedicate this book to:
My parents Late Ajit Kumar Bhattacharyya and Late Hashi Bhattacharyya, my beloved wife
Rashni and my revered teacher Prof. Bholananda Bhowmik
Mr. Hrishikesh Bhaumik would like to dedicate this book to:
My late father Major Ranjit Kumar Bhaumik and my mother Mrs. Anjali Bhaumik
Dr. Sourav De would like to dedicate this book to:
My father Mr. Satya Narayan De, my mother Mrs. Tapasi De, my wife Mrs. Debolina Ghosh, my
son Mr. Aishik De and my sister Mrs. Soumi De
Dr. Goran Klepac would like to dedicate this book to:
My beloved wife Antonija and children: Laura, Viktor, Oliver and Gabrijel

Editorial Advisory Board

Table of Contents

Detailed Table of Contents

Chapter 1
Foundations of Multimedia Information Processing 1
    Anindita Das Bhattacharjee, Swami Vivekananda Institute of Science and Technology, India

It is easy to understand image and video stream by a human being but a computer can't understand them at all. For that reason there are several methods to make the computer to understand about the media it is being talked about. The following writing discusses about how to analyze a video or an image by using several methods like scene analysis, and shot boundary detection and analysis, frame analysis, hypermedia representation, segmentation of media. All of these are the representation of the whole media that have been fed as input and these representation outputs are used by computer by computer vision algorithm to process a video or image and give the expected results. The main focus of this writing is discussing how to use the above mentioned methods in any of the media video or image and extract the information required to represent the whole media under process.

Chapter 2
Theoretical Concepts and Technical Aspects on Image Segmentation................................. 32
    Anju Pankaj, Mahatma Gandhi University, India
    Sonal Ayyappan, SCMS School of Engineering and Technology, India

Image segmentation is the process of partitioning a digital image into multiple segments (super pixels). Segmentation is typically used to locate objects and boundaries in images. The result of segmentation is a set of segments that collectively cover the entire image, or a set of contours extracted from the image. Each of the pixels in a region is similar with respect to some characteristic or computed property. Adjacent regions are significantly different with respect to the same characteristics. A predicate for measuring the evidence for a boundary between two regions using a graph-based representation of the image is defined. An important characteristic of the method is its ability to preserve detail in low-variability image regions and ignoring detail in high variability regions. This chapter discuss basic aspects of segmentation and an application and presents a detailed assessment on different methods in image segmentation and discusses a case study on it.

Chapter 3

Accessibility problem is relevant for audiovisual information, where enormous data has to be explored and processed. Most of the solutions for this specific type of problems point towards a regular need of extracting applicable information features for a given content domain. And feature extraction process deals with two complicated tasks first deciding and then extracting. There are certain properties expected from good features-Repeatability, Distinctiveness, Locality, Quantity, Accuracy, Efficiency, and Invariance. Different feature extraction techniques are described. The chapter concentrates of taking a survey on the topic of Feature extraction and Image formation. Here both image and video are considered to have their feature extracted. In machine learning, pattern recognition and in image processing has significant contribution. The feature extraction is one of the common mechanisms involved in these two techniques. Extracting feature initiates from an initial data set of measured data and constructs derived informative values which are non redundant in nature.

Chapter 4

Particle Swarm Optimization (PSO) is a well-known swarm optimization technique. PSO is very efficient to optimize the image segmentation problem. PSO algorithm have some drawbacks as the possible solutions may follow the global best solution at one stage. As a result, the probable solutions may bound within that locally optimized solutions. The proposed chapter tries to get over the drawback of the PSO algorithm and proposes a Modified Particle Swarm Optimization (MfPSO) algorithm to segment the multilevel images. The proposed method is compared with the original PSO algorithm and the renowned k-means algorithm. Comparison of the above mentioned existing methods with the proposed method are applied on three real life multilevel gray scale images. For this purpose, three standard objective functions are applied to evaluate the quality of the segmented images. The comparison shows that the proposed MfPSO algorithm is done better than the PSO algorithm and the k-means algorithm to segment the real life multilevel gray scale images.

Chapter 5

This chapter will focus on the concept of Content-based image retrieval. Searching of an image or video database based on text based description is a manual labor intensive process. Descriptions of the file are usually typed manually for each image by human operators because the automatic generation of keywords for the images is difficult without incorporation of visual information and feature extraction. This method is impractical in today's multimedia information era. "Content-based" means that the search will analyze the actual contents of the image rather than the metadata such as keywords, tags, and descriptions associated with the image. The term "content" in this context might refer to colors, shapes, textures, or any other information that can be derived from the image itself. Several important sections are highlighted in this chapter, like architectures, query techniques, multidimensional indexing, video retrieval and different application sections of CBIR.

Chapter 6

Swanirbhar Majumder, North Eastern Regional Institute of Science and Technology, India
Smita Majumder, Tripura University, India

Since 1960's digital image processing has been a popular field of research and applications. Among the various applications like physics, security, photonics, biomedical, astronomy, remote sensing, ecological, environmental, etc.; biomedical is one of the many important areas people are focusing on. So for the intelligent analysis of multimedia information like biomedical image has is the thrust area of this chapter. This chapter therefore would aid both biomedical engineers and non-technical people using the tools to get an overview. This chapter mainly concentrates on bio-medical imaging. The medical testing abbreviations and terms like X-ray, MRI, SPECT, PET, Ultrasonography, CFI, optical and IR Imaging SEM, TEM, etc. are discussed here. They mainly concentrate on images of internal structure of living organisms which are not accessible by standard imaging techniques. Moreover, this helps non-technically oriented people to get an overview of the bio-medical aspects.

Chapter 7

Petre Anghelescu, University of Pitesti, Romania

In this paper are presented solutions to develop algorithms for digital image processing focusing particularly on edge detection. Edge detection is one of the most important phases used in computer vision and image processing applications and also in human image understanding. In this chapter, implementation of classical edge detection algorithms it is presented and also implementation of algorithms based on the theory of Cellular Automata (CA). This work is totally related to the idea of understanding the impact of the inherently local information processing of CA on their ability to perform a managed computation at the global level. If a suitable encoding of a digital image is used, in some cases, it is possible to achieve better results in comparison with the solutions obtained by means of conventional approaches. The software application which is able to process images in order to detect edges using both conventional algorithms and CA based ones is written in C# programming language and experimental results are presented for images with different sizes and backgrounds.

Chapter 8

Kalyan Mahata, Government College of Engineering and Leather Technology, India
Subhasish Das, Jadavpur University, India
Rajib Das, Jadavpur University, India
Anasua Sarkar, Jadavpur University, India

Image segmentation among overlapping land cover areas in satellite images is a very crucial task. Detection of belongingness is the important problem for classifying mixed pixels. This paper proposes an approach for pixel classification using a hybrid approach of Fuzzy C-Means and Cellular automata methods. This new unsupervised method is able to detect clusters using 2-Dimensional Cellular Automata model based on fuzzy segmentations. This approach detects the overlapping regions in remote sensing images by uncertainties using fuzzy set membership values. As a discrete, dynamical system, cellular automaton explores uniformly interconnected cells with states. In the second phase of our method, we utilize a 2-dimensional cellular automata to prioritize allocations of mixed pixels among overlapping land cover areas. We experiment our method on Indian Ajoy river watershed area. The clustered regions are compared with well-known FCM and K-Means methods and also with the ground truth knowledge. The results show the superiority of our new method.

Chapter 9

Fuzzy classification techniques are used for image classification for quite a long time back by allowing pixels to have membership in more than one class. However, handling information at the pixel level is time consuming and there is a high chance of biased assessment of images if class labels are assigned by a single human observer. Even considering multiple observers' opinions don't able to reflect an individual's perception in assessing quality of images, if it is crisp. In this chapter, the fuzzy relational classifier (FRC) is used to assess quality of images distorted by information loss or noise, unlike the earlier methods where images are preprocessed to remove the noise before classification.

Chapter 10

eHealth is a set of systems and services that enable the sharing of medical diagnostic imaging data remotely. The application of eHealth solves the problem of the lack of specialized personnel, unnecessary execution of multiple diagnostic imaging and rapid exchange of information and remote diagnostics. Medical imaging generates large amounts of data. An MRI study can contain up to several Gigabytes (GB). The exchange of such large amounts of data in the local network facilities is a significant problem due to bandwidth sharing which is even more significant in mobile and wireless networks. A possible solution to this problem is data compression with the requirement that there is no loss of data. The goal of this chapter is a conceptual compression prototype that will allow faster and more efficient exchange of medical images in systems with limited bandwidth and communication speeds (cellular networks, wireless networks). To obtain this conceptual compression prototype we will use wavelets.

Chapter 11

During video editing, the shots composing the video are coalesced together by different types of transition effects. These editing effects are classified into abrupt and gradual changes, based on the inherent nature of these transitions. In abrupt transitions, there is an instantaneous change in the visual content of two consecutive frames. Gradual transitions are characterized by a slow and continuous change in the visual contents occurring between two shots. In this chapter, the challenges faced in this field along with an overview of the different approaches are presented. Also, a novel method for detection of dissolve transitions using a two-phased approach is enumerated. The first phase deals with detection of candidate dissolves by identifying parabolic patterns in the mean fuzzy entropy of the frames. In the second phase, an ensemble of four parameters is used to design a filter which eliminates candidates based on thresholds set for each of the four stages of filtration. The experimental results show a marked improvement over other existing methods.

#### Chapter 12

Music listening is one of the most common thing of human behaviors. Normally mobile music is downloaded to mobile phones and played by mobile phones. Today millennial people use mobile music in about all the age groups. Music recommendation system enhances personalized music classifications that create a profile with the service and build up a music library based on the choice preferences using mobile cloud services. Music recommendation through cloud is therefore an emerging field, and this can be done using various parameters like song genre similarity, human behavior, human mood, song rhythmic patterns, seasons etc. In this article an intelligent music recommender system that identifies the raga name of one particular song music and then mapping with the raga time database and classify the songs according to their playing time and create time slot based personalized music libraries.

Over the past decade, research in the field of Content-Based Video Retrieval Systems (CBVRS) has attracted much attention as it encompasses processing of all the other media types i.e. text, image and audio. Video summarization is one of the most important applications as it potentially enables efficient and faster browsing of large video collections. A concise version of the video is often required due to constraints in viewing time, storage, communication bandwidth as well as power. Thus, the task of video summarization is to effectively extract the most important portions of the video, without sacrificing the semantic information in it. The results of video summarization can be used in many CBVRS applications like semantic indexing, video surveillance copied video detection etc. However, the quality of the summarization task depends on two basic aspects: content coverage and redundancy removal. These two aspects are both important and contradictory to each other. This chapter aims to provide an insight into the state-of-the-art approaches used for this booming field of research.

Biometric system is used by many institution, organization and industry for automatic recognition of person. One of the main reason for popularity of used for biometric system is that the ability of the system to identify between an authorized person and unauthorized person. There are many challenges associated with the biometric system such as designing of human recognition algorithm, compression of biometric templates, privacy and security of biometric templates in biometric systems. This chapter gives an application of Compressive Sensing (CS) theory for solutions of the above mentioned challenges in biometric systems. Recent research and trends in a biometric system indicated that many challenging of biometric system problems are being solved using Compressive Sensing (CS) theory and sparse representation algorithms. This chapter gives an overview of sparsity property of various image transforms and application of compressive sensing and sparse representation with regards to biometric image compression, biometric image recognition and biometric image protection.

#### Chapter 15

This chapter will introduce methodology how to use analytical potential of multimedia contents like YouTube, Bing Videos or Vimeo for discovering behavioral consumer characteristics. Chapter will also show how to consolidate unstructured text data sources from blogs and Twitter with revealed knowledge from multimedia contents for better understanding consumer habits and needs. For this purposes Social Network Analysis will be used as well as text mining techniques on different internet data sources. Presented methodology has practical value where information about customer behavior, preferences and changes in preferences during different time periods is valuable information for campaign planning, campaign management and new product development. Presented methodology also captures different techniques for data crawling from different internet resources, as well as analytical consolidation of revealed results which aim is better understanding of client behavior.

#### Chapter 16

Nowadays, Multimedia contents such as images, videos, e-books and texts are easy to available for download through internet in worldwide. Duplication of multimedia contents is to create using different software. This type of operation some time created problem of copyright and ownership authentication. Digital watermarking techniques are one of the solutions for providing protection to multimedia contents. This chapter gives various watermarking techniques in transform domain and sparse domain for protection of multimedia contents. This chapter has demonstrated various watermarking techniques such as Discrete

Cosine Transform (DCT), Discrete Wavelet Transform (DWT), Singular Value Decomposition (SVD), Fast Discrete Curvelet Transform (FDCT), and CS theory based technique. All watermarking techniques can be applicable to every type of multimedia contents such as grayscale images or videos and color image or videos.

Preface

Multimedia refers to the representation of information in varied forms. Two broad categories of multimedia information are prevalent. These are (1) discrete media and (2) continuous media. Information becomes multimedia information if and only if it contains at least a continuous media. The most common and enormous continuous media type is the video. A lot of time-complex computing facility is required for processing video contents given its variety and enormity of underlying data.

Video content classification is an important task in the computer vision community as far as intelligent analysis of video content is concerned. Typical applications include video content mining, video indexing (for media industry), video surveillance and defense applications to name a few. A score of literatures exists in this regard providing a detailed comparative study of the different techniques in vogue. Video content classification primarily entails the detection of the cuts in the video sequences through classical as well as non-classical techniques. The non-classical techniques resort to computational intelligence perspectives in ascertaining the video shot boundaries by using the inherent information distribution of the video content. Hence, larger video frames/sequences obviously require a lot of computational overhead in the shot detection task. Since, video data are essentially continuous in nature, dynamic estimation of the data distribution is a prerequisite in the commonly used shot boundary detection and video analysis techniques.

This edited volume aims to open up a new realm of research in media industry helping practitioners to securely and faithfully process their multimedia data as is evident from the table of contents. Almost no book is existent in the market as of now in this related field. Moreover, the use of intelligent techniques for processing of multimedia data would give rise to robust and time efficient systems especially when multimedia data are very bulky in nature. Add to it, the book would also serve as a treatise for effective transmission of multimedia data across reliable networks.

This edited volume is intended to bridge the gap in the media-researchers' community by introducing newer avenues in the form of recent trends in research areas in continuous media processing and manipulation. In fact, the objectives of the proposed publication are many fold. These may be summarized according to their priorities.

1. Till date, the existing techniques for video segmentation are able to detect with high accuracy the hard cuts present in a video. This book seeks avenues for advancements in these techniques to be applied to live streaming videos for on-the-fly video segmentation.
2. The problem of setting an automatic threshold for video segmentation has to be addressed. The threshold is to be set dynamically without any a priori knowledge about the type, content or length

of the video. Newer research trends would surely target this untouched area and thereby open a new era of video summarization of real time events, such as producing highlights of sports videos.

3. Detection of representative frames (key-frames) which denote the semantic content of the shots in a video which are used for video indexing is also a challenging proposition. Redundancy reduction is an important step as it removes uninformative or redundant video frames/segments and retains the most informative parts which are concatenated to form a video summary. This book strives to seek newer research initiatives in this direction.

The intended readers of this book are the relevant research community and the media practitioners. To be precise, the book is aimed to establish the missing link between the research standing in the relevant field and that is upcoming. Infusing intelligent paradigms for multimedia information processing would surely and certainly help the readers grasp the essence and utility of the different intelligent techniques in vogue for faithful understanding of multimedia information.

This book would come to the benefits of several categories of students and researchers. At the students' level, this book can serve as a treatise/reference book for the special papers at the masters level aimed at inspiring possibly future researchers. Newly inducted PhD aspirants would also find the contents of this book useful as far as their compulsory coursework is concerned.

At the researchers' level, those interested in interdisciplinary research would also benefit from the book. The enriched interdisciplinary contents of the book would always be a subject of interest to the faculties, existing research communities and new research aspirants from diverse disciplines of the concerned departments of premier institutes across the globe. This is expected to bring different research backgrounds (due to its cross platform characteristics) close to one another to form effective research groups all over the world.

The edited volume comprises 16 well versed and self-contained chapters from diverse research domains ranging from fundamentals of multimedia to image, audio and video processing to data compression.

Chapter 1 discusses about how to analyze a video or an image by using several methods like scene analysis, and shot boundary detection and analysis, frame analysis, hypermedia representation, segmentation of media. The main focus of the chapter is to discuss as to how to use the above mentioned methods in any of the media video or image and extract the information required to represent the whole media under process.

Chapter 2 discusses the basic aspects of image segmentation and an application and presents a detailed assessment on the different methods in image segmentation and discusses a case study on it.

Feature extraction in a multimedia environment deals with two complicated tasks first deciding and then extracting. There are certain properties expected from good features viz., Repeatability, Distinctiveness, Locality, Quantity, Accuracy, Efficiency, and Invariance. Chapter 3 describes the different feature extraction techniques. It also concentrates on taking a survey on the topic of Feature extraction and Image formation.

Particle Swarm Optimization (PSO) is a well-known swarm optimization technique. It is very efficient to optimize the image segmentation problem. PSO algorithm has some drawbacks as the possible solutions may follow the global best solution at one stage. As a result, the probable solutions may be bound within locally optimized solutions. Chapter 4 tries to get over the drawback of the PSO algorithm and proposes a Modified Particle Swarm Optimization (MfPSO) algorithm to segment the multilevel images. The proposed method is compared with the original PSO algorithm and the renowned k-means algorithm. Comparison of the above mentioned existing methods with the proposed method are applied on three real life multilevel gray scale images and the results are demonstrated.

Chapter 5 focuses on the concept of Content based image retrieval. Searching of an image or video database based on text based description is a manual labor intensive process. Descriptions of the file are usually typed manually for each image by human operators because the automatic generation of keywords for the images is difficult without incorporation of visual information and feature extraction. This method is impractical in today's multimedia information era. "Content-based" means that the search will analyze the actual contents of the image rather than the metadata such as keywords, tags, and descriptions associated with the image. The term 'content' in this context might refer to colors, shapes, textures, or any other information that can be derived from the image itself. Several important sections are highlighted in this chapter, like architectures, query techniques, multidimensional indexing, video retrieval and different application sections of CBIR.

Among the various applications like physics, security, photonics, biomedical, astronomy, remote sensing, ecological, environmental, etc.; biomedical is one of the many important areas researchers are focusing on. So for the intelligent analysis of multimedia information like biomedical image, Chapter 6 covers this thrust area. This chapter therefore aids both biomedical engineers and non-technical people to get an overview of the basics of biomedical image processing and analysis.

In Chapter 7 different solutions are presented to develop algorithms for digital image processing focusing particularly on edge detection, which is one of the most important phases used in computer vision and image processing applications and also in human image understanding. In this chapter, implementation of classical edge detection algorithms is presented and also implementation of algorithms based on the theory of Cellular Automata (CA) is demonstrated.

Image segmentation among overlapping land cover areas in satellite images is a very crucial task. Detection of belongingness is the important problem for classifying mixed pixels. Chapter 8 proposes an approach for pixel classification using a hybrid approach of Fuzzy C-Means and Cellular automata methods. This new unsupervised method is able to detect clusters using 2-Dimensional Cellular Automata model based on fuzzy segmentations. This approach detects the overlapping regions in remote sensing images by uncertainties using fuzzy set membership values.

Fuzzy classification techniques are used for image classification for quite a long time back by allowing pixels to have membership in more than one class. However, handling information at the pixel level is time consuming and there is a high chance of biased assessment of images if class labels are assigned by a single human observer. An individual's perception in assessing quality of images is not reflected even if multiple observers' opinions are considered. In Chapter 9, the Fuzzy Relational Classifier (FRC) is used to assess quality of images distorted by information loss or noise, unlike the existing methods where images are preprocessed to remove the noise before classification.

eHealth is a set of systems and services that enable the sharing of medical diagnostic imaging data remotely. The application of eHealth solves the problem of the lack of specialized personnel, unnecessary execution of multiple diagnostic imaging and rapid exchange of information and remote diagnostics. Medical imaging generates large amounts of data. An MRI study can contain up to several Gigabytes (GB). The exchange of such large amounts of data in the local network facilities is a significant problem due to bandwidth sharing which is even more significant in mobile and wireless networks. A possible solution to this problem is data compression with the requirement that there is no loss of data. The goal of Chapter 10 is a conceptual compression prototype that will allow faster and more efficient exchange of medical images in systems with limited bandwidth and communication speeds (cellular networks, wireless networks). To obtain this conceptual compression prototype we will use wavelets.

During video editing, the shots composing the video are coalesced together by different types of transition effects. These transition effects are classified abrupt and gradual transitions based on the inherent nature of these transitions. In abrupt transitions, there is an instantaneous change in the visual content of two consecutive frames. Gradual transitions are characterized by a slow and continuous change in the visual contents occurring between two shots. In Chapter 11, the challenges faced in this field along with an overview of the different approaches are presented. Also, a novel method for detection of dissolve transitions using a two-phased approached is enumerated.

Music listening is one of the most common things of human behaviors. Normally mobile music are downloaded to mobile phones and played by mobile phones. Today millennial people use mobile music in about all the age groups. Music recommendation system enhances personalized music classifications that create a profile with the service and build up a music library based on the choice preferences using mobile cloud services. Music recommendation through cloud is therefore an emerging field, and this can be done using various parameters like song genre similarity, human behavior, human mood, song rhythmic patterns, seasons etc. Chapter 12 presents an intelligent music recommender system that identifies the raga name of one particular song music and then mapping with the raga time database and classifies the songs according to their playing time that create time slot based personalized music libraries.

Over the past decade, research in the field of Content-Based Video Retrieval Systems (CBVRS) has attracted much attention as it encompasses processing of all the other media types i.e. text, image and audio. Video summarization is one of the most important applications as it potentially enables efficient and faster browsing of large video collections. A concise version of the video is often required due to constraints in viewing time, storage, communication bandwidth as well as power. Thus, the task of video summarization is to effectively extract the most important portions of the video, without sacrificing the semantic information in it. The results of video summarization can be used in many CBVRS applications like semantic indexing, video surveillance copied video detection etc. However, the quality of the summarization task depends on two basic aspects: content coverage and redundancy removal. These two aspects are both important and contradictory to each other. Chapter 13 aims to provide an insight into the state-of-the-art approaches used for this booming field of research.

Biometric system is used by many institutions, organizations and industries for automatic recognition of person. One of the main reasons for popularity of used for biometric system is that the ability of the system to identify between an authorized person and unauthorized person. There are many challenges associated with the biometric system such as designing of human recognition algorithm, compression of biometric templates, privacy and security of biometric templates in biometric systems. Chapter 14 gives an application of Compressive Sensing (CS) theory for solutions of the above mentioned challenges in biometric systems.

Chapter 15 introduces a methodology on how to use analytical potential of multimedia contents like YouTube, Bing Videos or Vimeo for discovering behavioral consumer characteristics. The chapter also enumerates on to how to consolidate unstructured text data sources from blogs and Twitter with revealed knowledge from multimedia contents for better understanding consumer habits and needs.

Nowadays, multimedia contents such as images, videos, e-books and texts are easily available for download on the internet. Duplication of multimedia contents is done using different software. This type of operation sometimes creates problem of copyright and ownership authentication. Digital watermarking technique is one of the solutions for providing protection to multimedia contents. Chapter 16 gives various watermarking techniques in the transformation and sparse domain for protection of multimedia contents. This chapter demonstrates various watermarking techniques such as Discrete Cosine Transform (DCT), Discrete Wavelet Transform (DWT), Singular Value Decomposition (SVD), Fast Discrete Curvelet Transform (FDCT), and CS theory based technique.

The primary objective of the book is to bring a broad spectrum of multimedia application domains under the purview of intelligent techniques so that it is able to trigger further inspiration among various research communities and contribute in their respective fields of applications. Thereby, these application fields may be oriented towards using intelligence techniques.

Once the purpose stated above, is achieved, a larger number of research communities may be brought under one umbrella to ventilate their ideas in a more structured manner. Thus, the present endeavor may be seen as the beginning of such an effort in bringing various research domains close to one another.

Siddhartha Bhattacharyya
RCC Institute of Information Technology, India

Hrishikesh Bhaumik
RCC Institute of Information Technology, India

Sourav De
The University of Burdwan, India

Goran Klepac
University College for Applied Computer Engineering Algebra, Croatia & Raiffeisenbank Austria, Croatia

Chapter 1
Foundations of Multimedia Information Processing

Anindita Das Bhattacharjee
Swami Vivekananda Institute of Science and Technology, India

ABSTRACT

It is easy to understand image and video stream by a human being but a computer can't understand them at all. For that reason there are several methods to make the computer to understand about the media it is being talked about. The following writing discusses about how to analyze a video or an image by using several methods like scene analysis, and shot boundary detection and analysis, frame analysis, hypermedia representation, segmentation of media. All of these are the representation of the whole media that have been fed as input and these representation outputs are used by computer by computer vision algorithm to process a video or image and give the expected results. The main focus of this writing is discussing how to use the above mentioned methods in any of the media video or image and extract the information required to represent the whole media under process.

BACKGROUND

Implementation of proper interface between user and machine is primary concern of computer engineers and it is the most statistical area where the concept of multimedia arrives. The focus and concern is to represent information and its presentation techniques. And now at present emerged application of multimedia is visible in internet where multimedia concept is integrated with networked computers. And the reason for popularity of multimedia documents is basically its fluent rich representation form.

Multimedia devices are mainly considered as "information content" processing devices. The main aim here is to focus the area in which the researcher may able to know-how audio-visual contents are useful in wide variety of platform. The research in this field may enhance the design skills; also it is a learning process that helps in understanding the effective representation of information across different media system. Concept of "multimedia" is generally made, for any "live" performance. Multimedia devices are generally as a "storeroom" and "experience" of multimedia content. Multimedia devices are

DOI: 10.4018/978-1-5225-0498-6.ch001

represented as "electronic media" and the only difference that is visible form "mixed media" is that the multimedia device includes "audio".

The second major requirement is the area of resource management, environmental monitoring and so on. Basically in recent days there is scarcity of skilled manpower in the field of remote sensing, geographic information systems and many more fields. In this scenario, to train and increase the skilled manpower, multimedia is the only weapon by which classroom training for short intensive courses, distance education through telecast is possible.

In recent days a new trend of multimedia system is introduced where software consists of images, sample data, case studies that can be used for experiment with sample books on image processing are provided as study material, so that reader can experiment with given image to find out the working principle of the algorithm given. Hence, we can say that multimedia systems in our real life are very imperative to extract best technical benefits.

Now a day, multimedia system has extreme benefits in the educational fields. Form the above discussion it is understood that it provides learning opportunities to students and enables students to express themselves as designers, they are skilled in the field where they can use tools for analyzing the world also can interpret the information. Multimedia also helps the researcher to organize their personal knowledge, and also helps in representing the fact about what they know about others. In educational field, multimedia appears as computer-based systems and extensively uses associative linkage to permit the user for information retrieval and navigation. In this chapter, as an author I would like to focus on core techniques, of multimedia systems along with I would like to highlight on progress of image segmentation approaches, image enhancement, restoration, describe the process of modeling and feature extraction, and explain the core implementation details of image processing techniques. Fundamental and advanced concepts which are useful in bio-medical and image processing are also highlighted.

INTRODUCTION

Human beings can understand video and images better than any computer but computer can outperform a human in the means of computation. Say for instance from a live stream of video one specific face should be located and the person whose face is being tracked is also in motion is a crowd. It is almost impossible for a human being to detect that specific face in such a short time where the person is on the move and there are other people surrounding him. The computer if it has the proper algorithm written, can detect the face and track down the person with much higher probability of success than any human being. So the objective is not to make the computer understand a video stream or image better than human but to detect and separate objects better than any human being.

In general, concept of multimedia is defined as arrangement of two or more media such as image, text, video, animation, and sound. In this context the main relevance of multimedia is on the area of website design i.e. if we want to make dynamic and interactive website or else we want o make any traffic building tools and want to make them more attention-grabbing to online clients audio-video component of multimedia is the only option. For this purpose "streaming multimedia" is used in order to attach live-feeds with real time content in the web page. Hence, video is the most important concept in multimedia for recording, processing, and capturing electronic signals, digital media, and moving pictures. Videos, animations are used in general in e-learning courses. Digital video is significant and greater means of real world sound and image communication. Along with video another multimedia component audio is useful in e-learning ad training processes. The concept of audio is "vibration audible by human being". In general, compared to audio and graphical file format digital video occupies large bandwidth. MPEG, AVI are general file format used. AVI is "Audio video interleaved", in this audio and video encoding is mixed and this format is widely used in "multimedia CD". But recently, YouTube, tudou and so on video sites uses Flash Video or FLV format.

In this section of writing it has been discussed how to analyze a media whether is an image or a video stream.

1. IMAGE SCENE

Like we have methods to understand a scene in an image, computer also has methods to visualize a scene. It extracts the contents of the scene and analyzes the contents and makes a guess about the scene. Now there are already several methods to understand a scene namely, Support Vector Machine (SVM), image histogram, hidden Markov model etc. Segmentation of an image into regions also gives better analysis of an image than global image feature. Before following this, it is also important to know how the scene information has appeared, how they are classified. Since the image is segmented into several regions, computer after several training process is able to tell about the whole image after understanding the whole region. In order to train the system, when an image is fed to the system the image gives a wide variety of possible real scenes. Now each image is divided or segmented into regions. After this the main work is started. Each region according to their standard feature, they are extracted by means of procedures such as mean color, color histogram. After feature extraction each region is indexed. That is based on their features which are extracted are marked with index. Now using Fuzzy C-means algorithm clustering (of Bertrand Le Saux, Giuseppe Amato, 2006) of these indexed images is performed. Thus by clustering visually similar images are clustered.

The system is now trained with clustering algorithm, so when a new image is introduced to the system it is described by a presence vector. Presence vector is nothing but features that should be present in a region. Now based on the feature space, that is the clusters measure whether the region type is present in the image or not. That is presence vector which determines the presence of a region type depending on image feature space, displays only those components which directs towards features present in the image with respect to the image feature space. This way it can be concluded whether an image is a country side image containing blue sky and dark ground region spaces. Now, in order to represent an image mnemonic representation is preferred such as- people, countryside etc. For that as we have all the regions of an image analyzed, feature selection method determines which region(s) is best to describe the whole image. Secondly, a classifier such as Kernel classifier is used to make the system learn a decision rule on the basis of the selected region types and name the image. Since each region is associated with a feature, the filtering procedure rearranges the selected features by ranking them according to their predictive power.

Let us assume Y to be a Boolean random variable for the scene to associate with the image. Again, say $F_1, F_2, ..., F_p$ be the Boolean random variables with each region types. Now, as we choose relevant features we look to the entropy measure. Now entropy is an encoding scheme where, entropy is the measure of average number of bits required to encode the value of a random variable. Entropy of class Y is,

$$H(Y) = -\sum_y P(Y=y)\log P(Y=y) \tag{1}$$

Again, conditional entropy finds the number of bits required to describe Y when F_j is already known before. That is:

$$H(Y| F_j) = H(Y, F_j)-H(F_j). \tag{2}$$

So the mutual information shared is $I(Y, F_j) = H(Y)-H(Y|F_j)$ when feature F_j is considered. The feature which give largest $I(Y, F_j)$ is selected ones. Now to categorize a region and thus concluding an image with mnemonics Kerneladarton classification is necessary. Here training data set is denoted as $T=\{(x_1,y_1), …, (x_m,y_m)\}$. Now these xi is the reduced presence vector of only the selected features and yi is a parameter denoting true or false whether the image is an example to learn or not. Now the Kernel K algorithm ai and b are two parameters of decision rule which finds an unknown presence vector x that is presence vector of an unknown image and its region falls in the same cluster as derived while training or not.

$$F(x) = sign(\sum_{i=1}^n Y_i a_i K(xx_i)+b) \tag{3}$$

Above equation is the function of kernel adarton.

2. VIDEO SCENE

Unlike image scenes video scenes are dynamic or it can be stated as changing of images one after another at a very small interval of time to stop and look at the two images. It is comparatively easier to analyze an image scene rather than video scene. Since the elements of the video is always moving, changing direction, nonstop random change lighting effect are taking place, whereas the scene of an image particularly is always the same. Any video analysis process goes through some basic steps that are object recognition which helps in deciding the class of the scene. Along with recognition processing of the object and object segmentation for scene categorization is important. Generally, it is done through estimating the global information. Now the most important activity related to our lives are object identification and linking with prior knowledge through distinction. This provides ability for object recognition and interpretation of the environment around us. Highlighting the perception of content of information extraction technique will be another concern of this chapter, as this concept is very significant for dynamic multimedia data. And content extractions are applicable in text, video data.

According to Yang Yang, Jingen Liu, Mubarak Shah (2011), say multiple pixels of same key motion patterns are grouped together, with this the whole abstraction of the video is obtained. Following this method it becomes easier to detect any abnormality, it is useful to detect anyone from a crowded scene, and it is very much helpful for unsupervised learning and detecting a particular pattern of activity. It is very obvious as, if the pixels are grouped based on their key motion patterns any set of pixels moving in an unusual way will easily be detected. Also the grouped pixels can be used as a training data set to feed a learning model and thus making it taking its own decision to find the exact group to select while treating an unknown set of pixels.

Now it is really very hard job to analyze the whole video and group the pixels as the video length may range up to 90 minutes or 120 minutes or more than these. For this reason the video is divided into very small clips and then the apparent flow of pixel from one frame to another frame is observed. Now there are some flow vectors and they are of very small magnitude, they are noise and they are removed and the flow is strictly arranged and measured in the traditional four vectors- North, East, South, West. Now each clip is divided into small pieces of cuboids. Histograms of four motion directions are then computed for each cuboids. The process goes as minimizing the whole video as much as possible and then performing the computation to its basic core. The local histogram for direction is then computed for each cuboids and then they are recalculated altogether.

It is proposed in using to embed the cuboids in the diffusion maps to perform clusters in order to obtain motion patterns and their estimations in the scene which is being considered. The diffusion map framework takes onto consideration the main points and takes them in lower dimensional space. Now talking about the diffusion mapping firstly the points are organized in a graph distributed with weights and these weights are basically the similarities are a way of representing complex relationship between the feature points. Now as the weight matrix is finally obtained we can interpret pair wise relationship.

Diffusion matching as it forms clusters it follows its own method of clustering. Now as it was previously said that weights are the measure of similarity in features between the points so diffusion mapping sorts out semantically similar points into one cluster. The more diffusion is performed the more the size of the cluster increases and more precise and grouped points of patterns are found.

3. SHOTS

Shots are basically, the image taken by the camera, it is easy to understand if it is said this way, say a video is being recorded and a particular scene is under focus and the scene needs to be changed, now those scenes before it was changed can be called shot altogether. While processing a multimedia detecting of these sots are very important and for that it is important to detect shot boundary that is to separate shots from one from another. Now there are generally two types of change of shots one way where the shot changes abruptly that is at a sudden and the other is where a shot changes gradually including more visual effects. Gradual transformations use more frames to transform from one shot to another. Now there are several classifications of gradual change of these shots- cut transition, fade transition, dissolve transition, wipe transition. Cut transition is almost like abrupt transition where frame F_k belongs to one transition and frame F_{k+1} belongs to immediately other frame when the next shot is detected. This fade transition makes the transition looks gradual, when the shot changes, from the last frame of first shot of consideration it takes multiple monochromatic frames to enter into the next frame of the next shot. Description of dissolve transition sounds familiar but instead of adding multiple monochromatic frames between two frames of two different shots, here as one shot gradually disappears the second shot gradually appears, that is they overlap each other for a few frames. Wipe transition technique includes a set of shots appearing and disappearing at the same time that is one shot enters the scene while the other one leaves.

Now the algorithms to work on a video it needs to extracts features from a range of frames called region of interest. (According to Upesh Patel, Pratik Shah, Pradip Panchal," 2013.)Some particular features are selected to process and conclude to indicate probable shot boundary detection. These features include:

1. **Color:** It is the simplest feature as average grayscale color can be chosen for this region of interest.
2. **Color Histogram:** Robust feature while detecting shot boundaries. This is quite a robust one because it is easy to compute, and it remains insensitive to transitional, camera movement and zoom in zoom out motions.

3. **Image Edge:** Image edge is a good choice to include it in region of information as image edge predicts shot boundaries. The main advantage of image edge feature is that it is invulnerable to illumination changes and camera motions as well as it are related to human understanding of a scene. But the main disadvantage of this feature is computational cost and it is sensitive to noise.

4. **Motion:** It is the most unused but still is considered as a feature of the video. If motion is kept under study a sudden change in a continuous flow of motion may imply a shot transition. But in a single shot itself the motion may be discontinuous which can lead to a false conclusion to have a shot transition.

Along with the above mentioned features there is another feature type called spatial feature domain which is also important while considering shot detection. This feature determines the appropriate size of the region of interest which could be suitable. A small region will reduce shot detection and a large region may mislead to missed transition between similar shots. Some possible spatial feature domain can be as follows:

1. **Single Pixel:** Some algorithms tend to derive features for each pixels. These features can be any of the above mentioned features but this results in large feature set and it becomes sensitive to motion.

2. **Rectangular Block:** Here each frame is divided or segmented into equal sized blocks and a set of features are extracted from each of the blocks. With this method it becomes invulnerable to camera motion and discriminate for shot boundary detection.

3. **Arbitrary Shaped Region:** Here feature extraction can also be performed to an arbitrary shaped region derived by spatial segmentation algorithm. This way as the area has been determined by the algorithm features can be extracted from homogenous region which leads to better detection of temporal discontinuity. The main disadvantage is the computation is costly and instability in region.

4. **Whole Frame:** The algorithm is very robust which can extract features from the whole frame as it can easily deal with motion within a shot but falls into problem if it has to detect two similar shots.

In order to evaluate discontinuity between frames for the selected frames correct similarity measures are necessary to be taken. One similarity measure is defined as

$$D_{Ln}(i,j) = \sqrt[n]{\left(\sum_{k=1}^{K} |F_i(K) - F_j(k)|^n\right)} \tag{4}$$

The above example is of the difference between histogram and this is one way to measure the similarity between the frames.

Again there is another way to measure similarity and it is also with histograms, called chi square (χ^2). The measure is as follows

$$D_{\chi}^{2}(i,j) = \sum_{k=1}^{K} \left((F_i(K) - F_j(k))^2 / F_i(K)\right) \tag{5}$$

Another important approach for shot boundary detection is the temporal window which is performed to perform shot change detection. The temporal window must represent a suitable amount of video activity to perfectly distinguish between to shots whether they are similar or not. The temporal domain window metric includes as:

1. **Two Frames:** The simplest way to detect discontinuity between two frames is to look for the high value of the discontinuity metric between them. But this method is not as strong as it sounds to be but it fails when there is considerable variation in activity in the video. Thus it fails to distinguish between inter shot transformation and changes within a shot. Also there can be brief discontinuity in the video like a flash which is actually not a shot transition but can be falsely indicated as a change in shot that is a gradual transition.

2. **N-Frame Window:** The above problem can be avoided and discontinuity can be detected if features of all the frames are extracted within a suitable temporal window which eventually points towards the discontinuity.

3. **Interval from the Last Shot Change:** This method proposes that to detect a shot change it needs to compute some statistical data from the last shot change to current frame and it is also needed to check whether the next frame is also following the same statistical computation of data. But this method is not very much suitable as there are always some discontinuity, constantly changing behavior within a single shot. For this a shot transition may be declared by this method following the statistical data but where actually there is no shot transition but a single frame itself.

Based on the above discussions two methods are chosen to compute shot detection. One follows a measuring expression of the similarity and dissimilarity between two adjacent frames extracting appropriate features discussed above from the region of interest, and the other follows classifying the frames whether there is a ashot change or whether it has not by computing a robust measure and comparing between the frames of interest.

Two algorithms can be introduced to detect the shots Pixel-wise Difference with Adaptive Thresholding and Color Histogram Difference.

In Pixel-wise Difference with Adaptive Thresholding technique the difference in intensity or color values of the corresponding pixels are of two consecutive frames are evaluated. Then the difference is compared with a threshold.

$$D(i) = 1/(X*Y) \sum_{x=1}^{X} \sum_{y=1}^{Y} |f_{i+1}(x,y) - f_i(x,y)| \tag{6}$$

X,Y are the frame width and height respectively and $f_i(x,y)$ represents intensity value at the pixel (x,y). Calculation of mean μ and standard deviation σ of the feature vector is as follows $\mu = 1/(N-1)\sum_{i=1}^{N-1} D(I,i+1)$ and $\sigma = \sqrt{(1/(N-1)\sum_{i=1}^{N-1}[D(I,i+1)-\mu]^2)}$. $T_{cut} = \mu + k\sigma$. Where k is pre-specified constant and N is the number of frames in video sequence. If $D(i) > T_{cut}$ then i^{th} frame is declared to be cut boundary. The algorithm is only used to detect any abrupt changes in the video shots.

In Color Histogram Difference method the procedure is based on the calculations of detecting difference between color histograms between frames as a measure of change.

$$d_{RGB}(x,y) = \sum_{j=1}^{M} |h_x(i) - h_y(i)| \tag{7}$$

Where h_x is the color histogram of image X which contain M different bins. Now the shot boundary detection method is based on the difference between color histograms of frames which belong to a video sequence. The difference is computed as

$$HistDiff[i] =) = \sum_{j=1}^{M} |h_i(i) - h_{i-1}(j)|. \tag{8}$$

Where h_i the color histogram with M is bins of frame I corresponding to the video sequence.

To detect abrupt cut boundary detection the difference in color histogram method is calculated and then the threshold is calculated. Then the difference is compared with the threshold value if the difference is greater, then it is called to achieve the shot boundary. But sometimes it gives false alarm failing to give accurate result that is it indicates an abrupt cut has been detected where the cut hasn't occurred yet. For this reason second order derivative method is used to detect the correct result that is to detect the correct cut. Now it may fail due to camera motion, illumination changes so that the difference of histograms exceeds the threshold value giving false result. So the second order derivative method is defined as

$$HD2=d(x_{k+1},x_{k+2})-d(x_k,x_{k+1}) \tag{9}$$

Where HD2 is the second order derivative of the color histogram difference. Now this second order derivative is compared with the threshold to detect the cut. Now at gradual boundary detection there either there can be multiple monochromatic frames between last frame of first shot and the first frame of next shot or two shots can overlap each other or as one arrives the previous shot disappears, so no clear boundary exists between them. To detect boundaries the gradual changes are divided into two classes one which gradually but simultaneously affect every pixel of the image and those that abruptly affect the evolving pixels with the subset changing in each frame.

One of the most popular method is again comparing the histograms of the consecutive frames. It is assumed that consecutive frames will have same background and the objects in the frames move very little then the difference of their histograms will show negligible or very little change. The difference is calculated as

$$D(i,i+1)=\sum_{j=1}^{n}|H_i(j)- H_{i+1}(j)| \tag{10}$$

Where $H_i(j)$ is the jth element of the histogram of the ith frame and n is the number of bins.

Fade detection falls under the category of gradual boundary detection technique. The key characteristics of fading detection are to detect the monochromatic frames. The algorithm of fading detection is as follows

3.1. Algorithm

1. Input video is chosen.
2. Calculation of mean of pixel intensity in a frame is calculated.
3. Calculation of standard deviation of pixel intensity in a frame is performed.
4. The threshold value is also calculated.
5. If the standard deviation value is less than the threshold value then indicate that there is either cut or gradual cut, go to step 7.
6. If standard deviation value is not less than the threshold value then go to step 2.
7. Decide whether it is a cut or gradual cut.
8. If it is a cut go to step 2.
9. If it is gradual cut then detect the frame after which the gradual cut has been detected and declare a gradual cut has been detected, thus fade boundary is detected.

The threshold value has a calculation with standard deviation of all frames and the calculation is as follows

T_f= (Average of standard deviation X scaling factor)/100

The scaling factor varies according to the video. If the standard deviation of any video falls below the threshold value the frame is declared as monochromatic and it will be processed for fading detection.

(Ramin Zabih, Justin Miller & Kevin Mai, 1995) In this research cut detection falls into the category of abrupt cut where the shot changes at random. There are several algorithms to detect this like pixel based approach which has already been discussed, edge change fraction method where change in shot is detected by detecting the change in ratio of edges. The edge change ratio can be stated as

$$ECR(k)=\max(X_k^{in}/\sigma_k, X_{k-1}^{out}/\sigma_{k-1}) \tag{11}$$

Where X_k^{in} and X_{k-1}^{out} represents the numbers of incoming and outgoing edge pixels in frame k and k-1 respectively. σ_k and σ_{k-1} are total number of edge pixels in frames k and k-1 respectively. If the ECR is greater than a threshold T then a cut is said to be detected. This gives false result when there is a high speed motion in a video sequence.

For this reason, Yu-Jin Zhang (2006) 2D luminance histogram using an appropriate threshold method is used. Here the histogram difference works in a combined color space YV. Where, a frame is represented with its luminance component Y and brightness component V in the HSV color space. This was done to robustly detect the abrupt change in color of the shot to declare a sudden change in shot. Now this method is resistant to several illumination changes although it works on illumination. Which means change in illumination does not always mean to have a prediction of a shot is been changed but to understand whether only brightness has increased, that is why there is a component called V is there to measure the brightness component.

First of all each frame is converted into its brightness and illumination components before making any operations on them. After that the histogram difference is calculated between two consecutive frames following the equation to find a dissimilarity vector

$$HD_k=\sum_{j=1}^{B}|Y_k(j)-Y_{k-1}(j)|+|V_k(j)-V_{k-1}(j)| \tag{12}$$

Where, $Y_k(j)$ denotes the illumination histogram value of kth frame and $V_k(j)$ denotes the brightness histogram value of kth frame. A calculation of threshold is needed here. Because the features extracted from here will be compared with the threshold value and if the value of the dissimilarity vector is greater than the threshold then a cut is declared to be detected.

Two consecutive frames in the same shot will have smaller distance compared to the frames belonging to different shots. Now first threshold needs to be calculated to go further regarding comparison.

In the many proposed methods in the past several parameters and threshold was the key to find the shot boundaries. But still there was challenge as to detect the correct threshold which can work best among the varying distances among the frames. In this algorithm threshold is very much dependent on the data indicated by the distance vector. Here the distance vector indicated the value of how much a frame is similar to another consecutive frame or as mentioned before whether the distance between the two frames are very small as they belong to the same shot. If this distance vector is plotted it shows to follow a log normal distribution (Figure 1).

Figure 1. Histogram

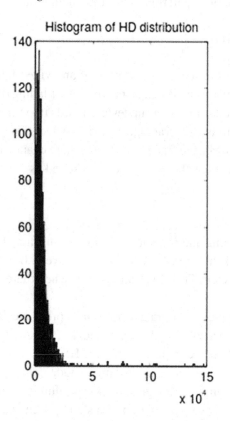
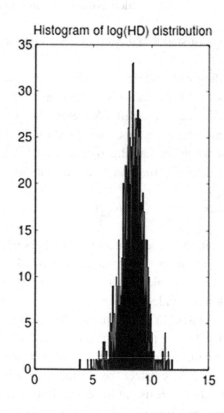

Now, if a random variable is normally distributed with N(μ,σ), then the interval μ±2σ is probable to cover the 95.5% of the whole distribution. Only 4.5% of the observations are left within the interval]0;μ-2σ]U[μ+2σ;+∞[. Since wide range of values have better scope of finding it is helpful to select interval I_c=[μ+2σ;+∞[. This way threshold will be able to detect any shot changes. The following procedure brings the overview of next stage of calculating the threshold value.

1. **Initial Threshold:** $T=\min(I_c)= x+2\sigma_x$
2. **General Threshold:** $T=x+\alpha\sigma_x$

Where x and σ_x are mean and standard deviation and α is a fitting parameter.
Now that the threshold value is calculated the algorithm to find the shots are described as follows:

1. Extraction of luminance and brightness from RGB color image.
2. Since successive frames are detected it is needed to find out the similarity vector or distance vector between them. This determines whether they fall in the same shot or not. If the value is high then they belong to different shots otherwise they belong to the same shot. The calculation of equation is as follows

$$HD_k=\sum_{j=1}^{B}|Y_k(j)-Y_{k-1}(j)|+|V_k(j)-V_{k-1}(j)| \tag{13}$$

Y and V parameters here are explained before. Here B is the representation of the number of bins. The equation can also be stated as the sum of pixels belonging to the color bin (y,v) in the frame k.

3. Repetition of steps 1 and 2 are requires until it is sure that there are no frames left in the given video sequence to find out the value of HD_k between all consecutive frames.
4. We have the threshold T already calculated and a shot is detected if the distance vector HD_k is greater than the threshold value. That is
    a) $HD_k > T$ then shot boundary detected
    b) $HD_k <= T$ then it is not shot boundary.

So, finally pictorially the whole procedure can be summed up as Figure 2.

Now it is also necessary to shift the focus on gradual cut detection while discriminating shot boundaries.

Zuzana, Cernekov´a, Pitas, and Nikou (2004) research states that a fade is included in gradual cut while detecting a shot. A fade can be described as a transition of gradual decrease of visual intensity which is also called fade-out and it also can be described as a transition of gradual increase of visual intensity which is also called fade-out (Figure 3).

A fade-out is the gradual darkening of a shot until the last frame becomes dark while fade-in follows the procedure of starting from a black frame to a completely illuminated frame.

Average intensity of frames does not change significant from time to time within a shot. Which means the difference of intensities between the starting frame and the ending frame of a same shot will have a huge difference, but within the same shot two consecutive frames do not show much difference in intensity values since this process is gradual and the name itself suggests that it fades-in or fades-out. The algorithm for fade detection algorithm is described as follows

Figure 2. Video cut detector

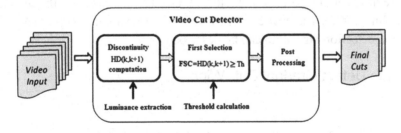

Figure 3. Video cut detector (a) fade-out (b) fade-in

Figure 4. Wipe detection

3.1.1. Algorithm to Detect Gradual Cut-Fade

Step 1: Searching of all monochromatic frames is performed in the video. A sequence of monochromatic frames $R_i = \{f_a, ..., f_e\}$ is found.

Step 2: Now for each of frames found in the sequence R_i do,

    1. Searching for a fade-in is done following the procedure below
        a. Setting of n=2 and calculation of line of regression over $\{\sigma(f_e),...,\sigma(f_{e+n})\}$ is performed.
        b. Incrimination of n is performed as well as re-computation of the line of regression is performed.
        c. If the correlation reduces by more than 3% or the slope is more than halved then if the minimum fade length has not been reached yet then go to b) else go to ii).
        d. The sequence $F_i = \{f_e,...,f_{e+n}\}$ can be considered of containing fade-in sequences.
    2. Searching for a fade-out sequence is performed following the procedure below
        a. Setting of n=2 and calculation of line of regression over $\{\sigma(f_{a-n}),...,\sigma(f_a)\}$ is performed.
        b. n is incremented and line of regression is computed as well.
        c. If the correlation decreases by 3% or the slope is more than halved then if the minimum fade length has not yet been reached the go to 2) else go to 2) b).
        d. The sequence $F_i = \{f_{a-n},...,f_a\}$ can be considered of containing fade-out sequences.

In wipe transition method pixels of one shot are replaced gradually by the pixels of the other shot step by step until the previous shot pixels are completely replaced by the pixels of the second shot (Shan Li, Moon-Chuen Lee, June 2007). The image can make a little sense about it (Figure 4).

The general wipe detection algorithm can be described as

3.1.2. Algorithm to Detect Gradual Cut- Wipe

```
Input the first frame f₁ from the video segment;
i=1;
continued=true;
while(i<Iₛ) //where Iₛ is the length of the video segment
        While(continued) //Find the start frame of the potential wipe
sequence
                Input the next frame f_{i+n from} the video segment;
                Detect scene changes between f_i and f_{i+n};
```

```
                    Compute r. //r is the ratio of scene changes region
to the total number  of regions in the frame
                    if(r>T_ratio) then continued=false;
                    else i=i+n;
              Set s=i and continued=true; //s is the first frame of the po-
tential wipe sequence
              while(continued)// Find the end frame of the potential wipe
sequence
                    Accumulate the detected scene change regions;
                    Input the next frame f_{i+n} from video segment;
                    Detect scene changes between f_i and f_{i+n};
                    Compute r. //r is the ratio of scene changes region
to the total number of regions in the frame
                    if(r>T_ratio) then continued=false;
                    else i=i+n;
              Set e=i; //e denotes the last frame of the potential wipe se-
quence
              Perform statistical inference on the potential wipe sequence
between s and e;
                    Output the inference decision;
                    Input the next frame f_{i+n};
                    i=i+n
```

(Upesh Patel, Pratik Shah, Pradip Panchal, 2013) research says that dissolve detection also falls under the category of gradual cut detection technique and this detection method uses twin comparison method. In dissolve method fade in and fade out occurs simultaneously. That means while one frame fades-out, simultaneously another frame starts to fade-in overlapping each other. (Shan Li, Moon-Chuen Lee, 2007) The following image represents the actual working of dissolve procedure (Figure 5).

The algorithm can be narrated as below

3.1.3. Algorithm for Gradual Cut Detection-Dissolve

Step 1: In this step the probable cuts are detected using the higher T_{cut}.
Step 2: Potential starting frame F_s of gradual transition is detected using the lower threshold value T_1.
Step 3: Then the subsequent frame is compared with the frame F_s.
Step 4: The end of transition is detected through a frame if
   1. The difference between successive frame falls below T_1 while the accumulated difference increases over T_{th}.
   2. If consecutive difference falls below the T_1 and cumulative difference reaches T_h.

Figure 5. Dissolve

4. FRAMES

While transmitting media that is images or videos, especially videos it is very much necessary to look at checking of the unwanted and invalid transmission along with it. Because of the transmission storage management and technique and video information becomes an issue. If there is an invalid or unwanted transmission the storage space is filled up with some unwanted video or image information. Although it might seem that space is not a factor these days but multimedia database needs huge amount of memory, so it is better not to occupy spaces with unwanted information. Now memory is not always the problem but if there is a wrong information stored in the database then while processing the database or deriving information from it will not give expected data rather faulty data.

Now for content based video retrieval and for analyzing a media video extracting key frames are very much important. Upon extraction of key frames from the video it provides suitable video summarization to index videos, for browsing videos, and to retrieve videos from the multimedia database based on the feature analysis of the extracted frame. Now as the key frames get extracted the important information required to represent the whole video reduces. Thus it requires less information to index a video and to represent the whole framework (According to Liu & Zhao, 2009).

The key frames must be able to represent the salient features of the shot. The key frames extracted should be able to make a summary of the content of the whole video and the image characteristics can be acquired from all the key frames taken at a specific time sequence. Now while extraction of key frames it is very much important to check whether there is any redundancy in the frame. That is multiple key frames showing same video characteristics is absolutely not desirable since it again goes back to the previously discussed issues regarding invalid or unwanted information. Before extracting the frames it should always be noted about the video type is being processed. If the video is decompressed and then searched for key frames it may introduce inefficiency and computational complexity. So it is better to apply the frame extraction algorithm on compressed video.

In case when extraction of frames is required firstly the video stream is segmented into several temporal shots. A shot contains several sequences of frames from a continuous recording. After that as the frame sequence of that shot is identified the key frames are extracted from it.

Now as discussed before segmentation of shots is the first step to extract the key frames from a video. So shot segmentation means detecting each shot transition and thus segmenting them. There are various segmentation algorithms available such as pixel based comparison method, template matching, and histogram based method. Pixel based method relies on the changes in features and thus detects shot transition, but this method is highly sensitive to motion so it may declare to have found a shot transition but actually it may be a motion in a single shot itself. Template matching is appropriate to detect error.

Histogram based method tend to lose the information of location of pixels but it is actually more robust than pixel based method and any other method known till date. A color histogram method is considered to segment the shots according to frame difference.

Histogram based method is the most common procedure to calculate the frame difference in a shot. Now since color histograms do not relate the spatial information with the pixel of a given color and only keeps a record of color information collected so far, it becomes a reason to construct a drifted image even if the same color histogram is provided that is reverse construction of an image from a color histogram may not be possible.

To solve this problem an improved histogram algorithm is applied. The color histogram difference $d(I_i,I_j)$ between two consecutive frames are calculated as

$$d(I_i,I_j)=\sum_{k=1}^{n} ((H_{ik}-H_{jk})^2/ H_{ik}+H_{jk}), H_{jk}\neq 0 \qquad (14)$$

Where, H_i and H_j stand for histograms of frames I_i and I_j respectively. A shot transition is declared to have been detected if the value of $d(I_i,I_j)$ is greater than a threshold value.

Now that shot segmentation is complete as well as frame sequencing with histogram method we need to extract the key frames. Now key frame extraction being a major role to determine the properties of a video there are several procedures are available to extract key frames. Some methods are briefed below

1.   Observing the activity inside a shot, key frames can be extracted. Some intra frame histograms and reference histograms are drawn for the frames inside a shot and on computing the activity measure key frames are selected.
2.   If there is a compressed video stream macro-block features are extracted from the stream and then analyzing the macro-block features the frame difference is computed.
3.   Key frames can also be extracted following the method of motion analysis. Here optical flow of each frame is computed. Now the change in optical flow is detected by a simple motion metric. Key frames are found where the computed metric converges to.

Now videos are in general are compressed and thus this compressed video processing has advantages. One advantage can be stated as macro block based feature extraction method reduces the temporal redundancy which means preventing same key frames to appear redundantly and the second advantage is that it follow domain based compression method to reduce spatial redundancy again which means to reduce the same number of key frames to appear.

In compressed video stream frames are assembled into sequences which can also called as sequential group of pictures because three types of frames are always in a group. The types of frames can be categorized as I frame, P frame, and B frame. These frames are evenly arranged in a video and constitute the group of sequential pictures. Within the group of frames it is being talked about I frames is the first frame and I frame and P frames are known as reference frames. I frames are intra coded. The frames are processed by discrete cosine transformation using 8*8 blocks and Discrete Cosine coefficients contain the information. P frames and B frames are inter frame coded. As said before P frames are reference frames, P frames refer to its preceding I frame or P frames; With forward motion compensation P frames are coded that is based on macro blocks. B frames are inter frame coded. It has forward motion prediction and backward motion prediction and bi-directional motion prediction scheme associated. After shot segmentation key frames are extracted by using the characteristics of I frame, P frame, and B frame in the video stream. If a scene cut takes place then the first I frame is chosen as key frame.

Now in the video stream P frames are encoded. The encoding for P frame includes forward motion compensation and so If a shot transition occurs at the P frame then a huge changes are very much possible to occur inside of that P frame in corresponds to other reference frames. There exists an equation to determine the calculation for finding out the ratio of macro blocks exclusive of motion compensation. It is used to check whether a P frame is selected as a key frame or not. The equation is stated as

$$R_p = no\_com/com \tag{15}$$

Where "no_com" means the number of the macro blocks exclusive of motion compensation and "com" means number of macro blocks subsequent to motion compensation.

When R_p appears as a peak value then it is denoted that P frame can be selected as a key frame.

Shot transition can as well occur on the B frame, and if that takes place then a huge changes are possible to take place in the content of B frames in corresponds to other preceding reference frames. A ratio of backward motion vector and forward motion is calculated to understand whether the B frame in consideration is the key frame or not. The equation is as

$$R_B = back/forw \tag{16}$$

Where back means number of backward motion vectors and forw means number of forward motion vector.

Key frames are supposed to reduce the amount of data carried in the video stream but only the important ones but it should also preserve the content of the original video data. It should always be noted that upon extraction of key frames if such happens that the representation of the key frames in combination does to represent the original video then there might be either a distortion while choosing the key frames or the correct key frames have not been chosen. Compression ration and fidelity are chosen to check the validity of the algorithm. Compression ratio measures the compactness of the key frames and fidelity is used to check the correlation between image set classifications.

Let us say that key frame set R consists of K frames such that $R=\{KF_j \mid j=1,2,3....,k\}$. Also let us assume that the shot frame set S consists of N frames in it. That is $S=\{F_i \mid i=1,2,3,....,k\}$. The distance between any two of the frames KF_j and F_i be denoted as $d(KF_j, F_i)$. Now defining d for each frame it becomes d_i and its measure for each frame F_i is

$$d_i = min(d(KF_j, F_i)) \tag{17}$$

Now the distance between key frame set R and shot frame set S can be written as

$$d_{sh} = max(d_i), i = 1, 2, 3, ..., N \tag{18}$$

Lastly the fidelity measure is defined as

$$fidelity = 1 - (d_{sh}/(max_i(max_j (d_{ij})))) \tag{19}$$

Where d_{ij} denotes the dissimilarity matrix of the shot set S. The more big is the fidelity measure by the above mentioned calculation the more is the accurate result in terms of key frames extracted by scanning all over the input video stream.

The algorithm of the whole procedure can be written as

4.1. Key Frame Extraction

1. Segment the input video into shots by detecting shot transition. Detection of shot is done by the improved histogram based method discussed above where the distance between two consecutive frames can be calculated as
$$d(I_i,I_j)=\sum_{k=1}^{n}((H_{ik}-H_{jk})^2/H_{ik}+H_{jk}), H_{jk}\neq 0. (20)$$
2. Key frame sequence are observed to be consisting of a sequence of I frame, P frame and B frame. Each of them are encoded either intra frame or inter frame. Some of them are reference frames.
3. Key frames are extracted from the sequence of frames I frame, P frame and B frame.
4. Compression ration and fidelity checking is performed to understand the accuracy of key frame extraction.

Dang, Kumar, and Radha, (2012) say that to extract key frames from unstructured video streams image epitome is applied where, image epitome is used as a feature vector and applied with the information divergence distance measure to find dissimilarity between the input video. Even being at a smaller size than the video it keeps valuable information such as color, edge, texture etc. The dissimilarity is measured using a min-max algorithm to take out the desired number of key frames from the input video.

Measuring visually dissimilar images in a video sequence is indeed a challenging one where it needs to extract the key frames from it. The min-max algorithm to extract the key frames are as below:

```
        Inputs: Number of key frames T, the total number of frames is N,
video sequence V={I_1,I_2,....., I_N}
        Outputs: Key frame sequence S={f_1, f_2,......, f_T}.
1.      Initialization S=ø
2.      Do from I for 1 to N-1
3.      Do for j for i+1 to N
4.      Compute D(I_i/ I_j)
end
end

        Detect first two key frames:
1.      { f_1, f_2}=Arg max D(I_i/ I_j)
2.      Update S={f_1, f_2}, n=2, V/S={g_1, g_2, g_3,......, g_{N-n}};
3.      V/S be the remaining number of frames without key frames.
Repeat
1.      Do for i from 1 to (N-n)
2.      a_i=min{D(g_i/f_k), k=1,2,3,....,n}
3.      imax=Arg max a_i
End
1.      Update n=n+1; f_n=g_{imax} ; S=SU{f_n};
```

```
2.          V/S={g_1, g_2, g_3,......, g_{N-n}};
3.          until n=T+1;
4.          return S={f_1, f_2,......, f_T}.
```

The min-max algorithm is a representation of a optimization tool powerful enough to use on many theories like game theory, statistics, decision theory etc. The above algorithm upon summarization it stands that, firstly the output set of key frames are set to be an empty set. Now two video sequences are compared till the end. At each iteration the dissimilarity is checked between them. The maximum dissimilarity between two video sequences are selected as the two key frames. Then the rest of the frames which do not contain the key frame sequences are arranged. The same procedure is applied to the rest of the frames available.

5. HYPERMEDIA

According to Sharma, Mioc, and Anton (2008), the computer vision algorithm firmly depends on the knowledge base of the system and the manipulation of knowledge base depends on manual hard work of knowledge engineers to develop it. Since the data are domain specific which it should be to identify and analyze data easily in case of a AI based approach, and they are described by objects which are related by general AI logics like predicate logic, object oriented rule base systems. These all leads to some typical problems such as, it is really hard for a knowledge engineer to follow down a huge knowledge base and its structures in terms of domains and their connections. It is also not sure whether the knowledge base will be consistent and complete while programming it manually. The procedure can be thought to follow to obtain interactive image features, to build domain oriented knowledge data by itself so that it does not require human intervention to have such complex knowledge base modifications.

Now since this is an Artificial Intelligence based approach it should give some facilities to improve the performance. The provided facilities are to give direct feature access to the image which is being analyzed. The geometrical and conceptual knowledge acquired from the observed image, the facility to determine the background to analyze an image to separate it based on domain specific separations, validation of knowledge base during acquisition of knowledge base. These all are to be done by the AI system rather than doing manually to avoid complexity while working with a huge knowledge base and its logical connectives.

5.1. Adaptive Hypermedia

Hypermedia is derived from hypertext that provides the concept of the hypertext link to contain links among any set of multimedia objects, such as sound, motion video. Adaptive hypermedia is a fresh approach of research in the line of multimedia. These systems create a model of a user and relate it to that user and his needs. Its aim is to acclimatize the content of a hypermedia page to the user's understanding and goals, or advise nearly all related links to track to ease the user, that is it personalizes the function of hypermedia. AH systems use intelligence to understand the user's needs and change the links to suit the user. This not only removes irrelevant links but is also used in areas where the hyperspace is huge and where a hypermedia application is likely to be used by individual users with diverse backgrounds, knowledge and goals. Users with different needs may be interested in diverse pieces of information or knowledge accessible on a hypermedia page and also may use other relevant links for navigation.

Peter Brusilovsky (1996) states that there are three basic things an Adaptive Hypermedia should have. They are:

1. It should be a hypermedia system (Figure 6).
2. It should have a user model.
3. It should be capable of adapting the hypermedia according to this model (i.e. the same system may appears to be different to the users with different models).

As we can see in the above diagram the system collects data about the user. It then processes the received data to form a user model. These two steps are called User modeling. This user model now has information about the user needs, and goals. The hypermedia is adapted according to this model and this step is called adaptation. These two steps are integral to converting a normal hypermedia to an adaptive and intelligent hypermedia.

5.2. Techniques of Adaptive Hypermedia

The methods of providing adaptation are referred by adaptation techniques in hypermedia systems (Brusilovsky, 1996). These techniques are a component of the execution level of an AH system. Each of these techniques can be classified as a particular category of knowledge demonstration and also as a specific adaptation algorithm (Figure 7).

The main question about a particular category of adaptive system is what are the characteristics of the user using the system that can be taken into consideration when providing adaptation. We have to keep in mind that the features that have to be adapted may be dissimilar for different users and may be dissimilar for the same user at different time. So far we have identified users' goals, knowledge, background, hyperspace, experience, and preferences, to be the five features which are used by existing adaptive hypermedia systems.

The most important characteristic of the user is considered to be the knowledge of the user of the subject represented in the hyperspace for adaptive hypermedia systems. User's knowledge is a variable.

Figure 6. Hypermedia system

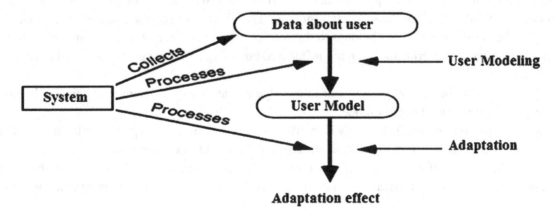

Figure 7. Hypermedia technique

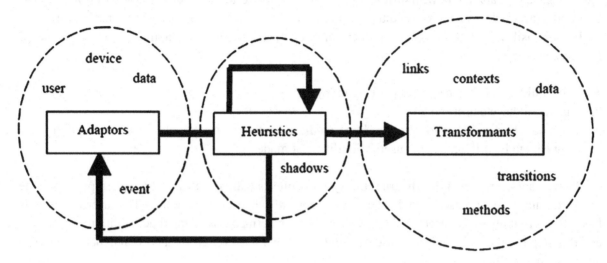

So this means that an adaptive hypermedia system has to identify the changes in the knowledge of user, state and update the user model accordingly that relies on user's knowledge. Overlay model is used for User's knowledge representation. Hypadapter, EPIAIM, KN-AHS, ELM-ART, SHIVA, Hyper Tutor, ITEM/PG, ISIS-Tutor are the overlay models. These models are generally based on structural model of the subject domain. The structural domain model notion is based on semantic network structure where concepts form network structure as they are related to each other for forming the structure of subject domain. The design of overlay model is basically used for representing individual knowledge of the user on specific subject just as an "overlay" of domain model where concepts seems to be a small segments or pieces of knowledge for a given domain. Here individual overlay models are used to store some specific values. These values are gathered as an estimation of the concept of the user knowledge level. These values in the domain model perception are simply binary values which are treated as the qualitative measure such as identifying goo, average or best quality and also these values are considered to be quantitative measure where quantitative measure implies probability that concept is known by the user. Overlay model always treats user knowledge as "concept-value" pair where each pair signifies individual domain concept i.e. each domain is associated with each concept-value pair. Overlay model is very popular as it is powerful and flexible in independently measuring different types of user's knowledge.

On the other hand the stereotypical model is useful in representing stereotypical value i.e. values without having only "true" or "false" representation. Technically stereotypical knowledge is used to represent whether the specific user belongs to the specific typecast or stereotype. This model is simple but in comparison with overlay model, it not influential but it requires low maintenance and provide an ease of initialization.

A difficulty with the stereotype model of knowledge is that many proficient adaptation techniques require a extra fine-grained overlay model.

One technique to resolve this difficulty is to offer a mapping from stereotype to overlay model. This is achieved by associating a fixed set of pairs of concept value with each stereotype.

In hypermedia, goal of user or task of user is considered as feature which is associated with the circumstance of work of user in hypermedia i.e. the kind or type of system determines whether, it can be the work's goal in application systems, goal of a search in information retrieval systems, and a problem solving or learning goal in educational systems. In all of the above situation the goal validates the reason the user is using the hypermedia system and defines the work the user actually wants to do. User's goal is considered to be the most unpredictable feature, it is always changing from session to session and it can often alter several times within one session of work.

In this type of systems it is better to differentiate local or low-level goals that can change pretty often and common or high level goals and tasks which are more steady. For an instance, in educational systems the goal of learning (i.e. what we want to learn) is a high-level goal, while the goal of problem-solving (i.e. how to learn) is a low-level goal which alters from one educational problem to another a number of times within a session. The user's goal can be measured as a very significant feature of the user for adaptive hypermedia systems. Nearly all of the techniques which rely on user goals are adaptive navigation support techniques. The user's present goal is typically modeled by a way which is fairly similar to overlay knowledge modeling.

Each system considers a set of probable user goals or tasks which it can distinguish. In some cases, the set of goals is very little and the goals are unrelated to each other. The most superior representation of possible user goals is a hierarchy or a tree of tasks.

Two features of the user which are alike to knowledge of user of the subject but functionally vary from it are user's background and user's skill in the given hyperspace. User's Background refers to all the information associated to the user's past knowledge or external skill beyond the subject of the hypermedia system, which is applicable enough to be measured. This embraces the user's profession, experience of work in associated areas, as well as the user's point of view and outlook. The term user's experience implies the fact that in the given hyperspace we signify how well-known is the user with the arrangement of the hyperspace and how easily can the user find the way in it.

One of the significant features of the user regarded by adaptive hypermedia systems is user's preferences which cannot be defined logically and can be absolute in nature. On the basis of different grounds the user can prefer some nodes and links in comparison to other and some part of a page than others.

The choice of User's preferences differs from other user model components in numerous aspects. Such as the preferences cannot be assumed by the system. It is the responsibility of the user to notify the system directly or indirectly by a feedback about such preferences.

The adaptive presentation mechanism is used to adapt the content of a page which is access by some particular user to the current knowledge, goals, and other characteristics of the user. For an instance, a qualified user may provide more detailed and profound information while a beginner needs additional effort of explanation to understand the profound subject details.

The adaptive navigation support mechanism helps user to locate their paths in hyperspace by the way of presenting links to goals adapting, along with the knowledge, and other individuality of an specific user.

This new research field has a number of motivating techniques. According to the way they use to adapt presentation of links, these techniques are classified in five groups: direct guidance, sorting, hiding, annotation, and map adaptation.

Hiding the user some parts of information about a specific concept which are not related to the user's level of knowledge about this concept is the objective of the most accepted method of content adaptation

The frame-based technique is most excellent with respect to all content adaptation mechanism (Hohl, Böcker & Gunzenhäuser, 1996), and EPIAIM. All the information about a particular concept is characterized in the form of a frame in this mechanism. Many explanation variants of the concept, links to other frames, examples, and so on. are contained inside Slots of a frame.

Specific rules are enforced to find out the order of shots while presenting it to user.

In EPIAIM these rules are considered to select one of the existing presentation schemes. Here each scheme is an ordered subset of slots and the scheme is used for the concept presentation. The "presentation priority" for each slot is calculated by the Hypadapter, rules. Then high priority subset of slots is submitted considering decreasing priority.

In the conditional parts of these rules contains not just the user knowledge level of a concept, but also feature represented in the user model. Specifically, both systems with this technique always considers the user's background. In Hypadapter and EPIAIM, the frame-based technique is used to implement all methods mentioned above except prerequisite and comparative explanation. However, the latter two methods also can be implemented with the frame-based technique by setting appropriate conditions on the knowledge level of related concepts.

Peter Brusilovsky (1996) says that a technique of Adaptive Hypermedia is Collaborative filtering. The user is involved in the process of user modeling and collaborates in gathering the information. It can be called collaborative user modeling. According to the three stages of user modeling process, we distinguish three approaches to involving the user in the process of user modeling. First, users can provide the data required for the user modeling mechanism. For example, rather than guessing whether a particular page is relevant to the user's goal using the time spent on it (as it was done in HYPERFLEX) the system can directly request this feedback from the user (as it was done in Adaptive HyperMan). Similarly, rather than guessing whether the user understands a particular page, the system can get feedback from the user. Such a feedback is a more reliable source of information and not very difficult for the user to provide. Data received from the user can be further processed by the system to update the user model.

Second, users can make the desired adaptation themselves, directly showing the system what they would like to see on the screen in the given context. To proceed according to this second approach the system has to provide users with special interface features to make the adaptation. The system should be user-adaptable. At the same time, the system has to be able to update the user model on the basis of the preferences established by the adaptation driven by user. As a result, the preferences demonstrated by the user in one context can be used to adapt the interface in other contexts. Third, the information in the user model can be updated directly by the information received from the users. The idea is involving the user in the process of user modeling to get additional information from the user and - as a result - to make user modeling simpler and more reliable.

Collaborative filtering is the process of filtering information or patterns using techniques involving collaboration among multiple agents, viewpoints and data sources. Many existing applications use filtering techniques to recommend items such as music, books, movies etc. Using artificial intelligence algorithms we can derive some user characteristics and store them in the user model. Similarly, we could add new features to the multidimensional matrix in the storage layer based on the characteristics of similar users. Collaborative filtering is based on the assumption that similar users have similar preferences. For example Amazon.com internet shop portal makes recommendations based on the items users have already bought. Some music portals recommend its users songs based on their recent playlist.

In adaptive hypermedia we use clustering based on the similarity of users that could help to solve the "cold start" problem. This means that if we don't have any information about the current user, we could use information about a similar user which we assume to be similar too.

There are many approaches and algorithms to compute the similarity of user preferences.

The commonly used algorithm for collaborative filtering tasks is the k-Nearest Neighbor (k-NN) algorithm. The k-NN algorithm is a method for classifying objects based on the closest training examples in the feature space. It belongs to a class of so called lazy learning algorithms. The following formula can be used to calculate the distance d of two users- ua and ub:

$$d(u_a, u_b) = \sqrt{\sum_{i=1}^{n} (P_a(o_i)\, P_b(o_i))^2} \tag{21}$$

where n is the number of compared objects o_i and $P(o_i)$ is the rating of the object.

After determining the distance of users, we can select K users with the lowest distance and calculate the unknown rating of item i for the user u_0 as the arithmetic mean of rating of the K nearest users:

$$P_o(o) = \sum_{i=1}^{K} P_i(o)/K \tag{22}$$

We can also use k-NN algorithm to calculate the similarity of two users as a value ranging from 0 to 1 as:

$$sim(u_a, u_b) = 1 - d(u_a, u_b) / \sqrt{n} \tag{23}$$

Another algorithm for determining the similarity of users uses the Pearson correlation coefficient. It ranges from -1 (a perfect negative relationship) to +1 (a perfect positive relationship), with 0 stating that there is no relationship whatsoever. The value of the coefficient can be computed as a quotient of covariance of variables and their standard deviations:

$$r = cov(X,Y)/ s_X s_y = E((X_i - E(X))\,(Y_i - E(Y))) = 1/(n-1) \sum_{i=1}^{n} (X_i - \bar{X}/s_X)\,(Y_i - \bar{Y}/s_Y) \tag{24}$$

where and are sample means and sx and sy are sample standard deviations. XY

Similarity can be also calculated using Spearman correlation coefficient. In principle, ρ is considered to be a special case of the Pearson product-moment coefficient. Here two sets of data X_i and Y_i are changed to rankings x_i and y_i before the coefficient is calculated. If there are no tied ranks:

$$\neg \exists i, j : i \neq j (X_i = X_j \vee Y_i = Y_j) \tag{25}$$

then ρ is given by:

$$\rho = 1 - (6\sum_{i=1}^{n} d_i^2 / n(n^2 - 1)) \tag{26}$$

Where, d_i is the rank difference of corresponding values X_i and Y_i and n represents the number of values in individual data set. The last algorithm that we used for our experiments uses the Kendall coefficient. Kendall τ coefficient is defined as:

$$\zeta = (n_c - n_d)/1/2\,(n\,(n-1)) \tag{27}$$

where n_c is the number of concordant pairs and n_d is the number of discordant pairs.

5.3. Application

The most popular application of adaptive hypermedia research is educational hypermedia system which has moderately small hyperspaces covering a particular course learning section material on a specific subject. The objective of the student is usually to study all this material. The hypermedia form supports student-driven design of the learning material, that is, the student only gets information on what he is learning or related to that topic. The user's knowledge is considered to be a one of the significant feature of the subject being taught. Adaptive hypermedia methods are popular in solving a number of the problems connected with the use of educational hypermedia.

Basically, the knowledge of different users is different and the growth of knowledge of a specific user varies from person to person. The same page content can be vague for a beginner and at the same time boring for an advanced learner.

Second, the beginners start the study of educational material without knowing anything about the subject. The offered links from any specific node guide to the material which is entirely new for the beginners. Hence beginners need navigational help to find the way through the hyperspace. Without such specification one may lost even in a small hyperspaces, or else bound to use very ineffective browsing policy.

Another application in the adaptive hypermedia field is on-line information systems from on-line documentation to electronic encyclopedias. These systems aim to provide reference access to information for the users with diverse knowledge level of the subject. Each node of the hyperspace represents one concept of the subject with several pages of information containment. The size of the hyperspace alters in the range from reasonably small to very large on the basis of the subject. Like educational hypermedia, an on-line information system suffers from the needs of very different users. Different information about a concept and at different levels of detail is required for different knowledge and background. User's usually have less or no time to browse the entire information about the concept. So adaptive hypermedia guides them to the exact part and amount of the information they need using the references. So that they don't have to read the whole document to extract the information required.

Individual user has different goals while information accessing in the system. In some cases concepts to access to achieve their goals are known and navigational support can be omitted. However, when the goal cannot be directly identified to the structure of the hyperspace or when the hyperspace is large, users needs guidance in navigation for finding relevant segments of information. The system has to know the user's goal to provide such guidance. We know that inferring the goal of user is a complicated problem in on-line information systems, if goal is provided directly by the user then inference will be easier.

These are the applications of adaptive hypermedia. Several other applications are also present but as we see the main application of adaptive hypermedia is to personalize hypermedia in such a way that it works according to the users objectives.

6. SEGMENTATION

The goal of image segmentation is to cluster pixels into specialized regions that is regions corresponding to individual surfaces, natural objects, objects etc.. Segmentation can be used for object recognition, boundary estimation, searching in multimedia database through the clustered pixels.

According to the research of Yu-Jin Zhang (2006), segmentation can be considered as a partition of the image and the segmentations generated must be non overlapping and together they represent the whole image back. Now part of the image can only be considered as segments if they follow some rules like the segments should be uniform and homogeneous based on the features they are selected, which also means that their inner parts should be without or very negligible number of holes, Adjacent regions must have different values so that each segments can be separated from the other ones, boundaries of each segment must be spatially accurate.

More formally image segmentation can be defined as that if the whole image is represented as a whole region R and each individual region is denoted as R_i, then it must follow the protocols as:

1. $U_{i=1}^{n} R_i = R$
2. $R_i \cap R_j = \emptyset$
3. $P(R_i) = True$
4. $P(R_i U R_j) = False$

Where $P(R_i)$ is uniformity predicate for all elements in the region R_i.

There are so many algorithms available to cluster a media- image or video that it is easier if it is classified and analyzed each class so to pick the best algorithm. Segmentation algorithm is classified into three categories such as

1. Thresholding
2. Clustering – it is multidimensional of the former category
3. Edge detection
4. Region extraction
5. Pixel classification
6. Neural network based approaches
7. Range image segmentation
8. Color image segmentation
9. Edge detection
10. Fuzzy methods- fuzzy clustering, fuzzy thresholding, fuzzy edge detection.

It seems clear that some of the methods above fall into a group but based on their slightest different approach they are classified different. Like range image segmentation and color image segmentation methods efforts to show how images are segmented. Also they are based on pixel classification, edge detection and thresholding techniques. Now since some algorithms falls under some groups so if the algorithms are classified as which algorithm belongs to which group to understand segmentation approach better, it must serve the following rules properly:

1. Every algorithm must be in a group.
2. All groups together must include all algorithms.
3. Algorithms in same group must share some common properties.
4. The algorithms residing in different groups must have clear distinguishable properties.

The above classification of algorithm was made how the algorithm should behave like a thresholding algorithm will any how will implement threshold technique but will not implement any fuzzy techniques. So based on what the algorithms implement to segment a video or an image is as follows:

1. Histogram shape based methods where peaks, valley, curvature etc properties of histograms are analyzed.
2. Cluster based methods where grey level samples are clustered in to two parts as background and foreground.
3. Entropy based methods where entropy between background and foreground regions or entropy between segmented and original image etc are calculated.
4. Attribute based methods where the measure of similarity between grey level image and segmented images like similarity of fuzzy similarity, shape, edges, number of objects detected etc. are investigated.

Now, if thinking is performed here the main requirement becomes how to segment an image and a video. Image segmentation is comparatively easier because image segmentation is a static process and it does not change. On segmenting the image and collecting necessary data and storing it can be used to train a system to conceptually predict a new image. Now in case of video things are difficult because the media constantly changes its state after a particular interval of time. The video includes many smooth motions as well as uneven motions. For video segmentations shots, pixel properties, frames all come into play and the aim becomes to correlate each of them. Now since segmentation of both image and video are considered here some method must be employed which be applied on any of the media- image or video.

For this if it is thought this way that when a media is fed to the system, the system will start with a pixel and look for its similar and almost similar pixels to categorize them together and make a segment of them to reconstruct the media snapshot. This way if any of the media is supplied as input whether it is video or an image it follows the same process and sorts the things like it should. Any other methods mentioned above is either works better for video or works better to segment images. Now the method thought to segment images and videos here follows the clustering procedure and it is necessary to have clustering as a procedure to segment media.

Jue Wang, Bo Thiesson, Yingqing Xu, Michael Cohen (2004) says since segmentation is performed through clustering procedure there are many clustering procedures available to perform clusters, such as a top down approach K-D tree to bottom up approach as K-means algorithm. Now segmentation falls under media analysis category. When a media- image or video is sent as input to the system, it segments the image, feeds the segmented image to analyze for object which it could represent and then it is sent for feature analysis to extract the features of the media detected. While clustering firstly the procedure mean shift algorithm starts at each pixel of the media whether it is image or video. Now as it selects one pixel it looks for the local density of similar type of pixel. Now here the confusion should be cleared, since this is a clustering procedure it should be decided whether to choose nearby or similar pixels are to be chosen or not. The mean shift algorithm performs evaluation of local density gradient of similar pixels. Now this gradient evaluation is done in the local density to find some peaks and all the pixels which are drawn upwards the peak are considered to be the similar pixels to the pixel chosen as data point.

The application of mean shift to an image segmentation or video segmentation generally consists of two steps. The first step is to define the kernel which deals with each pixel x_i. This kernel measures an intuitive distance between each pixel and the distance is either spatial for images or temporal for video.

This kernel chooses the distance of pixels which is similar to the selected pixel while clustering it as it is mentioned above.

Now for the second step of mean shift algorithm assigns a mean shift point to each pixel as M(xi). Now these mean shift points are moved upwards along the gradient of density function. This density function is defined by sum of all kernels and the mean shift points are moved upwards until they reach a stationary point. Pixels which reach at the same level of stationary points are selected in a segment. This way neighboring segments are also calculated this way. The multivariable kernel density function at pixel x is defined as:

$$f(x) = 1/n \sum_{i=1}^{n} K_H(x - x_i) \tag{28}$$

Where n is the number of data points and x_i is the ith pixel. Now the function $K_H(x)$ is defined as

$$K_H(x) = |H|^{-1/2} K(H^{-1/2}x) \tag{29}$$

Where H is a symmetric positive definite dxd matrix, and d is the number of variable consisting of a kernel function.

For image segmentation and video segmentation the feature space is composed of two independent domains mostly based on which segmentation is performed and they are spatial or lattice domain and range or color domain. A pixel is mapped into the feature space where p dimensional spatial lattice, where p=2 for image and p=3 for video and q dimensional color where q=3 for color. Now it is easier for the kernel to decide if the kernel is broken into two for two domains which are to be analyzed. So the kernel when broken into two parts for each domain looks like

$$K_{h_s,h_r}^{s,r}(x) = c/((_h{}^s)^p(_h{}^r)^q) k^s(|x_s/h_s|^2) k^r(|x_r/h_r|^2) \tag{30}$$

Where x_s and x_r are spatial part and range part of feature vector k^s and k^r are profiles used in the two domains h_s and h_r are two employed bandwidths in two domains and c is normalized constant. Now as the kernel is redefined here the kernel density function defined before will change too. The reflection of the change is as follows

$$f(x) = c/(n(_h{}^s)^p(_h{}^r)^q) \sum_{i=1}^{n} K^s(|(x_s - x_i{}^s)/h_s|^2) k^r(|(x_r - x_i{}^r)/h_r|^2) \tag{31}$$

As discussed before at each step of mean shift procedure the, mean shift points assigned to each pixel goes upward along the kernel density function. Since each pixel is different than the others so they are attracted by the kernel in different variations. Kernel that is sample pixels are at different distance apart from other pixels. Kernel somewhat represents a measure of likelihood by which nearby pixels which are attracted towards it if the measure of likelihood permits. The closer two pixels are in terms of likelihood the more probable they will be in the same segment.

There is another, more robust mean shift kernel algorithm available which is called as Anisotropic mean shift algorithm. In case of general mean shift kernel algorithm as the kernels are divided in different domains their functions overlap if the boundaries are irregular and make it look like in lack of temporal coherence in the video segments. But the anisotropic mean shift kernel solves this problem. Anisotropic mean shift algorithm, can adapt itself to the local condition of pixel arrangements near the kernel. Anisotropic mean shift algorithm is more robust and less sensitive to overlap of feature domains like any other kernel systems and this anisotropic mean shift kernel algorithm provides some handlers to handle the rate and requirements of segmentation. For instance it can be noted that a user can choose to segment the background of a video more coarsely that is into more piece of segments while the objects in the video to be preserved. This was not possible in general mean shift kernel algorithm as it segments everything in equal rate.

The kernel density function of anisotropic mean shift algorithm is as follows

$$f(x) = 1/n \sum_{i=1}^{n} 1/(h^r(H_i^s)^q) k^s(g(x_s, x_i^s, H_i^s)) K^r(|x_r - x_i^r|/h_r(H_i^s)|^2) \tag{32}$$

Where: $g(x_s, x_i^s, H_i^s)$ means $g(x_s, x_i^s, H_i^s) = (x_i^s - x^s)^T H_i^{s-1}(x_i^s - x^s)$

The algorithm of the means shift algorithm is stated below. But before that as discussed before the kernel is divided for each domain like spatial domain and color domain. The algorithm is as follows

1. Kernel initialization and input data selection
   a. Transfer of pixels into multidimensional feature points is performed. here as said in case of spatial domain p=2 for image and p=3 for video and for color domain q=3 for color.
   b. Initialization of spatial domain parameter h_0^s and range domain parameter h_0^r is performed.
   c. As kernels are assigned to these feature points mean shift points are assigned to these points $M(x_i)$.
   d. All spatial domain matrix is set as $H_i^s = (h_0^s)^2 I$ and all range domain matrix is represented as $h^r(H_i^s) = h_0^r$.
2. For each pixels points x_i determination of kernel and related color range is performed.
   a. All neighbors of the pixel x_i are searched which follow the kernel constraint are searched and selected. The constraint is

$$k^s(g(x_i, x_j, H_i^s)) < 1; \ k^r(|(x_r - x_i^r)/h_r(H_i^s)|^2) < 1 \tag{33}$$

3. Repeat step 2 for some iterations.
4. As mean shifts are performed with each pixel points x_i determination of x_j, the neighbor of x_i is determined, and then calculation of mean shift vector summing over the neighbors are performed to get $M_v(x_i)$. So the new mean shift point is obtained as $M(x_i) = M(x_i) + M_v(x_i)$.
5. Merge those pixels whose mean vectors are somewhat same as to produce homogeneous color regions.
6. Eliminate segments which contains less number of pixels than the same value given.

Thus on using the anisotropic mean shift algorithm clustering method is followed where spatial domain and color domain is divided and respective kernels are given the responsibility to maintain the clusters. Since in case of anisotropic mean shift algorithm does not get itself bothered like general mean shift algorithm when the boundaries between the two domains are irregular and overlapping in nature thus creating a confusion while selecting the feature points, it is more robust in nature. Since cluster points are stored in the media database predicting of future media segmentation becomes easier if the feature and characteristics follow the cluster properties.

6.1. Segmentation and Clustering

According to Dr. Sanjay Kumar, Er. Ankur Chauhan (2014) feature analysis of an image is the pattern analysis of images and differentiating if from its immediate neighborhood. Good feature must have repeatability which means images of same object taken in different situation then the similar pattern should be high. Distinctiveness in formativeness i.e. the intensity patterns found in detected features should show a lot of differences.

The locality feature should be local so that the differentiation of patterns is possible. The quantity feature should be large enough so that the number of detected features is large even in small objects. The main procedure of feature extraction is query which is given by the user as query image, and then the feature of the image is extracted. Now the image database is followed through and features are extracted. Now these extracted features are matched with the query feature and image(s) with same feature patterns are supplied as result.

Pixel values are calculated and the rule of comparison is defined. The calculation of similarity takes place by computing the difference in its feature components to its descriptors. These descriptors are color histograms for color shape feature, about curvature and so on. This feature extraction of image is divided into several regions. A single image may contain several distinguishing objects.

In region based image retrieval system same thing occurs except each image is divided into several regions, user queries about a region and features are extracted followed by the above mentioned procedure (Sharma, Mioc, & Anton, 2008). The procedure becomes easier if the image under process is segmented. Upon segmentation the image is segmented based on its color information and thus in one word a clear edge has been found for each image. There is an algorithm called mean shift algorithm that segments the image relying on its color properties forming a cluster. Initially the search window is considered and the center of the window is considered. Then a locally initial point is selected. Initially it is called local mean. Then it is calculated how much this local mean is deviated from the center of the window. The formula for calculating the deviation from the window center is as follows:

$$M_\lambda(x) = (\sum_{r \in R} {}^d K(r-x) r / \sum_{r \in R} {}^d K(r-x)) - x \tag{34}$$

Here from the above formula it is known as mean shift vector. It is the ratio of difference between local mean and the center of the window $K(x)$ to gradient of probability density at x. The algorithm regarding this mean shift clustering can be stated as follows

1. Choose the radius r of the window of consideration.
2. Choose the initial location of the window.
3. Calculate the mean shift and translate the search window by that amount.
4. Repeat until convergence.

Here convergence means that as the local mean gets shift each time it tends to converge. Now if we add feature domain and image domain with this algorithm it is clear that the image will be perfectly segmented following this clustering algorithm.

CONCLUSION

The concept of "multimedia" covers a large range of application as it considered as a grouping of numerous media into one unit. The most useful and common fields of multimedia applications are Hypermedia courseware, Video conferencing, Groupware, Home shopping, Digital video editing, Virtual reality, and so on. In this chapter I try to focus each relevant area of multimedia fundamental such as Hypermedia which is used preferably in rich media i.e. online multimedia presentation. "The learn more" concept i.e. when user click online on a link of website to choose certain topic for further reading is the place where hypermedia is used. Shot is defined along with segmentation and clustering. But the modern multimedia approaches like "virtual reality " implementation is not discussed in this chapter. Virtual reality is used to implement realistic and entertaining environment where participation of human being appears by controlling software behavior within synthetic world. The concept of online streaming and P2P file sharing is not provided. Using streaming concept playback in real time using real time protocols are possible i.e., user can star, pause stop digital audio or video. Multimedia application is entertainment field and in smart phone and portable devices (such as iPod), application is not a part of this chapter. In the upcoming future new devices, new forms of entertainment based on network availability are arising; hence new multimedia applications and inventions are also at our door steps.

As we consider multimedia system as one of the complex computing system class as the concept of multimedia can perform special tasks such as importing, creating, editing, deleting, storing multiple types of digital materials like audio, image, full motion video, and text information. Its application is increasing day by day and the most important, recent and modern approach towards multimedia application is business-oriented multimedia systems. The basic aim of this type of application is on advanced multimedia news system architecture implementation, document standards, implementing multimedia news system architecture on Web and so on. This type of applications provides a base on which news aggregation and manipulation may be done on World Wide Web. Hence the very well known research is done for the news community for high level semantic analysis solution.

REFERENCES

Brusilovsky. (n.d.). *Methods and Techniques of Adaptive Hypermedia*. Academic Press.

Dang, Kumar, & Radha. (n.d.). *Key frame extraction from consumer videos using epitome*. Michigan State University.

Kumar, & Chauhan. (2014). A Survey On Feature Extraction Techniques For Color Images. *International Journal of Scientific and Engineering Research, 5(9)*.

Le Saux & Amato. (n.d.). *Image classifiers for scene analysis*. Academic Press.

Li, S., & Lee, M.-C. (2007). *Effective Detection of Various Wipe Transitions. IEEE Transactions on Circuits and Systems for Video Technology, 17(6)*.

Lienhart. (n.d.). *Comparison of Automatic Shot Boundary Detection Algorithms*. Microcomputer Research Labs, Intel Corporation.

Liu & Zhao. (2009). Key Frame Extraction from MPEG Video Stream. *International Computer Science and Computational Technology*.

Patel, Shah, & Panchal. (2013). Threshold and Color Histogram Method in Compressed and Uncompressed Video. *International Journal of Computer Applications*.

Sharma, O., Mioc, D., & Anton, F. (2008). Polygon feature extraction from satellite imagery based on colour image segmentation and medial axis. The International Archives of the Photogrammetry, Remote Sensing and Spatial Information Sciences.

Wang, Thiesson, Xu, & Cohen. (n.d.). *Image and Video Segmentation by Anisotropic Kernel Mean Shift*. Microsoft Research.

Yang, Liu, & Shah. (n.d.). Video Scene Understanding Using Multi-scale Analysis. *Computer Vision Lab University of Central Florida*.

Zabih, R., Miller, J., & Mai, K. (1995). A Feature-Based Algorithm for Detecting and Classifying Scene Breaks. *ACM Multimedia*, *95*, 189–200.

Zhang, Y.-J. (2006). *An Overview of Image and Video Segmentation in the Last 40 Years*. Beijing, China: Tsinghua University. doi:10.4018/978-1-59140-753-9

Zuzana, Pitas, & Nikou. (2004). *Information Theory-Based Shot Cut/Fade Detection and Video Summarization*. Methods for Unified Multimedia Information Retrieval (MOUMIR) project - RTN-1999-00177 MOUMIR.

Chapter 2
Theoretical Concepts and Technical Aspects on Image Segmentation

Anju Pankaj
Mahatma Gandhi University, India

Sonal Ayyappan
SCMS School of Engineering and Technology, India

ABSTRACT

Image segmentation is the process of partitioning a digital image into multiple segments (super pixels). Segmentation is typically used to locate objects and boundaries in images. The result of segmentation is a set of segments that collectively cover the entire image, or a set of contours extracted from the image. Each of the pixels in a region is similar with respect to some characteristic or computed property. Adjacent regions are significantly different with respect to the same characteristics. A predicate for measuring the evidence for a boundary between two regions using a graph-based representation of the image is defined. An important characteristic of the method is its ability to preserve detail in low-variability image regions and ignoring detail in high variability regions. This chapter discuss basic aspects of segmentation and an application and presents a detailed assessment on different methods in image segmentation and discusses a case study on it.

INTRODUCTION

Image segmentation is a very significant area in computer vision. Image segmentation, partitions an image into multiple regions based on certain similarity constraints. This acts as the pre-processing stage in several image analysis problems like image compression, image recognition etc. Segmentation is the vital part for the successful extraction of image features and classification. Image segmentation can be defined as the partition of an image into several regions or categories. These regions can be similar in any features like color, texture, intensity etc. Every pixel in an image is assigned to any one of the categorised region. Quality of segmentation is described as pixels in the same region are similar in some

DOI: 10.4018/978-1-5225-0498-6.ch002

characteristics whereas pixels in different regions differ in the characteristics. The segmentation process includes restoration, enhancement, and representation of the image data in the required form.

Image segmentation techniques can be broadly classified based on certain characteristics. Basic classifications of image segmentation techniques include local and global image segmentation techniques. The segmentation method that is concerned with segmenting specific parts or region of image is known as local image segmentation. The segmentation method that is concerned with segmenting the whole image, consisting of very large number of pixels is known as global image segmentation.

The next category of image segmentation method is based on the properties of the images to be segmented. It is categorised as discontinuity detection based approach and similarity detection based approach. In discontinuity detection based approach, the segmentation is based on discontinuities in the images like edge based segmentation and similarity detection based approach is based on similarity of regions like Threshold based, Region growing, Region Splitting and Merging etc. The segmentation technique which is based on the information of the structure of required portion of the image is known as structural segmentation. Most of the segmentation methods are stochastic type, where the segmentation is completely depended upon the discrete pixel values of the image.

An undirected graph, set of vertices and a set of edges, are considered. Vertex represents the pixels in an image and edges denote the connection between the adjacent pixels. There exists a source and sink node which holds the foreground and background respectively. In graph cut method, each edge is assigned with a non-negative weight which coins the term cost [20]. A graph cut is actually the partitioning of the edge set into several component sets. Graph cut method can be either min cut or max cut. Min cut can be defined as cut through minimum cost and max cut can be defined as the cut through maximum cost. That is after the cut performed, the vertices are divided into two sets, source and sink, which holds the foreground and background pixels respectively.

Implementing graph cut method assigns value 1 to the pixels in the foreground and 0 to the pixels in the background. This is achieved through minimum graph cut method by minimizing the energy function.

BACKGROUND

Graph-based image segmentation techniques generally represent the problem in terms of a graph, G =(V,E) where each node $v_i \; \mathcal{E} \; V$ corresponds to a pixel inthe image, and the edges in E connect certain pairs of neighboring pixels. A weight is associated with each edge based on some property of the pixels that it connects, such as their image intensities. Depending on the method, there may or may not be an edge connecting each pair of vertices. The earliest graph based methods use fixed thresholds and local measures in computing segmentation.

Different cluster-structures can be detected using algorithms on minimum spanning tree. The dataset used by Zahn include Fisher Iris data in four dimensional space. The work of Zahn (1971) presents a segmentation method based on the minimum spanning tree (MST) of the graph. This method has been applied both to point clustering and to image segmentation. For image segmentation the edge weights in the graph are based on the differences between pixel intensities, whereas for point clustering the weights are based on distances between points. The segmentation criterion in Zahn's method is to break MST edges with large weights, which is inadequate. Differences between pixels within the high variability region can be larger than those between the ramp and the constant region. Thus, depending on the threshold, simply breaking large weight edges would either result in the high variability region being split into multiple regions, or would merge the ramp and the constant region together.

The algorithm proposed by Urquhart (1982) attempts to address this shortcoming by normalizing the weight of an edge using the smallest weight incident on the vertices touching that edge. When applied to image segmentation problems, however, this is not enough to provide a reasonable adaptive segmentation criterion. Early approach to image segmentation is that of splitting and merging regions according to some uniformity criterion. Generally these uniformity criteria obey a subset property, such that when a uniformity predicate $U(A)$ is true for some region A then $U(B)$ is also true for any $B \subset A$. Usually such criteria are aimed at finding either uniform intensity or uniform gradient regions.

A number of approaches to segmentation are based on finding compact clusters in some feature space. These approaches generally assume that the image is piecewise constant, because searching for pixels that are all close together in some feature space implicitly requires that the pixels be alike. A recent technique using feature space clustering by Siddiqui (2012), first transforms the data by smoothing it in a way that preserves boundaries between regions. This smoothing operation has the overall effect of bringing points in a cluster closer together. The method then finds clusters by dilating each point with a hyper sphere of some fixed radius, and finding connected components of the dilated points. This technique for finding clusters does not require all the points in a cluster to lie within any fixed distance.

Consider a class of segmentation methods based on finding minimum cuts in a graph, where the cut criterion is designed in order to minimize the similarity between pixels that are being split. Work by Wu and Leahy (2012) introduced such a cut criterion, but it was biased toward finding small components.

This bias was addressed with the normalized cut criterion developed by Shi and Malik (2012), which takes into account self-similarity of regions. These cut-based approaches to segmentation capture non-local properties of the image, in contrast with the early graph-based methods. However, they provide only a characterization of each cut rather than of the final segmentation.

The normalized cut criterion provides a significant advance. However, the normalized cut criterion also yields an NP-hard computational problem. While Shi and Malik develop approximation methods for computing the minimum normalized cut, the error in these approximations is not well understood. In practice these approximations are still fairly hard to compute, limiting the method to relatively small images or requiring computation times of several minutes. Recently Weiss (2012) has shown how the eigenvector-based approximations developed by Shi and Malik relate to more standard spectral partitioning methods on graphs. However, all such methods are too slow for many practical applications.

The author, Wang (2010) proposes a threshold based segmentation method. Threshold based level set approach combines threshold segmentation and fast marching approach by Yasmin (2012). This technique include, pre-processing stage using an anisotropic filter. Anisotropic filter is used to enhance the image edge and filter noise. As a next step threshold segmentation is done. This is done to control the diffusion coefficient of curve in the threshold limit kept. As a final step segmentation is done using fast marching method. Statistical similarity degree of the regions is used to define the speed function of fast marching method. The final experiments show that the segmentation method produce drastic segmentation results and improve the speed of segmentation.

In the area of online processing based on machine vision, the acquisition and processing of wheel set profile image remains as a key problem. The application lies in train safety. Clear wheel set profile curve can be obtained from different backgrounds by using threshold segmentation. The old threshold method used is Otsu algorithm, which is popular and efficient. In situations where, the target image is much lower than the background image, that is, the SNR is much lower, and then the segmentation effect is weak. To improve the image acquisition process in computer vision, threshold based segmentation method based on entropy criteria and genetic algorithm is mentioned by Kaihua (2011). The author Kaihua (2011), introduces an optimal threshold segmentation method which is based on the entropy scenario and genetic algorithm (GAEC). The factors that affect image acquisition include image histogram characteristics, light source life, CCD exposure time, environmental illumination and light reflection. Tests proved that, the proposed method can efficiently eliminate interferences in image acquisition. The quality of segmentation and its efficiency was improved.

Most of the segmentation algorithm results in a problem that, the result obtained will be limited for that particular application alone. The result will not be expandable for any other presentation. As a result of which comparison between the segmentation results of two algorithms are not possible. Edge based segmentation method is based on the sudden change of intensity values in an image. In image processing, object boundaries are represented using edge. Edge based segmentation works by identifying the region of abrupt intensity change in an image by Khalifa (2010) .The author, Khalifa (2010) proposes an innovative method through which the assessment of the efficiency of Region growing and edge detection segmentation method is performed. EXOR measure approach is used in the proposed evaluation metric. The EXOR measure is mainly used in the application of skin tumour borders. The proposed method scales in such a way that the two segmentation algorithms can be compared in a better manner. 300 images from the Berkley Segmentation Dataset are used for the experimentation. According to the order of dominance, the images were classified into seven groups. Through experimentation that can be concluded that the edge detection algorithms showed better results than the region growing and merging in several applications.

In order to perform multi scale image segmentation an edge based auto threshold generating method is introduced by author Zhang (2010) . Here, an improved multispectral high resolution image segmentation which is based on object is introduced. Object based high resolution technique is realized using optimal theory of minimum spanning tree. Band weight and Normalized Difference Vegetation Index (NDVI) were introduced to upgrade the formulation of edge weight. The auto threshold based on edge is used to perform multi scale image segmentation. Here scale parameters can be varied. The dataset used were Quick Bird multispectral images. This kind of segmentation resulted in high quality segmentation. The segmentation results include detail of object. The application of this method lies in remote sensing images. The method can be used for any kind of images and these kinds of methods can be easily controlled by the users.

Another method for edge detection using variance filter is introduced by author Fabijanska (2011). Here, the edge position is determined using variance filter. The dataset used here is of synthetic and real images. The results were analysed and proved that, the variance filter based edge detection method showed better and optimized result.

Theory based segmentation method uses derivatives from several fields. Several types of this kind of algorithm includes, Clustering based segmentation: In this method clusters are formed based on the similarity criteria (size, color, texture etc). Methods include k-means clustering, fuzzy clustering, hard clustering etc in the paper by the author Sulaiman (2010).

Clustering algorithms plays a significant role in image segmentation. Certain segmentation algorithms are specific for certain applications alone. The author Deng (2010), proposes an algorithm for segmentation, that works irrespective of the application. The algorithm is termed as Adaptive Fuzzy K means clustering (AFKM) algorithm. This algorithm works on the bases of the theory behind fuzziness. This algorithm provides better result for clustering based segmentation than any other method. This proposed method gives high quality segmentation result as compared to other methods.

Artificial Neural Network: In this method the neuron represents the pixels and segmentation is performed with the help of trained images. Methods using Wavelet Decomposition and Self Organization Map of artificial neural networks are proposed by author Zhang (2010). The author Zhang (2010) proposed a segmentation method for segmenting colour images. The concept of BP neural network is introduced here. The concept include, BP neural network has the ability of parallel computing, distributed saving, fault to learnt, self studying and non linear function approximation. BP neural networks was widely used for image segmentation, but due to its certain unavoidable defects a new method based on neural network is introduced. The new method include both Wavelet Decomposition and the concept of self organising map neural network (SOM NN). The main advantage of this method is it is highly resistant to noise which gradually improves the convergence. Color prototypes used generates a good estimate for object colors. Observation from various experiments can conclude that the method is useful for image segmentation in n number of application.

The author Kang (2012) proposes a method based on region growing. The method involves technique of image segmentation based on seeded region growing. This method mainly focussed the applications that include images having complicated background. The dataset include both color and gray scale images. The method is a combination of fuzzy edge detection method along with fuzzy image pixel similarity. Fuzzy edge detection method detects the connected edges, whereas using fuzzy image pixel similarity, initial seeds are selected automatically from a complicated background. The fuzzy distance is a measure that computes the change in difference among the pixel and region in the neighboring region growing and dissimilarity between the two regions during the region merging. The older region growing method is modified in this algorithm, by ensuring that the edge pixels are processed later than other additional pixels. Experiments showed that this proposed method based on region growing and merging produced good and better segmentation results than other segmentation methods. The advantage of region based method is that it is highly resistant to the effect of noise.

Region Growing: the collection of pixels is grouped into a region with similar properties in the paper by Barbosa (2012). Region Splitting and Merging: Here the image is further subdivided into several regions based on some pre-defined criteria. Graph cut image segmentation is a very significant technique of segmentation under region based segmentation.

As image segmentation plays a very important role in computer vision and pattern recognition several image segmentation algorithms have been emerged. The most important factor regarding these segmentation techniques is which algorithm can produce segmented results in lesser time. This always remains as a real time problem in image processing. The author Chen (2009) proposes a region based method improving the speed of segmentation. The older method of segmentation based on region growing method produces highly efficient result, but it is time consuming. In this method weight matrix is introduced so that objects can be detected faster which is based on least square method. A minimal error function is the key factor in this approach. Error function is generated based on approximating objects and background of input image. The object and background of the image is mapped to two constants. The weight matrix increases the weight of the object by reducing the weight of the background. This reduces the influence of background. Alternating iterations are done based on the least square method. The main focus of this proposed method is that efficient results are produced in a less time consumed manner with high accuracy.

Several techniques of region growing methods include techniques that combine edge and region based information using morphological watershed algorithms. In this method, initially a noise filter along with magnitude gradient is used and pre segmentation is performed through region merging. A region similarity graph is then produced and final segmentation is performed using Multi Class Normalized Cut. This technique overpowers the Spectral clustering method. As the method mentioned is a time consuming task, new method is presented by Moon (2012). For the purpose of detecting objects sharply, least square method is used for region based segmentation. Here the local information is also considered by calculating the weight matrix. This segmentation technique is optimum and fast.

IMAGE SEGMENTATION

Partitioning of an image into several segments can be termed as image segmentation. Image segmentation can else be defined as partitioning of an image pixel set into several small sets of pixels based on certain similarity functions or constraints. These sets of pixels are known as super pixels. Segmentation changes the representation of an image into more meaningful manner. This makes application in computer vision and pattern recognition to analyse images in a more meaningful manner. Through segmentation a researcher locates or finds the object and boundaries of an image. A label is assigned to every pixels of an image so that pixel with the same or similar label may share common characteristics.

Segmentation results in set of contours. That is, segments that cover the complete image. The similarity constraints that are computed for the segmentation process can be color, texture or intensity. Interpolation algorithms can be used to create 3D reconstructions from the segmented images.

Image segmentation and grouping remains as a great problem in computer vision. Image segmentation is a fundamental and challenging problem in computer vision and medical image analysis. Image segmentation is typically used to locate objects and boundaries (lines, curves, etc.) in images. Image segmentation is the process of assigning a label to every pixel in an image such that pixels with the same label share certain characteristics. The result of image segmentation is a set of segments that collectively cover the entire image, or a set of contours extracted from the image. Each of the pixels in a region are similar with respect to some characteristic or computed property, such as color, intensity or texture. It is important for an image segmentation method to have the following properties:

1. Capture perceptually important groupings or regions, which often reflect global aspects of the image.
2. Be highly efficient, running in time nearly linear in the number of image pixels.

Two central issues are to provide precise characterizations of what is perceptually important, and to be able to specify what a given segmentation technique does. A precise definition of the properties of a resulting segmentation is done in order to better understand the method and to compare with different methods. Segmentation methods should run at speeds similar to edge detection or other low-level visual processing techniques (linear time and with low constant factors). That is, a segmentation technique that runs at several frames per second can be used in video processing applications.

Types of Segmentation

Segmentation methods can be broadly classified into several types. They are:

1. Image based segmentation
2. Model based segmentation
3. Hybrid based segmentation
4. Threshold based segmentation
5. Edge based segmentation
6. Theory based segmentation
7. Region based segmentation

Image-based methods perform segmentation based only on information available in the image. Image-based method include thresholding, region growing, morphological operations, active contours, level sets, live wire (LW), watershed, fuzzy connectedness and graph cuts (GCs). These methods perform well on high-quality images. However, the results are not as good when the image quality is inferior or boundary information is missing. Model based method came into importance in recent years. One advantage of these methods is that, even when some object information is missing, such gaps can be filled by drawing upon the prior information present in the model. The model-based methods employ object population shape and appearance priors such as atlases, statistical active shape modes, and statistical active appearance models (AAMs). Hybrid approaches are most useful at present. The synergy that exists between the two approaches, i.e, purely image-based and model-based strategies, is clearly emerging in the segmentation field. Hybrid methods that form a combination of two or more approaches are emerging as powerful segmentation tools, where their superior performances and robustness over each of the components are beginning to be well done.

MODEL-BASED SEGMENTATION

Active Appearance Model

An active appearance model (AAM) is a computer vision algorithm for matching a statistical model of object shape and appearance to a new image. They are built during the training phase. A set of images, together with coordinates of landmarks that appear in all of the images, is provided to the training supervisor. The model was first introduced by Edwards, Cootes and Taylor in the context of face analysis at the 3rd International Conference on Face and Gesture Recognition, 1998. Cootes, Edwards and Taylor further described the approach as a general method in computer vision at the European Conference on Computer Vision in the same year. The approach is widely used for matching and tracking faces and for medical image interpretation. The algorithm uses the difference between the current estimate of appearance and the target image to drive an optimization process. By taking advantage of the least squares techniques, it can match to new images very swiftly.

Hybrid-Based Segmentation

Hybrid approaches are most useful at present. The synergy that exists between the two approaches, that is, purely image-based and model-based strategies, is clearly emerging in the segmentation field. Hybrid methods that form a combination of two or more approaches are emerging as powerful segmentation tools, where their superior performances and robustness over each of the components are beginning to be well done.

Threshold-Based Segmentation

Threshold based segmentation method is the simplest method of segmentation. The image pixels are segmented based on the intensity level. This kind of segmentation is more applicable for images where the objects are lighter than the background. This method is based on prior knowledge of the image features. There are mainly three types of threshold based segmentation. Global Thresholding: This method is done using a proper threshold value. The threshold value will be constant for the whole image. Output of the image is based on this threshold value. Variable Thresholding: In this type of segmentation method the value of threshold can vary in a single image. Multiple Thresholding: In this kind of thresholding, the output of segmentation is based on multiple threshold values. Threshold values can be computed from image histograms.

Edge-Based Segmentation

Edge based segmentation method is based on the sudden change of intensity values in an image. In image processing, object boundaries are represented using edge. Edge based segmentation works by identifying the region of abrupt intensity change in an image . Mainly there are two types of edge based segmentation methods. Grey Histogram Technique: In this method the foreground is separated from the background based on a threshold value. Choosing the correct threshold value creates a problem. Gradient Based Method: Gradient can be defined as the first derivate of the image near the edge. Higher change in the intensity values between two regions is depicted by the high value of gradient magnitude. In order to perform multi scale image segmentation an edge based auto threshold generating method is introduced by Zhang (2010). Another method for edge detection using variance filter is introduced in Fabijanska (2011).

Theory-Based Segmentation

Theory based segmentation method uses derivatives from several fields. Several types of this kind of algorithm includes, Clustering based segmentation: In this method clusters are formed based on the similarity criteria (size, color, texture etc). Methods include k-means clustering, fuzzy clustering, hard clustering etc . Artificial Neural Network: In this method the neuron represents the pixels and segmentation is performed with the help of trained images. Methods using Wavelet Decomposition and Self Organization Map of artificial neural networks are proposed by Deng (2010).

Region-Based Segmentation

. Region based segmentation methods are similar to edge based segmentation. The advantage of region based segmentation upon edge based is that, the former is more immune to noise. In this method, the region of an image is either splitted or merged into areas based on similarity. Region Growing: the collection of pixels is grouped into a region with similar properties. Region Splitting and Merging: Here the image is further subdivided into several regions based on some pre-defined criteria. Graph cut image segmentation is a very significant technique of segmentation under region based segmentation.

Several techniques of region growing methods include techniques that combine edge and region based information using morphological watershed algorithms. In this method, initially a noise filter along with magnitude gradient is used and pre segmentation is performed through region merging. A region similarity graph is then produced and final segmentation is performed using Multi Class Normalized Cut. This technique overpowers the Spectral clustering method. As the method mentioned is a time consuming task, new method is presented by Moon (2012). For the purpose of detecting objects sharply, least square method is used for region based segmentation. Here the local information is also considered by calculating the weight matrix. This segmentation technique is optimum and fast.

Image-Based Segmentation

There are different types of image based segmentation methods. They are:

1. Livewire
2. Graph cut method

Livewire

Livewire, is a segmentation technique that allows a user to select regions of interest to be extracted quickly and accurately, using simple mouse clicks. It is based on the lowest cost path algorithm, (Edsger W. Dijkstra). Initially, convolve the image with a Sobel Filter to extract edges. Each pixel of the resulting image is a vertex of the graph and has edges going to the 4 pixels around it, as up, down, left, right. The edge costs are defined based on a cost function. The user sets the starting point clicking on an images pixel, which is known as an anchor. Then, the smallest cost path is drawn from the anchor to the pixel where the mouse is over, changing itself if the user moves the mouse. In order to choose the path, the user simply clicks the image again. User can easily see the places where the user clicked to outline the desired region of interest, that are marked with a small square. It is also easy to see that the livewire has snapped on the images borders. LW is a user-steered 2-D segmentation method in which the user provides recognition help and in which the algorithm performs optimal delineation. The main limitation of LW stems from the recognition process, where the anchor points are to be selected on the boundary by a human operator.

Graph Cut

Graph cuts can be employed to efficiently solve a wide variety of low-level computer vision problems, such as image smoothing and many other computer vision problems that can be formulated in terms of energy minimization. Such energy minimizations problems can be reduced to instances of the maximum flow problem in a graph (and thus, by the max-flow min-cut theorem, define a minimal cut of the graph). The minimum energy solution corresponds to the maximum a posteriori estimate of a solution. The term graph cuts is applied specifically to those models which employ a max-flow/min-cut optimization. GC methods have the ability to compute globally optimal solutions and can enforce piecewise smoothness. They are interactive methods, and require labelling of the source and sink seeds by a human operator.

Types of Graph Cut-Based Algorithm

The graph cut based segmentation can be mainly divided into three types. They are Speed-up based graph cut, Interactive based graph cut and Shape prior based graph cut. The speed up based graph cut method is used to improve the speed of the graph cut method through parallel computing. Earlier implementation was based on CUDA code. The best way to speed up the computational time is to reduce the number of graph nodes while reconstructing the graph. Another method used for speed up based graph cut method is clustering based graph cut. Clustering based graph cut is based on reducing the number of nodes by grouping similar pixels into a single cluster and treating a cluster as a node. Watershed based method is another important speed up based approach where, gradient images are considered and the concept of catchment basins are used by author Sulaiman (2010).

Interactive based graph cut plays a very important role in segmentation of natural images and the situations where the segmentation requires high precision. In this kind of methods the seed points are selected and then segmentation is performed based on these points. Several methods are performed using the concept of bounding box, where the centre portion of the bounding box corresponds to the object and histogram is constructed. The area outside the bounding box is considered as the background region. Certain interactive segmentation is performed by choosing both the foreground and background region together. Iterative interactive graph cut segmentation is also performed.

Shape prior based graph cut segmentation finds its importance where the image to be segmented is affected by noise, diffuse edge, obstructed objects etc. In this kind of segmentation, the shape information is included as the energy function in paper Chen (2009).

Case Study Method

Initially form a graph G = (V,E) by considering all pixels to form the set V and choose a neighborhood around each pixel to find the edges around the pixels. Generally four neighborhood or eight neighborhood is chosen. The weights of the edges are defined to be the absolute intensity differences between the pixels forming the edges.

Algorithm 1: Graph-based Image segmentation
Input : $G = (V, E)$ and $w(v_i, v_j) \, \forall \, v_i, v_j \in V$ and $v_i \neq v_j$
Step 1: Sort E into $E' = (o_1, ..., o_m)$ by non-decreasing edge weight.
Step 2: Start with segmentation S^0 where each vertex v_i is in a component by itself.
Step 3: Let $o_q = (v_i, v_j)$. Repeat step 3 for $q = 1, ..., m$ to find S^q given S^{q-1}.
Step 4: If v_i and v_j are in disjoint components of S^{q-1} then
Step 4.1: If $w(o_q)$ is lesser than $MInt(C_i, C_j)$ where $v_i \in C_i$ and $v_j \in C_j$ then
Step 4.1.1: Merge C_i and C_j .

Step 4.2: end If
Step 5: end If
Output: S^m

Graph-Based Segmentation

Let $G = (V, E)$ be an undirected graph with vertices $v \mathcal{E} V$ and edges $(v_i, v_j) \mathcal{E} E$. Edges are between two vertices always. The set that needs to be segmented is the set of vertices V. Each edge has a corresponding weight $w(v_i, v_j)$ which is a non-negative measure of the dissimilarity between neighboring elements v_i and v_j. In the case of image segmentation, the elements in V are pixels and the weight of an edge is some measure of the dissimilarity between the two pixels connected by that edge. That is dissimilarity between the edges can be measured as the difference in intensity, color, motion, depth, location or any other local attribute.

Here weights of the edges are considered to be the L2 norm between the RGB values of the pixels. The goal of image segmentation is to find a partition of the set V such that each component of the partition is a connected graph $G = (V,E')$ where $E' \subseteq E$. The driving forces of such a partition are that the elements of each component are similar to other elements belonging to the same components and yet dissimilar to elements belonging to other components. Based on our guideline that the weights measure the amount of dissimilarity between two vertices, we can that the edges between vertices of the same component will have low weights whereas edges between vertices belonging to different components will have high weights.

Pairwise Region Comparison Metric

An absolute metric would not take into account the variability of the region. This would result in either merging together separate regions with low variability between them or separating high variability regions into several components. To avoid this, a metric is proposed which adapts itself based on the variability of the region under consideration. The metric is based on measuring the dissimilarity between elements along the boundary of two components relative to the measure of dissimilarity of the elements within each component. Define internal difference to be the largest edge weight in the minimum spanning tree of the component. That is,

$$Int\left(C\right) = \max_{e \in MST\left(C,E\right)} w\left(e\right) \tag{1}$$

Where $MST(C,E)$ is the minimum spanning tree of the sub graph $G = (C,E)$. A minimum spanning tree is the sub graph which connects all vertices C and has the least sum total of weights. The differences between two components are defined to be the minimum edge weight connecting the two components. That is,

$$Dif\left(C_i, C_j\right) = \min_{v_i \in C_i, v_j \in C_j, \left(v_i, v_j\right) \in E} w\left(v_i, v_j\right) \tag{2}$$

The region comparison predicate evaluates if there is evidence for a boundary between a pair or components by checking if the difference between the components, $Dif\left(C_i, C_j\right)$, is large relative to the internal difference within at least one of the components, $Int(C_1)$ and $Int(C_2)$. A threshold function is used to control the degree to which the difference between components must be larger than minimum internal difference. If there is no edge connecting C_i and C_j, then $Dif\left(C_i, C_j\right) = 1$. While this error metric could be made more robust to outliers by using some statistical measure like median, mean or quantile, it makes the problem NP-hard. The criterion for a merge between two components is to check if the difference between the two components is lesser than the internal difference of each of the components by a threshold function. Comparison of $Dif\left(C_i, C_j\right)$ and $MInt\left(C_i, C_j\right)$ is done where,

$$MInt\left(C_1, C_2\right) = \min\left(Int\left(C_1\right) + \lambda\left(C_1\right), Int\left(C_2\right) + \lambda\left(C_2\right)\right) \tag{3}$$

If the former is lesser than the later, the components are merged; otherwise, the components are not merged and conclude that there is a strong evidence of a boundary between the two components. The threshold function λ controls the degree to which the difference between two components must be greater than their internal differences in order for there to be evidence of a boundary between them (D to be true). For small components, $Int(C)$ is not a good estimate of the local characteristics of the data. In the extreme case, when $|C| = 1, Int\left(C\right) = 0$. Therefore, threshold function is used based on the size of the component. The threshold function is defined as:

$$\lambda\left(C\right) = k \Big/ |C| \tag{4}$$

Where $|C|$ denotes the size of C, and k is some constant parameter. That is, for small components stronger evidence for a boundary is required. In practice k sets a scale of observation, in that a larger k causes a preference for larger components. k is not a minimum component size. Smaller components are allowed when there is a sufficiently large difference between neighboring components. Any non-negative function of a single component can be used for λ. For instance, it is possible to have the segmentation method prefer components of certain shapes, by defining a λ which is large for components that do not fit some desired shape and small for ones that do. This would cause the segmentation algorithm to aggressively merge components that are not of the desired shape. Such a shape preference could be as weak as preferring components that are not long and thin or as strong as preferring components that match a particular shape model.

The threshold function implies that for small components; require a strong evidence for a boundary. A large k prefers larger components and vice versa. Instead of defining the λ (C) based on some constants and cardinality of the components, it is possible to define λ (C) based on prior information to favour some desired shape.

Implementation Details

The implementation of the graphs and components is best done by the disjoint set forest with union by rank and path compression. Both these strategies, union by rank and path compression are aimed at minimizing the parsing time from any node to the root node. In a tree data structure, each node holds a reference to its parent node. In a disjoint set forest, each set is represented by the root of set's tree. A merging operation is an operation that combines the trees of two sets into one tree. The parsing time from any node to root node mainly depends upon the depth of the tree, combine the trees in such a way that the resulting tree has the minimum depth possible.

So, the tree with a smaller depth gets added under the root of the deeper tree. If both trees have equal depth, then the choice of the root node doesn't matter and can pick either one. Whenever we traverse through a node to its root node, we would pass through a certain order of nodes. All these nodes belong to the same root and hence, they could all be attached to the node for the purposes of our algorithm. This practice is called path compression.

Properties

For any (finite) graph $G = (V, E)$ there exists some segmentation S, that is neither too coarse nor too fine.

A segmentation S, is said to be too fine if there exists some pair of regions C_1, $C_2 \in S$ for which there is no evidence for a boundary between them. Segmentation is said to be too coarse when there exists a proper refinement of S that is not too fine. If regions of segmentation can be split and yield segmentation where there is evidence for a boundary between all pairs of neighbouring regions, then the initial segmentation has too few regions. In general there can be more than one segmentation that is neither too coarse nor too fine, so such segmentation is not unique. There is always some segmentation that is both not too coarse and not too fine. Consider the segmentation where all the elements are in a single component. This segmentation is not too fine, because there is only one component.

Application

Certain applications of image segmentation include:

1. Medical Imaging
2. Computer guided surgery
3. Object detection
4. Object Tracking
5. Machine vision Application
6. Automated Inspection
7. Traffic control system
8. Content based image retrieval
9. Video Surveillance

Figure 1. (a) Input image, (b) segmented image

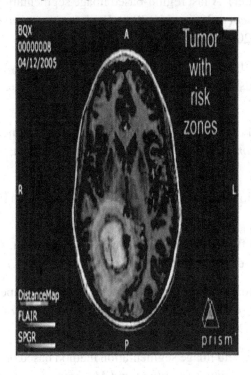 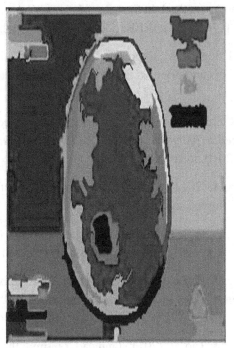

Figure 1: a. Input image   b.Segmented image

Experiments and Results

Experiments were conducted on the standard Berkeley Dataset. The experiments proved that the graph based segmentation produced highly efficient and accurate segmentation. The segmentation results were produced in much lesser time when compared with other segmentation algorithms (see Figure 1).

REFERENCES

Barbosa, D., Dietenbeck, T., Schaerer, J., D'hooge, J., Friboulet, D., & Bernard, O. (2012). B-spline explicit active surfaces: An efficient framework for real-time 3-D region-based segmentation. *Image Processing. IEEE Transactions on, 21*(1), 241–251.

Callan, C. G. Jr, Coleman, S., & Jackiw, R. (1970). A new improved energy-momentum tensor. *Annals of Physics, 59*(1), 42–73. doi:10.1016/0003-4916(70)90394-5

Chang, L. Y., & Hsu, W. H. (2009, June). Foreground segmentation for static video via multi-core and multi-modal graph cut. In *Multimedia and Expo, 2009. ICME 2009. IEEE International Conference on* (pp. 1362-1365). IEEE. doi:10.1109/ICME.2009.5202756

Chen, G., Hu, T., Guo, X., & Meng, X. (2009, October). A fast region-based image segmentation based on least square method. In *Systems, Man and Cybernetics, 2009. SMC 2009. IEEE International Conference on* (pp. 972-977). IEEE. doi:10.1109/ICSMC.2009.5346073

Chen, X., Udupa, J. K., Bagci, U., Zhuge, Y., & Yao, J. (2012). Medical image segmentation by combining graph cuts and oriented active appearance models. *Image Processing. IEEE Transactions on, 21*(4), 2035–2046.

Cui, W., & Zhang, Y. (2010, October). Graph based multispectral high resolution image segmentation. In *Multimedia Technology (ICMT), 2010 International Conference on* (pp. 1-5). IEEE. doi:10.1109/ICMULT.2010.5631004

Fabijanska, A. (2011). Variance filter for edge detection and edge-based image segmentation. In Perspective Technologies and Methods in MEMS Design.

Felzenszwalb, P. F., & Huttenlocher, D. P. (2004). Efficient graph-based image segmentation. *International Journal of Computer Vision, 59*(2), 167–181. doi:10.1023/B:VISI.0000022288.19776.77

Freedman, D., & Zhang, T. (2005, June). Interactive graph cut based segmentation with shape priors. In *Computer Vision and Pattern Recognition, 2005. CVPR 2005. IEEE Computer Society Conference on* (Vol. 1, pp. 755-762). IEEE. doi:10.1109/CVPR.2005.191

Kaihua, W., & Tao, B. (2011, January). Optimal threshold image segmentation method based on genetic algorithm in wheel set online measurement. In *Measuring Technology and Mechatronics Automation (ICMTMA), 2011 Third International Conference on* (Vol. 2, pp. 799-802). IEEE. doi:10.1109/ICMTMA.2011.483

Kang, C. C., Wang, W. J., & Kang, C. H. (2012). Image segmentation with complicated background by using seeded region growing. *AEÜ. International Journal of Electronics and Communications, 66*(9), 767–771. doi:10.1016/j.aeue.2012.01.011

Khalifa, A. R. (2010). Evaluating The Effectiveness of Region Growing And Edge Detection Segmentation Algorithms. *Journal of American Science.*

Khokher, M. R., Ghafoor, A., & Siddiqui, A. M. (2012, December). Multilevel Graph Cuts Based Image Segmentation. In *Digital Image Computing Techniques and Applications (DICTA), 2012 International Conference on* (pp. 1-8). IEEE. doi:10.1109/DICTA.2012.6411726

Lempitsky, V., Kohli, P., Rother, C., & Sharp, T. (2009, September). Image segmentation with a bounding box prior. In *Computer Vision, 2009 IEEE 12th International Conference on* (pp. 277-284). IEEE. doi:10.1109/ICCV.2009.5459262

Shi, J., & Malik, J. (2000). Normalized cuts and image segmentation. *Pattern Analysis and Machine Intelligence. IEEE Transactions on, 22*(8), 888–905.

Sulaiman, S. N., & Isa, N. A. M. (2010). Adaptive fuzzy-K-means clustering algorithm for image segmentation. *Consumer Electronics. IEEE Transactions on, 56*(4), 2661–2668.

Urquhart, R. (1982). Graph theoretical clustering based on limited neighbourhood sets. *Pattern Recognition, 15*(3), 173–187. doi:10.1016/0031-3203(82)90069-3

Vineet, V., & Narayanan, P. J. (2008, June). CUDA cuts: Fast graph cuts on the GPU. In *Computer Vision and Pattern Recognition Workshops, 2008. CVPRW'08. IEEE Computer Society Conference on* (pp. 1-8). IEEE.

Wang, H., Zhang, H., & Ray, N. (2013). Adaptive shape prior in graph cut image segmentation. *Pattern Recognition, 46*(5), 1409–1414. doi:10.1016/j.patcog.2012.11.002

Wu, X., Xu, W., Li, L., Shao, G., & Zhang, J. (2011, May). An interactive segmentation method using graph cuts for mammographic masses. In *Bioinformatics and Biomedical Engineering,(iCBBE) 2011 5th International Conference on* (pp. 1-4). IEEE. doi:10.1109/icbbe.2011.5780190

Xu, A., Wang, L., Feng, S., & Qu, Y. (2010, November). Threshold-based level set method of image segmentation. In *Intelligent Networks and Intelligent Systems (ICINIS), 2010 3rd International Conference on* (pp. 703-706). IEEE. doi:10.1109/ICINIS.2010.181

Yasmin, M., Sharif, M., Masood, S., Raza, M., & Mohsin, S. (2012). Brain image enhancement-A survey. *World Applied Sciences Journal, 17*(9), 1192–1204.

Yi, F., & Moon, I. (2012, May). Image segmentation: A survey of graph-cut methods. In *Systems and Informatics (ICSAI), 2012 International Conference on* (pp. 1936-1941). IEEE. doi:10.1109/ICSAI.2012.6223428

Yi, F., & Moon, I. (2012, May). Image segmentation: A survey of graph-cut methods. In *Systems and Informatics (ICSAI), 2012 International Conference on* (pp. 1936-1941). IEEE. doi:10.1109/ICSAI.2012.6223428

Yu, Z., Xu, M., & Gao, Z. (2011, August). Biomedical image segmentation via constrained graph cuts and pre-segmentation. In *Engineering in Medicine and Biology Society, EMBC, 2011 Annual International Conference of the IEEE* (pp. 5714-5717). IEEE.

Zahn, C. T. (1971). Graph-theoretical methods for detecting and describing gestalt clusters. *Computers. IEEE Transactions on, 100*(1), 68–86.

Zhang, L., & Deng, X. (2010, November). The research of image segmentation based on improved neural network algorithm. In *Semantics Knowledge and Grid (SKG), 2010 Sixth International Conference on* (pp. 395-397). IEEE. doi:10.1109/SKG.2010.68

KEY TERMS AND DEFINITIONS

Computer Vision: It is an area that contains procedures for obtaining, handling, examining, and understanding images and, high dimensional facts from the real world in order to produce mathematical or representational data.

Image Processing: Processes that receipts images as input and produces images as output. It performs some manipulations to improve image quality.

Object Recognition: Object recognition is concerned with decisive the identity of associate object being ascertained within the image from a collection of known labels.

Chapter 3
Feature Extraction

Anindita Das Bhattacharjee
Swami Vivekananda Institute of Science and Technology, India

ABSTRACT

Accessibility problem is relevant for audiovisual information, where enormous data has to be explored and processed. Most of the solutions for this specific type of problems point towards a regular need of extracting applicable information features for a given content domain. And feature extraction process deals with two complicated tasks first deciding and then extracting. There are certain properties expected from good features-Repeatability, Distinctiveness, Locality, Quantity, Accuracy, Efficiency, and Invariance. Different feature extraction techniques are described. The chapter concentrates of taking a survey on the topic of Feature extraction and Image formation. Here both image and video are considered to have their feature extracted. In machine learning, pattern recognition and in image processing has significant contribution. The feature extraction is one of the common mechanisms involved in these two techniques. Extracting feature initiates from an initial data set of measured data and constructs derived informative values which are non redundant in nature.

BACKGROUND

Extracting, analyzing, and understanding large scientific and non-scientific database of image available manually is very complex and tedious task for human brain. This type of knowledge discovery tasks are also contains some very decisive computational activities, hence always there is a requirement of automated activities that can be operated better than human brain by computers. But externally knowledge and experience input are provided to get improvised algorithms that can be used for any critical data analysis and extraction processes. This extraction process on image and video assists us to solve some high-level critical problems such as face and image recognition, medical and biological imaging, knowledge discovery, and so on. Also feature extraction minimizes and simplifies resource requirements, and describes large set of data accurately. Hence if we expect to achieve robust, adaptive and real time processing in multimedia application, then it is oblivious to use feature extraction mechanism. Very popular application of feature extraction involves image feature extraction with very useful mechanism to extract features are Average RGB, Color moments, Local color histogram and so on. These techniques

DOI: 10.4018/978-1-5225-0498-6.ch003

focus simply in extracting feature from test image given. There are many types of features present in an image and a video which can be exploited and extracted to understand the image and video segment. This procedure is followed either simplification of media that is images or videos or to extract only important parts of it. For instance, features of a video stream upon extracting and exploiting redundant and relatively unwanted clips of that video can be avoided to present the shorter version with only relatively necessary information of the given video. Videos are considered as sequential frames or simply sequence of images. In case of image formation real values are processed and fed into the calculations to make up and image of the representing real object. There are some specific features associated with image and video stream. The point is to extract those features and on exploiting them the properties of the image can be understood and later the image can be recreated back when needed. Videos also can be recreated if their features are extracted. Apparently extracted features of videos will be dynamic and different than images. Since computers are computationally robust it can extract feature from video and images and with that it is possible to detect objects at a significant rate of success. There are several features and their extraction procedures are available a survey of those procedure is stated below.

INTRODUCTION

Feature Extraction in Video Processing

Process of extracting features or informative characteristics are generally termed as feature extraction. In video processing these features are acquired from video frames which are usually independent of previous or future frames. Feature extraction is applicable for text, video data or any kind of multimedia data. Convenience in accessing dynamic multimedia data is the only reason for feature extraction.

Recent trend in video processing focuses on quality of video. The growth in development of high speed digital camera, video components took so much attention of users. The most promising application where video analysis is one of the significant areas is sports. Video processing has many applications areas in sports such as slow motion replay, pattern analysis, statistics collection, video archiving and so on. Sports video analysis is frequently used in tracking balls, players, referees, etc. Generally quality of video must be enhanced and improved before its processing. The two very basic problems are noise and segmentation problems in video frames and reduction of noise, with proper object segmentation is very important. The only way is video de-noising. The method of noise elimination from video signal is termed as video de-noising. Noise reduction takes place for each video frame. Video de-noising is divided into some specific categories spatial, temporal and spatio-temporal. Basically, concept of image de-noising is very popular. Linear models are used for image de-noising. Popular one is Gaussian filter. There are many types of noises exists such as Amplifier noise, Salt-and-pepper noise, Periodic noise. Depending on the type of video image noise reduction technique takes place such as Average filter, Median filter, Wiener filter, Rank order filter, Gaussian filter, Non- linear filter, Outlier filter. Linear and Non-linear filtering is used noise reduction generally. Linear filter is not effective with compared to non-linear filter as non-linear filter can effectively remove blur edges of images. Non-linear filters generally used in fuzzy techniques. To compute the performance of noise in a video, we use three types of noises. By adding up the various types of noise we try to clean the image source so as to get the extracted parameters of added noise. Filter initialization provide noise removal technique so that various noise can be applied and filtered simultaneously from video.

Machine Learning and Feature Extraction

Machine learning mechanism is based on analyzing and extracting patterns. In machine learning mechanism pattern is the only means by which data is recognized. The pattern analysis is the way-out for pattern extraction. To identify identifiable patterns, different mathematical models are used so that to diminish difference between data instances. The main difficulty exists in machine learning in its data set used; these data sets are random and uncertain in nature. Hence pattern recognition in the field of machine learning seems to be computationally complex. Generally to find out optimal properties of data many feature extraction techniques are used. Feature for an image is its differentiable properties from its immediate neighborhood. Technically, Feature extraction means a way of analyzing property of an image or a video by its current existing property like its pixel values, histogram charts etc. and categorizing them with its detected properties. Image formation uses feature extraction concept as main component, as in the real life situation image formation deals with extracting features of input. Further using those features as input and thus creating an image or image sequence. This concept is based on change of image properties along with many others such as intensity, color and texture which are indicated as basic image properties. In machine learning there exist some pre defined properties to identify good features such as repeatability, disjunctiveness, locality, quantity, accuracy, robustness and invariance.

Feature Extraction Components

There are two basic components exists for video feature extraction first is extracting features which is a good representation of the video segments, that leads to achieve good clustering. One key frame is extracted from individual shot, choosing median frame is the general practice. Color histograms with specific color spaces are also considered such as IHS, RGB, and HSV. In application along with a global color histogram, histogram for top, left, right regions of an image are also considered for extraction. Self-organizing map is used to train with vector merging concept of all partial histogram vectors which in turns used to define each shot.

The second component of feature extraction is temporal segmentation. In general video stream is automatically segmented into shots by identifying cuts. The job of temporal segmentation is done by detecting rapid changes of the distinction between colour histograms of succeeding frames with single threshold concept. Generally colours are represented in IHS space, as it is suitable for perceptual properties and provide independence between three color space components. A shot with less than 5 frames are considered to be insufficient and hence ignored. Numbers of false positives are removed by filtering and they do not have huge influence as similar shots generally assigned to same cluster.

1. GENERAL FEATURE EXTRACTION TECHNIQUES

Feature extraction means a way of analyzing property of an image or a video by its current existing property like its pixel values, histogram charts etc. and categorizing them with its detected properties. Image formation means taking the situation of a real life input and extracting its features and using those features as input and thus creating an image or image sequence. These techniques are used in various systems and have contributed a great deal in object recognition task. Future study and research work will signify it's performance a detailed analysis of which is provided here. There are various feature extraction techniques which can be listed as follows:

1.1. Grid Color Moment

One of the most commonly used features in low level feature extraction includes color feature. Color contributes more information; also color feature illustrates higher stability and it is more insensitive towards image rotation and zooming. In this technique following steps are followed to calculate the feature vector:

1.   Converting the image from RGB to HSV Color space
2.   Dividing the image equivalently into 3 X 3 blocks.
Calculating mean color for each of the blocks.

$$(x)' = 1/N \sum_{i=1}^{N} \binom{n}{k} x_i \tag{1}$$

Where N signifies the number of pixels in a block, xi_d epicts the pixel intensity in H/S/V channels.

4.   Calculating its variance

$$\sigma^2 = 1/N \sum_{i=1}^{N} \binom{n}{k}(x_i - x')^2 \tag{2}$$

Each block contains 3+3+3=9 features, and thus the entire image will have 9x9=81 features.

1.2. Canny Edge Detection

This is done to significantly reduce the amount of data in the images without destroying the structural properties. The steps of this algorithm are:

Step 1: Smoothing- Image blurring for noise elimination
Step 2: Finding gradients- Edges are marked for high magnitude gradients
Step 3: Non maximum suppression: A Local maximum is identified by edges.
Step 4: Double thresholding: Determines the potential edges.
Step 5: Edge tracking by hysteresis- Resolution of the final edges.

1.3. Gabor Wavelet Transform

Gabor function comprises of exponential localized around x = 0 by the cover with a Gaussian window shape (Barbu, Ciobanu & Costin, 2002) specifically in case 1D. Wavelets are basically an element belongs to a family of mutually similar Gabor functions. This function is called when they are created by dilation and it is shifted from one elementary Gabor function. To obtain a Gabor filter bank with L orientations and S scales, the Gabor function is rotated and dilated according to the following equation:

$$g_{a,\xi} = \sqrt{\alpha/\pi} e^{-\alpha x^2} e^{-i\xi x} \tag{3}$$

For $\alpha \in R+ \xi$, $x \in R$, where $\alpha = (2\sigma 2)-1$, σ signifies variance and ξ is a frequency.
Feature Extraction and Image formation have the following subtopics.

2. MOTION ESTIMATION

This technique focuses mainly in motion vector determination which defines the transformation of one 2D image to another image by considering contiguous frames in a video sequence. As the motion has three dimensions, hence it is one of the most ill-posed problems. We know images are generated from 3dimensional or 3D projection of the scene onto a 2dimension or 2D plane. The motion vectors which are related to the whole image known to be global motion estimation or definite parts. For instance rectangular blocks, patches of arbitrary shaped and so on. Many translational models are used for representing the motion vectors. These models approximates the motion corresponds to the real video camera. It uses rotation and translation in all three magnitudes and zooms. The temporal prediction mechanism of MPEG video is one of the areas where motion estimation is widely used. The essential concept of motion estimation is consecutive video frames will be similar and changes occurs by objects moving inside frames.

In the minor case of zero motion among frames (and no other dissimilarities originated by noise, and so on.), for the encoder it is simple to predict the current frame as a duplicate of the prediction frame proficiently. After this step, the information required is to send out to the decoder that becomes the syntactic overhead necessary to renovate the picture. This reconstruction is done from the original reference frame. When motion exists in the images, the situation becomes difficult (Rawat, & Singhai 2013; Ling-Yu Duan, & Jinqiao Wang 2008). Motion estimation solves this difficulty by comprehensive 2D spatial search ; it is executed for each luminance macro block. Motion estimation cannot be applied directly to chrominance in MPEG video, since motion in case of color can be effectively correspond to the same motion information as the luminance (an assumption). MPEG does not define the search performance. It depends on the system designer who can select the implementation in one of many probable ways.

In general, we know that a full, exhaustive search over an extensive 2D area offers the best matching results, but this performance requires tremendous computational cost to the encoder, because motion estimation is the most computationally expensive part of the video encoder. Generally, some low rated encoders might prefer to choose a limit for the pixel search range, or use alternative methods like telescopic searches, typically compromising the video quality.

2.1. Motion Estimation Techniques

Video Stabilization is used to enhance the quality of the input video. This quality improvement is done by eliminating the unwanted camera motions.

. Basic approaches for hand held mobile videos stabilization are either very complex or are not suitable for slow and smooth videos. So it is necessary to remove the undesired motion among the frames of the hand held mobile video. This research is done to analyze and estimate the various 2D and 3D motion models, to achieve stabilization and smoothening techniques in motion estimation. The direct pixel and feature based methods of estimating error between frames is done to get the differential motion estimation.

The overall video quality is affected mainly by slow and unwanted motions. This type of undesired component exists in hand held mobile cameras. The main aim here to achieve stabilization for that reason estimating and eliminating unwanted motions encountered between successive frames are necessary.

Video stabilization methods are classified as mechanical, optical and image post processing stabilization.

The mechanical image stabilization which is based on vibration feedback through sensors was developed in the early stage of camcorders. The basic principle is not to stabilize the image rather the entire camera by using Gyro that consists of gyroscope which is a motion sensor with two perpendicular spinning wheels and a battery pack. To move the wheels a signal is sent to the motors in order to sustain the stability when there is any movement. A tuning fork structure and a vibration amplitude feedback control were employed to improve vibration gyro sensors. Being heavy and consuming more power doesn't make it suitable for hand held mobile cameras.

After this technique, the optical image stabilization technique was developed and is based on a moveable lens assembly that variably adjusts the path of the light while travelling through the lens system. To sense the angle and speed of movement to counteract the image vibration, two vibration detecting sensors are used. Because in both horizontal and vertical directions image vibration occurs. But due its high cost and lack of compactness is not suitable for mobile phone camera.

The image post processing technique is basically digital stabilization method which has three stages as camera motion estimation, motion smoothening and image wrapping. These three stages are modified for different camera system under different environment for stabilizing captured videos. A modified video stabilization algorithm is proposed . This technique uses hierarchical differential global motion estimation along with Taylor series expansion for hand held camera videos.

2.1.1. Algorithms

(According to the research of D. Jagiwala, & Prof. Sah, 2012) Proficient reduction in temporal redundancy helps to achieve high performance of video compression. The increased performance is provided by Block matching algorithm. This algorithm is used for motion estimation technique for video compression standards. Generally, spatial redundancy implies redundancy between pixels; redundancy between frames implies temporal redundancy. Temporal redundancy basically a kind of Inter-frame redundancy. It is achieved by techniques of motion estimation (Rawat, 2013; Ling-Yu Duan, & Wang 2008) Pixel based methods (direct) and feature based methods (indirect) are the techniques for finding out motion vectors. Basically there is a block of N x N pixels from the candidate frame at position (r, s) and a search window of range $\pm w$ in both end direction. Foe each $(2p+1)2$ search positions the candidate block is compared with a block of N x N pixels and the motion vector only after $(2p+1)2$ search spaces are exhausted.

2.1.1.1. Indirect Methods

It uses the concept of corner detection and matches equivalent features among frames, using statistical function which is applied over a local or global area. This method is also termed as indirect parametric estimation technique. In the first phase of this approach indirectly calculates motion parameters from a dense motion field. This method does not prefer to compute parameters from pixel of images. Hence two distinct steps are used: first a dense motion field estimation and then fitting of parametric motion model on the obtained vectors of motion i.e. motion vectors. LMS technique i.e. Least Mean Square technique is considered for model filtering.

The main loophole of this approach lies in its performance estimation as it is completely dependent on correctness of the initial dense motion field. Technically, LMS concept is very perceptive to erroneous samples that may adversely impact estimating the model parameters.

2.1.1.2. Direct Methods

This method is termed as direct parametric method for motion estimation. This concept uses optical flow equation and as a equation it uses gradient based formulation. Always in this method an additional constraint is essential i.e. Horn-Schunck constraint, locally termed as smoothness constraint or else local uniformity constraint termed as Lucas-Kanade constraints.

2.1.1.2.1. Block Matching Algorithm

This algorithm mainly involves itself in locating matching macro blocks in a succession of digital video frames intended for motion estimation. Patterns correspond to objects and background within a frame of video sequence. This is one of the beliefs considered in motion estimation; which moves within the frame in order to form corresponding objects in the succeeding frame. This concept is used to determine temporal redundancy in the video sequence; it increases the effectiveness of inter-frame video compression by demonstrating the macro block contents. It is done by reference to the contents of a known macro block; that block must be minimally different.

2.1.1.2.2. Optical Flow

Pattern of apparent motion of objects, surfaces, and edges in a visual scene between an observer (an eye or a camera) and the scene, is caused by the relative motion. For a 2D+t dimensional case (3D or n-D cases are similar) a pixel at location (x, y, t) with intensity $I(x, y, t)$ moved by $\Delta x, \Delta y$ and Δt between the two image frames, and the following brightness constancy constraint can be given:

$$I(x, y, t) = I(x + \Delta x, y + \Delta y, t + \Delta t) \tag{4}$$

In this study the motion between two sequential frames are depicted as, f(x, y, t) and f(x, y, t −1) is modeled with a 6-parameter affine transform. Single affine transformation is used to find motion vectors between two images can be described by a as given by the following equation, where m_1, m_2, m_3, m_4 presents the 2 × 2 affine rotation matrix A, and m_5 and m_6 the translation vector.

$$f(x, y, t) = f(m_1 x + m_2 y + m_5, m_3 x + m_4 y + m_6, t - 1) \tag{5}$$

Where $A = \begin{pmatrix} m_1 & m_2 \\ m_3 & m_4 \end{pmatrix}$ and $\bar{\bar{T}} = \begin{pmatrix} m_5 \\ m_6 \end{pmatrix}$

For estimating the affine parameters, we define the following quadratic error function to be minimized

$$E(m) = \sum_{x,y \in \Omega} [f(x, y, t) - f(m_1 x + m_2 y + m_5, m_3 x + m_4 y + m_6, t - 1)]^2 \tag{6}$$

Where Ω indicates a user specific region of interest here it is the entire frame.

Apart from these two estimation scheme most recently robust estimation scheme is used. This technique is mainly invented in order to remove the outlier's impact. Outliers are basically samples that clearly deviate from the prevailing tendencies. Three classes of estimators are generally used: M-estimator which is simplification of maximum likelihood. Another one is L-estimator which is generally linear combination of order statistics. And finally R-estimator is based on rank test.

2.2. Global Motion Estimation

(Duan, & Wang 2008 states) Efficient methods to estimate global motion find applications in diverse fields. For example, in remote sensing and virtual reality, it is often necessary to build large images from partial views, i.e., to register, or align, the input images. The key step for the success of these tasks is the estimation of the global motion between the images.

2.2.1. Camera Motion Model

The eight-parameter perspective motion model is defined as:

$$x_i^{'} = (a_0 + a_2 x_i + a_3 y_i) / (a_6 x_i + a_7 y_i + 1) \tag{7}$$

$$y_i^{'} = (a_1 + a_4 x_i + a_5 y_i) / (a_6 x_i + a_7 y_i + 1) \tag{8}$$

Where $a_0, \ldots, a_7$ are known as the motion parameters, (x_i, y_i) are the spatial coordinates of the ith pixel in the current frame. $(x_i`, y_i`)$ represents coordinates of the corresponding pixel in the preceding frame. From this model many motion models can be derived.

2.2.2. Initial Estimation and Robust Estimation

An extremum can be either global or local in terms of minimization and maximization functions. A very general problem is finding a global extremum. Estimating the initial motion modal is essential in order to in select an appropriate start point to initiate the iteration procedure.

To accomplish block-based searching here a three-step search (TSS) algorithm [6] is utilized.. The search range is set to ±4, ±2, and ±1 in the first, second, and third step. TSS is popular for its design simplicity and also for its robustness and near optimal performance. To further improve robustness and efficiency, a hierarchical scheme is implemented. The estimated motion parameters at a given level are projected onto the level of higher resolution and they further considered as an initial value for computation. To expand robustness against outliers M-estimator is applied.

Tukey's bi-weight function is chosen as the weighting function:

$$\varnothing(z) = \begin{cases} z(1 - z^2 / C^2)^2, \bmod z < C \\ 0, \bmod z > C \end{cases} \tag{9}$$

Weights are greater for more deviant points. (Duan & Wang, 2008) The following block diagram will show the overview of the system concepts (see Figure 1).

Figure 1. System overview

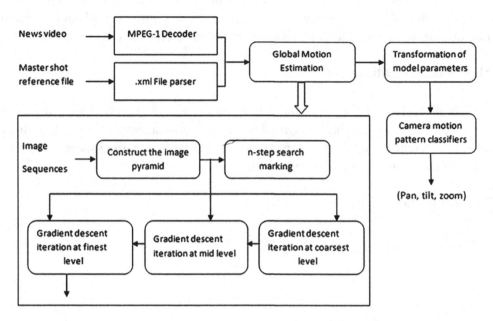

2.3. Applications

Motion estimation finds its maximum use in video coding. In order to synthesize the transformation to the next image to an image, the application of the motion vectors are popular. It is termed as motion compensation. Motion estimation and compensation are most significant parts of video compression; they are considered to be a path of developing temporal redundancy. Block-based motion estimation along with compensation such as the MPEG series includes the most recent HEVC which are commonly used by approximately every video coding standard.

3. SHOT

3.1. Shot is Termed as Temporal Segmentation Tool

Generally, a film or video will be segmented into disjoint segments of story unit sequence which are consequently segmented into successive shots. These story units are termed as shots which are a component of motion picture created in theatre. It is a job of any motion picture specialist to segments into hierarchy of partitions. Any scene which is continuous in nature and generally it is temporal and spatially cohesive component in nature. On the other direction motion cameras are the originators of shots which are longest continuous sequence. A single camera take will produce a shot for that reason camera image is uninterrupted. Computing appropriate continuity and similarity metric is important to perceive change in shot between two adjacent frames.

The most important mission for video analysis is to specify a unit set, within which the video temporal sequence may be organized. Generally, our prime focus is a different video transition which helps in video content identification. Video content identification aims mainly on the definition of the semantics of the video language. In this identification process usually two assumption are made i.e. the video segments must be spatially and temporally continuous and therefore boundary image must undergo major content alteration. This alteration depends on the type of the transition and can be measured. This entire technique reduces search space appropriate of different quantification metric of the original problem, with great probability, the transition temporal locations.

Segmentation is a separation process where a digital image is separated into sections of pixels. The main motive of segmentation is straightforward first is easy modification of image, then presenting image into some meaningful component which may help in easy examination and extraction. More precisely segmentation helps in locating objects, images along with their boundaries made up of lines, curves. Other promising sectors where Segmentation is used are object recognition, occlusion boundary evaluation within action or stereo systems, image compression, image editing, or image database look-up.

One of the important components of video processing is temporal segmentation which is known as shot boundary detection. Most important domain for Shot boundary detection is used for SPORTS VIDEO segmentation. As For user Video player made by Shot boundary detection gives provision to forward and rewind one shot at a time. Or else shot boundary detection is useful in browsing video contents by its key frame representation.

3.2. Reason for Shot Detection

In the present days there are huge progresses in the field of multimedia and web technology as different video data is available in various formats. The main focus of this advanced era is to achieve efficient browsing, searching and retrieval these enormous video data resources are the prime requirement. Also database is required as a repository of these huge video data resources. We can use any traditional method to support the work of video retrieval and indexing but unfortunately all traditional method lacks in efficiency and they are very time consuming. The main reason for time consuming behavior as these method uses intervention of human being for manually explaining the videos with text keyword. Hence there is a need of automatic indexing and retrieval technique which are directly based on video content. The main aim is to provide information related to video without overriding the time, also speed will be achieved. One of the most important pioneer techniques of this type of video content retrieval is shot boundary detection. This mechanism helps in segmenting a video by identifying boundaries between camera shots. A shot boundary mainly divides two successive shots when one shot transforms to another shots. This concept implies that if *n* number of shots are unavailable from different cameras with different Video shot boundary detection, it has different applications in diverse domains like video indexing, video compression, video access and others.

3.3. Shot Classification and Detection

If we classify shot transition then two major classes are achieved such as abrupt transition which generally occur in a single frame, and gradual transitions. The types fade, dissolve and wipe are classified types of gradual transition. The structure of shot transition is depicted in the above diagram. The most important reason for shot boundary analysis is abrupt (cut) and gradual (fades, dissolve, wipes) shots taken by camera. For that reason shot boundary detection is also termed as "cut detection". *Cut* is the classic quick change case, where one frame belongs to the diminishing shot and the next one to the appearing shot. A cut is an immediate transition from one scene to the subsequent one. There are no

Figure 2. Shot transition diagram

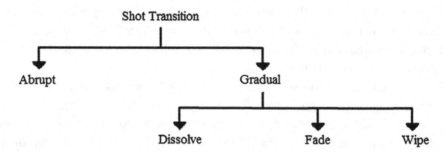

transitional frames between two shots. Hence classification of shot boundary analysis is based on these two reasons: abrupt transition and gradual transition (see Figure 2).

In order to define a video in terms of its content it needs partition to achieve its smallest unit known as shot (Patel, Shah, & Panchal, 2013). Video sequence is defined by the following diagram (see Figure 3). This diagram shows

Now for video segmentation to achieve shots, shot boundary is essential. It is a set of images (frames) taken from a single camera. A shot boundary separates two consecutive shots when one shot changes to another shot.

Boundary detection i.e. shot transition is performed to contrast the corresponding pixels between two consecutive frames. Other is using color histogram of two frames.

Regarding various methods, abrupt transition is a change of shot immediately to the subsequent frame and gradual transition is the change of shot gradually over multiple frames. Abrupt transition is swift transition from one shot to the succeeding shot. Gradual transition arises over multiple frames, which is produced through requisition of more detailed editing results involving numerous frames. Gradual transition can be further classified into fade out/in (FOI) transition; dissolve transition, wipe transformation, and others transformation, as per the characteristics of the different editing effects. They are required for further video analysis such as. Person tracking, identification and high level feature detection.

3.4. Shot Boundary Extraction

According to Patel, Shah, and Panchal, (2013) In general video segmentation requires shots which are a segmented part of video; hence shot boundary identification is needed. It is a set of images (frames) taken from a single camera. A shot boundary separates two consecutive shots when one shot changes to another shot. Boundary detection i.e. shot transition is performed to compare the corresponding pixels between two consecutive frames. Other is using color histogram of two frames.

Generally basic three pioneer steps are involved in shot boundary detection such as: Image segmentation, attention model, and matching the difference.

Figure 3. Video classification

The last technique is very popular and it is achieved by many types of histogram matching. Histograms are a measure of discontinuity, and shot boundary detection is done by calculating the difference of color histogram between frames. The attention model focuses on neurobiological power i.e. from visual viewpoint, contents are ranked according to their importance and based on the thought, one can assume pixel's different position as different contributor of shot boundary detection. Pixel resides on the edge has more importance than other pixel orientation. To distinguish shots along with shot boundary pixel-wise difference with adaptive threshold and color histogram are the only way out.

Regarding various methods, abrupt transition is a change of shot immediately to the subsequent frame and gradual transition is the change of shot gradually over multiple frames.

3.4.1 Colour Histogram-Based Approach

Shots are basically, the image taken by the camera, it is easy to understand if it is said this way, say a video is being recorded and a particular scene is under focus and the scene needs to be changed, now those scenes before it was changed can be called shot altogether. While processing a multimedia detecting of these sots are very important and for that it is important to detect shot boundary that is to separate shots from one from another. Now there are generally two types of change of shots one way where the shot changes abruptly that is at a sudden and the other is where a shot changes gradually including more visual effects. Gradual transformations use more frames to transform from one shot to another. Now there are several classifications of gradual change of these shots- cut transition, fade transition, dissolve transition, wipe transition. Cut transition is almost like abrupt transition where frame F_k belongs to one transition and frame F_{k+1} belongs to immediately other frame when the next shot is detected. This fade transition makes the transition looks gradual, when the shot changes, from the last frame of first shot of consideration it takes multiple monochromatic frames to enter into the next frame of the next shot. Description of dissolve transition sounds familiar but instead of adding multiple monochromatic frames between two frames of two different shots, here as one shot gradually disappears the second shot gradually appears, that is they overlap each other for a few frames. Wipe transition technique includes a set of shots appearing and disappearing at the same time that is one shot enters the scene while the other one leaves. Now the algorithms to work on a video it needs to extracts features from a range of frames called region of interest. Some particular features are selected to process and conclude to indicate probable shot boundary detection. These features include:

1. **Color:** It is the simplest feature as average grayscale color can be chosen for this region of interest.
2. **Color Histogram:** Robust feature while detecting shot boundaries. This is quite a robust one because it is easy to compute, and it remains insensitive to transitional, camera movement and zooms in zoom out motions.
3. **Image Edge:** Image edge is a good choice to include it in region of information as image edge predicts shot boundaries. The main advantage of image edge feature is that it is invulnerable to illumination changes and a camera motion as well as it is related to human understanding of a scene. But the main disadvantage of this feature is computational cost and it is sensitive to noise.
4. **Motion:** It is the most unused but still is considered as a feature of the video. If motion is kept under study a sudden change in a continuous flow of motion may imply a shot transition. But in a single shot itself the motion may be discontinuous which can lead to a false conclusion to have a shot transition.

Along with the above mentioned features there is another feature type called spatial feature domain which is also important while considering shot detection. This feature determines the appropriate size of the region of interest which could be suitable. A small region will reduce shot detection and a large region may mislead to missed transition between similar shots. Some possible spatial feature domain can be as follows:

1. **Single Pixel:** Some algorithms tend to derive features for each pixels. These features can be any of the above mentioned features but this results in large feature set and it becomes sensitive to motion.
2. **Rectangular Block:** Here each frame is divided or segmented into equal sized blocks and a set of features are extracted from each of the blocks. With this method it becomes invulnerable to camera motion and discriminate for shot boundary detection.
3. **Arbitrary Shaped Region:** Here feature extraction can also be performed to an arbitrary shaped region derived by spatial segmentation algorithm. This way as the area has been determined by the algorithm features can be extracted from homogenous region which leads to better detection of temporal discontinuity. The main disadvantage is the computation is costly and instability in region.
4. **Whole Frame:** The algorithm is very robust which can extract features from the whole frame as it can easily deal with motion within a shot but falls into problem if it has to detect two similar shots.

In order to evaluate discontinuity between frames for the selected frames correct similarity measures are necessary to be taken. One similarity measure is defined as

$$D_{Ln}(i,j) = \sqrt[n]{\left(\sum_{k=1}^{K}|F_i(K)-F_j(k)|^n\right)} \tag{10}$$

The above example is of the difference between histogram and this is one way to measure the similarity between the frames.

Again there is another way to measure similarity and it is also with histograms, called chi square (χ^2). The measure is as follows

$$D_{\chi}^{2}(i,j) = \sum_{k=1}^{K}((F_i(K)-F_j(k))^2 / F_i(K) \tag{11}$$

Another significant approach for shot boundary detection is the temporal window which is performed to perform shot change detection. The temporal window must represent a suitable amount of video activity to perfectly distinguish between two shots whether they are similar or not. The temporal domain window metric includes as

1. **Two Frames:** The simplest way to detect discontinuity between two frames is to look for the high value of the discontinuity metric between them. But this method is not as strong as it sounds to be but it fails when there is considerable variation in activity in the video. Thus it fails to distinguish between inter shot transformation and changes within a shot. Also there can be brief discontinuity in the video like a flash which is actually not a shot transition but can be falsely indicated as a change in shot that is a gradual transition.

2. **N-Frame Window:** The above problem can be avoided and discontinuity can be detected if features of all the frames are extracted within a suitable temporal window which eventually points towards the discontinuity.

3. **Interval from the Last Shot Change:** This method proposes that to detect a shot change it needs to compute some statistical data from the last shot change to current frame and it is also needed to check whether the next frame is also following the same statistical computation of data. But this method is not very much suitable as there is always some discontinuity, constantly changing behavior within a single shot. For this a shot transition may be declared by this method following the statistical data but where actually there is no shot transition but a single frame itself.

Based on the above discussions two methods are chosen to compute shot detection. One follows a measuring expression of the similarity and dissimilarity between two adjacent frames extracting appropriate features discussed above from the region of interest, and the other follows classifying the frames whether there is a a shot change or whether it has not by computing a robust measure and comparing between the frames of interest.

Two algorithms can be introduced to detect the shots Pixel-wise Difference with Adaptive Thresholding and Color Histogram Difference.

3.4.2. In Pixel-Wise Difference

With Adaptive Thresholding technique the difference in intensity or color values of the corresponding pixels are of two consecutive frames are evaluated. Then the difference is compared with a threshold.

$$D(i)= 1/(X*Y)\sum_{x=1}^{X}\sum_{y=1}^{Y} |f_{i+1}(x,y)-f_i(x,y) \tag{12}$$

Where x= frame width and y= frame height and $f_i(x,y)$ represents intensity value at the pixel (x,y). Calculation of mean μ and standard deviation σ of the feature vector is as follows $\mu=1/(N-1)\sum_{i=1}^{N-1}D(I,i+1)$ and $\sigma=\sqrt{(1/(N-1)\sum_{i=1}^{N-1}[D(I,i+1)- \mu]^2)}$. $T_{cut}= \mu + k \sigma$. Where k is pre-specified constant and N is the number of frames in video sequence. If $D(i) > T_{cut}$ then i^{th} frame is declared to be cut boundary. The algorithm is only used to detect any abrupt changes in the video shots.

3.4.3. Histogram

To characterize any frame of any region we need to use the histogram mechanism. This technique calculates the average gray scale illumination for the specific region. Basically color histogram technique is most popular one. The reason of huge popularity lies in good shot analysis feature. If we use color histogram for shot analysis we get cost effective, and ease in computation. But this mechanism is insensitive in camera zooming and motion, camera rotation, translation. In Color Histogram Difference method the procedure is based on the calculations of detecting difference between color histograms between frames as a measure of change.

$$d_{RGB}(x,y)=\sum_{j=1}^{M}|h_x(i)-h_y(i)| \tag{13}$$

Where, h_x is the color histogram of image X which contains M different bins. Now the shot boundary detection method is based on the difference between color histograms of frames which belong to a video sequence. The difference is computed as

$$\text{HistDiff}[i]=)=\sum_{j=1}{}^{M}|\,h_i(i)\text{-}h_{i\text{-}1}(j)|. \tag{14}$$

Where h_i the color histogram with M is bins of frame I corresponding to the video sequence.

To detect abrupt cut boundary detection the difference in color histogram method is calculated and then the threshold is calculated. Then the difference is compared with the threshold value if the difference is greater, then it is called to achieve the shot boundary. But sometimes it gives false alarm failing to give accurate result that is it indicates an abrupt cut has been detected where the cut hasn't occurred yet. For this reason second order derivative method is used to detect the correct result that is to detect the correct cut. Now it may fail due to camera motion, illumination changes so that the difference of histograms exceeds the threshold value giving false result. So the second order derivative method is defined as

$$\text{HD2}=d(x_{k+1},x_{k+2})\text{-}d(x_k,x_{k+1}). \tag{15}$$

Where HD2 is the second order derivative of the color histogram difference. Now this second order derivative is compared with the threshold to detect the cut. Now at gradual boundary detection there either there can be multiple monochromatic frames between last frame of first shot and the first frame of next shot or two shots can overlap each other or as one arrives the previous shot disappears, so no clear boundary exists between them. To detect boundaries the gradual changes are divided into two classes one which gradually but simultaneously affect every pixel of the image and those that abruptly affect the evolving pixels with the subset changing in each frame. One of the most popular method is again comparing the histograms of the consecutive frames. It is assumed that consecutive frames will have same background and the objects in the frames move very little then the difference of their histograms will show negligible or very little change. The difference is calculated as

$$D(i,i+1)=\sum_{j=1}{}^{n}|H_i(j)\text{-}H_{i+1}(j)| \tag{16}$$

Where $H_i(j)$ is the jth element of the histogram of the ith frame and n is the number of bins. Fade detection falls under the category of gradual boundary detection technique. The only important problem with fade detection is recognition of monochrome frame. Because there must be one monochrome frame exists in FOI transition. But monochrome rarely appears elsewhere. One leading characteristic of monochrome frame is its low standard deviation of pixel intensities. Fade detection process can be defined by the following diagram (see Figure 4).

The algorithm of fading detection is as follows

Step 1: Input video is chosen.
Step 2: Calculation of mean of pixel intensity in a frame is calculated.
Step 3: Calculation of standard deviation of pixel intensity in a frame is performed.
Step 4: The threshold value is also calculated.
Step 5: If the standard deviation value is less than the threshold value then indicate that there is either cut or gradual cut, go to step 7.

Figure 4. Fade detection process

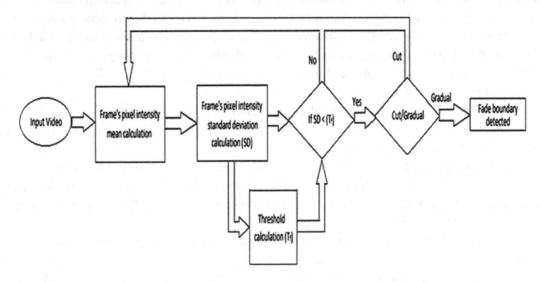

Step 6: If standard deviation value is not less than the threshold value then go to step 2.

Step 7: Decide whether it is a cut or gradual cut.

Step 8: If it is a cut go to step 2.

Step 9: If it is gradual cut then detect the frame after which the gradual cut has been detected and declare a gradual cut has been detected, thus fade boundary is detected.

The threshold value has a calculation with standard deviation of all frames and the calculation is as: T_f = (Average of standard deviation X scaling factor)/100

The scaling factor varies according to the video. If the standard deviation of any video falls below the threshold value the frame is declared as monochromatic and it will be processed for fading detection.

(Fa-Xin Yu, Zhe-Ming Lu, & Yue-Nan Li, 2011 states that)Dissolve detection also falls under the category of gradual cut detection technique and this detection method uses twin comparison method. The algorithm can be narrated as below

Step 1: In this step the probable cuts are detected using the higher T_{cut}.

Step 2: Potential starting frame F_s of gradual transition is detected using the lower threshold value T_l.

Step 3: Then the subsequent frame is compared with the frame F_s.

Step 4: The end of transition is detected through a frame if

    a.   The difference between successive frame falls below T_l while the accumulated difference increases over T_{th}.

    b.   If consecutive difference falls below the T_l and cumulative difference reaches T_h.

3.5. Hard Cut Detection

Shot transitions where abrupt transitions between adjacent frames take place are called hard cuts (Pardo, 2005). For this we need to understand shot boundary first. There are several existing methods to detect shot boundary- pixel, histogram, block matching, object segmentation and feature tracking based methods. Frame difference by pixel method can be detected in several color space. Its drawback is that pixels are sensitive to camera, object motion and noise. Filtering is applied before computation to filter out noise. Now in pixel based method two way differences can be calculated – distance based method and threshold based method. The former one computes a distance between frames called difference and in later case number of pixel difference above a given threshold. It is not very reliable so it is used to declare probable shot boundary.

In histogram based method, histograms of a pair of frames using a suitable histogram distance. Histogram based method is not vulnerable to camera and object motion. The limitation is different shot can have similar histograms so that the method will be

In block matching algorithm each frame is divided to blocks and then they are matched with a given set of feature blocks. The best match for each block in the source frame is found in the destination frame and similarities of these blocks are used as an indicator for shot boundary. These methods rely on a set of thresholds whether there is a shot boundary.

Now detection of hard cuts using only inter frame difference is quite simpler than previous ones. The key idea is to define a meaningful event as large deviation from the expected background process. Here a hard cut will be defined if the inter frame differences have little probability to be produced by a given mode of inter frame differences of non-cut frames.

In the first step of the algorithm computation of hard cut probability or meaningfulness is performed. I second step, an adaptive threshold technique that uses the information of the video sequence to find the hard cuts.

3.6. Dissolve Detection

According to the research of Lonescu, Vertan, and Lambert, 2011) A dissolve is the gradual transformation at pixel intensity level of a certain image into another. Several approaches to detect dissolve in a video sequence include pixel intensity based, feature based, transformation based and other approaches. Image differences approach inspired but cut detection method uses a twin threshold between intensities of two consecutive frames. Here accumulation of gradual transition should be above threshold and for consecutive frames the accumulation should be below second threshold.

In mathematical approach mean and variance of pixel intensities, show linear and quadratic behaviors respectively. Intensity based dissolve detection method is proposed in which it exploits pixel intensity in terms of amount of fading out and fading in pixels. During a dissolve transition it should be high.

The localization of the dissolve is carried out within the discontinuity function. Here since twin threshold dissolve detection is used, it reduces false detection and also to retrieve dissolve caught up in other visual effect and scene movements. The intensity information provided with the luminance component Y of the YCbCr color space is used. According to the authors FoP_k number of fading out, FIP_k number of fading in pixels. A normalized visual discontinuity function is determined by taking the mean of the two parameters thus: $FP_k=(FOP_k+FIP)/H.W.$ If in FP_k for current frame is greater than first threshold and this value is local maximum then a dissolve is found. If FP_k for image I_k is greater than second threshold but still beneath 1st threshold then the image is considered to be potential dissolve middle frame.

Fa-Xin Yu, Zhe-Ming Lu, & Yue-Nan Li, 2011 provides where we state that) A concept of dissolve is familiar with fade. The only difference is movement between a shot and solid color, i.e. it moves between two images. A dissolve occurs when the images of the first shot become dimmer and while the second shot get brighter, frames showing the transition as two images superimposed with each other.

The twin comparison shot detection scheme is very popular method to identify both abrupt and global transition. However, all kind of shot transitions cannot be detected with fixed thresholds. Proposed method here detects dissolves on the basis of two new characteristic parameters. One is that it can distinguish between gradual transition and fast object motion and two; it can omit the frames with growing brightness with subsequent cuts that are often incorrectly detected as gradual transition in general linear method. This method somewhat relies on histogram based dissolve detection method despite the fact frames from different shots may have same histograms. Now considering in a single shot consecutive frames have analogous histograms. Therefore histograms for dissolve candidate selection are given by the following:

$$HD_i = \sum_{j=1}^{J} | H_i(j) - H_{i-1}(j)| \quad i>0 \tag{17}$$

$H_i(j)$ histogram value of the jth bin for i^{th} frame. J is number of histogram bins. Here two threshold cut offs are used, the higher one for hard cut detection and the lower one for lower cut detection. When HD_i is larger than lower threshold but smaller than higher threshold it can be said that i^{th} frame is a potential start of a gradual transition and this frame is compared with subsequent frames following

$$HD'_k = \sum_{j=1}^{J} |H_k(j) - H_{start}(j)| \quad k \geq 0 \tag{18}$$

Here $H_{start}(j)$ denotes the jth bin histogram value of potential start of gradual transition.

End is declared when value HD_k is lower than threshold, while HD'_k exceeds the higher one. If HD_k value falls below lower threshold and HD'_k value is greater than higher threshold then drop the start point and the search for other transitions is executed.

3.7. Recent Algorithm on Shot Boundary Detection Using Neural Network

In recent days shot boundary detection on DC extraction technique is popular in the research field. The objective of this algorithm is straightforward that is to analyze input files such as MPEG, to detect shot boundaries efficiently. For that reason this algorithm attempts to identify shot boundaries directly from compressed data in order to avoid decoding the video file. The two basic approaches are used in this technique to accomplish efficiency: first DC sequence is generated from compressed data. And in the next stage the sequence generated in previous stage is used for training a feed forward neural network that is used afterwards in its recall phase for shot boundary detection.

3.7.1. Algorithm

The first stage of this algorithm focuses on DC sequence extraction from MPEG files. This extracted DC sequence is further used as an input in the NNM. In general for MPEG file encoding, original video file of each frame is divided in 8X8 blocks and DCT transformation is applied on individual blocks. The focus of the DC sequence is proposed by Shen and Delp & Yeo and Liu (1995). The extraction of the DC frame from an I frame is minor and can be considered for each block as:

DCI=1/8 Decoded ;

Where: *DCI:* Known as derived DC for a specific block. *DCencoded*: The encoded value in that specific block (the first coefficient of the DCT).

Now a preference for neural network model selection solely depends on the generalization and fault tolerant properties. Many neural network architectures are tested to find out the most effective one. Along with some properties such as dimension of the pattern space, because if pattern space is huge then it needs complex network with longer training and recall time. As a result if use large and complex neural network to support this kind of patterns, we may face problem for converging the program to satisfactory training error levels. Hence by considering many aspects the most efficient architecture is selected with (see Figure 5).

In the primary step, the network is trained by a combination of two video clips. The first clip is a soccer match video that contains one cut, while the next one is a wrestling clip that comprises two cuts. The network learned the classification task swiftly and stored the mapping between the inputs and outputs into its connection weights. This type of architecture uses the small training set but the convergence behavior of the network is very superior. Rumelhart, Hinton, & Williams, 1986 proposed the algorithm it decides the size of the network to be trained. This embraces the number of hidden layers and the number of neurons in each layer. The type of the activation function is determined too. The bipolar sigmoid activation function is used and is defined in the following equation

$$f(x) = (2/(1+\exp(-\lambda x))) - 1 \tag{19}$$

Figure 5. Neural network architecture for DC sequence generator

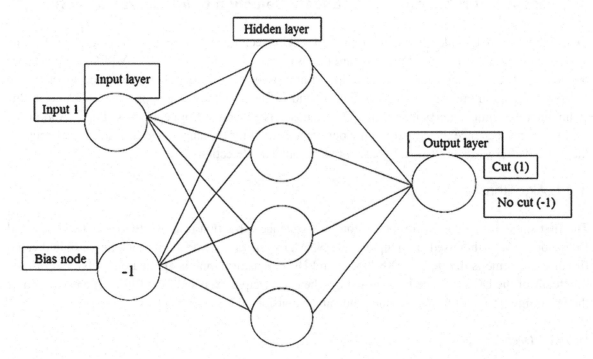

Where

l: The slope, steepness coefficient, of the activation function.

Establish the values of the training set and its size.
Establish the values of the momentum back-propagation algorithm parameters.
These are considered as the rate of learning (*h*) and coefficient of the momentum (*a*).
Random initialization of all weights and thresholds.
Present the first element of the training set to the network and initialize an error accumulator (*E*=0.0).
Calculate the actual output of each neuron in all layers using equation

$$Y_{pj} = f(\sum_{i=1}^{n} w_{ji} x_i) \tag{20}$$

Where

y_{pj}: Output of node j in any layer in response to presenting pattern p.
w_{ji}: The weight-connecting node i in the previous layer to node j in this layer.
xi: Output of node i in the previous layer.
f: The bipolar sigmoid activation function.
n: The number of nodes in the previous layer.

Use the responses of each layer as inputs to the next layer.
Accumulate the error due to the actual output of each neuron in the output layer using equation
$E=E+1/2(d_{pk} - o_{pk})^2$ (21) Where

dpk: Desired output of node k at the output layer in response to input pattern p.
opk: Actual output of node k at the output layer in response to input pattern p.

Calculate the error signal at any node j for a pattern p using equation for the output layer and equation for hidden layer(s).

$$\delta_{pj} = 1/2 \lambda(1-o^2_{pj})(d_{pj} - o_{pj}) \tag{22}$$

$$\delta_{pj} = 1/2 \lambda(1-o^2_{pj}) \sum_{k=1}^{K} \delta_{pk} w_{kj} \tag{23}$$

Where

pk: The error signal at node x as a result of presenting pattern p.
wkj: The weight connecting node j in this layer to node k in the next layer.
K: The number of the neurons in the next layer.

Adapt each layer weights:

$$w_{ji}(t+1)= w_{ji}(t) +\eta\delta_{pj}o_{pj} + \alpha\Delta w_{ji}(t) \tag{24}$$

Where

wji(t): Weight adaptation at time t.

For all of the remaining elements in the training set, go and repeat execution starting from equation (21). If *E* < *Emax*, then store the connection weights, then exit, otherwise proceed.

If the number of iterations exceeds a maximum value, stop declaring convergence failure, otherwise initialize the error accumulator (*E=0.0*) and repeat execution starting from equation (21).

To perform the recall phase of the network, a similar algorithm to the one just described is used, but without any weight adaptation. Instead, the resulting weights produced during the training phase will be used to calculate the output of the network in the feed forward direction via equation (21).

To establish proper values for the parameters of the back-propagation algorithm and the neural network, many combinations of different values have been experimented so that we can choose those values, that give better results. These parameters comprises of the number of hidden layers, number of neurons in every hidden layer, the learning rate, the momentum coefficient, the slope of the sigmoid function, and the number of nodes at the input and the output layers.

Detection of shot boundaries in a video stream is always a difficult task in particularly when we consider multiple video types such as action movie, romantic movies, sports, newscast, and so on with different characteristics of each type. Two extreme cases where many shot boundary detection algorithms fail is the fast camera or object motion or when a huge object occupies the whole scene for a while are termed as less robust algorithms.

3.8. Application

Shot boundary detection is concern about indexing, understanding, and categorizing video. Hence temporal segmentation of video is another most important application area of shot boundary detection. Shot boundary detection mostly concentrates on media for capturing information around us, so application such as multimedia information system, distance learning are highly dependent on enormous amount of video data hence dependent on shot boundary detection. Searching video media in web requires search interfaces, hence online video portals are another application area. YouTube provides keyword search concept and it is a market leader which manually generates meta information and tag. We can say that increased requirement of intelligent processing, intelligent video processing and analysis improves the demand of shot transition detection.

4 COLOR ANALYSIS

Color analysis is basically the process of finding colors of clothing and makeup to match a person's skin complexion, eye color, and hair color. The goal is to determine the colors that best suit an individual's natural coloring and the result is often used as an aid to wardrobe planning and style consulting. Color analysis has a great significance in feature extraction. Meaningful patterns are used to recognize data in machine learning process. The feature extraction consists of an image content analysis. As one knows, the image content is provided by its color, texture and shape information. Numerous color, texture and shape analysis techniques have been developed in recent years. The main aim of this paper is to discover various color analysis methods and thereby apply them t=for feature extraction.

Color analysis basically follows a storage strategy to specify the intensity of pixels. Color image is represented by three intensity components. These components generally correspond to red, green and blue (in accordance with the RGB model) although other color schemes may also be considered. In any mode, pixel's color can be specified in two ways. First, an integer value can be associated with each pixel that can be used as an index to a table that stores the intensity of each color component. This index is used to recover the actual color from the table. An alternative way of representing colors includes the use of several image planes to store the color components of each pixel. This is known as true color scheme. This paper looks forward to discover various such schemes and techniques and thereby draw an analysis with respect to feature extraction.

4.1. Lab Color Space

Barbu, Ciobanu, and Costin (2011) states that the characteristics of the LAB color space makes it suitable for extracting global color features from a digital image. Therefore we convert the analyzed RGB images into LAB format. The characteristic known as luminance or intensity is represented on the axis named L, that is perpendicular on a pile of "ab" planes, each one containing all the possible colors for a given luminance. The fact that the colors are uniformly distributed in an "ab" plane, from green to red along the "a" axis and from blue to yellow along the "b" axis is one of the most useful characteristics of color space. One color is defined by a point (a1, b1) in an "ab" plane of a given luminance L, and colors are changing gradually and uniformly in the plane around this point. It is to be noted that the human eye perceives this gradual change of color as an uniform one. A triplet (L, a, b) is used to define a precise color in the lab space. But in LAB the pair (a, b) can be viewed as a pure color, and the L coordinate depicts only how darker or lighter that color is observed by the human eye. In order to obtain global characteristics, a reduction in the number of colors is necessary. Such a reduction can be obtained by considering only several "ab" planes from the total of 256. As for simplicity 8 'ab' planes can be chosen with the following central L values: 16, 48, 80, 112, 144, 176, 208 and 240.

For each of the 8 selected "ab" planes, one planar histogram is constructed having [256 x 256] bins, one for every possible (a, b) color pair. Since there are 8 "ab" planes, 32 quadrants are used to identify the most important color. For each quadrant a list of (a, b) pairs with corresponding nonzero bins in the planar histogram is constructed. An ordering of the (a, b) are performed according to the bin values, the colors with a greater number of corresponding pixels in the image being on top of this ordered list. The top (a, b) pair is taken as the most important color in the corresponding quadrant. The following feature vector is obtained after collecting all the 32 important colors.

$$V(I_i) = \begin{pmatrix} a^i_1 & \cdots & a^i_{32} \\ \vdots & \ddots & \vdots \\ b^i_1 & \cdots & b^i_{32} \end{pmatrix} \tag{25}$$

where each column represents a winning (a_i, b_i) color pair. The 32 pairs in the feature matrix are ordered from low to high "ab" luminance planes, and every four values corresponding to the same luminance are ordered from quarter 1 to 4 of their corresponding place in the "ab" plane.

4.2. Crust Extraction Using Color Analysis

According to Sharmay, Miocz, and Antony (2009), the vertices of the Voronoi diagram approximate the medial axis of a set points sampled along the boundary of an object. In their research, vertices of the Voronoi diagram of the sample points were inserted into the original set of sample points and a new Delaunay triangulation was computed. The circumcircles of this new triangulation approximate empty circles between the original boundary of the object and its skeleton. This technique is used for crust extraction and segmentation of images. In this triangulation method, each Delaunay edge is adjacent to two triangles and the circumcircles of these triangles are the Voronoi vertices. It has been proved that a Delaunay edge is a part of the border if it has a circle passing through its extremities that does not contain any Voronoi vertex in its interior. This test is known as the standard In-circle test. Considering two triangles (p, q, r) and (r, q, s) sharing an edge (q, r) in a Delaunay triangulation and let v be the a vector orthogonal to edge (r - q) in clockwise order, then the test is performed as follows:

$$(s-q) . (s-r) * (p-q).(p-r) \geq - (s-r) .v * (p-q).v \tag{26}$$

For an edge in the border set, this test will be true.

4.3. Grid Color Moment Analysis

According to Kumar and Chauhan (2014), color adds more information and color feature shows superior stability and is more insensible to the rotation and zoom of image. In this technique following steps are followed to calculate the color feature vector-

1.   Converting the image from RGB to HSV Color space
2.   Dividing the image equivalently into 3 X 3 blocks.
Calculating mean color for each of the blocks.

$$(x)'= 1/N\sum_{i=1}^{N} \binom{n}{k} x_i \tag{27}$$

Where N is the number of pixels in a block, *xi* is the pixel intensity in H/S/V channels.

4.   Calculating it's variance

$$\sigma^2=1/N\sum_{i=1}^{N} \binom{n}{k}(x_i - x')^2 \tag{28}$$

Each block will have 3+3+3=9 features, and thus the entire image will have 9x9=81 features.

4.4. Seasonal Color Analysis

4.4.1. The Suzanne Caygill Method

This system relies on an in-person interview which reveals a range of clues. The most important indicators are the color, light, texture and pattern found in the skin, hair and eyes. Texture, color contrast levels, movement patterns, and facial and body characteristics are secondary indicators that help to determine basic seasonal type and subgroup within the season. The following preferences correspond to a person's seasonal group:

1. **Winter:** Includes colors that are pure pigments, or pigments with added black, or with so much white added as to create an icy, frosted pastel.
2. **Spring:** Colors are usually clear washes or tints, pigments that have white or water added.
3. **Summer:** Colors may have a blend of black, grey, white or brown added to their pure pigments.
4. **Autumn:** dominated by undertones of natural brown pigment, which may range from ochre, umber, or burnt sienna to browns darkened with black.

4.5. Applications

Modern UV spectrophotometers are portable, durable, and offer a low-cost, effective method of color analysis (Pachouri, 2015). Providing the ability to see beyond the human range of vision and into the ultra-violet range, it allows for a wider range of uses. The latest technology in color analysis provides a valuable resource for environmental chemists, with real-time data helping to determine clean water at nearly any source or location. This portable and real-time analysis is also highly utilized by law enforcement agencies for on-site forensic analysis of many various sample materials. Probably the most highly utilized form of color analysis is currently within pharmaceutical research and development. Here, the technology can detect slight differences in chemical composition based on reflectance and absorbance values in order to guarantee quality, purity, and safety for consumers. In addition to real-time and on-site analysis, UV spectrophotometry offers one of the only non-destructive forms of analysis through color measurement. Sample integrity can be preserved and fewer materials are wasted, which is extremely important for small sample sizes or in cases where sample resources are limited. The quick and reliable data that color analysis provides makes it the obvious choice for the many applications of analytical chemistry. The various color methods used for feature extraction and its advantages are as follows:

1. **Histogram:** Simple to compute.
2. **CM Model:** Compact and robust for usage.
3. **Correlogram:** Provides spatial information.
4. **CSD:** Provides spatial information.
5. **SCD:** Scalable and compact.
6. **DCD:** Compact, robust, and perceptual.

4.6. Limitations

The limits of color analysis are merely the grey areas that have not yet been discovered. Some of the newest technology uses spectral mapping to create precise and vivid geographical representations of geological landforms. Not only can these visual features be quantified through spectral data, but the chemical composition can also be differentiated using the same technology. The versatility color analysis continues to open up doors to new and various scientific applications. With the right equipment and support, almost anything is possible with spectrophotometric technology. Segmentation algorithms commonly used in color analysis may result in misclassification. For this purpose image preprocessing must be carried out.

This paper has aimed at exploring the various methods of color analysis and has focused on its applications and also highlighting the limitations which can be recovered with future research work. Color analysis has been greatly used in feature extraction which further emphasizes on its significant contribution in this regard. The various techniques which involve color analysis suggest the ways by which different features can be uniquely extracted. Further research will lead to more such innovative applications in this field.

5. DYNAMIC CONTENT GESTURE ANALYSIS

Gesture recognition and analysis mainly focuses on identifying and understanding human body language. Sign language is a very common form of gesture and in the long run many approaches have been made to interpret them using suitable computer vision algorithms (Turk, 2014; Glowinski, Camurri, & G Volpe, 2008). This further has enabled to build a richer bridge between the humans and the machine as compared to using traditional text interfaces or even GUIs. Without the use of mechanical devices humans can interact freely with the machine (HMI). Techniques from computer vision and image processing have contributed effectively in the field of gesture recognition and our main goal is to conduct a research study on it and thereby take this analysis a step further.

Two types of gestures can be distinguished in computer interfaces (Glowinski, Camurri, & Volpe, 2008).

1. **Offline Gesture:** Gestures which are processed after an interaction of user with the object.
2. **Online Gesture:** They are direct manipulation gestures used mainly to scale or rotate an object.

Broadly there can be three functional classifications of human gestures:

1. **Semiotic:** Communicating meaningful gestures.
2. **Ergotic:** Manipulating the environment.
3. **Epistemic:** Using tactile experience to discover the environment.

Gesture recognition involves some aspects which contain information about a particular gesture which can be further used as a tool for its recognition. These aspects include:

1. Spatial Information- indicating location of a gesture.
2. Pathic Information- indicating path that a gesture takes.

3.   Symbolic Information- indicating the sign made by the gesture.
4.   Affective Information- expressing the emotional quality of a gesture.

In order to conclude from these gesture aspects, appropriate human position, movement and their configuration must be sensed effectively.

5.1. Gesture Recognition Tools and Techniques

Besides representing gestures appropriately, building the proper recognition system is a crucial issue in this field of analysis. Implementations of both static as well as dynamic gestures involve certain tools and techniques which can be summarized briefly (Turk, 2014; Wojtczuk, Armitage, Binnie, & Chamberlain 2012).

5.1.1. Pen-Based Gesture Recognition Technique

In this technique, sensing and interpretation of gestures are straightforward compared to vision based systems. Several 2D input devices including pen, mouse has been considered in the recent works (Turk, 2014). Commercially available PDAs (Personal Digital Assistance) have also been in use which allows users to call operations by using various limited pen gestures thereby performing handwriting recognition. Although it is a promising technique in the field of gesture analysis yet the assumption of a readily available flat surface of screen pose as a constraint and has contributed to the need of better techniques. Figure 6 depicts the various events associated with this form of gesture analysis.

5.1.2. Tracker-Based Gesture Recognition

There are various tracking systems which are commercially available used as input to gesture recognition finding its use in tracking eye gaze, position of overall body or hand configuration (Turk, 2014). Here are some of the tools used in such tracking:

5.1.2.1. Instrumented Gloves

People generally use hands for communicating in most cases. Hands are extremely expressive and have the maximum degree of freedom in communicative tasks. Data gloves mounted on hands and fingers

Figure 6. Gesture analysis

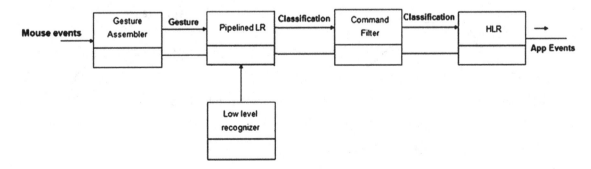

are widely in use for analyzing hand configuration with maximum accuracy and precision. It's easy to use and does not suffer from line of sight occlusion problem and is translation independent.

Latoschik and Wachsmuth (1997) present a multi-agent architecture for detecting pointing gestures in a multimedia application. Väänänen & Böhm (1992) developed a neural network system that recognized static gestures and allows the user to interactively teach

5.1.2.2. Body Suits

Complex movement patterns of human body including activities, identities and other aspects can be perceived by viewing only small number of strategically placed dots on the human body. By measuring the 3D position of such dots recognition of human movements become easier. Body suits provide reliable data and also at a high sampling rates.

Wexelblat (1994) implemented a continuous gesture analysis system using a data suit, "data gloves," and an eye tracker. In this system, data from the sensors is segmented in time (between movement and inaction), key features are extracted, motion is analyzed, and a set of special-purpose gesture recognizers look for significant changes. Marrin & Picard (1998) have developed an instrumented jacket for an orchestral conductor that includes physiological monitoring to study the correlation between affect, gesture, and musical expression. Figure 7 shows the various tracker based models associated with gesture recognition.

5.1.3. Passive Vision-Based Gesture Recognition

This recognition technique is real time based and overcomes the shortcoming of the previous ones (by Turk, 2014). Human motion is recognized using real time data and this techniques is non obtrusive. To meet the requirements of this technique, computer vision has a major role to play. Vision based interfaces use camera to capture one or more images to produce visual features which thereby can be used to interpret the activities of humans. Vision uses a multipurpose sensor which recognizes gestures as well as other objects in the environment. This technique recognizes and interprets the following nature of gestures:

Figure 7. Gesture analysis

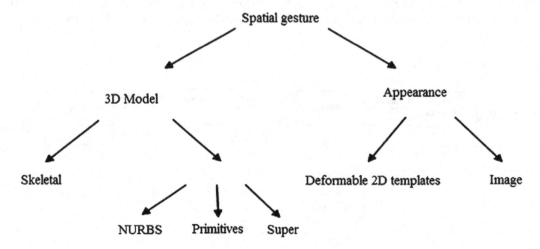

5.1.3.1. Hand and Face Gestures

While interacting, people very commonly use an assortment of cues from head to body to convey information. Some examples of hand and body gestures include:

1. Nodding head
2. Direction of eye stare
3. Raising of eyebrows
4. Winking
5. Anger, look of surprise, disgust

Moses et al. (1995) used fast contour tracking to determine facial expression from a mouth contour. Essa and Pentland (1997) used optical flow information with a physical muscle model of the face to produce accurate estimates of facial motion.

5.1.3.2. Hand and Arm Gestures

The most attention given to a particular form of gesture is hand and arm movement. Various automatic recognition systems focus on this form of gesture. Sign languages, pointing, hand poses and gestures in real time have been recognized using the vision based technique.

One of the first to use computer vision without requiring the user to wear anything special was built by Starner (1995), who used HMMs to recognize a limited vocabulary of ASL sentences. A more recent effort, which uses HMMs to recognize Sign Language of the Netherlands, is described by Assan and Grobel (1997).

5.1.3.3. Body Gestures

This section includes the tracking of full body motion which mainly considers on the following three aspects namely

1. Movement
2. Activity
3. Action

Davis and Bobick (1997) used a view-based approach by representing and recognizing human action based on "temporal templates," where a single image template captures the recent history of motion. This technique was used in the Kids Room system, an interactive, immersive, narrative environment for children.

The block diagram (Figure 8) shows the various steps associated with this technique.

5.1.3.4. Algorithms

Gesture analysis or gesture recognition is a very well-known aspect in the field of computer science and language technology whereby suitable algorithms are applied to interpret human gestures. Any bodily

Figure 8. *Gesture analysis*

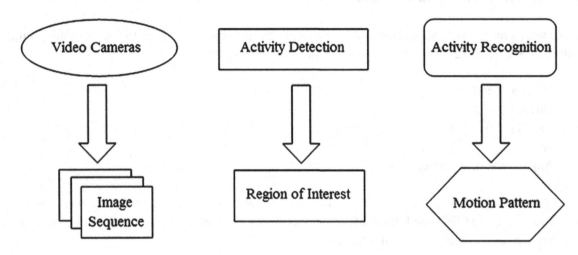

motion can thereby give rise to gestures; moreover gestures are more commonly seen to originate from face or hand. These are the basic modes of expressions commonly used by people during interactions. Our main aim of this study is to basically analyze and interpret these gestures using various effective techniques and suitable algorithms.

5.1.4. Simple Gesture Recognition Algorithm Using PIR Sensor Array

Wojtczuk, Armitage, and Binnie's (2012) stated technique is an inexpensive pyroelectric array detector is used for simple gesture control. The use of 16 element passive infrared sensor array responds to changing infrared signals. A prototype system is developed in this algorithm which can recognize hand movements in different directions in front of a detector.

5.1.4.1. PIR Array Architecture

It is an interesting technology widely used in settings like burglar alarms and automatic light switches. It uses dual element detectors whose principle is to generate a differential signal which thereby reduces effect of noise and drift. This passive array interestingly responds to temperature differences as well. The signal increasingly varies with such differences and the speed of the swipe motion of PIR array has an effect on the size of the signal.

5.1.4.2. Capture Device

A thin film passive infrared sensor with dimensions of 4X4 pixels is enclosed in a package with a broadband infrared filter. These elements have low thermal mass which in turn results in higher frequency of operations well suited for gesture recognition.

5.1.4.3. Performance

Each pixel is sensitive to changes in incident IR radiation. When a hand is swept in front of the detector, the radiation first increases and then decreases. A double peak is obtained corresponding to the sensitivity of pixels with respect to the differential of the radiation.

5.1.4.4. Direction Determination

The PIR array detector sums pixels in one section of the array and subtracts in the other in order to obtain a differential signal. While detection of image moving across the array, the peaks arrive in different sections in different times.

5.1.4.5. Processing of Signal

A tracking algorithm is applied to the sequence of frame and also a derived blob detection technique is used for the application of people counting. Tracking and localization of hotspots enables to determine the direction and process the signals.

5.1.4.5.1. Results Based on Experiments

Functionality of the system was tested in four main directions of hand swipe across the sensor using the blob detection software to deduce the direction of motion. Five participants were asked to perform a set of 100 hand movements each (25 per direction). The detection rate and accuracy of the system response (correct direction detected) were recorded as shown in Table 1.

5.1.5. Emotion Recognition Algorithm

There has been a recent interest in the ability of a computer vision system to detect behavioral expressions of interest, i.e. emotions. Several video analysis algorithms have been researched upon in order to extract and classify information based on emotional state (Glowinski, Camurri, & Volpe, n.d.).

A layered approach has been used to model human movements and gesture ranging from low level physical measures like position, speed or acceleration of body parts to overall motion of the body. In this approach a database of projected emotional expressions have been used and recorded. A selection has been made systematically on the basis of ratings given by experts and non experts. The emotions have been divided into categories based on two differing parameters shown in Table 2.

Two digital cameras has been used each possessing manual gain, constant shutter and focus and body movements has been recorded from both profile and frontal views.

Table 1. Detection rate and accuracy

	Direction Accuracy (%)	Detection Rate (%)
Up	93.6	72.8
Down	93.6	86.4
Left	93.6	88.0
Right	89.6	78.4
Average	92.6	81.4

Table 2. Positive and negative valence

	Positive Valence	Negative Valence
High-Arousal	Anger	Joy
Low-Arousal	Sadness	Relief

5.1.5.1. Extraction of Expressive Cues

From the video recordings, motion cues of the actors were extracted automatically. This form of gesture analysis was mainly based on the dynamics of hands and head position. For each gesture in the database two separate synchronized movies were used to determine the 3D position of the blobs' centroid. Based on its coordinates the velocity of the head and hand movements was also calculated. The modules of velocity of each extremity were summed up and were computed talking into account its horizontal, vertical and depth components.

5.2. Challenges

The purpose is to analyze real time gesture and follow the rules. For this a video camera is used to capture a wide scene from which hands are extracted and tracked. It is easier to capture gesture in low resolution. A 3-dimensional map of the scene is created from its infrared refection analysis, captured by an infrared array. Each pixel can read ranges, as with simple infrared image finders. The aim is to produce low cost low energy consumption device (Wojtczuk & Armitage, 2012).

The limitation in this process is that the hand temperature and background temperature has to be different i.e. hand temperature must be higher at a range so that the sensors can detect and distinguish the hand from background. In order to detect the infrared light, a thin film of passive infrared sensor, 4 pixel X 4 pixel array is enclosed in a package with a broadband infrared filter. That is a sensor die is a customizable structure with pixel pattern on a membrane. It is well suited to detect gesture, a detected object moves quickly across the field of view.

An infrared blocking film is mounted on the infrared filter, with a pinhole centered above the array to produce a low resolution infrared image of the scene in front of the sensor. Electrical signals from the infrared array are amplified, low pass filtered and digitized. The images are captured using an interface board. The distinguished image frames are sent to a computer to provide a uniform output.

Now each pixel senses the change in IR radiation and this change comes from the motion of the target. A stationary target cannot be detected but this is not a problem since dynamic gesture is being detected. A tracking algorithm is applied on the frame sequence and adaptation of the algorithm involves increase in the processing rate and adjustment for larger object size.

This research and analysis on gesture recognition faced several hindrances and have posed various challenges in its processing (Turk, 2014; Wojtczuk & Armitage, 2011; Glowinski, Camurri, & Volpe, 2011):

1. The response of PIR array is not identical for all pixels.
2. The detection scheme assumes that there is a considerable temperature difference between the hand and the background scene which may not be present.

3.   The prototype system mainly uses pin hole optics which is not suitable at all for radiation gathering properties.

4.   Use of higher quality lenses operating in the mid infrared range is expensive.

5.   Calibration can be difficult while using instrumented gloves.

6.   Data from inexpensive systems prove to be noisy.

7.   Use of tethered gloves for gesture recognition reduces comfort and the range of motion.

8.   Tracker based systems are cumbersome.

9.   The occlusion problem often makes full body tracking difficult.

10. For image-based gesture recognition there are limitations on the equipment used and image noise.

11. Images or video may not be under consistent lighting, or in the same location.

12. Items in the background or distinct features of the users may make recognition more difficult.

13. The variety of implementations for image-based gesture recognition may also cause issue for viability of the technology to general usage.

14. The amount of background noise also causes tracking and recognition difficulties, especially when occlusions (partial and full) occur.

15. The distance from the camera, and the camera's resolution and quality, also cause variations in recognition accuracy.

5.3. Applications

This dynamic gesture content analysis has found its usage in a wide variety of applications (Turk, 2014; Wojtczuk & Armitage, 2011; Glowinski, Camurri, & Volpe, 2011):

1.   Gesture recognizer can be used to change slides in a multimedia presentation.

2.   Widely used in the interpretation of kinesics, pen computing and handwriting recognition as well.

3.   Used in the automatic interpretation of sign languages.

4.   Used to recognize hand poses and automatically apply them in interactive video games.

5.   Amidst complex visual backgrounds, the recognition techniques can be applied greatly to identify hand postures.

6.   Finds its usage in temporal gesture recognition.

7.   Facial expressions can be detected from televisions and talk show guests.

8.   Tracking devices has led to the detection of fast and subtle movements of the fingers when a user is waving his hands.

9.   These techniques have also achieved establishment in detecting and recognizing faces, analyzing facial expressions, extracting lip and facial motion as well.

10. It is a complete aid to speech recognition and interpretation of human activities as well.

This analysis on dynamic content gesture recognition has provided a wide variety of aspect to focus on. It's immense application in today's scenario contributes to the need of further research on it to develop fast, effective and smarter techniques to achieve gesture recognition. Nevertheless, the discussed techniques and algorithms have also significantly contributed to development in this field. The concept of automated video analysis for gesture recognition projects the vast area we have covered starting from basic sign language, hand and arm gestures, body movements to detection of emotional expressions of individuals. Though several limitations have been encountered in the proposed systems, yet the advantages of the various techniques do not rule out the necessity of its implementation. A lot of future study and research work will definitely help us to improve the detection reliability working towards an increase in angular resolution which will enable to detect more gestures. Further optimization of the system applications will help us to develop more effective embedded system which will overcome all the existing limitations. New sensing technologies will arrive in near future which will further contribute in this field of study (Turk, 2014; Wojtczuk & Armitage, 2011; Glowinski, Camurri, & Volpe, 2011).

6. AUDIO VIDEO ANALYSIS

Modern technology is much more user centric and is developed much more for individuals rather than for a group of related people. The widely used communication medias including phones, computers and other electronic devices tend to provide more of an individual experience which further contributes to the need of that very technology which can overcome such barriers and thereby help to strengthen the interaction. The main purpose of this analysis is to effectively evaluate and combine the algorithms in order to build a system which can select relevant portions of audio and video elements and thereby build an unconstrained audio-visual environment (Barbu, Ciobanu & Costin, 2011).

Audiovisual (AV) basically possesses both sound and a visual component. The very aim of this analysis is to design and represent an effective system consisting of several audio and video processing components enabling multimode stream manipulation (example: Video conferencing applications) in open and unconstrained environments. Multiple people should be able to interact clearly within the observable scene facing no hindrances. Underlying algorithms are designed to allow them to do so. They include continuous localization of audio components and visual focus of attention, detection and localization of verbal and paralinguistic events. The association and amalgamation of these various events have contributed to the evaluation of the system's performance. The results so obtained project the effectiveness of the proposed design including utilization of the undertaken algorithms representing the overall scenario of this analysis.

6.1. Working and Architecture

In accordance with the underlying algorithms, the proposed system accepts audio and video inputs from separated sensors located within a place (Barbu, Ciobanu & Costin, 2011). The audio elements are placed closer to the participants for better localization and detection. Since video inputs are based on the coverage of an overall scene, it is much more widespread and hence placed a bit far to enhance its functionality. Thus the semantic and the audio object separation clearly enhance the performance using this architecture. For better audio and video capturing for event like teleconferencing both the sensors are separated spatially within a room. Figure 9 clearly demonstrates the placement of various processing elements in order to achieve the best and intelligent capture of both audio and video.

The architecture of the audio visual system can be greatly divided into four basic components including:

- ACE (Audio Communication Engine)
- VCDE (Video Cue Detection Engine)
- ACDE (Audio Cue Detection Engine)
- UCDE (Unified Cue Detection engine)

Figure 9. Video conferencing (audio + video)

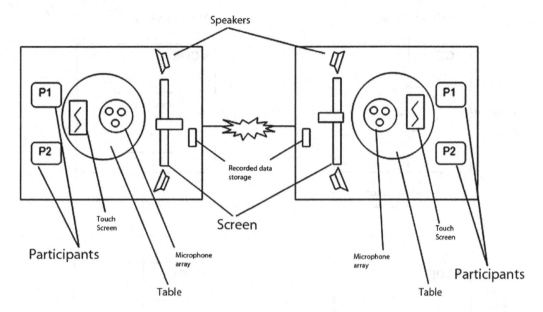

The output of this basic architectural system encompasses the distinct audio elements, semantic video objects, events and states. The system is based on a parametric representation of the recorded visual sound. This enables an effective extraction of sound sources in a particular room. This can be further transformed into object based representation using the underlying components of the four blocks of audio-visual architecture. The ACE block is mainly responsible for the continuous localization of the system. The audio objects so separated are passed on to the ACDE block which further performs speech and voice detection activity. On a similar way the visual inputs are fed to the VCDE block which focuses on the video objects and performs detection activity of the visual aspects of a scene. Both of these elements are passed on to the UCDE block. On synchronization of the various elements so obtained by the UCDE block distinctive semantic video objects are obtained which thereby after association results into semantic events and states depicting audio visual components. The block diagram (Figure 10) represents the effective audio capturing which extracts sound sources from various recordings thereby transforming them into distinctive audio objects.

6.2. Algorithms

Upon performing audio and video analysis summaries of a video is obtained. Video summaries are videos of reduced length than the original and are obtained on performing audio video analysis on the original video. Video summaries are produced with three different heuristic algorithms. One is oriented to the production of summaries and the other one is to produce summaries for the alternative of the original video. The third one is a trade of between the previous algorithms. The produced video must have low jerkiness. Jerkiness is whether a video is a continuous motion of frames or a sequence of distinct snapshots (Furini, & Ghini, 2006).

The definition of video summary must be achieved following the goals:

Figure 10. Basic architecture of audio-visual system

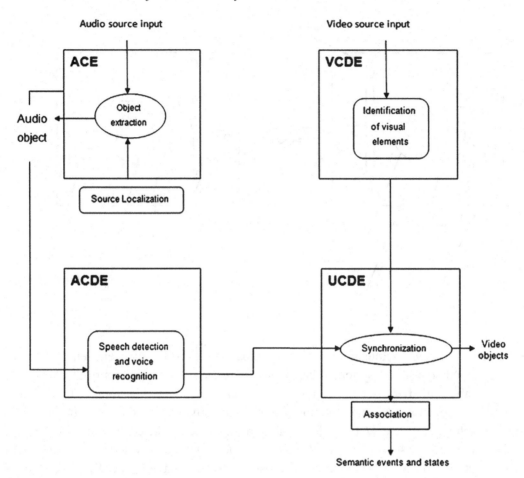

1. **Temporal Reduction:** Play out length must be less than the original video.
2. **Audio Continuity:** Audio is provided with the summary so it has to be intelligible.
3. **Video Continuity:** The video must be as smooth as possible.

Now the mechanism works as- audio analysis is performed on the whole video and all the silent video portions are identified and those portions of the video are dropped. Before performing a silence analysis the whole audio is decoded to PCM, and is divided into consecutive audio blocks. Each audio block has length equal to each video frame. This is done to have a complete synchronization between audio and video. Now silence analysis is performed. The set of silent are identified to drop the corresponding video frame. Now video may be encoded with inter-frame techniques the discard of a frame in this situation may cause problem in case of the next frame. For this reason the video file is temporarily decoded so that each frame can be treated independently.

Now, following the above theory goal 1 and goal 2 are achieved but goal 3 which says about video continuity is not achieved as it introduces discontinuity or jerkiness as video frames are dropped. Audio portion do not suffer jerkiness. So there has to be a reasonable tradeoff between goal 1 and goal 3, three different heuristic tradeoffs are:

1. **All:** It removes all silent video segments thus reducing temporal length but jerkiness is very high.
2. **2X:** It removes a video frame of two silent video frames in a video segment. The goal is to obtain smoothness. Temporal reduction is not as effective as 'All'.
3. **3X:** The goal here is to reduce temporal length as well as to obtain smoothness. The algorithm skips two frames out of three frames causing the user to perceive the play out of silent video segments as a speed factor of 3X. A perfect trade off appears to be found.

6.2.1. Regression Algorithm

Detection and analysis of observable behavior is a crucial step in audio-visual analysis system (Girarda & Cohna, 2014). It encompasses some behavior symptoms pertaining to individual expressions. Various automated methods are in use to analyze depression from audio visual data captured from microphones, telephones and video cameras.

The automated methods can be briefed as follows:

6.2.1.1. Visual Behavior Analysis

Facial expressions, body movements, gesture, etc. are means of visual communications. Firstly, the relevant body parts are detected within video frame. The video frame is basically searched for regions that match previously unidentified body parts and the process is repeated. Then features are extracted to quantify the shape or the appearance of the parts. Finally, a developed algorithm is applied for the interpretation of these features: classification algorithm or regression algorithm. It basically performs mapping between the features and various behavioral characteristics and dimensions. Further, the video frames are identified using this deduced mapping.

6.2.1.2. Acoustic Behavior Analysis

These include analysis of the audio components. Speech, Voice quality, tone etc. are communicated via audio signals which include much of the acoustic behavior. Here, main focus of attention is on the paralinguistic features. Listeners perceive them in terms of pitch, rhythm, note, speaking rate. They are basically measured from recordings of spontaneous speech and identified using various feature centric parameters. Some intra personal features (pausing between utterances in a speaking turn) and some intra personal features like (Switching of pauses between two speakers) are the basic quantitative measures for such analysis.

6.2.2. Classification Algorithm

This algorithm has a major role to play in the approach of automated depression analysis and uses high dimensional audio visual features for identifying behavioral and symptom oriented indicators of audio visual analysis (Girarda & Cohna, 2014). Classification algorithm finds its best use in automated depression analysis and greatly contributes to the operationalization of the behaviors. The typical and atypical behaviors of individuals can be effectively detected using this algorithm.

Figure 11. Automated audio-visual behavior analysis

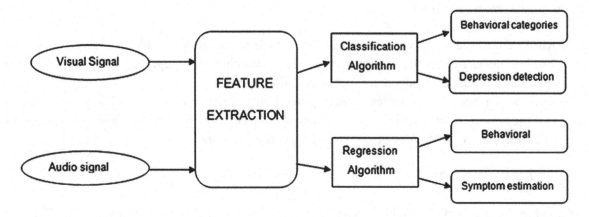

Figure 11 greatly depicts the structured analysis of audio-visual behavior.

6.2.3. Clustering Algorithm

The number of sound sources and the angular positions of these sources are calculated using an effective algorithm known as clustering (Motlicek et al., 2013). This is applied to the detected, filtered spatial audio-visual parameters. This algorithm basically requires no prior information on the number of sources. The steps include:

Step 1: Initial step: creating a vector V containing points with equal spacing.
Step 2: Update step: this step involves determining a local centre of gravity within a limited area around each point in the vector V.
Step 3: Assignment step: this step involves assigning the elements of the vector with the values of the determined centers of gravity respectively.
Step 4: Repeating the update and the assignment step until stopping criteria is achieved.

A crucial aspect of this algorithm involves the size of the area around each point which should be chosen such that the initial points in the vector V are overlapped by these areas. Hence, multiple points may meet at the same position. Moreover in the final step, when the filtered spatial parameters correspond to zero for individual points in the vector V, these points are removed as they are likely not to cover any sound source. Also, identical points are replaced by an average point since they are considered to cover same sound source. The remaining points indicate the number of sources and thereby their angular positions.

6.2.4. Information Extracting Algorithm

Several components are used in this algorithm for performing semantic information extraction. There is a face tracking component which aims at determining at a time how many persons are present in a particular visual scene. Since, it involves a higher-level task and owing to the efficiency of the algorithm much advanced method is in need which can track the faces of persons rather than their full bodies (Voges, M̈argnera, & Martin, 2006).

Multiple face tracking: This proposed tracking algorithm relies heavily on a face detector which encompasses models for front and profile views, frames which further enhances the efficiency of the algorithm. Anomalies like false detection is also minimized with the use of discrete model which only scans regions with skin-like colors by using face bounding boxes from the tracker output. The main aim of this extraction algorithm is to associate detections with the tracked objects and thereby estimate the number and position of visible faces at a particular time. For this tracking problem, a recursive Bayesian framework is used which determines state S_t at each time t, given some observations $O_{1:t}$ from time 1 to t: K = normalisation constant

$$P(S_t | O_{i:t)} = 1/K \times P(O_t | S_{t)} \times \int St-1 \; P(S_t | S_{t-1}) \; P(S_{t-1} | O_{i:t-1}) d \; S_{t-1} \qquad (29)$$

6.3. Evaluation and Conclusion Based on Recent Works

6.3.1. Performance Measures

Experiments have been performed on various real life data sets whereby one may include enabled echo suppression while the other may include disabled echo suppression (Motlicek et al., 2013). An enabled video chat of spatially separated people has been analyzed separately and various observations have been deduced. Achieved results are majorly represented in terms of precision and recall. Precision can be defines as the ratio of true positive test cases and sum of true and false positive test cases or events. Similarly, recall may be precisely defined as the ratio of true positive test events and sum of true positive and false negative test events.

6.3.2. Face Tracking Results

Face detection shows the precision and recall of a standard face detector and it is computed as an average over all the people. This improves the overall accuracy of the processing of video elements. Also, person identification algorithms are evaluated on the given datasets by measuring the amount of time for assigned identifiers for a given person. Also, a visual focus of attention evaluation has been performed on a subset of the data to determine whether a person in a particular scene is focused or where is it looking at. Frames containing focused objects are annotated whereas non annotated frames are ignored in the result statistics.

6.3.3. Speaker Match Results

Based on different localization approaches, speaker match evaluation is carried out. The dependency between recall and precision is depicted using fingerprint approach on individual datasets. Audio visual combinations of the individual streams are performed for effective speaker match accuracies.

Figure 12. Speech transcript analysis

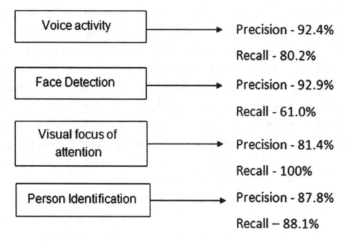

6.3.4. Voice Activity Results

Different audio-visual systems are considered based on the input audio and a visual motion is extracted from the video stream.

The results can be diagrammatically represented as follows (see Figure 12).

6.4. Challenges

Various challenges and limitations encountered in the audio-visual analysis include (Motlicek et al., 2013; Voges, M¨argnera, & Martin, 2006):

1. Faces may not be detected for longer periods of time.
2. The scene dynamics and the lighting conditions are not clear enough and less controlled especially in a living room environment.
3. Presence of two or more person makes person identification difficult in a visual scene thereby leading to frequent track interruptions.
4. The processing of the audio-visual elements must be in real time and should have low delay which is difficult to achieve.
5. The impact of experimental and social context further acts as a hindrance in identification of observable behavioral characteristics.
6. The enhancement of audio and video are further limited by the resolution of the recorded scene.
7. Low light conditions for video recordings and noisy environments are some common limiting factors in the audio-visual analysis.
8. Diverse samples and datasets make the analysis technique difficult and thereby lead to incorrect results.
9. Motion estimation techniques require precise localization of the body parts and in case of uncontrolled light conditions, it is a challenging task.

10. In multi-person tracking, real time scenario the detection of visual components is increasingly complex.

6.5. Applications

The audio visual analysis has got a variety of usage in various fields and has contributed to the need of the optimal and effective algorithms to achieve high-level audio visual stream manipulation overcoming the various limitations encountered (Motlicek et al., 2013; Voges, M¨argnera, & Martin, 2006). The widespread applications are:

1. Used as online multi face tracker with great precision.
2. It has an immense usage in the field of multimedia whose materials combine the audio components, still images and moving video images with the flexibility of a computerized presentation to present users with an interactive, informative medium.
3. It also finds its application in lasers and holograms which are generally used for presentations and displays in electoral education facilities. The audio visual components can be used as a part of pre recorded multimedia presentations for school groups.
4. In the field of DVD technology, the recordings combine the virtue of audio, video and multimedia presentations in a portable format.
5. Television is a very powerful medium for electoral advertising and the use of images as well as sound make it a very powerful medium.
6. It also finds its use in speaker diarization using semi discriminant analysis.
7. Speech recognition is another widespread area where audio visual analysis based techniques are applied.
8. Source separation, voice manipulation and object recognition are those areas where these techniques are also applied.
9. Audio-visual components are also applied in EEG analysis which is basically a study on brain recorded data.
10. Techniques are also applied for conversation scene analysis.
11. Robust sensor fusion has also incorporated audio visual analysis for its working.
12. Statistical analysis and modeling of audio-visual biometric signals find its way through audio visual analysis algorithms.
13. Audio-visual biometric authentications are solely based on the audio visual analytical principle.
14. Automated methods of audio visual analysis have the benefit of high repeatability which is difficult for humans to detect and quantify.
15. Widely used for depression analysis and thereby identify the behavioral indicators in a scene.

These varied applications are contributing more and more to the need of the audio-visual analysis and more research and insight into this topic is aimed at producing better, effective results based on experimental observations.

This audio visual analysis is aimed at presenting a system enabling higher level stream manipulation in multiple modes. This analysis has addressed various challenges and limitations which need to be overcome in order to facilitate better communication with low delay from spatially separated sensors. The main evaluated components of the proposed system include face tracking, speaker match, localization of sound sources, voice activity detection, estimation of visual focus of attention, object coding and information extraction with respect to negligible loss of quality. It is primarily important to generalize the results to diverse samples which would thereby enhance the comparability of the results. This very analysis was to develop suitable algorithms in order to locate a person by visual and acoustic localization techniques. Further developments are aimed at in near future which will significantly contribute in this analysis. It is clearly established that both audio and visual components play a major role in our life and implementation of suitable algorithms are bound to facilitate an effective communication.

7. SPEECH TRANSCRIPTS

The main goal of this analysis is to devise and formulate those effective algorithms which can significantly perform the speech transcription. This very representation of speech in written form can be that of an orthographic transcription or phonetic transcription. Various transcription software's have come into play and they perform transcription in the linguistic sense. This study focuses on such aspects and aims at building a wide view and a better understanding on this topic taking into account various recent research based works.

Speech recognition or speech transcription is another major field of interest in the field of computer science and electrical engineering. It basically refers to the transcript of spoken words into text. Basically the speech recognition systems analyze the person's specific voice and thereby use it to fine tune the recognition of that particular speech. Our main aim of this study is to project the well known and commonly used techniques and algorithms for speech transcription and thereby perform an effective analysis on it. Speech transcript has greatly contributed to video summarization whereby this approach breaks the video into small, coherent segments and then ranks them. The techniques which are generally used are largely drawn from the existing text analysis techniques.

7.1. Transcription Alignment and Analysis

Speech transcript analysis is basically analyzing the audio which is speech in video and upon analyzing them creation of appropriate summary of the video (Taskiran, Amir, Ponceleon, & Delp, 2002). Related to video summarization that the video is analyzed and divided into video segments using shot boundary detection algorithm, now the segments are assigned scores by using various combination of features.

Segments with highest scores are selected, summary is generated and visualization (static or dynamic) are generated based on summary. In static method some key frames are selected from the video and presented to the user and in case of dynamic method it generates a shorter version of the video to present to the user. Now coming back to the main topic, speech recognition may be performed on audio to obtain the transcript. Once the text corresponding to the video sequence is available, the summary of the text is found. There are two types of summarization techniques- statistical analysis based on information retrieval technique and natural language processing analysis based on information extraction technique.

In statistical analysis method various features are extracted from the text which are shown to be correlated with abstract worthiness of a sentence and ranking is done based on these extracted feature. In case of NLP, semantic detailed analysis the source text is performed to get a text representation. Then summary representation is performed and output summary text is synthesized. Statistical analysis suffers from lack of coherence between generated summaries. Also it suffers from dangling anaphor problem.

NLP gives better summary, but the knowledge base required for this is generally large and complex. Statistical analysis is done by the CureVideo system where it uses shot boundary detection and speech recognition and indexing. NLP is performed by IBM's ViaVoice with IBM's large vocabulary and it follows the process of speech recognition followed by text analysis and information retrieval tool.

As it is not wanted an audio phrase to begin at the middle of the summary, shot boundary to segment video is avoided and audio pause boundaries are looked upon. Long pause in an audio is detected with a heuristic using simple speech transcript file generated by Via Voice at the end of speech recognition step of the CueVideo indexing process. Score for each segmentation is calculated to rank them for text retrieval following the equation:

$$S_{i,w} = ((K+1) n_{i,w} / K[(1-b)+ bL_i/AL]) \log(N/ n_w)$$

$n_{i,w}$ = number of occurrences of word w in segment 'i'.
n_w = total number of occurrences of w.
L_i = no of words in segment i.
A_L = Average number of words per segment in the video sequence.
N = Total number of segments.
k, b = Tuning parameters .

As the score of each word is analyzed score for the whole segment is calculated as –

$$S_i = 1/ L_i \sum S_{i,w}$$

There is a large vocabulary of speech recognition in CueVideo with which it can attain high accuracy, but however it can run into difficulty if the video contains rare words and phrases. For that a second order analysis of word frequencies in the video is considered. Then as output the dominated word pares in each segment is listed.

Alignment links sound units with corresponding text units. Once an authoritative transcription for a speaker has been created a linguist can then compare the transcription with the previously transcribed speech of another speaker. At first an alignment is made between the word and the phone level between two transcriptions. The output from this part is a phone to phone alignment between two transcriptions. After completion of this alignment, the phonological speech pattern analysis is performed (Taskirany, Amirz, Ponceleonz, & Delp, 2001). This analysis is widely used in various video summarization techniques, details of which are explained below.

7.2. Video Summarization Using Speech Transcript

With the increasing advances of video streaming and emergence of low cost storage media, digital video has found its importance (Taskirany, Amirz, Ponceleonz, & Delp, 2001). It has become an important factor in the field of education, entertainment and commerce. Systems that organize and search video data based on content are being designed. In order to achieve this, certain summarization techniques are followed which uses script transcript analysis. Video involves a rich, sequential medium. It includes both audio and motion. This is the reason due to which the manipulation of video shots and scenes are

Figure 13. Speech transcript analysis

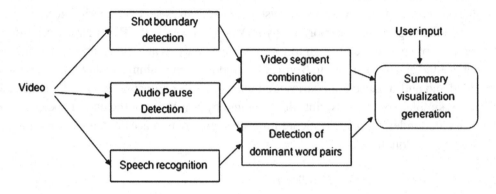

much more complex. Various methods have been proposed for effectively analyzing video and deriving a compact representation thereby enabling users to browse easily. Video summarization falls under one of these methods. The block diagram (Figure 13) will show the substantial steps of video summarization using speech transcript.

7.3. Related Work

Here are some of the works based on video summarization.

7.3.1. Static Visualization of Video Summaries

This basically refers to presentation of one frame from each video segment, which may or may not correspond to an actual shot. There is a major problem encountered while doing so and that is the representation which becomes impractically large for long videos. To overcome this approach followed is to rank the video segments and display only the representative key frames corresponding to the segments having maximum score. This approach has been followed significantly. The recent works have used time-constrained clustering to cluster shots. Representative frames from segments are arranged in a video poster" using a frame packing algorithm.

7.3.2. Dynamic Visualization of Video Summaries

Here, a selection of segments with the highest scores is made from the source video and concatenated to generate a video skim. One of the earliest systems for video summarization namely the MOCA project uses color and action of shots among other heuristics to obtain trailers for feature films. Another work namely the Informedia project constitutes a pioneer and one of the largest efforts in creating a large video database with search and browse capabilities. It uses integrated speech recognition, image processing, and natural language processing techniques for the analysis of video data.

7.3.3. Video and Speech Indexing

In this research, for video and speech indexing, shot boundary detection and speech recognition is used. Here, indexing is performed on digitized video (Taskirany, Amirz, Ponceleonz, & Delp, 2001). The video processing automatically detects shot boundaries, generates a shots table, and extracts representative frames as JPEG files from each of the shots. With respect to speech indexing, audio processing is also performed. It basically starts with speech recognition using appropriate system and which is followed by text analysis and information retrieval tools. Several searchable speech indexes are created, including an inverted word index, a phonetic index and a phrase glossary index.

7.3.4. Segmentation of Speech and Audio

In case of segmentation there is use of audio pause boundaries instead of using shot boundaries. Basically, there is no use of visual features for dividing video into segments of video frames. These are determined by detecting large inter word pauses of the speaker in the audio. In case of documentary the pauses are larger in contrast to seminar video. Various techniques are applied for detecting pauses in speech (Taskirany, Amirz, Ponceleonz, & Delp, 2001; Coden & Brown, 2001). Pauses are detected with a simple heuristic using the time stamped speech transcript file at the completion of the speech recognition step. A sliding window mechanism is applied for detecting pauses between the segments. At first the durations of the pauses between all the words in the video are computed using the time stamps and word lengths from the speech transcript. A symmetric window of size $2m + 1$ is placed around the ith pause and a segment boundary is declared between words i and i + 1 whenever

1. the length of the ith pause is the maximum within the window, and
2. it is also n times the value of the second maximum in the window.
    'n' is used to control detection sensitivity.

7.4. Computing Segment Weights

A score for each segment is computed after the video is segmented using pause boundaries. Determination is done using information about term frequencies within segments, as is usually done to rank the documents for text retrieval. Using the following formula for each word w in segment i, a score is computed which measures the statistical importance of w.

$$S_{i,w} = ((k + 1) n_{i,w} / K[(1 - b) + b^{Li/AL}] + n_{i,w}) \log N/N_w \qquad (30)$$

where

$n_{i,w}$ - number of occurrences of word w in segment i
N_w - total number of occurrences of word w in the video sequence
Li - number of words in segment i
AL - average number of words per segment in the video sequence
N - total number of segments in the video sequence
k, b - tuning parameters

Figure 14. Architecture overview of speech transcript

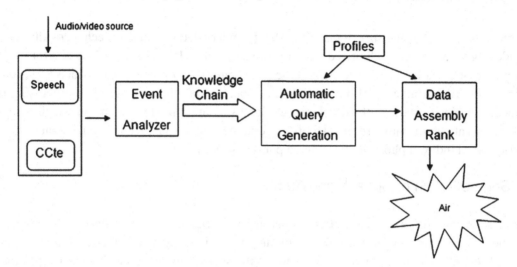

7.5. Architecture

The goal is to find collateral information for a live broadcast in real time (Coden & Brown, 2001). For this each part of the system must perform as close to real time as possible. For facilitating development of real time components, the components are separated from each other by a modular architecture with clearly defined interfaces. The input to the Real Time Feature Extractor is a live television broadcast. A module in the extractor can determine a particular feature in real time from a video/audio signal. The Speech module basically transcribes the audio signal into English. Figure 14 shows this basic transcription.

Here the input is a live television broadcast. The Speech module transcribes the audio signal into English and the CCText module extracts the closed caption text from the video. The operation of both the modules is in real time. The Feature Extractor produces ASCII Text, both in the form of transcribed text and closed caption text (CCText) if it is available. The Event Analyzer subsystem represents the most important and innovative part of the system. Each analyzer has a task to perform based on the ASCII text. The output of one analyzer can be the input to another analyzer. The output of an analyzer is again a time stamped ASCII string. The output events from the analyzers are stored on a linked list data structure, called the Knowledge Chain. The very next step is to find the collateral information that will be broadcast with the program. Finally the results are inserted into the broadcast stream.

7.6. Evaluation and Result

Based on the techniques of the research, an evaluation is done with respect to questions related to performance issues and other factors (Taskirany, Amirz, Coden, & Brown, 2001). There can be several performance related queries ranging from ranging from the speed and effectiveness of individual analyzers, to the overall usefulness of the system measured by end-user satisfaction. System usefulness and end-user satisfaction are best measured by a carefully designed user study. For evaluating the individual analyzers techniques from traditional information retrieval and natural language processing evaluation may be used. These evaluations are basically based upon a working prototype of the system.

7.7. Related Work

In the transcript generated by our IBM Via Voice recognition engine, 34 relevant named entities were detected, a 62% recognition rate, which is much higher than the recognition rate for the entire document. WASABI recognized 98% of the named entities in the transcript. WASABI typed the named entities correctly 97% of the time, the errors coming from inherent ambiguities in the names, for instance Tijuana being both a name and a place. To correctly type such words a more extensive analysis of the context has to be performed which cannot be done in a real-time system.

7.8. Applications

Speech recognition and transcription finds a wide variety of usage based on real life needs.

7.8.1. Playing Back Simple Information

If you have customers who need fast access to information. In many circumstances customers do not actually need or want to speak to a live operator. For example, if they have little time or they only require basic information then speech recognition can be used to cut waiting times and provide customers with the information they want. By deploying an intelligent speech recognition system, Dublin Airport was able to cope with a 30 per cent rise in passenger numbers without the need to increase staff levels. Incoming customer calls are filtered according to requirements and those wanting basic information, say on 'departures' or 'arrivals', are automatically directed to the speech recognition system that quickly evaluates the nature of the enquiry through a series of prompts. At all times there is an option to speak with a live operator, if necessary. The system has been fine-tuned to pick up the vagaries of the Irish accent. The average call time has been reduced to just 53 seconds, freeing up skilled agents for more complex calls.

7.8.2. Call Steering

Placing callers through to the right department, waiting in a queue to get through to an operator or, worse still, finally being put through to the wrong operator can be very frustrating to your customer, resulting in dissatisfaction. By introducing speech recognition, you can allow callers to choose a 'self-service' route or alternatively 'say' what they want and be directed to the correct department or individual. Standard Life is using speech recognition for its Life and Pensions business. The solution helps in three ways: it ascertains what the call is about; if necessary it takes the customer through security checks and then transfers the customer to the appropriate member of staff. The details that the customer has already provided appear on the screen so that they do not have to repeat the information. Using this technology Standard Life increased its overall call handling capacity by over 25 per cent and reduced their misdirected calls by 66 per cent. The system also gives them a better understanding of why customers are calling, because it allows the customer to 'voice' their request rather than forcing them to conform to an organisation's preconceptions on what the customer wants.

7.8.3. Automated Identification

When we need to authenticate someone's identity, over phone without using 'risky' personal data. Identity fraud is now one of the biggest concerns facing UK organizations and research by the UK's fraud prevention service (CIFAS) estimates that it is costing the UK £1.7bn a year. Some advanced speech recognition systems provide an answer to this problem using voice biometrics. This technology is now accepted as a major tool in combating telephone-based crime. On average it takes less than two minutes to create a 'voiceprint' based on specific text such as 'Name' and 'Account Number'. This is then stored against the individual's record, so when they next call, they can simply say their name and if the voiceprint matches what they have stored, then the person is put straight through to a customer service representative. This takes less than 30 seconds and also bypasses the need for the individual to have to run through a series of tedious ID checks such as passwords, address details and so on. Australia's 8th largest insurers, Health Management is successfully using voice biometrics to allow existing account holders to speak to customer service representatives quickly and securely. The company has enrolled more than 20,000 customers' voiceprints.

7.8.4. Removing IVR Menus

Replacing complicated and often frustrating 'push button' IVR, due to poorly implemented systems, IVR and automated call handling systems are often unpopular with customers. However, there is a way to improve this scenario, termed as 'intelligent call steering' (ICS), it does not involve any 'button pushing'. The system simply asks the customer what they want (in their words, not yours) and then transfers them to the most suitable resource to handle their call. Callers dial one number and are greeted by the message "Welcome to XYZ Company, how can I help you?" The caller is routed to the right agent within 20 to 30 seconds of the call being answered with misdirected calls reduced to as low as 3-5 per cent. By introducing Natural Language Speech Recognition (NLSR), general insurance company Suncorp replaced its original push button IVR, enabling the customer to simply say what they wanted. Using a financial services' statistical language model of over 100,000 phrases, the system can more accurately assess the nature of the call and transfer it first time to the appropriate department or advisor. The company reduced its call waiting times to around 30 seconds and misdirected calls to virtually nil.

7.8.5. Dealing with Spikes in Call Volumes

We need to handle high volumes of customer service enquiries from repeat customers. The betting industry is an example of a business that has very high volumes of calls from regular 'punters', most of which occur in irregular peaks and troughs. During a normal day, races occur every ten minutes with 80 per cent of calls occurring minutes before each race. To overcome this problem Ladbrokes was able to divert the calls depending simply on their nature, e.g. placing a bet, asking for odds, which were both handled automatically, or for more complex 'customized' best they could speak directly to an operator. The system is effective on all race days, but on big race days such as The Grand National or The Cheltenham Gold Cup it enables the company to increase the capacity of its call centers without the need to add additional staff. A large database of over 40,000 registered horses and 6,000 football players are part of an extensive database that is updated in real time.

We have successfully completed an analysis on speech transcription and recognition thereby focusing on the main techniques and types of feature extraction. Several challenges might have been encountered while performing such techniques, yet the widespread applications of each of them clearly signifies its importance. Future research and study on this topic will enable us to overcome the constraints and to carry out this process in real time using a text transcript generated by an automatic speech recognition system. In future research, we plan to explore the same problem without the real time constraints to discover whether more sophisticated text analysis tools can improve the quality of the retrieved material after transcription.

7.9. Related Work

The work of automated music analysis is very relevant work with speech transcript as music analysis includes perceptual information extraction such as notes and instruments and so on from music files (Coden & Brown, 2001). Also music analysis is another important part where feature extraction techniques is very important, as automated music analysis requires musical note extraction, instruments, emotion extraction is also part of automated musical extraction. Music analysis is also termed as multifaceted problem as it includes extraction, recognition and classification concepts together. Other apparently related topics are electrocardiogram analysis, speech recognition, and seismology and so on. Topic detection and tracking is the most popular research on speech transcript, known as TDT. The main aim of TDT is to analyze new broadcasts such as text articles and text transcripts which are automatically generated from audio and video. TDT is able to identify the previous unseen news events. Topic identification is another part of it which is used to recognize subsequent news stories.

8. OBJECT RECOGNITION

Object recognition basically refers to determining the identity of an object being observed in the image from a set of known labels. One of the most fascinating abilities that humans possess is object recognition. Humans are able to tell its identity or category despite of the appearance variation due to change in pose, illumination, texture, deformation, and under occlusion just by a simple glance on an object. They can easily generalize from observing a set of objects to recognizing objects that have never been seen before. It is indeed a very difficult task to develop vision systems that match the cognitive capabilities of human beings, or systems that are able to tell the specific identity of an object being observed. Factors which contribute to such difficulty includes- relative pose of an object to a camera, lighting variation, and difficulty in generalizing across objects from a set of exemplar images. The main aim of this paper is to explore and establish various object recognition techniques and signify its importance in the following discussion.

Every day we recognize a multitude of familiar and novel objects. We do this with little effort, despite the fact that these objects may vary somewhat in form, color, texture, etc. Objects are recognized from many different vantage points (from the front, side, or back), in many different places, and in different sizes. Objects can even be recognized when they are partially obstructed from view. While it may be obvious that people are capable of recognizing objects under many variations in conditions, it has been thought that pigeons may not possess the same range of capabilities. It has been proposed that pigeons act as "perceptrons," by analyzing simple features of objects and using those features to recognize objects. If the pigeon were a perceptron, then it would not be able to recognize an object that varied slightly in form or was seen from a novel viewpoint because the features would be altered. Moreover, a pigeon would be unable to discriminate between two objects that contained the same features, but with a different organization. Object recognition is basically a task of finding and identifying objects in an image or video sequence.

8.1. Algorithms

Object recognition is all about determining the identity of an object being observed in the image from a set of known labels. It is assumed that there is a single object in the image (Yang, 2007, 2002).

Humans recognize a multitude of objects in images with little effort, despite the fact that the image of the objects may vary somewhat in different viewpoints, in many different sizes and scales or even when they are translated or rotated. Objects can even be recognized when they are partially obstructed from view. This task is still a challenge for computer vision systems. Various approaches are followed for recognizing object or its parts based on several parameters. Various approaches have been followed for developing algorithms to be used for object recognition.

8.1.1. Appearance Based

In this approach, example images of the objects are used to perform the recognition. Objects look different under varying conditions like changes in lighting or color, changes in viewing direction, changes in size / shape.

Appearance based algorithms say to recognize objects, based on their appearance. The idea is to compute Eigen vectors where each represents one image as a raster scan vector of grey scale pixel value. Each Eigen vector captures certain variance among all the vectors, and thus a small set of Eigen vectors capture all the appearance variation of images in the training set. For a test image its identity is determined by finding the nearest neighbor of this vector after being projected onto a set of eigenvectors. For learning or training several cognitive algorithms such as RBF in artificial neural network, k-nearest neighbor algorithm, SVM etc. are used to recognize 3D objects from 2D images.

8.1.2. Edge Matching

It uses edge detection techniques, such as the Canny edge detection, to find edges. Changes in lighting and color usually don't have much effect on image edges. Strategy used in this approach is to Detect edges in template and image, compare edges images to find the template, consider range of possible template positions.

8.1.3. Divide and Conquer Search

Here we consider all positions as a set (a cell in the space of positions),determine lower bound on score at best position in cell. If bound is too large, we prune cell .If bound is not too large, we divide cell into sub cells and try each sub cell recursively, the process stops when cell is small enough. Unlike multi-resolution search, this technique is guaranteed to find all matches that meet the criterion. To find the lower bound on the best score, we look at score for the template position represented by the center of the cell. Then we subtract maximum change from the "center" position for any other position in cell.

8.1.3.1. Grayscale Matching

Edges are (mostly) robust to illumination changes; however, they throw away a lot of information. It should be noted that we must compute pixel distance as a function of both pixel position and pixel intensity, can be applied to color also.

8.1.3.2. Gradient Matching

Another way to be robust to illumination changes without throwing away as much information is to compare image gradients. Matching is performed like matching grayscale images.

8.1.3.3. Histograms of Receptive Field Responses

It avoids explicit point correspondences. Relationships between different image points are implicitly coded in the receptive field responses.

8.1.4. Feature Based

The very basic idea of this approach lies in finding interest points, often occurred at intensity discontinuity, that are invariant to change due to scale, illumination and affine transformation. The SIFT descriptor, commonly known as scale invariant feature transform descriptor is one of the widely used feature representation schemes. In this approach a search is used to find feasible matches between object features and image features. The primary constraint is that a single position of the object must account for all of the feasible matches. Here, the methods that extract features from the objects are to be recognized and the images to be searched.

Feature based algorithm marks, extracts and exploits the feature of an image to note objects. The scale invariant feature transform is arguably one of the most widely used for vision application. Here in SIFT approach the extreme in scale space for automatic scale selection with a pyramid of Gaussian filters is used and key points with low contrast are removed. A consistent orientation is applied to each key point and its magnitude is computed based on local image gradient histogram.

8.1.4.1. Interpretation Trees

A method for searching for feasible matches is to search through a tree. Each node in the tree represents a set of matches. Root node represents empty set. Each other node is the union of the matches in the parent node and one additional match. Wildcard is used for features with no match. Nodes are "pruned" when the set of matches is infeasible. A pruned node has no children.

8.2. Hypothesize and Test

A correspondence is hypothesized between a collection of image features and a collection of object features. Then this is used to generate a hypothesis about the projection from the object coordinate frame to the image frame. This projection hypothesis is used to generate a rendering of the object. This step is usually known as back projection. The rendering is compared to the image, and, if the two are sufficiently similar, accept the hypothesis.

8.2.1. Obtaining Hypothesis

There are a variety of different ways of generating hypotheses. When camera intrinsic parameters are known, the hypothesis is equivalent to a hypothetical position and orientation – pose – for the object. Geometric constraints are utilized. Finally a correspondence is constructed for small sets of object features to every correctly sized subset of image points. These are known as hypotheses.

8.2.2. Randomization

Examining small sets of image features until likelihood of missing object becomes small. For each set of image features, all possible matching sets of model features must be considered.

Formula: $(1 - W^c)^k = Z$

where

W = the fraction of image points that are "good" (w ~ m/n)
c = the number of correspondences necessary
k = the number of trials
Z = the probability of every trial using one (or more) incorrect correspondence.

So the image may contain a huge number of objects which are to be recognized. Firstly a threshold mechanism is applied. Here Threshold value for the image is defined (Kaur, Singh, Kundra, 2013). Then some morphological operation is performed on the binary image that is under consideration. With this, boundaries of regions of foreground pixels are made to be skipped from the image under test. Then the image is compared with the preloaded data set which is also called the training data set. So the training data set is compared with the data found on processing the image and thus objects are detected.

Now it follows certain steps of detecting the objects in the previous manner. The steps are as follows

Step 1
- a. First step is to read the image and convert it into grey scale on using multi threshold.
- b. Segmentation is needed to convert the image into a binary image.
- c. The boundaries of regions of foreground pixels are detected and shrunk in size.
- d. Extraction of features from the image is performed.

Step 2
- a. The features of the image which are extracted are matched with the preloaded data set and the actual objects are obtained from it and while doing that minimum distance from one training data set feature to detected feature is considered.

The algorithm of the procedure of detecting objects can be defined as follows:

1. Read an image.
2. Convert an RGB image into an grey scale image.
3. Define threshold value. New threshold value is defined as the average of z_1 and z_2. $N = (z_1 + z_1)/2$. Where, z_1=average value of $\{f(x,y):f(x,y)>N\}$ and z_2=average value of $\{f(x, y):f(x, y)\leq N\}$.
4. Apply operation to find edges and boundary values of boundary image.
5. Extract features.
6. Maintain a dataset of the predicted minimum distance of matched value. $dist=\sqrt{(m-x)^2+(n-y)^2}$ and min_val=min(dist).

8.3. Limitation

It is a challenging task to introduce cognitive computer vision to identify objects. The difficulty can be like relative pose of an object to a camera, lighting variation.

Geometry based approaches say that the geometric description of a 3D object allows the projected shape to be accurately predicted in 2D image under projective projection. Such primitives can only be reliably extracted under limited conditions controlled variation in lighting and view point with certain occlusion.

According to Ullman (1996), although object recognition finds its use in a wide variety of fields yet it faces certain limitations which might be encountered:

1. For faces, difference due to viewing conditions may be much larger than differences between individuals.
2. Using distance between faces based on pixel differences, machine recognition is poor.
3. Many objects do not decompose naturally into a union of clearly distinct parts.
4. Finding parts such as limbs, torso reliably is very difficult.

8.4. Application

Using Object recognition technology implementation of exciting applications is possible. In industry there exists a variety of computer vision products and services from the field of machine inspection to recent applications. Object recognition finds its usage in variety of applications. It is widely used in biometric recognition systems, optical character/digit/document recognition. Some more object recognition applications include surveillance, industrial inspection, content-based image retrieval (CBIR), robotics, medical imaging, human computer interaction, and intelligent vehicle systems (Yang, 2002; Ullman, 1996).

Our main goal of this paper was to retrieve information that is not apparent in the images we perceive. Recognition of common objects is way beyond capability of artificial systems proposed so far. This analysis has clearly depicted the importance and significance of object recognition and has devised the appropriate algorithms for identifying objects and its parts. With more reliable representation schemes and recognition algorithms being developed, tremendous progress has been made in the last decade towards recognizing objects under variation in viewpoint, illumination and under partial occlusion. Nevertheless, most working object recognition systems are still sensitive to large variation in illumination and heavy occlusion. In addition, most existing methods are developed to deal with rigid objects with limited intra-class variation. It is hoped that by overruling the limitations, various new tools and techniques can be devised on further research.

8.5. Advanced Research

The recent research on object recognition focuses on unsupervised methods known as two stage unsupervised method. This method uses ACM and FCM for image segmentation and object detection i.e. Active Contour Model and Fuzzy C means respectively. In the first stage to identify region of interest ACM is applied, by this process basically background is subtracted after that FCM based algorithm is applied for object detection in specific image. This method gain popularity over the existing methods as they require manually cluster number selection but this process aims at estimating the number of clusters automatically. This type of technique is very efficient for multi objects in occurrence of occlusion with image containing arbitrary number of unknown objects.

We must remember now days it is considered to be a open challenge to identify unknown objects in static images due to implementation complexity and difficulty in finding object classes and understanding the image.

8.5.1. Technique

8.5.1.1. Two-Stage Unsupervised Method for Multiple Object Detection

This algorithm is comprises of two steps described below (Memar, Ksantini, & Boufama, 2014):

Step 1: Using Active Contour Model Background Subtraction

Active Contour Model or (ACM) is well known as an edge based segmentation technique. This technique is very popular as it can extract object outline. The ACM implementation uses level set functions by means of an energy minimization concept. This type of energy functions are used to control shape and size of the curve and make the zero level set function to move towards boundaries of objects. ACM uses external and internal terms. Conventional level set methods are computationally complex and expensive for re-initialization during curve evolution. This ACM based method is re-initialization free concept and perform effectively in presence of intensity in-homogeneity. The energy function comes in the form of

$$\varepsilon(\Phi) = \mu R_p(\Phi) + \varepsilon_{g,\lambda,v} \tag{31}$$

Here the constant μ is >0, μ is known as distance regularization term which is used to control the derivation of the level set function from signed distance function, and $R_p(\varnothing)$ is internal function of ACM. In the above equation as external energy function, as edge indicator, the gradient is used as it is helpful in object detection with well defined gradient based edge. But the gradient is sensitive to textured and or noisy region, hence the curve will liable to stop before attaining the object boundaries. If the gradient has small local maxima on the object edge, in that case it may even pass through the edges.

Now to solve this problem the concept of image polarity is applied on the on external energy term as stopping criteria. The term polarity implies the feature of local image which is used to measure the extent of gradient vector orientation in some dominant direction around a specific pixel. Unfortunately in absence of texture, the polarity concept outperforms by gradient. Along with these two features, depth information is used as a good hint for salient object detection as in general pixels of the depth image correspond to a distance. As an alternative to ACM stopping criteria disparity map acquired from two images can be used as clue for depth. But for 3D sensors it is still a challenge to detect and differentiate objects located at same depth. As a alternate of this problem a solution is made automatic selection of best feature concept is made, which can be used in ACM and finally by merging these two techniques with semi-supervised classification method with Support Vector Machine (SVM) a new algorithm is designed.

At very first stage three features such as gradient (F_g), polarity (F_p) and depth(F_D) are taken as input and computed. Then in the next stage automatic election is done either of gradient or polarity base on noise indicator. This noise indicator is generally calculated over the mean of the gradient values in the target region. After this the histogram of depth of initial contour is taken out and analyzed. Here if the non-zero bin known as peaks are greater than 1then it indicates the availability of depth information which is used as stopping function of ACM after combining it to either with gradient or polarity. But if more than one term is selected as stopping criteria then the only way is to use SVM to combine them. The values of features such as gradient (F_g), polarity(F_p) and depth(F_D) are always between 0 and 1. Values close to edge are indicated as 0 and 1 indicates non edge areas. So basically we have two classes 0 class indicates edge and 1 class indicates non-edge, every pixel should be classified by these two class types. For this algorithm we need some training sets or samples as SVS is supervised technique. But in real life scenario class labels are not available for real image pixels.

Step 2: Object (Salient object) Identification with Fuzzy C Means Algorithm

This step provides detection technique of salient object and number of clusters are calculated automatically in this section. Basically ACM which is a preprocessing step produces some contours as a final set. But keep in mind when objects are occluded by each other then a single contour may contain more than one object as object may have similar color and creates difficulties while separation. For that reason depth calculation is used to explore the content of each and every final contour which lead us to find the actual number of clusters.

In this chapter I would like to focus on video feature extraction techniques but image is an implicit part of video contents hence the most common technique for image retrieval needs to be depicted for the readers.

9. POPULAR IMAGE RETRIEVAL TECHNIQUES

Content-based image retrieval (CBIR) is provided in this chapter. CBIR is a method that utilizes the visual content of an image, in order search for comparable images in large-scale image databases, in accordance with user interest. This scheme provide a up-to-date comparison of state-of-the-art low-level color and texture feature extraction methods. The concept of CBIR problem is influenced by the requirement of exponentially increasing search space for image and video databases proficiently and successfully. In

Figure 15. Image retrieval system

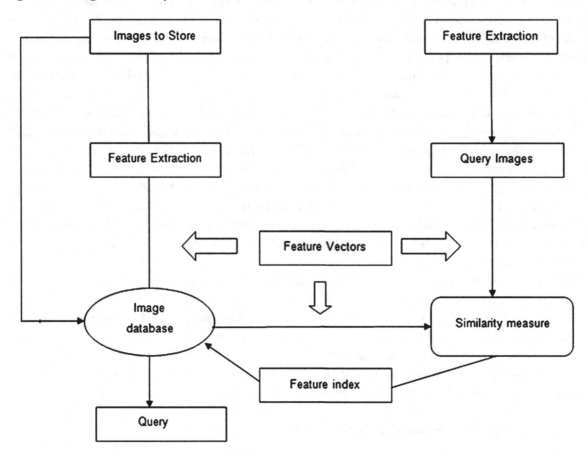

terms of low-level features the visual content of an image is analyzed; these features are extracted from the image. These mainly constitute color and texture features.

9.1. Content-Based Image Retrieval

Conventional information retrieval is dependent only on text, and textual information retrieval uses different techniques for image retrieval. It includes, as a vector of feature values, the representation of an image. However, "a picture is worth a thousand words." .Text based image retrieval is considered to be a non standardized mechanism as different users use different keywords for annotation. As mentioned before, manual systems require too much manpower taking into account the amount of image data available nowadays (see Figure 15).

Text descriptions are always considered to be Subjective and incomplete as it cannot portray difficult and complicated image feature very well. Alternatively content based image retrieval scheme exists as generally image contents are much more flexible or versatile with respect to text, and the amount of visual data is already enormous and still expanding very rapidly. However, this requires linear time with respect to the size of the database and quickly becomes impractical for large databases. Semi-automatic systems provide tools to accelerate the annotation process.

9.2. Synthetic Natural Hybrid System

The concept is all about processing images or video where one specific content is separated and synthetically recreated from other contents (Dugelay, Fintzel, & Valente, 1999). This procedure is used to process virtual teleconferencing system. Here aim is to provide the participants with a virtual common meeting space as if they were at the same physical room and synthesize the individual points of view they would naturally see.

This process approaches both speaker's representation and the meeting room background by mixing synthetic textured face models, built with specialized natural images resulting in a virtualized vision of the world.

Clearly, the above mentioned procedure includes face cloning. Face cloning is considered in animating a synthetic face model. It is done by analyzing the real speaker's video sequence. There exist some difficult challenging constraints on facial cloning which involves itself in analyzing face, frame rate synthesis, image processing delays and the very low bandwidth networks and so on. Now this face cloning and tracking method must work on the face without red tape on it and also it must deal with unknown lighting condition and background. The user must be allowed to move freely.

Now the above was the rule for face feature extraction regulations but practically it has to be done on video sequence. Video specialization for background control is based on un-calibrated 2D views. It is impossible to transmit and catch all necessary scene views. So the data compression for transmission is the only way to augment information for the creation of available mesh points of view rather.

On introduction of mesh oriented algorithm – in the analysis step using points equivalent to the nodes of the mesh in the original calibrated views, estimation of parameter is performed. In the synthesis step using the mesh of external image's nodes and the estimated parameters reconstruct the mesh of the central image is performed.

CONCLUSION

The concept of overall feature extraction guide us towards a notion of simplification of resource requirement that in turns results accuracy while defining huge set of data. Technically we realize the need for feature extraction where memory availability is one of the most important concerns. When we state that feature extraction helps in complex data analysis it basically indicates the number of variable involve in the complex data. Large number of variable needs more memory and huge computation in case of algorithm classification.

The research scope in this topic is growing day by day but mainly the most popular use of feature extraction is in the field of computer vision, computer graphics, photogrammetric, and image or pattern classification. In this chapter we learn about many feature extraction techniques but before using those techniques on specific application area the domain knowledge must be acquired properly, as this domain specific knowledge guides the researcher towards selecting appropriate techniques for specific application. Now modern researches of feature extraction include many diversified field such as visual tracking, handwritten Gurumukhi script analysis in Optical Character Recognition system (OCR) (Singh & Budhiraja, 2011) ECG feature extraction techniques (Karpagachelvi, Arthanari, & Shivakumar 2010) and so on. These research fields are applied in modern gadgets: for an instance visual tracking concept is used mainly for security surveillance, apart from this relevance visual tracking is very popular concept vehicle navigation, access control and computer-human interaction. Here the critical region is noise in image, information loss while 3-dimesional to 2-dimensional image projection. And this is the area where we need a proper feature extraction technique. Similarly ECE feature extraction technique is also useful in critical medical diagnosis and monitoring- preferably for cardiac disease. Here designing proper, accurate method is required for automatic ECG feature extraction to evaluate classification performance of an automatic classifier. In this case wavelet transformation for extracting coefficients for each ECG feature segment is appropriate. Also for OCR system in Gurumukhi script analysis histogram based feature extraction method is relevant as writing style of this script is left to write order and three types of projection histogram exists horizontal, vertical, left and write diagonal. Hence we can conclude that domain knowledge is one of the greatest implicit parameter for good feature extraction.

REFERENCES

Barbu, Ciobanu, & Costin. (2002). *Unsupervised Color - Based Image Recognition Using A Lab Feature Extraction Technique*. Academic Press.

Coden & Brown. (2001). *Speech Transcript Analysis for Automatic Search*. Academic Press.

Duan & Wang. (2008). *Shot-Level Camera Motion Estimation Based on a Parametric Model*. Academic Press.

Dugelay, J.-L., Fintzel, K., & Valente, S. (1999). Synthetic Natural Hybrid Video Processing for Virtual Teleconferencing Systems. *IEEE Picture Coding Symposium*.

Furini, M., & Ghini, V. (2006). *An Audio-Video Summarization Scheme Based on Audio and Video Analysis*. IEEE. doi:10.1109/CCNC.2006.1593230

Girarda & Cohna. (2014). *Automated Audiovisual Depression Analysis*. Academic Press.

Glowinski, Camurri, & Volpe. (2008). *Body gesture analysis: Technique for automatic emotion recognition*. Academic Press.

Ionescu, B., & Vertan, C. (2011). Dissolve Detection In Abstract Video Contents. IEEE.

Jagiwala, D. D., & Sah. (2012). Analysis of Block Matching Algorithm for Motion Estimation in H.264 Video CODEC. *International Journal of Engineering Research and Applications, 2*.

Karpagachelvi, Arthanari, & Shivakumar. (2010). *ECG feature extraction technique- A survey approach*. Academic Press.

Kaur, Singh, & Kundra. (2013). Algorithm for object recognition. *American International Journal of Research in Science, Technology, Engineering & Mathematics*.

Kumar & Chauhan. (2014). *A survey on feature extraction techniques for color images*. Academic Press.

Kumar & Chauhan. (2014). A Survey On Feature Extraction Techniques For Color Images. *International Journal of Scientific and Engineering Research, 5*(9).

Memar, Ksantini, & Boufama. (2014). *Multiple Object Detection With Occlusion using Active Contour Model and Fuzzy C Means*. Academic Press.

Motlicek, Duffner, Korchagin, Bourlard, Scheffler, Odobez, … Thiergart. (2013). *Real-Time Audio-Visual Analysis for Multiperson Videoconferencing*. Academic Press.

Pachouri. (2015). *A Comparative Analysis & Survey of various Feature Extraction Techniques*. Academic Press.

Pardo, A. (2005). *Simple and Robust Hard Cut Detection using Interframe Differences*. DIE, Facultad de Ingeniera y Tecnologas, Universidad Catolica del Uruguay IIE, Facultad de Ingeniera, Universidad de la Republica. doi:10.1007/11578079_43

Patel, Shah, & Panchal. (2013). Shot Detection using Pixel wise Difference with Adaptive Threshold and color Histogram Method in Compressed and Uncompressed Video. *International Journal of Computer Application, 64*(4).

Rawat & Singhai. (2013). *Review of Motion Estimation and Video Stabilization techniques for hand held mobile video*. Academic Press.

Sharma, O., Mioc, D., & Anton, F. (2008). Polygon feature extraction from satellite imagery based on colour image segmentation and medial axis. The International Archives of the Photogrammetry, Remote Sensing and Spatial Information Sciences.

Sharmay, O. (2009). Polygon Feature Extraction From Satellite Imagery Based On Colour Image Segmentation And Medial Axis. Academic Press.

Singh & Budhiraja. (2011). *Feature extraction and classification techniques in O.C.R systems for handwritten Gurumukhi script*. Academic Press.

Taskiran, Amir, Ponceleon, & Delp. (2002). *Automated Video Summarization Using Speech Transcripts*. IBM Almaden Research Center and Video and Image Processing Laboratory.

Taskirany, Amirz, Ponceleonz, & Delp. (2001). *Automated Video Summarization Using Speech Transcripts*. Academic Press.

Turk. (2014). *Gesture Recognition*. Academic Press.

Ullman. (1996). *High Level Vision: Object Recognition and Visual Cognition*. Academic Press.

Voges, M¨argnera, & Martin. (2006). *Algorithms for Audiovisual Speaker Localisation in Reverberant Acoustic Environments*. Academic Press.

Wojtczuk, Armitage, Binnie, & Chamberlain. (2012). *Simple Gesture Recognition using a PIR Sensor Array*. Research Gate.

Yang. (2002). *Object Recognition*. Academic Press.

Yang. (2007). *Object Recognition*. University of California at Merced.

Yu. (2011). Dissolve Detection Based On Twin-Comparison With Curve Fitting. *International Journal of Innovative Computing, Information, & Control, 7*(5).

Chapter 4
Multilevel Image Segmentation Using Modified Particle Swarm Optimization

Sourav De
The University of Burdwan, India

Firoj Haque
University of Kalyani, India

ABSTRACT

Particle Swarm Optimization (PSO) is a well-known swarm optimization technique. PSO is very efficient to optimize the image segmentation problem. PSO algorithm have some drawbacks as the possible solutions may follow the global best solution at one stage. As a result, the probable solutions may bound within that locally optimized solutions. The proposed chapter tries to get over the drawback of the PSO algorithm and proposes a Modified Particle Swarm Optimization (MfPSO) algorithm to segment the multilevel images. The proposed method is compared with the original PSO algorithm and the renowned k-means algorithm. Comparison of the above mentioned existing methods with the proposed method are applied on three real life multilevel gray scale images. For this purpose, three standard objective functions are applied to evaluate the quality of the segmented images. The comparison shows that the proposed MfPSO algorithm is done better than the PSO algorithm and the k-means algorithm to segment the real life multilevel gray scale images.

INTRODUCTION

The process of segregating a digital image into more than one meaningful regions or segments is known as image segmentation. The characteristics of the pixels in a single segment of an image have the same attributes though the attributes of the pixels in different segments are characteristically different to each other. The basic attributes of an image are color, shape, texture, position and similarity/dissimilarity between the regions. The objective of the image segmentation is to represent a digital image into meaningful and easy to understand components, so that any user can able to analyze that image. Image segmentation

DOI: 10.4018/978-1-5225-0498-6.ch004

is considered as a preliminary step in different types of image processing, moving and non-moving video related applications. The application areas of image segmentation are very much wider, like satellite image processing, machine vision, remote sensing, medical imaging, biometric measurement, feature extraction, object recognition, etc. to detect, recognize or track an object. The multiplicity of objects in a digital image and huge variation between them are the major challenges in the segmentation process. Different types of classical and non-classical image processing application are employed to handle the image segmentation problem.

Edge detection and region growing, thresholding, normalized cut, etc. are different types of classical image segmentation techniques to segment the multilevel gray scale images. The segmentation of the images by the detection of the object boundaries in that image is the main characteristics of the edge detection image segmentation algorithms. But an incorrect segmentation may be caused by this edge detection algorithms as these processes are not helpful for segmenting the blur images or any complicated images. Region growing techniques are not efficiently employed for multilevel image segmentation as the different regions of an image is not well segregated. The histogram of an image plays a vital role in image segmentation by thresholding techniques. The segmentation of an image that have the distinctive objects and the background is very much helpful using the thresholding techniques. This process may fail when the distribution of the pixels in the image are very much complex.

It has been observed that most of the real world problems can be devised as an optimization problem. Traditional heuristic algorithms are designed to solve differentiable functions. As most real world optimization problems are non-differentiable, it is too difficult to find a heuristic algorithm which will properly work on non-differentiable optimization functions. Many meta-heuristic approaches have been developed to solve non-differentiable optimization functions. Recently, meta-heuristic algorithms are becoming more attractive and useful tools to the researchers. Evolutionary algorithms (EAs) are the metaheuristic type of algorithms and they are effective enough to solve the problem of clustering. Genetic algorithms, differential evolution, particle swarm optimization, etc. are the example of evolutionary algorithms. The functional characteristics of these type of algorithms are inspired by the principle of natural genetics.

Particle Swarm Optimization (PSO), developed by Eberhart and Kennedy in 1995, is one of the population based meta-heuristic optimization technique imitating social behavior of bird flocking or fish schooling (Kennedy, 1995). The PSO algorithm is very much popular as this algorithm converges very quickly and easy to implement. The PSO algorithm is also known as an important evolutionary algorithm. Like any other evolutionary algorithms, PSO algorithm stores the fitter solutions with respect to a particular problem and the performance of a problem improves by upgrading the entire populations instead of the individual solution.

Basically, the PSO algorithm is applied to find out the best possible solution of a problem and the best solution is noted as the g_{best} solution. This best solution in each iteration of the PSO algorithm guides to get the ultimate solution of the problem. It is usually happened that the probable solutions in different iterations may follow the global solution. It may be possible that a solution in other region may give better result. Ultimately, the diversity of the probable solutions are lost as the solution may follow the global best solution. This problem can be solved if the diversity of the probable solutions are maintained. This chapter proposes a modified version of particle swarm optimization (MfPSO) algorithm to segment multilevel gray scale images into different segments. The proposed MfPSO algorithm tries to overcome the said problem of the PSO algorithm. For that reason, the proposed algorithm tries to modify the velocity updation formula of the particles in the original PSO algorithm. The proposed method is compared with the basic PSO method as well as with the well-known k-means algorithm to establish its efficiency.

The above mentioned algorithms are applied on three benchmark images to determine the performance of those algorithms. Three standard efficiency measure, the Peak Signal to Noise Ratio (PSNR) (Zayed, 2005), the correlation coefficient (ρ) (Bhattacharyya, 2008; De, 2012) and the empirical measure, F due to Liu and Yang (Liu, 2015; De, 2012) are applied as the evaluation functions to measure the quality of the segmented images. The experimental results show that the proposed MfPSO algorithm outperforms the other two algorithms to segment the multilevel gray scale images.

The outline of the chapter is as follows. The next section, named as the literature review, demonstrates a detailed review of different types of current image segmentation techniques those are proposed by different learnt researchers. The following section is known as the prerequisite techniques in which the k-means algorithm and the image segmentation quality evaluation metrics are described in two respective subsections. The peak signal to noise ratio (PSNR), correlation coefficient (ρ) and the empirical measure (F') are described in the image segmentation quality evaluation metrics subsection. A detailed analysis of the modified particle swarm optimization (MfPSO) is presented in the next section. The basic discussion and the mathematical formulations of particle swarm optimization (PSO) along with the drawback of PSO is also narrated in this section. The next section is followed by the detailed representation of the proposed methodology to segment the real life multilevel gray scale images as well as the real life magnetic resonance (MR) images. The image segmentation results, both in qualitative and quantitative nature, are detailed in the next section. The chapter ends with a brief concluding section.

LITERATURE REVIEW

The working principle of the well-known k-means algorithm (Jain, 1999; Kanungo, 2002) is based on the crisp approach. The initial selection of the cluster centroids is the primary key for the better performance of this algorithm. In this algorithm, a cluster is generated by measuring the distance between the cluster centroid and the data points. The nearer data points are used to create a cluster. The primary objective of this algorithm is to maximize the intercluster separation or minimize the intracluster separation. Generally, random selection of the clusters may not give the unique result as this algorithm follows the data-dependent greedy approach and it may converge to a suboptimal solution. Huge numbers of research are done to improve the quality of the k-means algorithm. The modification in the initialization of the cluster centers of this algorithm is done by Khan and Ahmad (Khan, 2004). Zalik (Zalik, 2008) presented a modified version of the k-means algorithm. Halder and Dasgupta (Halder, 2012) proposed rough set based k-means algorithm for gray scale image segmentation. In this method, spatial segmentation is done on the basis of the intensity values of the image pixels along with neighborhood relationships. A modified k-means algorithm with the help of rough set theory is applied in this method.

Different type of image and pattern segmentation problem can be handled by the Genetic algorithms (GAs) for their domain independent nature (De, 2012). In a large search space, the optimal or near optimal solutions can be derived easily by GAs. As an efficient search method, three operators i. e., selection, crossover and mutation are applied in the GAs. GAs may be applied for those problems that does not have any knowledge about the domain theories of the problem or it is difficult to formulate the problem (De, 2013). Without knowing the segmentation techniques applied, image segmentation problem can be solved by the GAs due to their generality characteristics. It only needs a segmentation quality measurement criterion. Janc *et al.* (Janc, 2013) applied genetic algorithm to segment the trabecular and cortical bone images. Hammouche *et al.* (Hammouche, 2008) proposed a multilevel image segmentation technique using genetic algorithm as well as wavelet transform. In this method, the proper threshold levels and the exact number of thresholds are determined with the help of the histogram of the multilevel test image. Reduction of the original histogram is done by the wavelet transform and after that, the genetic algorithm is applied to resolve the number of thresholds and the threshold values. A hybrid genetic algorithm is presented to segment the gray scale images on the basis of the q-state Potts spin glass model (Hauschild, 2012). After the conversion of the test image into a set of weights for a q-state spin glass, the genetic algorithm is employed to generate the suitable candidate solution. The Otsu method in combination with the genetic algorithm (Otsu-GA) is applied for gray scale image segmentation (Zhou, 2011; Xu, 2014). De *et al.* (De, 2010; De, 2008) applied genetic algorithm to segment the gray scale image with the help of multilayer self-organizing neural network (MLSONN) architecture. The genetic algorithm is applied to generate the optimized class levels to generate the optimized multilevel sigmoidal (OptiMUSIG) activation function. The image content heterogeneity is incorporated in this segmentation methodology. The OptiMUSIG activation function with variable threshold is also very effective for gray scale image segmentation (De, 2009). Three-level thresholding on the basis of maximum fuzzy entropy and genetic algorithm is applied for image segmentation (Tao, 2003). In this method, the genetic algorithm is employed to determine the optimal combination of all the fuzzy parameters those will be applied to design the fuzzy entropy.

Kennedy *et al.* (Kennedy, 1997) also proposed the binary PSO which is able to select the optimal number of segments/clusters. In this method, the k-means algorithm is applied to refine the centroids of the chosen segments/clusters. The PSO algorithm is capable to optimize the image segmentation problem. An image segmentation algorithm with the help of PSO is proposed by Orman *et al.* (Omran, 2005). In this algorithm, the number of centroids those are used to generate the clusters are user specified and the similar pixels are putted in a cluster. The quality of the partitioned image data are evaluated by a crisp logic based function. Zhang *et al.* (Zheng, 2009; Zheng, 2010) applied PSO algorithm to improve the gray scale image segmentation. In this method, the improvised 2D entropy is applied to segment the gray scale two head CT images. PSO algorithm with Kapur's entropy criterion method as fitness function is applied for image segmentation (Mishra, 2014). Liu *et al.* (Liu, 2015) presented a modified particle swarm optimization (MPSO) algorithm for multilevel threshold based image segmentation. In this approach, two new properties are introduced in the original PSO algorithm, i. e., adaptive inertia (AI) and adaptive population (AP), respectively. To improve the search efficiency and convergence speed, the inertia weight in the AI strategy is dynamic and it depends upon the iteration stage (Liu, 2015). The population size of MPSO of AP strategy is also dynamic to overcome the problem of local convergence (Liu, 2015). A modified PSO algorithm in combination with the Otsu's method is applied to segment the multilevel gray scale images (Hamdaoui, 2015). This method has attempted to improve the updating procedure of the velocity and position of the particles in PSO algorithm. Color images can also be segmented efficiently by different type of modified PSO algorithms and they are reported in (Li, 2014; Banerjee, 2015). Mishra *et al.* (Mishra, 2015) applied PSO algorithm to segment the medical images, like X-ray images.

PREREQUISITE TECHNOLOGIES

Before moving to the proposed methodology, some prerequisite technologies are discussed in this section. In the first subsection, the methodology and working principle of the k-means algorithm are discussed.

After that, three image segmentation quality evaluation metrics i. e. the PSNR (Zayed, 2005), the correlation coefficient (ρ) (Bhattacharyya, 2008; De, 2012) and the empirical measure, F (Liu, 1994; De, 2012) are illustrated in the remaining subsection briefly.

k-Means Algorithm

The term *k-means* was first used by MacQueen in 1967 (MacQueen, 1967) and this algorithm was first proposed by Stuart Lloyd in 1957 as a technique for pulse-code modulation. In *k*-means algorithm, number of cluster *k* is fixed. The algorithm uses an iterative technique to modify the initial random cluster centers. Let, P is the set of data points and $\left[m_1^{(0)} \quad m_2^{(0)} \quad \ldots \quad m_K^{(0)} \right]$ are the initial random $k \leq |P|$ cluster centers where, $m_i^0 \in P, \forall i$. A cluster $C_i^{(t)}$ at iteration t, associated with the cluster center $m_i^{(t)}$, is a set of data points defined as (MacQueen, 1967)

$$C_i^{(t)} = \{x : x \in P \text{ and } \| m_i^{(t)} - x \| < \| m_j^{(t)} - x \| \forall j\} \tag{1}$$

The algorithm updates a cluster center as follows (MacQueen, 1967)

$$m_i^{(t+1)} = \frac{1}{|C_i|} * \sum_{x \in C_i} x \tag{2}$$

k-means algorithm minimize the following criterion (MacQueen, 1967)

$$J(K) = \sum_{i=1}^{K} \sum_{x \in C_i} (\| m_i, x \|)^2 \tag{3}$$

The algorithm is composed of the following steps

Step 1: Randomly select *k* points from the set of the data points that are considered as initial cluster centers.
Step 2: Partition the data points into *k* clusters by assigning each points to its nearest cluster center.
Step 3: Calculate centroid of each cluster and replace the cluster center of each cluster by its centroid.
Step 4: Repeat Step 2 and Step 3 until the cluster centers no longer change.

k-means algorithm is fast, robust and easier to understand. It also gives the best result when the clusters are distinct or well separated from each other. But *k*-means also have many disadvantages as it requires a predefined fixed value of *k*. In many cases, *k*-means produces locally optimal solutions those are susceptible to noise and also biased towards the globular shape of the clusters.

Image Segmentation Quality Evaluation Metrics

Different type of algorithms are available to segment an image and they produce different results of an image. It is difficult to measure the quality of the segmented images. Several unsupervised approaches are available in different literatures (Zhang, 1996). In this subsection, we will throw some light on three image segmentation quality evaluation matrices.

Peak Signal to Noise Ratio (PSNR)

The Peak Signal to Noise Ratio (PSNR) is used to measure the distortion between original image and segmented image. The PSNR is defined as (Zayed, 2005)

$$PSNR = 20\log_{10}\frac{MAX_I}{\sqrt{MSE}} \; where, MSE = \frac{1}{M \times N}\sum_{x=1}^{M}\sum_{x=1}^{N}(I[x,y] - I'[x,y])^2 \tag{4}$$

$I[x, y]$ and $I'[x, y]$ denotes (x, y) pixel value of original image I and segmented image I' respectively. The size of the image is denoted as M×N. MAX_I is the maximum value of the signal and in most of the cases, its value will be 255 for an image. The higher value of PSNR means that the quality of the segmented image is better.

Correlation Coefficient

The standard measure of correlation coefficient (ρ) (Bhattacharyya, 2008; De, 2012; De, 2013) can be applied to assess the quality of segmentation achieved. It is given by (Bhattacharyya, 2008; De, 2012; De, 2013)

$$\rho = \frac{\frac{1}{n^2}\sum_{i=1}^{n}\sum_{j=1}^{n}(M_{ij} - \bar{M})(G_{ij} - \bar{G})}{\sqrt{\frac{1}{n^2}\sum_{i=1}^{n}\sum_{j=1}^{n}(M_{ij} - \bar{M})^2}\sqrt{\frac{1}{n^2}\sum_{i=1}^{n}\sum_{j=1}^{n}(G_{ij} - \bar{G})^2}} \tag{5}$$

where, M_{ij}, $1 \le i, j \le n$ and G_{ij}, $1 \le i, j \le n$ are the original and the segmented images respectively, each of dimensions n×n. The respective mean intensity values of the original and segmented images are denoted as $\bar{M}$ and $\bar{G}$, respectively. The quality of the segmentation will be better if the ρ value has the higher value.

Empirical Goodness Measure (F')

Before knowing the exact notation of the empirical goodness measure (F'), we have to know some basic notations.

Let an image (IM), having an area A_{IM}, can be segmented into N number of regions. The area of the kth region is denoted as $A_k = |R_k|$, where, R_k signifies the number of pixels in region k. The average value of the gray level intensity feature (ν) in region k is denoted as (Liu, 1994; De, 2012; De, 2013)

$$\hat{C}_\nu(R_k) = \frac{\sum\limits_{p \in R_k} C_\nu(p)}{S_k} \tag{6}$$

where, $C_\nu(p)$ represents the value of ν for pixel p. The squared color error of region k is represented as (Liu, 1994; De, 2012; De, 2013)

$$e_k^2 = \sum\limits_{\nu \in (r,g,b)} \sum\limits_{p \in R_k} (C_\nu(p) - \hat{C}_\nu(R_k))^2 \tag{7}$$

The quantitative evaluation function F' for image segmentation, proposed by Liu and Yang (Liu, 1994; De, 2012; De, 2013) is denoted as

$$F'(M) = \frac{1}{1000.S_{IM}} \sqrt{\sum\limits_{u=1}^{Maxarea} \left[N(u) \right]^{1 + \frac{1}{u}} \sum\limits_{r=1}^{N} \frac{e_k^2}{\sqrt{S_k}}} \tag{8}$$

where, S_{IM} is the area of an image (*IM*) to be segmented. *Maxarea* is represented as the area of the largest region in the segmented image. $N(u)$ denotes the number of regions in the segmented image having an area of exactly u. The lower values of F signifies the better segmentation.

MODIFIED PARTICLE SWARM OPTIMIZATION

Particle Swarm Optimization (PSO), developed by Eberhart and Kennedy in 1995, is one of the population based meta-heuristic optimization technique imitating social behavior of bird flocking or fish schooling (Kennedy, 1995). It is a population-based stochastic optimization technique. PSO was originally developed to solve non-linear problem with continuous valued search space. In many aspect, PSO and genetic algorithm (GA) are very much similar with respect to their functionalities. At the starting point of both the algorithms, the initial population is generated on the random basis. The ultimate solution is derived by iterating through generations in both the processes. Unlike Genetic Algorithm (GA), PSO does not apply any evolution operators such as selection, crossover and mutation operators.

The probable solutions are denoted as particles in PSO algorithm. PSO and all of its variants use a number of particles. These particles constitutes a swarm and moves around in K- dimensional search space looking for the optima. In the problem space, each particle maintains the record of its positions related with the best solution which is attained so far. This record keeping continues for all stages of the algorithm. The best solution is determined by the fitness value of that particle. For a particular particle, the stored fitness value is known as *pbest*. Another best position that has been achieved so far by the particle in the entire population is called global best position or *gbest*. As each particle is moving through the search space, they must have a velocity. Each particle tries to update its position based on the current position, the current velocity and also based on the personal best position and the global best position. The performance of each particle in a PSO is decided by how nearer it is from the global optimum

(Bhattacharyya, 2013). The fitness function of the optimization problem is considered as the metric for this purpose. Each Particle updates its position with the internal velocity. PSO is easy to implement and few parameters have to be adjusted. For this reason, it can be applied to solve the engineering problem as well as scientific research. PSO algorithm is a derivative free search algorithm and require lower computational cost. PSO algorithm is as follows

Let, $p_i^{(t)}$ is the position of the ith particle in the swarm at iteration t and it is denoted as (Kennedy, 1995)

$$p_i^{(t)} = [p_{i,1}^{(t)} \quad p_{i,2}^{(t)} \quad p_{i,3}^{(t)} \quad \cdots \quad p_{i,K}^{(t)}] \tag{9}$$

where, $i = 1, 2, 3, ...,N$ denotes the number of particles and K is the dimension of the particle position. Particle position in search space is updated by (Kennedy, 1995)

$$p_{i,j}^{(t+1)} = p_{i,j}^{(t)} + v_{i,j}^{(t+1)} \tag{10}$$

where, $v_i^{(t)}$ is considered as the velocity of ith particle at iteration t. The $v_i^{(t)}$ is denoted as (Kennedy, 1995)

$$v_i^{(t)} = [v_{i,1}^{(t)} \quad v_{i,2}^{(t)} \quad v_{i,3}^{(t)} \quad \cdots \quad v_{i,K}^{(t)}]` \tag{11}$$

Particle velocity is updated by the following equation (Kennedy, 1995)

$$v_{(i,j)}^{(t+1)} = w^{(t)} * v_{(i,j)}^{(t)} + c_1 * r_1 * [l_{best_{i,j}}^{(t)} - p_{i,j}^{(t)}] + c_2 * r_2 * [g_{best_j} - p_{i,j}^{(t)}] \tag{12}$$

In the above equation, w is the inertia weight which controls the flying of a particle by weighing the contribution of previous velocity. Basically, it controls the memory of the previous flight direction. The inertia constant can be either implemented as a fixed value or it can change dynamically changing [33, 34]. The calculation of w is performed as follows (Rao, 2009; Lee, 2010)

$$w^{(t)} = w_{max} - \frac{w_{max} - w_{min}}{t_{max}} * t \tag{13}$$

where w_{min} and w_{max} are the minimum and maximum inertia weight respectively. t_{max} is the maximum iteration number and t is current iteration.

Considering maximization problem, the personal best or local best position l_{best_i} visited by i^{th} particle at iteration $(t + 1)$ is calculated as (Kennedy, 1995)

$$l_{best_i}^{(t+1)} = \begin{cases} l_{best_i}^{(t)}, iff(p_{i,1}^{(t+1)}, ..., p_{i,K}^{(t+1)}) < f(l_{best_{i,1}}^{(t)}, ..., l_{best_{i,K}}^{(t)}) \\ f(p_{i,1}^{(t+1)}, ..., p_{i,K}^{(t+1)}), Otherwise \end{cases} \tag{14}$$

Where $f : \mathbb{R}^K \to \mathbb{R}$ represents as the fitness function. The global best position g_{best} at iteration t is calculated as (Kennedy, 1995)

$$g_{best}^{(t)} = l_{best_i}^{(t)}, \text{where } f(l_{best_{i,1}}^{(t)}, ..., l_{best_{i,K}}^{(t)}) > f(l_{best_{j,1}}^{(t)}, ..., l_{best_{j,K}}^{(t)}) \forall j, i \neq j \tag{15}$$

In equation (12), c_1 and c_2 are denoted as acceleration and r_1 and r_2 are two random variables in the range [0, 1]. The value of $v_{(i,j)}^{(t+1)}$ is within the range $[\nu_{min,j}, \nu_{max,j}]$. The velocity of particle is adjusted using following equation (Kennedy, 1995; Eberhart, 2001)

$$v_{i,j}^{(t)} = \begin{cases} v_{i,j}^{(t)}, if v_{min,j} \leq v_{i,j}^{(t)} \leq v_{max,j} \\ v_{max,j}, if v_{i,j}^{(t)} > v_{max,j} \\ v_{min,j}, if v_{i,j}^{(t)} < v_{min,j} \end{cases} \tag{16}$$

The following equations are used to calculate $\nu_{min,j}$ and $\nu_{max,j}$ (Abido, 2002)

$$\nu_{min,j} = (p_{min,j} - p_{max,j}) / \delta_j \tag{17}$$

$$\nu_{max,j} = (p_{max,j} - p_{min,j}) / \delta_j \tag{18}$$

where $p_{min,j}$ and $p_{max,j}$ are the minimum and maximum positions of the particle in the jth dimension and δ_j is the number of intervals in the jth dimension selected by the user. It may happened that a particle may go beyond the boundary of the search space. Then the position of the particle is adjusted as follows (Kennedy, 1995; Eberhart, 2001)

$$\text{If } p_{i,j}^{(t)} < p_{min,j}, \text{then } p_{i,j}^{(t)} = p_{min,j} \text{ and } v_{i,j}^{(t)} = -v_{i,j}^{(t)} \tag{19}$$

$$\text{If } p_{i,j}^{(t)} > p_{max,j}, \text{then } p_{i,j}^{(t)} = p_{max,j} \text{ and } v_{i,j}^{(t)} = -v_{i,j}^{(t)}$$

In PSO algorithm, it has been observed that all the particles used to follow g_{best} position as the social leader. As all the particles are influenced by single leader's direction, the leader may leads all the particle to a particular region. As a result, the particles are congested in a local region instead of the diversified solutions. That's why standard PSO algorithm can easily get trapped in the local optimal when solving complex multi modal problems. To overcome this problem, many variants of PSO has been proposed. The previously proposed methods, narrated in different articles, are mutation based to increase the diversity in the search space. In this chapter, a new approach has been narrated to maintain the diversity of the particles. In this proposed modified version of PSO, a set of best solutions S is maintained, where $|S| = per*N$ (where, $per \in [0.0, 1.0]$) and S is denoted as

$$S^{(t)} = \{s_1^{(t)}, s_2^{(t)}, s_3^{(t)}, ..., s_{|S|}^{(t)}\} \text{ where, } S \subset \{l_{best_j}^{(t)} : j = 1, 2, ..., N\}$$

and $\forall i$ if $l_{best_i}^{(0)} \notin S^{(0)}$ then $f(l_{best_{i,1}}^{(0)}, ..., l_{best_{i,K}}^{(0)}) < \min_{j=1}^{|S|} f(s_{j,1}^{(0)}, ..., s_{j,K}^{(0)})$ (20)

In the modified PSO, the velocity update is performed by the following equation

$$v_{(i,j)}^{(t+1)} = w^{(t)} * v_{(i,j)}^{(t)} + c_1 * r_1 * [l_{best_{i,j}}^{(t)} - p_{i,j}^{(t)}] + c_2 * r_2) * [s_{x,j}^{(t)} - p_{i,j}^{(t)}]$$

where $|| s_x^{(t)} - p_i^{(t)} || < || s_y^{(t)} - p_i^{(t)} ||, \forall y$ (21)

In the proposed method multiple leaders are selected to lead the particle into different promising region of search space. The modified PSO algorithm is narrated in Algorithm 1.

Algorithm 1 Modified Particles Swarm Optimization Algorithm

1: procedure MODIFIED-PSO
2: for $i = 1 \rightarrow N$ do
3: for $j = 1 \rightarrow K$ do
4: $p_{i,j}^{(0)} \sim U(p_{min,j}, p_{max,j})$
5: $v_{i,j}^{(0)} \sim U(v_{min,j}, v_{max,j})$
6: end for
7: $fit_{i,j} := f(p_{i,1,...,p_{i,K}})$
8: $l_{best_i} := p_i$
9: end for
10: $S^{(0)} = \{s_1^{(0)}, s_2^{(0)}, s_3^{(0)}, ..., s_{|S|}^{(0)}\} where, S \subset \{l_{best_j}^{(0)} : j = 1, 2, ..., N\}$

and $\forall i$ if $l_{best_i}^{(0)} \notin S^{(0)}$ then $f(l_{best_{i,1}}^{(0)}, ..., l_{best_{i,K}}^{(0)}) < \min_{j=1}^{|S|} f(s_{j,1}^{(0)}, ..., s_{j,K}^{(0)})$

11: $t = 0$
12: while $t < MAX\_ITER$ do
13: for $i = 0 \rightarrow N$ do
14: for $j = 1 \rightarrow K$ do
15: $v_{(i,j)}^{(t+1)} = w^{(t)} * v_{(i,j)}^{(t)} + c_1 * r_1 * [l_{best_{i,j}}^{(t)} - p_{i,j}^{(t)}] + c_2 * r_2) * [s_{x,j}^{(t)} - p_{i,j}^{(t)}]$
where, $|| s_x^{(t)} - p_i^{(t)} || < || s_y^{(t)} - p_i^{(t)} ||, \forall y$
16: if $v_{(i,j)}^{(t+1)} > v_{max,j}$ then
17: $v_{(i,j)}^{(t+1)} := v_{max,j}$

18: end if

19: if $\nu_{(i,j)}^{(t+1)} < \nu_{\min,j}$ then

20: $\nu_{(i,j)}^{(t+1)} := \nu_{\min,j}$

21: end if

22: $p_{(i,j)}^{(t+1)} = p_{i,j}^{(t)} + \nu_{(i,j)}^{(t+1)}$

23: if $p_{(i,j)}^{(t+1)} > p_{\max,j}$ then

24: $p_{(i,j)}^{(t+1)} := p_{\max,j}$

25: $\nu_{(i,j)}^{(t+1)} := -\nu_{(i,j)}^{(t+1)}$

26: end if

27: if $p_{(i,j)}^{(t+1)} > p_{\min,j}$ then

28: $p_{(i,j)}^{(t+1)} = p_{\min,j}$

29: $\nu_{(i,j)}^{(t+1)} := -\nu_{(i,j)}^{(t+1)}$

30: end if

31: end for

32: $fit_{i,j} := f(p_{i,1}^{(t+1)},...,p_{i,K}^{(t+1)})$

33: if $fit_{i,j} > f(l_{best_{i,1}}^{(t)},...,l_{best_{i,K}}^{(t)})$ then

34: $l_{best_i}^{(t+1)} := p_i^{(t+1)}$

35: else

36: $l_{best_i}^{(t+1)} := l_{best_i}^{(t)}$

37: end if

38: $S^{(t+1)} = \{s_1^{(t+1)}, s_2^{(t+1)}, s_3^{(t+1)},...,s_{|S|}^{(t+1)}\}$ where, $S \subset \{l_{best_n}^{(t+1)} : j = 1,2,...,N\}$

and $\forall m$ if $l_{best_m}^{(t+1)} \notin S^{(t+1)}$ then $f(l_{best_{m,1}}^{(t+1)},...,l_{best_{m,K}}^{(t+1)}) < \min_{n=1}^{|S|} f(s_{n,1}^{(t+1)},...,s_{n,K}^{(t+1)})$

39: end for

40: $t := t + 1$

41: end while

42: Return $s_i^{(t)}$ where, $f(s_{i,1}^{(t)},...,s_{i,K}^{(t)}) > f(s_{j,1}^{(t)},...,s_{j,K}^{(t)}), \forall j$

43: end procedure

PROPOSED METHODOLOGY

In this chapter, the multilevel gray scale images are intended to segment by the modified PSO algorithm. The different steps of the proposed method is narrated in the following subsections step by step manner.

Consider a $H \times W$ sized gray level image (I) with minimum and maximum gray levels $L_{\min}$ and $L_{\max}$. A pixel intensity at (x, y) co-ordinate is denoted as $I[x, y]$ and it is also within the range i. e., $L_{\min} \leq I[x, y] \leq L_{\max}$. Multilevel image segmentation is the process of partitioning image into K number of classes where $K \geq 2$. Assume, C is the set of class levels and it is represented as

$$C = [c_1 \quad c_2 \quad ... \quad c_K] \text{ where, } L_{\min} \leq c_i \leq L_{\max} \text{ and } c_i \text{ is an integer} \tag{22}$$

The segmented image I' is also a gray level image of size $H \times W$, and a pixel at (x, y) co-ordinate is given by

$$I'[x, y] = c_i \text{ where } |c_i - I[x, y]| < |c_j - I[x, y]|, \forall j \tag{23}$$

Particle's Position Representation

The swarm size or number of particles in the swarm is denoted as N. Position of particle i at iteration t is represented as $p_i = [p_{i,1}^{(t)} \quad p_{i,2}^{(t)} \quad ... \quad p_{i,K}^{(t)}]$ and initially all the particle's positions will be initialize randomly such that $p_{i,j}^{(0)} \sim U(p_{\min,j}, p_{\max,j})$, where, $p_{\min,j} = L_{\min}$ and $p_{\max,j} = L_{\max}, \forall i$ and $j = 1, ..., K$.

Particle's Velocity Representation

The ith particle at iteration t is denoted as $v_i^{(t)} = [v_{i,1}^{(t)} \quad v_{i,2}^{(t)} \quad ... \quad v_{i,K}^{(t)}]$. Initially, the velocities of all the particles also will be initialized randomly and it is done as follows $v_{i,j}^{(0)} \sim U(v_{\min,j}, v_{\max,j})$. The selection procedure of the parameters $v_{\min,j}$ and $v_{\max,j}$ have been described in equation the (17) and (18).

Fitness Computation

At iteration t, particle position $p_i = [p_{i,1}^{(t)} \quad p_{i,2}^{(t)} \quad ... \quad p_{i,K}^{(t)}]$ represent a set of cluster labels $C = [c_1 \quad c_2 \quad ... \quad c_K]$ where $c_j = \lfloor p_{i,j}^{(t)} + 0.5 \rfloor$. Using C, segmented image I' can be calculated from image I using equation (23). In this chapter the quality of I' has been calculated using three image quality evaluation metrics i. e. PSNR, ρ and F, using the equations 4, 5 and 8, respectively.

Multilevel Image Segmentation Using MfPSO

The quality of the segmented images using each particle is determined using the image segmentation quality evaluation functions. The particle having the better fitness value is considered as the global best solution (*gBest*). Then all the particles go for the proposed MfPSO algorithm. The velocity of each particle is updated using the equation 21. The position of the particles are also updated. After the updation, the fitness of the modified particles are evaluated and the population of the solutions are updated. This process continues for a certain amount of iteration.

Experimental results and analysis

In this chapter, multilevel image segmentation using MfPSO is demonstrated with two multilevel real life images viz., Lena and Peppers and one real life Brain Neuroanatomy (MRI) image (De, 2014). The dimensions of each images are 256×256. Results are also reported for the segmentation of the multi-level test images using the k-means and PSO algorithm and the same three above-mentioned images are applied for the experiment. The population size is taken as 100 solutions for all algorithms. The multi-level images are segmented into $K=$ {6, 8, 10} classes but the results with the $K=$ {8, 10} are reported in this chapter. Different parameters are used in the PSO and MfPSO algorithm. The PSO and proposed modified PSO have been implemented using following parameters $c_1 = 2, c_2 = 2, \delta = 50, w_{min} = 0.1$ and $w_{max} = 0.5$. In modified PSO, pr has been chosen 0.1 that means 10% of total swarm size. Three evaluation functions (PSNR, ρ, F') have been employed to measure the quality of the segmented images. The MfPSO based optimization procedure generates the optimized sets of class boundaries (cl_{MfPSO}) on the basis of three evaluation functions (PSNR, ρ, F') for different number of classes. They are tabulated in Tables 1-9 for the test image. In the first column of these tables, the number of class levels *(# of segments)* is noted and the name of the methods *(Algo)* is mentioned in the second column of these tables. The derived class levels and the corresponding fitness value (FI_{val}) are tabulated in the fourth and fifth columns of these tables. The last columns of all tables show the quality measures κ [graded on a scale of 1 (best) onwards] obtained by the segmentation of the test images based on the corresponding set of optimized class levels and the best results on the basis of the particular algorithm is marked in **bolded** font. The derived class levels and the corresponding fitness values by three algorithms for Lena image are reported in Tables 1 - 3. In Tables 4 - 6, the deduced class boundaries and their fitness values for Peppers image are tabulated after employing the above mentioned algorithms. The results for MR Brain image are accounted in Tables 7 - 9. We have run all the algorithms for 50 times each for each images and their corresponding class levels. Only six good results of each case are reported in these tables.

The segmented gray scale output images derived for the $K=$ {8, 10} classes, with the proposed optimized approach vis-a-vis with the k-means and the original PSO algorithm are presented afterwards.

The first four better results of each algorithm set are applied to deduce the output images. The segmented multilevel gray scale test images obtained by the k-means algorithm and the original PSO are shown in the first and second row each figure. In the third row of each figure, the segmented multilevel gray scale test images by the proposed MfPSO algorihm are depicted. That means, the segmented images by the k-means algorithm are shown in (a)-(d), the segmented images by the original PSO algorithm are depicted in (e)-(h) and the MfPSO based multilevel segmented images are pictured in (i) – (l) of each figure, respectively. In Figure 1, the first four better class levels ($K=8$) of Table 1, derived by the proposed approach and other two algorithms, are applied to get the segmented output of the Lena image. In this case, PSNR is used as the evaluation function. The first four better results from the same table with $K=10$ are employed to generate the multilevel segmented outputs of the same image and that are shown in Figure 2. Figures 3 and 4 are generated by the first four better results of each algorithm with $K = 8$ and 10, respectively of the Lena image. The fitness function, ρ is used as the evaluation criteria in these cases. The empirical measure, F' is applied as the fitness function to generate the segmented Lena images those are presented in Figures 5 and 6 using $K = 8$ and 10 class levels, respectively.

The multilevel segmented outputs of Peppers image are presented in Figures 7 – 12. The first four better class levels ($K=8$) of Table 4, gained by the proposed approach as well as other two algorithms, are applied to get the segmented output of the Peppers image in Figure 7. In this case, PSNR is employed as the evaluation function. In Figure 8, the multilevel segmented outputs of the Peppers image are generated using the first four better results from the Table 4 with $K=10$ class levels. Using $K = 8$ and 10

Table 1. Different algorithm based class boundaries and evaluated segmentation quality measures, PSNR, for 8 and 10 classes of Lena image

# of Segments	Algo	#	Class Levels	FI$_{PSNR}$	κ
8	k-means	1	49, 72, 96, 115, 134, 154, 175, 204	32.0004	2
		2	**50, 73, 96, 115, 134, 154, 175, 204**	**32.0059**	**1**
		3	49, 67, 87, 105, 127, 149, 171, 204	31.7350	5
		4	**50, 73, 96, 115, 134, 154, 175, 204**	**32.0059**	**1**
		5	51, 80, 104, 129, 150, 169, 190, 209	31.7908	3
		6	46, 61, 84, 106, 130, 153, 176, 205	31.7695	4
	PSO	1	**44, 80, 111, 133, 147, 170, 171, 208**	**31.1948**	**1**
		2	50, 89, 115, 137, 160, 179, 191, 218	31.1012	2
		3	36, 61, 91, 128, 136, 152, 169, 211	30.6862	4
		4	47, 83, 99, 106, 137, 164, 207, 230	30.6263	5
		5	48, 53, 85, 87, 101, 129, 161, 211	29.9875	6
		6	65, 88, 104, 131, 149, 169, 188, 217	31.0122	3
	MfPSO	1	44, 53, 74, 117, 131, 149, 163, 210	32.1239	3
		2	**61, 83, 101, 132, 164, 194, 201, 204**	**32.1291**	**1**
		3	34, 61, 98, 101, 132, 154, 167, 212	32.1070	5
		4	67, 93, 115, 136, 148, 163, 190, 213	32.1199	4
		5	45, 75, 112, 128, 152, 169, 206, 210	32.1199	4
		6	34, 58, 92, 107, 118, 138, 172, 218	32.1241	2
10	k-means	1	50, 74, 96, 112, 127, 138, 150, 162, 180, 206	33.3950	2
		2	45, 56, 70, 86, 102, 122, 138, 155, 176, 205	33.3120	3
		3	43, 53, 65, 82, 100, 116, 133, 152, 174, 204	33.0175	5
		4	43, 53, 67, 85, 102, 122, 138, 155, 176, 205	33.2852	4
		5	45, 56, 70, 86, 102, 122, 138, 155, 176, 205	33.3120	3
		6	**45, 58, 77, 95, 109, 127, 143, 159, 180, 206**	**33.6758**	**1**
	PSO	1	37, 52, 54, 68, 101, 120, 130, 159, 198, 210	31.7014	5
		2	33, 50, 63, 66, 86, 109, 117, 128, 153, 198	31.2189	6
		3	**31, 41, 65, 91, 106, 123, 147, 168, 208, 232**	**32.1199**	**1**
		4	34, 36, 51, 73, 98, 102, 131, 160, 173, 201	31.8812	4
		5	49, 93, 99, 126, 136, 151, 157, 186, 212, 225	32.0716	2
		6	29, 36, 56, 98, 114, 129, 131, 159, 168, 201	31.9885	3
	MfPSO	1	27, 60, 88, 111, 128, 150, 157, 158, 174, 183	34.5529	6
		2	17, 34, 66, 88, 102, 119, 144, 166, 198, 202	34.5633	5
		3	61, 87, 90, 91, 108, 129, 149, 171, 185, 192	34.5785	4
		4	36, 54, 83, 108, 137, 150, 158, 176, 183, 205	34.5953	2
		5	**39, 61, 88, 109, 113, 133, 146, 150, 174, 186**	**34.5961**	**1**
		6	25, 31, 74, 90, 98, 121, 136, 163, 183, 210	34.5933	3

Table 2. Different algorithm based class boundaries and evaluated segmentation quality measures, ρ for 8 and 10 classes of Lena image

# of Segments	Algo	#	Class Levels	FIρ	κ
8	*k*-means	1	46, 61, 83, 104, 127, 149, 171, 204	0.9902	3
		2	**50, 76, 98, 116, 133, 152, 174, 204**	**0.9907**	**1**
		3	50, 73, 96, 112, 131, 151, 173, 204	0.9906	2
		4	51, 79, 103, 127, 146, 162, 184, 208	0.9906	2
		5	48, 66, 86, 105, 127, 149, 171, 204	0.9902	3
		6	50, 73, 96, 112, 131, 151, 173, 204	0.9906	2
	PSO	1	**52, 71, 93, 114, 134, 150, 162, 187**	**0.9901**	**1**
		2	39, 75, 106, 109, 141, 160, 168, 205	0.9881	3
		3	49, 84, 99, 124, 144, 168, 209, 210	0.9896	2
		4	37, 71, 99, 122, 154, 167, 195, 227	0.9877	4
		5	41, 81, 108, 138, 153, 174, 200, 232	0.9873	5
		6	42, 54, 59, 87, 111, 136, 164, 196	0.9870	6
	MfPSO	1	**49, 75, 104, 105, 135, 170, 197, 229**	**0.9910**	**1**
		2	54, 74, 82, 100, 134, 150, 166, 204	0.9903	4
		3	32, 46, 71, 95, 140, 156, 173, 215	0.9909	2
		4	30, 54, 89, 122, 137, 162, 195, 208	0.9903	4
		5	51, 94, 111, 138, 140, 168, 200, 205	0.9906	3
		6	49, 80, 86, 113, 151, 164, 191, 213	0.9909	2
10	*k*-means	1	43, 53, 65, 82, 100, 116, 133, 152, 174, 204	0.9927	4
		2	50, 76, 98, 116, 130, 144, 158, 173, 192, 210	0.9936	2
		3	50, 76, 98, 116, 130, 144, 158, 173, 192, 210	0.9936	2
		4	**50, 74, 97, 113, 129, 142, 156, 172, 190, 209**	**0.9937**	**1**
		5	43, 53, 67, 85, 102, 122, 138, 155, 176, 205	0.9932	3
		6	43, 53, 65, 82, 100, 116, 133, 152, 174, 204	0.9927	4
	PSO	1	41, 70, 80, 94, 98, 99, 123, 145, 168, 204	0.9912	4
		2	56, 68, 82, 88, 125, 138, 148, 166, 190, 206	0.9923	3
		3	42, 53, 83, 92, 103, 127, 127, 152, 183, 214	0.9924	2
		4	41, 65, 69, 89, 117, 129, 132, 151, 162, 198	0.9901	5
		5	**47, 68, 100, 105, 115, 133, 156, 173, 183, 210**	**0.9928**	**1**
		6	41, 58, 104, 111, 126, 132, 143, 164, 191, 218	0.9914	3
	MfPSO	1	48, 73, 99, 135, 154, 165, 170, 188, 217, 224	0.9936	3
		2	**27, 48, 50, 61, 99, 126, 145, 167, 171, 202**	**0.9939**	**1**
		3	**50, 64, 78, 102, 125, 152, 156, 163, 203, 225**	**0.9939**	**1**
		4	35, 55, 82, 107, 116, 124, 128, 150, 171, 205	0.9938	2
		5	**31, 43, 71, 100, 122, 139, 166, 173, 200, 229**	**0.9939**	**1**
		6	31, 54, 92, 98, 122, 155, 163, 184, 190, 202	0.9938	2

*Table 3. Different algorithm based class boundaries and evaluated segmentation quality measures, F',
for 8 and 10 classes of Lena image*

# of Segments	Algo	#	Class Levels	$FI_{F'}$	κ
8	k-means	1	**47, 63, 84, 104, 128, 150, 173, 204**	**0.0066**	**1**
		2	50, 75, 100, 120, 137, 155, 175, 204	0.0064	3
		3	**46, 61, 84, 106, 130, 153, 176, 205**	**0.0066**	**1**
		4	51, 80, 105, 130, 151, 170, 191, 210	0.0065	2
		5	51, 78, 102, 124, 141, 157, 177, 205	0.0063	4
		6	**46, 61, 83, 104, 127, 149, 171, 204**	**0.0066**	**1**
	PSO	1	**47, 70, 80, 114, 129, 155, 168, 233**	**0.0067**	**1**
		2	**64, 72, 90, 131, 155, 172, 184, 208**	**0.0067**	**1**
		3	**56, 62, 89, 134, 135, 165, 170, 197**	**0.0067**	**1**
		4	61, 70, 122, 123, 141, 172, 182, 226	0.0066	2
		5	29, 70, 80, 104, 125, 151, 174, 221	0.0062	4
		6	52, 69, 107, 121, 144, 161, 185, 194	0.0064	3
	MfPSO	1	48, 60, 105, 121, 130, 167, 185, 207	0.0055	3
		2	**49, 70, 77, 114, 121, 154, 172, 203**	**0.0063**	**1**
		3	59, 84, 101, 126, 140, 145, 191, 193	0.0054	4
		4	65, 87, 102, 108, 134, 137, 193, 196	0.0054	4
		5	59, 67, 94, 94, 132, 152, 177, 207	0.0062	2
		6	37, 67, 70, 121, 135, 154, 155, 212	0.0054	4
10	k-means	1	**41, 51, 63, 81, 99, 116, 133, 152, 174, 204**	**0.0069**	**1**
		2	50, 74, 96, 112, 127, 138, 150, 162, 180, 206	0.0065	2
		3	50, 74, 97, 113, 129, 142, 156, 172, 190, 209	0.0061	4
		4	46, 59, 76, 92, 106, 124, 140, 156, 177, 205	0.0063	3
		5	**41, 51, 63, 81, 99, 116, 133, 152, 174, 204**	**0.0069**	**1**
		6	**43, 53, 65, 82, 100, 116, 133, 152, 174, 204**	**0.0069**	**1**
	PSO	1	47, 71, 91, 100, 107, 137, 144, 158, 198, 210	0.0065	3
		2	52, 57, 87, 89, 127, 135, 159, 165, 198, 210	0.0060	5
		3	42, 60, 68, 83, 101, 133, 138, 184, 191, 220	0.0066	2
		4	45, 63, 82, 82, 93, 123, 138, 150, 181, 215	0.0063	4
		5	**60, 75, 110, 119, 130, 146, 171, 187, 213, 233**	**0.0067**	**1**
		6	**30, 74, 77, 96, 100, 129, 141, 150, 199, 205**	**0.0067**	**1**
	MfPSO	1	**52, 65, 88, 103, 121, 130, 133, 163, 184, 196**	**0.0059**	**1**
		2	45, 48, 59, 71, 113, 130, 145, 153, 170, 208	0.0053	2
		3	32, 71, 100, 116, 116, 136, 146, 161, 185, 204	0.0053	2
		4	43, 51, 89, 104, 126, 157, 162, 181, 186, 233	0.0053	2
		5	42, 72, 96, 101, 117, 131, 162, 170, 182, 204	0.0053	2
		6	48, 53, 58, 66, 103, 126, 138, 167, 186, 205	0.0053	2

Table 4. Different algorithm based class boundaries and evaluated segmentation quality measures, PSNR, for 8 and 10 classes of Peppers image

# of Segments	Algo	#	Class Levels	FI$_{PSNR}$	κ
8	*k*-means	1	10, 38, 62, 86, 114, 141, 165, 200	30.6063	2
		2	10, 36, 61, 84, 113, 141, 165, 200	30.5939	3
		3	**10, 38, 62, 87, 115, 143, 166, 201**	**30.6256**	**1**
		4	9, 34, 56, 72, 106, 138, 164, 200	30.3268	4
		5	10, 38, 62, 86, 114, 141, 165, 200	30.6063	2
		6	10, 36, 61, 84, 113, 141, 165, 200	30.5939	3
	PSO	1	22, 26, 57, 113, 132, 152, 165, 202	29.6044	4
		2	11, 65, 103, 121, 126, 166, 201, 219	28.6268	3
		3	**18, 34, 61, 103, 143, 153, 170, 199**	**30.1192**	**1**
		4	17, 42, 74, 104, 136, 161, 200, 207	29.7592	2
		5	21, 63, 104, 114, 134, 158, 168, 178	29.1383	6
		6	4, 25, 69, 90, 110, 144, 181, 190	29.3345	5
	MfPSO	1	20, 40, 59, 73, 91, 137, 163, 197	30.6382	6
		2	13, 44, 71, 72, 125, 140, 171, 202	30.6871	4
		3	9, 38, 56, 92, 117, 143, 180, 224	30.6875	3
		4	25, 66, 79, 95, 100, 137, 165, 179	30.6876	2
		5	**8, 25, 68, 99, 137, 148, 169, 207**	**30.6914**	**1**
		6	34, 59, 78, 114, 134, 158, 200, 220	30.6418	5
10	*k*-means	1	10, 38, 62, 85, 110, 133, 151, 167, 185, 208	32.4323	2
		2	10, 38, 62, 85, 110, 133, 151, 167, 185, 208	32.4323	2
		3	8, 26, 40, 54, 68, 92, 118, 142, 165, 200	31.6773	5
		4	10, 38, 62, 81, 104, 123, 138, 154, 172, 203	32.3862	4
		5	**9, 32, 51, 66, 90, 116, 140, 158, 176, 205**	**32.4829**	**1**
		6	9, 33, 55, 71, 101, 129, 149, 166, 184, 208	32.4196	3
	PSO	1	**13, 30, 51, 78, 114, 128, 141, 158, 164, 193**	**31.5040**	**1**
		2	19, 25, 55, 77, 104, 120, 139, 163, 192, 196	30.8561	5
		3	7, 45, 66, 108, 134, 154, 169, 179, 208, 209	31.1704	2
		4	0, 1, 29, 48, 62, 87, 109, 148, 157, 202	30.7030	6
		5	10, 13, 37, 58, 74, 82, 93, 142, 170, 192	31.0477	3
		6	17, 55, 74, 82, 106, 111, 133, 157, 179, 214	31.0248	4
	MfPSO	1	13, 38, 68, 95, 136, 154, 176, 184, 212, 226	32.6904	4
		2	15, 42, 53, 55, 75, 109, 146, 169, 191, 218	32.4700	5
		3	14, 24, 34, 57, 73, 113, 132, 167, 188, 214	32.4548	6
		4	16, 38, 46, 64, 86, 98, 136, 163, 212, 218	32.7013	2
		5	**7, 44, 54, 62, 73, 103, 145, 170, 174, 202**	**32.7035**	**1**
		6	6, 29, 50, 90, 115, 125, 131, 154, 175, 208	32.6927	3

Table 5. Different algorithm based class boundaries and evaluated segmentation quality measures, ρ for 8 and 10 classes of Peppers image

# of Segments	Algo	#	Class Levels	FIρ	κ
8	k-means	1	10, 36, 61, 84, 113, 141, 165, 200	0.9911	2
		2	9, 34, 56, 72, 106, 138, 164, 200	0.9906	3
		3	**12, 44, 67, 98, 126, 148, 168, 202**	**0.9912**	**1**
		4	**12, 44, 67, 98, 126, 148, 168, 202**	**0.9912**	**1**
		5	9, 34, 56, 72, 106, 138, 164, 200	0.9906	3
		6	9, 34, 56, 72, 106, 138, 164, 200	0.9906	3
	PSO	1	4, 62, 95, 116, 150, 167, 206, 224	0.9872	4
		2	12, 46, 53, 68, 85, 131, 155, 217	0.9870	5
		3	**12, 48, 71, 109, 112, 140, 166, 224**	**0.9902**	**1**
		4	13, 38, 54, 86, 92, 132, 170, 194	0.9893	2
		5	36, 56, 99, 123, 149, 164, 180, 210	0.9857	6
		6	9, 52, 97, 112, 112, 145, 175, 193	0.9882	3
	MfPSO	1	**25, 60, 73, 113, 133, 161, 173, 192**	**0.9913**	**1**
		2	**8, 42, 49, 79, 110, 128, 163, 180**	**0.9913**	**1**
		3	12, 36, 53, 66, 80, 119, 157, 194	0.9912	2
		4	**10, 22, 42, 60, 92, 137, 167, 199**	**0.9913**	**1**
		5	**18, 60, 91, 96, 102, 128, 160, 187**	**0.9913**	**1**
		6	**21, 65, 84, 95, 99, 147, 168, 217**	**0.9913**	**1**
10	k-means	1	8, 26, 40, 54, 68, 92, 118, 142, 165, 200	0.9931	4
		2	**9, 32, 51, 65, 84, 108, 131, 150, 170, 202**	**0.9945**	**1**
		3	8, 26, 40, 56, 70, 97, 123, 145, 167, 201	0.9934	3
		4	**9, 31, 50, 65, 84, 108, 131, 150, 170, 202**	**0.9945**	**1**
		5	10, 38, 62, 84, 108, 131, 147, 161, 176, 205	0.9942	2
		6	10, 38, 62, 85, 110, 133, 150, 165, 182, 208	0.9942	2
	PSO	1	12, 16, 44, 63, 97, 121, 131, 155, 160, 205	0.9928	3
		2	**10, 29, 58, 70, 102, 114, 125, 150, 168, 203**	**0.9937**	**1**
		3	4, 11, 42, 64, 79, 125, 148, 187, 215, 216	0.9911	6
		4	15, 19, 44, 67, 100, 125, 157, 173, 192, 223	0.9924	4
		5	5, 30, 46, 59, 105, 137, 157, 189, 210, 217	0.9917	5
		6	9, 43, 54, 75, 91, 107, 134, 150, 187, 216	0.9929	2
	MfPSO	1	**21, 24, 48, 54, 82, 120, 137, 152, 166, 188**	**0.9945**	**1**
		2	**4, 46, 60, 83, 98, 135, 156, 187, 189, 202**	**0.9945**	**1**
		3	21, 40, 68, 92, 114, 144, 163, 166, 196, 204	0.9942	2
		4	**5, 9, 31, 59, 82, 120, 146, 164, 185, 223**	**0.9945**	**1**
		5	**4, 20, 58, 79, 104, 112, 140, 169, 181, 193**	**0.9945**	**1**
		6	20, 58, 79, 104, 112, 140, 169, 181, 193	0.9942	2

*Table 6. Different algorithm based class boundaries and evaluated segmentation quality measures, F',
for 8 and 10 classes of Peppers image*

# of Segments	Algo	#	Class Levels	FI$_{F'}$	κ
8	k-means	1	12, 45, 68, 101, 129, 150, 170, 202	0.0089	2
		2	10, 38, 62, 87, 115, 143, 166, 201	0.0089	2
		3	**9, 34, 56, 72, 106, 138, 164, 200**	**0.0093**	**1**
		4	**9, 34, 56, 72, 106, 138, 164, 200**	**0.0093**	**1**
		5	12, 45, 68, 101, 131, 152, 171, 203	0.0089	2
		6	10, 38, 62, 87, 115, 143, 166, 201	0.0089	2
	PSO	1	16, 19, 38, 64, 108, 140, 173, 195	0.0089	4
		2	13, 25, 66, 108, 131, 165, 183, 214	0.0089	4
		3	7, 25, 59, 86, 110, 148, 196, 204	0.0092	3
		4	27, 29, 51, 82, 110, 133, 169, 210	0.0093	2
		5	4, 40, 72, 96, 122, 145, 163, 207	0.0088	5
		6	**31, 41, 63, 82, 115, 136, 176, 209**	**0.0095**	**1**
	MfPSO	1	19, 38, 76, 92, 110, 135, 164, 200	0.0086	2
		2	**15, 33, 63, 90, 117, 147, 184, 206**	**0.0087**	**1**
		3	8, 43, 46, 56, 116, 131, 165, 200	0.0086	2
		4	27, 54, 62, 91, 112, 154, 166, 200	0.0086	2
		5	**6, 26, 43, 70, 97, 154, 158, 208**	**0.0087**	**1**
		6	**14, 40, 61, 120, 126, 146, 147, 223**	**0.0087**	**1**
10	k-means	1	9, 32, 52, 65, 84, 108, 131, 150, 170, 202	0.0081	3
		2	**10, 38, 62, 85, 110, 133, 150, 165, 182, 208**	**0.0083**	**1**
		3	9, 31, 50, 65, 85, 109, 133, 153, 172, 203	0.0081	3
		4	9, 31, 50, 65, 84, 108, 131, 150, 170, 202	0.0081	3
		5	9, 33, 53, 67, 90, 115, 137, 155, 173, 204	0.0082	2
		6	**10, 38, 62, 85, 110, 133, 150, 165, 182, 208**	**0.0083**	**1**
	PSO	1	4, 31, 57, 94, 109, 120, 142, 176, 195, 196	0.0083	5
		2	14, 31, 74, 75, 107, 135, 143, 160, 166, 205	0.0080	6
		3	**3, 20, 45, 55, 55, 97, 101, 146, 150, 220**	**0.0089**	**1**
		4	19, 27, 62, 62, 72, 116, 126, 157, 175, 186	0.0088	2
		5	18, 22, 51, 60, 74, 92, 111, 153, 154, 210	0.0087	3
		6	9, 30, 59, 79, 104, 108, 130, 153, 162, 201	0.0084	4
	MfPSO	1	**13, 34, 58, 86, 97, 147, 153, 176, 187, 204**	**0.0081**	**1**
		2	**9, 36, 59, 59, 80, 89, 107, 144, 161, 193**	**0.0081**	**1**
		3	6, 37, 38, 85, 99, 129, 132, 160, 164, 215	0.0072	2
		4	**9, 45, 73, 96, 109, 137, 170, 176, 199, 225**	**0.0081**	**1**
		5	2, 20, 35, 66, 94, 109, 127, 141, 179, 185	0.0071	3
		6	**7, 45, 56, 92, 98, 98, 125, 155, 169, 219**	**0.0081**	**1**

Table 7. Different algorithm based class boundaries and evaluated segmentation quality measures, PSNR, for 8 and 10 classes of MR brain image

# of Segments	Algo	#	Class Levels	FI_{PSNR}	κ
8	*k*-means	1	**2, 36, 67, 93, 114, 134, 182, 228**	**34.3184**	**1**
		2	2, 38, 71, 96, 116, 134, 182, 228	34.3054	2
		3	0, 3, 37, 73, 100, 128, 175, 224	32.9002	5
		4	2, 35, 67, 92, 112, 133, 182, 228	34.2959	4
		5	2, 38, 71, 96, 116, 134, 182, 228	34.3054	2
		6	2, 34, 67, 92, 112, 133, 181, 228	34.2895	3
	PSO	1	6, 29, 86, 86, 98, 112, 131, 213	32.8253	4
		2	4, 59, 94, 125, 137, 177, 237, 245	32.8101	5
		3	3, 4, 43, 85, 106, 144, 211, 223	32.5080	6
		4	4, 27, 74, 99, 112, 125, 133, 201	33.2723	2
		5	4, 15, 40, 94, 117, 134, 171, 191	33.1159	3
		6	**2, 44, 47, 90, 117, 134, 208, 220**	**33.4582**	**1**
	MfPSO	1	1, 31, 87, 113, 160, 179, 225, 228	34.3286	3
		2	2, 65, 101, 112, 118, 151, 211, 212	33.1182	6
		3	8, 67, 83, 112, 136, 159, 202, 223	34.3311	2
		4	1, 39, 88, 109, 150, 206, 207, 208	33.5544	5
		5	3, 57, 80, 110, 134, 191, 202, 239	34.3273	4
		6	**3, 49, 90, 110, 134, 182, 205, 220**	**34.3316**	**1**
10	*k*-means	1	0, 3, 23, 45, 69, 91, 109, 131, 181, 228	34.8817	6
		2	2, 32, 61, 85, 102, 119, 135, 165, 202, 240	35.9415	2
		3	1, 30, 59, 84, 101, 117, 134, 164, 202, 240	35.7441	4
		4	**2, 34, 65, 87, 104, 120, 135, 165, 202, 240**	**35.9848**	**1**
		5	1, 26, 52, 75, 93, 108, 122, 136, 183, 228	35.7668	3
		6	0, 3, 29, 54, 77, 95, 113, 133, 182, 228	35.2050	5
	PSO	1	7, 27, 53, 84, 88, 102, 133, 136, 140, 209	33.9625	5
		2	**1, 43, 77, 96, 100, 131, 149, 181, 209, 249**	**35.0671**	**1**
		3	2, 46, 90, 107, 126, 138, 169, 178, 189, 249	34.4663	3
		4	6, 16, 42, 61, 67, 102, 113, 135, 172, 227	34.3576	4
		5	2, 45, 52, 71, 73, 95, 104, 130, 181, 234	34.6743	2
		6	2, 15, 46, 108, 129, 145, 145, 182, 199, 238	33.9314	6
	MfPSO	1	2, 26, 32, 80, 86, 111, 122, 166, 214, 235	35.9088	6
		2	0, 5, 9, 28, 65, 106, 135, 166, 213, 230	35.9611	3
		3	4, 5, 71, 84, 87, 121, 143, 148, 174, 200	35.9359	5
		4	3, 16, 26, 55, 80, 89, 115, 129, 154, 208	35.9418	4
		5	1, 17, 50, 68, 95, 126, 133, 162, 231, 244	35.9730	2
		6	**3, 64, 72, 81, 98, 120, 148, 182, 236, 252**	**36.0038**	**1**

Table 8. Different algorithm based class boundaries and evaluated segmentation quality measures,ρ, for 8 and 10 classes of MR brain image

# of Segments	Algo	#	Class Levels	FIρ	κ
8	k-means	1	0, 3, 37, 73, 100, 128, 175, 224	0.9950	2
		2	**2, 38, 72, 97, 117, 135, 183, 228**	**0.9963**	**1**
		3	**2, 38, 71, 97, 117, 135, 182, 228**	**0.9963**	**1**
		4	**2, 38, 70, 94, 113, 133, 181, 228**	**0.9963**	**1**
		5	**2, 35, 68, 94, 114, 133, 182, 228**	**0.9963**	**1**
		6	**2, 35, 67, 92, 112, 133, 182, 228**	**0.9963**	**1**
	PSO	1	5, 27, 80, 99, 114, 127, 154, 196	0.9953	2
		2	**9, 46, 74, 103, 129, 132, 199, 240**	**0.9955**	**1**
		3	3, 52, 82, 95, 116, 169, 217, 240	0.9951	3
		4	9, 68, 91, 118, 130, 173, 212, 239	0.9950	4
		5	7, 13, 76, 107, 138, 180, 209, 224	0.9947	5
		6	12, 45, 69, 93, 116, 144, 214, 220	0.9947	5
	MfPSO	1	**5, 10, 19, 72, 104, 127, 187, 251**	**0.9963**	**1**
		2	**8, 35, 54, 70, 96, 101, 127, 195**	**0.9963**	**1**
		3	9, 11, 33, 62, 94, 135, 148, 205	0.9960	2
		4	**1, 69, 95, 115, 124, 134, 169, 238**	**0.9963**	**1**
		5	**10, 22, 56, 69, 83, 116, 141, 191**	**0.9963**	**1**
		6	**7, 12, 62, 87, 117, 139, 201, 238**	**0.9963**	**1**
10	k-means	1	2, 35, 67, 92, 113, 133, 158, 193, 219, 248	0.9970	3
		2	1, 30, 59, 84, 101, 117, 134, 164, 202, 240	0.9974	2
		3	2, 36, 67, 92, 113, 133, 158, 193, 219, 248	0.9970	3
		4	1, 30, 59, 84, 101, 117, 134, 164, 202, 240	0.9974	2
		5	1, 29, 58, 82, 99, 116, 133, 159, 196, 234	0.9974	2
		6	**1, 26, 52, 75, 93, 108, 123, 137, 186, 231**	**0.9975**	**1**
	PSO	1	3, 35, 69, 109, 117, 121, 128, 140, 173, 188	0.9966	2
		2	**1, 16, 50, 67, 92, 106, 113, 131, 192, 226**	**0.9971**	**1**
		3	10, 44, 55, 58, 89, 117, 124, 126, 136, 205	0.9958	6
		4	4, 26, 63, 65, 87, 98, 126, 147, 219, 223	0.9962	4
		5	1, 11, 46, 53, 65, 69, 105, 132, 191, 206	0.9963	3
		6	12, 47, 63, 75, 101, 130, 174, 217, 221, 243	0.9959	5
	MfPSO	1	4, 14, 66, 87, 119, 138, 168, 197, 217, 228	0.9974	2
		2	**4, 40, 86, 98, 119, 139, 176, 176, 213, 237**	**0.9975**	**1**
		3	**7, 35, 50, 72, 97, 121, 121, 128, 222, 227**	**0.9975**	**1**
		4	0, 15, 23, 70, 92, 113, 118, 132, 159, 212	0.9974	2
		5	**0, 38, 58, 68, 95, 99, 117, 161, 177, 215**	**0.9975**	**1**
		6	**6, 43, 66, 74, 81, 107, 140, 186, 188, 241**	**0.9975**	**1**

*Table 9. Different algorithm based class boundaries and evaluated segmentation quality measures, F',
for 8 and 10 classes of MR brain image*

# of Segments	Algo	#	Class Levels	FI$_{F'}$	κ
8	*k*-means	1	2, 37, 69, 94, 114, 133, 181, 228	0.0064	2
		2	2, 35, 68, 94, 114, 134, 181, 228	0.0064	2
		3	2, 38, 71, 97, 117, 135, 182, 228	0.0064	2
		4	**2, 36, 68, 93, 114, 134, 182, 228**	**0.0063**	**1**
		5	**2, 36, 68, 94, 114, 133, 181, 228**	**0.0063**	**1**
		6	**2, 48, 86, 110, 132, 161, 201, 240**	**0.0063**	**1**
	PSO	1	**9, 63, 74, 106, 130, 180, 190, 251**	**0.0058**	**1**
		2	16, 44, 78, 112, 138, 200, 236, 252	0.0060	3
		3	8, 39, 54, 71, 103, 138, 223, 253	0.0060	3
		4	16, 43, 61, 98, 138, 180, 183, 246	0.0060	3
		5	**1, 35, 54, 92, 105, 141, 201, 209**	**0.0058**	**1**
		6	36, 43, 90, 113, 134, 164, 189, 239	0.0059	2
	MfPSO	1	**6, 51, 73, 100, 116, 140, 210, 220**	**0.0055**	**1**
		2	**1, 41, 82, 108, 111, 199, 202, 248**	**0.0055**	**1**
		3	**21, 70, 92, 119, 124, 208, 209, 240**	**0.0055**	**1**
		4	13, 59, 86, 105, 145, 154, 172, 245	0.0057	2
		5	**10, 49, 81, 90, 109, 147, 191, 253**	**0.0055**	**1**
		6	**11, 43, 43, 102, 105, 147, 198, 247**	**0.0055**	**1**
10	*k*-means	1	**2, 34, 65, 87, 102, 119, 135, 164, 201, 240**	**0.0057**	**1**
		2	2, 35, 65, 89, 105, 120, 135, 162, 198, 234	0.0059	3
		3	**2, 34, 65, 87, 102, 119, 135, 164, 201, 240**	**0.0057**	**1**
		4	**2, 32, 61, 85, 102, 119, 135, 165, 202, 240**	**0.0057**	**1**
		5	1, 26, 52, 75, 93, 108, 123, 137, 186, 231	0.0065	4
		6	2, 36, 67, 94, 114, 133, 158, 192, 218, 248	0.0058	2
	PSO	1	**23, 42, 72, 105, 120, 127, 177, 195, 233, 250**	**0.0054**	**1**
		2	26, 52, 70, 88, 112, 143, 187, 209, 216, 240	0.0057	2
		3	4, 42, 53, 93, 96, 124, 134, 159, 184, 233	0.0057	2
		4	13, 27, 54, 95, 101, 121, 152, 177, 242, 253	0.0057	2
		5	21, 46, 50, 58, 84, 117, 122, 200, 202, 244	0.0059	3
		6	26, 33, 64, 86, 113, 121, 138, 190, 196, 214	0.0059	3
	MfPSO	1	15, 41, 94, 95, 128, 131, 170, 179, 251, 255	0.0053	2
		2	30, 37, 68, 69, 102, 128, 143, 188, 220, 251	0.0053	2
		3	13, 20, 62, 77, 117, 125, 165, 200, 240, 241	0.0053	2
		4	9, 68, 75, 107, 123, 137, 160, 212, 223, 253	0.0053	2
		5	**9, 49, 62, 93, 117, 127, 141, 187, 227, 251**	**0.0052**	**1**
		6	18, 27, 82, 90, 109, 141, 179, 193, 236, 241	0.0053	2

Figure 1. 8-class segmented 256×256 gray scale Lena image with the class levels derived by (a-d) k-means (e-h) PSO (i-l) MfPSO algorithm of first four better results of Table 1 with PSNR as the quality measure.

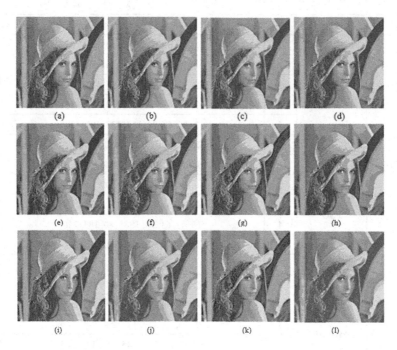

Figure 2. 10-class segmented 256×256 gray scale Lena image with the class levels derived by (a-d) k-means (e-h) PSO (i-l) MfPSO algorithm of first four better results of Table 1 with PSNR as the quality measure.

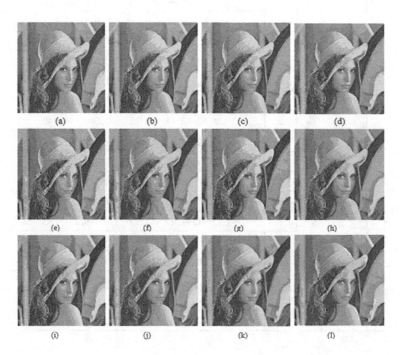

Figure 3. 8-class segmented 256×256 gray scale Lena image with the class levels derived by (a-d) k-means (e-h) PSO (i-l) MfPSO algorithm of first four better results of Table 2 with ρ as the quality measure.

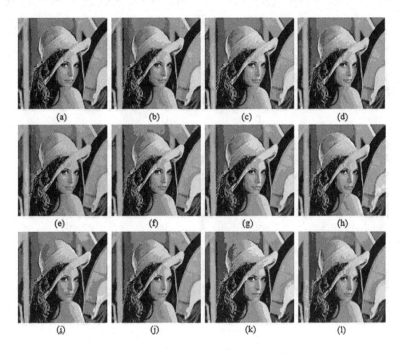

Figure 4. 10-class segmented 256×256 gray scale Lena image with the class levels derived by (a-d) k-means (e-h) PSO (i-l) MfPSO algorithm of first four better results of Table 2 with ρ as the quality measure.

Figure 5. 8-class segmented 256×256 gray scale Lena image with the class levels derived by (a-d) k-means (e-h) PSO (i-l) MfPSO algorithm of first four better results of Table 3 with F' as the quality measure.

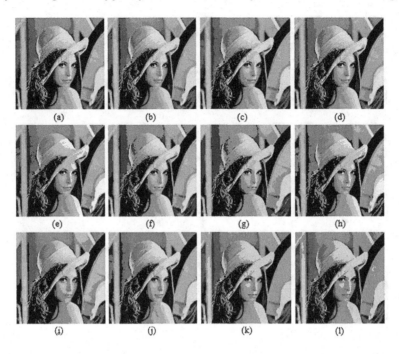

Figure 6. 10-class segmented 256×256 gray scale Lena image with the class levels derived by (a-d) k-means (e-h) PSO (i-l) MfPSO algorithm of first four better results of Table 3 with F' as the quality measure.

class levels, the ρ fitness function based multilevel segmented outputs of Peppers image is presented in Figures 9 and 10, respectively. The empirical measure, F' is employed as the fitness function to generate the segmented images those are shown in Figures 11-12 using $K = 8$ and 10 class levels, respectively.

In Figures 13 – 18, the multilevel segmented MR Brain images are shown. The first four better class levels ($K=8$) of Table 7, deduced by the above mentioned three approaches, are used to generate the segmented output of the MR Brain image in Figure 13. PSNR is employed as the evaluation function in this regard. In Figure 14, the multilevel segmented outputs of the MR Brain image are generated using the first four better results by all the algorithms from the Table 7 with $K=10$ class levels. Using $K = 8$ and 10 class levels, the ρ fitness function based multilevel segmented outputs of MR Brain image by three algorithms are depicted in Figures 15 and 16, respectively. The empirical measure, F' is used as the fitness function to generate the segmented MR Brain images by the above discussed algorithms and they are shown in Figures 17 - 18 using $K = 8$ and 10 class levels, respectively.

It is evident from the results of the Lena image in Table 1 that the MfPSO algorithm does better than the k-means and PSO algorithm. The PSNR is used as the fitness function in Table1 and it known from the previous discussion that the PSNR function is a maximization function. In this table, the PSNR value derived by the MfPSO algorithm is better than other two algorithms though the k-means has done better than the PSO algorithm. It is also observed from the Figures 1-2 that the proposed approach gives better segmented outputs than the same derived by other two approaches.

In Table 2, the ρ is applied as the fitness function to get the class levels of the multilevel Lena image and the corresponding fitness values by the proposed as well as other two algorithms. It can be said after examining the results in Table 2 that the results deduced by the k-means and PSO algorithm are not as

Figure 7. 8-class segmented 256×256 gray scale Peppers image with the class levels derived by (a-d) k-means (e-h) PSO (i-l) MfPSO algorithm of first four better results of Table 4 with PSNR as the quality measure.

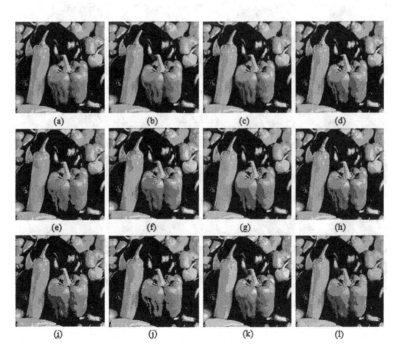

Figure 8. 10-class segmented 256×256 gray scale Peppers image with the class levels derived by (a-d) k-means (e-h) PSO (i-l) MfPSO algorithm of first four better results of Table 4 with PSNR as the quality measure.

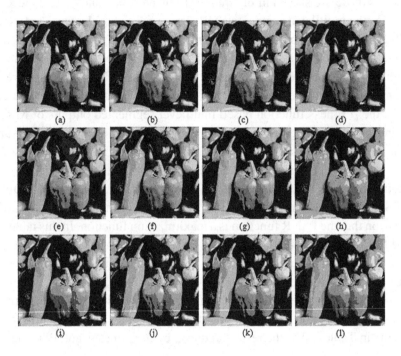

Figure 9. 8-class segmented 256×256 gray scale Peppers image with the class levels derived by (a-d) k-means (e-h) PSO (i-l) MfPSO algorithm of first four better results of Table 5 with ρ as the quality measure.

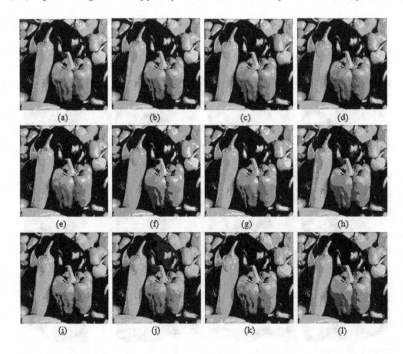

Figure 10. 10-class segmented 256×256 gray scale Peppers image with the class levels derived by (a-d) k-means (e-h) PSO (i-l) MfPSO algorithm of first four better results of Table 5 with ρ as the quality measure.

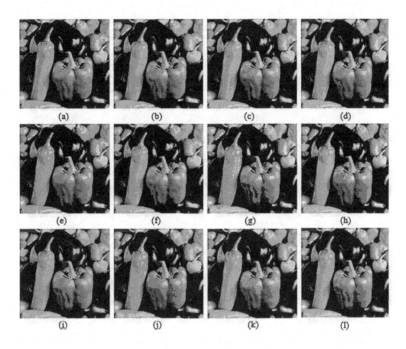

Figure 11. 8-class segmented 256×256 gray scale Peppers image with the class levels derived by (a-d) k-means (e-h) PSO (i-l) MfPSO algorithm of first four better results of Table 6 with F' as the quality measure.

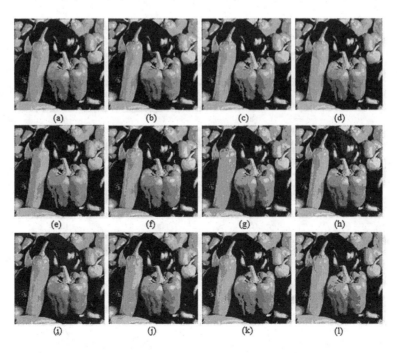

Figure 12. 10-class segmented 256×256 gray scale Peppers image with the class levels derived by (a-d) k-means (e-h) PSO (i-l) MfPSO algorithm of first four better results of Table 6 with F' as the quality measure.

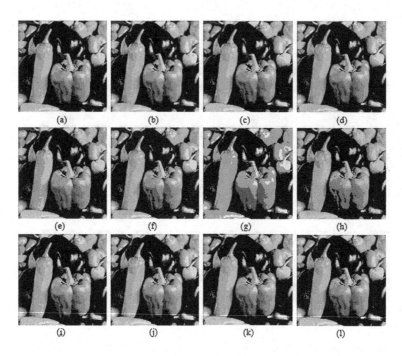

Figure 13. 8-class segmented 256×256 gray scale MR Brain image with the class levels derived by (a-d) k-means (e-h) PSO (i-l) MfPSO algorithm of first four better results of Table 7 with PSNR as the quality measure.

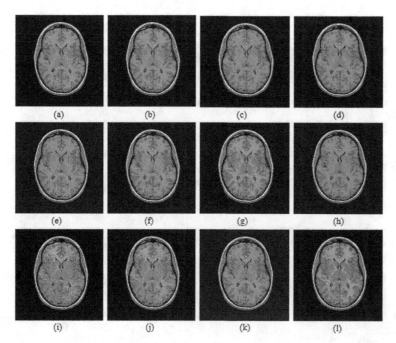

Figure 14. 10-class segmented 256×256 gray scale MR Brain image with the class levels derived by (a-d) k-means (e-h) PSO (i-l) MfPSO algorithm of first four better results of Table 7 with PSNR as the quality measure.

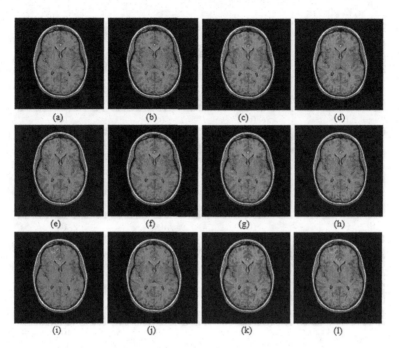

Figure 15. 8-class segmented 256×256 gray scale MR Brain image with the class levels derived by (a-d) k-means (e-h) PSO (i-l) MfPSO algorithm of first four better results of Table 8 with ρ as the quality measure.

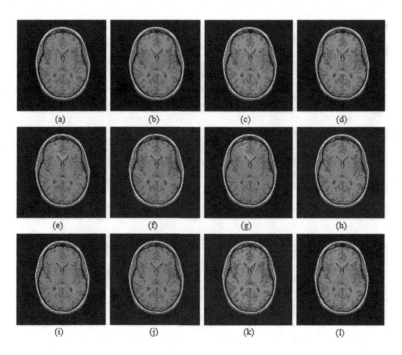

Figure 16. 10-class segmented 256×256 gray scale MR Brain image with the class levels derived by (a-d) k-means (e-h) PSO (i-l) MfPSO algorithm of first four better results of Table 8 with ρ as the quality measure.

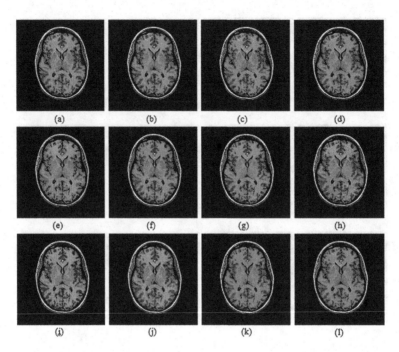

Figure 17. 8-class segmented 256×256 gray scale MR Brain image with the class levels derived by (a-d) k-means (e-h) PSO (i-l) MfPSO algorithm of first four better results of Table 9 with F' as the quality measure.

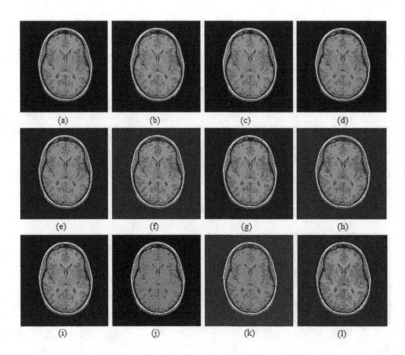

good enough with respect to the MfPSO algorithm. The multilevel segmented images by the proposed MfPSO algorithm are segmented in better way than the segmented imaged deduced by other two approaches and it is clear from Figures 3-4.

The derived class levels of the multilevel Lena image and the corresponding fitness values are tabulated in Table 3 and the empirical measure, F' is applied as the fitness function in that table. It is to be noted that F' is a minimization function. The results show that the proposed MfPSO algorithm gives better result than the same derived by other two approaches. From Figures 5-6, it can be said that the multilevel Lena image is better segmented by the proposed MfPSO algorithm than the k-means and PSO algorithm.

The PSNR based fitness values and the corresponding class levels of Peppers and MR Brain images are tabulated in Table 4 and 7, respectively. It is evident from both the Tables that the fitness values those are derived by the proposed MfPSO algorithm are really better than the same deduced by other two algorithm. The corresponding segmented outputs of Peppers and MR Brain images are shown in Figures 7-8 and 13-14, respectively. Both the images are segmented in good fashion by the proposed MfPSO algorithm than the same by the k-means and PSO algorithm.

The corresponding class levels and the ρ based fitness values of Peppers and MR Brain images are presented in Table 5 and 8, respectively. It is clear from those Tables that the fitness values those are derived by the proposed MfPSO algorithm are really better than the same deduced by other two algorithm. The fitness values, derived by the k-means algorithm are good than the same gained by the PSO algorithm. The fitness value deducted by the proposed MfPSO algorithm are good than the same derived by the k-means algorithm. The corresponding segmented outputs of Peppers and MR Brain images are shown in Figures 9-10 and 15-16, respectively.

In Table 6 and 9, the empirical measure, F', based fitness values and the corresponding class levels of Peppers and MR Brain images are produced, respectively. The F' values those are deduced by the proposed MfPSO algorithm are really better than the same derived by other two algorithm. The corresponding segmented outputs of Peppers and MR Brain images are presented in Figures 11-12 and 17-18, respectively. Both the images are segmented in good fashion by the proposed MfPSO algorithm than the same by the k-means and PSO algorithm.

We have already mentioned that each process has been examined for 50 times on the basis of different fitness functions. The mean and standard deviation are derived for each case and they are tabulated in Table 10. In the first and second column of that table, the respective images (*Image*) and the fitness function (*Fitness fn*) are tabulated. The number of segments (*# segments*), name of the algorithms and the corresponding mean and standard deviation (*Mean ± Std. Div.*) are columned in third, fourth and fifth column of Table 10, respectively. The better results are in **boldfaced**. It has been observed from Table 10 that the proposed MfPSO algorithm is superior to other two algorithms.

At the end, it can be concluded that the proposed MfPSO algorithm overwhelms the k-means and PSO algorithm in respect of quantitatively and qualitatively.

CONCLUSION

In this chapter, the multilevel gray scale image segmentation approaches are discussed. In this regard, a modified version of the particle swarm optimization (MfPSO) algorithm is proposed to segment the multilevel gray scale images. The k-means and the PSO algorithm are also narrated briefly and they are also applied to segment the same multilevel gray scale images. The drawback of the original PSO

Figure 18. 10-class segmented 256×256 gray scale MR Brain image with the class levels derived by (a-d) k-means (e-h) PSO (i-l) MfPSO algorithm of first four better results of Table 9 with F' as the quality measure.

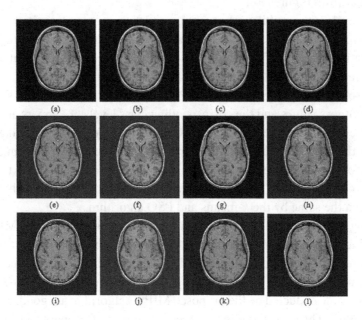

Table 10. Different images of different algorithm based mean and standard deviation using different type of fitness functions

Image	Fitness fn.	# Segments	Algorithm	Mean ± Std. Div.
Lena	*PSNR*	8	*k*-means	31.8911 ± 0.1447
			PSO	30.9133 ± 0.4659
			MfPSO	**32.0765 ± 0.1451**
		10	*k*-means	33.3351 ± 0.2350
			PSO	32.3030 ± 0.4653
			MfPSO	**33.8365 ± 0.0236**
	ρ	8	*k*-means	0.9905 ± 0.0003
			PSO	0.9879 ± 0.0015
			MfPSO	**0.9908 ± 0.0002**
		10	*k*-means	0.9934 ± 0.0004
			PSO	0.9916 ± 0.0006
			MfPSO	**0.9939 ± 0.0005**
	F'	8	*k*-means	0.0065 ± 0.0001
			PSO	0.0066 ± 0.0002
			MfPSO	**0.0060 ± 0.0004**
		10	*k*-means	0.0067 ± 0.0003
			PSO	0.0064 ± 0.0001
			MfPSO	**0.0058 ± 0.0004**

continued on following page

Table 10. Continued

Image	Fitness fn.	# Segments	Algorithm	Mean ± Std. Div.
Peppers	*PSNR*	8	*k*-means	30.4940 ± 0.1441
			PSO	29.5991 ± 0.2567
			MfPSO	**30.6840 ± 0.0167**
		10	*k*-means	32.2742 ± 0.3156
			PSO	31.0861 ± 0.5526
			MfPSO	**32.5805 ± 0.1206**
	ρ	8	*k*-means	0.9909 ± 0.0003
			PSO	0.9883 ± 0.0011
			MfPSO	**0.9912 ± 0.0006**
		10	*k*-means	0.9941 ± 0.0005
			PSO	0.9927 ± 0.0007
			MfPSO	**0.9944 ± 0.0001**
	F'	8	*k*-means	0.0090 ± 0.0002
			PSO	0.0090 ± 0.0004
			MfPSO	**0.0087 ± 0.0003**
		10	*k*-means	0.0082 ± 0.0001
			PSO	0.0086 ± 0.0003
			MfPSO	**0.0079 ± 0.0003**
MR Brain	*PSNR*	8	*k*-means	34.0691 ± 0.5727
			PSO	32.998 ± 0.3481
			MfPSO	**34.9985 ± 0.5312**
		10	*k*-means	35.5873± 0.4437
			PSO	34.4099 ± 0.4329
			MfPSO	**35.9541 ± 0.0329**
	ρ	8	*k*-means	0.9941 ± 0.0005
			PSO	0.9951 ± 0.0003
			MfPSO	**0.9963 ± 0.0001**
		10	*k*-means	0.9963 ± 0.0002
			PSO	0.9964 ± 0.0004
			MfPSO	**0.9975 ± 0.00005**
	F'	8	*k*-means	0.0064 ± 0.00005
			PSO	0.0059 ± 0.00009
			MfPSO	**0.0055 ± 0.00008**
		10	*k*-means	0.0059 ± 0.0003
			PSO	0.0057 ± 0.0001
			MfPSO	**0.0053 ± 0.00004**

algorithm is also pointed out in this chapter quite efficiently. The way to get rid from the drawback of the PSO algorithm is also discussed elaborately by proposing the MfPSO algorithm. The solutions derived by the MfPSO algorithm are globally optimized solutions. Different image segmentation quality measures are employed to get the optimized class levels in this procedure. The performance of the proposed MfPSO algorithm for real life multilevel gray scale image segmentation is superior in most of the cases as compared to other two segmentation algorithms.

REFERENCES

Abido, A. (2002). Optimal power flow using particle swarm optimization. *International Journal of Electrical Power & Energy Systems*, *24*(7), 563–571. doi:10.1016/S0142-0615(01)00067-9

Banerjee, S., Saha, D., & Jana, N. D. (2015). Color image segmentation using cauchy-mutated PSO. *Advances in Intelligent Systems and Computing*, *343*, 239–250. doi:10.1007/978-81-322-2268-2_26

Bhattacharyya, S., Dutta, P., & Maulik, U. (2008). Self organizing neural network (SONN) based gray scale object extractor with a multilevel sigmoidal (MUSIG) activation function. *Foundations of Computing and Decision Sciences*, *33*(2), 131–165.

Bhattacharyya, S., & Maulik, U. (2013). *Soft Computing - Image and Multimedia Data Processing*. Heidelberg, Germany: Springer. doi:10.1007/978-3-642-40255-5

De, S., Bhattacharyya, S., & Chakraborty, S. (2012). Multilevel Image Segmentation by a Multiobjective Genetic Algorithm Based OptiMUSIG Activation Function. In Handbook of Research on Computational Intelligence for Engineering, Science and Business. IGI Global.

De, S., Bhattacharyya, S., & Chakraborty, S. (2013). Efficient Color Image Segmentation by a Parallel Optimized (ParaOptiMUSIG) activation Function. In Global Trends in Intelligent Computing Research and Development. IGI Global.

De, S., Bhattacharyya, S., & Chakraborty, S. (2014). Application of Pixel Intensity Based Medical Image Segmentation Using NSGA II Based OptiMUSIG Activation Function. *2014 Sixth International Conference on Computational Intelligence and Communication Networks*.

De, S., Bhattacharyya, S., & Datta, P. (2008). OptiMUSIG: An Optimized Gray Level Image Segmentor. In *Proceedings of 16th International Conference on Advanced Computing and Communications*.

De, S., Bhattacharyya, S., & Dutta, P. (2009) Multilevel Image Segmentation using OptiMUSIG Activation Function with Fixed and Variable Thresholding: A Comparative Study. In Applications of Soft Computing: From Theory to Praxis, Advances in Intelligent and Soft Computing. Springer.

De, S., Bhattacharyya, S., & Dutta, P. (2010). Efficient grey-level image segmentation using an optimised MUSIG (OptiMUSIG) activation function. *International Journal of Parallel, Emergent and Distributed Systems*, *26*(1), 1–39. doi:10.1080/17445760903546618

Eberhart, R., Shi, Y., & Kennedy, J. (2001). *Particle swarm optimization: Developments, applications and resources*. San Mateo, CA: Morgan Kaufmann.

Halder, A., & Dasgupta, A. (2012). Image segmentation using rough set based k-means algorithm. *Proceedings of the CUBE International Information Technology Conference.* doi:10.1145/2381716.2381728

Hamdaoui, F., Sakly, A., & Mtibaa, A. (2015). An efficient multi level thresholding method for image segmentation based on the hybridization of modified PSO and otsus method. *Studies in Computational Intelligence, 575,* 343–367. doi:10.1007/978-3-319-11017-2_14

Hammouche, K., Diaf, M., & Siarry, P. (2008). A multilevel automatic thresholding method based on a genetic algorithm for a fast image segmentation. *Computer Vision and Image Understanding, 109*(2), 163–175. doi:10.1016/j.cviu.2007.09.001

Hauschild, M., Bhatia, S., & Pelikan, M. (2012). Image segmentation using a genetic algorithm and hierarchical local search. *Proceedings of the 14th International Conference on Genetic and Evolutionary Computation.* doi:10.1145/2330163.2330253

Jain, A. K., Murty, M. N., & Flynn, P. J. (1999). Data Clustering: A Review. *ACM Computing Surveys, 31*(3), 264–323. doi:10.1145/331499.331504

Janc, K., Tarasiuk, J., Bonnet, A. S., & Lipinski, P. (2013). Genetic algorithms as a useful tool for trabecular and cortical bone segmentation. *Computer Methods and Programs in Biomedicine, 111*(1), 72–83. doi:10.1016/j.cmpb.2013.03.012 PMID:23602574

Kanungo, T., Mount, D. M., Netanyahu, N. S., Piatko, C. D., Silverman, R., & Wu, A. Y. (2002). An efficient k-means clustering algorithm: Analysis and implementation. *IEEE Transactions on Pattern Analysis and Machine Intelligence, 24*(7), 881–892. doi:10.1109/TPAMI.2002.1017616

Kennedy, J., & Eberhart, R. C. (1995). Particle swarm optimization. *Proc. of the 1995 IEEE International Conference on Neural Networks.*

Kennedy, J., & Eberhart, R. C. (1997). A discrete binary version of the particle swarm algorithm, *Proceedings of the 1997 Conference on Systems, Man, and Cybernetics.* doi:10.1109/ICSMC.1997.637339

Khan, S. S., & Ahamed, A. (2004). Cluster center initialization algorithm for K-means clustering. *Pattern Recognition Letters, 25*(11), 1293–1302. doi:10.1016/j.patrec.2004.04.007

Lee, K.Y. & Park, J.B. (2010). Application of Particle Swarm Optimization to Economic Dispatch Problem: Advantages and Disadvantages. *Power Systems Conference and Exposition,* 188–192.

Li, P., & Li, Z. (2014). Color image segmentation using PSO-based histogram thresholding. *WIT Transactions on Information and Communication Technologies, 52,* 1601–1607. doi:10.2495/SSSIT132142

Liu, J., & Yang, Y. H. (1994). Multi-resolution color image segmentation. *IEEE Transactions on Pattern Analysis and Machine Intelligence, 16*(7), 689–700. doi:10.1109/34.297949

Liu, Y., Mu, C., Kou, W., & Liu, J. (2015). Modified particle swarm optimization-based multilevel thresholding for image segmentation. *Soft Computing, 19*(5), 1311–1327. doi:10.1007/s00500-014-1345-2

MacQueen, J. (1967). Some Methods for classification and Analysis of Multivariate Observations. *Proceedings of 5th Berkeley Symposium on Mathematical Statistics and Probability.* University of California Press. Retrieved from http://projecteuclid.org/euclid.bsmsp/1200512992

Mishra, D., Bose, I., Chandra De, U., & Pradhan, B. (2014). A multilevel image thresholding using particle swarm optimization. *IACSIT International Journal of Engineering and Technology*, *6*(2), 1204–1211.

Mishra, D., Bose, I., De, U. C., & Das, M. (2015). Medical Image Thresholding Using Particle Swarm Optimization. *Advances in Intelligent Systems and Computing*, *308*(1), 379–383. doi:10.1007/978-81-322-2012-1_39

Omran, M., Engelbrecht, A., & Salman, A. (2005). Particle swarm optimization method for image clustering. *International Journal of Pattern Recognition and Artificial Intelligence*, *19*(3), 297–322. doi:10.1142/S0218001405004083

Rao.Singiresu, S. (2009). *Engineering Optimization Theory and Practice* (4th ed.). John Wiley and Sons.

Tao, W. B., Tian, J. W., & Liu, J. (2003). Image segmentation by three-level thresholding based on maximum fuzzy entropy and genetic algorithm. *Pattern Recognition Letters*, *24*(16), 3069–3078. doi:10.1016/S0167-8655(03)00166-1

Xu, Z. B., Chen, P. J., Yan, S. L., & Wang, T. H. (2014). Study on Otsu threshold method for image segmentation based on genetic algorithm. *2014 International Conference on Applied Sciences, Engineering and Technology*. doi:10.4028/www.scientific.net/AMR.998-999.925

Zalik, K. R. (2008). An efficient *k*-means clustering algorithm. *Pattern Recognition Letters*, *29*(9), 1385–1391. doi:10.1016/j.patrec.2008.02.014

Zayed, H. H. (2005). A High Hiding Capacity Technique for Hiding data in Image based on K-bit LSB substitution. *The 30th International Conference on Artificial Intelligence Applications* (ICAIA- 2005).

Zhang, Y. (1996). A survey on evaluation methods for image segmentation. *Pattern Recognition*, *29*(8), 1335–1346. doi:10.1016/0031-3203(95)00169-7

Zheng, L., Li, G., & Bao, Y. (2010). Improvement of grayscale image 2D maximum entropy threshold segmentation method. *2010 International Conference on Logistics Systems and Intelligent Management*. doi:10.1109/ICLSIM.2010.5461410

Zheng, L., Pan, Q., Li, G., & Liang, J. (2009). Improvement of Grayscale Image Segmentation Based on PSO Algorithm. *Fourth International Conference on Computer Sciences and Convergence Information Technology*. doi:10.1109/ICCIT.2009.68

Zhou, S., Yang, P., & Xie, W. (2011). Infrared image segmentation based on Otsu and genetic algorithm. *2011 International Conference on Multimedia Technology*. doi:10.1109/ICMT.2011.6003109

KEY TERMS AND DEFINITIONS

Genetic Algorithm: A probabilistic search technique for achieving an optimum solution to combinatorial problems that works in the principles of genetics.

Image Segmentation: A collection of image pixels, similar to one another within the same segment, dissimilar to the objects in other segments with respect to some features.

Optimization: A technique for determining single or more feasible solutions which corresponds to minimum or maximum values of single or more objectives.

Chapter 5
Retrieval of Multimedia Information Using Content– Based Image Retrieval (CBIR) Techniques

Anupam Mukherjee
Siliguri Institute of Technology, India

ABSTRACT

This chapter will focus on the concept of Content-based image retrieval. Searching of an image or video database based on text based description is a manual labor intensive process. Descriptions of the file are usually typed manually for each image by human operators because the automatic generation of keywords for the images is difficult without incorporation of visual information and feature extraction. This method is impractical in today's multimedia information era. "Content-based" means that the search will analyze the actual contents of the image rather than the metadata such as keywords, tags, and descriptions associated with the image. The term "content" in this context might refer to colors, shapes, textures, or any other information that can be derived from the image itself. Several important sections are highlighted in this chapter, like architectures, query techniques, multidimensional indexing, video retrieval and different application sections of CBIR.

INTRODUCTION

There is something in this world that no word can convey it. It has to be seen. The facial expressions of an actor while playing Charlie Chaplin. Try to imagine a doctor describing the Angiogram report without seeing them. It is beyond words. Interpretation of what we see is hard to characterize. Pictures have to be seen and searched as pictures: by object, style and purpose (Smeulders et al., 2000).

T. Kato (1992) introduced the term *Content-Based Image Retrieval* (CBIR), to explain his research work on automatic retrieval of images from a database by color and shape features. Content-Based Image Retrieval (CBIR), a technique which uses visual contents to search images from large scale image

DOI: 10.4018/978-1-5225-0498-6.ch005

databases has been an active research area. Increasing popularity the internet and field of digital imaging have resulted in an exponential raise in the volume of digital images. The need to find a desired image from a collection of databases has wide applications, such as, in crime prevention by automatic face detection, finger print, medical diagnosis, to name a few. Early techniques of image retrieval were based on the manual textual annotation of images, a cumbersome and also often a subjective task. Texts alone are not sufficient because of the fact that interpretation of what we see is hard to characterize by them. Hence, contents in an image, color, shape, and texture, started gaining prominence (Wang, et al., 1998).

In content-based image retrieval we are focusing on *content* of the image not the total part of the image. *Content-based* means that the search will analyze the actual contents of the image rather than the metadata such as keywords, tags, and descriptions associated with the image. The term *content* in this context might refer to colors, shapes, textures, or any other information that can be derived from the image itself. During the retrieval procedure features and the descriptors of the query are compared to those of the image in the database in order to rank of the each index image according to its distance to the query.

Content-Based Image Retrieval (CBIR) is the application of computer vision to the image retrieval problem. Some of the major areas of application are Art collections, Medical diagnosis, Crime prevention, Military, Intellectual property, Architectural and engineering design and Geographical information and Remote sensing systems (Eakins et al., 1999).

CBIR involves the subsequent four parts in system designing, collection of data, feature extraction and build up feature database, searching in the database, process index wise and generate the result.

1. **Data Collection:** In case of Content-based image retrieval images are treated as data, and data collection is processed using Internet spider program that can collect webs automatically to interview Internet and do the gathering of the images on the web site, then it will go over all the other webs through the URL, repeating this process and collecting all the images it has reviewed into the server. In an Internet web resources are treated as a node and hyperlink of that web resources are treated as edges and the overall concept is called web graph.

2. **Feature Extraction and Build up Feature Database:** The query image can be analyzed to extract the visual features and can be compared to find matches with the index of the images stored in the database. The extracted image features are stored as meta-data, and images are indexed based on these meta-data information.

3. **Searching in the Database:** This meta-data information comprises some measures of the extracted image features. Then the extracted features of the example image are compared with the features of the images stored in the metadata database. Then the difference will be calculated and the values which are less than some defined threshold produced as output.

4. **Index Wise Processing and Result Generation:** Index the image obtained from searching due to the similarity of features, and then returns the retrieval images to the user and allows the user select those images. If the user is not pleased with the searching result, he/she can regenerate the retrieval query and searches the database again.

In the past decade, several image retrieval systems have been successfully developed, such as the IBM QBIC System (Flickner et al., 1995), developed at the IBM Almaden Research Center, the VIRAGE System (Gupta & Jain, 1997), developed by the Virage Incorporation, the Photobook System (Pentland et al., 1996), developed by the MIT Media Lab, the VisualSeek System (Smith et al., 1996), developed at Columbia University, the WBIIS System (Bebis et al., 2007) developed at Stanford University, and the Blobworld System (Carson et al., 2002), developed at U.C. Berkeley and SIMPLIcity System (Wang et al., 2001). Since simply color, texture and shape features cannot sufficiently characterize image semantics, semantic-based image retrieval is still an open problem (Singha et al., 2012).

Different Image Retrieval Approaches

An image is a representation of a real object or scene. Internet is rapidly developed and at the same time image capturing devises are also improved, so huge numbers of images are captured and processed day by day in different areas including remote sensing, crime prevention, publishing, medicine, media industries, architecture, etc. so we need to develop efficient and effective methodologies to manage large scale image database. Several general purpose image retrieval systems are implemented; some of them are given below:

1. Text-based Image Retrieval
2. Content-Based Image Retrieval
3. Hybrid Approach

1. Text-Based Image Retrieval (TBIR)

In today's world almost every retrieval system are based on text based. Each image is stored and retrieved from image database based on textual annotation. Many web search engines are currently developed, among them Google, Yahoo Image Search engines are most famous. These search engines are fast and robust but many times they failed to retrieve relevant images. Some advantages and disadvantages of this type of search engine are given bellow:

Advantages

1. Easy to implement. Simply add a caption to identify an image. Based on this caption search will progress by generating simple SQL queries.
2. Fast retrieval.

Disadvantages

1. In case of large database, manual annotation is impossible.
2. Personalized human annotation: viewers can annotate the same image in distinct way.
3. Lots of time and effort are required.
4. Classify images by few keyword is complex task. Because class of searching depends on users understanding, skillfulness and capability to define proper query.
5. Polysemy problem (more than one object can be referring by the same word).
6. Sensory and semantic gap.

2. Content-Based Image Retrieval (CBIR)

Content-Based means that the search will analyze the actual contents of the image rather than the metadata such as keywords, tags, and descriptions associated with that image. The term *content* in this context might refer to colors, shapes, textures, or any other information that can be derived from an image itself. During the retrieval procedure features and the descriptors of the query are compared to those images in the database in order to rank of each index image according to its distance.

Advantages

1. In CBIR the features employed by the image retrieval systems include color, texture, shape and spatial are retrieve automatically.
2. Similarities of images are based on the distances between features.

Types of CBIR-Based Image Retrieval

1. **Example-Based Image Retrieval:** In example based image retrieval system users provide a simple image or part of an image as an input. Where the system uses this input image as a base object. Then the system finds images that are similar to the base object.
2. **Feedback-Based Image Retrieval:** In that method system provides a sample pictures to the user and asks a user rating. Based on these rating, system generate re queries and repeats that queries until the desire image is found.
3. **Object-Based Image Retrieval:** In object based image retrieval system retrieval of images are done based on the appearance of the physical objects. The object can be any symbol, human face, arrow sign, sun, tree or anything that user need to find. Image segmentation is the best method to extract objects from an image frame. Segmentation of foreground object from the background is done by color or texture features.
4. **Region-Based Approach:** In this approach region of interest (ROI) of an image is provided by the user as a query image. Based on the features of that region required output is generated.

3. Hybrid Approach

As the name suggest, it is the combination of the above two approaches. Images are searched based on textual context and visual features for retrieval. The simplest approach for this method is based on counting the frequency-of-occurrence of words for automatic indexing. This hybrid approach attempts to find out the correlation between textual words and visual features on an unsupervised basis. These hybrid features are also enhanced the retrieval techniques.

LITERATURE REVIEWS

Da Silva Torres, and Falcao (2006) introduce the problems and challenges concerned with the creation of CBIR systems. They uses two types of query techniques *K-nearest neighbor query (KNNQ) where* the user specifies the number *K* of images to be retrieved that are closest to the query pattern and *range query (RQ)*, the user defines a search radius *r* and wants to retrieve all database images whose distances to the query pattern are less than *r*. Singha and Hemachandran, (2012) presented a novel approach for Content-based Image Retrieval by combining the color and texture features called Wavelet-Based Color Histogram Image Retrieval (WBCHIR). From the experimental result they found that the proposed method outperforms the other retrieval methods in terms of average precision. Moreover, the computational steps are effectively reduced with the use of Wavelet transformation. As a result, there is an increase in the retrieval speed. Lin et al. (2009) proposed a color-texture and color-histogram based image retrieval system (CTCHIR). They proposed image features based on color, texture and color distribution, as color co-occurrence matrix (CCM), difference between pixels of scan pattern (DBPSP) and color histogram for K-mean (CHKM), they also mentioned a method for image retrieval by integrating CCM, DBPSP and CHKM to enhance image detection rate and simplify computation of image retrieval. From the experimental results they found that, their proposed method outperforms the Jhanwar et al. (2004) and Huang and Dai (2003) methods. Haridas, Antony, Selvadoss, and Thanamani (2014) introduces a Content-based image retrieval System, they work on RGB Color Histogram, Tamura Texture and Gabor Features. The methods are implemented and tested based on three parameters like Precision value, Recall value and Accuracy rate. From the experimental results they found that Gabor Feature method is more efficient when comparing with other methods. Hemaltha (2012) proposed a research to find out the accurate images while mining an image (multimedia) database and developed an innovative technique for mining images by means of LIM dependent image matching method with neural networks. Hiremath and Pujari (2007) proposed Content-based Image Retrieval based on Color, Texture and Shape features using Image and its complement. Color, texture and shape information have been the primitive image descriptors in Content-based Image Retrieval systems. Yang et al. (2010) have proposed research on Content-based Image Retrieval in medical images like X-ray images collected from plain radiography. Efficient relevance feedback for Content-based Image Retrieval by mining user navigation pattern is proposed by Ja-Huangsu et al. (2011) and Müller et al. (2004) who have done a review work of content-based image retrieval systems in medical applications, they have proposed With digital imaging and communications in medicine (DICOM), a standard for image communication has been set and patient information can be stored with the actual image(s). Gudivada et al. (1995) explains how CBIR techniques are implemented in defense and civilian satellites, military reconnaissance and surveillance flights, fingerprinting and mug-shot-capturing devices, scientific experiments, biomedical imaging, and home entertainment systems. They have explained NASA's Earth Observing System will generate about 1 terabyte of image data per day when fully operational. They are focusing on the application areas in which CBIR is a principal activity are numerous and diverse. With the recent interest in multimedia systems, CBIR has attracted the attention of researchers across several disciplines. Hermes et al. (1995) described a research project IRIS (Image Retrieval for Information Systems) combines well-known methods and techniques in computer vision and AI in a new way to generate content descriptions of images in a textual form automatically. The text retrieval is done by IBM SearchManager for AIX. The system is implemented on IBM RISC Sytem/6000 using AIX. It has already been tested with 1200 images. Pass and Zabih (1996) describe a technique for comparing images called histogram refinement, which imposes added constraints on histogram based similarity measure. Histogram refinement splits the pixels in a given bucket into many classes, based on some local characteristic. Within a given bucket, only pixels in the same class are compared. They also explain a split histogram called a Color Coherence Vector (CCV), which partitions each histogram bucket based on spatial coherence. Color coherence vector can be calculated at over 5 images per second on a standard workstation. Belongie et al. (1998) introduce a new problems and challenges concerned with the of image representation which provides a transformation from the raw pixel data to a small set of image regions which are coherent in color and texture space. This termed as "blobworld" representation is based on segmentation using the expectation-maximization algorithm with the combination of color and texture features. The texture features they use for the segmentation occur from a new approach to texture description and scale selection. From that view point they construct a system that uses the blobworld representation to retrieve images. Most important and unique aspect of the system is that, in the context of similarity-based querying, the user is permitted to view the inner depiction of the submitted image and the query results. Kato (1992) describes visual interaction mechanisms for image database systems. Different mechanisms for visual interactions are query by visual example and query by subjective descriptions. That paper explains both image model and a user model to interpret and operate the contents of an image. In this paper he describes the image model and user model for visual perception processes of the users. These models automatically created by image analysis and statistical learning. He proposed an algorithm that worked on experimental database system, the TRADEMARK and the ART MUSEUM. Chen and Wang (2002) proposed a fuzzy logic approach, UFM (unified feature matching), for region-based image retrieval. In that system, an image is represented by a set of segmented regions and individual region is characterized by a fuzzy feature (fuzzy set) reflecting color, texture, and shape properties. The similarity of two images is then defined as the overall resemblance between two families of fuzzy features and quantified by a similarity measure. The UFM measure greatly reduces the influence of inaccurate segmentation and provides a very intuitive quantification. Their experimental result created SIMPLIcity image retrieval system. Petkovic (2000) provides a framework for automatic mapping from features to semantic concepts, integrating audio and video primitives. This paper also made a contrast between domain independent features, like color histograms, shapes, textures and domain dependent high-level concepts such as objects and events. This paper describes the layered structure of video model that guides the process of translating raw video data into efficient internal representation. Proposed model of this paper has formal foundation and layered structure that enables using of different techniques at different layers as well as combining different techniques at the same layer. This model also supports flexible video. Zhang et al. (1997) presents an integrated system solution for computer assisted video parsing and content-based video retrieval and browsing. The usefulness of this solution lies in its use of video content information derived from a parsing process by using visual feature analysis. This paper explain segmentation of parsing and video source abstract based on low-level image analyses; then retrieval and browsing of video will be based on key-frame, temporal and motion features. Ghodeswar et al. (2010) describes a Content-based video Retrieval approach where collections of videos in the database are segmented into several frames. Then from collection of frames, one or more key frames are selected, and then a feature vector for each key frame is computed. As every database video contains a sequence of key frames, there exists a sequence of feature vectors for the database video. The sequences of feture vectors of database videos are stored in the feature database. Then, this paper uses a dynamic programming approach to compute the similarity between the sequence of feature vectors of the query video and each sequence of feature vectors in the feature database. Chang et al. (1998) proposed a fully automated content-based video search engine for supporting spatiotemporal queries. In this paper, they proposed a novel, interactive system on the Web, based on the visual paradigm, with spatiotemporal attributes playing a key role in video retrieval. This paper also explain some innovative algorithms for automated video object segmentation and tracking, and use real-time video editing techniques while responding to user queries. The generated system, called VideoQ, is the first on-line video search engine supporting automatic object-based indexing and spatiotemporal queries. Kawashima et al. (1998) proposed a method to index baseball telecast for content-based video retrieval. Assumptions specific to baseball telecast are used to index video-recordings. Initially that paper detect domain specific scene in a baseball video based-on image similarity. These basic scenes are the shots which include a single pitching in each. After extracting these scenes they try to identify location of pitching and batting action using continuous dynamic programming matching for fixed areas in the image. If the batter swings the bat, they determine the end point of the play from the camera view after batting to recognize the batting result. They also recognize the caption to confirm the recognition result. The percentages of correct spotting for pitching and batting are 96% and 89%, respectively. Lew et al. (2006) made a survey reviews of more than 100 recent articles on content-based multimedia information retrieval and discusses their role in current research directions which include browsing and search paradigms, user studies, affective computing, learning, semantic queries, new features and media types, high performance indexing, and evaluation techniques. Chen and Chua (2007) presents a novel match-and-tiling approach to retrieve video sequences. The approach considers two levels of video similarity matching first one is the shot and second one is the sequence levels. At the shot level, transformation matching of similar shots into a problem of matching video feature trajectories using a longest sub-sequence matching technique. At the sequence level, they view sequence matching as a clustering problem and employ an effective sliding window algorithm to locate multi-occurrences of similar video sequences in the database. Finally the resulting technique is able to achieve both exact and similar video sequences with different durations and shot ordering. Dimitrova and Abdel-Mottaleb (1999) presents a novel approach for video retrieval from a large archive of MPEG or Motion JPEG compressed video clips. They introduce a retrieval algorithm that takes a video clip as a query and searches the database for clips with similar contents. Video clips are constructed from DC coefficients and motion information (`DC+M' signatures). The similarity between two video clips is determined by using their respective signatures. This method facilitates retrieval of clips for the purpose of video editing, broadcast news retrieval, or copyright violation detection. Shyu et al. (1999) presented a paper on content-based retrieval system for HRCT image databases. In this paper they focus on medical radiology. This paper explain that clinically useful information in an image typically consists of gray level variations in highly localized regions of the image is not always possible to extract these regions by automatic image segmentation techniques. To address this problem, we have implemented a human-in-the-loop (a physician-in-the-loop, more specifically) approach. In addition, the system records attribute that capture relational information such as the position of a PBR with respect to certain anatomical landmarks. An overall multidimensional index is assigned to each image based on these attribute values. Verma et al. (2012) presented a novel approach using canny and sobel edge detection algorithm for extracting the shape features for the images. In order to retrieve relevant images from the database extracting classified images are indexed and labeled. In their work, retrieval of the images from the huge image database as required by the user can get perfectly by using canny edge detection technique according to results. Choras (2007) contributes their work for the recognition of the problems existing in CBIR and biometrics systems. They proposed different approach based on the image content in low level features. In their paper they focus on number of different color, texture and shape features for image retrieval in CBIR and Biometrics systems. Kannan et al. (2010) have proposed Clustering and Image Mining Technique for quick retrieval of Images. The main objective of the image mining is to remove the data loss and extracting the meaningful information to the human expected needs. The images are clustered based on RGB Components, Texture values and

Fuzzy C mean algorithm. Entropy technique is used to compare the images with some threshold constraints. Lee et.al. (1996) in the year 1996 have present the analysis of the CBIR system. They made a contrast between human controlled and the machine controlled relevance feedback, over different network topologies including centralized, clustered, and distributed content search. In the interactive relevance feedback using RBF, they observe a higher retrieval precision by introducing the semi-supervision to the non-linear Gaussian-shaped RBF relevance feedback. Cho and Lee (2002) has published a paper on image retrieval system based on human preference and emotion by using an Interactive Genetic Algorithm (IGA). In that paper they used wavelet transform to extract image features and IGA to search the image that the user has in mind. Several experiments have been performed to evaluate the performance of this system. The resultant value of their approach allows one to search not only an explicitly expressed image, but also an abstract image such as "cheerful impression image", "gloomy impression image," and so on. Jaswal and Kaul (2009) in their paper they reviewed the main components of a content-based image retrieval system, including image feature representation, indexing, and system design, at the conclusion portion they concluded that content-based image retrieval is not a replacement of, but rather a complementary component to text based image retrieval. Tangelder and Veltkamp (2008) have published a survey paper of content-based 3D shape retrieval method. They explain that 3D shapes are often represented as a surface, in particular polygon mesh, often this model contains holes, intersecting polygon, are not manifold. This paper survey the literature on methods for content-based 3D retrieval, the methods are evaluated based on several requirements of content-based 3D shape retrieval, like shape representation requirements, efficiency, property of dissimilarity measure, discrimination ability, ability to perform partial matching, robustness and necessity of pose normalization. Lastly this paper also focused on the advantages and disadvantages of content-based 3D retrieval. Lai and Chen (2011) proposed an interactive genetic algorithm (IGA) to reduce the gap between the retrieval results and the users' expectation. They have used different color properties like the mean value, standard deviation, and image bitmap. They have also used different texture features, such as entropy based on the gray level co-occurrence matrix and the edge histogram. This paper compared this methods with others approaches and achieved better results. Madugunki et al. (2011) describe detailed classification of CBIR Systems. This paper focus on the Global color histogram, Local Color histogram, HSV method for extracting the color feature and matched the result by using Euclidean distance, Canbera distance. Ardakany and Joula (2012) provides classification using a simple feature extraction which performs geometric and appearance features at the same time. This feature extraction is carried out by computing the derivative in all pixels of face images and then constructing a histogram based on edges magnitudes and directions. The experiments are clear evidence that presented method is quite competitive with 95.67% accuracy on FERET database. Jin et al. (2005) proposed a novel approach which is augmenting the classical model with generic knowledge based. This approach attempts to trim irrelevant keywords by the usage of Word Net. To categorize irrelevant keywords, investigation on various semantic similarities of keywords and to fuse the outcomes of all these measures together to make a final decision with the help of Dempster Shafer evidence combination. Various models have implemented by them to associate visual tokens with keywords based on knowledge based, Word Net and evaluated performance using precision, and recall using benchmark dataset. The results show that by augmenting knowledge based with classical model they can improve precision of annotation by taking out irrelevant keywords.

MAIN FOCUS OF THE CHAPTER

Architecture of a Content-Based Image Retrieval System

The architecture of CBIR system is divided into two parts. In the first part, the images from the image database are processed off-line. The features from each image in the image database are extracted to form the metadata information of the image, in order to describe the image using its visual content features. These extracted features are used to index the image, and they are stored into the meta-data database along with the images.

The Second part query image is analyzed to extract the visual features, and these features are used to retrieve the analogous images from the image database. Rather than directly comparing two images, similarity of the visual features of the query image is measured with the features of each image stored in the meta-data database as their signatures. The similarity of two images is measured by computing the distance between the feature vectors of the two images (Mitra, & Acharya, 2005).

As an illustration of *Figure 1*, an image can be represented by an N - dimensional feature vector whose first $n1$ components may represent color, the next $n2$ components may represent shape, the following $n3$ components may represent some image topology, and finally n4 components may represent texture of the image, so that there are $N = n1 + n2 + n3 + n4$ components. As a result, an example image can simply be used as a query using visual content-based indexing.

The query image can be analyzed to extract the visual features and can be compared to find matches with the indices of the images stored in the database. The extracted image features are stored as meta-data, and images are indexed based on these meta-data information. This meta-data information comprises some measures of the extracted image features. Then the extracted features of the example image in compared with the features of the images stored in the metadata database. Then the difference will be calculated and the values which are less than some defined threshold produced as output. An example of a CBIR system is given in *Figure 2*, where the images are stored in image database. Based on the image features image meta-database will be generated.

Figure 1. Architecture of a content-based image retrieval system (Mitra & Acharya, 2005)

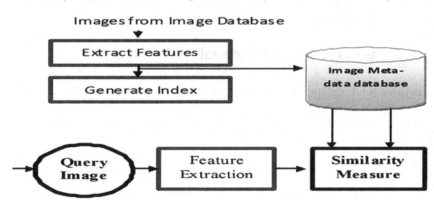

Figure 2. Example of content-based image retrieval techniques

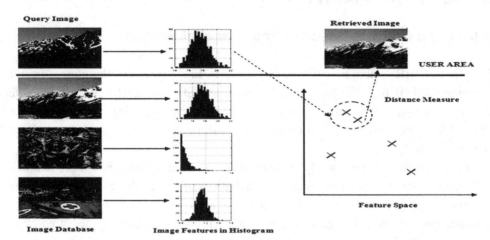

Techniques of Content-Based Image Retrieval

The Content-based image Retrieval techniques explain that how query image are retrieved from collection of stored images by comparing features automatically. The common features are color, shape and textures. Typical Content-based image Retrieval system used different types of input, it may be stored or captured images or sketch images provided by the user. Then the system identifies those stored images whose feature vector matches and closely with each other and display thumbnails of these images on screen (Long, Zhang, & Feng, 2003). A generic Content-based image Retrieval system is shown in *Figure 3. Relevance feedback* is a feature of information retrieval systems. The idea behind relevance feedback is to take the results that are initially returned from a given query and to use information about whether or not those results are relevant to perform a new query. Relevance Feedback (RF) is a frequently used method to improve the effectiveness of retrieval systems. It consists of three phases, first an initial search is made by the system. The search is based on user supplied query pattern and returning a small number of image. In second phases, the user then indicates which of the retrieved images are useful or relevant then finally, the system automatically reformulates the original query based upon user's relevance judgments. This process can continue until the user is satisfied. RF strategies help to improve the semantic gap problem, because it allows the CBIR system to learn user's image Perceptions. RF algorithms should be fast enough to Support real-time user interaction.

Modules of Content-Based Image Retrieval

In general there is three fundamental module of content-based image retrieval.

1. Feature Extraction or visual contents.
2. Multidimensional indexing.
3. Retrieval methods.

Images which are stored in image database are indexed based on extracted visual content or features such as color, shape, texture, patterns, shape of object and their location within the image. The feature vector actually acted as a signature of an image. The feature vector is assumed as a point in the multidimensional space.

Figure 3. Diagram for content-based image retrieval system (Long, Zhang, & Feng, 2003)

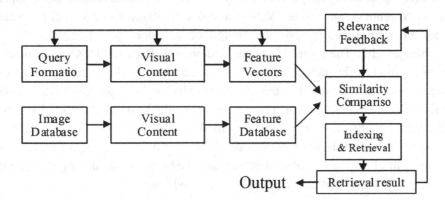

FEATURE EXTRACTION OR VISUAL CONTENTS

Color

Color is most frequently used visual features in content-based image retrieval. While we can perceive only a limited number of gray levels, our eyes are able to distinguish thousands of colors and a computer can represent even millions of distinguishable colors in practice. A color pixel in a digital image is represented by three color channels, i.e. Red, Green and Blue (Pass, & Zabih, 1996; Stricker, Orengo, 1995; Swain, & Ballard, 1991; Zhang, & Shong, 1995).

Although we can use any color space for computation of a color histogram HSV (Hue, Saturation, and Value), HLS (Hue, Lightness, and Saturation), CIE color spaces (such as CIELAB, CIELUV) were found to convey better results as compared to the RGB space. Since these color spaces are visually (or perceptually) consistent compared to the RGB, they are found to be more efficient to measure color similarities between images.

The color of the image is represented through some color model. The commonly used color models are Chromacity color model, RGB color model, HSV color model, CMYK color model and YUV color model.

Color Model

1. **Chromacity Color Model:** The Chromacity model is one of the earliest models. It is three dimensional model, with two dimensions *x* and *y* represents the color and the third direction defining luminance component. It is an additive color model, since x and y are added to generate different colors.
2. **RGB Color Model:** Most traditional color model is RGB composed of *red, green* and *blue* color components. It is used by television monitors, image capturing devices like digital cameras. Since by adding different color components of *red, green* and *blue* any color can be generated. RGB is a additive color model.
3. **HSV Color Model:** The HSV color model is mostly used in the CBIR community. The Hue Saturation and value (HIV) represents an artist's impression of tint, shade, and tone. This model

is used for image processing purpose. Hue of a color represents the relative color appearance; that is, 'redness', 'greenness,' and so on, Value indicates the darkness of the color (or the perceived luminance), and saturation represents the strength of the color.

4. **CMYK Color Model:** The Cyan, Magenta, Yellow and Black (CMYK) color model is used in desktop publishing printing devices. It is color subtractive model. Primary color of this model is cyan, magenta and when these colors are mixed then black color is produced. The secondary colors of CMYK model are the same as the primary colors of the RGB Model and vice versa. So, these two models are also known as complimentary model.

5. **YUV Color Model:** YUV is 3-D colors model. Y is the luminance component, UV is the chrominance components. Luminance component contains the black and white or gray-scale information. Chrominance component contains color information where,

$$U = R\left(red\right) - C\left(cyan\right)$$

$$V = M\left(magenta\right) - G\left(green\right)$$

So, YUV model is a subtractive model.

If the red, green, and blue component values of a color pixel in the RGB space are R, G, and B respectively, they can be linearly normalized to fractions r, g, and b in the range [0, 1] and these normalized values r, g, and b are used to transform into the HSV space. Transformation of RGB to HSV color space can be accomplished by the following set of equations (Chanda, B., Majumder, D. D.).

$$H = \cos^{-1}\left[\left(R - G\right) + \frac{G - B}{2\sqrt{\left(R - G\right)^2 + \left(R - B\right)\left(G - B\right)}}\right] \tag{1}$$

$$S = 1 - \frac{\min\left(R, G, B\right)}{V} \tag{2}$$

$$V = \frac{R + G + B}{3} \tag{3}$$

The color features can be described by color moments, color histogram, color coherence vectors.

Color Moments

Color moments are measures that can be used to distinguish images based on their features of color (Noah Keen, 2005). They provide a measurement for color similarity between images. Similarity value can then be compared to the values of images indexed in a database for tasks like image retrieval.

The basis of color moments lays in the assumption that the distribution of the color is represented using probability distribution. Probability distributions are characterized by a number of unique moments. Stricker and Orengo (1995) described three essential moments of an image's color distribution. They are *Mean, Standard deviation* and *Skewness*. As color can be defined by 3 values or channels (e.g. RGB or HSV) moments are calculated for each of these channels in an image. An image therefore is characterized by 9 moments that is 3 moments for each of the 3 color channels. Let P_{ij} is the ith Color channel at the jth image pixel. Then three Color moments can be defined as:

Mean: It provides average Color value in the image. It is calculated using following statics:

$$Mean\left(\mu\right) = \sum_{N}^{j=1} \frac{1}{N} P_{ij} \text{ Where, N is the total number of pixels in the image.}$$

Standard Deviation: The standard deviation is the square root of the variance of the distribution. It is calculated using following statics:

$$Std.Deviation\left(\sigma\right) = \sqrt{\left(1/N \sum_{j=1}^{N} \left(P_{ij} - E_i\right)^2\right)}$$

Skewness: It gives measure of the degree of asymmetry in the distribution. It is calculated using following statics:

$$Skewness\left(s\right) = \sqrt[3]{\left(\frac{1}{N} \sum_{j=1}^{N} \left(P_{ij} - E_i\right)^3\right)}$$

Color Histogram

This is one of the most important features used by CBIR system. Color histogram is very efficient and important feature for image characterization. In color histogram the color space is quantized into a finite number of discrete levels. Each of these levels becomes a bin in the histogram. The color histogram is then computed by calculating the number of pixel in each of this bin. Using the color histogram, we can find the images that have similar color distribution. Similarity measure approaches used by color histogram to compute the distance between two histograms.

$$H1 = \left\{h_1, h_2, h_3, \ldots\ldots\ldots, h_k\right\}$$

$$H2 = \left\{h_1, h_2, h_3, \ldots\ldots\ldots, h_k\right\}$$

Let us consider that $H1$ and $H2$ are two feature vectors generated from the color histograms of two images, where h_j for $H1$ and h_j for $H2$ are the count of pixels in the jth bin of the two histograms respectively, and k is the number of bins in each histogram. We can define a simple distance between two histograms as

$$D = \sum_{j=1}^{k} |h_j(1) - h_j(2)|$$

Color Coherence Vector

There is a problem of color histogram based similarity measure approach; global color distribution doesn't reflect the spatial distribution of the color pixels locally in the image. This cannot distinguish whether a particular color is sparsely scattered all over the image or it appears in a one large region in the image.

The color coherence vector based approach was designed to provide the information of spatial color into the color histogram. Here the classification of each pixel in an image is based on whether it belongs to a large uniform region or not. In this approach, each bin of the histogram is divided into two sections. First section contains the count of pixels belonging to a large uniformly colored region and the second section contains the same colored pixels belonging to a sparse region (Mitra, & Acharya, 2005; Shyu, et al., 1999).

Texture Feature

Texture is a very interesting image feature that has been used for characterization of images in content-based image retrieval. There is no single formal definition of texture in the literature. However, a major characteristic of texture is the repetition of a pattern or patterns over a region in an image (Mitra, & Acharya, 2005).

Several texture features such as entropy, energy, contrast, and homogeneity, can be extracted from the co-occurrence matrix $(C(i, j))$ of gray levels of image. The co-occurrence matrix $(C(i, j))$ is computed for several values of displacement $d_{x, y,}$ and the one which maximizes a statistical measure is used.

$$Entropy = -\sum_i \sum_j C(i,j) \log C(i,j)$$

$$Energy = \sum_i \sum_j C^2(i,j)$$

$$Contrast = \sum_i \sum_j (i-j)^2 C(i,j)$$

$$Homogeneity = \sum_i \sum_j \frac{C(i,j)}{1 + |i - j|}$$

The major two types of feature extractions strategies are grey-level co-occurrence matrix (GLCM) and other the other extraction is based on grey-level run-length matrix (GLRLM).

Grey-Level Co-Occurrence Matrix

In a statistical texture analysis, texture features were computed on the basis of statistical distribution of pixel intensity. Depending on the number of pixels or dots in each combination present in an image matrix, we have the first-order statistics, second-order statistics or higher-order statistics. Feature extraction based on grey-level co-occurrence matrix. (GLCM) is the second-order statistics that can be use to analyzing image as a texture. GLCM is also called gray tone spatial dependency matrix.

The *Figure 4* represents the formation of the GLCM of the grey-level (4 levels) image at the distance d = 1 and the direction of 0°.

Now the question comes in our mind how we can calculate the direction?

From the center (o) to the pixel 1 representing direction = 0° with distance d =1, to the pixel 2 direction = 45° with distance d = 1, to the pixel 3 direction = 90° with distance d = 1, and to the pixel 4 direction = 135° with distance d = 1. In addition to the horizontal direction (0 °), GLCM can also be formed for the direction of 45 °, 90 ° and 135 ° as shown in *Figure 5*.

Figure 4. (a) Example of image matrix with 4 gray levels. (b) GLCM for distance 1and direction 0°

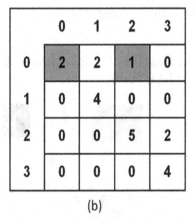

Figure 5. Directions of GLCM generation

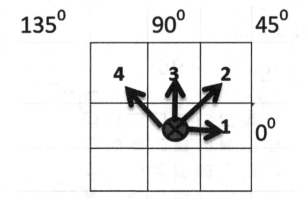

Gray-Level Run-Length Matrix

Grey-level run-length matrix (GLRLM) is a matrix from which the texture features can be extracted for texture analysis. Texture is understood as a pattern of grey intensity pixel in a particular direction from the reference pixels. Run length is the number of adjacent pixels that have the same grey intensity in a particular direction as shown in *Figure 6*.

Gray-level run-length matrix is a two-dimensional matrix where each element $p(i, j \mid \Theta)$ is the number of elements j with the intensity i, in the direction Θ.

In addition to the 0° direction, GLRL matrix can also be formed in the other direction, i.e. 45°, 90° or 135° which is explained in *Figure 7*.

Shape Features

Shape features play an important role in Content-based Image retrieval. Shape of an object can be defined as the description of an object minus its position, orientation and size; it should be invariant to translation, rotation, and scale when the arrangements of the objects in the image are not known in advance.

Some essential properties of shape features are described below (Yang, Kpalma, & Ronsin, 2008):

- **Identifiability:** Shapes which are found perceptually similar by human have the same features that are different from the others.

Figure 6. (a) Example of image matrix with 4 gray level. (b) Length calculation of gray levels. (c) Formation of GLRLM matrix

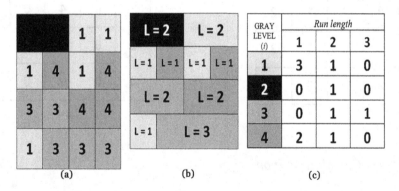

Figure 7. Directions of GLRLM generation

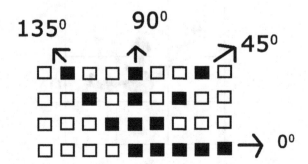

- **Translation, Rotation, and Scale Invariance:** The location, the rotation and the scaling changing of the shape must not affect the extracted features.
- **Affine Invariance:** The affine transform performs a linear mapping from coordinates system to other coordinates system that preserves the "straightness" and "parallelism" of lines. Affine transform can be constructed using sequences of translations, scales, flips, rotations and shears. The extracted features must be as invariant as possible with affine transforms.
- **Noise Resistance:** Features must be as robust as possible against noise, i.e., they must be the same whichever be the strength of the noise in a give range that affects the pattern.
- **Occultation Invariance:** When some parts of a shape are occulted by other objects, the feature of the remaining part must not change compared to the original shape.
- **Statistically Independent:** Two features must be statistically independent. This represents compactness of the representation.
- **Reliability:** As long as one deals with the same pattern, the extracted features must remain the same.

Techniques for shape characterization can classify into two major categories.

- **Boundary-Based Approach**
- **Region-Based Approach**

The first category *boundary-based*, using the edge detection concept to detect the outer contour of the shape of an object as shown in *Figure 8*. Edge detection is an important part of digital image processing, it is not only reduces the amount of data but also maintain useful structural information (Gonzalez, Woods, & Eddins, 2004). Edge is the boundary between two homogeneous regions, which will help us to detect the object by using segmentation technique. Edge detection is also important part of object recognition. Image segmentation partition an image into meaningful regions. Second category is region-based approach, to use shape as an image feature, it is essential to segment the image to detect object or region boundaries; and this is a challenge.

Figure 8. Original image and edge detected image

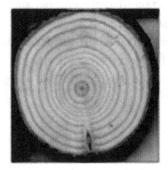 

MULTIDIMENSIONAL INDEXING

Multidimensional indexing is an important part of Content-based Image Retrieval. Indexing techniques is an active research area in the field of database management, computational geometry and pattern recognition. In traditional database management (relational database), the indexing refers to the access structure of the database files with respect to record organization. These record and file structures are supported by an access structure such as hashing, B-tree etc. in Information Retrieval system the organized documents are retrieved using phrases or keywords or descriptors. The indexing technique of Content-based Image Retrieval is similar with IR. The primary concern of indexing is to assign a suitable description to the data in order to detect the information content of the data (Mitra, & Acharya, 2005).

The key issues in indexing for content-based image retrieval are

1. Reduction of high dimensionality of the feature vectors,
2. Finding an efficient data structure for indexing,
3. Finding suitable similarity measures.

In CBIR, the dimensionality of features vectors is normally too large. Dimensionality is typically of the order of 10^2. With the rapid growth of multimedia content, this order may increase in future. So before indexing, it is very important to reduce the dimensionality of the feature vectors. The well known approach to reduce this dimensionality is application of principal component analysis which is based on singular decomposing of feature matrices.

After dimensionality reduction, it is very necessary to select an appropriate multidimensional indexing data structure and algorithm to index the feature vectors. Most popular approach are multidimensional binary search trees (Bentley, 1980), R-Tree (Guttman, 1984), variants of R-Tree such as R*-Tree (Beckmann, Kriegel, 1990), SR-tree (Katamaya, & Satoh, 1997), SS-tree (David, & Ramesh, 2002), K-d tree (Overmars, 1997) etc.

Most of these tree-based indexing techniques have been designed for traditional database queries, but not for similarity queries for multimedia data retrieval. There have been some limited efforts in this direction.

RETRIEVAL METHOD

After indexing of images in the image database, it is important to apply a proper similarity measure for their retrieval from the database. Similarity measures based on statistical analysis have been dominant in CBIR. Distance measures such as Euclidean distance, Mahalanobis distance, Manhattan distance (Devijver, & Dekesel, 1987), and similar techniques have been used for similarity measures. Distance of histograms and histogram intersection methods have also been used for this purpose, particularly with color features (Mitra, & Acharya, 2005).

Figure 9. Image retrieval process

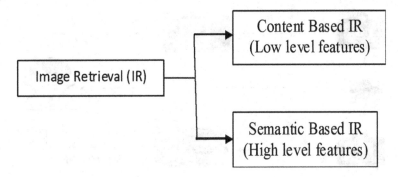

IMAGE RETRIEVAL (IR)

Content-based image retrieval system retrieved the images based on their low level features like texture, shape spatial information or color (Gao, et al., 2007). In early period of this emerging filed the image was retrieved by text description called as Text Based Image Retrieval [TBIR]. All text based image retrieval systems require the text description with images in large scale data bases and manually this task is not feasible. As a result, text based image retrieval systems were not relevant for task dependent queries (Rafiee, et al., 2004). Image retrieval process can be visualized as in *Figure 9*.

SEMANTIC GAP

Traditionally human vision are able to distinguished both low level features (color, shape, texture and object detection) and high level semantics (abstract objects, an event). However, computer vision is only able to interpret images based on low level image features. But users prefer to articulate high level queries (Kherfi, et al., 2004; Smeulders, et al., 2000); indexing of CBIR system is made using low level features. Hence, introducing an interpretation inconsistency between image descriptors and high level semantics that is known as the semantic gap (Liu, et al., 2007; Smeulders, et al., 2000). The semantic gap is the lack of correlation among the semantic categories that a user requires and the low level features that CBIR systems offer. The semantic gap between the low level visual features (color, shape, texture, etc.) and semantic concepts identified by the user remains a major problem in content-based image retrieval (Idrissi, Martinez, & Aboutajdine, 2009).

SENSORY GAP

Sensory gap is the difference between an object visualized in the real world and its computer interpretation. This interpretation can be visualized by either via sensors and displays, or can be used by computers in the learning process. In the latter case, sensory gap influences the semantic gap. Sensory gap is caused by either the parameters of the scene (e.g., clutter, occlusion, illumination, etc.) or the parameters of the sensors (e.g., viewpoint, perceptual spectra, etc.) (Liu, & Song, 2011; Smeulders, et al., 2000).

A conceptual diagram of this semantic and sensory gap is shown in *Figure 10*.

Figure 10. Conceptual diagram of sensory and semantic gap

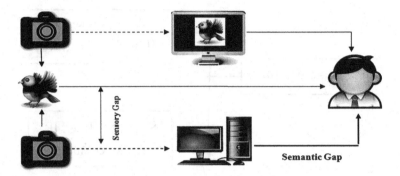

QUERY TECHNIQUES FOR CBIR

Different types of query techniques are used by the CBIR system.

- **Query by Content:** The most common method for comparing two images in content-based image retrieval is using an image distance measure. An image distance measure compares the similarity of two images in various dimensions such as color, texture, shape, and others.
- **Query by Example:** In this technique query image is supplied by the user or chosen from a random set and the system find similar images based on low-level criteria.
- **Query by Sketch:** In this technique user draws a rough approximation of the image, e.g., blobs of color or shapes locate in images whose layout matches the sketch.
- **Other Methods:** In this techniques user specify proportions of colors (e.g. "80% red, 20% blue"). Searching is done using these proportions of color.

IMAGE RETRIEVAL SYSTEM

Since the early 1990s, content-based image retrieval has become a very active research area. Many image retrieval systems both commercial and research, have been built. Now some well known system with their characteristics is described below:

QBIC (Query By Image Content)

Developed by: IBM Almaden Research Center, San Jose, CA

URL: http://wwwqbic.almaden.ibm.com/_.

QBIC (David, 2002; Equitz, 1994; Faloutsos, 1994; Flickner, 1995; Lee, 1994; Scassellati, 1994; Rui, 1999), stands for Query by image content. It is the first commercial CBIR system. In QBIC system users prepare sketches and drawings; these are treated as a input query. The color feature used in QBIC are the average (R, G, B), (Y, i, q), (L, a, b), and MTM (mathematical transform to Munsell) coordinates, and a k-element color histogram (Faloutsos, 1994). The texture feature of QBIC is an improved version of the Tamura texture representation (Smeulders, et al., 2000); i.e. combinations of coarseness, contrast, and directionality (Equitz, 1994). The shape features of QBIC consist of shape area, circularity, eccentricity, major axis orientation, and a set of algebraic moment invariants (Scassellati, 1994; Faloutsos, 1994). Most important part of QBIC is its high dimensional feature indexing. In its indexing subsystem, first time KLT is used to perform reduction of dimension and then R^*-tree is introduced as the multidimensional indexing structure (Lee, 1994; Faloutsos, 1994).

Virage

Developed by: Virage Inc.
URL: http://www.virage.com/cgi-bin/query-e_.

Virage (Bach, et al.; Gupta, & Jain, 1997) supports visual queries based on color, composition (color layout), texture, and structure (object boundary information). But Virage goes one step further than QBIC. Virage, Inc. was formed in April of 1994 by Professor Ramesh Jain, Director of the Visual Computing Laboratory at the University of California, San Diego. The company's core academic research team research in multimedia information system technology and has developed a new model for such systems, called the Visual Information Management System (VIMSYS) model. Virage (Bach, et al.; Gupta, A., & Jain, R.,1997) supports visual queries based on color, composition (color layout), texture, and structure (object boundary information). Virage also support random combination of the atomic queries. Various observation shown that this model recognize the most users prefer to search image and video content rather than by keywords or descriptions associated with the visual information. In traditional database system information or data is stored as a file name or raw image data which is useful to display images but not describing it. Many times textual annotation is not sufficient to describing detail information of the raw file or binary large object (BLOB), simply because the same image might be described in different ways by different people. The content represents most of what the user needs in order to organize, search, and locate necessary visual information (Gupta, 1997; Rui, et al., 1999)

RetrievalWare

Developed by: Excalibur Technologies Corp.
URL: http://www.searchtechnologies.com/retrievalware-support_

RetrivalWare is an enterprise search engine used for retrieving the content of the information developed by Excalibur Technologies Corp. RetrievalWare incorporate natural language processing and semantic network for information retrieval. Its more recent search engine uses color, shape, texture, brightness, color layout, and aspect ratio of the image, as the query features. In RetrivalWare system users can adjust the weights associated with each feature (Rui, et al., 1999).

Photobook

Developed by: MIT Media Lab.
URL: http://vismod.media.mit.edu/vismod/demos/photobook/_

Photobook is a collection of interactive application tools for searching and browsing images (Pentland et al., 1996). Photobook consists of three sub-books from which shape, texture, and face features are extracted. Users can then generate query, based on the corresponding features in each of the three sub-books. Picard *et al.* (Minka et al., 1996; Picard, 1995) proposed in his research work that there was no single feature which can best model images from each and every domain, and human perception is subjective. Photobook includes *Four Eyes,* an interactive learning agent which selects and combines models based on examples from the user. They proposed a "society of model" approach to incorporate the human factor. Experimental results show that this approach is effective in interactive image annotation (Minka et al., 1996). Different query Examples uses by Photobook are Texture modeling, Face recognition, Shape matching, Brain matching, Interactive segmentation and annotation.

VisualSEEk and WebSEEk

Developed by: Columbia University.
   URL: http://www.ee.columbia.edu/ln/dvmm/researchProjects/MultimediaIndexing/VisualSEEk/VisualSEEk.htm_
   VisualSEEk (Smith, Chang, 1996, 1997) is a Content-based Image Retrieval system based on visual feature and WebSEEk is a World Wide Web oriented text/image search engine. In visualSEEk user made a query based on diagramming spatial arrangements of color regions (Chang, 1995; Chen, & Wang, 2002). The visual features used in their systems are color set and wavelet transform based texture feature (Smith, & Chang, 1994; Chang, 1995). Binary tree based indexing method is used by the system for the purpose of information retrieval (Chang, 1995; Smith, 1996). WebSEEk is a web oriented search engine. It consists of three main modules, i.e. image/video collecting module, subject classification and indexing module, and search, browse, and retrieval module (Rui, 1999). In WebSEEk query may be in form of key word or visual content.

NeTra

Developed by: UCSB Alexandria Digital Library (ADL)
   URL: *http://vivaldi.ece.ucsb.edu/Netra*
   NeTra, a prototype image retrieval system that uses color, texture, shape and spatial location information in segmented image regions to search and retrieve similar regions from the database (Ma, & Manjunath, 1999, 1996). The main features of NeTra system are its Gabor filter based texture analysis, neural net-based image thesaurus construction and edge flow-based region segmentation (Ma et al., 1999, 1997, 1995).

MARS

Developed by: University of Illinois at Urbana-Champaign
   URL: http://www.ifp.illinois.edu/~qitian/MARS.html_
   MARS stands for multimedia analysis and retrieval system was developed at University of Illinois at Urbana-Champaign (Rui, 1997; Mehrotra, 1997; Ortega, 1997). MARS involve multiple interdisciplinary communities, such as computer vision, database management system (DBMS), and information retrieval (IR). Based on the rank retrieval the research features of MARS are integrated using database management system and information retrieval (Ortega, 1997; Rui, 1999).

JustVisual (formerly known as Superfish)

Description: pure image-to-image search

URL: http://www.justvisual.com/

In the year 2006 California-based advertising company lunches this web site. Previously it was known as Superfish. That web site currently known as JustVisual. It is purely based on CBIR techniques. That search engine support external image query and as well as meta-data query. Billions of images are indexed. That search engine has different segments, like Plant, Style, Furniture and Pets. JustVisual & Augmented Reality (AR) API allows AR developers to utilize visual similarity for AR data identification and retrieval (http://www.justvisual.com/) shown in *Figure 11*.

Picalike

Developed by: German LLC

URL: http://www.picalike.com

Picalike was founded in August 2010.They offer state of the art solutions catering to user needs. Picalike offers high level software as a service (SaaS) solutions to search and match product pictures. This technology assists e- and m-commerce clients, product search engines or picture data base offering or enabling search solutions. Picalike support different application like dating companies, geo-analysis for mining companies as well as pharmaceutical, diagnostic, biotechnology services. Picalike mainly focus on image content. Picalike algorithms build a system looks at images like a human would. The learning system of Picalike tries to understand the image and extracts the most important visual features (www.picalike.com) shown in *Figure 12*.

Google Image Search

Developed by: Google in July 2001

URL: https://images.google.com/

You can use a picture as your search to find associated images from around the web. In Google image search, the search result may include: Similar images, Sites that include the image, other sizes of the image you searched for. Google image search support the following web browsers: Chrome 5+, Internet Explorer 9+, Safari 5+, Firefox 4+. There are four ways to search by image in Google search, these are

Figure 11. JustVisual (www.justvisual.com)

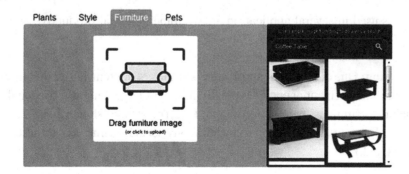

Figure 12. Picalike (www.picalike.com)

Figure 13. Google Image search (www.images.google.com)

Drag & Drop, Upload an Image, Copy and paste the URL for an image and right click an image on the web (www.images.google.com) shown in *Figure 13*.

Idmypill

Description: Instant pill identification
   URL: http://www.idmypill.com/
   The ID My Pill iPhone app automatically identifies your prescription pill and provides drug fact information, including the name of the pill, manufacturer, and if there is potential for abuse and addiction. Compare the drug name to your prescription bottle to ensure the pharmacist gave you the right medication! Protect yourself and your family, click on the "Available on the App Store" button below to download the ID My Pill iPhone app shown in *Figure 14*. One of the main goals when creating the ID My Pill API was to make it *platform independent* with zero libraries or packages to install. Instantly identifying prescription pills is as simple as a call to the ID My Pill cloud (www.idmypill.com).

APPLICATIONS OF CONTENT-BASED IMAGE RETRIEVAL:

A CBIR technique is used in several application areas. Some potential productive areas are discussed bellow.

1.   **Crime Prevention:** One of the major application sections of content-based image retrieval is crime prevention. Law enforcement agencies typically maintain large database of visual evidence. That evidence includes criminals' facial photograph, fingerprints and shoeprints, images or pattern of tire threads etc. These images are used to match if any serious crime is committed. (Sharma, Ekta Walia & Sinha, n.d.)

Figure 14. Idmypill (www.idmypill.com)

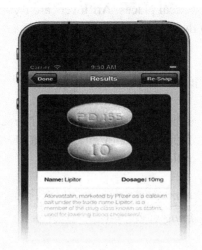

2. **Medical Diagnosis:** The exponential increase of medical data in digital libraries, it's becoming more complex task to execute certain analytical work. The use of CBIR can result in powerful services that can benefit medical information systems. Different techniques like radiology, computerized tomography has resulted in an explosion in the field of medical imaging and this type of medical images now stored by many hospitals. The prime requirement for medical imaging systems is to be able to exhibit images and to assist diagnosis by identifying similar past cases.

3. **Military Applications:** Most important application of CBIR techniques is in the field of Military sections, though least publicized. There are various example of content-based image retrieval in the field of military application, such as identification of target from satellite photographs, recognition of enemy aircraft from radar screens, provision of guidance for missile lunching system (Eakins, & Graham, 1999).

4. **Digital Libraries:** Several digital libraries that support services based on image content. One example is the digital museum of butterflies (Hong, Chen, & Hsiang 2000) that contain several collections of butterflies. Image retrieval is based on color, texture and pattern. Zhu et al., in 2000 describes a content-based image retrieval approach of digital library that supports geographical image retrieval. This paper explains how system manages air photos which can be retrieved through texture descriptors. Name of the places are associated with retrieved images that can be displayed by cross-referencing with a Geographical Name Information System (GNIS).

5. **Intellectual Property:** Copyright protection is an essential application of content-based image retrieval. Trademark is also a potentially significant application area of CBIR. Trademark is recognizable symbol, design or appearance which distinguished products of a particular dealer from the similar products of other dealers. (Wikipedia, Sharma)

6. **Fashion and Interior Designing:** Another application of CBIR system is in the field of fashion and interior designing. Retrieving of pattern, particular combination of color and textures provides important aids in designing process. (Sharma, D., Ekta Walia & Sinha)

7. **Preserving Cultural Heritage Information:** CBIR system is also important to preserving information of Museum and historical places. Art lovers are trying to perceive further examples of sculptures, painting based on the similarity measure. (Sharma, D., Ekta Walia & Sinha)

PERFORMANCE EVALUATION

To assess the retrieval efficiency can be measured in terms of its recall and precision. Precision, P, is defined as the ratio of the number of retrieved relevant images to the total number of retrieved images. Precision P measures the accuracy of the retrieval.

$$Precision = \frac{Number\ of\ relevant\ images\ retrieved}{Total\ number\ of\ images\ retrieved} = \frac{X}{X + Y}$$

Recall, R, is defined as the ratio of the number of retrieved relevant images to the total number of relevant images in the whole database.

$$Recall = \frac{Number\ of\ relevant\ images\ retrieved}{Total\ number\ of\ relevant\ images} = \frac{X}{X + Z}$$

Where X represent the number of relevant images that are retrieved, Y, the number of irrelevant items and the Z, number of relevant items those were not retrieved. The number of relevant items retrieved is the number of the returned images that are similar to the query image in this case. The total number of items retrieved is the number of images that are returned by the search engine (Singha, & Hemachandran, 2012).

The efficiency of the retrieval, namely recall precision and accuracy were calculated for color images from image database. Standard formulas have been used to compute accuracy rate (Haridas, & Thanamani, 2014).

$$AccuracyRate = \frac{Precision + Recall}{2}$$

FUTURE RESEARCH DIRECTIONS

Content-Based Video Retrieval System

There is a rapid growth in the field of Digital Video data in recent years. But no such types of well established tools are available to retrieve those data. It is most challenging filed in area of multimedia information retrieval. We can easily capture and store video, we can compress it, transmit it, and we can easily render it on fixed or mobile platforms. What remains our greatest technical challenge is being able to navigate it, to be able to browse it and search it in order to find clips which are of interest or of value to us.

Different steps of Content-based Video Retrieval (CBVR) System:

1. **Video Segmentation:** Segments the video into shots,
2. **Key Frame Selection:** Selects the key frame to represent the shot using Euclidian Distance Algorithm.
3. **Feature Extraction:** Features are extracted for the key frame and stored into feature vector.

Features can be classified in two types' spatial features and temporal features. Color, shape and edges are the major issue of spatial feature selection process and motion and audio are the temporal features.

Architectural Block Diagram of Content-Based Video Retrieval System:

Data inform of video and audio can be inserted in two ways, first on is off-line and second is on-line processing represented in *Figure 15*.

1. **Off-Line Processing:** In this method system administrator will upload the video content off-line and process it to the media descriptors. The media descriptor performs the feature extraction function of that video file and then the key frame is selected from the available set of frames, after this procedure indexing is done on the key frame.
2. **On-Line Processing:** In this method user prepared a short video clip and submit it to the query system then query media transfer the control to media descriptor. Media descriptor performs feature extraction function and collect the features that are proceed to search engine, then search engine request to Meta-data database match features of requested video with the stored video on database and finally matched result is given to the user.

Figure 15. Architectural block diagram of content-based video retrieval system

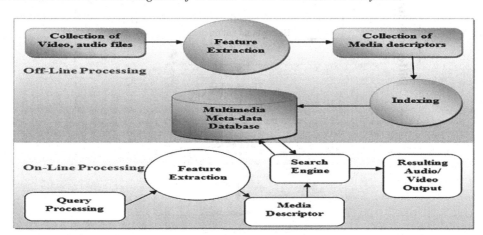

Video Segmentation: Video segmentation has become one of the foundation areas in visual signal processing research. Video segmentation is initial step towards the content-based video search aiming to segment moving objects in video sequences. In video segmentation the complete video is first converted into scenes, then scenes are converted into shots and finally shots are converted into various frames (Girgensohn, 2001).

Key Frame Selection: Generally key frames are the starting and ending frames of any video animation. As we know that the video or motion pictures consist of lots of still images. Many applications extract one or more of these still images, termed key frames, as useful graphical representations of the video data (Gitte, 2014). Select the key frame among the extracted frames is an important task.

Background Subtraction: In video segmentation background subtraction is an important method of subtracting foreground image from its background, this techniques is used in the field of image processing and computer vision. In background subtraction techniques sample images are collected from sequence of video frames then image filtering ((which may include image de-noising) task is done. Capture the sample image at time t - 1 and t and then subtract these two different matrices to generate the difference image shown in *Figure 16*. The rationale in the approach is that of detecting the moving objects from the difference between the current frame and a reference frame, often called "background image", or "background model". Background subtraction is mostly done if the image is a part of a video stream (Mukherjee, & Kundu, 2013).

Figure 16. Flow chart of background subtraction

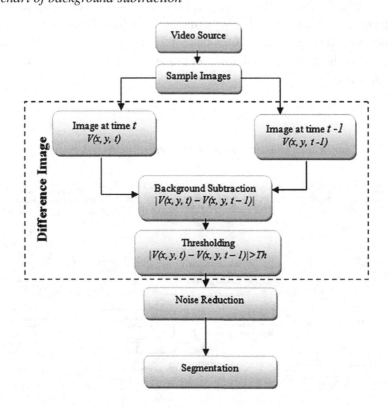

CHALLENGES OF CONTENT-BASED IMAGE RETRIEVAL SYSTEM

The implementation of CBIR systems raises several research challenges, such as:

1. The semantic gap is the lack of coincidence between the information that one can extract from the visual data and the interpretation that the same data have for a user in a given situation. Traditionally human vision are able to distinguished both low level features (color, shape, texture and object detection) and high level semantics (abstract objects, an event). User seeks semantic similarity, but the database can only provide similarity by how to represent visual content of images.
2. As the Internet grows rapidly the amount of data or images will also increase tremendously. So the algorithm should be fair enough to deal with this type of huge amount of objects to search.
3. The image retrieval techniques should be strongly developed to retrieve images efficiently. Because several problems may arise in different situations like incomplete query specification or incomplete image description. The system should be fair enough to deal with this type of problems.
4. Other great challenges of CBIR system is to efficiently maintain the database and should have proper searching techniques.

CONCLUSION

This chapter presented a brief overview on work related to an exciting field of content-based image retrieval covering over 100 of publications. A separate literature review has been done where more than 25 papers are reviewed. This chapter also has a great impact in the future trends of multimedia information retrieval. The architecture of CBIR system is divided into two parts. In the first part, the images from the image database are processed off-line. The Second part query image is analyzed to extract the visual features, and these features are used to retrieve the analogous images from the image database. Typical Content-based image Retrieval system used different types of input, it may be stored or captured images or sketch images provided by the user. This chapter also explains the fundamental modules of content-based image retrieval. Images which are stored in image database are indexed based on extracted visual content or features such as color, shape, texture, patterns, shape of object and their location within the image. The feature vector actually acted as a signature of an image. Sensory gap and semantic gap is an important factor in image retrieval. Traditionally human vision are able to distinguished both low level features (color, shape, texture and object detection) and high level semantics (abstract objects, an event). However, computer vision is only able to interpret images based on low level image features. The semantic gap between the low level visual features (color, shape, texture, etc.) and semantic concepts identified by the user remains a major problem in content-based image retrieval. This chapter also made some overview of several real life image retrieval systems, such as QBIC, Virage, RetrievalWare, Photobook, VisualSEEk, WebSEEk and NeTra. CBIR technique is used in several application areas. Some potential fruitful areas are also discussed in that chapter. Other focusing areas of this chapter are recall and precision, which are used for performance evaluation. There is amazing growth in the amount of digital video data in recent years, universally accepted video retrieval and indexing technique are not well defined or available. This is another emerging area of that chapter. The Video Retrieval system includes various steps: Video Segmentation, Key frames Selection, Feature Extraction. The future of this field depends on the collective focus and overall progress in each aspect of image retrieval, and how much the ordinary individual stands to benefit from it.

REFERENCES

Alexandrov, A. D., Ma, W. Y., El Abbadi, A., & Manjunath, B. S. (1995, March). Adaptive filtering and indexing for image databases. In *IS&T/SPIE's Symposium on Electronic Imaging: Science & Technology* (pp. 12-23). International Society for Optics and Photonics.

Ardakany, A. R., & Joula, A. M. (2012). Gender recognition based on edge histogram. *International Journal of Computer Theory and Engineering*, *4*(2), 127–130. doi:10.7763/IJCTE.2012.V4.436

Bach, J. R., Fuller, C., Gupta, A., Hampapur, A., Horowitz, B., Humphrey, R., . . . Shu, C. F. (1996, March). Virage image search engine: an open framework for image management. In Electronic Imaging: Science & Technology (pp. 76-87). International Society for Optics and Photonics.

Bebis, G., Boyle, R., Parvin, B., Koracin, D., Paragios, N., Tanveer, S.-M., & Malzbender, T. et al. (Eds.). (2007). *ISVC, Part II, LNCS 4842. Springer-Verlag Berlin Heidelberg*.

Beckmann, N., Kriegel, H. P., Schneider, R., & Seeger, B. (1990). The R*-tree: an efficient and robust access method for points and rectangles: Vol. 19. *No. 2*. ACM.

Belongie, S., Carson, C., Greenspan, H., & Malik, J. (1998, January). Color-and texture-based image segmentation using EM and its application to content-based image retrieval. In *Computer Vision, 1998. Sixth International Conference on* (pp. 675-682). IEEE. doi:10.1109/ICCV.1998.710790

Bentley, J. L. (1980). Multidimensional divide-and-conquer. *Communications of the ACM*, *23*(4), 214–229. doi:10.1145/358841.358850

Carson, C., Belongie, S., Greenspan, H., & Malik, J. (2002). Blobworld: Image segmentation using expectation-maximization and its application to image querying. *Pattern Analysis and Machine Intelligence. IEEE Transactions on*, *24*(8), 1026–1038.

Chanda, B., Majumder, D.D. (n.d.). *Digital Image Processing and Analysis*. PHI Publication.

Chang, S., Smith, J. R., Meng, H. J., Wang, H., & Zhong, D. (1997). *Finding Images/Video in Large Archives: Columbia's Content-Based VisualQuery Project*. Academic Press.

Chang, S. F. (1995, October). Compressed-domain techniques for image/video indexing and manipulation. In *Image Processing, 1995. Proceedings., International Conference on* (Vol. 1, pp. 314-317). IEEE.

Chang, S. F. (1996). Compressed-domain content-based image and video retrieval. In Multimedia Communications and Video Coding (pp. 375-382). Springer US. doi:10.1007/978-1-4613-0403-6_46

Chang, S. F., Chen, W., Meng, H. J., Sundaram, H., & Zhong, D. (1998). A fully automated content-based video search engine supporting spatiotemporal queries. *Circuits and Systems for Video Technology. IEEE Transactions on*, *8*(5), 602–615.

Chang, S. F., & Smith, J. R. (1995, October). Single color extraction and image query. In *Image processing, 1995. Proceedings., International conference on* (Vol. 3, pp. 528-531). IEEE.

Chang, S. F., & Smith, J. R. (1995, April). Extracting multidimensional signal features for content-based visual query. In *Visual Communications and Image Processing'95* (pp. 995–1006). International Society for Optics and Photonics. doi:10.1117/12.206632

Chen, Y., & Wang, J. Z. (2002). A region-based fuzzy feature matching approach to content-based image retrieval. *Pattern Analysis and Machine Intelligence. IEEE Transactions on, 24*(9), 1252–1267.

Cho, S. B., & Lee, J. Y. (2002). A human-oriented image retrieval system using interactive genetic algorithm. *Systems, Man and Cybernetics, Part A: Systems and humans. IEEE Transactions on, 32*(3), 452–458.

Choras, R. S. (2007). Image feature extraction techniques and their applications for CBIR and biometrics systems. *International Journal of Biology and Biomedical Engineering, 1*(1), 6-16.

da Silva Torres, R., & Falcao, A. X. (2006). Content-Based Image Retrieval: Theory and Applications. *Research Initiative, Treatment Action, 13*(2), 161–185.

Daneels, D., Van Campenhout, D., Niblack, C. W., Equitz, W., Barber, R., & Fierens, F. (1993, April). Interactive outlining: An improved approach using active contours. In *IS&T/SPIE's Symposium on Electronic Imaging: Science and Technology* (pp. 226-233). International Society for Optics and Photonics.

Devijver, P. A., & Dekesel, M. M. (1987). Learning the parameters of a hidden Markov random field image model: A simple example. In *Pattern Recognition Theory and Applications* (pp. 141–163). Springer Berlin Heidelberg. doi:10.1007/978-3-642-83069-3_13

Dimitrova, N., & Abdel-Mottaleb, M. (1997, January). Content-based video retrieval by example video clip. In *Electronic Imaging'97* (pp. 59–70). International Society for Optics and Photonics.

Eakins, J. P., & Graham, M. E. (1999). *Content-based image retrieval, a report to the JISC Technology Applications programme.* Academic Press.

Equitz, W., & Niblack, W. (1994). *Retrieving images from a database: using texture algorithms from the QBIC system, IBM Research Division.* Research Report 9805.

Faloutsos, C., Barber, R., Flickner, M., Hafner, J., Niblack, W., Petkovic, D., & Equitz, W. (1994). Efficient and effective querying by image content. *Journal of Intelligent Information Systems, 3*(3-4), 231–262. doi:10.1007/BF00962238

Flickner, M., Sawhney, H., Niblack, W., Ashley, J., Huang, Q., Dom, B., & Steele, D. et al. (1995). Query by image and video content: The QBIC system. *Computer, 28*(9), 23–32. doi:10.1109/2.410146

Gao, Y., Chan, K. L., & Yau, W. Y. (2007, December). Learning in content-based image retrieval-a brief review. In *Information, Communications & Signal Processing, 2007 6th International Conference on* (pp. 1-5). IEEE.

Ghodeswar, S., & Meshram, B. B. (2010). Content-based video retrieval.*Proceedings of ISCET*, 135.

Girgensohn, A., Boreczky, J., & Wilcox, L. (2001). Keyframe-based user interfaces for digital video. *Computer, 34*(9), 61–67. doi:10.1109/2.947093

Gitte, M., Bawaskar, H., Sethi, S., & Shinde, A. (2014). Content-based video retrieval system. *Int J Res Eng Technol, 3*(6).

Gonzalez, R. C., Woods, R. E., & Eddins, S. L. U. (2004). Digital Image Processing Using MATLAB. Pearson Prentice Hall.

Gudivada, V. N., & Raghavan, V. V. (1995). Content-based image retrieval systems. *Computer, 28*(9), 18–22. doi:10.1109/2.410145

Gupta, A., & Jain, R. (1997). Visual information retrieval. *Communications of the ACM, 40*(5), 70–79. doi:10.1145/253769.253798

Guttman, A. (1984). R-trees: a dynamic index structure for spatial searching: Vol. 14. *No. 2* (pp. 47–57). ACM.

Haridas, K., & Thanamani, A. S. (2014). Well-Organized Content-based Image Retrieval System in RGB Color Histogram, Tamura Texture and Gabor Feature. *International Journal of Advanced Research in Computer and Communication Engineering, 3*(10).

Hemaltha, M. (2012). Similar Image Retrieval using DWT and LIM based Image Matching Technique. *International Journal of Advanced Research in Computer Science, 3*(2).

Hermes, T., Klauck, C., Kreyss, J., & Zhang, J. (1995, March). Image retrieval for information systems. In *IS&T/SPIE's Symposium on Electronic Imaging: Science & Technology* (pp. 394-405). International Society for Optics and Photonics.

Hiremath, P. S., & Pujari, J. (2007, December). Content-based image retrieval using color, texture and shape features. In *Advanced Computing and Communications, 2007. ADCOM 2007. International Conference on* (pp. 780-784). IEEE. doi:10.1109/ADCOM.2007.21

Hong, J. S., Chen, H. Y., & Hsiang, J. (2000, June). A digital museum of Taiwanese butterflies. In *Proceedings of the fifth ACM conference on Digital libraries* (pp. 260-261). ACM. doi:10.1145/336597.336694

Huang, P. W., & Dai, S. K. (2003). Image retrieval by texture similarity. *Pattern Recognition, 36*(3), 665–679. doi:10.1016/S0031-3203(02)00083-3

Idrissi, N., Martinez, J., & Aboutajdine, D. (2009). Bridging the semantic gap for texture-based image retrieval and navigation. *Journal of Multimedia, 4*(5), 277–283. doi:10.4304/jmm.4.5.277-283

Jaswal, G., & Kaul, A. (2009). Content-Based Image Retrieval-A literature Review. In *National Conference on Computing Communication and Control*.

Jhanwar, N., Chaudhuri, S., Seetharaman, G., & Zavidovique, B. (2004). Content-based image retrieval using motif cooccurrence matrix. *Image and Vision Computing, 22*(14), 1211–1220. doi:10.1016/j.imavis.2004.03.026

Jin, Y., Khan, L., Wang, L., & Awad, M. (2005, November). Image annotations by combining multiple evidence & wordnet. In *Proceedings of the 13th annual ACM international conference on Multimedia* (pp. 706-715). ACM. doi:10.1145/1101149.1101305

Kannan, A., Mohan, V., & Anbazhagan, N. (2010, December). Image clustering and retrieval using image mining techniques. In *IEEE International Conference on Computational Intelligence and Computing Research* (Vol. 2).

Katayama, N., & Satoh, S. I. (1997, June). The SR-tree: An index structure for high-dimensional nearest neighbor queries. *SIGMOD Record, 26*(2), 369–380. doi:10.1145/253262.253347

Kato, T. (1992, April). Database architecture for content-based image retrieval. In *SPIE/IS&T 1992 Symposium on Electronic Imaging: Science and Technology* (pp. 112-123). International Society for Optics and Photonics.

Kawashima, T., Tateyama, K., Iijima, T., & Aoki, Y. (1998, October). Indexing of baseball telecast for content-based video retrieval. In *Image Processing, 1998. ICIP 98. Proceedings. 1998 International Conference on* (Vol. 1, pp. 871-874). IEEE. doi:10.1109/ICIP.1998.723657

Keen, N. (2005). *Color moments*. School Of Informatics, University Of Edinburgh.

Kherfi, M. L., Ziou, D., & Bernardi, A. (2004). Image retrieval from the world wide web: Issues, techniques, and systems. *ACM Computing Surveys, 36*(1), 35–67. doi:10.1145/1013208.1013210

Lai, C. C., & Chen, Y. C. (2011). A user-oriented image retrieval system based on interactive genetic algorithm. *Instrumentation and Measurement. IEEE Transactions on, 60*(10), 3318–3325.

Lee, D., Barber, R., Niblack, W., Flickner, M., Hafner, J., & Petkovic, D. (1994, October). Indexing for complex queries on a query-by-content image database. In *Pattern Recognition, 1994. Vol. 1-Conference A: Computer Vision & Image Processing.,Proceedings of the 12th IAPR International Conference on* (*Vol. 1*, pp. 142-146). IEEE. doi:10.1109/ICPR.1994.576246

Lee, I., Muneesawang, P., & Guan, L. (1996). Automatic Relevance Feedback for Distributed Content-based Image Retrieval.*International Congress for Global Science.*

Lew, M. S., Sebe, N., Djeraba, C., & Jain, R. (2006). Content-based multimedia information retrieval: State of the art and challenges. *ACM Transactions on Multimedia Computing, Communications, and Applications, 2*(1), 1–19. doi:10.1145/1126004.1126005

Lin, C. H., Chen, R. T., & Chan, Y. K. (2009). A smart content-based image retrieval system based on color and texture feature. *Image and Vision Computing, 27*(6), 658–665.

Liping, C. H. E. N., & Tat-Seng, C. H. U. A. (2001, August). A match and tiling approach to content-based video retrieval. In null (p. 77). IEEE. doi:10.1109/ICME.2001.1237716

Liu, C., & Song, G. (2011, October). A method of measuring the semantic gap in image retrieval: Using the information theory. In *Image Analysis and Signal Processing (IASP), 2011 International Conference on* (pp. 287-291). IEEE.

Liu, Y., Zhang, D., Lu, G., & Ma, W. Y. (2007). A survey of content-based image retrieval with high-level semantics. *Pattern Recognition, 40*(1), 262–282. doi:10.1016/j.patcog.2006.04.045

Smith, J. R., & Chang, S. F. (1996, May). Automated binary texture feature sets for image retrieval. In *Acoustics, Speech, and Signal Processing, 1996. ICASSP-96. Conference Proceedings., 1996 IEEE International Conference on* (Vol. 4, pp. 2239-2242). IEEE. doi:10.1109/ICASSP.1996.545867

Long, F., Zhang, H., & Feng, D. D. (2003). Fundamentals of content-based image retrieval. In *Multimedia Information Retrieval and Management* (pp. 1–26). Springer Berlin Heidelberg.

Ma, W. Y., & Manjunath, B. S. (1995, November). Image indexing using a texture dictionary. In *Photonics East'95* (pp. 288–298). International Society for Optics and Photonics; doi:10.1007/978-3-662-05300-3_1

Ma, W. Y., & Manjunath, B. S. (1996). A pattern thesaurus for browsing large aerial photographs. *Department of Electrical and Computer Engineering, University of Califórnia, ECE Technical Report 96, 10.*

Ma, W. Y., & Manjunath, B. S. (1996, June). Texture features and learning similarity. In *Computer Vision and Pattern Recognition, 1996. Proceedings CVPR'96, 1996 IEEE Computer Society Conference on* (pp. 425-430). IEEE. doi:10.1109/CVPR.1996.517107

Ma, W. Y., & Manjunath, B. S. (1997, June). Edge flow: a framework of boundary detection and image segmentation. In *Computer Vision and Pattern Recognition, 1997. Proceedings., 1997 IEEE Computer Society Conference on* (pp. 744-749). IEEE. doi:10.1109/CVPR.1997.609409

Ma, W. Y., & Manjunath, B. S. (1999). Netra: A toolbox for navigating large image databases. *Multimedia Systems, 7*(3), 184–198. doi:10.1007/s005300050121

Madugunki, M., Bormane, D. S., Bhadoria, S., & Dethe, C. G. (2011, April). Comparison of different CBIR techniques. In *Electronics Computer Technology (ICECT), 2011 3rd International Conference on* (Vol. 4, pp. 372-375). IEEE. doi:10.1109/ICECTECH.2011.5941923

Manjunath, B. S., & Ma, W. Y. (1996). Texture features for browsing and retrieval of image data. *Pattern Analysis and Machine Intelligence. IEEE Transactions on, 18*(8), 837–842.

Mehrotra, S., Rui, Y., Ortega-Binderberger, M., & Huang, T. S. (1997, June). Supporting content-based queries over images in MARS. In *Multimedia Computing and Systems' 97. Proceedings., IEEE International Conference on* (pp. 632-633). IEEE. doi:10.1109/MMCS.1997.609791

Minka, T. P., & Picard, R. W. (1996, June). Interactive learning with a "society of models". In *Computer Vision and Pattern Recognition, 1996. Proceedings CVPR'96, 1996 IEEE Computer Society Conference on* (pp. 447-452). IEEE.

Mitra, S., & Acharya, T. (2005). *Data mining: multimedia, soft computing, and bioinformatics.* John Wiley & Sons.

Mukherjee, A., & Kundu, D. Motion analysis in video surveillance using edge detection techniques. *IOSR Journal of Computer Engineering.*

Müller, H., Michoux, N., Bandon, D., & Geissbuhler, A. (2004). A review of content-based image retrieval systems in medical applications—clinical benefits and future directions. *International Journal of Medical Informatics, 73*(1), 1–23. doi:10.1016/j.ijmedinf.2003.11.024 PMID:15036075

Ortega, M., Rui, Y., Chakrabarti, K., Mehrotra, S., & Huang, T. S. (1997, November). Supporting similarity queries in MARS. In *Proceedings of the fifth ACM international conference on Multimedia* (pp. 403-413). ACM. doi:10.1145/266180.266394

Pass, G., & Zabih, R. (1996, December). Histogram refinement for content-based image retrieval. In *Applications of Computer Vision, 1996. WACV'96., Proceedings 3rd IEEE Workshop on* (pp. 96-102). IEEE.

Pentland, A., Picard, R. W., & Sclaroff, S. (1996). Photobook: Content-based manipulation of image databases. *International Journal of Computer Vision, 18*(3), 233–254. doi:10.1007/BF00123143

Petkovic, M. (2000). *Content-based video retrieval*. Academic Press.

Picard, R. W. (1995). *Digital libraries: Meeting place for high-level and low-level vision*. Springer Berlin Heidelberg.

Picard, R. W. (1996). A society of models for video and image libraries. *IBM Systems Journal, 35*(3-4), 292-312.

Picard, R. W., Minka, T. P., & Szummer, M. (1996, September). Modeling user subjectivity in image libraries. In *Image Processing, 1996. Proceedings., International Conference on* (Vol. 1, pp. 777-780). IEEE. doi:10.1109/ICIP.1996.561018

Rui, Y., Huang, T. S., & Chang, S. F. (1999). Image retrieval: Current techniques, promising directions, and open issues. *Journal of Visual Communication and Image Representation, 10*(1), 39–62. doi:10.1006/jvci.1999.0413

Rui, Y., Huang, T. S., & Mehrotra, S. (1997, October). Content-based image retrieval with relevance feedback in MARS. In *Image Processing, 1997. Proceedings., International Conference on* (Vol. 2, pp. 815-818). IEEE. doi:10.1109/ICIP.1997.638621

Scassellati, B. M., Alexopoulos, S., & Flickner, M. D. (1994, April). Retrieving images by 2D shape: a comparison of computation methods with human perceptual judgments. In *IS&T/SPIE 1994 International Symposium on Electronic Imaging: Science and Technology* (pp. 2-14). International Society for Optics and Photonics.

Sherlock, G. (2000). Analysis of large-scale gene-expression data. *Current Opinion in Immunology, 12*(1), 201–205. doi:10.1016/S0952-7915(99)00074-6 PMID:10712947

Shyu, C. R., Brodley, C. E., Kak, A. C., Kosaka, A., Aisen, A. M., & Broderick, L. S. (1999). ASSERT: A physician-in-the-loop content-based retrieval system for HRCT image databases. *Computer Vision and Image Understanding, 75*(1), 111–132. doi:10.1006/cviu.1999.0768

Singha, M., & Hemachandran, K. (2012). Content-based image retrieval using color and texture. *Signal & Image Processing: An International Journal, 3*(1), 39–57.

Smeulders, A. W., Worring, M., Santini, S., Gupta, A., & Jain, R. (2000). Content-based image retrieval at the end of the early years. *Pattern Analysis and Machine Intelligence. IEEE Transactions on, 22*(12), 1349–1380.

Smith, J. R., & Chang, S. F. (1994, November). Transform features for texture classification and discrimination in large image databases. In *Image Processing, 1994. Proceedings. ICIP-94., IEEE International Conference* (Vol. 3, pp. 407-411). IEEE. doi:10.1109/ICIP.1994.413817

Smith, J. R., & Chang, S. F. (1996). *Searching for images and videos on the world-wide web*. IEEE Multimedia Magazine.

Smith, J. R., & Chang, S. F. (1996, May). Automated binary texture feature sets for image retrieval. In *Acoustics, Speech, and Signal Processing, 1996. ICASSP-96. Conference Proceedings., 1996 IEEE International Conference on* (Vol. 4, pp. 2239-2242). IEEE. doi:10.1109/ICASSP.1996.545867

Smith, J. R., & Chang, S. F. (1997, February). VisualSEEk: a fully automated content-based image query system. In *Proceedings of the fourth ACM international conference on Multimedia* (pp. 87-98). ACM.

Smith, J. R., & Chang, S. F. (1997). Visually searching the web for content. *IEEE MultiMedia, 4*(3), 12–20. doi:10.1109/93.621578

Smith, J. R., & Chang, S. F. (1997, February). VisualSEEk: a fully automated content-based image query system. In *Proceedings of the fourth ACM international conference on Multimedia* (pp. 87-98). ACM.

Stricker, O., M. (1995). Similarity of color images.*Proceedings of SPIE Storage and Retrieval for Image and Video Databases III*. doi:10.1117/12.205308

Su, J. H., Huang, W. J., Yu, P. S., & Tseng, V. S. (2011). Efficient relevance feedback for content-based image retrieval by mining user navigation patterns. *Knowledge and Data Engineering. IEEE Transactions on, 23*(3), 360–372.

Swain, M. J., & Ballard, D. H. (1991). Color indexing. *International Journal of Computer Vision, 7*(1), 11–32. doi:10.1007/BF00130487

Tamura, H., Mori, S., & Yamawaki, T. (1978). Textural features corresponding to visual perception. *Systems, Man and Cybernetics. IEEE Transactions on, 8*(6), 460–473.

Tangelder, J. W., & Veltkamp, R. C. (2008). A survey of content-based 3D shape retrieval methods. *Multimedia Tools and Applications, 39*(3), 441–471. doi:10.1007/s11042-007-0181-0

Verma, P., Mahajan, M., & Mohali, P. (2012). *Retrieval of better results by using shape techniques for content-based retrieval*. Academic Press.

Wang, J., Wiederhold, G., Firschein, O., & We, S. (1998). Content-based Image Indexing and Searching Using Daubechies' Wavelets. *International Journal on Digital Libraries, 1*(4), 311–328. doi:10.1007/s007990050026

Wang, J. Z., Li, J., & Wiederhold, G. (2001). SIMPLIcity: Semantics-sensitive integrated matching for picture libraries. *Pattern Analysis and Machine Intelligence. IEEE Transactions on, 23*(9), 947–963.

White, D. A., & Jain, R. (1996, February). Similarity indexing with the SS-tree. In *Data Engineering, 1996.Proceedings of the Twelfth International Conference on* (pp. 516-523). IEEE. doi:10.1109/ICDE.1996.492202

Yang, M., Kpalma, K., & Ronsin, J. (2008). A survey of shape feature extraction techniques. *Pattern Recognition*, 43–90.

Zhang, H., & Zhong, D. (1995, March). Scheme for visual feature-based image indexing. In *IS&T/SPIE's Symposium on Electronic Imaging: Science & Technology* (pp. 36-46). International Society for Optics and Photonics. doi:10.1016/B978-155860651-7/50110-8

Zhang, H. J., Wu, J., Zhong, D., & Smoliar, S. W. (1997). An integrated system for content-based video retrieval and browsing. *Pattern Recognition*, *30*(4), 643–658. doi:10.1016/S0031-3203(96)00109-4

Zhu, B., Ramsey, M., & Chen, H. (2000). Creating a large-scale content-based airphoto image digital library. *Image Processing. IEEE Transactions on*, *9*(1), 163–167.

KEY TERMS AND DEFINITIONS

Chrominance: Chrominance (chroma or C for short) is the signal used in video systems to convey the color information of the picture, separately from the accompanying luma signal (or Y for short). Chrominance is usually represented as two color-difference components: $U = B' - Y'$ (blue − luma) and $V = R' - Y'$ (red − luma).

Color Moments: Color moments are measures that can be used to distinguish images based on their features of color. They provide a measurement for color similarity between images.

Features: In image processing field features describes as an attributes or characteristic of an image.

Image Segmentation: Image segmentation is the process of partitioning a digital image into multiple segments. The goal of segmentation is to simplify and/or change the representation of an image into something that is more meaningful and easier to analyze.

Key Frame: A key frame in animation and filmmaking is a drawing that defines the starting and ending points of any smooth transition. The drawings are called "frames" because their position in time is measured in frames on a strip of film.

Luminance Component: Luminance is a photometric measure of the luminous intensity per unit area of light travelling in a given direction. It describes the amount of light that passes through, is emitted or reflected from a particular area, and falls within a given solid angle.

Meta-Data: It is data that describes other data. Meta is a prefix that in most information technology usages means "an underlying definition or description." Metadata summarizes basic information about data, which can make finding and working with particular instances of data easier.

Precision: Precision is defined as the ratio of the number of retrieved relevant images to the total number of retrieved images. Precision P measures the accuracy of the retrieval.

Recall: Recall is defined as the ratio of the number of retrieved relevant images to the total number of relevant images in the whole database.

Relevance Feedback: Relevance feedback is a feature of some information retrieval systems. The idea behind relevance feedback is to take the results that are initially returned from a given query and to use information about whether or not those results are relevant to perform a new query.

Semantic Gap: The semantic gap characterizes the difference between two descriptions of an object by different linguistic representations, for instance languages or symbols. In computer science, the concept is relevant whenever ordinary human activities, observations, and tasks are transferred into a computational representation.

Sensory Gap: Sensory gap is the difference between an object visualized in the real world and its computer interpretation. This interpretation can be visualized by either via sensors and displays, or can be used by computers in the learning process.

Thresholding: Image *thresholding* is a simple, yet effective, way of partitioning an image into a foreground and background.

Chapter 6
Biomedical Image Processing and Analysis

Swanirbhar Majumder
North Eastern Regional Institute of Science and Technology, India

Smita Majumder
Tripura University, India

ABSTRACT

Since 1960's digital image processing has been a popular field of research and applications. Among the various applications like physics, security, photonics, biomedical, astronomy, remote sensing, ecological, environmental, etc.; biomedical is one of the many important areas people are focusing on. So for the intelligent analysis of multimedia information like biomedical image has is the thrust area of this chapter. This chapter therefore would aid both biomedical engineers and non-technical people using the tools to get an overview. This chapter mainly concentrates on bio-medical imaging. The medical testing abbreviations and terms like X-ray, MRI, SPECT, PET, Ultrasonography, CFI, optical and IR Imaging SEM, TEM, etc. are discussed here. They mainly concentrate on images of internal structure of living organisms which are not accessible by standard imaging techniques. Moreover, this helps non-technically oriented people to get an overview of the bio-medical aspects.

INTRODUCTION

The different biomedical imaging modalities have been discussed here. Most of these techniques are very common in our day to day lives but in spite of using them we are not aware of the mechanism of these systems and the image analysis procedures. So, brief explanations are provided here to the extent that is needed to understand the imaging properties of the individual modalities and their requirements with respect to processing and analysis of measured data. No attempt has been made to go deeper into the physical background of these individual modalities, nor has the technical construction been described of the respective imaging systems. The purpose here is solely to explain those features of each modality that determine its imaging properties and limitations, and to comment on intrinsic signal and image data processing and analysis, as well as on typical parameters of the provided image data. This should lead the reader to an understanding of the reasons behind the application of this or another data processing approach in the frame of every modality. Moreover, as this chapter is targeted to the general audience

DOI: 10.4018/978-1-5225-0498-6.ch006

who might not be too accustomed to high level of mathematics involved in these modalities and their image analysis techniques. Therefore very negligible amount of mathematical terms have been involved in this chapter (Bijnens, 1997; Dawant & Zijdenbos, 2000; Fenster & Downey, 2000; Hrivnák, 1986; Kilian, Jan, & Bijnens, 2000; Reiber, 2000; Sheehan, Wilson, Shavelle, & Geiser, 2000; Stegmann, Wepf, & Schroder, 1999; Wahl, 2002; Woodward, 1995; Xu, Pham, & Prince, 2002; Bloch, 1946; Purcell, Torrey, & Pound 1946; Lauterbur, 1973; Hahn, 1950; Mansfield, 1977; Anger, 1958; Namekava, Kasai, Tsukamoto, & Koyano, 1982; Petrán, Hadravsky, Egger, & Galambos, 1968; Hounsfield, 1973).

The biomedical imaging systems can be classified into the following categories according to basic imaging criteria:

- X-ray projection radiography
- Digital subtractive angiography (DSA)
- X-ray computed tomography (CT)
- Magnetic resonance imaging (MRI) tomography
- Nuclear imaging (planar gamma-imaging, SPECT, PET)
- Ultrasonography (USG)
- Optical and Infrared (IR) Imaging
- Electron microscopy
- Electrical impedance tomography (IT)

All these modalities are not used exclusively in medicine; many of them find applications in other areas too i.e. in technology and industry (material engineering, micro- and nanotechnology, nondestructive testing), as well as in research and science, such as in biology, ecology, archaeology, etc. (Boone, 2000; Bronzino, 1995; Bushberg, Seibert, Leidholdt, & Boone, 2002; Cho, Jones, & Singh, 1993; Krestel, 1990; Rowlands, & Yorkston, 2000; Yaffe, 2000). Here in this chapter these modalities are briefly discussed, providing some overview in this field.

X-Ray Projection Radiography

Since Roentgen's discovery of the x-rays in the last decade of the 19th century, x-ray projection radiography is the oldest and simplest medical imaging modality as far as the imaging principle concerns. It is normally considered as a point radiator as the source of radiation is of negligible dimension. Here the image is formed of intensity values of the x-rays modified by passing through the imaged object, e.g., a part of the patient's body. The resulting image contains information on the complete three-dimensional volume projected on the two-dimensional plane of the detecting panel (originally a fluorescent screen, film, or image amplifier, currently also a type of digital flat-panel detector). Every pixel in the resulting image ideally represents the intensity of the incident x-ray that carries the information on the total attenuation along the respective ray. The resulting image can be interpreted as a mixture of images of planes parallel with the projection plane (Boone, 2000).

Normally the individual planes are imaged in different scales. It is impossible to separate the image information on the individual planes algorithmically, as the information of individual contributions to ray attenuation is missing. Usually, this is a (principally difficult) task for the radiologist analyzing the image to use his imagination in combination with a priori anatomical knowledge, in order to evaluate and classify the image information properly, taking into account the imaging properties and a few subtler ones. Principle of X-ray projection imaging is shown in Figure 1.

Figure 1. Principle of X-ray projection imaging

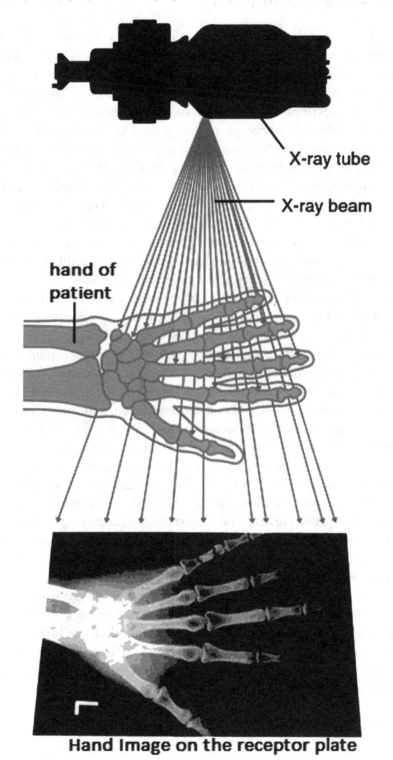

Hand Image on the receptor plate

Digital Subtractive Angiography (DSA)

Subtractive angiography—often called digital subtractive angiography (DSA)—is in fact not an individual imaging modality, but rather a specialized type of projection radiography, which uses a pre-imaging modification of the imaged object by adding a contrast agent to some of its structures and consequently comparing the artificially contrasted images with the non-contrasted ones. Though it is used primarily for visualizing vessel structures (thence its name) and, based on sequences of images, also for evaluation of blood flow and tissue perfusion, its principle is quite general and can be used for other purposes as well. It is a conceptually simple approach, enhancing visualization of structures normally hardly visible, which can be filled with an x-ray-attenuating contrast agent. Basically two images are provided—one before the application of the contrast agent (pre-injection image, often called the mask), and the other when the agent is properly distributed in the structure to be visualized (e.g., in vascular structures). The mask is then subtracted from the contrast image; this way, the structures that are common to both images (fixed anatomy) are suppressed, leaving only the enhanced image of the contrast-filled structures. Naturally, the precision of the algorithm of this system is limited by neglecting the influence of attenuation dependence on the x-ray frequency (photon energy); in other words, the analysis is precise only for monochromatic x-rays. Nevertheless, it can reasonably be used in practice, as the nonlinearity caused by the wideband character of radiation, related also to the hardening effect on the radiation, does not reach a level that would disqualify the linearity hypothesis (Reiber, 2000).

Though the principle is simple, the complete procedure of DSA is more complicated. It consists of providing the images (the precontrast mask and one or more contrast images), followed by the conversion of the obtained intensity images into attenuation images by the point-wise logarithmic contrast transform. The next, very important step is the image registration, which must ensure that the corresponding structures are precisely located at the same positions in both images to be subtracted. If this is not fulfilled perfectly, perhaps due to movement of the patient or his organs during the imaging, the subtraction would enhance not only the contrast-filled structures, but also (and perhaps predominantly) just the differences caused by the imperfect match. This may lead to very disturbing plasticity of the difference images, if not to improper conclusions as to blood flow concerns. The misregistration must therefore be prevented by special presubtraction registration procedures that themselves represent a complex computation and still a challenging problem. Due to the complicated character of the local shifts, often a rigid registration (consisting of mere shift and rotation) is insufficient and more efficient but more complicated flexible registration approaches must be applied. The perfectly matched images are then subtracted, and the contrast scale of the difference image should usually be normalized to the full display extent, as the differences have usually relatively low dynamics. A typical DSA images are presented in Figure 2. Of course, the same mask can be subtracted sequentially from a series of consecutive contrast images describing, e.g., progressive filling of a vessel structure. In this case, the registration step usually has to be repeated, as the movements in individual images of an image sequence usually differ mutually (Bijnens, 1997).

X-Ray Computed Tomography (CT)

his X-ray computed tomography (CT) was the first tomographic modality entirely based on digital reconstruction of images. It has qualitatively changed the field of medical imaging. Contemporarily, it is probably the most common computerized tomographic modality, with excellent spatial resolution, fast

Figure 2. Example of iodine-based contrast in DSA

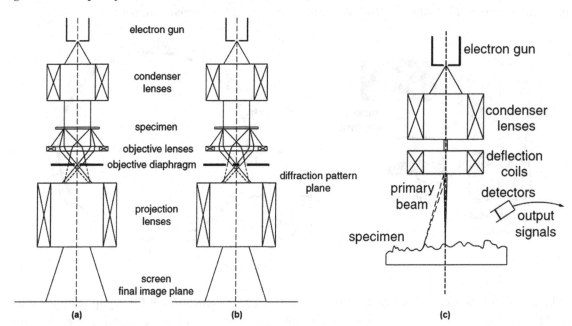

image acquisition enabling even real-time imaging, and rather generic application (Fenster & Downey, 2000).

As discussed above, the x-ray radiography provides attenuation images that are combinations of projections of all layers forming the thickness of the object. There is no way to separate the information from different layers, except by subjective evaluation using a priori anatomical knowledge. It is possible to enhance the image of an individual layer by blurring images of other layers on special x-ray equipment, where the radiation source and detection plane are moved simultaneously with respect to the patient during exposition in a proper way (classical x-ray tomography). Nevertheless, besides other drawbacks, this does not enable the determination of the spatial attenuation distribution, which would allow the reconstructing of images for any desired plane exactly. Computed tomography (CT) solves the problem of determining this inner distribution by measuring individual object-influenced intensity values for many differently oriented rays, and subsequently reconstructing the data on internal attenuation distribution computationally.

The basic principle of CT measurement can be seen in Figure 3. The x-ray source, together with primary collimators, provides a fine beam of radiation (ideally an infinitesimally narrow ray) that passes the object, the intensity of the beam is then measured by a detector. Even with a good primary collimation, the beam is always slightly divergent, thus increasing the diameter of the measured volume of the object when approaching the detector side. This is compensated for by the secondary (detector) collimator, which excludes all the rays outside of the desired beam, in this way also suppressing the radiation scattered along the way through the object. The effective diameter of the resulting beam may be in the range of about 0.5 to 10 mm. This linear arrangement (source–detector) can be moved in the imaged plane with respect to the object perpendicularly to the beam so that the intensity is measured on different parallel rays.

Figure 3. Principle of measurement of projections—(a) Basic rectangular arrangement, schematic view of the third-generation CT scanner (b) View of the slice plane. (c) Perpendicular view

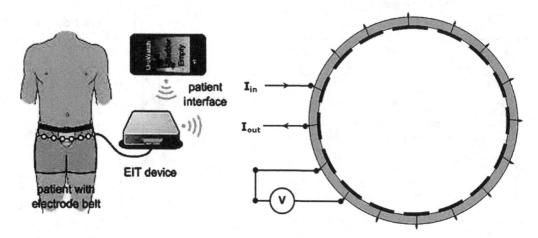

The arrangement depicted in Figure 3(a) represents the first generation of CT equipment that made use of a single pair of the x-ray source and detector. This "pencil ray" probe scanned linearly across the object to provide a projection, and was rotated by about 1° before scanning for another projection, in the angle range of 180° to 240°. The main disadvantage of the first generation was a long scanning time (several minutes), besides the large dose for the patient. The second-generation systems improved the situation partially by using a narrow fan beam and a short linear array of detectors, but the linear scanning was still necessary. Most of the presently used CT systems belong to the third generation, of which the most prominent feature is the use of a thin (about 1 to 10 mm) but wide fan beam (30° to 60°) covering the complete slice of the object, as shown in Figure 3 (b) and (c). The detector array, curved into a circular segment with the center in the radiation focus, is encompassing several hundred to a thousand detectors. Spacing of the detectors is equiangular with respect to the radiation focus, which is advantageous from the image reconstruction viewpoint.

The lines connecting the focus with the detectors thus define the individual equiangular rays of the fan. No lateral translation is needed, as the entire slice is scanned at once; thus, only rotational movement is needed. The complete rigid fan arrangement — the x-ray source and the detector array—rotates around a fixed axis, which crosses the object space. Naturally, the inner part of the fan is empty to allow placing of the object — a patient; the bearings are sufficiently far away so that the axial object shift is enabled as needed for scanning of different slices of the patient's body. This concept is complicated mechanically as, apart from others, the energy supply and all measuring signals have to be transferred via a slide ring arrangement to allow continuous rotation. Also, the centrifugal forces are enormous, thus requiring special construction solutions.

The fourth- and fifth-generation fan beam systems are similar to those of the third generation as far as the image forming concerns. The concept of the fourth generation differs from the previous generation primarily in having a stationary circular array of equidistantly spaced detectors, which eliminates the need of complicated transfer of measuring signals. Only the radiation source is rotating, either inside the detector ring as depicted or possibly also outside, provided that the rays can somehow pass around the detector ring when entering the object space. The fans, forming individual projections, are defined in the opposite way as in the third generation: the vertex of a fan is at a detector and the projection data are acquired gradually, during the x-ray source rotation; obviously, many different fans can be served simultaneously. Nevertheless, the imaging situation is less favorable than that of the third generation because the secondary collimators cannot be efficiently applied since the detectors must accept rays from different angles; thus, the influence of scattered radiation cannot be suppressed that well. Another drawback is the non-equi-angular spacing of the rays in a fan, so that some additional interpolation providing the uniform spacing is necessary.

The fifth generation uses the same imaging arrangement, with the only difference being that the x-ray source is not rotating mechanically. Instead, a large circular metallic anode is situated in place of the radiation source track and the electron beam is electronically swept to reach the anode in the desired instantaneous position of the focus. This naturally requires a huge vacuum envelope, but there are no mechanically moving parts so that the scanning can be very fast. The reconstruction algorithm principle for both the fourth and fifth generations remains practically equivalent to that used in the third generation, with some minor modifications (more interpolation to provide for equiangular sampling of fan projections, a need for more efficient compensation of scatter influence) (Jan, 2006).

Two substantial improvements, concerning three-dimensional data acquisition in the form of sets of parallel slices, can be implemented in CT systems of the third to fifth generations: helical and multi-slice scanning.

- **Helical Scanning:** Here the object is axially moved during the scanning procedure while the measuring fan is rotating. This can easily be arranged for by automatically moving the patient support with respect to the gantry of the scanner.
- **Multi-Slice Systems:** These provide more than one slice during a single rotation, usually four slices. It is enabled by using a two-dimensional field of detectors: instead of a single row, several parallel rows of detectors are used, separated in the z-direction by about 0.5 to 2 mm.

Magnetic Resonance Imaging (MRI) Tomography

Magnetic resonance imaging (MRI) is based on a rather complex physical phenomenon of nuclear magnetic resonance (Bloch 1946); (Purcell et al., 1946), which is basically the exchange of energy between elementary particles placed in a strong magnetic field and the irradiating electromagnetic field of a particular frequency. It is, precisely taken, governed by laws of quantum mechanics and should be described in corresponding terms. Nevertheless, from the viewpoint of medical image data acquisition, processing, and interpretation, the description at the level of individual atoms or their nuclei is, in most respects, not necessary. We will thus present a macroscopic approximation, introduced originally by Bloch (1946), where large sets of nuclei are the subject of observation or measurement. These sets (sc., or spin iso-chromats i.e. the nuclei in the group are processing at the same frequency) can often be considered to encompass a volume of a voxel—a three-dimensional space element of the discrete image data (3D version of a pixel). In some cases, when some of the parameters influencing the behavior of the group are not homogeneous throughout the voxel volume, a sub-voxel view is necessary; nevertheless, even such a smaller sub-volume still contains a huge number of particles, allowing the acceptance of the macroscopic view when analyzing the external magnetic behavior of the subgroup.

Magnetic resonance imaging (MRI) is done for various reasons. An MRI scan can be done for the:

- **Head:** MRI can look at the brain for tumors, an aneurysm, bleeding in the brain, nerve injury, and other problems, such as damage caused by a stroke. MRI can also find problems of the eyes and optic nerves, and the ears and auditory nerves.
- **Chest:** MRI of the chest can look at the heart, the valves, and coronary blood vessels. It can show if the heart or lungs are damaged. MRI of the chest may also be used to look for breast cancer.
- **Blood Vessels:** Using MRI to look at blood vessels and the flow of blood through them is called magnetic resonance angiography (MRA). It can find problems of the arteries and veins, such as an aneurysm, a blocked blood vessel, or the torn lining of a blood vessel (dissection). Sometimes contrast material is used to see the blood vessels more clearly.
- **Abdomen and Pelvis:** MRI can find problems in the organs and structures in the belly, such as the liver, gallbladder, pancreas, kidneys, and bladder. It is used to find tumors, bleeding, infection, and blockage. In women, it can look at the uterus and ovaries. In men, it looks at the prostate.
- **Bones and Joints:** MRI can check for problems of the bones and joints, such as arthritis, problems with the temporomandibular joint, bone marrow problems, bone tumours, cartilage problems, torn ligaments or tendons, or infection. MRI may also be used to tell if a bone is broken when X-ray results are not clear. MRI is done more commonly than other tests to check for some bone and joint problems.
- **Spine:** MRI can check the discs and nerves of the spine for conditions such as spinal stenosis, disc bulges, and spinal tumors.

MRI is entirely dependent on digital processing of the measured data that have to be converted to the image form by means of algorithms based on the theory underlying this book. While it is impossible here to go into details of many branches of the highly developed MRI field, the purpose of this chapter is to give a consistent and comprehensible explanation of the principles of MRI data acquisition and processing, which are generally considered difficult (and often described in an obscure or vague way) (Jan, 2006).

The main the image-forming procedures involving MRI to interpret the image properties are mainly:

- **Magnetic Resonance Phenomena:** It involves mainly the magnetization of nuclei, stimulated NMR response and Free Induction Decay (FID) followed by relaxation.
- **Response Measurement and Interpretation:** As single FID signal cannot determine parameters of the analyzed tissue other than the proton density due to low contrast in biomedical images so techniques like Saturation Recovery (SR), spin-echo and gradient-echo techniques are used.
- **Basic MRI Arrangement:** The basic MRI arrangement must be assembled providing the necessary magnetic fields and RF excitation, enabling response measurement, and also allows spatial localization of the response components. The contemporary MRI systems use interesting high-technology solutions based on long-term physical and technological research and development.
- **Localization and Reconstruction of Image Data:** As the RF signal measured in MRI is always acquired from a large volume of the imaged object; it is not feasible to focus the signal acquisition to individual pixels or voxels. It is therefore necessary to use mechanisms that would define the total acquisition volume as well as possible, and provide means for detailed localization of the acquired

information inside this volume. Both of these tasks can be accomplished utilizing the frequency-selective properties of the MR phenomena. Therefore the following are used:

- ◦ Gradient Fields
- ◦ Spatially Selective Excitation
- ◦ RF Signal Model and General Background for Localization
- ◦ One-dimensional frequency encoding and two-dimensional reconstruction from projections
- ◦ Two-Dimensional Reconstruction via Frequency and Phase Encoding
- ◦ Three-Dimensional Reconstruction via Frequency and Double Phase Encoding
- ◦ Fast MRI(F-MRI) techniques involving:
  - ▪ Multiple-Slice Imaging
  - ▪ Low Flip-Angle Excitation
  - ▪ Multiple-Echo Acquisition
  - ▪ Echo-Planar Imaging

- **Image Quality and Artifacts:** Image quality is mainly enhanced by dealing with noise properties for improving signal to noise ratio (SNR) by enhancement of the signal strength by adjusting the physical conditions of imaging taking into account the technique and parameters of signal acquisition and noise suppression via averaging of the individual uncorrelated noise components. In general, image parameters, point-spread function and resolving power based image quality analytics are used. Other than these imaging artifacts in MRI can be divided in to the following three groups:
  - ◦ Discretization effects
  - ◦ Effects related to object chemical composition, susceptibility distribution, and time variance
  - ◦ System-related imperfections

Nuclear Imaging (Planar Gamma-Imaging, SPECT, PET)

Nuclear imaging portrays distribution of radio-nuclides inside the patient's body by external measurement of γ-rays emanating from the body; this gave the modality its alternative generic name of γ-imaging or gammagraphy (the latter is usually used only for planar imaging). Radioactive substances of short half-lives in the range of minutes to weeks are administered to patients intravenously, orally, or inhaled. The radiopharmaceuticals then circulate in the organism and concentrate gradually in diagnosed regions, from where they are consequently excreted depending on the activities of the observed regions. The information to be obtained by an external measurement consists of generally time-dependent spatial distribution of the radioactive substance. This way, not only the shape of organs or lesions can be estimated, but also the local activity-dependent time-course of radioactivity density (Sheehan, et. al. 2000).

Of the radioactive decay products, only high-energy photons forming the γ-component of radiation (ranging in energy from about 50 keV to over 500 keV) are capable of penetrating the surrounding tissue and reaching the external detectors; the a and b radiation only contributes to the patient dose and should be avoided as much as possible. Obviously, the γ-photon energy range is about the same as that of diagnostic. X-rays; physically, the photons are not distinguishable. Nevertheless, the measured intensities of γ-rays, given by the low density of radioactive substances, are generally very weak, being limited by the maximum allowable dose to patients. Thus, the only difference in the character of rays, besides the different mechanism of generation, is in the photon flux density, which is several orders lower in nuclear imaging than in x-ray imaging. At these intensities, the rays do not constitute a continuous flux, but rather they consist of discrete photons that must be individually detected; the intensities are expressed by the counts of detected photons that are stochastically generated. This probabilistic character of the measurements causes problems with a high relative variance of counts and, consequently, a low signal-to-noise ratio (SNR). The photons are generated in all directions, of which only a very small part, on the order of 10–3 to 10–4, can be measured in any projection acquisition (see below); this contributes substantially to the very low detected intensities.

It is clear that the photons are subject to the same quantum mechanisms of attenuation and scatter. This contributes to complications of the measurement evaluation too: besides the required local density of the applied radionuclide, the measurement is also influenced by the unknown attenuation and scattering, which influences the photon on its way from the point of generation to the detector. It should be understood that the attenuation means a loss of a certain percentage of photons due to interactions with the matter, but the γ-photon, reaching the detector without interacting on the way, always has the exact energy characteristic for a particular used radionuclide. A lower energy of a detected γ-photon means that it is a product of Compton scattering; this is used to discriminate direct photons from the scattered ones. Naturally, if the radionuclide produces γ-photons of two or more energies, a scattered originally high-energy photon may be confused for a direct one with a lower energy.

Two types of radio-nuclides are used in nuclear imaging. The first type encompasses those for which the radioactive decay directly produces the individual γ-rays (single photons) in the energy range, usually not exceeding 200 keV. The other type is constituted by radio-nuclides producing primarily positrons, which consequently, when colliding with electrons, produce an annihilation couple of two 511-keV photons traveling in almost exactly opposite directions. The first type is used in single-photon emission imaging that may be either the simpler planar imaging (i.e., the two-dimensional projection imaging) or the more sophisticated single-photon emission computed tomography (SPECT) based on reconstruction of spatial data from many planar projections. The positron emission-based imaging utilizes the production of the photon pair to improve substantially the collimation definition of the measured beam. This advanced method is applied namely in positron emission tomography (PET). We shall deal with the three mentioned modalities from the image data generation viewpoint in the following sections. For a more detailed study or for further references, see (Bushberg, et. al., 2002; Cho, et. al. 1993; Krestel, 1990; Budinger, & VanBrocklin, 1995; Croft, & Tsui, 1995; Kak, & Slaney, 2001). The main nuclear imaging techniques are: Simple planar gamma imaging, single-photon emission computed tomography (SPECT) and positron emission tomography (PET).

- **Planar Gamma Imaging:** Ideally, planar γ-imaging is a parallel projection of the radionuclide spatial density in the patient; the image pixel values are ideally the line integrals of the density. Similarly, as in x-ray planar projection, it is then up to the radiologist to use his a-priori anatomical knowledge and three-dimensional imagination to evaluate and classify the image. Unfortunately, in reality, it is not possible to obtain an image corresponding exactly to the plain geometry of Figure 4(a) due to several reasons, which may be subdivided into two groups:
- **Deterministic phenomena:** Firstly, due to the measured counts are given by both the radioactivity distribution ideally integrated and the spatially dependent attenuation. The imperfect collimations contributing to a nonpoint, depth dependent point-spread function (PSF) of the system too, contribute to the same. Finally, interpolation-based localization of a γ-photon interaction on the detector plane providing limited intrinsic resolution as well as widening of the total system PSF.
- **Stochastic phenomena:** Stochastic (Poisson) processes like radioactive decay results to very low detection efficiency and suffer with a high variance, with a strong noise component; thus the im-

age appears mottled. Due to scatter phenomena, some γ-photons of lower energies may arrive from other directions than would correspond to the point of origin. Due to Compton scattering in the crystal localization of a detected photon and amplitude response discrimination may be falsified by accidental coincidence of more simultaneously detected photons, by stochastic distribution of emitted light photons among photomultipliers, and by multiple light-emitting locations per a γ-photon. Higher counts may be distorted due to dead time of the detectors, causing some photon interactions to pass undetected. All the stochastic phenomena are contributing to the error of measurement. While it is possible to predict the mean and variance of the errors, the concrete error components of a pixel value are random, thus contributing to the image noise.

Due to all those distorting phenomena, the interpretation of the obtained images is less straightforward than in planar x-ray imaging. Further on, we shall briefly analyze the above-mentioned influences taking into account the principles of the measuring equipment conventional today—the gamma camera, which can produce a digitized two-dimensional output. It mainly comprise of the gamma detectors and gamma camera. Inherent data processing and imaging properties that are considered are:

- Data Localization and System Resolution
- Total Response Evaluation and Scatter Rejection
- Data Post-processing

- **Single-Photon Emission Tomography:** Gamma imaging is generally based on measuring one-dimensional or two-dimensional projections of three-dimensional radionuclide distribution. In principle, it is possible to measure a high number of such projections sufficient for consequential reconstruction of the source function—the radionuclide distribution—by means of the respective methods. The single-photon emission computed tomography (SPECT), as an individual imaging modality, is based on this idea. Basically, it is possible to provide the measurements by any arrangement of gamma detectors; even a single detector would do if it is moving in a proper way, thus providing projections as sets of line (ray) integrals—see the principle of x-ray tomography. As the cameras have achieved a high degree of sophistication, most contemporary SPECT imaging uses such cameras, either modern single-camera arrangements intended primarily for planar gamma imaging that also allow tomographic positioning, or systems designed primarily for tomographic imaging, with two or more cameras as in Figure 4 (b). Unfortunately, the real situation in SPECT is far from ideal, in contrast with the case of CT. The problems of SPECT imaging are partly given by the deficiencies of the used gamma cameras (collimation, scatter influence, non-uniformity of sensitivity, geometric distortion).

- **Positron Emission Tomography:** Positron emission tomography (PET) is a sophisticated imaging method enabling the provision of relatively precise two-dimensional or three-dimensional data on spatial distribution of a radionuclide inside the object, e.g., a patient's body. It utilizes radioactive decay of a particular type that involves positron emission. An individual phenomenon of such decay consists of several phases important from the imaging aspect. Initially, a nucleus undergoes a decay producing (besides other decay products) a positron with a certain kinetic energy. Though positrons, as antimatter particles, tend to annihilate in the environment of matter particles, this cannot be accomplished before the positron loses the kinetic energy by colliding with the surrounding medium, thus traveling a certain distance from the place of its origin. The distance is random and its mean value, dependent on the type of the radionuclide as well as on the surrounding matter, is called mean positron range (about 1.4 to 4 mm for different radio-nuclides in water or soft tissue; less in bones, but much more in lungs). Because the position of the decaying nucleus should be imaged while the location of the annihilation is obtained instead, this uncertainty causes a blur in the resulting image denoted as positron range blurring. The positron finally meets with an electron, which leads to annihilation, producing two high-energy (511-keV) photons traveling in exactly opposite directions as in Figure 4(c). The movement of the positron and electron before annihilation leads to the result that, in the imaging coordinate system, the angle between both photon trajectories need not be exactly 180°, but may differ randomly in the range of about ±0.5°. This angle is neither measurable nor predictable; thus, the best estimate is the zero mean, i.e., the assumption that the photon trajectories lie on a single line—a ray—crossing the annihilation point. Nevertheless, the related uncertainty contributes to the blur of the image as noncollinearity blurring (Jan, 2006).

Here the imaging arrangements of the PET are very important. Then the post processing of raw data and Imaging properties are to be taken into account taking care of the distorting phenomena like:

- Attenuation Correction
- Random Coincidences
- Scattered Coincidences
- Dead-Time Influence
- Resolution Issues
- Ray Normalization

The most prominent difference between SPECT and PET modalities is in the definition of rays (or better said, of volumes that contribute to ray counts). In SPECT, the ray volume is determined by the

Figure 4. Different Nuclear imaging techniques (a) Planer Gamma Ray Imaging (b) Single-Photon Emission Computed Tomography (SPECT) and (c) Positron Emission Tomography(PET)

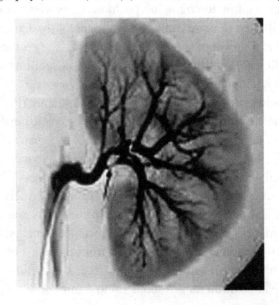

collimator properties and basically has the form of a cone widening with the depth; this unavoidably leads to poor resolution inside the object. On the other hand, PET imaging has the ray of an essentially constant cross-section determined by the size of the small input windows of detectors. This leads to the superior spatial resolution in PET (typically 3 to 5 mm), best in the center of image, while SPECT resolution, generally worse (~10 mm), is deteriorating rapidly with the depth and, consequently, is dependent on the shape and size of the camera orbit; the center of the reconstructed image has the worst resolution. On the other hand, the PET range of usable radio-nuclides is limited to positron-emitting types only, while SPECT can use a wide spectrum of γ-emitters in a broad range of photon energies (with best results for 100 to 200 keV), both single-photon and annihilation couple types. Both modalities are affected by in-object attenuation; the influence is more severe (but easier to exactly compensate for) in PET than in SPECT. The overall imaging properties of PET are favorable (when disregarding the system and data processing complexity, leading to a higher price).

Ultrasonography (USG)

Ultrasonography (USG) utilizes ultrasonic waves as the information carrier; these are mechanical longitudinal waves of high inaudible frequencies in the approximate range of 1 to 10 MHz, propagating in tissues. They are emitted artificially by a probe that acts usually as both the emitter and, in time multiplex, the receiver of the ultrasonic energy. The ultrasonic imaging may be based on detecting reflected and scattered waves that are responses to the emitted wave (like in radar or sonar systems); then it is called echo imaging. Alternatively, it is possible to detect the waves penetrating through the imaged object, in which case it is referred to as transmission imaging. The transmission concept, similar in principle to projection tomography, such as computed tomography (CT) or positron emission tomography (PET), enables good specification of the imaged parameter (e.g., ultrasound attenuation or velocity) extracted from the measured data; also, some kinds of artifacts (nonlinear paths due to refraction, reflection or diffusion, or shadows behind highly attenuating tissues) can be better suppressed this way than in the echo mode. The transmission imaging thus has definite advantages over echo imaging—a better possibility of quantitative imaging and the possibility of applying computational tomographic techniques, at least in principle. However, it is rarely used owing to long imaging times and complicated positioning of probes, with severe practical obstacles in obtaining a reliable acoustic coupling on opposite surfaces of the object.

Echo imaging is practically much simpler to apply, but regarding the physics of the measured signals, it is more complicated. Without going into details, let us state that consequently, most standard echo imaging (traditionally called B-scan imaging) is only qualitative, describing only the shape and position, but not any concrete tissue parameters, of the anatomic structures. The information, so far utilized in commercial systems, is, besides the spatial coordinates, only the intensity of the detected echo. This intensity, however, is dependent on the imaged scene, on the imaging system properties and adjustment, and on the particular circumstances of the measurement in a very complex manner, so that it cannot be considered to describe a particular tissue parameter. The main varieties of USG are:

- Two-Dimensional Echo Imaging
- Flow Imaging
- Three-Dimensional Ultrasonography
- Three-Dimensional and Four-Dimensional Data Post processing and Display

Two-Dimensional Echo Imaging

Ultrasonic imaging in the common sense means echo imaging, which is in principle similar to radar or sonar action. The probe emits a short ultrasonic wave impulse that propagates in the medium (e.g., tissue) through the imaged space approximately only along a ray of a certain direction. When touching an object of properties differing from the medium (i.e., an organ of different acoustic impedance), the wave is reflected, refracted, or scattered, depending on the size of the object and the character of the impedance interface. A part of the wave energy returns back to the probe, where it is detected as an impulse. The delay τ of the received impulse with respect to the emission time determines the radial distance r between the probe and the interface, $\tau=r/2c$, where c = is the (supposedly constant) velocity of the ultrasound in the tissue (about 1540 m/sec). As the direction of the ray is known thanks to a particular construction of the probe, the spatial coordinates of the point of interaction (i.e., of the object surface) are known and may be utilized when reconstructing the image. The velocity c determines, together with the used frequency f, the wavelength of the ultrasonic energy in the imaged tissue, $\lambda=c/f$, which influences the theoretical resolution limit that is of the same order as λ. Nevertheless, the practical resolution is influenced by other factors too, and generally is considerably worse. The basic arrangement for echo measurement is depicted in Figure 5.

A piezoelectric crystal supplied temporarily by electrical energy from the system transmitter acts as the transducer that generates the impulse of ultrasound. The duration of the impulse in imaging applications is rather short—a few cycles of the used frequency, due to high artificial damping of the crystal. The shape of the real impulse envelope is similar to that depicted: a short rise period followed by a slightly longer decay. This single-line investigation is historically called A-mode; although this mode as such has been practically abandoned, it forms a basis for two- and basically also three-dimensional imaging. It mainly depends on:

- **Ultrasonic Transducers:** Ultrasonographic probes have a dual purpose: primarily they emit short impulses of ultrasound, and consequently they convert the incoming echoes into measurable volt-

Figure 5. Basic single-line ultrasonic measurement. The probe and the ideal ultrasonic ray penetrating through tissue interfaces

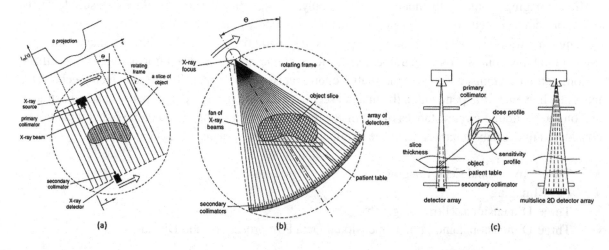

ages. The approximate map of ultrasound intensity in the beam emitted by a simple circular probe of the diameter D is depicted. In the near-field (Fresnel) zone of the length D2/4λ, the beam is approximately of the same diameter as the probe, slightly narrowing near to the outer border (thanks to Fresnel focusing); in the far-field (Frauenhofer) zone, distinct directional lobes are formed.

- **Ultrasound Propagation and Interaction with Tissue:** The ultrasound, when propagating in tissue, is subject to phenomena common to all wave fields: reflection, refraction, diffraction or scatter, and attenuation.
- **Echo Signal Features and Processing:** Ultrasound is differently attenuated in the various imaged tissues, and also the portion returned by targets is very different; the signal, as received by the transducer from differently effective and distant targets, thus has an enormous dynamic range. The time-gain compensation (TGC) plays an important role in this regard.

B-Mode Imaging is the 2 dimensional version of the A-Mode imaging. The different configurations of rays forming the two-dimensional scans: parallel scan, fan scan and curved scan. The line (ray) data, provided in the above-described manner, constitute the elements of which the resulting image is formed. The imaged area—in this section a two-dimensional slice through the object— must be sampled by the rays densely enough to cover the region of interest. This means that the distances between the lines (or, more generally, between the locations of available image data) should not exceed the resolution limits given by the physics of imaging and parameters of the used system. Technically, the sampled image data, as provided by the line acquisitions, are obviously obtained on a rectangular sampling grid and therefore form directly the image matrix in Cartesian coordinates. Such a matrix can be displayed directly (or with only simple separable one-dimensional interpolation and aspect ratio correction) on common rectangular monitors using the standard hardware. On the other hand, the fan scans suffer from diverging rays so that the lateral coverage density decreases with radial depth; however, this may reasonably correspond to the unavoidable lateral resolution decrease along a ray due to beam widening with depth, thus not impairing the effective resolution. The main advantage of the fan scan is the small interface area needed as the window to the imaged slice, necessary when the approach to the imaged internal organs is restricted by structures impenetrable by ultrasound (like bones or air in lungs). Nevertheless, modern imaging probes (Figure 6) provide for automatic acquisition of complete scans; they can be classified into linear arrays (sequential, parallel), curvilinear arrays, and fan-scan probes; each has its better and worse features, as partly discussed above.

Most signal and image data processing involved in two-dimensional ultrasonography belongs to one-dimensional ray examination. The format conversion is elementary in the case of linear (parallel) arrays. The data matrix of a rectangular slice area is provided column by column, and the only modification that might be needed is a change in pixel size of the displayed image from the acquired one. Then, obviously only two independent one-dimensional backward interpolations may be needed to obtain the values on a different rectangular grid, possibly with a different aspect ratio, as needed for the realistic display on common monitors or printers. With the inclusion of small necessary delays (in the range of several times that of a column's acquisition time) in order to consider future values in the interpolation, this may easily be implemented in real time. The situation is more complex in the case of curvilinear arrays (providing a part of a fan scan) or true fan-slice scanners.

The standard USG images of cross-sectional slices of the object can be characterized as qualitative in the sense that the imaged parameter represented by the shade of gray (brightness) in the image are not well defined. As already mentioned the echo signal to which the brightness corresponds is given by

Figure 6. Main forms of two-dimensional ultrasonic scan probes: (a) plain linear array and its transducer, (b) focused linear array and its curvilinear transducer, (c) fan probe with wobbling crystal and its mechanical sectored transducer, and (d) phased array and its phased array sector transducer

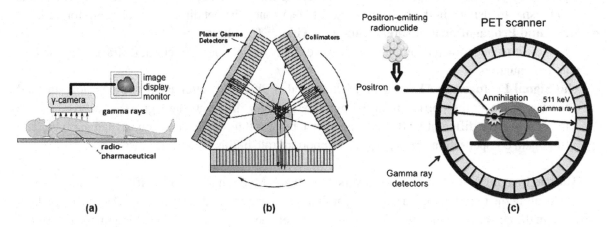

(a)   (b)   (c)

complex and combined phenomena that cannot be easily decomposed into clearly defined influences of particular tissue parameters. Thus, only the spatial description of the object structures (tissue areas, organs, lesions) is offered; nevertheless, it may give a clear picture of the concrete anatomy to an experienced ultrasonographer.

Contrast imaging utilizes contrast agents, administered to patients usually intravenously, that enable better tracing of blood flow and delineation of blood-filled volumes, like large arteries or heart cavities. Also, the blood labeled by a contrast agent may fill an organ (e.g., a muscle like myocardium); thus, perfusion of the organ and its time development may be assessed from the developing echo-geneity of the corresponding area in the USG image sequence.

It has been found that the harmonic signals are partly generated in tissues even without contrast agents, thanks to a certain degree of nonlinearity in tissue properties. Thus, the harmonic imaging becomes a recognized alternative even in non-contrast two-dimensional imaging. Generally, it complements the information of the standard imaging; it has slightly lower radial resolution, but visibly increased lateral resolution (the effective beam thickness contracts, as only the central higher-power part of the beam generates the harmonics). The harmonic imaging, both contrast based and non-contrast, suffers much less from the influence of secondary reflections and scatter, as well as from the effects of directional side lobes of the transducer than the fundamental frequency imaging, because the harmonic signals are not generated by the transducer, but in the imaged objects. The harmonics are produced only when the original ultrasound is strong enough, which is the case almost solely, near the main beam axis.

Flow Imaging

There are mainly two different principles of flow imaging. They are:

1.   Doppler blood velocity measurement (the narrowband approach)
2.   Cross-correlation blood velocity measurement (the wideband approach)

The Doppler Effect concerns the change of the observed frequency of a wave field if there is a relative movement between the field and the observer. In ultrasonography, the Doppler Effect is used for measuring the blood velocity. Both mentioned partial phenomena are involved: the moving blood particles are insonified with a frequency modified due to particle movement in the ultrasonic field of the fixed transducer; consequently, due to scattering, every particle acts as a moving source of this modified frequency field, which is then detected by the transducer. A completely different approach to flow estimation is based on the direct radial movement measurement in the space domain. When a target response can be identified on the measured ray in two consequential measurements (A-scans), set apart by a radial velocity is obviously the ratio of position difference per unit time difference. This principle has some advantages over the Doppler method: primarily, it does not suffer with the aliasing problem; also, when used for flow imaging, it is better compatible with wideband transducers designed for B-scanning. On the other hand, it is computationally very intensive, exceeding the requirements of the Doppler approach by more than two decimal orders.

Dedicated blood flow measurement usually provides the velocity profile along an ultrasonic ray, or the sonogram for a chosen spatial element on the ray. It turned out to be very advantageous, besides the mentioned quantitative measurement, to combine the more qualitative two-dimensional flow imaging with standard B-scan imaging that provides auxiliary information on the anatomy of the imaged region. Commonly, the gray-scale anatomic image is combined with the color-coded flow image (usually available only on a part of the imaged area, in order to maintain a reasonable frame rate); this mode is generally called color flow imaging (CFI). Independently of the method of flow imaging, algorithms must be applied that decide on the level of flow data for a particular pixel, so that the pixel is displayed with either anatomic or flow image content. This way, only the pixels with a certain minimum level of detected flow (e.g., velocity or flow-related power) are displayed in color, while the others, depicting anatomic tissues, remain in gray, providing important support in localization and interpretation of the flow image data. Other than that, for the color flow imaging (CFI) the popular methods are:

1. Autocorrelation-based Doppler imaging
2. Movement estimation imaging
3. Contrast-based flow imaging

The detailed spectral estimates described there are based on numerous samples (several tens or hundreds) per a depth level, which are not available in flow imaging should a reasonable frame rate be preserved, since each sample means a new impulse to be transmitted. With respect to this limitation, only several (3 to 16) impulses per image line are transmitted; hence, only the same number of samples per depth level is available, not enough for classical spectral estimates. A different approach, suggested by Namekava et al. (Namekava, et. al., 1982), limits its interest to only three quantities: the mean local power of the Doppler signal, the mean Doppler frequency, corresponding to the mean local radial velocity, and the variance of the velocity that describes the degree of local turbulence. These three local values can be estimated based on the mere few available samples, at the cost of sacrificing other details.

The cross-correlation principle yields the optimum time delay differences corresponding to the spatial shifts of blood clusters during the time between successive pulses. The time delay finally determines the sought radial velocities (including direction). An important advantage of this mode is that it does not suffer from aliasing due to insufficient pulse repetition frequency, which is often difficult to prevent (or to interpret properly) in Doppler CFI of more complicated anatomic structures. The power of the velocity signal is not readily available via correlation, so that the power Doppler imaging should be arranged on the spectral basis (as the name indicates), i.e., using properly filtered signal.

Using contrast agents in the flow imaging is generally profitable, as it increases enormously the Doppler components of the echo signals. This leads to a notable improvement in SNR and, consequently, to suppression of ambiguities in decisions on whether to display the color flow information. Combined with special techniques, such as, e.g., disruption imaging, it may give results not available otherwise.

Flow imaging suffers from several typical phenomena observed in the final images, mainly due to the rather stochastic character of the flow signal. Primarily, it leads to dropouts of colored values in flow-containing areas as well as to some colored pixels in stationary tissues, both randomly changing from frame to frame. Generally, the appearance of the flow image, especially of the velocity (CFI) image, is influenced by the stochastic changes between following frames, thus causing both disagreeable flicker and ambiguities as to decisions on whether the gray-scale B-image or colored flow information should be displayed. This in turn has the consequence of frayed time-variable borders, which are rather unpleasant and disturbing to the observer. Another possibility for suppressing the noise and ambiguities, and consequently the flickering, is to use some kind of temporal (interframe) processing. A partial suppression of the flickering of individual pixels may be expected from temporal uniform or exponential averaging or median filtering.

Three-Dimensional Ultrasonography

Ultrasonography provides basically tomographic data, which can be arranged into three-dimensional data blocks describing the interior of the imaged object, so that the analysis and display methods used for three-dimensional imaging in other modalities may be applied adequately. In principle, data may be collected ray by ray and compiled into a three-dimensional data block taking into account the instantaneous position of the transducer and the image data format determining the ray geometry. However, several problems appear when trying to apply this simple principle:

- Long acquisition times, as given by physical limits of the USG modality
- Precision of transducer probe localization, and consequently proper positioning of measured data in the set
- Anisotropic and inhomogeneous image data as provided by the ultrasonic modality, which nevertheless should be combined in a consistent data block
- Unequally dense space sampling, which is connected with the methods of ray positioning, and hence also with the transducer scan format
- Consequently, the need of rather complicated interpolation with re-sampling
- Low signal-to-noise ratio due to strong three-dimensional speckle texture

Even though the three-dimensional data acquisition based on a single-ray transducer would be in principle possible, the procedure would be obviously too heavy going, and thus impractical. The three dimensional ultrasonic imaging may therefore be reasonably based either on sequentially collected two-dimensional scans with gradually repositioned slices (tomographic planes) or on providing directly the three-dimensional data by means of specially designed three dimensional transducers.

Diverse possibilities of three-dimensional data acquisition based on two dimensional scans (slices) are schematically depicted in Figure 7. If the imaged scene is stationary, the third dimension can be gradually investigated by many types of systematic slice movement: the linear shift perpendicular to the slice planes (panel a), which may be combined (panel c) with an in-plane movement that effectively increases the cross-sectional (slice) area (panel b), or an inclination providing a pyramidal block of slices (panel d), or a rotation along the longitudinal axis of the transducer (panel e). All of these movements can be provided by mechanical supports guaranteeing via electronic control identical distance or angle differences among the slices, thus simplifying the following data processing. Endoscopic probes may offer additional (not depicted) possibilities by means of their shift and rotation. Panel (f) of the figure depicts an example of a random scanning as provided typically by freehand scanning. This is perhaps the most acceptable method for an experienced echo-radiologist, as such a three-dimensional examination does not differ in principle from a standard procedure: the radiologist collects (and evaluates) the best available images by moving the probe (possibly taking care of certain regularity in the movement). During the examination, the image data are stored together with the transducer position data and gradually compiled into the three-dimensional block. Afterwards, i.e., offline, the data are processed to obtain a consistent data block, from which differently oriented slices or reconstructed three-dimensional views may be generated. Providing the precise information on the instantaneous position of the probe (six parameters—three spatial coordinates plus three spatial angles of rotation/swing) is a self-standing problem (Jan, 2006).

Three-Dimensional and Four-Dimensional Data Post Processing and Display

The obtained USG data can be processed in basically two ways. It is possible to analyze each two-dimensional scan independently, thus identifying and localizing particular features or borders; these would in turn be used in three-dimensional space (matrix) to build a spatial structure describing more or less roughly the anatomy. Obviously, the information contained in the spatial relations among the scan data is not utilized then, which not only is a definite loss anyway, but also may lead to inconsistencies in the reconstructed

Figure 7. Schematic arrangements of two-dimensional scans as three-dimensional data sources: (a) regular parallel scans, (b) in-plane scans, (c) combined in-plane and shift, (d) tilt scanning, (e) rotational scanning, and (f) irregular (freehand) scanning

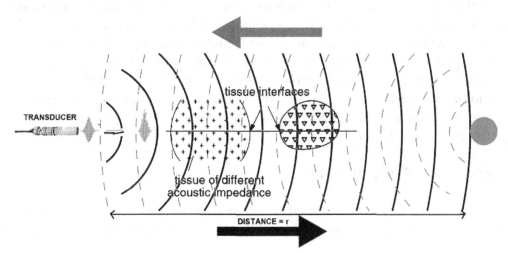

scene. Hence, to compile all the acquired data into a three-dimensional (or four-dimensional, with time development) block of data, and to base any subsequent analysis on this complete spatial information appears to be a better approach. It turns out that this seemingly elementary step of compiling the data structure from numerous *B-scans*, is a rather demanding action, the quality of which is decisive for the success of the final reconstruction. There are several problems involved in this procedure.

The measured scan data are randomly positioned with respect to the nodes of the three-dimensional rectangular sampling grid. A kind of image data interpolation is thus needed, which may be done in a single process with the data homogenization. The interpolation is complicated by the fact that the resulting samples at the grid nodes will be obviously derived from a variable number of randomly positioned input data with a different quality. The quality may be taken into account by weighting the input data correspondingly when interpolating; however, determining the quality is itself a difficult problem related to homogenization.

Finally, in case of moving object imaging (e.g., cardiological applications), a longer series of measurements is needed, filling the four-dimensional space by data covering the complete space volume of FOV and the time extent covering the complete movement (e.g., a heart cycle). As it may be difficult or impossible to cover a particular phase of the movement completely by the spatial data in a single cycle of the movement, several cycles should be measured and the data synchronized with the cycle phase. Above the high acquisition time and difficulty of measurement, inclusion of the fourth coordinate also adds to the complexity of the homogenization and interpolation task.

Once the three-dimensional (or four-dimensional) data block is provided, all the techniques used in the display of tomographic data can in principle be used, although the low ultrasonic image data quality complicates the situation in comparison with such modalities as x-ray CT or MRI. This does not impose many restrictions on the two-dimensional (multi-plane) viewing, consisting of synthesizing arbitrarily positioned tomographic planes where the noise, primarily speckles, is an expected feature. However, in the true three-dimensional volume reconstruction (though projected on two-dimensional display), the speckles may be rather disturbing, as they severely complicate proper segmentation of the imaged spatial objects. As already mentioned, this may be the reason why methods of volume rendering based on spatial ray tracing are more commonly used than the surface-based methods, requiring the preliminary spatial segmentation. Moreover, the ray-tracing methods provide images in which the speckles are partly suppressed by spatial averaging. An example of a typical three-dimensional reconstruction from ultrasonographic data is how the doctor or ultrasonographer can show an expecting mother the face of her baby in the womb via the present day USG in sepia mode. Moreover, this can be used to determine the sex of the child before birth by concentrating on the newly formed sexual organ on the child. An often used and perhaps preferred display mode in three-dimensional USG is a combination of multi-plane viewing with three-dimensional rendering of a polyhedron, the walls of which are formed by the two-dimensional tomographic images. This way, the simplicity of the multi-plane imaging is combined with the visually comprehensible (often revolving) spatial display of the polyhedron, which can be properly oriented in space (Jan, 2006).

Optical and Infrared (IR) Imaging

Optical imaging is not a very frequently used system for diagnosing medical issues. It normally does not fall in the popular variants of medical imaging. This is because the information carrier in this case is light. Both visible and infrared light are unable to penetrate in most tissue structures (except for very thin ones). Thereby extraction of information by the usage of light is a problem.

But still there are some vital areas of medical technology where optical imaging does have some role to play. On thin layers of tissue optical microscopy is used to provide image information. These days even three-dimensional data is obtained via optical microscopy. For translucent or transparent structures to be diagnosed as in the working nature of ophthalmologists, optical imaging does play a significant role. Optical surface related imaging applications are widely used by dermatologists. While for internal structures endoscopic probes mediate optical images for various modern medical applications used in laparoscopy, cystoscopy, gastroscopy, rectoscopy, etc. Finally, tiny differences in the temperature of body surface, detected by infrared imaging may help in providing information indicating internal changes.

Thus the field of light is transformed via prisms, lenses and mirrors or any other form of optical element to form images on the plane of the sensor or on the retina for human beings. Fourier based wave optics for real systems or geometrical optics may be the basis for approximate analysis of such optical systems (Jahne, Haussecker, & Geissler, 1999; Scott, 1998). Proceeding along the path of light, the spectral representation via 2D Fourier Transform or in image form of representation for original spatial domain is analyzed as information of the optical system, from the signal processing aspect.

The imaging quality is described in terms of system PSF (point-spread function) and its (an)isoplanarity, FOV (Field of view) and magnification (or scale), geometric distortions, contrast suppression and image dynamic extent, and signal nonlinearity including camera screen and film based sub systems. FTF (frequency transfer function) describe the iso-planer systems in frequency domain representation of PSF via Fourier transform, or by MTF (modulation transfer function), which is the absolute value of FTF. Therefore, these characteristics cannot be influenced. These are either be identified before correcting the image imperfections or provided by the manufacturer of optical system on the digital domain.

There is always a tendency of digitized storing or archiving of images captured via optical imaging system. Thus the digital camera is presently a standard part of optical system even though the information is still directly observed for diagnosis and evaluated without digitization. The standard method is of converting the optical images provided by the optical system via solid state sensor matrix (CMOS based light sensing matrix or CCD stricture) to digital data by passing the signal through ADCs (analogue-to-digital converters). Thereby based on the size of the sensor structure an image data matrix is obtained from the ADC of the system. The sensing element primarily determines other parameters like SNR (signal to noise ratio), bit depth of the image data, color resolution (in case of color images), etc. These parameters may also be influenced by the preceding optical systems, contrast agents used, illumination, etc. The underlying internal structure of the sensors and physical mechanisms has not been discussed in details but can be found in (Jan, 2006).

As per Petran et al., 1968 (Petrán, et. al. 1968), a tomographic modality determined for macroscopic cells or eye structures i.e. transparent or partially transparent objects is called confocal imaging. Here, a certain kind of sequential scanning is done utilizing the optical projection by a lens system to provide the perpendicular tomographic slices to the optical axis of the imager (Stelzer, 1999). As shown in Figure 8, in confocal imaging, the pinhole allows unrestricted passage of the focused beam. A light source, which may not necessarily be a LASER, illuminates the object point wise via this pin-hole. Its light beam is focused first on the illumination diaphragm on the collimator lens's common focus plane. The beam is reflected by the dichroic mirror in to the objective lens to be focused on the image plane after being collimated by the following lens initially. It then gets scattered, emitted or reflected form the illumination point of the object to the objective lens. The projection system then processes and focuses the remnant light onto image plane's proper point after a negligible partial amount of loss on the dichoric mirror. A light detector constantly measures the available light energy at another detection diaphragm placed with entry point being another pinhole in the path. The intensity of the light at the focus point, originated in the object space is described by the output of the detector. If through the pinhole, only a small part of the available light passes, the detection diaphragm trace is wide. This is if the scattering or light emitting object spot lies above or below the focused object plane. Thus, the smaller light part is, greater is the axial shift. So in the measurement, the light components due to structures are substantially suppressed if not on the image plane.

Estimation of spatial distribution of body surface temperature is mainly detected via Infrared (IR) imaging. Radiation energy produced by the body is used here as a passive medical imaging modality. With the wavelength range $\lambda = 2...10\,\mu m$, a skin surface has emissivity ≈ 0.98 to 0.99 i.e. it optimally radiates and behaves as a black body. Therefore, by localizing the sources of heat in blood vessels, inflammatory or pathologic areas near the body surface, by interpretation in terms of surface temperature the intensity image obtained may be simple. But practically the heat transfer in tissues is complex. Thereby leading to convoluted surface temperature patterns due to a combination of many factors, making the interpretation complicated. Influence of multiple sources, non- Lambertinian character of the body radiator, external temperature and uneven external cooling of the body surface, shorter end of the wavelength range leading to partial skin tissue transparency, etc. are a few popular common factors. Infrared imaging is not widely clinically used as the attempts to obtain more definite images by blind deconvolution and similar approaches were not particularly successful. Cases like early detection of mamma carcinoma as shown in Figure 9 aiming at evaluation of IR imaging capabilities on experimental images is slowly picking up.

Here a precisely air-conditioned environment is needed along with sensitive and stable equipment as the measured differences small and the body temperature is rather low for such type of detection via IR imaging. Either a semiconductor photo-resistive or bolometric type or at least a photovoltaic detector type single detector with prisms or oscillating/rotating mirrors to cover the FOV by shifting the IR image

Figure 8. Schematic concept of a scanning confocal microscope

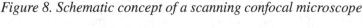

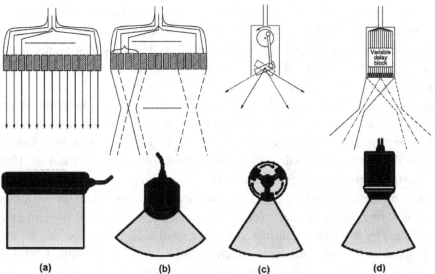

Figure 9. Schematic concept of an infrared imaging for early detection of mamma carcinoma

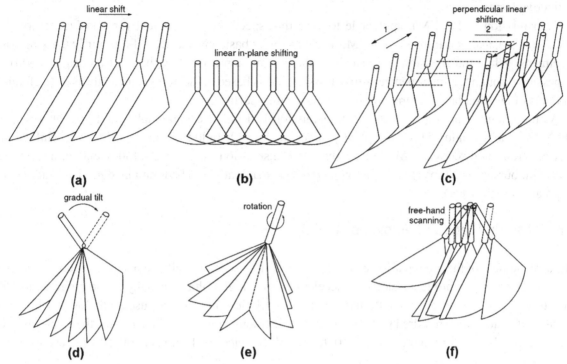

two-dimensionally in front of the detector based on the scanning principle may be the basis of the IR camera. Liquid nitrogen or other coolant based intensive cooling is needed for these types of systems. The capability of absolute IR radiation evaluation based on a known reference radiator using comparative measurement along with ease in calibration are the main advantages of the single-detector cameras. Only one-dimensional scanning is needed if in case an integrated line of semiconductor detectors is used. Spectral sensitivity and temperature resolution along with the spatial resolution are the basic parameters of the imaging system. Before any analysis or interpretation of the measured image data is performed, they are either to be identified experimentally, or should be specified by technical parameters guaranteed by the manufacturer (Dereniak, & Boreman, 1996).

Electron Microscopy (EM)

Electron microscopy (EM) appeared in about 1930 (Glaser and Scherzer, Knoll, and Ruska, see (Hawkes, 1985)) as a logical extension of light microscopy, which reached its physical limits of spatial resolution (fraction of a micrometer) as determined by the wavelength of the visible light. The information carriers in EM, the electrons of practicable energies, have substantially lower effective wavelengths on the order of 10^{-9} m, and the electron-based imaging can thus in principle achieve many orders higher resolution. Practically, the resolution is determined by the quality of the used electron optics, particularly by the objective lens aperture; the practicable resolution may reach the nanometer range (up to about 0.2 nm). It should be mentioned that EM is used also in low-magnification applications where the resolution of otherwise simpler light microscopy would suffice; besides the possibility of imaging different parameters, the incomparably larger depth of focus is often highly appreciated. Electron microscopy has two distinctive forms:

Transmission EM (TEM), applicable to very thin specimens transparent (or translucent) for the electron beam, and non-transmission EM, which analyzes basically surfaces of arbitrarily thick opaque specimens. While transmission EM visualizes the information carried by the electron beam, modified by passing through the specimen, non-transmission EM is based on detection and analysis of (different) products of electron beam interaction with the specimen surface.

As the scanning principle is used in transmission EM rather exceptionally (and then abbreviated STEM), the abbreviation TEM is implicitly understood as full-field transmission imaging, while scanning electron microscopy (SEM) denotes the non-transmission mode. In the following comments, we shall limit ourselves to those two common modes. Further details can be found in, e.g., (Hrivnák, 1986; Stegmann, et. al., 1999).

Transmission Electron Microscopy (TEM)

The arrangement of the transmission electron microscope is schematically depicted in Figure 10 (a) and (b). The electron gun produces electrons accelerated by a high voltage, usually in the range 50 to 150 kV, but with rare exceptions on both margins: high-resolution microscopes use up to 3 MV, while low voltages of up to several hundred volts are also possible (though more in SEM). Hence, the electrons gain the corresponding energy in the range of 10^2 to 10^6 eV. The electron beam generated by the electron gun

Figure 10. Scheme of a transmission electron microscope(TEM) (a) bright-field imaging and (b) dark-field imaging and (c) Principle arrangement of a scanning electron microscope(SEM)

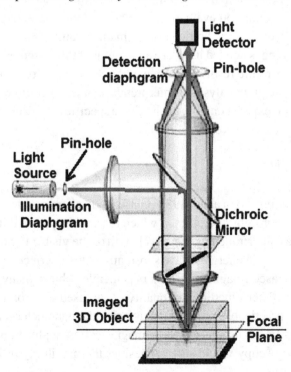

is collimated by the condenser using magnetic lenses, thus ideally providing a constant (possibly—with some arrangements—even coherent) illumination of the specimen.

The incident beam is influenced by passing the specimen, which may be described in terms of particle physics as scattering of individual electrons (see above) so that the output (postspecimen) beam consists of electrons traveling in differing directions with uneven velocity. Whether the scattered electron is utilized in forming the image by the following projection system depends on its individual scatter angle with respect to the projection objective aperture. As the magnetic lenses would have too large aberrations with wider apertures, the typical aperture value is rather low, 0.3 to 1.5° (5×10^{-3} to 25×10^{-3} rad). Thus only electrons scattered less than this will be processed, the other being refused by the diaphragm placed in the objective back-focus plane (see Figure 10a). The image contrast is then explained as being a consequence of locally different degrees of scatter in the specimen, leading to smaller or greater loss of part of the electrons stopped by the limited aperture (scattering contrast).

The described processing is the standard mode, denoted as the bright-field imaging. A complementary mode, called dark-field imaging, is based primarily on electrons with greater scatter angles, while the little scattered electrons are refused; the discrimination is provided for by a wider but centrally opaque diaphragm (Figure 10b). The alternative modality may provide additional information, e.g., by emphasizing the highly scattering areas.

The output image in TEM, historically visualized by a fluorescent screen or registered on photographic emulsion or another medium, can nowadays be directly discretized by a (often cooled) semiconductor light detector field (CCD or MOS type) with the resolution of several megapixels and a rather high dynamic range of about 10^5. The input plane of the sensor is separated from the harmful electron beam image by a scintillation layer converting the electron energy into light photons (and unfortunately, also partly lessening the resolution due to lateral leakage of light in the layer). The embedded (or external) A/D converter provides the data that can be stored in the standard matrix form.

Scanning Electron Microscopy (SEM)

The principle arrangement of a scanning electron microscope is depicted in Figure 10 (c). The electron gun provides the beam of electrons accelerated to the energy of about 10 to 50 keV, which is focused by the condenser lens system, in this case to the plane of the object (specimen). It is an important property of the focused beam that the convergence angle is very small (on the order of 1 mrad = 0.05°), so that the lateral beam width is almost constantly narrow (up to 1 to 3 nm) in a relatively large range of axial depth (~100 times the beam diameter or more). The quality of focusing the electron beam is critical, as it determines the resolution and depth of focus of the microscope.

The beam is deflected by the auxiliary magnetic field of the deflection coils, which provides for two-dimensional scanning of the chosen area on the specimen surface, usually in the non-interlaced rectangular manner (line by line across the FOV, several hundreds of lines, each sampled at up to ~1000 points). The instantaneous response, measured by the detectors positioned above the specimen, thus characterizes a tiny sample area—the just illuminated spot, approximately of the cross-sectional size of the beam. The acquisition of data on the chosen parameter (see below) is thus sequential and must be synchronized with the currents in the deflection coils. The depicted conventional type of SE microscope suffers from a high background of disturbing secondary and backscattered electrons generated outside of the illuminated spot or even outside of the specimen, due to secondary and tertiary effects. This can be prevented in the in-lens type of the SE microscope, where the specimen is situated between the pole pieces of the immersion lens, while the detectors are located above the lens.

As mentioned above, the detected quantity may be the count rate of secondary electrons (*secondary electron imaging (SEI)*), of backscattered electrons (*backscattered electron imaging (BEI)*), or x-ray photons (possibly with energy discrimination, allowing chemical element determination based on spectral analysis of the characteristic radiation—see below); other less frequently used quantities are the Auger electron rate, photoemission, or resulting current through the specimen. The detector of x-ray photons should be capable of wavelength recognition, based either on the less discriminative, but faster *energy dispersive x-ray analysis (EDX)*, i.e., on amplitude classification of detection pulses, or on diffraction of x-rays on a suitable crystal followed by a variably positioned counting detector (more sensitive *wave-dispersive analysis (WDX)*).

Electrical Impedance Tomography (EIT)

Electrical impedance tomography (EIT) is a modality aiming at imaging the spatial distribution of electrical conductivity σ (x, y, z) (S m–1) in tissue. Though it is seemingly a clearly defined physical parameter of tissue, the complex microscopic structure makes its realization less straightforward, see, e.g., (Barber, 2000).

Because of disturbing polarization phenomena, the measurement cannot be done by means of direct current (DC), and therefore, the measured quantities are derived from (frequency-dependent) impedances Z at the measuring frequency f of the used alternating current (AC), rather than from the pure resistances R. However, due to stray capacitances in the measuring arrangement, it is infeasible to measure precisely the imaginary part of Z, and hence only the real part is usually measured via synchronous detection. Even these quantities, though determined by the resistivity $\rho=1/\sigma$, are frequency dependent, as is the conductivity itself due to complicated conductive mechanisms. The known frequency dependence may, on the other hand, be utilized for multiple measurements, enabling partial suppression of the measurement errors.

The conductivity is usually physically defined as a scalar quantity, thus isotropic in the sense that the current of any direction is conducted (or impeded) equally. This may be right on the microscopic level of tissues, not available to EIT measurement, but on the measured macroscopic level, there is important anisotropy (e.g., obvious difference between the conductivities of muscles along and across fibers that are significantly different). Should this be taken into account, the imaged parameter is no more scalar, but rather a vector quantity. So far considered a limitation, it may carry a potential for improving the diagnostic value of the images by a more complex measurement, enabling reconstruction of the vector-valued image with the orientation and degree of directivity presented in false color (color EIT). Nevertheless, in the following outline we shall neglect this phenomenon (see Figure 11).

FUTURE RESEARCH DIRECTIONS

For biomedical Image processing and analysis, the past, present, and future paradigms are as in below Figure 12 (Deserno, 2011). Previously (till around 1985), the focus of research was mainly on the pragmatic issues of image processing, generation, presentation, and archiving in biomedical image processing. This was because computers of that time had issues with handling large image data in memory in

Figure 11. Principle of EIT measuring arrangement

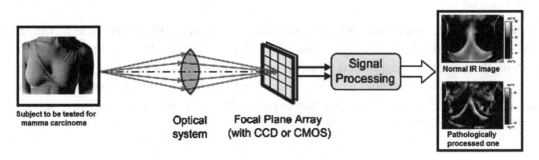

terms of capacity to hold and modify. Thus only offline calculations were allowed for image processing at proper computation speed. Real-time automatic interpretation of biomedical images is till date an area of research with lots of improvements coming up every day. Since validation depends on larger volume of experimental studies with higher volumes of data, continuous improvements and more accurate validations of biomedical images are being done via recent methods of segmentation, classification, and measurements. Future developments in this field would be with integration of algorithms and applications in mobile apps, medical routines and diagnosis on the go as soon as the test is done or the data is fed to the system. Therefore, treatment planning, procedures to support diagnosis and therapy should be usable and accessible to physicians so that clinical use based necessary interoperability is further standardized.

Figure 12. Changing paradigms in medical image processing

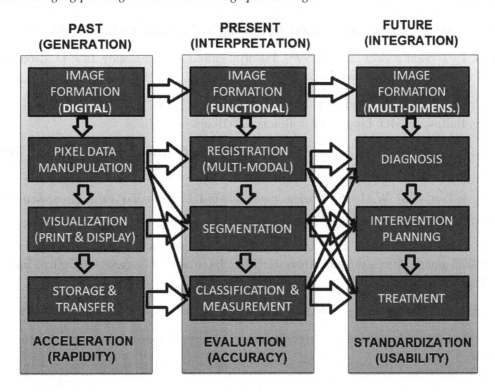

CONCLUSION

Biomedical Images are very important for any type of disease identification and detection. They are very important for diagnosis of internal organs and physical abnormalities. Here an engineering approach for analysis of biomedical images and their different processing methodologies are discussed. Different attributes of the different modalities have been discussed here. Along with these the different problems and aspects of the different modalities and their depiction have been provided. Brief descriptions of the different techniques are also covered with relevant references.

REFERENCES

Anger, H. O. (1958). Scintillation camera. *The Review of Scientific Instruments*, *29*(1), 27–33. doi:10.1063/1.1715998

Barber, D. C. (2000). Electrical impedance tomography. In J. D. Bronzino (Ed.), *Biomedical Engineering Handbook* (2nd ed.; Vol. 1). Boca Raton, FL: CRC Press/IEEE Press.

Bijnens, B. (1997). *Exploiting Radiofrequency Information in Echocardiography*. (Ph.D. dissertation). Catholic University of Leuven, Belgium.

Bloch, F. (1946). Nuclear induction. *Physical Review*, *70*(7-8), 460–474. doi:10.1103/PhysRev.70.460

Boone, J. M. (2000). X-ray production, interaction and detection in diagnostic imaging. In J. Beutel, H. L. Kundel, & R. L. Van Metter (Eds.), *Handbook of Medical Imaging* (Vol. I). Washington, DC: SPIE Press. doi:10.1117/3.832716.ch1

Bronzino, J. D. (1995). *Biomedical Engineering Handbook*. Boca Raton, FL: CRC Press/IEEE Press.

Budinger, T. F., & VanBrocklin, H. F. (1995). Positron emission tomography. In J. D. Bronzino (Ed.), *Biomedical Engineering Handbook*. Boca Raton, FL: CRC Press.

Bushberg, J. T., Seibert, J. A., Leidholdt, E. M., & Boone, J. M. (2002). *The Essential Physics of Medical Imaging*. Baltimore, MD: Lippincott Williams & Wilkins.

Cho, Z. H., Jones, J. P., & Singh, M. (1993). *Foundations of Medical Imaging*. New York: John Wiley & Sons.

Croft, B. Y., & Tsui, B. M. W. (1995). Nuclear medicine. In J. D. Bronzino (Ed.), *Biomedical Engineering Handbook*. Boca Raton, FL: CRC Press.

Dawant, B. M., & Zijdenbos, A. P. (2000). Image segmentation. In Handbook of Medical Imaging, Vol. 2, Medical Image Processing and Analysis. SPIE, International Society for Optical Engineering. doi:10.1117/3.831079.ch2

Dereniak, E. L., & Boreman, G. D. (1996). *Infrared Detectors and Systems*. New York: John Wiley & Sons.

Deserno, T. M. (Ed.). (2011). *Fundamentals of Biomedical Image Processing*. Springer. doi:10.1007/978-3-642-15816-2

Fenster, A., & Downey, D. B. (2000). Three-dimensional ultrasound imaging. In J. Beutel, H. L. Kundel, & R. L. van Metter (Eds.), *Handbook of Medical Imaging* (Vol. I). Washington, DC: SPIE Press.

Hahn. (1950). E. Spin echoes. *Phys. Rev., 20*(4), 580–594.

Hawkes, P. (Ed.). (1985). The beginnings of electron microscopy. Academic Press.

Hounsfield, G. N. (1973). Computerized transverse axial scanning (tomography): Part I. *The British Journal of Radiology, 46,* 1016–1022. doi:10.1259/0007-1285-46-552-1016 PMID:4757352

Hrivnák, I. (1986). *Electron Microscopy of Steels*. Bratislava, Slovakia: Veda.

Jahne, B., Haussecker, H., & Geissler, P. (Eds.). (1999). *Handbook of Computer Vision and Applications* (Vol. 1). New York: Academic Press.

Jan, J. (2006). *Medical Image Processing Reconstruction and Restoration: Concepts and Methods*. Taylor and Francis.

Kak, A. C., & Slaney, M. (2001). *Principles of Computerized Tomographic Imaging*. Paper presented at SIAM Society for Industrial and Applied Mathematics, Philadelphia, PA.

Kilian, P., Jan, J., & Bijnens, B. (2000). Dynamic filtering of ultrasonic responses to compensate for attenuation and frequency shift in tissues.*Proceedings of the 15th EURASIP Conference BIOSIGNAL* (pp. 261–263).

Krestel, E. (Ed.). (1990). *Imaging Systems for Medical Diagnostics*. Berlin, Germany: Siemens Aktiengesellschaft.

Lauterbur, P. (1973). Image formation by induced local interactions: Examples employing nuclear magnetic resonance. *Nature, 242,* 190–191.

Mansfield, P. (1977). Multi-planar image formation using NMR spin echoes. *Journal of Physical Chemistry, 10,* L55–L58.

Namekava, K., Kasai, C., Tsukamoto, M., & Koyano, A. (1982). Real time blood flow imaging system utilizing autocorrelation techniques. In R. A. Lerski & P. Morley (Eds.), *Ultrasound '82* (pp. 203–208). New York: Pergamon.

Petrán, M., Hadravsky, M., Egger, M. D., & Galambos, R. (1968). Tandem scanning reflected-light microscope. *Journal of the Optical Society of America, 58*(5), 661–664. doi:10.1364/JOSA.58.000661

Purcell, E. M., Torrey, H. C., & Pound, R. V. (1946). Resonance absorption by nuclear magnetic resonance in a solid. *Physical Review, 69*(1-2), 37–38. doi:10.1103/PhysRev.69.37

Reiber, J. H. C. (2000). Angiography and intravascular ultrasound. In Handbook of Medical Imaging, Vol. 2, Medical Image Processing and Analysis. SPIE, International Society for Optical Engineering. doi:10.1117/3.831079.ch13

Rowlands, J. A., & Yorkston, J. (2000). Flat panel detectors for digital radiography. In J. Beutel, H. L. Kundel, & R. L. Van Metter (Eds.), *Handbook of Medical Imaging* (Vol. I). Washington, DC: SPIE Press.

Scott, C. (1998). *Introduction to Optics and Optical Imaging*. Washington, DC: IEEE Press.

Sheehan, F., Wilson, D. C., Shavelle, D., & Geiser, E. A. (2000). Echocardiography. In Sonka, M. & Fitzpatrick, J.M. (Eds.), Handbook of Medical Imaging, Vol. 2, Medical Image Processing and Analysis. SPIE, International Society for Optical Engineering.

Stegmann, H., Wepf, R., & Schroder, R. R. (1999). Electron microscopic image acquisition. In B. Jahne, H. Haussecker, & P. Geissler (Eds.), *Handbook of Computer Vision and Applications* (Vol. 1). New York: Academic Press.

Stelzer, E. H. K. (1999). Three-dimensional light microscopy. In B. Jahne, H. Haussecker, & P. Geissler (Eds.), *Handbook of Computer Vision and Applications* (Vol. 1). New York: Academic Press.

Wahl, R. L. (Ed.). (2002). *Principles and Practice of Positron Emission Tomography*. Baltimore, MD: Lippincott Williams & Wilkins.

Woodward, P. (Ed.). (1995). *MRI for Technologists* (2nd ed.). New York: McGraw-Hill.

Xu, C., Pham, D. L., & Prince, J. L. (2002). Image Segmentation Using Deformable Models. In Handbook of Medical Imaging, Vol. 2, Medical Image Processing and Analysis. SPIE, International Society for Optical Engineering.

Yaffe, M. J. (2000). Digital mammography. In J. Beutel, H. L. Kundel, & R. L. Van Metter (Eds.), *Handbook of Medical Imaging* (Vol. I). Washington, DC: SPIE Press.

KEY TERMS AND DEFINITIONS

Angiography: Angiography or arteriography is a medical imaging technique used to visualize the blood vessels with particular interest in the arteries, veins, and the heart chambers. An angiogram uses a radiopaque substance, or dye, to make the blood vessels visible under X-rays. It is used to detect abnormalities or blockages throughout the circulatory system, identify atherosclerosis, diagnose heart disease, evaluate kidney function, detect an aneurysm, arteriovenous malformations in the brain etc.

CFI: Color flow imaging (CFI) is a merging of gray-scale and motion-detection processing to produce an image that depicts soft tissue in gray scale and blood flow in color. CFI comes in three forms: synchronous signal processing, asynchronous signal processing and time domain analysis. All three forms of CFI break the image into multiple sampling segments and process amplitude and motion information.

EIT: It is a non-invasive medical imaging technique in which an image of the conductivity or permittivity of part of the body is inferred from surface electrode measurements. Typically, a number of electrodes are attached to the surface of the body, and electric currents are fed into the body through those electrodes. Applications of EIT include monitoring lung and heart function, detecting breast cancer underground prospecting and industrial process monitoring etc.

IR: Infrared imaging detect radiation in the long-infrared range of the electromagnetic spectrum (roughly 9–14 μm) and produce images of that radiation, called thermograms. It finds usage in both non-medical and medical fields as is sensitive to a broader range of wavelengths. The common uses are as digital infrared thermal imaging, non-contact thermography, contact thermography dynamic angiothermography, peripheral vascular disease screening, thyroid gland abnormalities, night vision" goggles etc.

MRI: Magnetic resonance imaging (MRI) is a test that uses a magnetic field and pulses of radio wave energy to make pictures of organs and structures inside the body. MRI gives more clear information about a problem in the body than can be seen with an X-ray, ultrasound, or computed tomography (CT) scan. It is used to find problems such as tumors, bleeding, injury, blood vessel diseases, or infection.

Nuclear Imaging: A branch of medical imaging that uses low doses of radioactive material to diagnose and treat a variety of diseases, including cancer, heart disease, gastrointestinal, endocrine, neurological disorders and other abnormalities within the body. Because the procedure is able to pinpoint molecular activity within the body, they offer the potential to identify disease in its earliest stages. Two major instruments of nuclear imaging used for cancer imaging are PET and SPECT scanners.

SEM: A scanning electron microscope (SEM) scans a focused electron beam of high energy over a surface which interacts with the sample producing various signals that can be used to obtain information about the surface topology, chemical composition and orientation of materials making up the sample. Areas ranging from approximately 1 cm to 5 microns in width can be imaged in a scanning mode using conventional SEM techniques.

TEM: Transmission electron microscopy (TEM) is a technique in which a beam of electrons is transmitted through an ultra-thin specimen. An image is formed from the interaction of the electrons transmitted through the specimen that is magnified and focused onto an imaging device. It operates on the same basic principles as the light microscope but the resolution is thousand times better as it uses electrons instead of light.

Tomography: Any of several radiologic techniques for making detailed three-dimensional images of a plane section of a solid object, such as the body, while blurring out the images of other planes. Tomography as the computed tomographic (CT) scanner was invented by Sir Godfrey Hounsfield. The method is used in radiology, archaeology, biology, geophysics, oceanography, and other sciences. In most cases it is based on the mathematical procedure called tomographic reconstruction.

Ultrasonography: It can be defined as a radiologic technique in which deep structures of the body are visualized by recording the reflections (echoes) of ultrasonic waves directed into the tissues. The ultrasonic waves are confined to a narrow beam that may be transmitted through or refracted, absorbed, or reflected by the medium toward which they are directed, depending on the nature of the surface they strike.

X-RAY: X-rays are signals with wavelength between 0.03 - 3 nm, having energies in the range 100 eV to 100 keV. It was first discovered by German physicist W. C. Roentgen, in 1895. Due to their penetrating ability X-rays are used for medical imaging via radiographs, Computed tomography Radiotherapy, microscopic analysis, fluorescence, crystallography, security purpose, for restoring paintings via pigment radiographs etc.

Cellular Automata Algorithms for Digital Image Processing

Petre Anghelescu
University of Pitesti, Romania

ABSTRACT

In this paper are presented solutions to develop algorithms for digital image processing focusing particularly on edge detection. Edge detection is one of the most important phases used in computer vision and image processing applications and also in human image understanding. In this chapter, implementation of classical edge detection algorithms it is presented and also implementation of algorithms based on the theory of Cellular Automata (CA). This work is totally related to the idea of understanding the impact of the inherently local information processing of CA on their ability to perform a managed computation at the global level. If a suitable encoding of a digital image is used, in some cases, it is possible to achieve better results in comparison with the solutions obtained by means of conventional approaches. The software application which is able to process images in order to detect edges using both conventional algorithms and CA based ones is written in C# programming language and experimental results are presented for images with different sizes and backgrounds.

INTRODUCTION

Digital images are intensively used in automated applications for object detection or various decisional systems based on information from the visible or invisible spectrum. Image processing is important in data transmission and data storage and has many applications in surveillance, medicine, biometrics, automatic identification data capture and many more. In this context, analysis and image processing techniques have become more and more popular, and among the methods used for image processing are thinning, edge detection, segmentation and texture processing. Based on these operations, can be made different measurements, object recognition and other parameters can be interpreted such as distances, areas, and perimeters and so on.

The goal of edge detection is to process a two-dimensional image and computationally determine where there are edges or boundaries in the image. The edges are a part of an image that contain important visual information since they correspond to geometrical variations of the objects. The human vision system easily picks out edges in an image, but finding an edge computationally is a challenging problem. The front end of many computer vision systems consists of an edge detection module and the high interest in edge detection uses the conjecture that boundaries manifest as intensity changes. Although there exists a lot of edge detection algorithms, a problem is that quantitative evaluation is realized on synthetic images and this is an accepted practice in order to compare different edge detectors by presenting visual results. On the other side, one of the biggest challenges for the nowadays informational and technological society is near a paradox: the desire of construct machines that can decide like a human being. These machines need to be efficient enough so they can be trustworthy. In these conditions and having in mind the above mentioned problems, the research presented in this chapter is based on the using of digital image edge detection techniques that works accordingly with bio-inspired systems (cellular automata) theory. The essence of the theoretical and practical research which are done in the image processing domain is justified by the opinion that cellular automata based edge detection techniques are capable to have similar performances regarding the classical edge detection methods based on gradient and Laplacian.

This chapter is organized in six sections as follows. The *background section* provides all the needed mathematical information on the basic concepts of both digital images & edge detection and cellular automata, including surveys on earlier work about digital image edge detection techniques. This section is organized into four subsections which deal with the following issues: digital images, literature review of classical edge detection techniques, basics of cellular automata and literature review of cellular automata based edge detection techniques. In section three, software implementation of CA edge detection techniques, the CA based model for edge detection are described in detail, including the most important source code for the CA evolution rules. In section four, testing and results, using different original images, the results derived from the classical edge detection techniques and CA based edge detection method is presented. Finally, section five sets some goals for future research directions and section six draws a conclusion of this study.

BACKGROUND

Digital Images

The computer representation, transmission and storage of an image is generally discrete, as opposed to images in the real world which are typically continuous. A digital image consists of discrete values arranged in a two-dimensional matrix.

For a color image, each pixel is typically represented by three values: a red value, a green value and a blue value. Each value is typically represented as an integer with values between 0 and 255 or, for example in OpenGL, as a floating-point values between 0.0 and 1.0. The representation of some sample colors are: red (255, 0, 0), green (0, 255, 0), blue (0, 0, 255), white (255, 255, 255), yellow (255, 255, 0), black (0, 0, 0). Because each value is an integer between 0 and 255, eight bits are necessary to store a value. Thus, 24 bits are required to store the color for each pixel of the digital image and a total of 2^{24} (more than 16 million) different colors can be represented on the computer display. In some cases, in function of the image format, an additionally 8 bits are used in order to store the transparency value (usually known as alpha value) of each pixel of the image. Here, as an example, if alpha value is 0 that means completely transparent and a value of 255 is completely opaque.

On the other hand, in a grayscale image, each pixel has only one value associated to it. This value doesn't carry the information about color, the only difference between the pixels of such and image being the intensity. These images are also known as black and white images, but they shouldn't be confused binary images (that only have two colors black and white) as gray scale images also have many shades of gray in between. The value of each pixel usually occupies 8 bits, but this value, though convenient for programming purposes, having the length of exactly 1 byte, is barely enough to correctly represent the equivalent of a color image. For higher precision up to 16 bits can be used. A color image can be converted into a gray scale equivalent by calculating the new value for each pixel using the equation (1).

$$Y = 0.289 * R + 0.587 * G + 0.114 * B \tag{1}$$

where

Y is the new value for the pixel and R, G and B are the previous three values of the pixel for the corresponding red, green and blue components.

Literature Review of Classical Edge Detection Techniques

Edge detection techniques transform digital images into edge images without encountering any changes in physical qualities of the main image (Destrempes et al., 2006; Yang et al., 2006). The objects from a digital image consists of multiple parts of different color levels and, after conversion to grayscale, the shape of the image can be recognized as step edge, ramp edge, line edge and roof edge.

Edge detection techniques contain usually three steps as shown in Figure 1.

In *step 1*, the initial image is converted into a grayscale image using equation (1).

In *step 2*, are obtained the gradient values for each pixel (Martinkauppi et al., 2001). In order to easy the detection of edges, is very important to determine changes in intensity in the neighborhood of a pixel. To highlight the pixels where there is a significant change in the local intensity values will compute the gradient magnitude. For a pixel, the gradient is composed of two values: the gradient magnitude and the gradient direction.

The gradient magnitude can be calculated in two steps:

1. Applying gradient operators on two or more directions. The number of operators differs depending on the algorithm that is used. For example, *classic operators* as Sobel (Sobel, 1970) and Prewitt (Prewitt, 1970) compute the gradient of two directions: horizontal and vertical. The Sobel operators for each direction are as follows:

Figure 1. Edge detection steps

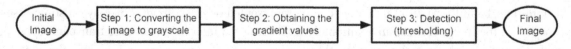

$$O_x = \begin{bmatrix} -1 & 0 & 1 \\ -2 & 0 & 2 \\ -1 & 0 & 1 \end{bmatrix} \qquad O_y = \begin{bmatrix} -1 & -2 & -1 \\ 0 & 0 & 0 \\ 1 & 2 & 1 \end{bmatrix}$$

The Sobel operator coefficients are not fixed. For this reason, there is a possibility of applying more weight to the mask depending on the requirements of the application.

The Prewitt operator uses a logic very similar to the Sobel operator. The principal difference between them being the fact that Prewitt's coefficients are fixed and uses the below masks for edge detection.

$$O_x = \begin{bmatrix} -1 & 0 & 1 \\ -1 & 0 & 1 \\ -1 & 0 & 1 \end{bmatrix} \qquad O_y = \begin{bmatrix} -1 & -1 & -1 \\ 0 & 0 & 0 \\ 1 & 1 & 1 \end{bmatrix}$$

Compass operators compute the gradient in eight directions, starting at 0^0, in increments of 45^0. An example of operator in this category is Kirsch (Kirsch, 1971) that uses the following masks.

$$O_0 = \begin{bmatrix} -3 & -3 & 5 \\ -3 & 0 & 5 \\ -3 & -3 & 5 \end{bmatrix} \quad O_{45} = \begin{bmatrix} -3 & 5 & 5 \\ -3 & 0 & 5 \\ -3 & -3 & -3 \end{bmatrix} \quad O_{90} = \begin{bmatrix} 5 & 5 & 5 \\ -3 & 0 & -3 \\ -3 & -3 & -3 \end{bmatrix}$$

$$O_{135} = \begin{bmatrix} 5 & 5 & -3 \\ 5 & 0 & -3 \\ -3 & -3 & -3 \end{bmatrix} \quad O_{180} = \begin{bmatrix} 5 & -3 & -3 \\ 5 & 0 & -3 \\ 5 & -3 & -3 \end{bmatrix} \quad O_{225} = \begin{bmatrix} -3 & -3 & -3 \\ 5 & 0 & -3 \\ 5 & 5 & -3 \end{bmatrix}$$

$$O_{270} = \begin{bmatrix} -3 & -3 & -3 \\ -3 & 0 & -3 \\ 5 & 5 & 5 \end{bmatrix} \quad O_{315} = \begin{bmatrix} -3 & -3 & -3 \\ -3 & 0 & 5 \\ -3 & 5 & 5 \end{bmatrix}$$

2. Obtaining gradient magnitude of each pixel. This value is calculated using different techniques in function of the operator that is applied.

    For *classic operators*, the gradient magnitude of the pixel will be computed using equation (2).

$$G = \sqrt{Gx^2 + Gy^2} \tag{2}$$

where,

G is the gradient of the pixel,

Gx is the horizontal gradient image and

Gy is the vertical gradient image.

For *compass operators*, the gradient magnitude is computed as the maximum absolute value of the previously obtained results. The equation is presented in (3).

$$G = \max\left\{ |Gk| \right\}, \qquad k = 0...7 \tag{3}$$

where,

G is the gradient of the pixel and

k represents the eight directions starting at 0^0, in increments of 45^0.

The **gradient direction** will be calculated different in function of the classic or compass operators used:

1. In the case of classic operators, the equation is presented in (4).

$$\theta = \tan^{-1} \frac{Gy}{Gx} \tag{4}$$

where,

θ is the direction of the gradient,

Gx is the horizontal gradient image and

Gy is the vertical gradient image.

2. In the case of compass operators, the gradient direction will be a value associated with one of the gradient operators. The equation is presented in (5).

$$\theta = k * \frac{\pi}{4} \tag{5}$$

where,

k could be any of 0, 1, ..., 7 and represents the maximum absolute value of the previously obtained results for compass gradient magnitude.

In edge detection techniques one step is applied for edge thinning that is named non-maximum suppression. In this step, the unwanted extra pixels from the edges of an image are removed, resulting edges that have a thickness of one pixel. This step is applied in Canny edge detection method (Canny, 1986), and the algorithm has two steps that are applied for each pixel in the image: (1) compare the edge strength of the current pixel with the strength of the neighboring pixels in the same direction of the gradient; (2) draw a decision using the following logic: if the current pixel's edge strength is higher, the value is kept, otherwise the value is suppressed.

In *the last step*, the detection is produced using thresholding. Multiple points in an image will have a nonzero value for the gradient, and not all of them are edges for different applications. Frequently, thresholding provides the decisive criterion used for detection (Perez et al., 2002).

The simplest thresholding method uses a single value of intensity and, depending on it, every pixel can belong to one of two categories:

- If the intensity of the pixel is lower than the threshold value then the pixel is set to black.
- If the intensity of the pixel is higher than the threshold value then the pixel is set to white.

The algorithm in itself is simple but the problem that appears in making the process automatic is having a method of calculating the optimal threshold value for the respective image.

There are six types of thresholding methods, as categorized by Sezgin and Sankur in (Sezgin, & Sankur, 2004):

- Histogram shape-based methods, where, certain aspects of the smoothed histogram are analyzed.
- Clustering-based methods, where the pixels are clustered in two parts, either background or foreground.
- Entropy-based methods, that use the expected value of the information contained in each message received.
- Object attribute-based methods, based on the similarities between the newly obtained image and the grayscale one, such as edge coincidences and so on.
- Spatial methods, that use the higher-order probability distribution or the correlation between pixels.
- Local methods, where a threshold value is computed for each pixel, based on the neighboring pixels (the local image).

A particular algorithm used for thresholding is Otsu's method (Otsu, 1979). This algorithm is based on the assumption that the image contains two types of pixels, either background or foreground pixels. After doing so it calculates the optimum threshold for separating the two classes so that their combined spread is minimal.

Another histogram-based thresholding method is the balanced histogram threshold. It starts from the same assumption as Otsu's method, separating the pixels in the two categories. The next step is checking which of the two sides is heavier, removing some weight from it and repeating the process until the edges of the weighting scale meet.

Aside from simple thresholding there is double thresholding that uses two values, a high threshold and a low threshold. Depending on their value relative to the two thresholds pixels can be:

- Strong pixels, when their value is higher than the high threshold, strong pixels will be set to white in the final image.
- Weak pixels, when their value is higher than the low threshold but lower than the high threshold, the color of these pixels can't be determined at this point, edges made out of such pixels will be kept

only if they are connected with a strong edge. The process used for determining the final value of a weak pixel by checking its neighbors is called hysteresis.

• Pixels with a value lower than the low threshold will be suppressed, meaning that their value will be set to 0, as they will be black pixels in the final image.

Basics of Cellular Automata (CA)

CAs, proposed for the first time by von Neumann and Stanislav Ulam (Neumann, 1966) in the '50s, are mathematical idealizations of physical systems in which space and time are discrete, and each cell can assume the value either 0 or 1. CA are models for physical systems where space and time are discrete and interactions are only local. CA models have been applied to fluid dynamics, plasma physics, chemical systems, growth of dendrite crystals, economics, two-directional traffic flow, image processing and pattern recognition, parallel processing, random number generation, and have even been used as a model for the evolution of spiral galaxies (Adamatzky, 1994; Ilachinski, 2001; Wolfram, 2002). In spite of their structural simplicity, CA exhibit complex dynamical behavior and can describe many physical systems and processes.

CA are a particular class of dynamical systems characterized by parallelism, locality of interactions and simple components, that can be used to describe the evolution of a complex systems with simple rules, without using partial differential equations.

A CA consists of a regular uniform n-dimensional lattice (or array). At each site of the lattice (cell), a physical quantity takes values. This physical quantity is the global state of the CA, and the value of this quantity at each cell is the local state of this cell. Each cell is restricted to local neighborhood interactions only, and as a result it is incapable of immediate global communication. The neighborhood of the cell is taken to be the cell itself and some or all of the immediately adjacent cells. Typical examples of neighborhoods are depicted in Figure 2. Von Neumann Neighborhood has 3 cells for one-dimensional CA and respective 5 cells for bi-dimensional CA, consisting of the central cell and its four adjacent horizontal and vertical neighbors. This type of neighborhood has a radius of one. Moore neighborhood has 3 cells for one-dimensional cellular automata respective 9 cells for bi-dimensional cellular automata, consisting of the central cell and its eight neighbors. This type of neighborhood has a radius of one. Extended Moore neighborhood has 3 cells for one-dimensional cellular automata respective twenty-five cells for bi-dimensional cellular automata, consisting of the central cell and its twenty-four neighbors. This type of neighborhood has a radius of two.

A cellular automaton evolves in discrete steps, with the next value of one site determined by its previous value and that of a set of sites called the neighbor sites. The state of each cell is updated simultaneously at discrete time steps, based on the states in its neighborhood at the preceding time step. The algorithm used to compute the next cell state is referred to as the CA local rule.

Typically, a cellular automaton consists of a graph where each node is a finite state automaton (FSA) or cell. This graph is usually in the form of a two-dimensional lattice whose cells evolve according to a global update function that could be applied uniformly over all the cells (Figure 3).

The next-state function describing a rule for a three neighborhood CA cell where assuming that

i is *position of an individual cell in an one dimensional array*,

t is *time step*, and

Figure 2. CA typical neighborhoods (a) – von Neumann Neighborhood, (b) Moore Neighborhood, (c) Extended Moore Neighborhood

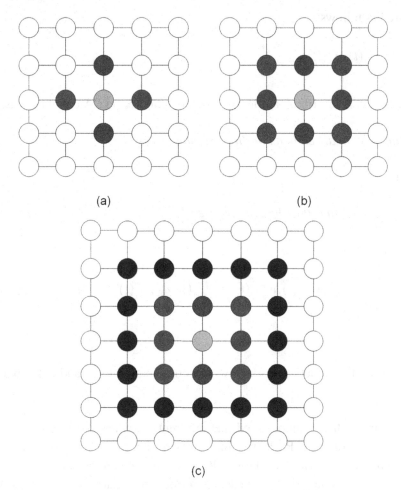

Figure 3. Example of CAs transitions

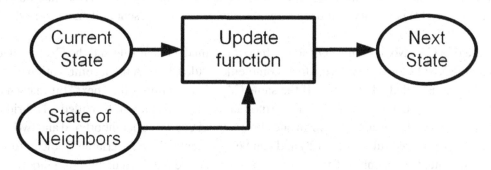

$a_i(t)$: *output state* of the *i-th cell* at *the t-th time step*

can be expressed as follows:

$$a_i(t+1) = f[a_i(t), a_{i+1}(t), a_{i-1}(t)] \tag{6}$$

The next-state function describing a rule for a nine neighborhood CA cell where assuming that

i, j is *position of an individual cell in an bi-dimensional array*,

t is *time step*, and

$a_{i,j}(t)$: *output state* of the *i,j-th cell* at *the t-th time step*

can be expressed as follows:

$$a_{i,j}(t+1) = f[a_{i,j}(t), a_{i,j-1}(t), a_{i,j+1}(t), a_{i-1,j}(t), a_{i-1,j-1}(t), a_{i-1,j+1}(t), a_{i+1,j}(t), a_{i+1,j-1}(t), a_{i+1,j+1}(t)] \tag{7}$$

where

f denotes the local transition function realized with a combination logic and is known as a rule of the CA.

For the CA marginal cells, it can be noted that different boundary conditions can be imposed such as Null, Periodic, Fixed, Adiabatic, Reflexive, Intermediate, etc. In case of Fixed boundary the extreme cells are connected by a pre-assigned fixed logic 0/1 states. If the extreme cells are connected by logic 0 states then it is called Null boundary CA. In case of Periodic boundary the extreme cells are connected to each other and form a cycle. In case of Adiabatic boundary the missing neighbors states (or virtual neighbors) are duplicate of the boundary cell values. In case of Reflexive boundary the value of left and right neighbors are same with respect to the boundary cell. In case of Intermediate boundary the value of the left (right) boundary will be the same as the cell value present at its next to next (previous to previous) cell.

If the rule of a CA involves only XOR logic, then it is called a linear rule and the CA is called linear. Rules involving XNOR logic are referred to as complement rules. If a CA use a combination of XOR and XNOR rules then is called additive CA. If the same CA rule determines the "next" bit in each cell of a CA, the CA will be called a Uniform Cellular Automaton; otherwise it will be called a Hybrid Cellular Automaton. For example, in case of uniform one-dimensional CA, three neighborhood and two-state cell, the number of all possible rules is 256 (2^8) and can be represented by a 3-variable Boolean function. In Table 1 are presented an example of five evolution rules that are obtained using 3-neighborhood. Each rule for this three cell neighborhood must contain 8 bits.

Must be pointed out that the space of evolution rules depends on the number of possible states of the current cell and the number of its neighbors. From Table 2 we see that this leads to an exponential growing of the rules space and the CA become very difficult to be analyzed and interpreted.

Table 1. Example of CA evolution rules (decimal and binary representation)

Rules (decimal number)	7 111	6 110	5 101	4 100	3 011	2 010	1 001	0 000
30	**0**	**0**	**0**	**1**	**1**	**1**	**1**	**0**
51	0	0	1	1	0	0	1	1
60	0	0	1	1	1	1	0	0
90	0	1	0	1	1	0	1	0
102	0	1	1	0	0	1	1	0
	2^7	2^6	2^5	2^4	2^3	2^2	2^1	2^0

Table 2. The size of the rules in function of neighborhood dimension

Size of the cell neighborhood	Decimal rule size (maximum value)	Rule bit size
2	16	4
3	256	8
4	65536	16
5	4294967296	32
6	18446744073709551616	64
7	3,40E+38	128
8	1,16E+77	256
9	1,34E+154	512

In conclusion, we can say that the CAs are completely defined with the help of five parameters: Number of States; Size of Neighborhood; Length of the CA; Evolution Rules Types (uniform or hybrid); Number of evolution times.

Based on the statistical properties of the CAs, S. Wolfram in (Wolfram, 2002) classified 1-D CAs into four categories:

Class 1: CAs that evolve to a homogeneous final global state.
Class 2: CAs in which each state lies in some cycle (periodic behavior).
Class 3: CAs that exhibit chaotic or pseudo-random behavior.
Class 4: CAs having complicated localized and propagating structures. CA of this class are capable of universal computation.

Classes 1 and 2 are more or less self-explanatory. However, the temporally periodic evolution of a spatially disordered configuration ("spatial chaos") falls into class 2. In class 3, "chaotic" is taken to mean "spatio-temporal disorder", in the sense that the number of distinct space-time patches growth exponentially with the linear size of the patch along both the spatial and temporal axes. Class 4 has been the subject of speculation about its possible computational capacity. It has been suggested that CA in this class may be capable of universal computation, that is, of implementing a universal Turing machine. Class 4 was defined by the presence of spatially isolated transients of many shapes evolving for arbitrarily long times.

We can regard these cellular automata as a metaphor of a universe whose physics is reduced to some fundamental simple laws. Regarding the Universe we live in, it seems for the physicists not to have managed until now to discover a set of fundamental simple lows, but it is possible for them to do that taking into account their efforts made in this direction. The inventors of the cellular automata, S. Ulam and John von Neumann, probably intended to show that the most elementary evolution rules could lead to too complex consequences for someone to guess them.

Literature Review of Cellular Automata (CA) Edge Detection Techniques

There are several edge detection techniques, each having its own strength, that can be grouped into three categories: gradient based and Laplacian based edge detection (presented in details in this paper in paragraph named: "Classical edge detection techniques") and CA based edge detection techniques. We note that edge detection techniques based on gradient and Laplacian operators requires a lot of computing time. With an increasing demand for high speed real time edge detection (and image processing in general) the need for simple and parallel algorithm instead of sequential algorithms is become a strong necessity. This need could be accomplished by using some massive parallel systems as cellular automata. Interesting is the fact that the strong relation between CAs and image processing is commented by S. Wolfram in (Wolfram, 1983) when he concluded saying that: "The development of a new methodology is a difficult but important challenge. Perhaps tasks such as image processing, which are directly suitable for cellular automata, should be considered first."

(Fasel, & Khan, 2012) and (Mohammed, & Nayak, 2013) proposed a version of edge detection that is based on a bi-dimensional CA that works based on the linear evolution rules. Thus, from the 2^9 linear rules (that use the XOR function), the authors identified 4 rules that can be used to edge detection and with performances similar to the computational detectors. Other similar versions to those presented above are described in (Dhillon, 2012) and (Nayak, et al., 2013) but, in this case, a rule of evolution that takes into account 25 neighboring pixels is used. In (Popovici, & Popovici, 2014) it is presented a CA based edge detection technique that takes into consideration the removal of noise and is based on a bi-dimensional CA. The transition rule of the CA is dynamic and takes into account the state of the neighbors of a given cell and a threshold that changes based on the application. (Wongthanavasu, 2011) presents a bi-dimensional uniform CA with an evolution rule that takes into consideration a von Neumann neighborhood. The model is used for edge detection in medical images, but the results reported are inferior to those obtained by classical computational methods. (Gharehchopogh, & Ebrahimi, 2012) proposes an edge detection method that works according with the cellular learning automata theory. In this case, each pixel of the digital image is mapped into the cellular automata cells and each learning automata has two possible states: edges or non-edges. The results reported by the authors, for different images, are superior as the time spent in comparison with Sobel edge detector.

Taking into account the great potential of using CAs in image processing – edge detection, results obtained until now by the CAs based methods suggest that this type of bio-inspired systems could be suitable for this type of information processing.

Figure 4. Bi-dimensional CA rule convention

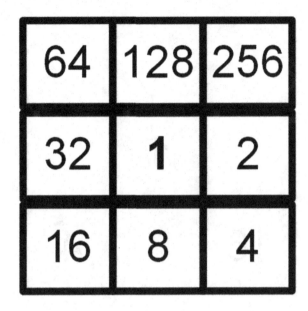

Software Implementation of CA Edge Detection Techniques

In this section is presented the CA based algorithm proposed to detect edges from digital images. The method is based on a bi-dimensional CA with nine neighborhood as depicted in Figure 4.

In 2-D Nine Neighborhood CA the next state of a particular cell is affected by the current state of itself and eight cells in its nearest neighborhood also referred as Moore neighborhood as shown in Figure 2 (b). Such dependencies are accounted by various rules. For the sake of simplicity, we take into consideration only the linear rules, i.e. the rules, which can be realized by XOR operation only. The middle cell marked "1" is the cell under consideration. In 2D CA, the state of the cell under consideration depends upon its own state and the state of its neighboring cells. Now each of the cells can be taken as a variable and thus for 2-D CA there are 9 variables to be considered. The number of linear rules can be realized by XOR operation only. The number of such rules generated by a combination of these 9-variables is 512 which include rules characterizing no dependency. Now, these 512 linear rules have been previously classified by taking into account the number of cells under consideration. The grouping has been Group-N for N=1, 2.... 9, includes the rules that refer to the dependency of current cell on the N neighboring cells amongst top, bottom, left, right, top-left, top-right, bottom-left, bottom-right and itself. Thus group 1 includes 1, 2, 4, 8, 16, 32, 64, 128, and 256. Group 2 includes 3, 5, 6, 9, 10, 12, 17, 18, 20, 24, 33, 34, 36, 40, 48, 65, 66, 68, 72, 80, 96, 129, 130, 132, 136, 144, 160, 192, 257, 258, 260, 264, 272, 288, 320 and 384. Similarly, rules belonging to other groups have been obtained. It can be noted that number of 1's present in the binary sequence of a rule is same as its group number.

The CA used in this paper to construct the edge detection algorithm is based on linear evolution rule number 29 (use only XOR operations) and uses for marginal cells adiabatic condition. Rule 29 is represented in terms of basic rule matrices in equation (8) and in Figure 5.

$$R_{29} = R_1 \oplus R_4 \oplus R_8 \oplus R_{16} \tag{8}$$

Figure 5. Bi-dimensional CA with rule 29

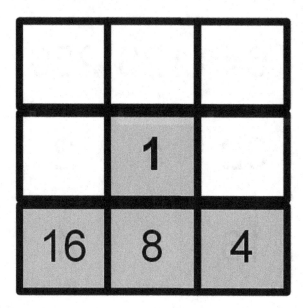

For the marginal CA cells (e.g. first and last rows and columns), it can be noted that different boundary conditions can be imposed such as Null, Periodic, Fixed, Adiabatic, Reflexive, Intermediate, etc.

Among the boundary conditions, adiabatic boundary is used in this paper to realize the edge detection algorithm.

In Equation 9, presents an example that shows the application of the rule 29 to a CA whose initial configuration is an image by size 4x4.

$$\xrightarrow{\text{Initial CA configuration}} \begin{bmatrix} 0 & 0 & 0 & 0 \\ 0 & 1 & 1 & 0 \\ 0 & 1 & 0 & 0 \\ 0 & 0 & 0 & 0 \end{bmatrix} \xrightarrow{\text{Rule 29 with adiabatic boundary condition}} \begin{bmatrix} 1 & 0 & 0 & 1 \\ 1 & 1 & 1 & 0 \\ 0 & 0 & 0 & 0 \\ 0 & 0 & 0 & 0 \end{bmatrix} \tag{9}$$

The CA based algorithm to solve digital image edge detection problem using the 29 CA rule and adiabatic boundary condition is presented in Figure 6.

The most important function of the CA based edge detect application, apply rule 29 with adiabatic boundary condition, that implement the effect of the rule within each cell to cause the cells state to change in the next time step is as follows:

```
public void ApplyRule29(Bitmap bp)
{
Bitmap bp2 = new Bitmap(bp);
int[] pos = new int[6]; //relative positions to the central CA cell
pos[0] = -1;  //x1
pos[1] = 1;   //y1
```

Figure 6. The diagram of the CA edge detection

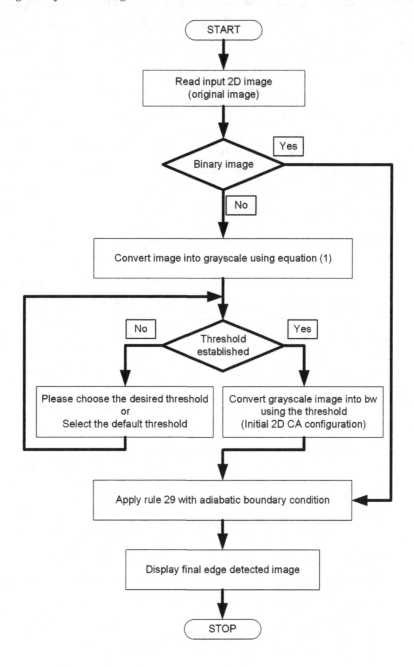

```
        pos[2] = 0;    //x2
        pos[3] = 1;    //y2
        pos[4] = 1;    //x3
        pos[5] = 1;    //y3
int k = 0;
BitmapData data = bp.LockBits(new Rectangle(0, 0, bp.Width, bp.Height), Im-
ageLockMode.ReadWrite, PixelFormat.Format24bppRgb);
```

```
BitmapData data2 = bp2.LockBits(new Rectangle(0, 0, bp2.Width, bp2.Height),
ImageLockMode.ReadWrite, PixelFormat.Format24bppRgb);
      int stride = data.Stride;
      int stride2 = data2.Stride;
      unsafe
{
byte* ptr = (byte*)data.Scan0;
            byte* ptr2 = (byte*)data2.Scan0;
            for (int i = 1; i < bp.Width-1; i++)
                  for (int j = 1; j < bp.Height - 1; j++)
                  {
                        for (k = 0; k < 6; k=k+2)
                        {
                              ptr[(i * 3) + j * stride] = (byte)(ptr[(i * 3) + j
* stride] ^ ptr2[((i + pos[k]) * 3) + (j + pos[k+1]) * stride]);
                              ptr[(i * 3) + j * stride + 1] = (byte)(ptr[(i * 3)
+ j * stride + 1] ^ ptr2[((i + pos[k]) * 3) + (j + pos[k+1])*stride + 1]);
                              ptr[(i * 3) + j * stride + 2] = (byte)(ptr[(i * 3)
+ j * stride + 2] ^ ptr2[((i + pos[k]) * 3) + (j + pos[k+1]) * stride+2]);
                        }
                  }
for (int j = 0; j < bp.Height; j++)
            {
                  ptr[j * stride] = ptr[3 + j * stride];
                  ptr[j * stride] = ptr[3 + j * stride + 1];
                  ptr[j * stride] = ptr[3 + j * stride + 2];
                  ptr[((bp.Width - 1) * 3) + j * stride] = ptr[((bp.Width - 2)
* 3) +j * stride];
                  ptr[((bp.Width - 1) * 3) + j * stride + 1] = ptr[((bp.Width
- 2) * 3) + j * stride + 1];
                  ptr[((bp.Width - 1) * 3) + j * stride + 2] = ptr[((bp.Width
- 2) * 3) + j * stride + 2];
}
for (int i = 0; i < bp.Width; i++)
            {
                  ptr[i * 3] = ptr[i * 3 + stride];
ptr[i * 3 + 1] = ptr[i * 3 + stride + 1];
                  ptr[i * 3 + 2] = ptr[i * 3 + stride + 2];
                  ptr[i * 3 + (bp.Height - 1) * stride] = ptr[i * 3 + (bp.
Height - 2) * stride];
                  ptr[i * 3 + (bp.Height - 1) * stride + 1] = ptr[i * 3 + (bp.
Height - 2) * stride + 1];
                  ptr[i * 3 + (bp.Height - 1) * stride + 2] = ptr[i * 3 + (bp.
Height - 2) * stride + 2];
```

```
}
}//unsafe - necessary in C# to obtain high speed
bp.UnlockBits(data);
     bp2.UnlockBits(data2);
}
```

The algorithm discussed here to detect edges in digital images has two main phases. First, if appropriate, the initial image is converted into binary image using a threshold that is calculated in function of the image or is applied by the user. The binarization is needed in order to convert any non-black and white image to its corresponding binary image using a suitable threshold value. This process is required if the image is not in binary form. If the original/input image is already in binary form, then go directly to the CA detection rules. The obtained binary image represents the initial state of the cellular automaton. Second, add adiabatic boundary conditions to the image and then apply rule 29 to the cellular automaton obtained at first phase (practically to the matrix generated). In the end, after the linear rule was successfully applied to the image an edge detected image is produced and displayed to the user.

TESTING AND RESULTS

The classical and the CA based image edge detection algorithms were fully implemented in software using C# programming language. The main interface of the application is presented in Figure 7.

The results of the classical edge detection algorithms such as Canny, Prewitt, Sobel and Kirsch applied to the picture from Figure 7 are shown in Figure 8 (a), (b), (c) and (d).

The results of the CA based edge detection algorithm applied to the picture from Figure 7 are shown in Figure 9 (a), (b) and (c).

Figure 7. Edge detection application – main interface

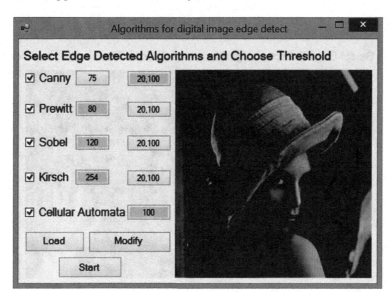

Figure 8. Edge detection of Lena image using classical methods – (a) Canny, (b) Prewitt, (c) Sobel, and (d) Kirsch

Another picture example is shown in Figure 10. In this Figure is presented the main application interface and, in the right side, the picture used for edge detection.

Figure 11 (a), (b), (c) and (d) shows the results of the classical edge detection algorithms such as Canny, Prewitt, Sobel and Kirsch applied to the picture from Figure 10.

Figure 9. Edge detection of Lena image using CA based algorithm – (a) Gray scale image, (b) Black and white image, (c) CA with Rule 29 – final image

Figure 10. Application main interface

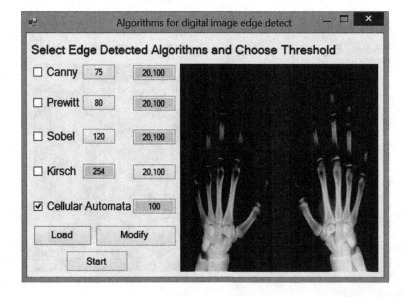

Figure 11. Edge detection of X-ray hands image using classical methods – (a) Canny, (b) Prewitt, (c) Sobel, and (d) Kirsch

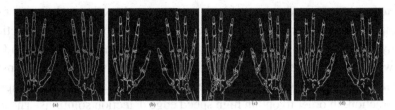

In Figure 12 (a), (b), and (c) are presented the results of the CA based edge detection algorithm applied to the picture from Figure 10.

For comparison purpose, the experimental results of the CA based algorithm are compared with some classical methods namely Canny, Prewitt, Sobel and Kirsch. The source code for the edge detection techniques mentioned above was written in C# programming language and we consider the same input images for all algorithms. From the visualization of the above figures (and other experiments that were carried out throughout the development of the edge detection application), demonstrates that it is possible to use cellular automata to carry out the tasks such as finding, recording and then displaying the edges in a digital image.

FUTURE RESEARCH DIRECTIONS

In the near future, in order to assure the best results for CA based edge detection, will be developed a module to control dynamically the threshold in function of the digital image used. The threshold can vary depending on many factors such as illumination image, so using a variable threshold depending on the image is recommended. Also, in order to obtain high speed, the CA based solution will be implemented in hardware, in FPGA (Field Programmable Gate Arrays) devices. In this way will be exploited the massive parallelism of the CA.

Figure 12. Edge detection of X-ray hands image using CA based algorithm – (a) Gray scale image, (b) Black and white image, (c) CA with Rule 29 – final image

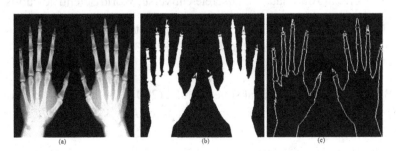

CONCLUSION

In this paper, we make a categorized survey of both image edge detection techniques: classical methods and cellular automata methods. Furthermore, was selected a subset of five edge detection methods (Sobel, Prewitt, Canny, Kirsch and cellular automata) which have been implemented in C# programming language and for which the results are presented and analyzed. In this way, it is demonstrated the ability of cellular automata based algorithms to combine the simple individuals following simple evolution rules and only local interaction, in order to obtain high speed edge detection solutions. The cellular automata based digital image edge detection algorithm performs competitively among known state-of-the-art edge detection techniques and remains simple, very easy parallelizable and general enough to be applied to different computer graphics applications.

According to the results obtained with respect to finding edges in digital images, the method investigated in this paper shows that cellular automata have huge potential in the image processing domain and is expected to be useful for real-time computer vision applications and can be very helpful by using it as a plug-in in available graphics packages.

REFERENCES

Adamatzky, A. (1994). *Identification of Cellular Automata*. London: Taylor & Francis Ltd.

Canny, J. (1986). A computational approach to edge detection. *IEEE Transactions on Pattern Analysis and Machine Intelligence*, 8(, 6), 679–698. doi:10.1109/TPAMI.1986.4767851 PMID:21869365

Destrempes, F., Angers, J. F., & Mignote, M. (2006). Fusion of hidden Markov random field models and its Bayesian estimation. *IEEE Transactions on Image Processing*, 15(10), 2920–2935. doi:10.1109/TIP.2006.877522 PMID:17022259

Dhillon, P. K. (2012). A Novel framework to Image Edge Detection using Cellular Automata. *IJCA*.

Fasel, Q., & Khan, K. A. (2012). Investigations of Cellular Automata Linear Rules for Edge Detection. *International Journal Computer Network and Information Security*, 47-53.

Gharehchopogh, F. S., & Ebrahimi, S. (2012). A Novel Approach for Edge Detection in Images Based on Cellular Learning Automata. *International Journal of Computer Vision and Image Processing*, 2(4), 51–61. doi:10.4018/ijcvip.2012100105

Ilachinski, A. (2001). Cellular Automata – A Discrete Universe. World Scientific Publishing Co. Pte. Ltd.

Kirsch, R. (1971). Computer determination of the constituent structure of biological images. *Computers and Biomedical Research, an International Journal*, 4(3), 315–328. doi:10.1016/0010-4809(71)90034-6 PMID:5562571

Martinkauppi, J. B., Soriano, M. N., & Laaksonen, M. H. (2001). Behavior of skin color under varying illumination seen by different cameras at different color spaces.*Proc. SPIE, Machine Vision Applications in Industrial Inspection IX*. doi:10.1117/12.420902

Mohammed, J., & Nayak, D. R. (2013). *An Efficient Edge Detection Technique by Two Dimensional Rectangular Cellular Automata*. Retrieved from http://arxiv.org/ftp/arxiv/papers/1312/1312.6370.pdf

Nayak, D. R., Sumit, K. S., & Jahangir, M. (2013). A Cellular Automata based Optimal Edge Detection Technique using Twenty-Five Neighborhood Model. *International Journal of Computer Applications, 84*(10).

Otsu, N. (1979). A Threshold Selection Method from Gray-Level Histograms. *IEEE Transactions on Systems, Man, and Cybernetics, 9*(1), 62–66. doi:10.1109/TSMC.1979.4310076

Perez, P., Hue, C., Vermaak, J., & Gangnet, M. (2002). Color-based probabilistic tracking.*Proc. Eur. Conf. Computer Vision.*

Popovici, A., & Popovici, D. (2014). *Cellular Automata in Image Processing*. Retrieved from http://www-ics.acs.i.kyoto-u.ac.jp/mtns2002/papers/17761_4.pdf

Prewitt, J. M. S. (1970). Object enhancement and extraction. In Picture Analysis and Psychopictorics. Academic Press.

Sezgin, M., & Sankur, B. (2004). Survey over image thresholding techniques and quantitative performance evaluation. *Journal of Electronic Imaging, 13*(1), 146–165. doi:10.1117/1.1631315

Sobel, I. (1970). *Camera Models and Perception*. (Ph.D. Thesis). Stanford University, Stanford, CA.

von Neumann, J. (1966). *Theory of Self-Reproducing Automata*. Univ. of Illinois Press.

Wolfram, S. (1983). A Universal Computation Class of Cellular Automata. *Los Alamos Science*.

Wolfram, S. (2002). *A new kind of science*. Champaign, IL: Wolfram Media Inc.

Wongthanavasu, S. (2011). Cellular Automata for Medical Image Processing. *Cellular Automata - Innovative Modelling for Science and Engineering*. InTech. Retrieved from: http://www.intechopen.com/books/cellular-automata-innovative-modelling-for-science-and-engineering/cellular-automata-for-medical-image-processing

Yang, A. Y., Wright, J., Sastry, S., & Ma, Y. (2006). Unsupervised segmentation of natural images via lossy data compression. Berkeley, CA: Elect. Eng. Comput. Sci. Dept. Univ. Available from http://www.eecs.berkeley.edu/Pubs/TechRpts/2006/EECS-2006-195.html

KEY TERMS AND DEFINITIONS

Edge Detection: Computationally determining the position of edges in a digital image.

Hysteresis Thresholding: A technique based on a weak and strong threshold to determine edges. An edge will be started when a pixel's intensity value is larger than the strong threshold and the edge will continue if the pixel's intensity value is larger than the weak threshold.

Non-Maximum Suppression: The process of removing parts of an edge that do not have a higher intensity value than their neighbors.

Radius of a Neighborhood: Maximum distance from the central cell, horizontally or vertically, to cells in the neighborhood.

Chapter 8
Indian River Watershed Image Analysis Using Fuzzy–CA Hybrid Approach

Kalyan Mahata
Government College of Engineering and Leather Technology, India

Subhasish Das
Jadavpur University, India

Rajib Das
Jadavpur University, India

Anasua Sarkar
Jadavpur University, India

ABSTRACT

Image segmentation among overlapping land cover areas in satellite images is a very crucial task. Detection of belongingness is the important problem for classifying mixed pixels. This paper proposes an approach for pixel classification using a hybrid approach of Fuzzy C-Means and Cellular automata methods. This new unsupervised method is able to detect clusters using 2-Dimensional Cellular Automata model based on fuzzy segmentations. This approach detects the overlapping regions in remote sensing images by uncertainties using fuzzy set membership values. As a discrete, dynamical system, cellular automaton explores uniformly interconnected cells with states. In the second phase of our method, we utilize a 2-dimensional cellular automata to prioritize allocations of mixed pixels among overlapping land cover areas. We experiment our method on Indian Ajoy river watershed area. The clustered regions are compared with well-known FCM and K-Means methods and also with the ground truth knowledge. The results show the superiority of our new method.

INTRODUCTION

Cogalton and Green in 1999 defined Remote sensing as "the art and science of obtaining information about an object without being in direct physical contact with the object" (Cogalton, 1999). Canopy of methods exist for classifying pixels into known classes (for example, an urban area or turbid water) in satellite images. Theoretically, a remote sensing image can be defined as a set,

DOI: 10.4018/978-1-5225-0498-6.ch008

$$P = \left\{ p_{ijk} \middle| 1 \leq i \leq r, 1 \leq j \leq s, 1 \leq k \leq n \right\} \tag{1}$$

of $r \times s \times n$ information units for pixels, where $p_{ij} \in \left\{ p_{ij1}, p_{ij2}, ..., p_{ijk} \right\}$ is the set of spectral band values for n bands related with the pixel of coordinate *(i,j)*. In order to find similar regions, this image has been segmented by fuzzy sets, that consider both the spatial image objects and the imprecision attached to them.

Let P (usually $d_F(x, y)$ or $\mathbb{Z}^n$) denotes the space of the remote sensing image. Consequently, the points of P (pixels or voxels) are the spatial variables x, y. Let $d_P(x, y)$ denotes the spatial distance between two pixels $\left\{ x, y \right\} \in P$. In existing works, d_P is taken as the Euclidean distance on P (Maulik, 2012), (Bandyopadhyay, 2005).

In the remote sensing image, a crisp object C is a subset of $P, C \subseteq P$. Henceforth, a fuzzy object is defined as a fuzzy subset F of $P, F \subseteq P$. This fuzzy object F is defined bi-univoquely by its membership function, μ. $\mu_F(x) \in (0, 1]$, which represents the membership degree of the point x to the fuzzy set F. When the value of $\mu_F(x)$ is closer to *1*, the degree of membership of *x* in *F* will be higher. Such a representation allows for a direct mapping of mixed pixels in overlapping land cover regions in remote sensing images. Let F denotes the set of all fuzzy sets defined on P. For any two pixels *x,y*, $d_F(x, y)$ is denoted by their distance in fuzzy perspective. The definition of a new method utilizing the cellular automata over fuzzy segmentation solutions is the scope of this chapter.

Clustering is an unsupervised classification method, based on maximum intra-class similarity and minimum inter-class similarity. State-of-the-art clustering methods for pixel classification in remote sensing images are - self-organizing map (SOM) (Spang, 2003), K-Means clustering (Tavazoie, 2001), (Hoon, 2004), simulated annealing (Lukashin, 1999), graph theoretic approach (Xu, 1999), fuzzy c-means clustering (Dembele, 2003) and scattered object clustering (de Souto, 2008). Different similar approaches like clustering based on symmetry (Maulik, 2009) or supervised multi-objective learning approach (Maulik, 2012), also efficiently detect arbitrary shaped land cover regions in satellite images.

The membership functions of soft computing approaches like rough sets and fuzzy sets, also efficiently detect overlapping partitions. Therefore, recently rough set theory is being used for clustering (Bandyopadhyay, 2008), (Cordasco, 2007), (Gonzalez, 1992), (Dembele, 2003), (Qin, 2003). Hirano and Tsumoto (Cordasco, 2007) proposed an indiscernibility based clustering method to handle relative proximity. Lingras and others (Xu, 1999), (Dembele, 2003), (Qin, 2003) used rough set theory to develop interval representation of clusters without crisp boundaries.

Fuzzy set theory is a methodology to illustrate how to handle uncertainty and imprecise information in the dataset. The fuzzy models have been experimented for land cover detection of remote sensing images and pattern recognitions (Bandyopadhyay, 2005), (Dave, 1989). Applying the concepts of fuzzy membership function (Wang, 1997), (Pappis, 1993), fuzzy clustering (Huang, 2008), fuzzy-rule based systems (Bardossy, 2002), fuzzy entropy (De Luca, 1972) and fuzzy integrals (Kumar, 1997) in algorithms, the remote sensing image identification becomes more feasible.

In the literature, earlier distances proposed comparing fuzzy membership functions do not include spatial information and therefore were not used in remote sensing (Chen, 1995) (Jain, 1995). The belongingness and non-belongingness of one pixel to one cluster can be measured as the approximated existence of the pixel using Entropy theory on fuzzy sets. Luca and Termini (De Luca, 1972) defines a fuzzy entropy pseudo metric as an objective function for convergence in their algorithm. However, their metric fails to satisfy the separability condition (Bloch, 1999). In decision problems, the entropy functions have been combined with membership comparison approach earlier (Coppia, 2005), (Yager, 1992), (Bouchon-Meunier, 1993). (Bhandari, 1992) introduces the method of fuzzy divergence, mimicking Kulback's approach. However, this distance does not satisfy triangular inequality.

A cellular automaton is a discrete, dynamical system composed of very simple, uniformly interconnected cells. A cellular automaton is a well-known method to detect states in cellular spaces. Therefore, to predict pixel classification of remote sensing imagery, we propose a 2-dimensional cellular automata to fuzzy set based initial clustering.

The present study focuses on the integration of fuzzy-set theoretic optimal classification with cellular automata based neighbourhood priority correction for pixel classification in remote sensing imagery. Clusters are associated with indiscernibility classes containing different land cover regions that occur in remote sensing images. The most widely used clustering algorithms for pixel classification analysis includes K-Means clustering clustering (Tavazoie, 2001; Hoon, 2004) and SOM (Spang, 2003).

The performance of the new distance metric in pixel classification of a chosen LANDSAT remote sensing image of the catchment area of one Indian river has been demonstrated. The quantitative evaluation over three existing validity indices indicates the satisfactory performance of our new hybrid Fuzzy set based and Cellular Automata (CA) corrected algorithm (FCA) to detect imprecise clusters. Therefore, the obtained solutions have been compared with those of K-Means and FCM algorithms to verify with the ground truth knowledge. The statistical tests also demonstrate the significance of our new FCA algorithm over K-Means and FCM algorithms.

Fuzzy C-Means Algorithm

Clustering is an unsupervised pattern classification method based on maximum intra-class similarity and minimum inter-class similarity. In a well-known partitional clustering approach, named fuzzy clustering, points may belong to more than one cluster. Therefore, for each point in a cluster, one set of membership levels is associated. This set of levels indicates the amount of association between the point and each of the clusters. One of the most widely used fuzzy clustering algorithms is the Fuzzy C Means algorithm. Fuzzy set theory was introduced in 1965 by Zadeh (Zadeh, 1965) as an approach to model the vagueness and ambiguity in complex systems. Fuzzy set theory handles the concept of partial membership to a set, with real valued membership degrees ranging from 0 to 1.

Introduced by Ruspini (Ruspini, 1970) and improved by Dune and Bezdek (Dunn, 1974) (Bezdek, 1981)], the Fuzzy C-means (FCM) algorithm partitions a finite dataset $X = \{x_1, x_2, ..., x_N\}$ into a collection of K fuzzy clusters, satisfying criterions (Reddi, 1984). Let m be the exponential weight of membership degree, $m \in (1, \infty]$. The objective function $W_{m\mu}$ of FCM is defined as:

$$W_m(U, C) = \sum_{i=1}^{N} \sum_{j=1}^{K} (\mu_{ij})^m (d_{ij})^2 \tag{2}$$

where μ_{ij} is the membership degree of point x$_i$ to centroid c$_j$ and d$_{ij}$ is the distance between x_i and c_j. Let $U_j = \left(\mu_{1j}, \mu_{2j}, ..., \mu_{Kj}\right)^T$. Then $U = \left(U_1, U_2, ..., U_N\right)$ is the membership degree matrix and $C = \left\{c_1, c_2, ..., c_K\right\}$ is the set of cluster centroids. W_m indicates the compactness and uniformity degree of clusters. Generally, a smaller W_m reflects a more compact cluster set.

The algorithm of FCM is an iteration process mathematically described as follows:

1. Initialize *m, M* and initial cluster centroid set $C^{(0)}$. Set the iteration terminating threshold ε to a small positive value and iteration time *q* to zero. Calculate $U^{(0)}$ according to $C^{(0)}$ with the following equation:

$$\mu_{ij} = \frac{1}{\sum_{k=1}^{K} \left(\frac{d_{ij}}{d_{ik}}\right)^{\frac{2}{(m-1)}}}$$

(3)

where $\sum_{j \in C_k, k=1,...,K} \mu_{ij} = 1$. If $d_{ij} = 0$, then and sets $\mu_{ij} = 1$ $\mu_{ik, k \neq j} = 0$ for membership of this pixel to other clusters.

2. Update $c^{(q+1)}$ according to $U^{(q)}$ with the following equation:

$$c_j = \frac{\sum_{i=1}^{N} \left(\mu_{ij}\right)^m x_i}{\sum_{i=1}^{N} \left(\mu_{ij}\right)^m}$$

(4)

3. Calculate $P = \left\{p_{ijk} \big| 1 \leq i \leq r, 1 \leq j \leq s, 1 \leq k \leq n\right\}$ according to $c^{(q+1)}$.

4. Compare $U^{(q+1)}$ with $U^{(q)}$. If $\left\|U^{(q+1)} - U^{(q)}\right\| \leq \varepsilon$, stop iteration. Otherwise, go to step (2).

Cellular Automata Method

Cellular Automata (CA) are defined to be the discrete spatially-extended dynamically defined systems to study models of physical systems (Smith, 1971). It evolves the computational devices in discrete space and time. A CA, which is seeded with any state from the set of states with all 0 and single 1 at different position, generates a fixed number of unique patterns.

Stephen Wolfram (Wolfram, 1986) proposed the simplest CA in a form of a spatial lattice of cells. Each cell stores a discrete variable at time *t* that refers to the present state of the cell. The next state of the cell at *(t+1)* is affected by its state and the states of its neighbors at time *t*. In the current work, 3-neighborhood (self, left and right neighbors) CA is considered, where a CA cell is having two states, either 0 or 1. The next state of each cell of such a CA is

$$S_i^{t+1} = f\left(S_{i-1}^t, S_i^t, S_{i+1}^t\right) \tag{5}$$

where f is the next state function. S_{i-1}^t, S_i^t and S_{i+1}^t are the present states of the left neighbor, self and right neighbor of the i th CA cell at a time t. The f can be expressed as a look-up table as shown in Table 1. The decimal equivalent of the 8 outputs in Table 1, is called 'Rule' R_i (Wolfram, 1983). In a two-state 3-neighborhood CA, there can be a total of 28 (256) rules.

One such rule is 30 in Table 1. Rule 30 CA can generate a sequence of random patterns. Scientists observed in their experiments that an n-cell rule 30 CA, seeded with a state all 0 and single 1, generates a state with fair distribution of 0 and 1 after n iterations. However, it is not guaranteed that after n iterations no all 0 pattern will come. It can be proved that for every, $n > 1$, an n-cell Rule 30 CA seeded with any state with all 0 and single 1 at different positions, generates a non-zero states after $n/2$ iterations.

Using Wolfram's classification scheme, Rule 30 is a class III rule (Wolfram, 1986), displaying aperiodic, chaotic behavior. Rule 30 of the elementary cellular automata (CA) was among the first rules, in which Stephen Wolfram noticed the appearance of intrinsic randomness in a deterministic system. When initialized with a single black pixel there is a pattern behavior down both sides of the unfolding CA which gives way to the randomly patterned center, as shown in Figure 1. This rule is of particular interest because it produces complex, seemingly-random patterns from simple, well-defined rules. In fact, Mathematica uses the center column of pixel values as one of its random number generator.

If the leftmost and right most cells are neighbors of each other, the CA is defined to be with periodic boundary; otherwise it is a null boundary CA. Cellular automata can further be divided as deterministic and probabilistic (or, stochastic). Elementary CA as stated above is deterministic in nature. On the other hand, in case of probabilistic CA, the next state of each cell is updated based on not only the present states of its neighbors but also on a predetermined probability.

Table 1. Look-Up Table for Rule 30

Present State	111	110	101	100	011	010	001	000
Rule	(7)	(6)	(5)	(4)	(3)	(2)	(1)	(0)
Next State	0	0	0	1	1	1	1	0

Figure 1. Example of Wolfram Rule 30.

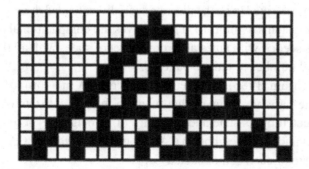

HYBRID FUZZY-CA CLUSTERING ALGORITHM

The new hybrid FCA algorithm consist of two phases – initial FCM clustering of remote sensing image to generate Fuzzy membership matrix U and fine-tuning using the cellular automata based neighborhood priority correction method, as shown in Figure 2. Initial random assignment put N pixels in K clusters for initializing FCM algorithm, as described in previous subsection.

Then the initial cluster centroids $C^{(0)}$ is obtained. The iteration terminating threshold value is set to 1E-05. The membership degree matrix U is initialized from the initial random allocations. Then the centroid updation method is repeated iteratively and compute the membership degree matrix $U^{(q)}$ for

Figure 2. The flowchart of FCA algorithm for remote sensing classification

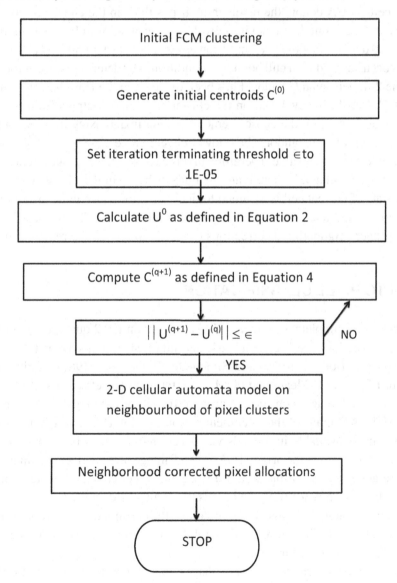

each of the q iterations. The iterations converge and stop, when the difference between the membership degree matrix in previous and current iterations becomes less than the iteration-terminating threshold.

After the first phase of FCM algorithm, new cellular automata based neighborhood priority correction method has been computed over all pixels as described in next subsection. Depending on final CA-corrected solutions, the validity indices values are calculated.

CELLULAR AUTOMATA BASED NEIGHBORHOOD PRIORITY CORRECTION METHOD

In our 2-dimensional CA model for neighborhood based priority correction, the states of the cells have been considered in each CA according to the clustering allocations from the fuzzy set based initial clustering phase. The cells in CA denote the pixels in their positions in the chosen remote sensing image. The state numbers of the cells in the model initially denote the assigned clusters from the first phase of our algorithm. State 0 denotes that the pixel has been assigned to cluster 0 in first phase. In the proposed model, the CA has been adopted with null boundary condition. The deterministic CA for our experiments has been used. The 2-dimensional CA model has been depicted in the flowchart in Figure 2.

The first stage CA has been developed on the cluster allocations outputs from the initial fuzzy set based clustering method FCM on the chosen remote sensing image. Now if among 4 neighbors (left, right, top, bottom), at least two neighbors show lower cluster values, the priority of current cell

decreases to be of lower cluster value. Therefore, in this case, the present state of current cell decreases by 1 towards 0 priority. Similarly, if more than 2 neighbors have similar cluster values other than current cell, the next state of current cell is assigned to that value, to reduce number of outliers depending on neighborhood pixels and reducing number of cluster outliers. The CA matrices have been iterated through to obtain proper neighborhood corrections for pixels in the chosen remote sensing image.

APPLICATION TO PIXEL CLASSIFICATION

The new FCA algorithm is implemented using MATLAB 7.0 on HP 2 quad processor with 2.40 GHz. The solutions are compared with well-known K-Means and FCM methods. Dunn (Dunn, 1973), Davies-Bouldin (DB) (Davies & Bouldin, 1979) and Silhouette (Rousseeuw, 1987) validity indices evaluate the effectiveness of FCA over K-Means and FCM quantitatively. The efficiency of FCA is also verified visually from the clustered images considering ground truth information of land cover areas.

The chosen LANDSAT image of the catchment region of Ajoy River, which has been extracted for further research works, is available in 3 bands viz. green, red and blue bands with original image as shown in Figure 3. Figure 3 shows the original LANDAST image of Ajoy river catchment with histogram equalization. There are 7 classes: turbid water (TW), pond water (PW), concrete (Concr.), vegetarian (Veg), habitation (Hab), open space (OS), and roads (including bridges) (B/R).

The river Ajoy cuts through the image, in the middle of the catchment area. From the upper left corner of the catchment area the river flows through the middle part of the selected area. The river is shown as a thin line in the middle of the catchment area.

The segmented catchment area of Ajoy river images obtained by K-Means and FCM algorithms respectively are shown in Figures 4 and 5 for (K = 7). In Figure 3, K-Means algorithm fails to classify the

Figure 3. Original image of the catchment area of Ajoy river

catchment area from the background. FCM clustering results as shown in Figure 5 also fails to detect the catchment area properly from the background in the middle part. Some waterbodies and the background are mixed in both K-Means and FCM clustering solutions in Figure 4 and 5 respectively. However, our new FCA algorithm in Figure 6 is able to separate all catchment areas from the background. These indicate that FCA algorithm detects the overlapping arbitrary shaped regions significantly with better efficiency than K-Means and FCM algorithms.

QUANTITATIVE ANALYSIS

The clustering results have been evaluated objectively by measuring validity measures Davies-Bouldin (DB) and Dunn index, as defined in (Dunn, 1973) and (Davies & Bouldin, 1979) respectively, for K-

Figure 4. Pixel classification of Ajoy river catchment area obtained by K-Means algorithm (with K=7)

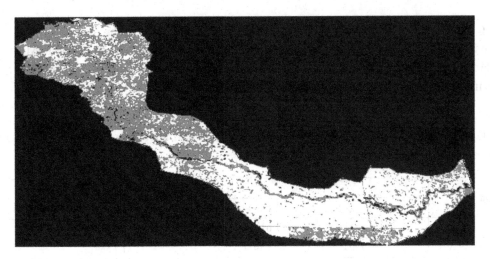

Figure 5. Pixel classification of Ajoy river catchment area obtained FCM algorithm (with K=7)

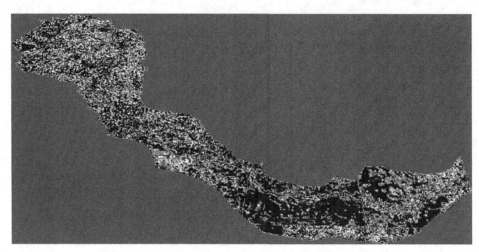

Figure 6. Pixel classification of Ajoy river catchment area obtained by FCA algorithm

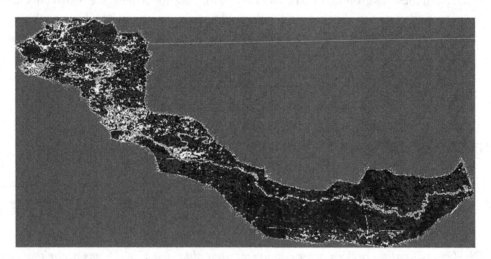

Means, FCM and FCA algorithms on the Ajoy river catchment remote sensing image in Table 2. It can be noticed that, FCA produces best final value for minimized DB index as 0.6438, while K-Means obtains a DB value of 0.7342 and FCM obtains 0.7180. Similarly, the Dunn index produced by FCA algorithm (maximizing Dunn) is 1.5691, but K-Means algorithm provides smaller Dunn value.

Table 2. Validity indices values of the classified remote sensing image provided by K-means, FCM and FCA algorithms

Index	Shanghai Image		
	K-Means	FCM	FCA
Davies-Bouldin index	0.7342	0.7180	0.6438
Dunn index	0.7053	1.1933	1.5691

These results imply that FCA optimizes DB and Dunn indices more than both K-Means and FCM. Hence, it is evident that FCA is comparable in goodness of solutions to K-Means and FCM algorithms and even FCA sometimes outperform to obtain superior fuzzy clustering results.

STATISTICAL ANALYSIS

A non-parametric statistical significance test called Wilcoxon's rank sum for independent samples was conducted at 5% significance level (Hollander & Wolfe, 1999). Two groups have been created from the performance scores DB index values produced by 10 consecutive runs of K-Means, FCM and FCA algorithms on the chosen remote sensing Image. From the medians of each group on the dataset in Table 3, it is observed that FCA provides better median values than K-Means and FCM algorithms.

Table 4 shows the P-values and H-values produced by Wilcoxon's rank sum test for comparison of two groups, FCA-K-Means and FCA-FCM. All the P-values reported in the table are less than 0.005 (5% significance level). For the chosen remote sensing Image on the catchment area of Ajoy, comparative P-value of rank sum test between FCA and K-Means is very small 2.00E-003, indicating the performance metrics produced by FCA to be statistically significant. Similar results are obtained for other group with FCM algorithm also. Hence, all results establish the significant superiority of FCA over K-Means and FCM algorithms.

FUTURE RESEARCH DIRECTIONS

As a scope of future research, the time-efficiency of FCA algorithm may be improved further by mapping it to the distributed environment (Sarkar & Maulik, 2009; Sarkar & Maulik, 2009a). Moreover, incorporation of spatial information in the feature vector in FCA method as earlier shown in (Bandyopadhyay, 2005), in lieu of intensity values at different bands, constitutes an important direction for further research.

Table 3. Median values of performance parameter DB index over 10 consecutive runs on different algorithms

Data	Algorithms		
	K-Means	FCM	FCA
Catchment Area of Ajoy river Image	0.7921	0.6008	0.6850

Table 4. P-values produced by rank sum while comparing FCA with k-means and FCA with fcm respectively

Algorithm	Comparison with FCA	
	H	P-value
K-Means	1	2.00E-003
FCM	1	3.9 E-003

CONCLUSION

In the realm of the remotely sensed imagery, the mixed pixel problems are common. This problem denotes the presence of multiple and partial class memberships for them. Therefore, the conventional crisp methodology fails to map land covers properly to different regions similar to the ground truth information. The soft computing theory may overcome this problem. Therefore, fuzzy sets may be applied to map overlapping regions in the image.

The contribution of this article lies in better detection of overlapping land cover regions in the remote sensing image than other crisp partitioning methodology by utilizing new fuzzy set based pixel segmentation in our FCA clustering algorithm. The primary contributions are – to utilize one new fuzzy set based initial clustering in remote sensing images with CA based neighborhood correction. The neighborhood correction phase helps to correct the wrong allocation of a single pixel to a cluster. It verifies the overall allocations with respect to the neighborhood, to obtain improved land cover regions.

The efficiency of the new FCA algorithm is demonstrated over one chosen remote sensing image of the catchment region of Ajoy River. Superiority of new FCA clustering algorithm over the widely used K-Means and FCM algorithms is established quantitatively over two validity indices. The verification with ground truth information also shows significant efficiency of new FCA algorithm over other two existing methods. Statistical tests also establish the statistical significance of FCA over K-Means and FCM algorithms.

REFERENCES

Bandyopadhyay, S. (2005). Satellite image classification using genetically guided fuzzy clustering with spatial information. *International Journal of Remote Sensing, 26*(3), 579–593. doi:10.1080/01431160 512331316432

Cordasco, G., Scara, V., & Rosenberg, A. L. (2007). Bounded-collision memory-mapping schemes for data structures with applications to parallel memories. *IEEE Transactions on Parallel and Distributed Systems, 18*(7), 973–982. doi:10.1109/TPDS.2007.1024

Davies, D. L., & Bouldin, D. W. (1979). A Cluster Separation Measure, *IEEE Transactions on Pattern Analysis and Machine Intelligence. PAMI, 1*(2), 224–227. doi:10.1109/TPAMI.1979.4766909

de Hoon, M. J. L., Imoto, S., Nolan, J., & Miyano, S. (2004). Open source clustering software. *Bioinformatics (Oxford, England), 20*(9), 1453–1454. doi:10.1093/bioinformatics/bth078 PMID:14871861

de Souto, M. C. P., Soares, R.G.F., de Araujo, D.S.A., Costa, I.G., Ludermir, T.B., & Schliep, A. (2008) Ranking and Selecting Clustering Algorithms Using a Meta-Learning Approach. In *Proc. of IEEE International Joint Conference on Neural Networks*. IEEE Computer Society. doi:doi:10.1109/ IJCNN.2008.4634333 doi:10.1109/IJCNN.2008.4634333

Dembele, D., & Kastner, P. (2003). Fuzzy c-means method for clustering microarray data. *Bioinformatics (Oxford, England), 19*(8), 973–980. doi:10.1093/bioinformatics/btg119 PMID:12761060

Dunn, J. C. (1973). A Fuzzy Relative of the ISODATA Process and Its Use in Detecting Compact Well-Separated Clusters. *Journal of Cybernetics, 3*(3), 32–57. doi:10.1080/01969727308546046

Eisen, M., Spellman, P., Brown, P., & Botstein, D. (1998). Cluster analysis and display of genome-wide expression patterns. *Proceedings of the National Academy of Sciences of the United States of America*, *95*(25), 14863–14868. doi:10.1073/pnas.95.25.14863 PMID:9843981

Gawrys, M., & Sienkiewicz, J. (1994). Rsl–the rough set library version 2.0. ICS Research Report 27/94. Institute of Computer Science.

Gonzalez, R. C., & Woods, R. E. (1992). *Digital image processing*. Addison-Wesley.

Hollander, M., & Wolfe, D. (1999). *Nonparametric statistical methods* (2nd ed.). Weily.

Lukashin, A., & Futchs, R. (1999). Analysis of temporal gene expression profiles, clustering by simulated annealing and determining optimal number of clusters. *Nature Genetics*, *22*(3), 281–285. doi:10.1038/10343 PMID:10391217

Maulik, U., Mukhopadhyay, A., & Bandyopadhyay, S. (2009). Combining Pareto-Optimal Clusters using Supervised Learning for Identifying Co-expressed Genes. *BMC Bioinformatics*, *10*(1), 27. doi:10.1186/1471-2105-10-27 PMID:19154590

Maulik, U., & Sarkar, A. (2012). Efficient parallel algorithm for pixel classification in remote sensing imagery. *GeoInformatica*, *16*(2), 391–407. doi:10.1007/s10707-011-0136-5

Pawlak, Z. (1982). Rough sets. *International Journal of Computer and Information.*, *11*(5), 341–356. doi:10.1007/BF01001956

Pawlak, Z. (1991). *Rough sets, Theoretical aspects of reasoning about data*. Kluwer Academic Publishers.

Qin, J., Lewis, D., & Noble, W. (2003). Kernel hierarchical gene clustering from microarray gene expression data. *Bioinformatics (Oxford, England)*, *19*(16), 2097–2104. doi:10.1093/bioinformatics/btg288 PMID:14594715

Rousseeuw, P. J. (1987). Silhouettes: A Graphical Aid to the Interpretation and Validation of Cluster Analysis. *Computational & Applied Mathematics*, *20*, 53–65. doi:10.1016/0377-0427(87)90125-7

Sarkar, A., & Maulik, U. (2009) Parallel Point symmetry Based Clustering for Gene Microarray Data, In *Proceedings of Seventh International Conference on Advances in Pattern Recognition-2009 (ICAPR, 2009)*. IEEE Computer Society. doi:doi:10.1109/ICAPR.2009.40 doi:10.1109/ICAPR.2009.40

Sarkar, A., & Maulik, U. (2009). Parallel Clustering Technique Using Modified Symmetry Based Distance. In *Proceedings of 1st International Conference on Computer, Communication, Control and Information Technology (C3IT 2009)*. MacMillan Publishers India Ltd.

Smith, A. R. III. (1971). Two-dimensional Formal Languages and Pattern Recognition by Cellular Automata. In *IEEE Conference Record of 12th Annual Symposium on Switchinh and Automata Theory*. doi:10.1109/SWAT.1971.29

Spang, R. (2003). Diagnostic signatures from microarrays, a bioinformatics concept for personalized medicine. *BIOSILICO*, *1*(2), 64–68. doi:10.1016/S1478-5382(03)02329-1

Tavazoie, S., Hughes, J., Campbell, M., Cho, R., & Church, G. (2001). Systematic determination of genetic network architecture. *Bioinformatics (Oxford, England)*, *17*, 405–414. PMID:11331234

Wolfram, S. (1983). Statistical mechanics of cellular automata. *Reviews of Modern Physics*, *55*(3), 601–644. doi:10.1103/RevModPhys.55.601

Wolfram, S. (1986). Cryptography with cellular automata. *Lecture Notes in Computer Science*, *218*, 429–432. doi:10.1007/3-540-39799-X_32

Xu, Y., Olman, V., & Xu, D. (2002). Clustering gene expression data using a graph theoretic approach, an application of minimum spanning trees. *Bioinformatics (Oxford, England)*, *18*, 536–545. PMID:12016051

ADDITIONAL READING

Al-Shahrour, F., Diaz-Uriarte, R., & Dopazo, J. (2004). FatiGO: A web tool for finding significant associations to gene ontology terms with groups of genes. *Bioinformatics (Oxford, England)*, *20*(4), 578–580. doi:10.1093/bioinformatics/btg455 PMID:14990455

Bandyopadhyay, S., Mukhopadhyay, A., & Maulik, U. (2007) An improved algorithm for clustering gene expression data. Bioionformatics.Oxford University Press. 23(21), 2859–2865.

Bandyopadhyay, S., & Saha, S. (2007). GAPS: A clustering method using a new point symmetry-based distance measure. *Pattern Recognition*, *40*(12), 3430–3451. doi:10.1016/j.patcog.2007.03.026

Bandyopadhyay, S., & Saha, S. (2008). A point symmetry based clustering technique for automatic evolution of clusters. *IEEE Transactions on Knowledge and Data Engineering*, *20*(11), 1–17. doi:10.1109/TKDE.2008.79

Chen, L., & Pan, Y. (2004). Scalable and efficient parallel algorithms for euclidean distance transform on the LARPBS model. *IEEE Transactions on Parallel and Distributed Systems*, *15*(11), 975–982. doi:10.1109/TPDS.2004.71

Chen, Y. L., & Hu, H. L. (2006). An overlapping cluster algorithm to provide non-exhaustive clustering. *European Journal of Operational Research*, *173*(3), 762–780. doi:10.1016/j.ejor.2005.06.056

Cho, R. J., Campbell, M. J., Winzeler, E. A., Steinmetz, L., Conway, A., Wodicka, L., & Davis, R. W. et al. (1998). A genome-wide transcriptional analysis of the mitotic cell cycle. *Molecular Cell*, *2*(1), 65–73. doi:10.1016/S1097-2765(00)80114-8 PMID:9702192

Chu, S. (1998). The transcriptional program of sporulation in budding yeast. *Science*, *282*(5389), 699–705. doi:10.1126/science.282.5389.699 PMID:9784122

DeRisi, J., Iyer, V., & Brown, P. (1997). Exploring the metabolic and genetic control of gene expression on a genome scale. *Science*, *278*, 257–264. PMID:9381177

Dhilon, I., Marcotte, E., & Roshan, U. (2003). Diametrical clustering for identifying anticorrelated gene clusters. *Bioinformatics (Oxford, England)*, *19*(13), 1612–1619. doi:10.1093/bioinformatics/btg209 PMID:12967956

(Gene Ontology, 2000) The Gene Ontology Consortium (2000) Gene ontology: tool for the unification biology. *Nat. Genet. 25,* 25–29.

Hollander, M., & Wolfe, D. (1999). *Nonparametric statistical methods* (2nd ed.). USA: Wiely.

Horn, D., & Axel, L. (2003). Novel clustering algorithm for microarray expression data in a truncated svd space. *Bioinformatics (Oxford, England)*, *19*(9), 1110–1115. doi:10.1093/bioinformatics/btg053 PMID:12801871

Hvidsten, T. R., Laegreid, A., & Komorowski, J. (2003). Learning rule-based models of biological process from gene expression time profiles using gene ontology. *Bioinformatics (Oxford, England)*, *19*(9), 1116–1123. doi:10.1093/bioinformatics/btg047 PMID:12801872

Iyer, V. R. (1999). The transcriptional program in the response of human fibroblasts serum. *Science*, *283*(5398), 83–87. doi:10.1126/science.283.5398.83 PMID:9872747

Jiang, K., Thorsen, O., Peters, A. E., Smith, B. E., & Sosa, C. P. (2008). An efficient parallel implementation of the hidden markov methods for genomic sequence-search on a massively parallel system. *IEEE Transactions on Parallel and Distributed Systems*, *19*(1), 15–23. doi:10.1109/TPDS.2007.70712

Kalyanaraman, A., Aluru, S., Brendel, V., & Kothari, S. (2003). Space and time efficient parallel algorithms and software for EST clustering. *IEEE Transactions on Parallel and Distributed Systems*, *14*(12), 1209–1221. doi:10.1109/TPDS.2003.1255634

Kanungo, T., Mount, D., Netanyahu, N., Piatko, C., Silverman, R., & Wu, A. (2002). An efficient k-means clustering algorithm: Analysis and implementation. *IEEE Transactions on Pattern Analysis and Machine Intelligence*, *24*(7), 881–892. doi:10.1109/TPAMI.2002.1017616

Kim, S. Y. (2006). Effect of data normalization on fuzzy clustering of DNA microarray data. *BMC Bioinformatics*, *7*, 309–318. PMID:16533412

Liu, W., & Schmidt, B. (2006). Parallel pattern-based systems for computational biology: A case study. *IEEE Transactions on Parallel and Distributed Systems*, *17*(8), 750–763. doi:10.1109/TPDS.2006.109

Rajasekaran, S. (2005). Efficient parallel hierarchical clustering algorithms. *IEEE Transactions on Parallel and Distributed Systems*, *16*(6), 497–502. doi:10.1109/TPDS.2005.72

Rajko, S., & Aluru, S. (2004). Space and time optimal parallel sequence alignments. *IEEE Transactions on Parallel and Distributed Systems*, *15*(12), 1070–1081. doi:10.1109/TPDS.2004.86

Sharan, R., Maron-Katz, A., & Shamir, R. (2003). CLICK and EXPANDER: A system for clustering and visualizing gene expression data. *Bioinformatics (Oxford, England)*, *19*(14), 1787–1799. doi:10.1093/bioinformatics/btg232 PMID:14512350

Tou, J. T., & Gonzalez, R. C. (1974). *Pattern recognition principles*. Reading, MA: Addison-Wesley.

Wen, X., Fuhrman, S., Michaels, G. S., Carr, D. B., Smith, S., Barker, J. L., & Somogyi, R. (1998). Large-scale temporal gene expression mapping of central nervous system development. *Proceedings of the National Academy of Sciences of the United States of America*, *95*(1), 334–339. doi:10.1073/pnas.95.1.334 PMID:9419376

KEY TERMS AND DEFINITIONS

Cellular Automata: A discrete, dynamical system composed of very simple, uniformly interconnected cells

Clustering: Assigning similar elements to one group, which increases intra-cluster similarity and decreases inter-cluster similarity.

Fuzzy Set: Set of elements with membership values between 0 and 1 for each of the clusters to which it belongs according to fuzzy set theory by Zadeh.

K-Means Algorithm: Clustering algorithm to classify n elements in k clusters, which iteratively computes the cluster centroids as the means of all elements in one cluster.

Validity Index: Index to estimate compactness of the clusters, leading to properly identified distinguishable clusters.

Chapter 9
A Fuzzy Relational Classifier Based Image Quality Assessment Method

Indrajit De
MCKV Institute of Engineering, India

ABSTRACT

Fuzzy classification techniques are used for image classification for quite a long time back by allowing pixels to have membership in more than one class. However, handling information at the pixel level is time consuming and there is a high chance of biased assessment of images if class labels are assigned by a single human observer. Even considering multiple observers' opinions don't able to reflect an individual's perception in assessing quality of images, if it is crisp. In this chapter, the fuzzy relational classifier (FRC) is used to assess quality of images distorted by information loss or noise, unlike the earlier methods where images are preprocessed to remove the noise before classification.

1. INTRODUCTION

Fuzzy classification techniques (Spearman, 1904) are used for image classification for quite a long time back by allowing pixels to have membership in more than one class. However, handling information at the pixel level is time consuming and there is a high chance of biased assessment of images if class labels are assigned by a single human observer. Even consideration multiple observers' opinions is not able to reflect an individual's perception in assessing quality of images, if it is crisp (Chakraborty et al, 2008, Gilles, 1998, Huang & Wang, 1995). In subjective image quality assessment methods, the human subjects are utilized to evaluate the image for assessing its visual quality. The method is most reliable and provides better understanding of mechanisms underlying the quality perception of human beings. The methodology used depending on the opinions of human observers regarding quality of an image and mapping the opinion as image quality metric. In the procedure, a set of images are displayed to a group of human observers and asked to rate the quality on a particular scale. The mean rating for an image is referred to as the mean opinion score (MOS) and is representative of the perceptual quality of that visual

DOI: 10.4018/978-1-5225-0498-6.ch009

stimulus. Such assessment of quality of image is referred to as subjective quality assessment. Another prominent approach to assess subjective quality of an image is based on stimulus namely, single stimulus (SS) and double stimulus (DS) method (ITU-R BT.500-13,2012). In SS procedure, a set of stimuli is taken one at a time and include a reference image in that set without the knowledge of the observers. Observer evaluates the quality and score is expressed in a numerical category rating. Single judgment is required per assessment and then the average score has been calculated. The quality range will be spanned by the stimuli. However, this method generally induces inconsistency in findings.

In Double Stimulus (DS) method the panel of subjects is watching two images in the same time: one is the reference, the other one is the test. If the format of the images is SIF (standard image format) or smaller, the two images can be displayed side by side on the same monitor, otherwise two aligned monitors should be used. Subjects are requested to check the differences between the two images and to judge the fidelity of the signal information by moving the slider of a handset-voting device. When the fidelity is perfect, the slider should be at the top of the scale range (coded 100), and in case of null fidelity, the slider should be at the bottom of the scale (coded 0).

Subjects are aware of which is the reference and they are requested to express their opinion while viewing the sequences, throughout the total duration. A non stimulus based subjective IQA method is Quality Ruler (QR) composed of a series of reference images whose scale is already known and they are closely spaced in quality, but span a wide range of quality all together. It detects the quality difference between them. The observer find the reference image closest in the quality to the test stimulus by visual matching and quality score is noted. Compared to SS method it is more consistent and QR scores are highly correlated to objective measure of distortions than the SS scores.

Fuzzy based approaches (Fan & Xie, 1999) have long been used to model human perception about the given tasks by transforming human observations into mathematical understanding. In general, the basic difference between perceptions and measurements is that, measurements are crisp whereas perceptions are fuzzy. One of the fundamental aims of science is to progress from perceptions to measurements. Pursuit of this aim has led to brilliant successes. So it may be inferred that fuzziness of perceptions reflects finite ability of sensory organs and the brain to resolve detail and store information. A concomitant of fuzziness of perceptions is the preponderant partiality of human concepts in the sense that the validity of most human concepts is a matter of degree, therefore not exact but approximate. For example, we have partial knowledge, partial understanding, partial certainty, and partial belief and accept approximate solutions, approximate truth and approximate causality. Furthermore, most human concepts have a granular structure and are context-dependent. In essence, a granule is a clump of physical or mental objects (points) drawn together by indistinguishable behavior, similarity, proximity or functionality. A granule may be crisp or fuzzy, depending on whether its boundaries are sharply defined or not. For example, age may be granulated crisply into years and granulated fuzzily into fuzzy intervals labeled very young, young, middle aged, old and very old.

In this chapter, the fuzzy relational classifier (FRC) is used to assess quality of images distorted by information loss or noise, unlike the earlier methods (Kuncheva, 2005, Nakashimaa et al, 2007) where images are preprocessed to remove the noise before classification.

Any image quality assessment method which does not require reference image for comparison with test image is known as no reference image quality assessment method. A no-reference image quality assessment technique has been developed in the work using entropy of significant features, captured based on local information variation in training images. The proposed quality metric is estimated by a fuzzy relational classifier (FRC) where variations of human perceptions to assess a particular image are incorporated by assigning a class label based on weighted mean opinion score(MOS) matrix. First different scale invariant local features are extracted and after removing redundancy, significant features are selected using principal component analysis (PCA) algorithm. To remove uncertainty in assigning different class labels to images, fuzzy c-means (FCM) clustering algorithm is applied using entropy of features. As a next step, logical relation has been established by designing the FRC. The relationship between information contained in the images obtained using a fuzzy partition matrix (FCM based) and human perception about the visual quality of the images obtained based on continuous weighted MOS matrix are determined using φ-composition of fuzzy implication rule (Ishibuchi and Nakashimaa, 1999) and conjunctive aggregation methods. Quality of test images is assessed or predicted in terms of degree of membership of the pattern in the given classes by applying fuzzy relational operator. The flow diagram of designing the FRC is described in Figure 1.

2. FEATURE SELECTION

Scale Invariant Feature Transform (SIFT) is an approach for detecting and extracting local feature descriptors, reasonably invariant to changes in illumination, noise, rotation, scaling and small changes in viewpoint. The SIFT approach, for image feature generation, takes an image and transforms it into a "large collection of local feature vectors". Each of these feature vectors is invariant to any scaling, rotation or translation of the image. This approach shares many features with neuron responses in primate vision. To aid the extraction of these features the SIFT algorithm applies a four stage filtering approach:

Scale-Space Extrema Detection

This stage of the filtering attempts to identify those locations and scales that are identifiable from different views of the same object. This can be efficiently achieved using a "scale space" function. Further it has been shown under reasonable assumptions it must be based on the Gaussian function. The scale space is defined by the function:

$$L\left(x, y, \sigma\right) = G\left(x, y, \sigma\right) * I\left(x, y\right)$$

where * is the convolution operator, G(x, y, σ) is a variable-scale Gaussian and I(x, y) is the input image.

Various techniques can then be used to detect stable keypoint locations in the scale-space. Difference of Gaussians is one such technique, locating scale-space extrema, D(x, y, σ) by computing the difference between two images, one with scale k times the other. D(x, y, σ) is then given by:

$$D\left(x, y, \sigma\right) = L\left(x, y, k\sigma\right) - L\left(x, y, \sigma\right)$$

To detect the local maxima and minima of D(x, y, σ) each point is compared with its eight neighbours at the same scale, and its nine neighbours up and down one scale. If this value is the minimum or maximum of all these points then this point is an extrema.

Figure 1. Feature entropy based image quality classification

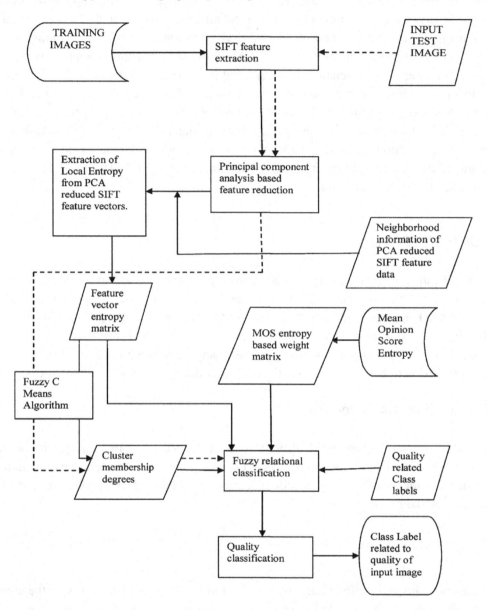

Keypoint Localistaion

This stage attempts to eliminate more points from the list of keypoints by finding those that have low contrast or are poorly localised on an edge. This is achieved by calculating the Laplacian, value for each keypoint found in stage 1. The location of extremum, z, is given by:

$$z = -\frac{\partial^2 D^{-1}}{\partial x^2} \frac{\partial D}{\partial x}$$

If the function value at z is below a threshold value then this point is excluded. This removes extrema with low contrast. To eliminate extrema based on poor localisation it is noted that in these cases there is a large principle curvature across the edge but a small curvature in the perpendicular direction in the defference of Gaussian function. If this difference is below the ratio of largest to smallest eigenvector, from the 2x2 Hessian matrix at the location and scale of the keypoint, the keypoint is rejected.

Orientation Assignment

This step aims to assign a consistent orientation to the keypoints based on local image properties. The keypoint descriptor, described below, can then be represented relative to this orientation, achieving invariance to rotation. The approach taken to find an orientation is:

Use the keypoints scale to select the Gaussian smoothed image L, from above.

Compute gradient magnitude, m.

$$m\left(x,y\right) = \sqrt{\left\{L\left(x+1,y\right) - L\left(x-1,y\right)\right\}^2 + \left\{L\left(x,y+1\right) - L\left(x,y-1\right)\right\}^2}$$

Compute orientation, θ.

$$\theta(x,y) = tan^{(-1)}\left\{L\left(x,y+1\right) - L\left(x,y-1\right)\big/L\left(x+1,y\right) - L\left(x-1,y\right)\right\}$$

Form an orientation histogram from gradient orientations of sample points.

Locate the highest peak in the histogram. Use this peak and any other local peak within 80% of the height of this peak to create a keypoint with that orientation. Some points will be assigned multiple orientations.

Fit a parabola to the three histogram values closest to each peak to interpolate the peaks position.

Keypoint Descriptor

The local gradient data, used above, is also used to create keypoint descriptors. The gradient information is rotated to line up with the orientation of the keypoint and then weighted by a Gaussian with variance of 1.5 * keypoint scale. This data is then used to create a set of histograms over a window centred on the keypoint.

Keypoint descriptors typically uses a set of 16 histograms, aligned in a 4x4 grid, each with 8 orientation bins, one for each of the main compass directions and one for each of the mid-points of these directions. This results in a feature vector containing 128 elements.

These resulting vectors are know as SIFT keys and are used in a nearest-neigbours approach to identify possible objects in an image. Collections of keys that agree on a possible model are identfied, when three or more keys agree on the model parameters this model is evident in the image with high probability. Due to the large number of SIFT keys in an image of an object, typically a 500x500 pixel image will generate in the region of 2000 features, substantial levels of occlusion are possible while the image is still recognised by this technique.

In this work first dimensionality of the features are reduced by applying principal component analysis (PCA) algorithm (Pearson, 1901) and then membership grade of the reduced feature space is obtained using fuzzy clustering method (Pal & Dasgupta 1992).

PCA is a way of identifying patterns in data, and expressing the data in such a way as to highlight their similarities and differences. Since patterns in data can be hard to find in data of high dimension, where the luxury of graphical representation is not available, PCA is a powerful tool for analysing data. The other main advantage of PCA is that once data patterns are found, it is compressed, ie. by reducing the number of dimensions, without much loss of information. The steps of PCA can be broadly described as:

- Input data into the PCA algorithm.
- Subtracting the mean from the input data set.
- Calculating the covariance matrix of the data set.
- Calculating the eigenvectors and eigenvalues of the covariance matrix thus obtained.
- Choosing components and forming a feature vector out obtained eigenvector set.
- Deriving the new data set.

It turns out that the eigenvector with the *highest* eigenvalue is the *principle component* of the data set. In general, once eigenvectors are found from the covariance matrix, the next step

is to order them by eigenvalue, highest to lowest. This gives the principal components in order of significance.

As a next step logical relation between the feature and the quality class label of the image is evaluated using φ-composition (Zadeh, 1973,1965) and conjunctive aggregation methods (Zadeh, 1973, Łukasiewicz & Tarski, 1930). Quality of a new image is predicted using fuzzy relational operator like max product and Lucasiewicz relational composition (Łukasiewicz and Tarski, 1930) applied on the membership grades of the features and MOS weight matrix. The proposed fuzzy MOS weight matrix is based on the entropy of MOS, distributed between various image quality classes.

Here, different scale invariant local image features are extracted from gray level (PGM format) training images of TAMPERE database (Chandler & Hemami, 2005) by applying David Lowe's (Lowe, 2004) algorithm. However, all extracted features are not equally important and redundant, so might not play significant role in assessing quality of images. Significant features are selected by applying Principal Component analysis (PCA) algorithm that effectively reduces the dimension of SIFT feature vector corresponding to each training images. Approximately twenty thousand features have been reduced to one twenty eight only considering TAMPERE database.

3. ENTROPY OF FEATURES

Entropy of features is calculated by forming a feature matrix (F) with number of rows corresponds to number of training images and number of columns representing the dimension of each feature vector. Information contained in each feature is obtained using local Shannon entropy (Takagi & Sugeno, 1985) as defined in equation (1).

$$E_j = -\left(p_j \log p_j\right) \tag{1}$$

where p_j represents probability of occurrence of j-th feature in a particular training image.

To compute the local entropy of each feature vector, the feature matrix F is considered as a representation of an image and each element of F denotes pixel value of the image. The F matrix has been scanned from left hand top corner pixel to the right hand bottom corner pixel using a 9×9 neighborhood pixel window, shown in figure 2. Each pixel is considered as a reference pixel that corresponds to a particular feature in an image. The frequency of occurrence of each reference pixel in the neighboring pixel region (9×9) is calculated and the process is repeated for n number of reference pixels ($j = 1 ... n$). Finally, entropy of a feature vector for a particular image (i-th image) is calculated using equation (2).

$$E_i = - \left\{ {}^{(81)}_{(k=1)} p_k log \left(p_k \right) \right\} \tag{2}$$

The probability distributions of the selected SIFT features extracted from ten different images are shown in figure 3, exhibiting exponential nature of variation of features in different training images. The result implies that information contained in different features is wide apart and so effective to partition the images using FCM clustering algorithm.

Probability distribution of local entropy of feature vectors of different training images is shown in figure 4. The distribution result shows the step functional nature at lower entropy values while becoming smooth and exponential in nature at higher local entropy values. Moreover, distinct characteristics amongst training images are evident when local entropy values of selected SIFT features (Figure 3) are considered compare to SIFT feature values (Figure 4). Therefore, in the proposed method local entropy of selected SIFT features are used to partition the images.

Figure 2. Feature entropy calculation procedure

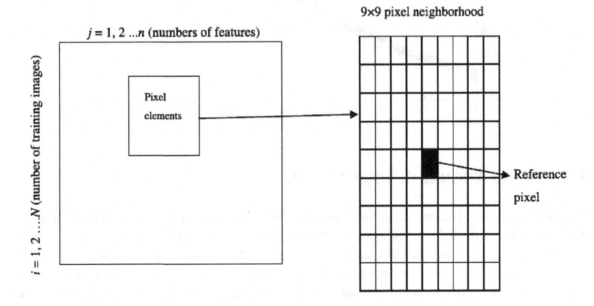

Algorithm 1. Entropy of features

```
Input: Feature matrix F of dimension 10 (no. of images) ×16384 (no. of feature
vectors)
Output: Local Entropy Matrix
Begin
 Step 1 Scan F from left to right and top to bottom.
    Step1.1 Select the first matrix element and keep it at the centre of the
9×9 window.
    Step1.2 Compute local entropy of the selected matrix element using equa-
tion (3.2) and store in the output matrix.
    Step1.3 Repeat step 1.2 for the entire matrix F.
End.
```

Figure 3. Probability distribution of selected SIFT features

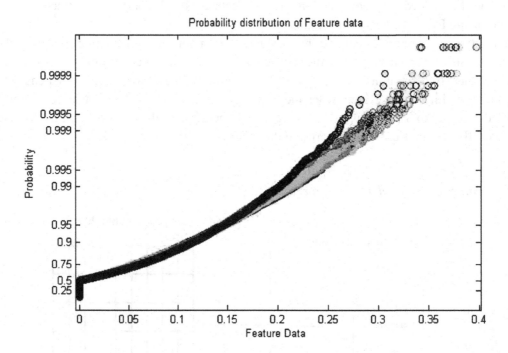

4. FUZZY RELATIONAL CLASSIFICATION

Fuzzy relational classification (Setnes and Babuska, 1999) establishes correspondence between structures in feature space of the training instances and the class labels. Using fuzzy logic in classification, one avoids the uncertainty of hard labelling the prototypes and easily captures the partial sharing of structures among several classes. In the training phase, two steps are performed to build the proposed classifier: (i) exploratory data analysis using unsupervised fuzzy clustering, (ii) establishing a logical relation between the structures of the feature space and the class labels using fuzzy mean opinion score(MOS)

Figure 4. Probability distribution of local entropy features

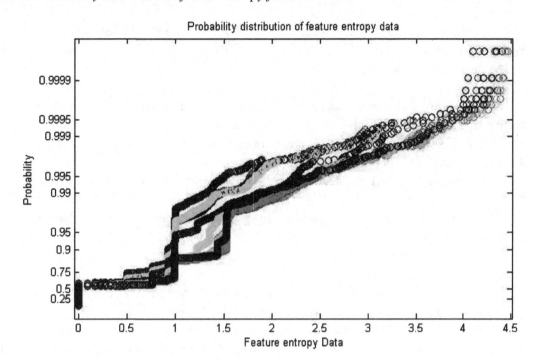

based weight matrix. Simultaneously, a MOS weight matrix W ($N \times C$) is formed by incorporating human perception on each training images where each element w_{ij} represents degree of belongingness of i-th image in j-th class.

4.1. MOS Entropy Based Weight Matrix

Utilizing human perception about the visual quality of the images, MOS entropies are computed and classified using algorithm 2 and equation (3).

$$w_{iq} = E_{x_i} \text{ for class } q \text{ and}$$

$$w_{il} = \frac{1 - E_{x_i}}{C - 1} \text{ for other classes } (l \neq q) \tag{3}$$

where x_i is the MOS of i-th image, w_{il} represents the membership of i-th image to class l, C is the total number of classes and N represents total number of images.

E_{x_i} stands for Shannon's entropy of image i, is defined in equation (4).

$$E_{x_i} = -p_{x_i} \log(p_{x_i}) \text{ where } p_{x_i} = \frac{x_i}{\sum_{i=1}^{N} x_i} \tag{4}$$

Algorithm 2. Classifying MOS entropies

```
Input: Five class labels: "excellent", "good", "average", "bad" and "poor"
with rank high to low.
Output: Weight matrix W
Begin
Step 1  MOS entropy values of images are sorted in descending order.
Step 2  Compute mean (M) of the entropy data sets.
Step 3  Denote maximum value of the data as E_max and minimum value as E_min.
Step 4  If entropy value of an image >= M and <= E_max then
        Assign Class label to the image > "average" // (i.e. "excellent",
"good")
        Else assign Class label to the image <= "average" //(i.e. "average",
"bad", "poor")
Step 5  Set E_min=M and compute new mean (m1) of the data having range E_max to E_min
If entropy value of an image >= m1 and <= E_max then
                Assign Class label to the image > "good" //(i.e. "excellent")
        Else Assign Class label to the image <= "good"
//(i.e. "good" as classification under "average" category is already done)
Step 6  Set E_max = M and repeat step 5 with assignment of the class label of the
image being changed to "bad".
Step 7  Repeat step 5 and step 6 until all Entropy values are covered.
End.
```

The output matrix W provides the MOS entropy based classification weight which is used to design fuzzy relational matrix considering sample training images of figure 5. Two more approaches, which consist of binary value and real value based on Keller et. al.s' (Keller et al, 1985) work to obtain MOS weight matrices are used to design the fuzzy relational matrix. The weights using the work of Keller et. al. is described by equation (5).

$$y_{li} = \begin{cases} 0.51+0.49(n_{li}/k), if j=i \\ 0.49(n_{li}/k), if j \neq i \end{cases} \tag{5}$$

5. IMAGE PARTITIONING

Sample training images (figure 5) from TAMPERE databases (Ponomarenko et al, 2009, 2011) are collected and different kinds of distortion with corresponding MOS value is listed in table 1. Images are partitioned using FCM (Xie and Beni, 1991) algorithm based on the entropy of feature sets. The element μ_{ij} of the partition matrix P specifies degree of membership of i-th image ($i = 1.... N$) into j-th cluster ($j=1 .. c$). Number of clusters is set to four ($c=4$) with fuzziness exponent value 2.5 ($m=2.5$) as determined experimentally. Number of clusters vs. classification entropy using Bezdek's classification entropy index

Figure 5. Training images, (a) Image1,(b) Image2,(c) Image3,(d) Image4,(e) Image5,(f) Image6, (g) Image7,(h)Image8,(i)Image9 and (j) Image10

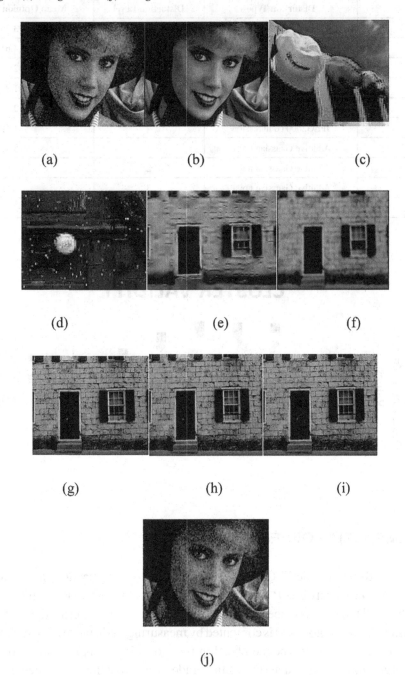

(Bezdek, 1980; Shannon, 1948; Fan & Xie, 1999) is shown in figure 6 for different fuzziness exponents (m)(Łukasiewicz & Tarski, 1930; Chakraborty et al, 2008). Xie-Beni index is also tried but it fails to predict optimal number of clusters for very large number of clusters (Bezdek, 1980). Experimentally it has been observed (Figure 6) that classification entropy is minimized for 4 clusters.

Table 1. Features extracted from TAMPERE database with varied level of distortion

Image Name	Distortion Type	Distortion Level	Mean Opinion Score (MOS)
Image 1	Spatially correlated noise	3	3.3529
Image 2	Additive Gaussian Noise	3	4.6176
Image 3	JPEG transmission errors	4	2.3333
Image 4	JPEG transmission errors	4	1.8710
Image 5	Gaussian blur	4	2.1765
Image 6	JPEG2000 compression	4	1.0000
Image 7	Additive Gaussian noise	1	5.9706
Image 8	Additive Gaussian noise	2	5.4167
Image 9	Additive Gaussian noise	3	4.5556
Image 10	Spatially correlated noise	4	3.1176

Figure 6. Bezdek's cluster validity measure for different 'm'

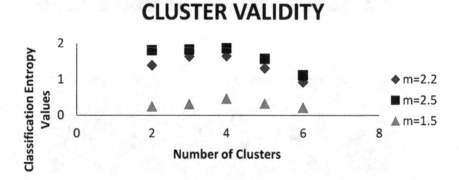

6. CLASS MEMBERSHIP GENERATION

In the second step of designing the FRC, φ-composition (a fuzzy implication) and conjunctive aggregation operators are applied between **P** and **W**, specifying the logical relationship between the cluster membership matrix and the class membership matrix. To classify new patterns, the membership of each pattern in the clusters (fuzzy prototypes) is computed by measuring its distance from the respective cluster centers, giving a fuzzy set of prototype membership functions. Relational composition operator is applied to obtain output fuzzy set that determines the grade of membership of the new pattern belonging to four different classes. The procedure is described using figure 7.

The partition matrix (**P**) is combined with the MOS weight matrix (**W**) using product implication method to obtain fuzzy relational matrix (**R**) as given in equation (6) (Xie and Beni, 1991).

$$\left(r_{ij}\right) = \min_{k=1,2,\dots N}\left[\left(r_{ij}\right)_k\right] \qquad (6)$$

Figure 7. Fuzzy relational classifier

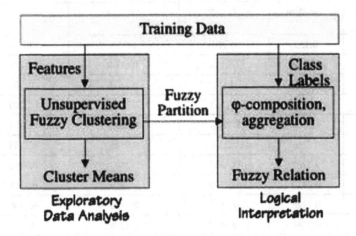

where $(r_{ij})_k = {}_{ik} + w_{jk} - {}_{ik} \times w_{jk}$

r_{ij} represents degree of relation between i-th cluster and j-th class ($i = 1 \ldots c, j = 1 \ldots C$), μ_{ik} is the element of P representing degree of membership of k-th image in i-th cluster where $k = 1 \ldots N$) and w_{jk} is the element of W (MOS weight matrix) provides weight of image k in class j.

For a particular image, say s, the class membership Ω_j in a specific class j is computed using the proposed method as given in equation (7).

$$_j = \max_{i=1\ldots c} \left[\mu_{is} \times r_{ij} \right] \tag{7}$$

Finally, the class membership value is converted to linguistic information to obtain the *quality* metric of the test images.

8. RESULTS OF FUZZY RELATIONAL CLASSIFIER

The MOS weight matrix (W) is given in Table 2 calculated using MOS value of Table 1.

Generally the output matrix W obtained using algorithm 2 provides the MOS entropy based classification weight, which has been used to design fuzzy relational matrix in the work. Two different types of MOS weight matrix have also been used in the work for experimentations. They are binary value based MOS weight matrix (table 3), which is formed on the principle that after descending order sorting of MOS values, the images with highest value of MOS, are assigned class labels starting from "excellent". Accordingly its MOS weight is assigned the binary value 1. The weights of that image for other classes are assigned the binary value 0. Ranges of MOS are fixed as described in algorithm 2 for assigning a particular class label to a set of images. Another approach of determining the MOS weight is based on Keller et al.s formula (equation 5), given in table 4.

The fuzzy relational matrix R is built to establish relation between the clusters and existing class labels of images. The common process of building such matrix is Lucasiewicz implication method and

Table 2. MOS Weight Matrix W

Images \ Class Labels	Excellent	Good	Average	Bad	Poor
Image 7	**0.132**	0.217	0.217	0.217	0.217
Image 8	**0.1264**	0.2184	0.2184	0.2184	0.2184
Image 9	0.2207	**0.117**	0.2207	0.2207	0.2207
Image 2	0.2209	**0.1163**	0.2209	0.2209	0.2209
Image 1	0.2254	0.2254	**0.0985**	0.2254	0.2254
Image 10	0.2263	0.2263	**0.0945**	0.2263	0.2263
Image 5	0.2302	0.2302	0.2302	**0.0792**	0.2302
Image 3	0.2310	0.2310	0.2310	**0.0758**	0.2310
Image 4	0.2328	0.2328	0.2328	**0.0688**	0.2328
Image 6	0.2388	0.2388	0.2388	0.2388	**0.0447**

Table 3. MOS weight matrix W using Binary weight

Images \ Class Labels	Excellent	Good	Average	Bad	Poor
Image 1	1	0	0	0	0
Image 2	1	0	0	0	0
Image 3	0	1	0	0	0
Image 4	0	1	0	0	0
Image 5	0	0	1	0	0
Image 6	0	0	1	0	0

Table 4. MOS weight matrix using Keller el al.s' formula

Images \ Class Labels	Excellent	Good	Average	Bad	Poor
Image 1	0.5916	0.0816	0.0816	0.0816	0.0816
Image 2	0.5986	0.0816	0.0816	0.0816	0.0816
Image 3	0.0816	0.5916	0.0816	0.0816	0.0816
Image 4	0.0816	0.5916	0.0816	0.0816	0.0816
Image 5	0.0816	0.0816	0.5916	0.0816	0.0816
Image 6	0.0816	0.0816	0.5916	0.0816	0.0816

the class membership for a new input image is given by its strong conjunction. A new implication method has been proposed in the work for generating the fuzzy relational matrix (R). Lucasiewicz implication method and product implication method are also experimented to develop the relational matrix (R). Table 5 provides the fuzzy relation matrix R computed by the proposed method while Table 6 (Binary MOS weight matrix) and Table 7 (Keller et al's MOS weight matrix) illustrates R computed using Lu-

Table 5. Fuzzy relational matrix (R)

Class Labels / Clusters	Excellent	Good	Average	Bad	Poor
Cluster1	0.0223	0.01	0.0208	0.0126	0.0223
Cluster2	0.01	0.0208	0.0126	0.0223	0.0281
Cluster3	0.0208	0.0126	0.0223	0.01	0.0208
Cluster4	0.0126	0.0388	0.01	0.0393	0.0306

Table 6. Fuzzy Relational matrix using Binary MOS weight matrix

Class Labels / Clusters	Excellent	Good	Average	Bad	Poor
Cluster1	0.0745	0.0745	0.6234	0.0745	0.0745
Cluster2	0.7721	0.0369	0.0369	0.0369	0.0369
Cluster3	0.0375	0.0375	0.7377	0.0375	0.0375
Cluster4	0.0653	0.6085	0.0653	0.0653	0.0653

Table 7. Fuzzy Relational matrix using Keller et al's MOS weight matrix

Class Labels / Clusters	Excellent	Good	Average	Bad	Poor
Cluster1	0.156061	0.156061	0.666061	0.156061	0.156061
Cluster2	0.628505	0.118505	0.118505	0.118505	0.118505
Cluster3	0.119078	0.119078	0.629078	0.119078	0.119078
Cluster4	0.146929	0.656929	0.146929	0.146929	0.146929

casiewicz implication method. The sample class membership matrix obtained by applying the proposed conjunction process is given in Table 8 while Table 9 provides the same using Lucasiewicz conjunction.

The class memberships of the test images (figure 8)(Ponomarenko et al, 2009, 2011; Schneiderman) are computed using equation (7) and accordingly its quality label is determined. Examples of computation of such class membership matrices are provided in table 8 and table 9. The class label of the test image is assigned to a particular quality class corresponding to the element of the matrix having highest value. Table 10 shows comparison between the proposed quality metric and othert no-reference quality metrics.

Table 8. Class membership matrix using proposed conjunction method

Class Labels / Image Name	Excellent	Good	Average	Bad	Poor
Img 132	0.0178	0.0058	0.0061	0.018	0.014

Table 9. Class membership matrix using Lucasiewicz method

Class Labels Image Name	Excellent	Good	Average	Bad	Poor
Img 132	0.1097	0	0.0709	0	0

Figure 8. Test images, from left to right and top to bottom- Img132, Img162, I04, I01, chinacongress distorted, chinacongress original, Bernstein distorted, Annan original, Afghan distorted and compressed Lena image

The highest element in Table 8 and Table 9 is corresponding to "excellent" class label and therefore, Img132 is treated as excellent quality image.

9. SUMMARY

The concept of fuzzy relational classifier has been utilized in the work to develop a no-reference image quality assessment technique of distorted and decompressed images. Important scale invariant local features are selected and then partitioned based on the entropy of features, thereby reducing dimensionality

Table 10. Comparison between the proposed quality metric with other quality metrics

Image Taken from Different Databases, Indicated in Parentheses	Fuzzyness Exponent Value (m)	Fuzzy Relation Based Image Quality in Linguistic Variable Term	Blind Image Quality Index (Linguistic Variable) (Krishnamoorthy Bovik)	Jpeg quality Score (Linguistic Variable) (Wang et. al.)	JP2KNR (Linguistic Variable) (Sheikh et. al.)
Img162 (LIVE)	2.5	excellent	good	excellent	good
Img132 (LIVE)	2.5	excellent	average	average	good
Chinacongress distorted (PROFILE)	0.75	poor	average	average	good
Chinacongress original (PROFILE)	2.5	excellent	good	excellent	good
Annan original (PROFILE)	0.75	excellent	good	excellent	good
Lena image decompressed with codebook size 1024	2.5	excellent	good	average	good
I01 (TAMPERE)	2.5	excellent	good	excellent	good
I04 (TAMPERE)	2.5	excellent	good	excellent	good
Afghangaussian distorted (PROFILE)	2.5	average	average	average	good
Bernstein distorted (PROFILE)	0.75	poor	poor	average	good

and complexity of the system and at the same time avoiding information loss. The variation of selected features are wide enough for capturing important information from the images. To avoid human biasing in assigning class label to the test images, variation of human observations are incorporated by estimating continuous weight based on entropy of MOS in different classes. The effect of fuzziness exponent on classification process is also studied in assessing quality of image. The proposed no reference image quality metric has been compared with the existing quality metric producing satisfactory result.

REFERENCES

Bezdek, J. C. (1980). A Convergence theorem for fuzzy ISODATA clustering algorithm. *IEEE Transactions on Pattern Analysis and Machine Intelligence*, 2(1), 1–8. doi:10.1109/TPAMI.1980.4766964 PMID:22499617

Chakraborty & Chakraborty. (2008). Fuzzy linear and polynomial regression modelling of IF-THEN fuzzy rulebase. *IJUFKBS, 16*(2), 219-232.

Chandler, D. M., & Hemami, S. S. (2005). Dynamic contrast-based quantization for lossy wavelet image compression. *IEEE Transactions on Image Processing*, 14(4), 397–410. doi:10.1109/TIP.2004.841196 PMID:15825476

Dunn, J. C. (1973). A Fuzzy Relative of the ISODATA Process and Its Use in Detecting Compact Well-Separated Clusters. *Journal of Cybernetics, 3*(3), 32–57. doi:10.1080/01969727308546046

Fan, J., & Xie, W. (1999). Distance measure and induced fuzzy entropy. *Fuzzy Sets and Systems, 104*(2), 305–314. doi:10.1016/S0165-0114(99)80011-6

Gilles, S. (1998). *Robust Description and Matching of Images.* (PhD thesis). University of Oxford.

Huang, L. K., & Wang, M. J. (1995). Image Thresholding by minimizing the measure of fuzzyness. *Pattern Recognition, 28*(1), 41–51. doi:10.1016/0031-3203(94)E0043-K

Ishibuchi, H., & Nakashimaa, T. (1999). Performance evaluation of fuzzy classifier systems for multidimensional pattern classification problems. *IEEE Transactions on Systems, Man, and Cybernetics. Part B, Cybernetics, 29*(5), 601–618. doi:10.1109/3477.790443 PMID:18252338

ITU-R BT.500-13(2012) recommendation, 18.

Keller, J. M., Gray, M. R., & Givens, J. A. (1985). A fuzzy k-nearest neighbour algorithm. *IEEE Transactions on Systems, Man, and Cybernetics, 15*(4), 580–585. doi:10.1109/TSMC.1985.6313426

Kuncheva, L. I. (2005). *Combining Pattern Classifiers, Methods and Algorithms.* New York, NY: Wiley Interscience.

Lowe, D. G. (2004). Distinctive image features from scale-invariant keypoints. *International Journal of Computer Vision, 60*(2), 91–110. doi:10.1023/B:VISI.0000029664.99615.94

Łukasiewicz, J., & Tarski, A. (1930). Untersuchungen über den Aussagenkalkül [Investigations into the sentential calculus]. Comptes Rendus des séances de la Société des Sciences et des Lettres de Varsovie, 23, 31–32.

Nakashimaa, T., Schaefer, G., Yokota, Y., & Ishibuchi, H. (2007). A weighted fuzzy classifier and its application to image processing tasks. *Fuzzy Sets and Systems, 158*(3), 284–294. doi:10.1016/j.fss.2006.10.011

Pal, S. K., & Dasgupta, A. (1992). Special fuzzy sets and soft thresholding. *Information Sciences, 65*(1-2), 65–97. doi:10.1016/0020-0255(92)90078-M

Pearson, K. (1901). On Lines and Planes of Closest Fit to Systems of Points in Space. *Philosophical Magazine, 2*(11), 559–572. doi:10.1080/14786440109462720

Ponomarenko, N., Lukin, V., Zelensky, A., Egiazarian, K., Carli, M., Battisti, F. (2009). TID2008 - A Database for Evaluation of Full-Reference Visual Quality Assessment Metrics. *Advances of Modern Radio electronics, 10*, 30-45.

Ponomarenko, N., Jin, L., Lukin, V. V., & Egiazarian, K. (2011). *Self-Similarity Measure for Assessment of Image Visual Quality.* Advanced Concepts for Intelligent Vision Systems (ACIVS).

Schade, O. H. (1956). Optical and photoelectric analog of the eye. *Journal of the Optical Society of America, 46*(9), 721–739. doi:10.1364/JOSA.46.000721 PMID:13358013

Schneiderman, H., & Kanade, T. (n.d.). *CMU/VASC Image database.* Retrieved from http://vasc.ri.cmu.edu/idb/html/face/profile_images/

Setnes, M., & Babuska, R. (1999). Fuzzy relational classifier trained by fuzzy clustering. *IEEE Transactions on Systems, Man, and Cybernetics. Part B, Cybernetics*, *29*(5), 619–625. doi:10.1109/3477.790444 PMID:18252339

Shannon, C. E. (1948). A Mathematical Theory of Communication. *The Bell System Technical Journal*, *27*(3), 379–423. doi:10.1002/j.1538-7305.1948.tb01338.x

Spearman, C. (1904). The proof and measurement of association between two things. *The American Journal of Psychology*, *15*(1), 72–101. doi:10.2307/1412159 PMID:3322052

Takagi, T., & Sugeno, M. (1985). Fuzzy Identification of Systems and Its Applications to Modelling and Control. *IEEE Transactions on Systems, Man, and Cybernetics*, *15*(1), 116–132. doi:10.1109/TSMC.1985.6313399

Xie, X. L., & Beni, G. (1991). A Validity Measure for Fuzzy Clustering. *IEEE Transactions on Pattern Analysis and Machine Intelligence*, *13*(8), 841–847. doi:10.1109/34.85677

Zadeh, L. A. (1965). Fuzzy Sets. *Information and Control*, *8*(3), 338–353. doi:10.1016/S0019-9958(65)90241-X

Zadeh, L. A. (1973). Outline of a New Approach to the Analysis of Complex Systems and Decision Processes. *IEEE Transactions on Systems, Man, and Cybernetics*, *3*(1), 28–44. doi:10.1109/TSMC.1973.5408575

Chapter 10
Data Compression as a Base for eHealth Interoperability:
3D FWT Applied on Volumetric Neuroimages

Martin Žagar
University of Applied Sciences, Croatia

Branko Mihaljević
Rochester Institute of Technology, Croatia

Josip Knezović
University of Zagreb, Croatia

ABSTRACT

eHealth is a set of systems and services that enable the sharing of medical diagnostic imaging data remotely. The application of eHealth solves the problem of the lack of specialized personnel, unnecessary execution of multiple diagnostic imaging and rapid exchange of information and remote diagnostics. Medical imaging generates large amounts of data. An MRI study can contain up to several Gigabytes (GB). The exchange of such large amounts of data in the local network facilities is a significant problem due to bandwidth sharing which is even more significant in mobile and wireless networks. A possible solution to this problem is data compression with the requirement that there is no loss of data. The goal of this chapter is a conceptual compression prototype that will allow faster and more efficient exchange of medical images in systems with limited bandwidth and communication speeds (cellular networks, wireless networks). To obtain this conceptual compression prototype we will use wavelets.

INTRODUCTION

Despite the economic crisis, the market potential of eHealth is strong. The global telemedicine market reached $14.3 billion in 2013, is expected to grow to $35.1 billion in 2018 representing a compound annual growth (CAGR) of 16.9% (Kovač, 2014). The wellbeing market enabled by digital technologies (mobile applications, devices) is rapidly growing. The convergence between wireless communication

DOI: 10.4018/978-1-5225-0498-6.ch010

technologies and healthcare devices and between health and social care is creating new businesses where interoperability is the key enabler.

There are many benefits of eHealth systems as an effective complement to routine clinical care. Since health care is based not only on textual data, but also on image and video data, it is important to define algorithms and protocols which will analyse and compress such data in appropriate way so they can be base for interoperability of electronic healthcare record (EHR) as a central point of personal health information.

To fully understand the challenges of creating secure, interconnected electronic health records, it is important to review the content and purpose of a medical record, regardless of the form it takes. Every time a patient is treated by a health care provider, a record is made of the encounter. This record includes information that the patient provides, such as medical history, as well as the physician's assessment, diagnosis, and treatment plan. Medical records beside textual data also contain diagnostic images and videos, and metadata connected with them that indicate the results and other medical procedures. This chronological electronic health record is an important business and legal document. It is used to support clinical treatment decisions, to document services provided to patients for billing purposes, and to document patient conditions and responses to treatment should a legal case arise.

BACKGROUND

Application of ICT in health care and improving the overall health system and services are nowadays defined in most national strategies for the development of health in the world. Following this, eHealth as a set of systems and services that enable the sharing of medical diagnostic imaging data remotely is an important factor in the achievement of these strategies. The application of eHealth solves the problem of the lack of specialized personnel, unnecessary execution of multiple diagnostic imaging and rapid exchange of information and remote diagnostics. The increased availability of medical imaging technologies that yield 4D data (3D + time), combined with the low-bandwidth requirements of telemedicine, generate demands for new medical image compression methods. Medical imaging generates large amounts of data. An MRI study can contain up to several gigabytes (GB). The obtained image data together with other metadata (about the patient) packed in standardized formats such as DICOM and NIfTI are stored in a centralized data repository. From there the needed data are sent to the client device (PC) and presented to a specialist who performs diagnostics. The exchange of such large amounts of data in the local network facilities is a significant problem due to bandwidth sharing which is even more significant in mobile and wireless networks (Žagar, 2012). The application of mobile devices (e.g. tablet) as client devices in recent years has also become possible and interesting due to their increasing computational capabilities. It allows reading of diagnostic data and diagnostics at any place and at any time without restriction (Žagar, 2011). In such applications, the need for data compression is even more stressed because of the limited communication opportunities (cellular networks, wireless networks), and the limited storage capacity of the current study data for these client devices. The goal of this chapter is a conceptual compression prototype that will allow faster and more efficient exchange of medical images in systems with limited bandwidth and communication speeds (cellular networks, wireless networks). Communicated data are meant to be finally decompressed and displayed on mobile devices with limited computational capabilities *(Knezović, 2011)*.

Considerable amount of research was aiming to the subject of image denoising as a base for data compression, and many different mathematical tools have been proposed. Various established denoising methods using variable coefficient linear filters (Ojo, 2000), (Rieder, 2001), adaptive nonlinear filters (Meguro, 2001), discrete cosine transform (DCT) based solutions (Kim, 1999), etc., have been introduced to the literature. For many natural signals, the wavelet transform is a more effective tool than the Fourier transform. The wavelet transform provides a multi-resolution representation using a set of analyzing functions that are dilations and translations of a few functions (wavelets) (Daubechies, 1992).

We will focus here just on exploring spatial (frequency) and this should be done after removing temporal redundancies by methods proposed in (Žagar, 2011). To obtain this conceptual compression prototype we will use wavelets. In wavelet analysis theory, signals have different characteristics in time and frequency domains. High-frequency components have shorter duration than low-frequency components. Therefore, wavelet analysis represents a windowing technique that proposes the use of variable-sized regions. Longer intervals are used where more precise low frequency information is needed and shorter where high frequency information is needed. In wavelet analysis, approximations and details are often used. Approximations are low-frequency components and details are high-frequency components of the signal. For many signals the low frequency information is the most important. It is what gives the signal its identity. The high frequency information, on the other hand, adds variations or noise as observed by. This produces wavelet coefficients which are then coded and ready for transmission or storage.

Storing the wavelet coefficients of an image, rather than the image itself, has a number of advantages. For example, often a large number of detail coefficients turn out to be very small in magnitude. Truncating or removing these small coefficients from the representation introduces only small errors in the reconstructed image, giving a form of lossy compression which is used to compress experimental volumetric neuroimage. Comparing to other 3D compression techniques, such as JPEG 2000, fast 3D wavelet transform is much faster and with higher compression ratio (Stollnitz, 1996).

In this chapter fast wavelet transform will be defined on three dimensions in order to reduce frequency redundancies of volumetric neuroimages. The fast wavelet transform is computed with three-dimensional (3D) filters that are separable products of the one-dimensional low-pass and high-pass filters. The wavelet coefficients are the voxel (3D pixel) values of eight images after the transform calculated with three-dimensional separable convolutions and subsamplings. High-resolution components are spread into different decomposition levels. The decomposition formula is obtained by applying the one-dimensional convolution formula to the separable three-dimensional wavelets and scaling functions. During each level of the transform, the scaling function and the seven wavelet functions are applied, respectively, to the original object at that level, forming a total of eight images, one smooth and seven detailed images. Since the wavelet transform components provide an efficient representation of the original image for compression purposes, different levels of representation can be encoded based on different wavelet bases adapted to different regions of interest.

CONSTRUCTION OF COMPRESSION METHODS

In wavelet analysis theory, signals have different characteristics in time and frequency domains. High-frequency components have shorter duration than low-frequency components. Therefore, wavelet analysis represents a windowing technique that proposes the use of variable-sized regions. Longer intervals are used where more precise low-frequency information is needed and shorter where high-frequency information is needed.

In wavelet analysis, approximations and details are often used. Approximations are low-frequency components and details are high-frequency components of the signal. For many signals the low frequency information is the most important. It is what gives the signal its identity. The high-frequency information, on the other hand, adds variations or noise (Burrus, 1998). Storing the wavelet transform of an image, rather than the image itself, has a number of advantages. For example, often a large number of detail coefficients turn out to be very small in magnitude. Truncating or removing these small coefficients from the representation introduces only small errors in the reconstructed image, giving a form of lossy compression which is used to compress experimental volumetric neuroimage. Comparing to other 3D compression techniques, such as JPEG 2000, fast 3D wavelet transform is much faster and with higher compression ratio.

Multiresolution approximations have important applications in image processing at different levels of details. Lower resolution images are indeed represented by fewer voxels and might still carry enough information to perform a recognition task. The original signal passes through two complementary filters, which results in two signals. Two output signals hold twice as much data compared to the original signal. Analyzing the computation, we can keep every other sample without losing any information. This is known as downsampling by two. This decomposition process represents the discrete wavelet transform (DWT) and the resulting samples are called discrete wavelet transform coefficients (Debnath, 2002).

The decomposition process can be iterated, with decomposed signals being decomposed further, so that one signal is decomposed into many lower resolution components. Theoretically, this iterative process can be repeated indefinitely. In real applications, the decomposition can iterate until the decomposed signal consists of a single sample, in the case of 3D, voxel (Žagar, 2011). To any wavelet orthonormal basis $\left\{\psi_{j,n}\left(x\right)\right\}_{(j,n)\in Z^2}$ of $L^2\left(R\right)$, with $\left(j,n\right)$ being wavelet coefficients, it can be associated a separable wavelet orthonormal basis of $L^2\left(R^2\right)$ (Wickerhauser, 1994):

$$\left\{\psi_{j_1,n_1}\left(x_1\right)\psi_{j_2,n_2}\left(x_2\right)\right\}_{(j_1,n_1,j_2,n_2)\in Z^4} \tag{1.1}$$

The functions $\psi_{j_1,n_1}\left(x_1\right)\psi_{j_2,n_2}\left(x_2\right)$ mix information at two different scales 2^{j_1} and 2^{j_2} along x_1 and x_2 dimensions. Separable multi-resolutions lead to another construction of separable wavelet bases whose elements are products of functions dilated at the same scale.

As in one dimension, the notion of resolution is formalized with orthogonal projections in spaces of various sizes. The approximation of an image $f\left(x_1,x_2\right)$ at the resolution c is defined as the orthogonal projection of f on a space V_j^2 that is included in $L^2\left(R^2\right)$. The space V_j^2 is a set of all approximations at the resolution 2^{-j}. When the resolution decreases, the size of V_j^2 decreases as well. The formal definition of a multiresolution approximation $\left\{V_j^2\right\}_{j\in Z}$ of $L^2\left(R^2\right)$ is a straightforward extension of the definition that specifies multi-resolutions of $L^2\left(R\right)$. The same causality, completeness and scaling properties must be satisfied. A particular case of separable multi-resolutions is a separable two-dimensional multiresolution composed of the tensor product spaces

$$V_j^2 = V_j \otimes V_j \tag{1.2}$$

with V_j being a multiresolution of $L^2(R)$.

If $\{V_j\}_{j \in Z}$ is a multiresolution approximation of $L^2(R)$, then $\{V_j^2\}_{j \in Z}$ is a multiresolution approximation of $L^2(R^2)$ (Stollnitz, 1996). There exists a scaling function ϕ such that $\{\phi_{j,n}\}_{j,n \in Z}$ is an orthonormal basis of V_j. Since, for

$$x = (x_1, x_2); n = (n_1, n_2) \tag{1.3}$$

is an orthonormal basis of V_j^2. It is obtained by scaling by 2^j the two-dimensional separable scaling function $\phi^2 = \phi(x_1)\phi(x_2)$ and translating it on a two-dimensional square grid with intervals 2^j. Multiresolution algorithms implement search for important high-resolution data into the software. Algorithms, from coarse to fine, analyze first the lower resolution image and selectively increase the resolution in regions where more details are needed (Debnath, 2002).

Wavelet Bases in Higher Dimensions

Separable wavelet orthonormal bases of $L^2(R^2)$ are constructed for any $p > 2$, with the following extension procedure. Let ϕ be a scaling function and ψ a wavelet that yields an orthogonal basis of $L^2(R)$. If it is denoted that $\theta^0 = \phi$ and $\theta^1 = \psi$, then any integer $0 \leq \varepsilon < 2^p$ written in binary form $\varepsilon = \varepsilon_1 \ldots \varepsilon_p$ can be associated to the p-dimensional functions defined in $x = (x_1, \ldots x_p)$ by

$$\psi^\varepsilon(x) = \theta^{\varepsilon_1}(x_1) \ldots \theta^{\varepsilon_1}(x_p) \tag{1.4}$$

For $\varepsilon = 0$ this is transformed into $\psi^0(x) = \phi(x_1) \ldots \phi(x_p)$. Non-zero indexes ε correspond to $2^p - 1$ wavelets. At any scale 2^j and for $n = (n_1, \ldots, n_p)$ it is denoted that

$$\psi_{j,n}^\varepsilon(x) = 2^{-pj/2} \psi^\varepsilon \left(\frac{x_1 - 2^j n_1}{2^j}, \ldots, \frac{x_p - 2^j n_p}{2^j} \right) \tag{1.5}$$

The family obtained by dilating and translating the $2^p - 1$ wavelets for $\varepsilon \neq 0$, $\{\psi_{j,n}^\varepsilon\}_{1 \leq \varepsilon < 2^p, (j,n) \in Z^{p+1}}$, is an orthonormal basis of $L^2(R^p)$. For coding volumetric images, the dimension p can be set as $p = 3$. The construction of separable wavelet orthonormal bases of $L^2(R^3)$ will now be proven.

The scaling function ϕ is associated to a one-dimensional multiresolution approximation $\{V_j\}_{j \in Z}$ where ψ is the corresponding wavelet generating a wavelet orthonormal basis of $L^2(R)$ (Stollnitz,

1996). Let $\left\{V_j^3\right\}_{j \in Z}$ be the separable three-dimensional multiresolution approximation defined by $V_j^3 = V_j \otimes V_j \otimes V_j$. Let W_j^3 be the detail space equal to the orthogonal complement of the lower resolution approximation space V_j^3 in V_{j-1}^3:

$$V_{j-1}^3 = V_j^3 \otimes W_j^3 \tag{1.6}$$

To construct a wavelet orthonormal basis of $L^2\left(R^3\right)$, the following procedure builds a wavelet basis of each detail space W_j^3. For $p = 3$, it must be verified that the basis includes the following seven elementary wavelets:

$$
\begin{aligned}
\psi^1\left(x\right) &= \phi\left(x_1\right)\phi\left(x_2\right)\psi\left(x_3\right) \\
\psi^2\left(x\right) &= \phi\left(x_1\right)\psi\left(x_2\right)\phi\left(x_3\right) \\
\psi^3\left(x\right) &= \phi\left(x_1\right)\psi\left(x_2\right)\psi\left(x_3\right) \\
\psi^4\left(x\right) &= \psi\left(x_1\right)\phi\left(x_2\right)\phi\left(x_3\right) \\
\psi^5\left(x\right) &= \psi\left(x_1\right)\phi\left(x_2\right)\psi\left(x_3\right) \\
\psi^6\left(x\right) &= \psi\left(x_1\right)\psi\left(x_2\right)\phi\left(x_3\right) \\
\psi^7\left(x\right) &= \psi\left(x_1\right)\psi\left(x_2\right)\psi\left(x_3\right)
\end{aligned}
\tag{1.7}
$$

Now it must be proven that the wavelet family

$$\left\{\psi_{j,n}^1, \psi_{j,n}^2, \psi_{j,n}^3, \psi_{j,n}^4, \psi_{j,n}^5, \psi_{j,n}^6, \psi_{j,n}^7\right\}_{n \in Z^3} \tag{1.8}$$

is an orthonormal basis of W_j^3 and

$$\left\{\psi_{j,n}^1, \psi_{j,n}^2, \psi_{j,n}^3, \psi_{j,n}^4, \psi_{j,n}^5, \psi_{j,n}^6, \psi_{j,n}^7\right\}_{(j,n) \in Z^4} \tag{1.9}$$

is an orthonormal basis of $L^2\left(R^3\right)$ (Jaffard, 2001). The equation (1.6) is rewritten

$$V_{j-1} \otimes V_{j-1} \otimes V_{j-1} = \left(V_j^3 \otimes V_j^3 \otimes V_j^3\right) \oplus W_j^3 \tag{1.10}$$

The one-dimensional multiresolution space V_{j-1} can also be decomposed into $V_{j-1} = V_j \oplus W_j$. By inserting this in (1.10), the distributivity of $\oplus$ with respect to $\otimes$ proves that

$$(V_j \oplus W_j) \otimes (V_j \oplus W_j) \otimes (V_j \oplus W_j) = \left(V_j^3 \otimes V_j^3 \otimes V_j^3\right) \oplus W_j^3 \tag{1.11}$$

with

$$W_j^3 = \left(V_j \otimes V_j \otimes W_j\right) \oplus \left(V_j \otimes W_j \otimes V_j\right) \oplus \left(V_j \otimes W_j \otimes W_j\right) \oplus \left(W_j \otimes V_j \otimes V_j\right) \oplus$$
$$\oplus \left(W_j \otimes V_j \otimes W_j\right) \oplus \left(W_j \otimes W_j \otimes V_j\right) \oplus \left(W_j \otimes W_j \otimes W_j\right)$$

(1.12)

Since $\left\{\phi_{j,n}\right\}_{n \in Z}$ and $\left\{\psi_{j,n}\right\}_{n \in Z}$ are orthonormal bases of V_j and W_j, we derive that

$$\left\{\begin{matrix}
\phi_{j,n_1}\left(x_1\right)\phi_{j,n_2}\left(x_2\right)\psi_{j,n_3}\left(x_3\right)\\
\phi_{j,n_1}\left(x_1\right)\psi_{j,n_2}\left(x_2\right)\psi_{j,n_3}\left(x_3\right)\\
\phi_{j,n_1}\left(x_1\right)\psi_{j,n_2}\left(x_2\right)\psi_{j,n_3}\left(x_3\right)\\
\psi_{j,n_1}\left(x_1\right)\phi_{j,n_2}\left(x_2\right)\phi_{j,n_3}\left(x_3\right)\\
\psi_{j,n_1}\left(x_1\right)\phi_{j,n_2}\left(x_2\right)\psi_{j,n_3}\left(x_3\right)\\
\psi_{j,n_1}\left(x_1\right)\psi_{j,n_2}\left(x_2\right)\phi_{j,n_3}\left(x_3\right)\\
\psi_{j,n_1}\left(x_1\right)\psi_{j,n_2}\left(x_2\right)\psi_{j,n_3}\left(x_3\right)
\end{matrix}\right\}_{\left(n_1,n_2,n_3\right)\in Z^3}$$

(1.13)

is an orthonormal basis of W_j^3. As in the one-dimensional case, the overall space $L^2\left(R^3\right)$ can be decomposed as an orthogonal sum of the detail spaces at all resolutions: $L^2\left(R^3\right) = \oplus_{j=-\infty}^{\infty} W_j^3$. Hence (1.13) is an orthonormal basis of $L^2\left(R^3\right)$, and the proof ends here.

The seven wavelets extract three-dimensional object details at different scales and orientations. Over positive frequencies, $\hat{\phi}$ and $\hat{\psi}$ have energy mainly concentrated on $[0,\pi]$ and $[\pi,2\pi]$ respectively. The separable wavelet expressions imply that

$$\hat{\psi}^1\left(\omega_1,\omega_2,\omega_3\right) = \hat{\phi}\left(\omega_1\right)\hat{\phi}\left(\omega_2\right)\hat{\psi}\left(\omega_3\right)$$
$$\hat{\psi}^2\left(\omega_1,\omega_2,\omega_3\right) = \hat{\phi}\left(\omega_1\right)\hat{\psi}\left(\omega_2\right)\hat{\phi}\left(\omega_3\right)$$
$$\hat{\psi}^3\left(\omega_1,\omega_2,\omega_3\right) = \hat{\phi}\left(\omega_1\right)\hat{\psi}\left(\omega_2\right)\hat{\psi}\left(\omega_3\right)$$
$$\hat{\psi}^4\left(\omega_1,\omega_2,\omega_3\right) = \hat{\psi}\left(\omega_1\right)\hat{\phi}\left(\omega_2\right)\hat{\phi}\left(\omega_3\right)$$
$$\hat{\psi}^5\left(\omega_1,\omega_2,\omega_3\right) = \hat{\psi}\left(\omega_1\right)\hat{\phi}\left(\omega_2\right)\hat{\psi}\left(\omega_3\right)$$
$$\hat{\psi}^6\left(\omega_1,\omega_2,\omega_3\right) = \hat{\psi}\left(\omega_1\right)\hat{\psi}\left(\omega_2\right)\hat{\phi}\left(\omega_3\right)$$
$$\hat{\psi}^7\left(\omega_1,\omega_2,\omega_3\right) = \hat{\psi}\left(\omega_1\right)\hat{\psi}\left(\omega_2\right)\hat{\psi}\left(\omega_3\right)$$

(1.14)

The above wavelet expressions have the following features:

$\left|\hat{\psi}^1\left(\omega_1,\omega_2,\omega_3\right)\right|$ is large at low horizontal frequencies ω_1, low vertical frequencies ω_2 and high depth frequencies ω_3

$\left|\hat{\psi}^2\left(\omega_1,\omega_2,\omega_3\right)\right|$ is large at low horizontal frequencies ω_1, high vertical frequencies ω_2 and low depth frequencies ω_3

$\left|\hat{\psi}^3\left(\omega_1,\omega_2,\omega_3\right)\right|$ is large at low horizontal frequencies ω_1, high vertical frequencies ω_2 and high depth frequencies ω_3

$\left|\hat{\psi}^4\left(\omega_1,\omega_2,\omega_3\right)\right|$ is large at high horizontal frequencies ω_1, low vertical frequencies ω_2 and low depth frequencies ω_3

$\left|\hat{\psi}^5\left(\omega_1,\omega_2,\omega_3\right)\right|$ is large at high horizontal frequencies ω_1, low vertical frequencies ω_2 and high depth frequencies ω_3

$\left|\hat{\psi}^6\left(\omega_1,\omega_2,\omega_3\right)\right|$ is large at high horizontal frequencies ω_1, high vertical frequencies ω_2 and low depth frequencies ω_3

$\left|\hat{\psi}^7\left(\omega_1,\omega_2,\omega_3\right)\right|$ is large at high horizontal frequencies ω_1, high vertical frequencies ω_2 and high depth frequencies ω_3

Fast Three-Dimensional Wavelet Transform

Let $f[n]$ be an input a 3-dimensional discrete signal sampled at intervals 2^L. The wavelet coefficients of f at scales $2^j > 2^L$ are computed with separable convolutions and subsamplings along all three signal dimensions. For $n = \left(n_1, n_2, n_3\right)$ it can be denoted that (Debnath, 2002):

$$a_j[n] = \left\langle f, \psi_{j,n}^0 \right\rangle \tag{1.15}$$

$$d_j^k = \left\langle f, \psi_{j,n}^k \right\rangle, 1 \le k \le 7 \tag{1.16}$$

The fast wavelet transform is computed with filters that are separable products of one-dimensional low-pass filter h and high-pass filter g. The separable 3-dimensional low-pass filter is

$$h^0[n] = h[n_1]h[n_2]h[n_3] \tag{1.17}$$

Denote that $u^0[n] = h[n]$ and $u^1[n] = g[n]$. Any integer $\varepsilon = \varepsilon_1 \ldots \varepsilon_p$ written in a binary form, can be associated to a separable 3-dimensional high-pass filter:

$$g^\varepsilon[n] = u^{\varepsilon_1}[n_1]u^{\varepsilon_2}[n_2]u^{\varepsilon_3}[n_3] \tag{1.18}$$

The wavelet coefficients at the scale 2^{j+1} are calculated from a_j with three-dimensional separable convolutions and subsamplings. The decomposition formulae are obtained by applying the one-dimensional convolution formula to the separable three-dimensional wavelets and scaling functions for $n = \left(n_1, n_2, n_3 \right)$. If it is denoted that $\bar{u}^\varepsilon \left[n \right] = g^\varepsilon \left[-n \right]$, then it can be verified that

$$a_{j+1} \left[n \right] = a_j * \bar{h}^0 \left[2n \right] \tag{1.19}$$

$$d_{j+1}^\varepsilon \left[n \right] = a_j * \bar{g}^\varepsilon \left[2n \right] \tag{1.20}$$

In an extended way, this can be rewritten as:

$$
\begin{aligned}
a_{j+1} &= a_j * \overline{hhh} \left[2n \right] \\
d_{j+1}^1 &= a_j * \overline{hh\bar{g}} \left[2n \right] \\
d_{j+1}^2 &= a_j * \overline{h\bar{g}h} \left[2n \right] \\
d_{j+1}^2 &= a_j * \overline{h\bar{g}g} \left[2n \right] \\
d_{j+1}^4 &= a_j * \overline{\bar{g}hh} \left[2n \right] \\
d_{j+1}^5 &= a_j * \overline{\bar{g}h\bar{g}} \left[2n \right] \\
d_{j+1}^6 &= a_j * \overline{g\bar{g}h} \left[2n \right] \\
d_{j+1}^7 &= a_j * \overline{ggg} \left[2n \right]
\end{aligned}
\tag{1.21}
$$

Separable three-dimensional convolution can be factored into one-dimensional convolutions along the rows and columns of the volumetric image (Jaffard, 2001). With the factorization illustrated in Figure 1, these eight convolution equations are computed with 14 groups of one-dimensional convolutions. The rows of a_j are first convolved with h and g and downsampled by two. The columns of these two output volumes are then convolved with h and g respectively and downsampled by two. Finally, the depth component of these four output volumes is then convolved with h and g respectively and downsampled by two which provides the following eight subsampled images

$$a_{j+1} \left[n \right], d_{j+1}^1 \left[n \right], d_{j+1}^2 \left[n \right], d_{j+1}^3 \left[n \right], d_{j+1}^4 \left[n \right], d_{j+1}^5 \left[n \right], d_{j+1}^6 \left[n \right], d_{j+1}^7 \left[n \right] \tag{1.22}$$

The reconstruction process in inverse fast 3D wavelet transform begins with denoting $\breve{a}_{j+1} \left[n \right]$ the signal obtained by adding a zero between any two samples (upsampling by two) of $a_{j+1} \left[n \right]$ that are adjacent in the three-dimensional lattice $n = \left(n_1, n_2, n_3 \right)$. The approximation a_j is recovered from the coarser scale approximation a_{j+1} and the wavelet coefficients d_{j+1} and the reconstruction is performed with

Figure 1. Three-dimensional decomposition and downsampling along rows, columns and depth

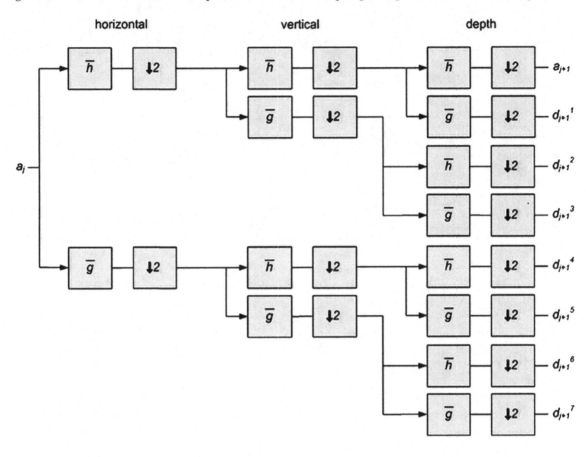

$$a_j[n] = \breve{a}_{j+1} * h^0[n] + \sum_{j+1}^{\varepsilon} d_{j+1}^{\varepsilon} * g^{\varepsilon}[n] \tag{1.23}$$

The procedure is shown in Figure 2. During each level of the transform, the scaling function and the seven wavelet functions are applied respectively to the original image at that level, forming a total of eight images, one smooth and seven detailed images (Mallat, 1999). The wavelet coefficients are the voxel values of eight images after the transform. Figure 3 shows two levels of 3D wavelet transform on an image volume data set. The first level decomposes the data into eight components: f_1 is the low (smooth) resolution portion of the image data, and the remaining blocks $f_1^{'}$ are high (detailed) resolution components. f_1 can be further decomposed into eight smaller volumes labelled f_2 and $f_2^{'}$. The detailed images $f_1^{'}$ on level 1 contain higher frequency components than those $f_2^{'}$ on the level 2.

With properly chosen wavelet functions, the low-resolution component in the j level is 2^{-3j} of the original image size after the transformation, but contains about 90% of the total energy in the j level. It is clear that the high-resolution components are spread into different decomposition levels. For these reasons, the wavelet transform components provide an efficient representation of the original image for compression purposes, while different levels of representation can be encoded differently to achieve a desired compression ratio (Tang, 2001).

Figure 2. Reconstruction by inserting zeros and filtering the output

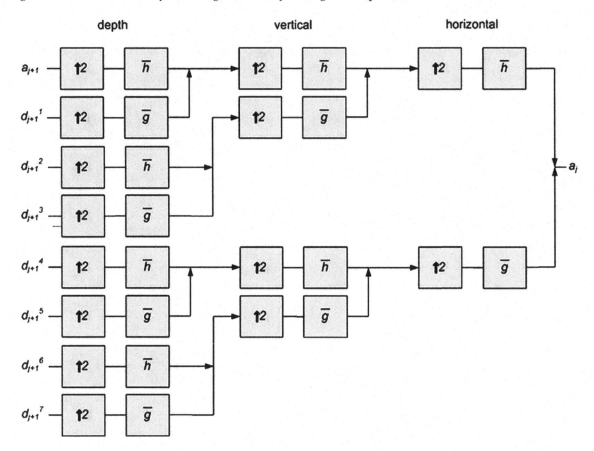

Figure 3. A two-level 3D wavelet transform on an image volume data set

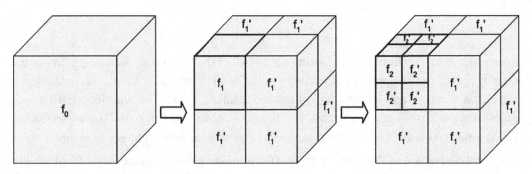

SOLUTIONS AND RECOMMENDATIONS

Exploring frequency redundancies in experimental volumetric neuroimages is based on fast wavelet transformation. To explore frequency redundancy, the original dataset is decomposed into low and high frequency coefficients using wavelet transformation. To obtain the standard decomposition of a single 3D object, one-dimensional wavelet transform is first applied to each row of voxel values, then to each column and then in depth dimension. The wavelet coefficients are derived by reversing the order of the scaling function coefficients and then reversing the sign of every second one.

3D decomposition function is repeated for a given number of transformation stages to complete the 3D transformation. The results of using fast 3D wavelet transform and inverse fast 3D wavelet transform on experimental medical data with Daubechies D2, Daubechies D10, Daubechies D20 and Cohen-Daubechies-Feauveau 5/3 wavelet are shown in Figure 4, Figure 5, Figure 6 and Figure 7 respectively.

In first example (Figure 4), simple Haar basis i.e. Daubechies D2 wavelet with coefficients (1,1) was used as a filter basis for wavelet transformation. The Haar wavelet has the shortest support among all orthogonal wavelets. It is not well adapted to approximating smooth functions because it has only one vanishing moment. It can be seen that the transformed data have viewable errors and it is noticeable noisy. Peak signal-to-noise ratio (PSNR) (Jiang, 2005) in case of using the Haar basis is 32,2 dB.

In second example instead of the Haar basis, we use Daubechies D10 wavelet with coefficients for the scaling functions (0.2264, 0.8539, 1.0243, 0.1958, -0.3427, -0.0456, 0.1097, -0.0088, -0.0178, 0.0047), which provides more smoothness and gives output data with no viewable errors (Figure 5). In this case peak signal-to-noise ratio is 60,7 dB.

Third example (Figure 6) shows use of Daubechies D20 wavelet with scaling coefficients (0.0377, 0.2661, 0.7455, 0.9736, 0.3976, -0.3533, -0.2771, 0.1801, 0.1316, -0.1010, -0.0417, 0.0470, 0.0051, -0.0152, 0.0020, 0.0028, -0.0010, -0.0002, 0.0001, -0.0001). Viewable output data are same as with using of Daubechies D10 wavelet. PSNR and compression ratio are higher, but execution time (on Intel i3 CPU, 2.1 GHz and 4 GB RAM) grows compared with Daubechies D10 wavelet.

Cohen-Daubechies-Feauveau 5/3 wavelet shown in Figure 7 is used in the JPEG 2000 3D (JP3D) compression standard. Although biorthogonal wavelets are not same as the orthogonal Daubechies wavelets, they can be compared in the context of features for lossless compression. PSNR, compression ratio, and execution time ratio for D2, D10, D20 and CDF 5/3 wavelet are compared in Table 1.

Figure 4. Original experimental medical data (a), compared to Daubechies D2 wavelet (b)

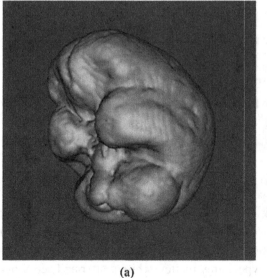 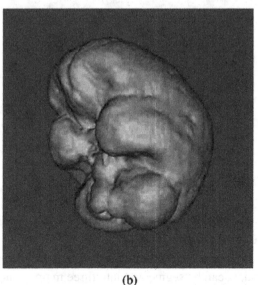

(a)   (b)

Figure 5. Original experimental medical data (a), compared to Daubechies D10 wavelet (b)

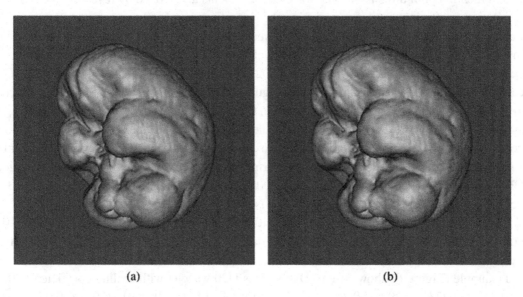

(a)   (b)

Figure 6. Original experimental medical data (a), compared to Daubechies D20 wavelet (b)

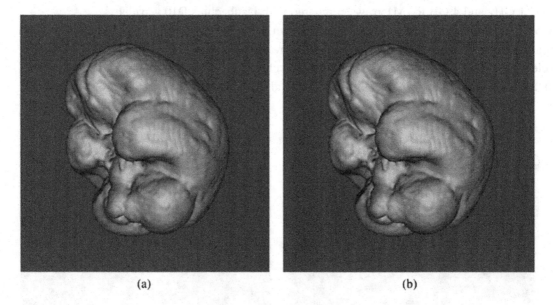

(a)   (b)

FUTURE RESEARCH DIRECTIONS

By assigning each voxel of an image to a codebook vector and each codebook vector to a tissue class, all the voxels of the 3D data set can be attributed to a tissue class and local shapes can be estimated. Object registration is based on the anatomical location (voxel location) with accurate intensity values. Neurodata can be segmented into three main tissue types: grey matter, white matter and cerebro-spinal

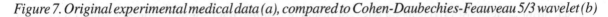

Figure 7. Original experimental medical data (a), compared to Cohen-Daubechies-Feauveau 5/3 wavelet (b)

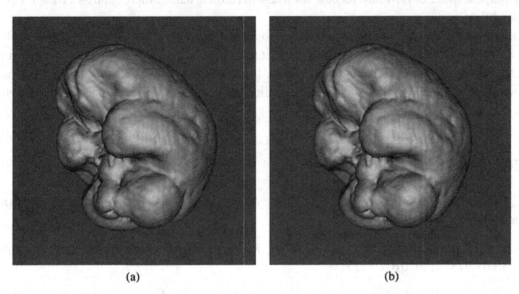

(a)   (b)

Table 1. Performance comparison of D2, D10, D20 and CDF 5/3 wavelet used for the compression of original data

	Original Data	Data Compressed with D2	Data Compressed with D10	Data Compressed with D20	Data Compressed with CDF 5/3
Size (MB)	103,6	0,71	1,99	3,24	2,3
PSNR (dB)	-	38,2	58,7	60,2	57,7
Compression ratio	-	1:146	1:52	1:32	1:45
Execution time (ms)	-	53	210	320	196

fluid. Future work will be focused towards building more sophisticated models of local shapes, which will allow more direct and interesting questions to be asked at the voxel level, as well as improving quality of visual experience.

CONCLUSION

In this chapter we have developed framework for construction of compression methods, built on wavelet bases in higher dimensions, and we applied it on experimental volumetric neuroimage. We have proofed the construction of orthonormal basis of $L^2\left(R^3\right)$ and we have verified wavelet expressions for fast 3D wavelet transform. We applied Daubechies D2, D10, D20 and Cohen-Daubechies-Feauveau 5/3 wavelet bases and concluded that with Haar (D2) wavelet we can achieve very high compression ratio but with not enough accuracy of details. Compared to JP3D (i.e. CDF 5/3) D20 wavelet gives better compression ratio but it is slower and D10 has better performance with almost same execution time, so as a conclusion we propose usage of D10 wavelet base for usage in medical data compression as a Base for eHealth Interoperability.

Limitation of proposed method is generally based on limitation of fast wavelet transform which is shown in (*Orban, 2008*) and that is that fast wavelet transform has good performance only when working on low noise environment and is not suited for low quality data. This is working for medical data where assumption is data acquired data is high quality, but generally this method cannot be adopted for low-quality videos.

REFERENCES

Burrus, C. S., Gopinath, R. A., & Guo, H. (1998). *Introduction to Wavelets and Wavelet Transforms*. Prentice Hall.

Daubechies, I. (1992). *Ten Lectures on Wavelets*. Rutgers University and AT&T Bell Labaratories. doi:10.1137/1.9781611970104

Debnath, L. (2002). *Wavelet Transforms and Their Applications*. Boston: Birkhauser. doi:10.1007/978-1-4612-0097-0

Jaffard, S., Meyer, Y., & Ryan, R. D. (2001). *Wavelets – Tools for Science & Technology*. Philadelphia: SIAM. doi:10.1137/1.9780898718119

Jiang, M., Yi, X., & Ling, N. (2005) On enhancing H.264 rate control by PSNR-based frame complexity estimation.*Proceedings of ICCE 2005 International Conference on Consumer Electronics* (pp. 231-238).

Kim, S. D., Jang, S. K., Kim, M. J., & Ra, J. B. (1999). Efficient block-based coding of noise images by combining prefiltering and DCT. *Proc. IEEE Int. Symp. Circuits Syst.*

Knezović, J., Kovač, M., Žagar, M., Mlinarić, H., & Hofman, D. (2011). Novel Based Prediction Technique for Efficient Compression of Medical Imaging Data. In G. Graschew (Ed.), *Telemedicine Techniques and Applications* (pp. 169–184). Rijeka, Croatia: INTECH. doi:10.5772/18126

Kovač, M. (2014). E-Health Demystified: An E-Government Showcase. IEEE Computer, 47(20), 34-42.

Mallat, S. (1999). *A Wavelet Tour of Signal Processing*. London: Academic Press.

Meguro, M., Taguchi, A., & Hamada, N. (2001). Data-dependent weighted median filtering with robust motion information for image sequence restoration. IEICE Trans. Fundamentals, 2, 424–428.

Ojo, O., & Kwaaitaal-Spassova, T. G. (2000). An algorithm for integrated noise reduction and sharpness enhancement. *IEEE Transactions on Consumer Electronics*, *46*(3), 474–480. doi:10.1109/30.883396

Orban, R., Faheem, M.T., & Sarhan, A. (2008). *Comparison between Discrete Wavelet Transform and Dual-Tree Complex wavelet Transform in Video Sequences Using Wavelet-Domain*. Faculty of Computers & Information-Cairo University.

Rieder, P., & Scheffler, G. (2001). New concepts on denoising and sharpening of video signals. *IEEE Transactions on Consumer Electronics*, *47*(8), 666–671. doi:10.1109/30.964161

Stollnitz, E. J., Derose, T. D., & Salesin, D. H. (1996). *Wavelets for Computer Graphics, Theory and applications*. San Francisco: Morgan Kaufmann Publishers.

Tang, Y. Y., Wickerhauser, V., Yuen, P. C., & Li, G. H. (2001). *Wavelet Analysis and Its Applications*. Berlin: Springer-Verlag. doi:10.1007/3-540-45333-4

Wickerhauser, M. V. (1994). *Adapted Wavelet Analysis from Theory to Software*. IEEE Press.

Žagar, M. (2011). *4D Medical Data Compression Architecture*. Saarbrucken: LAP Lambert Academic Publishing GmbH.

Žagar, M., Kovač, M., & Hofman, D. (2012). Framework for 4D Medical Data Compression. *Technical Gazette, 1*(19), 99-106.

KEY TERMS AND DEFINITIONS

Downsampling by Two: Analyzing the computation of two output signals and keeping every other sample without losing any information.

eHealth: Set of systems and services that enable the sharing of medical diagnostic imaging data remotely.

Electronic Healthcare Record: Central point of personal health information.

Fast Wavelet Transform: Wavelet transform computed with three-dimensional (3D) filters that are separable products of the one-dimensional low-pass and high-pass filters.

Medical Imaging: Acquiring and analyzing often large amounts of medical data.

Wavelet Analysis: Windowing technique that proposes the use of variable-sized regions in order to reduce frequency redundancies of volumetric neuroimages.

Wavelet Bases: Elements that are products of wavelet functions dilated at the same scale.

Chapter 11
Detection of Gradual Transition in Videos:
Approaches and Applications

Hrishikesh Bhaumik
RCC Institute of Information Technology, India

Siddhartha Bhattacharyya
RCC Institute of Information Technology, India

Manideepa Chakraborty
RCC Institute of Information Technology, India

Susanta Chakraborty
Indian Institute of Engineering Science and Technology, India

ABSTRACT

During video editing, the shots composing the video are coalesced together by different types of transition effects. These editing effects are classified into abrupt and gradual changes, based on the inherent nature of these transitions. In abrupt transitions, there is an instantaneous change in the visual content of two consecutive frames. Gradual transitions are characterized by a slow and continuous change in the visual contents occurring between two shots. In this chapter, the challenges faced in this field along with an overview of the different approaches are presented. Also, a novel method for detection of dissolve transitions using a two-phased approach is enumerated. The first phase deals with detection of candidate dissolves by identifying parabolic patterns in the mean fuzzy entropy of the frames. In the second phase, an ensemble of four parameters is used to design a filter which eliminates candidates based on thresholds set for each of the four stages of filtration. The experimental results show a marked improvement over other existing methods.

1. INTRODUCTION

Technological development in the field of multimedia and advances in internet technology along with low cost accessibility to computing resources has led to an increased interest in research on digital videos. This has also been augmented by the fact that memory and capturing devices have witnessed a downward surge in cost. Thus video processing and analysis has become an open area of research for the last few decades. Many new and innovative concepts are being proposed regularly so as to enrich

DOI: 10.4018/978-1-5225-0498-6.ch011

the field of content-based video retrieval (CBVR). The approaches and algorithms developed for CBVR, help to align computer vision in line with human perceptions. In course of defining content-based video retrieval, "content" stands for some features of images such as color, texture, shapes etc. and the term "retrieval" refers to intricate mathematical functions or techniques which can fetch results, relevant for the end user. Thus, content-based video retrieval can be elaborated as the search for videos, where the semantic content matches the query given by a user. In fact, the query given may be using any one of the media types, i.e. text, image, audio and video. In this era, there is an abundant amount of digital information in the form of videos related to music albums, news, documentaries, sports, movies etc. These are available publicly through online digital libraries and repositories. The main problem lies with the amorphous databases or repositories in which these videos are stored. This manifests the immense need for superior search engines which are capable of searching and retrieving videos based on any query media type i.e. text, image, audio, video or a combination of these. This sets the context for the goals with which content-based video retrieval systems are built. Also it enumerates the challenges that may be faced in this research domain.

The basic step towards video content analysis is the automated segmentation of a video into its constituent shots by applying algorithms developed for the purpose. This process is referred to as temporal video segmentation and forms the basis for applications related to video summarization, indexing etc. In other words, video segmentation can be defined as the process of grouping the contents of a video stream into meaningful and manageable fragments. Fragmentation of any video sequence into its constituent units is the prerequisite step for any video processing task. A video stream may be visualized as a conglomeration of a set of different scenes. Scenes in a video are clusters of successive shots having visual similarities. Hence, scenes are composed of shots having semantic similarity. Further scenes can be divided into its composing shots. A shot in a video is a sequence of consecutive frames captured continuously from a single camera having visual continuity. A shot consists of a sequence of temporally related frames. A set of representative frames may be selected which portray the visual content of the shot. These representative frames form the summary of the shot and are called key-frames. The hierarchical elucidation of video segmentation is given below in Figure 1. Shot boundary is the demarcation point which marks the end of one shot and the beginning of another shot. A shot boundary signifies distinct change in the visual contents of consecutive shots and represent discontinuity in high level features including edges, shapes etc. of objects in the spatial and temporal domains. Shot boundaries represent transitions in visual content which are incorporated at the editing stage of the video. The transition effects are categorized into two major categories i.e. abrupt and gradual transitions. In an abrupt transition there is an instantaneous transformation between two consecutive frames elucidated by a sudden change in the visual content of the video. Such abrupt transitions resulting from a change of camera are known as hard cuts and portray points of visual discontinuity. On the other hand, gradual transitions are the editing effects in which two or more shots are combined to enable a smooth changeover from one shot to the next. The change in visual content takes place slowly and continuously over a few frames. Fade-in, fade-out, wipe, whirls and dissolves are some of the types of gradual transitions. In case of wipe, one shot is gradually replaced by another shot using a geometric pattern moving across the screen. There are many types of wipe transitions such as, straight lines, complex shapes, split-screens, horizontal line wipes running from left, right or into the middle of frame. Fade-out transition is one in which one image is gradually replaced by a black screen or by some other image. Fade-in is just the opposite of fade-out in which a solid color or an image gradually gives way to a new image.

Figure 1. Hierarchical representation of video units

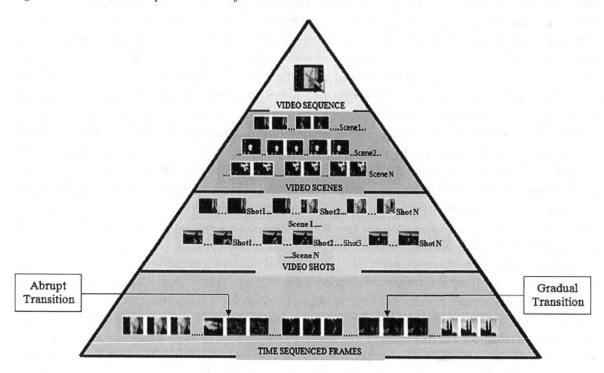

Dissolve is a type of gradual transition from one shot to another, in which the current shot fades out and the next shot fades in. In other words, dissolve is the gradual transformation at pixel-intensity level of one image into another. In such cases, the end frames of one shot are combined with the start frames of another shot so that the transition from one shot to the other occurs smoothly. A dissolve effect is characterized by a linear combination of several frames at the end of one shot $S_1 = f_1 \otimes f_2 \otimes f_3 \otimes \dots\dots \otimes f_p$ and the beginning of another shot $S_2 = g_1 \otimes g_2 \otimes g_3 \otimes \dots\dots \otimes g_q$. The resultant of such overlap gives rise to the following sequence:

$$D = f_1 \otimes f_2 \otimes \dots. \otimes d_{p-k+1} \otimes d_{p-k+2} \otimes \dots. \otimes d_p \otimes g_{p+1} \otimes \dots. \otimes g_q,$$ where, d_j is the jth dissolve frame in a sequence of k such frames. A dissolve frame is thus a linear combination of the matrix values representing two frames, one taken from each shot. Thus, the j_{th} dissolve frame may be expressed as $d_j = \alpha * f_{p-k+j} + \beta * g_j$, where α, β lie in the range [0,1]. As α decreases from 1 to 0 and β increases from 0 to 1, the units of the first shot fade away while the components of the second shot gain prominence. Depending on the editing effect, the values of α and β may or may not take a linear form. The rate of shot change is thus dictated by the rate of change of α and β. This also determines the number of frames over which the dissolve transition occurs.

Gradual transitions are hard to detect due to the continuous nature of these effects. Since the advent of Content Based Video Retrieval as a research field, detection of shot boundaries has been a major field of interest for the researchers. Since temporal video segmentation (shot boundary analysis) is the basic step for any Content Based Video Retrieval System, this research domain has attracted much attention ever since exploration in video analysis commenced. It is tough to split gradual transitions in the temporal domain as it is hard to find a clear boundary between two consecutive frames. In such transitions, the low-level and high-level features retrieved from the frames composing the transition, change gradually in the temporal domain. Thus detection of such transitions presents a major challenge to researchers. Among all types of transitions, dissolve is the most complex one to deal with. This is due to the fact that in dissolve, two images are present in superimposed manner and both fade-in and fade-out take place simultaneously. During the course of dissolve detection, there are many parameters which show a distinct pattern for gradual transitions. These parameters include entropy, numbers of edges, standard deviation etc. However, relying on these parameters alone could trigger false detections as well. For instance, when local/global motions are mixed up with other non-dissolve events, it can be easily mistaken and identified as legal dissolves due to their combined characteristics. Detection of abrupt transitions (hard cuts) is now considered to be a solved problem as many approaches with high accuracy have already been designed. However, accurate identification of the duration and points of gradual transitions in a video stream is still an open challenge for researchers.

The motivation behind this chapter is to focus on the approaches and paradigms developed for the detection of gradual transitions. Also a novel two-phased approach for detection of dissolve sequences is presented. During the first phase, candidates for the dissolves are identified. This phase aims at maximizing recall. The second phase involves a filtration stage which eliminates false candidates based on four parameters. Hence, in this stage, precision is maximized without affecting the recall.

The rest of the chapter is organized as follows. In section 2, a background is presented which includes the existing works. The conventional methods developed for transition detection and the soft computing approaches have been discussed in two separate sub-sections of section 2. Section 3 discusses the types of gradual transition. The issues and challenges faced in detection of gradual transition are presented in section 4. The low-level parameters used in dissolve detection are detailed in section 5, while the pitfalls of the parameters and reasons for these are discussed in section 6. A novel method for detection of dissolve sequences is presented in section 7. The experimental results pertaining to the proposed method are enumerated in section 8. The concluding remarks are given in section 9.

2. BACKGROUND

Over the past few decades, there has been an exponential rise in the number of videos available in online repositories. This is due to the decrease in the cost of multimedia devices. Since videos engulf the other three forms of media types i.e. text, image and audio, research in the field of content-based video retrieval (CBVR) has gained momentum. CBVR is a sub-domain of content-based information retrieval. A video can be considered as a set of images having a temporal relationship. Advancements in the field of content-based image retrieval have propelled and complemented extensive research in the domain of CBVR. CBVR stands as a culmination of the various sub-fields of video processing like video indexing, classification, summarization and retrieval. As mentioned in the previous section, video segmentation is the basic step for any video analysis application. It can be classified into two types i.e. spatial and temporal. Spatial video segmentation is mainly concerned with the tracking of objects present in the video. Temporal segmentation of video involves partitioning the video into temporal slices where each slice represents either a shot or a scene. This gives rise to temporal segmentation which entails research domains called shot boundary analysis and scene change detection. Shot boundaries are generated due to coalescing of shots during the editing process. The different edit effects that are incorporated may be abrupt transitions or gradual transitions. Since the advent of research in content-based video retrieval systems, a large number of techniques have been developed for temporal video segmentation. This engulfs algorithms for all types of shot change detection. The different approaches for shot boundary analysis can be broadly categorized into methods which fall under classical approaches and those which employ techniques built on the soft computing paradigm. The next two sub-sections deal with methods under classical and soft computing approaches respectively.

2.1 Classical Approaches to Shot Boundary Analysis

Some of the early works (Boreczky & Wilcox, 1998; Xiong et al., 1997) on shot boundary detection are part of approaches where conventional techniques have been used. In (Boreczhy & Wilcox, 1998) hidden Markov model (HMM) is used for video segmentation. Features for shot boundary detection considered in this work include an image-based distance between consecutive frames of the video, the audio level difference between the pre-frame and post-frame and also motion estimation between frames. These features are integrated on the HMM framework. The method also eliminates the use of threshold as the trained HMM take their place. (Xiong et al., 1997) deal with the problem of video partitioning, key frame computing and key frame pruning. Statistical and spatial information of an image is used for video partitioning. To deal with the problems of key-frame computation and pruning, wavelet decomposition is used to derive parameter vectors. The work also demonstrates a novel image similarity measure which is also used for inter-shot redundancy reduction. In (Abdeljaoued et al., 2000), feature points extracted from images have been used for shot boundary detection. The rate of change of feature points is used as a similarity measure for detecting these transitions. (Truong et al., 2000) developed a mechanism for detection and classification of shot transitions. The work focuses on identifying the points of transition rather than the temporal length of such transitions. (Mich et al., 1999) enumerate the video indexing techniques of these early works in a survey. A detailed analysis of the latest techniques in visual content-based video indexing and retrieval is presented in (Hu et al., 2011). The survey focuses mainly on methods for video structure analysis which include shot boundary detection, key frame extraction and scene segmentation. The approaches for extraction of features used for static summarization, video annotation and video retrieval are also discussed.

The problem of computing a threshold for the various extracted features has been the objective of research for a long time. Many conventional approaches designed for the purpose of shot boundary detection rely on development of a threshold. An approach based on average inter-frame correlation coefficient and block-based motion estimation was proposed in (Porter et al., 2001). This was used to track the image blocks in the video sequence and detect the shot transitions. (Boccignone et al., 2005) used a consistency measure of the eye fixation sequences generated by a human subject looking at the video. The approach detected both abrupt and gradual transitions between shots using a single method. Another approach which focused on a unified model for transition detection was proposed in (Bescós et al., 2005). The approach is based on mapping the inter-frame distances onto a new space which is based on determining a sequence-independent threshold. This mapping also incorporates frame ordering information in the threshold determining process. (Nam and Tewfik, 2005) devised a method based on polynomial data interpolation to detect gradual transitions. B-spline interpolation curve fitting is used to determine the goodness of fit.

(Liu et al., 2004) designed a shot boundary detection method based on constant false-alarm ratio (CFAR). The threshold for determining a cut was based on CFAR. (Liu and Chen, 2002) used temporal statistics based on features extracted from frames of the video. The current frame is matched with the created model. A cut is detected if the features of the current frame do not properly fit the model. Principal Component Analysis (PCA) is primarily used for model creation from the features. (Qi et al., 2003) take a different approach towards the problem of video segmentation. The problem is transformed into a multiple class categorization issue through supervised learning. A manually labeled training dataset is used for classification purposes. The approach achieves better performance than threshold based methods. The work in (Hanjalic, 2002) is based on minimizing the average detection-error probability. The method takes into account apriori knowledge relevant to shot-boundary detection. The factors taken into consideration are shot-length distribution, visual discontinuity patterns at shot boundaries, and characteristic temporal changes of visual features. The approach taken in (Miene et al., 2003) is to combine the results from three features extracted from images. The features taken into consideration are FFT-features, image luminance values, and gray level histogram differences. Adaptive thresholds based on all the three features are taken for determining the shot boundaries. A K-step slipped window and adaptive threshold was used for shot boundary detection in (Qin et al., 2010). (Lefevre et al., 2003) present a review of the video segmentation methods based on time complexity. In the earlier reviews, only recognition rate and ability to categorize the shot transitions were taken into consideration. The review is helpful for researchers since it deals with image features like pixel, histogram, block characteristics, motion, etc. A survey on temporal video segmentation is detailed in (Koprinska & Carrato, 2001). It describes the steady development of techniques for the uncompressed domain methods which were modified and applied into the compressed domain. The review also deals with the topic of camera operation recognition.

Gabor filtering technique was used for video cut detection in (Barbu, 2009). In this approach, tridimensional images are computed from 2D Gabor filtering. The use of a threshold was eliminated by using an unsupervised automatic distance classifier method. A real-time adaptive threshold technique was proposed in (Yasira & Natarajan, 2009). The proposed algorithm has a low computational complexity (which is imperative for application in real-time systems) and can deal with changing light effects. Another method proposed in (Liu et al., 2008) was reported to be effective for flashlight and fast background changes. These effects often cause false alarms. To counter this, a post refinement strategy using local feature analysis was used in the work. A linear transition detector was designed in (Grana & Cucchiara, 2007) which provided a unified approach for shot boundary analysis. The method was tested on publicly available videos of sports and also the TRECVID 2005 dataset.

(Cerneková et al., 2006) focused on detection of abrupt transitions, fade-in and fade-outs by taking into consideration the mutual information and joint entropy on the set of video frames. The method was tested on the TRECVID 2003 benchmark having videos containing high object and camera motion. The approach is reported to work well for detecting abrupt transitions and fades. Another approach which used the mutual information computed on the components of the HSV color model was proposed in (Bai et al., 2008). In this work a Petri-Net model was used to denote the boundary frames of the shots. The method can be applied for the detection of both hard cuts and gradual transitions.

The significant features of the 3D structure of a scene are modeled and tracked over the frames of a video in (Donate & Liu, 2010) for detecting the shot boundaries. The SLAM technique is used for the purpose. Shot transitions are detected by observing the feature tracking ability of the system. Color coherence change was used in (Tsamoura et al., 2008a) for detecting gradual transitions. The method shows lower sensitivity to local or global motion. Also this approach eliminates the need for threshold selection. Multiple features are used in (Tsamoura et al., 2008b) by the authors resulting in a meta-segmentation scheme. Each of the features used in the work could separately be employed for the detection of gradual shot transitions. Conditional Random Fields (CRFs) are useful for parameter estimation and inference. CRF was employed for the detection of gradual transitions in (Yuan et al., 2007). The approach developed in (Šarić et al., 2008), utilizes twin comparison method and absolute difference between frames for computing the ratio of dominant colored pixels to total number of pixels. The detection of gradual transitions was carried out using fractal analysis. The classifier used for the work is based on Clonal Selection Algorithm. (Chavez et al., 2006) used a kernel-based SVM classifier to detect shot boundaries. The method gets rid of the need for a threshold or any pre-processing step to compensate motion or post-processing filtering in order to eliminate falsely detected transitions. A high speed approach was devised in (Kawai et al., 2007) in which the detection was based on using multiple features. In this work, only those parts of the video were analyzed which are the likely candidate regions for a dissolve. The algorithm was tested on videos taken from the TRECVID 2007 dataset. A formal study of color-structure descriptors used for shot boundary detection is presented in (Abdelali et al., 2009). A comprehensive study of the shot boundary detection techniques has been enumerated in (Yuan et al., 2007). The study elaborates three techniques i.e. visual content representation, construction of signal based on similarity and classification of similarity values. The work also presents a general framework for detection of transitions. It conglomerates various shot boundary detection techniques using a graph partition model.

An intensity-based method was proposed in (Ionescu et al., 2011) for dissolve detection which was able to cope with constraints of the animated movie domain. In this method the concept of twin threshold was used in place of a global threshold. The approach allows to reduce false detections caused by steep intensity fluctuations as well as to retrieve dissolve caught up in other visual effects. Temporal segmentation of video using frame and histogram space was introduced in (Joyce & Liu, 2006). In this method, certain properties of a dissolves' trajectory in image-space are used to implement a simple threshold-based detector. A motion tolerant method for dissolve detection was proposed in (Su et al., 2005). In this approach, detection of dissolve occurs through manifestation of disturbance caused by the motions of the objects. Thereafter, a filter is used to eliminate confusion in the detected dissolved frames. Moreover, to model the behavior of a dissolve transition, classification of the pixels are done in three different categories i.e. proponents, fence sitters and opponents. Proponent pixels are those in which the intensity change is either monotonously increasing or decreasing. Pixels fall in the fence sitter category if the intensity of these pixels remains unchanged in an observation window. Opponents are those pixels which do not fall into the above two categories.

Morphological operators were used in (Naranjo et al., 2007) for the detection of gradual transitions. The algorithm for determining dissolve sequences is based on the computation of a simple metric between frames. In combination with the variance between the frames, morphological filtering is used to detect the dissolve effects. (Volkmer et al., 2004) used average frame similarity and adaptive threshold for detection of gradual transitions. In this approach the frames were grouped into two different sets, pre-frames and post-frames. For each of the two sets, the distance between each frame in that set and the current frame are determined. The average of these intra-set distances gives a final value, which is the average distance between that set and the current frame. The computation results in two values, one each for the pre- and post-frame sets. The ratio of these values are calculated, which is referred to as the Pre-Post ratio. The value of this ratio is used to detect gradual transitions. A chromatic video edit model for gradual transitions detection was portrayed in (Song et al., 1997). This was based on the assumption that discontinuity values belonging to a transition consist of two piece-wise linear functions of time. One function is monotonically decreasing and the other one is increasing. Such linearity is not present outside the transition area. A search for segments which are close-to-linear in the series of discontinuity values is carried out by investigating the first and second derivatives of the slope with respect to time. A close-to-linear segment is found if the second derivative is less than a pre-specified percentage of the first derivative.

An algorithm for detection of gradual transitions was proposed in (Yoo et al., 2006) which was based on the fact that most of gradual curves can be characterized by variance distribution of edge information in the frame sequences. Average edge frame sequence was obtained by performing Sobel edge detection. Features were extracted by comparing variance with those of local blocks in the average edge frames. These features were further processed by the opening operation to obtain smooth variance curves. The lowest variance in the local frame sequence was chosen as a gradual transition point. (Apostolidis and Mezaris, 2014) proposed a method for fast shot segmentation by combining global and local visual descriptors. In this approach, both abrupt and gradual transitions could be detected. The detection was based on the visual similarities of the neighboring frames of a video. For assessing frame similarity, SURF is used for local descriptor and HSV histograms are used for global descriptor. GPU-based processing is used for accelerating the analysis. Firstly, abrupt transitions are detected between the consecutive frames where there is a huge change in the visual content, expressed by a very low similarity value. Thereafter, gradual transitions are detected by computing the value of similarities in the identification of frame-sequences where a progressive change of the visual content is present. Finally, a post-processing step is performed which aims at identifying outliers due to object/camera movement and flash-lights. A concept based on accumulating histogram difference (AHD) and support points was proposed in (Ji et al., 2010). The algorithm is able to detect fades and dissolves. Another advantage of this method is that it can eliminate false detection caused by flashlight.

(Drew et al., 2000) introduced a method for detecting dissolve and wipe transitions. The approach was based on spatio-temporal images of chromatic histogram differences. According to this method all the pixels are used to create spatio-temporal images and each column of the frame is used to form a chromatic histogram. This histogram is then intersected with the histogram from previous frames. At the time of wipes, the edges appear very strong. For dissolve detection, another approach was proposed which was based on color-distance based on the 2D Cb-Cr histograms. In another work, (Rong et al., 2005) Expectation Maximization (EM) curve fitting was used on the frame to frame difference curve for detecting the gradual transitions. The peak contours are approximated by a combination of Gaussian and uniform distributions. The weight of uniform component, the average height and the relative height of the peaks are given as input features to the decision tree classifier in order to discriminate between gradual transitions and cuts. Also the method is able to differentiate between different types of gradual transitions i.e. wipes, fades and dissolves based on the flexibility of the EM curve.

Hilbert transform and feature vectors from Gray Level Co-occurrence Matrix (GLCM) are used for shot boundary detection in (Priya and Domnic, 2012). Contourlet Transform is employed by (Rao and Patnaik, 2014) for shot transition detection where features from each sub-band are extracted for determining the shot boundary. In (Lu and Shi, 2013), an approach was devised for fast detection of shot boundaries. Adaptive thresholds were used in the work for predicting the shot boundaries and width of gradual transitions. The candidates for gradual transitions are selected and singular value decomposition (SVD) is used to speed up SBD. In several approaches the problem of detecting gradual video transitions is viewed as a classification problem. In one such work (Koumousis et al., 2012), Iterative Self Organized Data Analysis (ISODATA) classification algorithm is used. The value of the kappa coefficient is computed from the confusion matrix and is used to identify the transitions. (Manjunath et al., 2011) proposed a nonparametric shot boundary detection technique which could be applied to real time systems. Eigen gap analysis was performed to detect the shot boundaries. (Sowmya and Shettar, 2013) analyzed block based histogram method and block based Euclidean distance methods by varying the block sizes. Two important conclusions were derived from the work. Firstly, the performance of the histogram method improves with increase in block size. Secondly, Euclidean distance approach performs better than the histogram method. Feature selection is an important step in Content Based Video Retrieval (CBVR). The efficacy of the retrieval algorithm is directly related to the features chosen for the purpose. (Patel and Meshram, 2012) elaborate some of the interesting features that can be extracted from video data. Several similarity measurement techniques are also described which are used in video indexing and retrieval. Also some of the predominant research issues in the area of CBVR are discussed.

Pixel value differences of consecutive frames are computed for determining an automatic threshold in (Kundu and Mondal, 2012). The method described in the work integrates an outlier removal algorithm and a false alarm elimination scheme for accurate detection of shot boundaries. Pixel-wise difference was also used in (Patel et al., 2013). In addition, color histogram method is included in the approach to improve performance. Some of the methods for video segmentation take into consideration the motion information of objects. One important work in this direction is (Poleg et al., 2014). The researchers work on egocentric videos (Poleg et al., 2014) which involve videos where the camera is under constant motion. Motion vectors are used to compute Cumulative Displacement Curves which help in temporal segmentation of such videos. A major point of concern for researchers in the field of shot boundary detection is the number of false detections due to rapid object motion. This issue was addressed in the work (Yu et al., 2011). Twin-comparison was used for approximate detection of dissolve sequences. Curve fitting is done in accordance with two parameters i.e. percentage of dissolve-supporters in a frame and the variance of coefficients in the dissolve model. The curve is used to remove non-dissolve transitions. Daubachy 4 Wavelet was integrated along with HSV Color Space for the detection of shot boundaries in (Tariq et al., 2014). Wavelet transform was also used in the work (Thakare, 2012) for temporal video segmentation. The detection of transition sequences in videos of the compressed domain present its own challenges. A fast method for detection of shot boundaries in MPEG videos was proposed in (Ma et al., 2012). The I frames in the MPEG videos are first decoded to generate the DC images components. The histogram differences are computed for detecting the approximate shot boundaries. Using the movement information of B frames, the abrupt transitions are captured precisely. The gradual transitions are located using difference values of N successive I frames. (Mahesh and Kuppusamy, 2012) perform hybridization of the frame difference as well as consecutive frame intersection methods for achieving better results. The efficacy of the method is analyzed by computing statistical measures and kappa coefficient. Tracking of figure-ground segmentation method was proposed in (Li et al., 2013) for unsupervised video segmentation. (Zajić et al., 2011) propose a method for shot boundary detection method using Multifractal Analysis (MA). In the proposed method, low-level features such as color and texture are extracted from the frames of the video. Thereafter, a feature matrix is constructed by concatenating the features. Each row of the feature matrix corresponds to feature vector of a frame. Multifractal analysis is then applied to detect the shot boundaries.

2.2 Soft Computing Approaches to Shot Boundary Analysis

Soft computing has been used extensively by researchers for detection of shot boundaries and several methods have been developed over time. A news video parsing system (Gao and Tang, 2002) was developed for temporal video segmentation as well as detection of news reader. In order to detect the shots in the video, fuzzy c-means algorithm is used. The shots are classified into two categories i.e. those containing the news reader and the other having shots of news footage. This is implemented by means of a graph-theoretical approach. The concept of fuzzy logic has been used for detection of shot boundaries in (Küçüktunç et al., 2010; Bhaumik et al., 2014). Fuzzy color histogram was used in (Küçüktunç et al., 2010) for video segmentation. The work was targeted at copy video detection as a CBVR application. The color histogram is generated with a fuzzy function on the L*a*b* color space. (Bhaumik et al., 2014) use spatio-temporal fuzzy hostility index on the pixels of the frames composing a video to find dissimilarity patterns for detection of abrupt transitions. A fuzzy logic based approach to integrate several features for shot boundary analysis is demonstrated in (Fang et al., 2006). The approach consists of two modes, one for detection of hard cuts and another for detection of gradual transitions. A mode-selector is used to switch between the two modes for efficient detection of shot boundaries. (Jadon et al., 2001) proposed a fuzzy logic based framework for temporal video segmentation. The frame-to-frame property difference values are fuzzified using Rayleigh distribution. The difference values were characterized by fuzzy terms which were used to design fuzzy rules for detecting abrupt and gradual changes. The discrimination power of rough sets was harnessed in (Shirahama et al., 2012) for event retrieval in video archives. In this approach, multiple classification rules are extracted using rough set theory to retrieve parts of event shots. Partial supervised learning is used to train the classifiers for extracting rules and achieving a higher accuracy of retrieval.

(Chan and Wong, 2011) demonstrate an approach for shot boundary detection based on Genetic Algorithm by optimizing a traditional scoring based metrics. The approach eliminates the use of thresholds which have always proved to be a bottleneck in maximizing both precision and recall. The method is based on the edge-change ratio metric. A different approach using genetic algorithm is adopted in (Chiu et al., 2000). A series of string representation is manipulated by the algorithm. The segmentations are evaluated by defining a similarity adjacency function.

Support Vector Machine (SVM) is the most popular and widely used soft computing paradigm for temporal video segmentation. (Ngo, 2003) demonstrated a robust dissolve detector based on SVM. The method extracts multi-resolution temporal slices from the frames of the video. At low resolution, the problem of dissolve detection is reduced to detection of abrupt transitions. Gabor wavelet features are extracted in the high resolution space surrounding the position of hard cuts in low resolution space. These output features are fed to a support vector machine for pattern classification. (Li et al., 2009) present a method based on a multi-class SVM to categorize the shots into cut transition, gradual transition and normal sequences. The algorithm extracts color and edge features in different directions from wavelet transition coefficients. The classification is based on the feature vectors taken from all frames within a temporal window. SVM has also been used in (Chasanis et al., 2009) for detection of both abrupt cuts and dissolve sequences in videos. A learner based strategy is adopted using a set of features which have discrimination power to differentiate between abrupt and gradual transitions. Features based on colour histogram, variation between consecutive frames and the contextual information at a time were taken into consideration. The SVM is capable of locating and characterizing transitions. (Sun et al., 2011) organize the features into a multi-dimension vector by using the method of sliding window. The approach for shot boundary detection is based on SVM and is optimized by particle swarm and Tabu searches respectively. The work demonstrates that optimization by Tabu search is more efficient than particle swarm optimization. (Ling et al., 2008) devised another method for rapid detection of shot boundaries based on SVM. The smooth intervals in the original video sequence are eliminated by detecting changes in gray level variance. Thereafter, the new frame sequence is called reordered frame sequence (RFS). Feature vectors are formed from parameters like intensity pixel-wise difference, color histogram differences in HSV space and edge histogram differences in X and Y direction. These vectors are given as input to the SVM to detect the cuts. Temporal multi-resolution is applied to the frames in RFS in order to detect gradual changes.

Methods for hardware implementation of the various algorithms have been developed for shot boundary detection. To this effect, (Hsu et al., 2009) implemented a FPGA based fully parallel digital Support Vector Machine (SVM) classifier which was used to detect shot boundaries in a continuous video stream. Particle Swarm Optimization based classifier for detection of abrupt and gradual transitions was devised in (Meng et al., 2009). Difference curves of U-component histograms from YUV model are taken as features. A sliding window mean filter is used to filter the difference curves. Further a KNN Classifier based on PSO is used to detect and classify the shot transitions. An unsupervised shot transition detection method based on Auto-associative Neural Network (AANN) was proposed in (Geetha & Palanivel, 2012). The AANN was able to classify the type of transition i.e. abrupt or gradual. The approach is tested on different genres of videos to determine its efficiency.

Although shot boundary detectors based on soft computing paradigms have proven efficacy, researchers have embarked on hybridization of the various soft computing paradigms in order to achieve better results. A fuzzy clustering neural network for detection of abrupt transition in videos was developed in (Shen & Cao, 2011). An amalgamation of genetic algorithm and SVM was presented in (Sun et al., 2011). In this work, a multi-dimensional vector was prepared from features of the pixel and compressed domains. GA was used to optimize the parameters of the SVM kernel. The main feature of the model is that it overcomes the difficulty of parameter selection for the SVM. Feature selection is a problem which has triggered enormous research over the last two decades. (Gao et al., 2005) proposed a method for selection of appropriate features from the entire gamut of the video feature space. For this purpose, rough sets and fuzzy c-means clustering was used for feature reduction and rule generation. A drawback of the fuzzy c-means algorithm is that it assumes a consistent contribution from each feature of the samples. To overcome this, a feature weighting technique was developed in (Bao et al., 2006) using Variable Precision Rough-Fuzzy Sets and incorporated into the fuzzy c-means algorithm. Fuzzy set theory and Adaboost for the detection of shot transition in videos was used in (Zhao & Cai, 2006). Videos were classified into six categories based on camera motion and color changes. Several features from the compressed domain were used to classify the shots into three categories i.e. abrupt cut, gradual transition and shots with no changes. Several techniques were proposed to increase the performance of Adaboost. The approach taken by (Lienhart, 2001) for detecting dissolve transition is mainly based on multi resolution detection approach and machine learning algorithms such as neural networks, support-vector machines etc. The detection is based on three principal ideas. A dissolve synthesizer was created for emulating dissolves of any duration from videos. The method incorporates two new features for extracting the characteristics of dissolves. Finally, the concepts of machine learning were utilized for reliable object detection.

3. TYPES OF GRADUAL TRANSITIONS

A video is created by the amalgamation of different types of scenes. The transformation from one scene to other is a result of incorporating various types of transition effects between the different scenes of the video. The two main classes of transition effects are abrupt and gradual transition. A classification of different types of transition effects is given below in Figure 2.

According to the above mentioned categorization, a brief insight into the different types of transition effects are given in further sub-sections.

3.1 Abrupt Transition

Abrupt transition refers to a sudden change in frame contents that takes place between successive frames of a video. Abrupt transitions make up almost 98% of the edit effects. Abrupt transitions are also termed as "hard cuts". During a hard cut, there is a substantial change in the visual contents occurring abruptly. The last frame before the hard cut is called the pre-cut frame and the first frame of the next shot after the hard cut is termed as post-cut frame. Pictorial depiction of a hard cut is given below in Figure 3.

3.2 Gradual Transition

Gradual transition is one in which the conversion from one shot to another takes place progressively over a set of frames. Gradual transition is often a contextual change occurring over a period of time. During the editing stage, these transitions are introduced and have different lengths. The various types of gradual transitions have been dealt with in further sub-sections.

Figure 2. Categorization of different types of transition effects

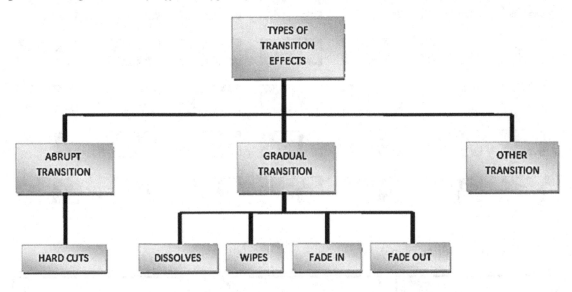

Figure 3. An abrupt transition

3.2.1 Dissolve

Dissolve is a type of gradual transition in which the last few frames of the vanishing shot temporally overlap with the fast few frames of the appearing shot. During the process of overlapping, the intensity of the vanishing shot decreases gradually and simultaneously the intensity of the appearing shot increases linearly. At the end of the transition the appearing shot gains prominence and the vanishing shot disappears completely. A dissolve transition is illustrated in Figure 4.

3.2.2 Wipes

Wipe is another type of gradual transition in which both the appearing frames of one shot and the disappearing frame of the other shots coexist in different spatial regions within two or more intermediate frames between a pair of different shots. This transition gives a concept of entering image and exiting image within the frames of the transition (the intermediate frames). At the end, the entering image is present and the exiting image gets completely removed as depicted in Figure 5.

Figure 4. Dissolve transition

Figure 5. Gradual transition (wipe)

3.2.3 Fade-in

Fade-in is a gradual transition which initiates with a few black or single colored frames. Gradually, the black or single colored frame disappears and the frames of the appearing shot gets prominent. In this transition the black frames and the starting frames of the next shots are superimposed. The intensity of the black frame decreases steadily and the frames of the next shot become prominent. The fade-in transition is depicted in Figure 6.

3.2.4 Fade-out

Fade-out is just the reverse of fade-in transition. Here the frames of a shot loose intensity and gradually turn into black or any other single colored frame. The visual content of the frames during a fade-out transition thus disappears. Figure 7 illustrates a fade-out transition.

Figure 6. Gradual transition (fade-in)

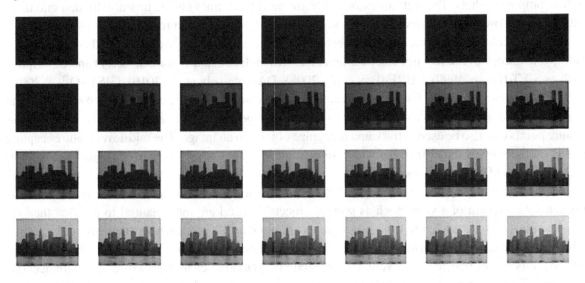

Figure 7. A fade-out gradual transition

3.2.5 Other Types of Gradual Transition

There are some special and rare transition effects that are used in some videos. These fall into the class of other transition effects. Swirl is an example of such transition where the pixels spin like a twister while a transition from one scene to the next occurs.

4. ISSUES AND CHALLENGES OF GRADUAL TRANSITIONS

The gradual transition takes place over a certain number of consecutive time sequenced frames. The contents of the video frames change progressively from one scene to another since the transition region is composed of the last few frames of one shot and an equal number of frames taken from the beginning of the next shot. In some videos, more complex edits are inserted such that a transition region is the conglomeration of frames taken from more than two shots. Determining the frames which compose the transition region become tough since the contents of frames in such regions is the combination of composing shots. The properties of the frames in the gradual transition region are close to the frames of the composing shots. The features extracted from the video frames can be broadly divided into three categories i.e. low-level, mid-level and high-level features. Low-level features include RGB values, HSV components, color histograms, statistical features like mean, variance, skewness of the pixel values, entropy, texture, wavelet features etc. Mid-level features include feature point detectors and descriptors such as SIFT (Lowe, 1999), SURF (Bay et al., 2008), DAISY (Tola et al., 2010), GIST (Oliva, 2001), BRIEF (Calonder, 2010) etc. Given an image, these feature point detectors can be used to extract salient positions in the image which could be used to capture the medium level semantics of the image. These feature points can also be used to track and recognize objects in an image. The mid-level features capture points on the objects rather than the whole semantic meaning. On the other hand, high-level features include shapes of objects, edges in the frames, optical flow (Barron et al., 1994), motion vectors (Wang et al., 2007), event modeling (Li & Sezan, 2001), etc. The high-level features are closely connected to the semantic content of a video such as scenes, objects etc. and are more natural to humans than the low-level features. As such, the low-level features are not capable of clearly distinguishing the frames which lie in the gradual transition region. Using low-level features such as color, histograms, intensity or statistical measures may lead to several false detections. The other challenges associated with accurate detection of dissolves pertain to object and camera movement. Several features have been extracted which compensate for object and camera movements. These ensure that false alarms caused due to these effects are minimized. The problem of flash light compensation has also been discussed in the literature and several methods relevant to it have been developed. Many approaches have been devised over the years to detect dissolve transitions. However, the efficiency of these approaches has not been satisfactory. In case of gradual transition detection, the appraisal of the algorithms depends on its ability to determine the location and duration of such transition. Another important factor to be considered is its capacity to judge the type of gradual transition such as dissolve, fade-in, fade-out, wipe etc. Other important issues include the robustness of the algorithm for application to various encoded file types in the compressed and uncompressed domains. The ability of the approaches developed for application to real-time systems is also an important criterion. A repository of such algorithms in web-executable format will be helpful for easy analysis and comparison of the developed methods as suggested in (Gargi et al., 2000). The reviews presented in (Sao and Mishra, 2014; Thakre, 2014; Saini and Gupta, 2015; Mittalkod et al., 2011) provide an insight into the challenges faced in this domain of research.

5. PARAMETERS FOR DETECTING GRADUAL TRANSITIONS

There are certain parameters that show distinct characteristics and behaviors when applied to the videos having gradual transitions. Based on these parameters, the gradual transitions can be detected. Some of these parameters have been elaborated in further sub-sections.

5.1. Fuzzy Hostility Index (FHI)

The measure of the amount of homogeneity or heterogeneity of a pixel with its neighborhood is termed as the Fuzzy Hostility Index (Bhattacharyya et al., 2009) of that pixel. In a fuzzy system, all elements have a certain degree of membership to a fuzzy set. A pixel having a gray level value in the range [0, 255] can be mapped to the range [0, 1]. The value in the range [0, 1] denotes the membership of that pixel to the fuzzy set WHITE denoted by μ_p. The degree of homogeneity or heterogeneity in the nth-order neighborhood of a pixel can be enumerated by the fuzzy hostility index (FHI).

The FHI (ζ) of a pixel in its $n-$order neighborhood is given by the following equation:

$$\zeta = \frac{3}{2^{n+1}} \sum_{i=1}^{2^{n+1}} \frac{\left| \mu_p - \mu_{qi} \right|}{\left| \mu_p + 1 \right| + \left| \mu_{qi} + 1 \right|} \tag{1}$$

where μ_p is the fuzzy membership value of the candidate pixel and μ_{qi}; i =1, 2, 3, . . ., 2^{n+1} are the fuzzy membership values of its neighbors in an $n-$order neighborhood. The value of the fuzzy hostility index ζ lies in [0, 1]. Higher value of ζ indicates lower neighborhood homogeneity and lower value of ζ indicates the higher neighborhood homogeneity. If $\zeta = 1$, then heterogeneity is maximum. If $\zeta = 0$ then there is total homogeneity in the neighborhood. The fuzzy hostility map (FHM) is the visual representation of the FHI values of pixels in an image. In a FHM, the edges of objects become prominent because the edges represent heterogeneous regions on an image. The same is illustrated in Figure 8 and Figure 9.

The mean FHI of the images where the gradual transitions are present i.e. the regions of gradual transition are lower than the mean FHI corresponding to pure frames. This is due to the fact that the pixel values are more homogeneous in frames of the dissolve region. The frames have lower contrast than a pure frame. This occurs as more than one image contributes to the gradual transition. If the mean FHI of all the pixels in an image is computed and plotted, then a sharp dip would occur in the regions of gradual transition. The same can be observed in the graph enumerated in Figure 10.

Figure 8. Original image

Figure 9. Fuzzy hostility map

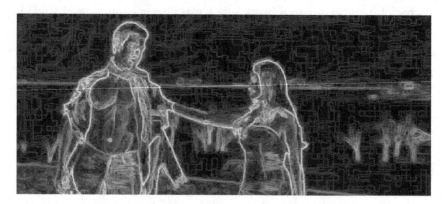

Figure 10. Mean FHI curve showing the dips during gradual transition

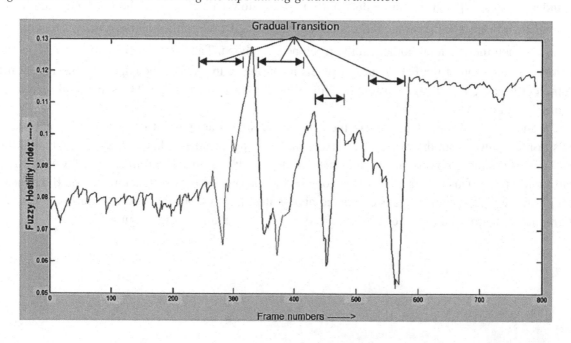

5.2. Edge Change Ratio (ECR)

Edge Change Ratio (Zabih et al., 1999) is a technique which was applied to detect shot boundaries. It takes into account the number of incoming and outgoing edges between each pair of consecutive frames in a video sequence. If the amount of change is greater than a specified threshold, a shot boundary is detected. For determining the ECR between a pair of frames, a number of intermediate steps are followed. The first step involves edge detection of the pair of frames from the gray scale converted image of the original one. The number of edge pixel is counted in the edge detected consecutive frames and are stored as p_{n-1} and p_n. In the next step, dilation is performed on the pair of frames followed by inversion of background. Thereafter AND operation is done between the dilated image of frame f_n and image of frame f_{n-1} obtained after edge detection. The resulting image denotes the outgoing edge pixels. The number of edge pixels is represented by EC_{n-1}^{out}. The same operation is performed between the dilated image of frame f_{n-1} and the image of frame f_n obtained after edge detection. The number of edge pixels in this case is represented by EC_n^{in} which denotes the number of incoming edge pixels. Edge Change Ratio of the frames under consideration is given by the maximum of $\dfrac{EC_{n-1}^{out}}{p_{n-1}}$ and $\dfrac{EC_n^{in}}{p_n}$.

ECR is computed from the following equation:

$$ECR_n = \max\left(ECR_n^{in}, ECR_{n-1}^{out}\right) = \max\left(\frac{\Sigma EC_n^{in}}{\Sigma p_n}, \frac{\Sigma EC_{n-1}^{out}}{\Sigma p_{n-1}}\right) \tag{2}$$

The pictorial representation of the method is given below in Figure 11. The value of ECR is larger at places where a gradual transition effect is present. As the number of edge changes is more at these places due to a combination of two or more images, the ECR is observed to be high.

5.3. Fuzzy Entropy

A measure of the amount of disorder in a system can be termed as entropy (Baber et al., 2011). In case of an 8-bit image, entropy can be defined as the spread of state corresponding to the gray level values which individual pixels can adopt. If an 8-bit pixel is taken into consideration, there are 256 spread of states. If all such states are equally occupied, as in the case of images which have been histogram equalized perfectly, the spread of states is a maximum. The entropy of images in such cases is maximum. On the other hand, if the image has pixel values concentrated on two states, then the entropy is low. If all the pixels have identical values, the entropy of the image is zero. If the entropy of an image decreases the information content of the image also decreases. The information content and the quality of the information content in an image can be computed as the logarithm of the probability of the amount of information conveyed by an image. The average entropy level of dissimilar shots resides at different levels. At the time of a gradual transition in a video, the entropy level shifts from the earlier level (of the disappearing shot) following a parabolic path and stabilizes at the new level (occupied by the appearing shot). This is illustrated in Figure 12. This is due to the fact that there is an increase in disorder in pixel

Figure 11. Steps of edge change ratio

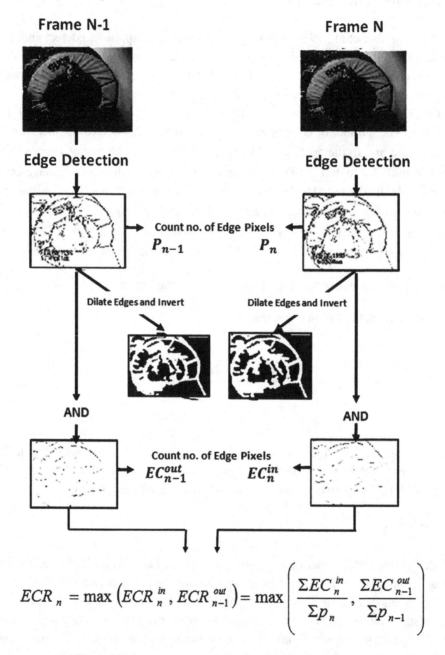

$$ECR_n = \max\left(ECR_n^{in}, ECR_{n-1}^{out}\right) = \max\left(\frac{\Sigma EC_n^{in}}{\Sigma p_n}, \frac{\Sigma EC_{n-1}^{out}}{\Sigma p_{n-1}}\right)$$

values during a dissolve transition which can be attributed to the intermingling of the image fading in and the one fading out. For a set of images participating in a dissolve, the entropy reaches maximum when the images are combined in equal proportions i.e. at the point where the intensity of the frame is exactly midway between the participating frames of the shots. At this point, the visual content portrayed by the frame is minimum.

If the pixel values of a gray scale image are mapped to the range [0, 1] by dividing each of the elements by 255, the values represent the membership of the pixels to two complementary fuzzy sets,

Figure 12. Variation of fuzzy entropy during dissolve sequence

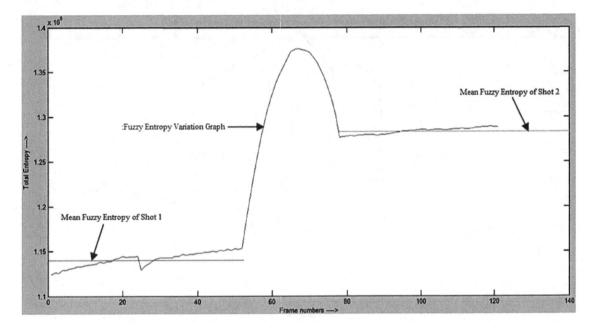

WHITE and *BLACK*. The membership function to *WHITE* is given by μ_W, where $\mu_W = pixelvalue \, / \, 255$. The membership value of *BLACK* is given by $\mu_B = 1 - \mu_W$. The fuzzy entropy (η) of an image having resolution $n \times m$ may be measured by the equation:

$$\eta = \sum_{i=1}^{n} \sum_{j=1}^{m} I(i,j) * \log \frac{1}{I(i,j)} + (1 - I(i,j)) * \log \frac{1}{1 - I(i,j)} \tag{3}$$

where, $I(i,j)$ is the fuzzy value of the pixel at position (i,j) in the fuzzy matrix.

During a dissolve transition, one shot gains prominence over the other. For a time, sequenced set of images obtained after disintegrating a video, the fuzzy entropy plot takes a form which is illustrated in Figure 13. The curve takes a parabolic nature at places where a dissolve transition occurs. The general equation of a 2nd degree curve may be represented as $y = ax^2 + bx + c$. which is useful for detecting candidate dissolve transitions.

5.4. Standard Deviation of Pixel Intensities

A gray scale image can be represented as a 2D matrix consisting of pixel values of an image. In case of a dissolve sequence or any other gradual transition, the matrix is a combination of two or more image matrices. Due to blending of these pixel values, the resultant images have a lower contrast than the original images combined to form such a transition. Thus, the variance of pixel values in the dissolve image is lower than the original images. If the values of standard deviation (Lienhart, 1999) are plotted, it will result in a sharp dip at places which imply the presence of gradual transitions in the video sequence. The same is evident from Figure 14.

Figure 13. Parabolic nature of fuzzy entropy during gradual sequence

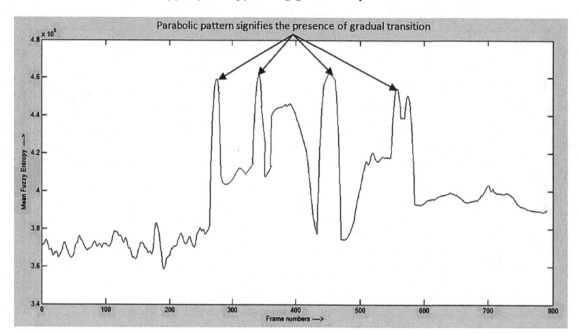

Figure 14. Plot of standard deviation of pixel intensities

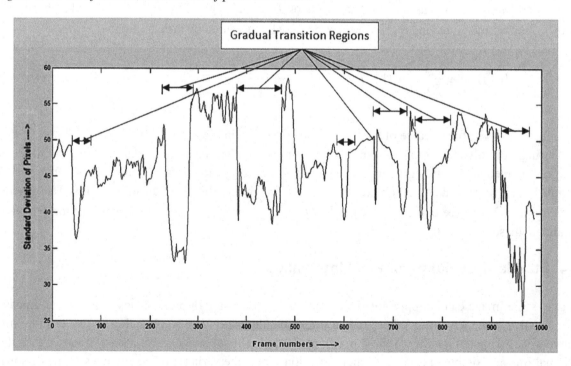

5.5. Count of the Edge Pixels

Edges are basically the line segments or curved line segments formed by set of points. These occur at places of high contrast within an image. These high contrast or high frequency regions usually occur at the boundaries of objects. Edges can also be viewed as places of discontinuity where the pixel neighborhood represents heterogeneity. Detecting such edges by some set of mathematical methods which aim to categorize the set of points in digital images, at which the image intensity changes sharply or has discontinuities, is known as edge detection. Edge detection is a deep-seated tool in image processing. One such edge detector is Canny Edge Detector. Canny Edge Detector (Canny, 1986) is a multi-stage algorithm used to detect a wide range of edges in an image. Canny edge detection algorithm is mainly biased on five steps. Primarily a Gaussian filter is introduced to eradicate the noise in an image and make the image smoother. Thereafter the intensity gradient of the image is determined and non-maximal suppression is applied to get rid of spurious response to edge detection. To determine the potential of edges, double threshold is used, and then the edges are tracked by hysteresis. Lastly, all the edges that are weak and not connected to strong edges are suppressed. Hence the remaining edges are finalized as the result of the Canny edge detection algorithm.

The number of edges will be more in the frames containing dissolve transitions than the pure frames because the dissolve transition frames are formed by the overlapping of two or more frames. Thus, if there is an abrupt change in the number of edge pixels in a sequence of frames, then it becomes a candidate for dissolve transition.

6. PITFALLS OF PARAMETERS IN DETECTING GRADUAL TRANSITIONS

The parameters enumerated in section 5 show distinct characteristics for enabling the detection of dissolve transition sequences. These parameters are useful in detecting dissolve sequences to a limited extent. The problems in relying on a single parameter are multi-fold. Although a parameter can provide an indicative pattern for a candidate dissolve, the precision level may fall due to false alarms in different situations. Also the problem of providing a decent threshold automatically is a major problem. The further subsections discuss some cases where false detection is possible due to different situations.

6.1 False Detection of Gradual Transition Based On Standard Deviation of Pixels

As discussed in section 5.4, the standard deviation of pixel values corresponding to the frames in a video falls due to presence of dissolve transitions as contrast of the frames decreases. However, there are cases where this property may lead to false detection. Figure 15 and Figure 16 depict an example of a false positive from the video "What's love got to do with it" by Tina Turner where the standard deviation value dips due to a close-up on the hair portion of the singer. Since most pixels have nearly the same value, so a fall in the standard deviation value of the pixel intensities triggers a dip in the plot.

Figure 15. Sequence from Tina Turner video

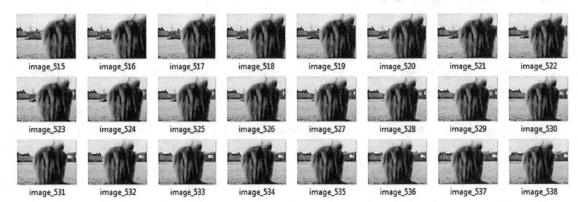

Figure 16. Standard deviation of pixel intensities dip during sequence in Figure 15

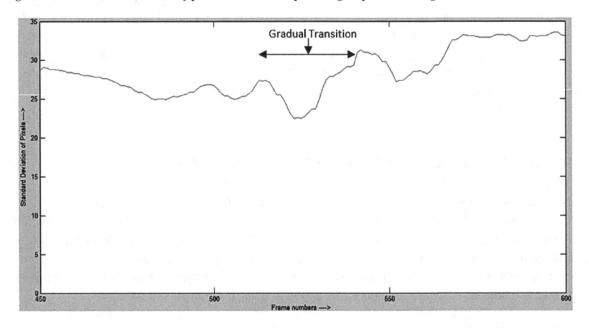

6.2 False Detection of Gradual Transition Based On Count of Edge Pixels

The number of edges increases during the occurrence of a gradual transition due to the combination of multiple images during a video sequence. Although this concept is found to be true for most video sequences, there are incidences of it being false. The false detection can occur due to various reasons. Such a false positive is demonstrated from the video "What's love got to do with it" by Tina Turner. The sequence shown in Figure 17 portrays such a situation where the number of edges rises rapidly due to appearance of buildings in the background. The rise in the number of edges and edge pixels thereof is attributed to the emergence of the various structural composites of the buildings in the scene. The graph plotted for the number of edges against the frame numbers is shown in Figure 18.

Figure 17. Sequence from Tina Turner video

Figure 18. Rise in number of edges during sequence of Figure 17

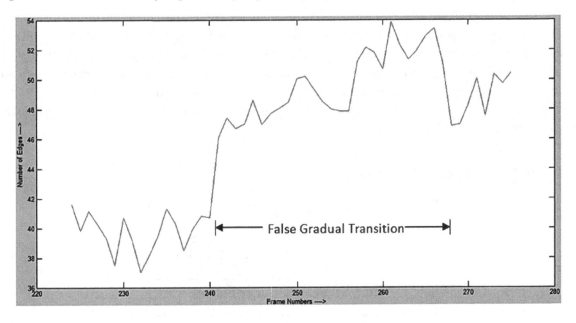

7. PROPOSED METHOD

In this section, a method for detection of dissolve sequences is elaborated. The concept used here is to employ a sequence of filters based on various low-level parameters extracted from the video sequence. In order to achieve high accuracy, a two-phased approach is used. The main target in the first phase is to increase the recall to 1 without being concerned about the precision of detection. Achieving a good recall ensures that all dissolve sequences are identified along with few other candidates which may not be legal dissolve sequences. The second phase involves an ensemble of filters which serve to eliminate the spurious dissolve sequences which were introduced in the first phase. Based on a particular low-level parameter, each filter is designed to remove fake dissolve sequences introduced in Phase 1. Thus, the second phase serves to increase precision without sacrificing recall. The design of the filters in the second phase is such that each filter employs a very conservative threshold. This ensures that after each filtration stage some of the spurious dissolve sequences that were introduced in the first phase are eliminated progressively after each filtration stage. Hence, the precision of the system improves after each stage of filtration without affecting the high recall achieved in the first phase. The two-phased dissolve detection approach is elaborated in further subsections.

7.1 First Phase

Initially, videos are fragmented into frames by means of a codec. As explained in section 5.3, the fuzzy entropy of the time sequenced frames is computed individually. The fuzzy entropy sequence generated from the frames is then analyzed for detecting parabolic sequences. A parabola is a second degree polynomial characterized by two properties:

The gradient on the curve (dy / dx) decreases monotonically as the curve is traversed in a direction of increasing x.

The change of gradient (d^2y / dx^2) is negative all along the curve in the direction of increasing x.

The above two properties are tested for the fuzzy entropy sequence. This helps in detecting all the dissolve sequences present in the video. However, there may be many false positives which may be introduced in this stage. The main target here is to include all the dissolve transitions even though all identified sequences may not be correct. These are termed as "candidate dissolves". In Figure 19, the flow of Phase 1 is enumerated. The output of Phase 1 is given as input to Phase 2, i.e the "candidate dissolves" are filtered in Phase 2.

Figure 19. Flow diagram of the first phase

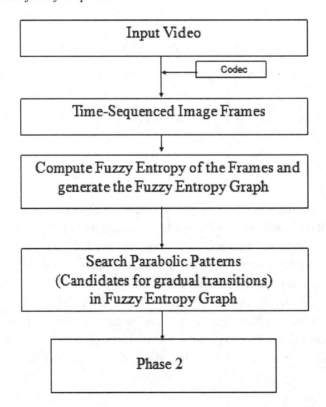

7.2 Second Phase

The second phase is the filtration stage for elimination of sequences which were wrongly identified as dissolves. This phase consists of four stages and each stage is based on a particular parameter. The four parameters which are considered include number of edge pixels, fuzzy hostility index, standard deviation of pixel intensities and edge change ratio. The purpose of this phase is to improve the precision at each stage of filtration. It is pertinent to mention here that if the true positives are filtered out unintentionally, it would lead to a fall in the recall value. The target of this phase is to curtail the false positive caused due to the first phase, as far as possible. The flow diagram of phase two is shown in Figure 20.

7.2.1 Filtration and Elimination Using Edge Detector

Edge detection is performed on the time sequenced image frames of the video by a Canny Edge Detector as explained in section 5.5. The number of edges increases abruptly during a dissolve transition. For

Figure 20. Flow diagram of Phase 2 of the proposed method

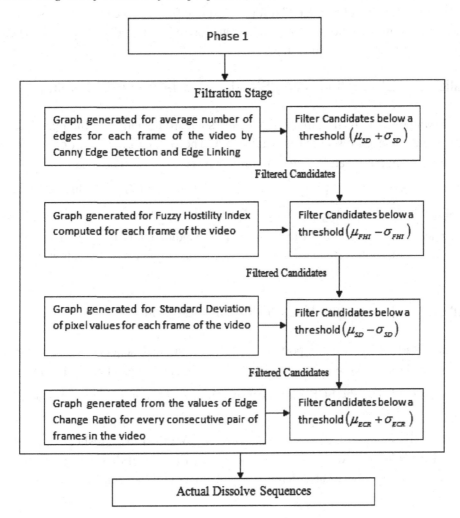

computing the threshold, the mean (μ_{ED}) and standard deviation (σ_{ED}) of the number of edges over all frames is computed. In this work, a low threshold has been selected at every stage of the filtration process to ensure that the true dissolve candidates are not eliminated. At the same time, it is ensured that the precision value increases as the selected candidates pass each stage of the filtration process. As each dissolve candidate is a collection of frame numbers, the values corresponding to each frame are tested against the threshold $\left(\mu_{ED} + \sigma_{ED}\right)$. A dissolve candidate is eliminated if none of the values corresponding to the frames in it cross the threshold.

7.2.2 Filtration and Elimination Using Fuzzy Hostility Index

The candidate dissolve sequences which pass the previous stage are fed into this stage. The average fuzzy hostility index is computed for all frames and stored in a row matrix (M_{FHI}). The mean (μ_{FHI}) and standard deviation (σ_{FHI}) of the values in M_{FHI} is calculated for determining the threshold. As explained in section 5.1, the average FHI value of the frames in the gradual transition region is lower than pure frames. Hence, in this stage, the threshold taken is $\left(\mu_{FHI} - \sigma_{FHI}\right)$. It may be seen that such a threshold is very conservative and value of average FHI for at least one frame of a candidate dissolve region must be equal or lower than this threshold in order to be categorized as a gradual transition. The candidates which do not meet the criteria are eliminated.

7.2.3 Filtration and Elimination Using Standard Deviation of Pixel Values

Due to multiple frames participating in a dissolve, the standard deviation of the pixel intensity values decrease. The same has been discussed in section 5.4. The standard deviation of the pixel intensity values for each frame in the video is stored in a row matrix $\left(M_{STD}\right)$. The mean $\left(\mu_{STD}\right)$ and standard deviation $\left(\sigma_{STD}\right)$ of the values in $\left(M_{STD}\right)$ is computed for determining the threshold. The threshold taken in this stage of filtration is $\left(\mu_{STD} - \sigma_{STD}\right)$. The candidates of dissolve transition filtered from the earlier stage are fed into this stage for further filtration. A candidate for dissolve transition is eliminated if no frame of the candidate has standard deviation of the pixel intensity values lower than or equal to $\left(\mu_{STD} - \sigma_{STD}\right)$.

7.2.4 Filtration and Elimination Using Edge Change Ratio

The Edge Change Ratio (ECR) is an important indicator for dissolve sequences as explained in section 5.2. During a gradual transition sequence, the ECR plot shows an abrupt change. The mean $\left(\mu_{ECR}\right)$ and standard deviation $\left(\sigma_{ECR}\right)$ of the ECR for successive frames of the video are computed. The dissolve candidates filtered from the earlier stage are tested against a threshold $\left(\mu_{ECR} + \sigma_{ECR}\right)$. If the ECR value for any two successive frames of a candidate dissolve is more than the threshold, it is retained in the candidate list, else eliminated. At the end of this stage, the final set of dissolve sequences is obtained. The final set of dissolve sequences are such that all members in it have passed the threshold levels set for the different parameters.

8. EXPERIMENTAL RESULTS AND ANALYSIS

The proposed method for gradual transition detection was tested on a video data set consisting of eight videos. The source code for the proposed method was written using MATLAB. The characteristics of the data set are given in Table I. All the videos in the dataset are in MP4 file format (ISO/IEC 14496-14:2003), commonly named as MPEG-4 file format version 2. For evaluating the performance of the proposed method, recall (*R*) and precision (*P*) are computed as follows:

$$\text{Recall} = (D_d - D_f) / D_t$$

$$\text{Precision} = (D_d - D_f) / D_d$$

where,

D_d : Dissolve sequences detected by algorithm.

D_f : False dissolve sequences detected.

D_t : Actual dissolve sequences present in the video.

The above two parameters are also taken to evaluate the performance of the proposed method to the existing methods.

8.1 The Video Dataset

Out of the eight videos in the dataset, V1 is a highlights video of a Wimbledon tennis match. The videos labeled V2-V6 are Hindi movie songs. The dataset also contains two documentary videos V7 and V8. Originally these videos contained mostly abrupt transitions (hard cuts). To test the robustness of the proposed method, dissolve sequences of various lengths were introduced into the videos at places where hard cuts originally existed. The details of the dataset are given in Table 1.

8.2 Experimental Results

The proposed method for dissolve detection is a two-phased method in which the first phase is used for parabolic pattern detection. The candidates detected in the first phase are filtered out based on threshold fixed for different parameters. The number of candidates detected in the first stage and filtered in the next stage is enumerated in Table 2. Further, Table 3 shows the details of precision and recall values obtained by running the algorithm on the videos of the test set. The span of the dissolve detected by the algorithm is within an error range of one frame on either side of the dissolve span.

8.3 Comparison with Other Existing Methods

The proposed method for dissolve detection was compared with three other existing methods like Edge Change Ratio (ECR) (Qi et al., 2010), Entropy and Local Descriptor (ELD) (Hanjalic,2002) and Edge-

Table 1. Test video dataset

Video	Length (mm:ss)	Resolution	FPS	No. of Frames	No. of Dissolves Sequences
V1	02:58	640 × 360	25	4468	43
V2	02:42	640 × 360	25	4057	70
V3	04:10	640 × 360	25	6265	172
V4	03:27	640 × 360	25	4965	77
V5	03:31	640 × 360	25	5053	138
V6	05:58	1280 × 544	24	8602	83
V7	51:20	640 × 360	25	74020	941
V8	44:14	480 × 360	25	66339	626

Table 2. Results on test video dataset

Video	Actual Dissolves Sequences	Parabolic Patterns Detected (1st Phase)	Dissolves Detected after Filtration Phase	Correct Detections	False Alarms
V1	43	666	46	43	3
V2	70	1449	76	68	8
V3	172	2751	177	170	7
V4	77	2154	81	75	6
V5	138	1922	135	133	2
V6	83	2573	89	82	7
V7	941	1876	952	939	13
V8	626	11146	633	625	8

Table 3. Recall and precision

Video	Actual Dissolves Sequences	Correct Detections	False Alarms	Recall	Precision
V1	43	43	3	1.0	0.934
V2	70	68	8	0.971	0.894
V3	172	170	7	0.988	0.960
V4	77	75	6	0.974	0.926
V5	138	133	2	0.963	0.985
V6	83	82	7	0.988	0.921
V7	941	939	13	0.997	0.986
V8	626	625	8	0.998	0.987

Table 4. Comparison with other methods

Video	ECR		ELD		EC		Proposed Method	
	R	P	R	P	R	P	R	P
V1	0.71	0.55	0.81	0.76	0.58	0.43	**1.0**	**0.93**
V2	0.54	0.63	0.76	0.64	0.62	0.56	**0.97**	**0.89**
V3	0.75	0.81	0.89	0.80	0.79	0.68	**0.98**	**0.96**
V4	0.44	0.41	0.92	0.87	0.46	0.32	**0.97**	**0.92**
V5	0.69	0.87	0.85	0.79	0.53	0.70	**0.96**	**0.98**
V6	0.59	0.51	0.94	0.91	0.62	0.46	**0.98**	**0.92**
V7	0.62	0.73	0.72	0.62	0.68	0.61	**0.99**	**0.98**
V8	0.56	0.76	0.81	0.77	0.70	0.55	**0.99**	**0.98**

based Contrast (EC) (Miene *et al.*, 2003). For each of the existing methods, the recall and precision values are computed for videos in the dataset. The proposed method is seen to outperform all the existing methods compared. A summary of the comparison is shown in Table 4.

9. CONCLUSION

Detection of dissolve transitions involve a lot of complexity because of the inherent structure of these edit effects. Although the method discussed here was seen to work well for detection of dissolves involving two shots, it is yet to be tested on transitions involving more than two shots. The method was seen to outperform traditional methods used for dissolve detection. As this method uses an ensemble of low-level features, the time taken for execution is relatively high. The method in its present form is not suitable for application in real-time systems. Detection of gradual transitions still remains an area of research as the methods developed do not show consistent performance for all types of video. As detection of edit effects has a great impact on the overall advances in the domain of video analysis, therefore research in this field will continue for some time to come.

REFERENCES

Abdelali, A. B., Nidhal Krifa, M., Touil, L., Mtibaa, A., & Bourennane, E. (2009). A study of the color-structure descriptor for shot boundary detection. *International Journal of Sciences and Techniques of Automatic control and computer engineering*, 956-971.

Abdeljaoued, Y., Ebrahimi, T., Christopoulos, C., & Ivars, I. M. (2000, September). A new algorithm for shot boundary detection.*Proceedings of the 10th European Signal Processing Conference* (pp. 151-154). SPIE.

Apostolidis, E., & Mezaris, V. (2014, May). Fast shot segmentation combining global and local visual descriptors. *Proceedings of 2014 IEEE International Conference on Acoustics, Speech and Signal Processing (ICASSP)* (pp. 6583-6587). IEEE. doi:10.1109/ICASSP.2014.6854873

Baber, J., Afzulpurkar, N., Dailey, M. N., & Bakhtyar, M. (2011, July). Shot boundary detection from videos using entropy and local descriptor. *Proceedings of the 2011 17th International Conference on Digital Signal Processing (DSP)* (pp. 1-6). IEEE. doi:10.1109/ICDSP.2011.6004918

Bai, L., Lao, S. Y., Liu, H. T., & Bu, J. (2008, July). Video shot boundary detection using petri-net. *Proceedings of the 2008 International Conference on Machine Learning and Cybernetics* (Vol. 5, pp. 3047-3051). IEEE.

Bao, Z., Han, B., & Wu, S. (2006). A novel clustering algorithm based on variable precision rough-fuzzy sets. In *Computational Intelligence* (pp. 284–289). Springer Berlin Heidelberg. doi:10.1007/978-3-540-37275-2_36

Barbu, T. (2009). Novel automatic video cut detection technique using Gabor filtering. *Computers & Electrical Engineering*, *35*(5), 712–721. doi:10.1016/j.compeleceng.2009.02.003

Barron, J. L., Fleet, D. J., & Beauchemin, S. S. (1994). Performance of optical flow techniques. *International Journal of Computer Vision*, *12*(1), 43–77. doi:10.1007/BF01420984

Bay, H., Ess, A., Tuytelaars, T., & Van Gool, L. (2008). Speeded-up robust features (SURF). *Computer Vision and Image Understanding*, *110*(3), 346–359. doi:10.1016/j.cviu.2007.09.014

Bescós, J., Cisneros, G., Martínez, J. M., Menéndez, J. M., & Cabrera, J. (2005). A unified model for techniques on video-shot transition detection. *IEEE Transactions on* Multimedia, *7*(2), 293–307.

Bhattacharyya, S., Maulik, U., & Dutta, P. (2009). High-speed target tracking by fuzzy hostility-induced segmentation of optical flow field. *Applied Soft Computing*, *9*(1), 126–134. doi:10.1016/j.asoc.2008.03.012

Bhaumik, H., Bhattacharyya, S., & Chakraborty, S. (2014, April). Video Shot Segmentation Using Spatio-Temporal Fuzzy Hostility Index and Automatic Threshold. *Proceedings of the 2014 Fourth International Conference on Communication Systems and Network Technologies (CSNT)* (pp. 501-506). IEEE. doi:10.1109/CSNT.2014.106

Boccignone, G., Chianese, A., Moscato, V., & Picariello, A. (2005). Foveated shot detection for video segmentation. *IEEE Transactions on* Circuits and Systems for Video Technology, *15*(3), 365–377.

Boreczky, J. S., & Wilcox, L. D. (1998, May). A hidden Markov model framework for video segmentation using audio and image features. *Proceedings of the 1998 IEEE International Conference onAcoustics, Speech and Signal Processing* (Vol. 6, pp. 3741-3744). IEEE. doi:10.1109/ICASSP.1998.679697

Calonder, M., Lepetit, V., Strecha, C., & Fua, P. (2010). Brief: Binary robust independent elementary features. *Computer Vision–ECCV*, *2010*, 778–792.

Canny, J. (1986). A computational approach to edge detection. *IEEE Transactions on Pattern Analysis and Machine Intelligence*, (6), 679-698.

Černeková, Z., Pitas, I., & Nikou, C. (2006). Information theory-based shot cut/fade detection and video summarization. *IEEE Transactions on* Circuits and Systems for Video Technology, *16*(1), 82–91.

Chan, C., & Alexander, W. (2011). Shot boundary detection using genetic algorithm optimization. *Proceedings of the 2011 IEEE International Symposium on Multimedia (ISM)* (pp. 327-332). IEEE. doi:10.1109/ISM.2011.58

Chasanis, V., Likas, A., & Galatsanos, N. (2009). Simultaneous detection of abrupt cuts and dissolves in videos using support vector machines. *Pattern Recognition Letters, 30*(1), 55–65. doi:10.1016/j.patrec.2008.08.015

Chavez, G. C., Precioso, F., Cord, M., Philipp-Foliguet, S., & Araujo, A. D. A. (2006). Shot boundary detection at TRECVID 2006.*Proc. TREC Video Retrieval Evaluation.*

Chiu, P., Girgensohn, A., Polak, W., Rieffel, E., & Wilcox, L. (2000). A genetic algorithm for video segmentation and summarization. *Proceedings of the 2000 IEEE International Conference on Multimedia and Expo ICME '00* (Vol. 3, pp. 1329-1332). IEEE. doi:10.1109/ICME.2000.871011

Donate, A., & Liu, X. (2010, June). Shot boundary detection in videos using robust three-dimensional tracking. *Proceedings of the 2010 IEEE Computer Society Conference on Computer Vision and Pattern Recognition Workshops (CVPRW)* (pp. 64-69). IEEE. doi:10.1109/CVPRW.2010.5543811

Drew, M. S., Li, Z. N., & Zhong, X. (2000). Video dissolve and wipe detection via spatio-temporal images of chromatic histogram differences. *Proceedings of the 2000 International Conference on Image Processing* (Vol. 3, pp. 929-932). IEEE. doi:10.1109/ICIP.2000.899609

Fang, H., Jiang, J., & Feng, Y. (2006). A fuzzy logic approach for detection of video shot boundaries. *Pattern Recognition, 39*(11), 2092–2100. doi:10.1016/j.patcog.2006.04.044

Gao, X., & Tang, X. (2002). Unsupervised video-shot segmentation and model-free anchorperson detection for news video story parsing. *IEEE Transactions on* Circuits and Systems for Video Technology, *12*(9), 765–776.

Gao, X. B., Han, B., & Ji, H. B. (2005). A shot boundary detection method for news video based on rough sets and fuzzy clustering. In *Image Analysis and Recognition* (pp. 231–238). Springer Berlin Heidelberg.

Gargi, U., Kasturi, R., & Strayer, S. H. (2000). Performance characterization of video-shot-change detection methods. *IEEE Transactions on* Circuits and Systems for Video Technology, *10*(1), 1–13.

Geetha, M. K., & Palanivel, S. (2012). Unsupervised Approach for Retrieving Shots from Video. *International Journal of Computers and Applications, 60*(6).

Grana, C., & Cucchiara, R. (2007). Linear transition detection as a unified shot detection approach. *IEEE Transactions on Circuits and Systems for Video Technology, 17*(4), 483–489. doi:10.1109/TC-SVT.2006.888818

Hanjalic, A. (2002). Shot-boundary detection: Unraveled and resolved? *IEEE Transactions on* Circuits and Systems for Video Technology, *12*(2), 90–105.

Hsu, C. F., Ku, M. K., & Liu, L. Y. (2009, September). Support vector machine FPGA implementation for video shot boundary detection application. *Proceedings of theIEEE InternationalSOC Conference SOCC '09* (pp. 239-242). IEEE. doi:10.1109/SOCCON.2009.5398049

Hu, W., Xie, N., Li, L., Zeng, X., & Maybank, S. (2011). A survey on visual content-based video indexing and retrieval. *IEEE Transactions on* Systems, Man, and Cybernetics, Part C: Applications and Reviews, *41*(6), 797–819.

Ionescu, B., Vertan, C., & Lambert, P. (2011, May). Dissolve detection in abstract video contents. *Proceedings of the 2011 IEEE International Conference on Acoustics, Speech and Signal Processing (ICASSP)* (pp. 917-920). IEEE. doi:10.1109/ICASSP.2011.5946554

Jadon, R. S., Chaudhury, S., & Biswas, K. K. (2001). A fuzzy theoretic approach for video segmentation using syntactic features. *Pattern Recognition Letters, 22*(13), 1359–1369. doi:10.1016/S0167-8655(01)00041-1

Ji, Q. G., Feng, J. W., Zhao, J., & Lu, Z. M. (2010, September). Effective dissolve detection based on accumulating histogram difference and the support point. *Proceedings of the 2010 First International Conference on Pervasive Computing Signal Processing and Applications (PCSPA)* (pp. 273-276). IEEE. doi:10.1109/PCSPA.2010.73

Joyce, R. A., & Liu, B. (2006). Temporal segmentation of video using frame and histogram space. *IEEE Transactions on* Multimedia, *8*(1), 130–140.

Kawai, Y., Sumiyoshi, H., & Yagi, N. (2007, November). Shot Boundary Detection at TRECVID 2007. Proceedings of TRECVID '07.

Koprinska, I., & Carrato, S. (2001). Temporal video segmentation: A survey. *Signal Processing Image Communication, 16*(5), 477–500. doi:10.1016/S0923-5965(00)00011-4

Koumousis, K. I., Fotopoulos, V., & Skodras, A. N. (2012, October). A new approach to gradual video transition detection. *Proceedings of the 2012 16th Panhellenic Conference on Informatics* (pp. 245-249). IEEE. doi:10.1109/PCi.2012.85

Küçüktunç, O., Güdükbay, U., & Ulusoy, Ö. (2010). Fuzzy color histogram-based video segmentation. *Computer Vision and Image Understanding, 114*(1), 125–134. doi:10.1016/j.cviu.2009.09.008

Kundu, M. K., & Mondal, J. (2012, December). A novel technique for automatic abrupt shot transition detection. *Proceedings of the 2012 International Conference on Communications, Devices and Intelligent Systems (CODIS)* (pp. 628-631). IEEE. doi:10.1109/CODIS.2012.6422281

Lefèvre, S., Holler, J., & Vincent, N. (2003). A review of real-time segmentation of uncompressed video sequences for content-based search and retrieval. *Real-Time Imaging, 9*(1), 73–98. doi:10.1016/S1077-2014(02)00115-8

Li, B., & Sezan, M. I. (2001). Event detection and summarization in sports video. *Proceedings of the IEEE Workshop on Content-Based Access of Image and Video Libraries (CBAIVL '01)* (pp. 132-138). IEEE. doi:10.1109/IVL.2001.990867

Li, F., Kim, T., Humayun, A., Tsai, D., & Rehg, J. (2013). Video segmentation by tracking many figure-ground segments. *Proceedings of the IEEE International Conference on Computer Vision* (pp. 2192-2199). doi:10.1109/ICCV.2013.273

Li, J., Ding, Y., Shi, Y., & Zeng, Q. (2009, August). DWT-based shot boundary detection using support vector machine. *Proceedings of the Fifth International Conference on Information Assurance and Security IAS'09* (Vol. 1, pp. 435-438). IEEE. doi:10.1109/IAS.2009.16

Lienhart, R. W. (1999). Comparison of automatic shot boundary detection algorithms. *Proc. of SPIE Conf. Image and Video Processing VII*, (pp. 290-301).

Lienhart, R. W. (2001, January). Reliable dissolve detection. In Photonics West 2001-Electronic Imaging (pp. 219-230). International Society for Optics and Photonics.

Ling, X., Yuanxin, O., Huan, L., & Zhang, X. (2008, May). A method for fast shot boundary detection based on SVM. Proceedings of the Congress on Image and Signal Processing CISP'08 (Vol. 2, pp. 445-449). IEEE. doi:10.1109/CISP.2008.605

Liu, S., Zhu, M., & Zheng, Q. (2008, October). Video shot boundary detection with local feature post refinement. *Proceedings of the 9th International Conference on Signal Processing ICSP '08* (pp. 1548-1551). IEEE.

Liu, T. Y., Lo, K. T., Zhang, X. D., & Feng, J. (2004). A new cut detection algorithm with constant false-alarm ratio for video segmentation. *Journal of Visual Communication and Image Representation*, *15*(2), 132–144. doi:10.1016/j.jvcir.2003.10.001

Liu, X., & Chen, T. (2002, May). Shot boundary detection using temporal statistics modeling. *Proceedings of the 2002 IEEE International Conference on Acoustics, Speech, and Signal Processing (ICASSP)* (Vol. 4, pp. IV-3389). IEEE. doi:10.1109/ICASSP.2002.5745381

Lowe, D. G. (1999). Object recognition from local scale-invariant features. *Proceedings of the seventh IEEE international conference on Computer vision* (Vol. 2, pp. 1150-1157). IEEE. doi:10.1109/ICCV.1999.790410

Lu, Z. M., & Shi, Y. (2013). Fast video shot boundary detection based on SVD and pattern matching. *IEEE Transactions on* Image Processing, *22*(12), 5136–5145.

Ma, C., Yu, J., & Huang, B. (2012). A rapid and robust method for shot boundary detection and classification in uncompressed MPEG video sequences. *Int. J. Comput. Sci. Issues, 5*, 368-374.

Mahesh, K., & Kuppusamy, K. (2012). A New Hybrid Algorithm for Video Segmentation. In *Advances in Computer Science, Engineering & Applications* (pp. 587–595). Springer Berlin Heidelberg. doi:10.1007/978-3-642-30157-5_59

Manjunath, S., Guru, D. S., Suraj, M. G., & Harish, B. S. (2011, March). A non parametric shot boundary detection: an eigen gap based approach.*Proceedings of the Fourth Annual ACM Bangalore Conference* (p. 14). ACM. doi:10.1145/1980422.1980436

Meng, Y., Wang, L. G., & Mao, L. Z. (2009, July). A shot boundary detection algorithm based on particle swarm optimization classifier. *Proceedings of the 2009 International Conference on Machine Learning and Cybernetics,* (Vol. 3, pp. 1671-1676). IEEE. doi:10.1109/ICMLC.2009.5212297

Mich, O., Brunelli, R., & Modena, C. M. (1999). A survey on the automatic indexing of video data. *Journal of Visual Communication and Image Representation*, *10*(2), 78–112. doi:10.1006/jvci.1997.0404

Miene, A., Hermes, T., Ioannidis, G. T., & Herzog, O. (2003, November). Automatic shot boundary detection using adaptive thresholds.*Proc. TRECVID Workshop* (pp. 1-7).

Mittalkod, S. P., & Srinivasan, G. N. (2011). Shot Boundary Detection Algorithms and Techniques: A Review. *International Journal of Computer System Engineering*.

Nam, J., & Tewfik, A. H. (2005). Detection of gradual transitions in video sequences using b-spline interpolation. *Multimedia. IEEE Transactions on, 7*(4), 667–679.

Naranjo, V., Angulo, J., Albiol, A., Mossi, J. M., Albiol, A., & Gomez, S. (2007). Gradual transition detection for video partitioning using morphological operators. *Image Analysis & Stereology, 26*(2), 51–61. doi:10.5566/ias.v26.p51-61

Ngo, C.-W. (2003). A robust dissolve detector by support vector machine.*Proceedings of the eleventh ACM international conference on Multimedia*. ACM. doi:10.1145/957013.957072

Oliva, A., & Torralba, A. (2001). Modeling the shape of the scene: A holistic representation of the spatial envelope. *International Journal of Computer Vision, 42*(3), 145–175. doi:10.1023/A:1011139631724

Patel, B. V., & Meshram, B. B. (2012). *Content based video retrieval systems*. arXiv preprint arXiv:1205.1641

Patel, U., Shah, P., & Panchal, P. (2013). Shot Detection Using Pixel wise Difference with Adaptive Threshold and Color Histogram Method in Compressed and Uncompressed Video. *International Journal of Computers and Applications, 64*(4).

Poleg, Y., Arora, C., & Peleg, S. (2014). Temporal segmentation of egocentric videos.*Proceedings of the IEEE Conference on Computer Vision and Pattern Recognition* (pp. 2537-2544).

Porter, S. V., Mirmehdi, M., & Thomas, B. T. (2001, September). *Detection and Classification of Shot Transitions*. BMVC.

Priya, G., & Domnic, S. (2012). Transition detection using Hilbert transform and texture features. *American J. of Signal Proc., 10*, 35–40. doi:10.5923/j.ajsp.20120202.06

Qi, Y., Hauptmann, A., & Liu, T. (2003, July). Supervised classification for video shot segmentation. *Proceedings of the 2003 International Conference on Multimedia and Expo ICME'03* (Vol. 2, pp. II-689). IEEE.

Qin, T., Gu, J., Chen, H., & Tang, Z. (2010, September). A fast shot-boundary detection based on k-step slipped window. *Proceedings of the 2010 2nd IEEE International Conference on Network Infrastructure and Digital Content* (pp. 190-195). IEEE. doi:10.1109/ICNIDC.2010.5657841

Rao, P. C., & Patnaik, M. R. (2014). Contourlet Transform Based Shot Boundary Detection. *International Journal of Signal Processing. Image Processing and Pattern Recognition, 7*(4), 381–388. doi:10.14257/ijsip.2014.7.4.36

Rong, J., Ma, Y. F., & Wu, L. (2005, January). Gradual transition detection using em curve fitting. *Proceedings of the 11th InternationalMultimedia Modelling Conference MMM '05*(pp. 364-369). IEEE.

Saini, S., & Gupta, P. (2015). Video Shot Boundary Detection Using Various Techniques. *International Journal of Emerging Technologies and Innovative Research*, 2(4), 1109–1115.

Sao, N., & Mishra, R. (2014). A survey based on video shot boundary detection techniques. *International Journal of Advanced Research in Computer and Communication Engineering*, 3(4).

Šarić, M., Dujmić, H., & Baričević, D. (2008). Shot boundary detection in soccer video using twin-comparison algorithm and dominant color region. *Journal of Information and Organizational Sciences*, 32(1), 67–73.

Shen, S., & Cao, J. (2011, March). Abrupt shot boundary detection algorithm based on fuzzy clustering neural network. *Proceedings of the 2011 3rd International Conference on Computer Research and Development.*

Shirahama, K., Matsuoka, Y., & Uehara, K. (2012). Event retrieval in video archives using rough set theory and partially supervised learning. *Multimedia Tools and Applications*, 57(1), 145–173. doi:10.1007/s11042-011-0727-z

Song, S. M., Kwon, T. H., Kim, W. M., Kim, H., & Rhee, B. D. (1997, December). Detection of gradual scene changes for parsing of video data. In Photonics West'98 Electronic Imaging (pp. 404-413). International Society for Optics and Photonics.

Sowmya, R., & Shettar, R. (2013). Analysis and verification of video summarization using shot boundary detection. *Am Int J Res Sci Technol Eng Math*, 3(1), 82–86.

Su, C. W., Liao, H. Y. M., Tyan, H. R., Fan, K. C., & Chen, L. H. (2005). A motion-tolerant dissolve detection algorithm. *IEEE Transactions on* Multimedia, 7(6), 1106–1113.

Sun, X., Zhang, Y., Hao, X., & Min, W. (2014). Shot Boundary Detection Based on SVM Optimization Model. *Open Automation and Control Systems Journal*, 6(1), 393–397. doi:10.2174/1874444301406010393

Sun, X., Zhao, L., & Zhang, M. (2011, August). A Novel Shot Boundary Detection Method Based on Genetic Algorithm-Support Vector Machine. *Proceedings of the 2011 International Conference on Intelligent Human-Machine Systems and Cybernetics (IHMSC)* (Vol. 1, pp. 144-147). IEEE. doi:10.1109/IHMSC.2011.41

Tariq, A., Flail, N., & Ghazi, A. (2014). Using Daub achy Wavelet for Shot Boundary Detection. *IOSR Journals*, 1(16), 66–70.

Thakare, S. (2012). Intelligent processing and analysis of image for shot boundary detection. *International Journal of Emerging Technology and Advanced Engineering*, 2(2), 208–212.

Thakre, K. S. (2014). Analysis and Review of Formal Approaches to Automatic Video Shot Boundary Detection. *Analysis*, 3(1).

Tola, E., Lepetit, V., & Fua, P. (2010). Daisy: An efficient dense descriptor applied to wide-baseline stereo. *IEEE Transactions on* Pattern Analysis and Machine Intelligence, 32(5), 815–830.

Truong, B. T., Dorai, C., & Venkatesh, S. (2000, October). New enhancements to cut, fade, and dissolve detection processes in video segmentation.*Proceedings of the eighth ACM international conference on Multimedia* (pp. 219-227). ACM. doi:10.1145/354384.354481

Tsamoura, E., Mezaris, V., & Kompatsiaris, I. (2008a, October). Gradual transition detection using color coherence and other criteria in a video shot meta-segmentation framework. *Proceedings of the 15th IEEE International Conference on Image Processing ICIP '08* (pp. 45-48). IEEE. doi:10.1109/ICIP.2008.4711687

Tsamoura, E., Mezaris, V., & Kompatsiaris, I. (2008b, June). Video shot meta-segmentation based on multiple criteria for gradual transition detection. *Proceedings of the International Workshop on Content-Based Multimedia Indexing CBMI '08* (pp. 51-57). IEEE. doi:10.1109/CBMI.2008.4564927

Volkmer, T., Tahaghoghi, S. M., & Williams, H. E. (2004, June). Gradual transition detection using average frame similarity. *Proceedings of theConference onComputer Vision and Pattern Recognition Workshop CVPRW'04* (pp. 139-139). IEEE. doi:10.1109/CVPR.2004.357

Wang, T., Wu, Y., & Chen, L. (2007, April). An approach to video key-frame extraction based on rough set. *Proceedings of the International Conference on Multimedia and Ubiquitous Engineering MUE'07* (pp. 590-596). IEEE. doi:10.1109/MUE.2007.65

Xiong, W., Lee, C. M., & Ma, R. H. (1997). Automatic video data structuring through shot partitioning and key-frame computing. *Machine Vision and Applications, 10*(2), 51–65. doi:10.1007/s001380050059

Yasira Beevi, C. P., & Natarajan, S. (2009). *An efficient video segmentation algorithm with real time adaptive threshold technique.* Citeseer.

Yoo, H. W., Ryoo, H. J., & Jang, D. S. (2006). Gradual shot boundary detection using localized edge blocks. *Multimedia Tools and Applications, 28*(3), 283–300. doi:10.1007/s11042-006-7715-8

Yu, F., Lu, Z., & Li, Y. (2011). Dissolve detection based on twin-comparison with curve fitting. *International Journal of Innovative Computing, Information, & Control, 7,* 2417–2426.

Yuan, J., Li, J., & Zhang, B. (2007, September). Gradual transition detection with conditional random fields.*Proceedings of the 15th international conference on Multimedia* (pp. 277-280). ACM. doi:10.1145/1291233.1291291

Yuan, J., Wang, H., Xiao, L., Zheng, W., Li, J., Lin, F., & Zhang, B. (2007). A formal study of shot boundary detection. *IEEE Transactions on* Circuits and Systems for Video Technology, *17*(2), 168–186.

Zabih, R., Miller, J., & Mai, K. (1999). A feature-based algorithm for detecting and classifying production effects. *Multimedia Systems, 7*(2), 119–128. doi:10.1007/s005300050115

Zajić, G. J., Reljin, I. S., & Reljin, B. D. (2011). Video shot boundary detection based on multifractal analysis. *Telfor Journal, 3*(2), 105–110.

Chapter 12
Time–Slot Based Intelligent Music Recommender in Indian Music

Sudipta Chakrabarty
Techno India Salt Lake, India

Samarjit Roy
Techno India Silli, India

Debashis De
Maulana Abul Kalam Azad University of Technology, India

ABSTRACT

Music listening is one of the most common thing of human behaviors. Normally mobile music is downloaded to mobile phones and played by mobile phones. Today millennial people use mobile music in about all the age groups. Music recommendation system enhances personalized music classifications that create a profile with the service and build up a music library based on the choice preferences using mobile cloud services. Music recommendation through cloud is therefore an emerging field, and this can be done using various parameters like song genre similarity, human behavior, human mood, song rhythmic patterns, seasons etc. In this article an intelligent music recommender system that identifies the raga name of one particular song music and then mapping with the raga time database and classify the songs according to their playing time and create time slot based personalized music libraries.

1. INTRODUCTION

Music Information Retrieval (MIR) is a contemporary research discipline of Computer Science and Information Technology that aims at retrieving semantic information from musical data sources. Those involved in MIR may have a background in musicology, music study, signal processing, machine intelligence and learning or several combinations of these. One of the most important features of Indian Classical Music is the assignment time slot of a particular day for each music and that is depend on the

DOI: 10.4018/978-1-5225-0498-6.ch012

ragas of that particular music. There are some ragas are attractive for listening in the early mornings, or mornings, or before noon, or noon, or after noon, or evening, or night, or late night, etc. This relation of time of the day or night with the raga is based on daily cycle of changes of different moments that occur in our own body and mind of the day and stimulate different moods and emotions. It is believed that the human body is dominated by three phases in Indian Music – Kaph, Pitta, and Vata. These elements work in a cycle order of rise and fall during the 24-hour period. Also the reaction of these three elements differs with the seasons. Hence it is said that performing or listening to music at the proper allotted time can affect the health of human being.

Therefore, listeners of Indian Classic Music must have to know the playing time of a particular music. It requires a Music Recommendation System that generates list of music for a particular time slot from the whole collection of music library. This article presents the representation of music recommendation system based on these time slots using mobile cloud services.

Music recommendation systems help users find music from large music databases, and an effective system is one that consistently matches a user's preference. Existing music recommendation systems rely on collaborative filtering or content-based technologies to satisfy users' long-term music playing needs. Normally a full day consists of eight time slots or beats each of which length is three hours. The first beat is starting from 3 AM to 6 AM and it is known as Early Morning. The second beat is starting from 6 AM to 9 AM and it is known as Morning. The third beat is starting from 9 AM to 12 Noon and it is known as Before Noon. The fourth beat is starting from 12 Noon to 3 PM and it is known as Near Noon. The fifth beat is starting from 3 PM to 6 PM and it is known as After Noon. The sixth beat is starting from 6 PM to 9 PM and it is known as Evening. The seventh beat is starting from 9 PM to 12 Midnight and it is known as Night. The eight or last beat is starting from 12 Midnight to 3 AM and it is known as Late Night.

Music Recommendation System on mobile depends on different time slots or beats of a day is one of the greatest work for listeners of Indian or Hindustani Classical Music. Although many mobile play music as ringtones, allow users to stream music or download music files, import audio files over the cloud. Mobile music being stored within the memory of the mobile phone like traditional business models applicable in the music industry. The user can either purchase the music or access entire music libraries via a subscription model using mobile cloud services. Music playing depends on various factors, like human mood, human behavior, places, seasons, cultures, different time domains of a particular day, and some other biological factors. Therefore, time is very important for listening music for a particular listener. Time slots of a particular day can change the music choices of any particular listener or the user of this system. In this chapter a method is proposed that creates a personalized music library depends on the different time slots of a day according to listener's perspective. This article focuses this intelligent approach and creates a significant era in the multimedia audio application and therefore the title of the chapter is highly appropriate. Another very important measure of this intelligent recommender is that there is no requirement of storage for huge musical data for different time slots of listener as storage is fully maintained by cloud.

The availability of influential computing systems escorts to extraordinary development of multimedia information. The recommended term, "multimedia" refers now-a-days not only restricted in traditional multimedia information such as images and videos, but also promising media such as audio signal and speech processing systems like Musical pattern recognition and information retrieval. Music Information Retrieval (MIR) is a contemporary research discipline of Computer Science and Information Technology that aims at retrieving semantic information from musical data sources. Those involved in MIR may have a background in musicology, music study, signal processing, machine intelligence and learning or several combinations of these. In this contribution computational modeling, analysis on musical pattern recognition and data retrieval, knowledge depiction and real-time applications in human-machine interaction, audio mining, perception, cognition, emotion, effects on sociology etc. will be illustrated. The schemes such as Soft Computing, Machine Intelligence, Object-Oriented Analysis, Petri Nets etc. will also be exemplified how they might be deal with musical features and patterns.

Object-Oriented Analysis in Music: Every piece of music has two imperative ingredients- rhythm and melody. An additional significant obsession for music composition is rhythms that give harmonic form to a melody and also important are performance instructions that are words or symbols that help the musician interpret the notes they are reading. Therefore, quality music composition depends on various musical elements and the relationship between their super classes and sub classes and music composition is the aggregation of these musical elements. In this chapter, a new method for composing music has been demonstrated using abstraction mechanism concept of software engineering. Two central components of any musical composition – Vocal and Instrumental and these two comprehensive patterns or information are tightly combined to create the aggregation point of music composition that also be initiated. The chief focus of this effort is to explore the efficiency of Abstraction mechanism – Generalization, Specialization, and Aggregation to search for the best possible arrangement between vocal and different instrumentals with their different tempo to improve the superiority of music composition. In the context of Indian Classical Music, there is a lot of challenging orientations in researches to be intended and analyzed the precise paths to be elaborated the musical patterns and their elementary characteristics. The ICM is not as popular as the cord-based music or western musical compositions. In Indian music, there is no such stipulation and calculation to set up music with cord. Hence, the identification of notes used in ICM is really a sturdy job and the music signal can never be calculated the linear expressions or equations only. Even though, the contemporary technologies and systems are already specified the smooth and sharp thought in pattern recognition and information retrieval disciplines with some of the special characteristics using object-oriented modeling.

Object-oriented modeling is a method where a set of objects can be grouped into one or more different classes depending upon several distinctive properties and features. The entire the substances of the analogous features are placed in the similar class and the objects of different distinctiveness are classified into other distinct types of classes based on their characteristics. The specialty of this perception is that it supports the hierarchical classification. The inheritance conception also provides the thought of code reusability where abundant supplementary features can moreover be complemented to an accessible class without transforming it. The new class have the collective attributes of both the classes. Thus the genuine influence of the Object-Oriented concept allows a software developer to reuse the characteristics with further ones with any damaging possessions into the remaining existing classes in the models. Polymorphism is one of the unique properties of object-oriented programming where the multiple sub-class methods are indifferently related to one interface. By this property it is easily possible to design a generic interface to a group of related activities (Schildt, 2011). The standard interface is considered as parent class or super class and the methods based on capturing some different features are the sub-classes from where the methods of classification are merely inherited from the parent class.

Quite a few years ago, there was a digital signal processing (DSP) tools accessible for generating the audio signals. Recently, the machine's computational efficiency of is so powerful by which the literal audio features and speech features processing tools are doable from these relating audio or music.

Raga is a conception of melodic structure in Indian music, working between the levels of scale and melody as these expressions are implicit in Western music. Numerous ragas may allocate the same scale; each raga can provide as the basis for an infinite number of melodic compositions or improvisations. Raga is central concept to Indian musical theory; but it also links musical sounds associated with cultural thoughts, and thus has important connections among the visual arts, literature, drama, film, etc. It is an innermost property of the Indian classical music tradition. Raga is usually offered in the form of a pre-composed song or instrumental melody, set in any appropriate rhythmic cycle with pre-composed or improvised variations.

The prime objective of Raga information analysis is to generate an automated system that will identify each and individual Raga and to represent classical music using object oriented modeling. Raga can be identified by particular set of note structures; first notes are extracted from a sample music file sung by performer. Raga is a combination of different note sequences both in ascending and descending order. The ascending and descending notes categorization generate melody and no two ragas are alike; that is, they do not have the same set of notes in the ascending and descending scales in order. Hence Raga name identification of any Indian Classical Music is very crucial task. There can be various initiatives and corresponding analysis to turn up at the decision of perfection and uniqueness of a particular raga. Three visions namely musical vision, object oriented vision and programmers vision have been explored in working out the details in this effort. Raga is not only the innermost concept of Indian music but it also association musical sounds with associated cultural meanings, and therefore very important for the visual arts, literature, drama, film, multimedia objects, etc. Raga origin class is a dependent class which depends on the class "group of notes". The prime objective for the reader is to generate an automated system that will identify each and individual Raga and to represent classical music using fundamental frequency mapping technique.

According to the musical perspective, it is a system that can hold a raga pattern or information. Automatic Raga Identifier (ARI) may also symbolize the percentage of accuracy. Secondly in object oriented paradigm Automated Raga Identifier is a classifier and pictorial representing mechanism of Raga as well as musical data. In programmers' vision, ARI is a set of instructions that assist to identify a raga. The aim of this chapter is to normalize musical features like notes, raga origin, raga using object oriented method and hence may be represented these fundamentals blocks using Unified Modeling Language.

Modeling musical patterns using Petri Nets: Petri Nets are the modeling tools for designing multimedia information which are explored in a large number of real-world simulations, systems modeling and scientific researches. The prime objective of this contribution is being ascertained that the Petri Net is the significant tool which keeps up a correspondence to the high performance quality analysis of musical compositions with its expressive graphical and analytical approaches as Petri nets have broad acceptance in the computational model perspective. In this effort, the method by which music structures and musical patterns has been demonstrated through a more conceptual revelation and consent to unambiguously illustrate the procedure of computational modeling of Musicology will be represented which present the attempt on music composition from the elementary musical objects like vocal and rhythmic cycles usage using Petri Nets. Due to quite a few complexities on the purposes of numerous musical features extractions and analysis mechanisms on Classical Music, the features or musical attributes are modeled in Petri Net meta-data modeling perceptions.

The quality overview of Petri Nets is conferred in this section. Petri Nets are a particular breed of graphs which can be the directed, bipartite and weighted. The fundamental concept is the regulation for data or token transition enabling and firing. The nodes used generally in these graphs are of two manners like the places (strained as circles) and transitions (drawn as boxes or bars). The arcs are the connectors of these nodes by initializing either in a place and terminating in a transition, or these are initializing by a transition and terminating with a place vice versa (Trček & Trček, 2013).

A very elementary perception that Petri Nets expand and self-modify is the concept of marking or labeling the position, documented by the tokens in Place. Any place uses to embrace at a provided time of the participant process a non-negative number of tokens, signified by the upper numerical value inside the place. The lower value inside places specifies the maximum capacity of the domiciled tokens. Tokens can be relocated from one place to another enabling the system according to guidelines known as the 'Firing rules'. The rules are mentioned as under:

1. A transition process will be enabled when all the incoming places of the system of that transition there a number of tokens greater or equal to the weights of the consequent incoming arcs, and – after the fire of the transition – the marking of all the output places will be less than or equal to their capacities.
2. When a transition will be enabled as above-mentioned, the fire plummet from the incoming places several tokens equal to the weights of the incoming arcs and adds to each outgoing place numerous tokens equal to the weights of the corresponding outgoing arc or edges.

Owing to avoid the possible complexities about the extractions of introductory features belong to musical patterns this pieces of works present the attempt on music composition from the fundamental musical patterns like vocal and rhythmic cycles usage using Petri Net. This attempt has been obtained to answer the query: whether the ordinary Petri Net is an adequate tool for modeling such a complex process as a complete composition of music composed from the fundamental rudiments is.

Evolutionary Computing and Intelligent Systems for extracting musical rhythmic features: As discussed earlier, Pattern recognition in rhythm of any instrument in music is very complex task that is the perfect combination of speech, audio, and their signal processing techniques. In this chapter a system that identify the basic source rhythm and then modify the rhythm to improve the quality of source rhythm will be proposed using Evolutionary Computing. The relationships of musical instruments with pervasive music education will also be elaborated entitled as m-learning or music learning based on Genetic Algorithm. The primary goal of m-learning is to provide the users with a learning environment which is not restricted to a precise location or session. With comparison to a traditional classroom system, m-learning enlarge the mobility of a learner, allowing learners to be trained. The ultimate objective of this study will highly escort to create a context awareness intelligent system tool for music rhythm creation for the application in Pervasive Teaching-Learning process. Music rhythmology as a context awareness learning process and applicable in the pervasive education as a huge number of students are interested to gather music knowledge.

The concept of the system brings in XML schema as sensor data through sensor devices. A context rhythm editor is also designed by employing schema creating adaptable rhythms using genetic Algorithm for sustaining intelligent context mapping between sensor devices and context model. As genetic algorithm is easy to understand, supports multi-objective optimization, superior for noisy environment, always give the outcomes get better with time, and trouble-free to exploit the alternate clarification, this technique can be chosen for rhythm parent pattern selection of music for producing better offspring rhythmic structures.

In order to identify the patterns of rhythms, the knowledge about rhythm notation is needed to be known. Rhythm occurs within the framework of meter, which is basically a repetitive pattern of strong and weak beats. The meter of a song is indicated by its time signature. Rhythms are represented using notes and rests.

The concept of Genetic Algorithm, introduced by J.H. Holland, USA, who described the basic idea and the implementation of Genetic Algorithm in his book *Adaptation in natural and artificial systems* in 1975. This mechanism is the same as modeling Darwinian's natural system.

Genetic Algorithm can be measured as multi-objective optimization techniques that equip optimization by simulating the biological natural law of evolution. This should be initiated with a population of randomly generated expressions. Each of these solutions is evaluated to measure the fitness value. A terminating condition is tested, if the solutions are optimum then terminate otherwise these have to be optimized the solutions again. Hence the best solutions from the initial population will be selected. Then the good solutions will be allowed to exchange their information, in order to get even better consequences. Some small percentage of the solutions might be muted randomly thus obtained after crossover. Again, each of the solutions are evaluated, and check the termination condition. The same mechanism can be obtained for genetic algorithm optimization to produce better rhythm that carries more rhythmic sound effects to a complete music composition.

This study about music rhythm is a wide acceptable region of all the learners of Musicology as well as the educators. A pervasive education learning surroundings is the framework by which pupils can come about entirely engrossed in the learning course of action. Pervasive learning of rhythmic materials might be multimedia objects, PowerPoint presentations, notes or application software. In a typical classroom, the instructor is the central source of information, and pupils are obligatory to be in the same place at a time, whereas Pervasive education alters the traditional classroom perception of teaching and e-learning process.

Context awareness is classified complementary to but location awareness. Context awareness instigates as a term from pervasive computing. In computer science and multimedia application context awareness means the inspiration that computers can sense and react based on their environment. This research utilizes the context-awareness knowledge structures to represent the learning background; to identify the learning objectives that the user is in reality interested in; to recommend learning activities to the user and to lead the user around the learning environment consist of various computing devices like PDA, wireless sensors, and servers.

Music Information Retrieval: Eventually the entire music information retrieval system and procedure will be discussed. This will suggest the classifications of vocal performance has been attempted to display by explaining unique musical features and pattern matching. This contribution might be represented how music structures can be advanced through a more conceptual demonstration and consent to unambiguously describe process of computational modeling of Musicology which signify the challenge on complete musical composition from the elementary vocal and rhythmic objects of music usage using Neural Networks.

The musical data retrieval and pattern analysis over multimedia information retrieval supposed to be led in academic and professional front for creation, manipulation and categorization of music for instance Music generation, Transcription, features extraction, track and instruments separation and recognition, developing music recommendation systems and others.

The Raga in Indian Classical music is explained as earlier as the extraordinary amalgamation of the set of notes arranged in a unique sequence which has been created the undergoing musical emotion to the audiences. If all the ragas and their corresponding features will be contemplated in object-oriented manner, then it must be belonged to sub-class under a parent or super class which is known as 'Thhat' in Indian Classical music. The Thhat is nothing but the numerous distributions of musical notes and the note-structures. In Indian Classical Music, there are ten thhats and twelve notes. Among the twelve notes there are seven pure notes and five scratched notes available. Each thhat exactly consists of seven notes out of entire twelve notes and the notes are used to be arranged in ascending orders. All the ragas must belong to any one of the ten thhats. The Structures of the notes in a particular raga can be shown discrepancies due to the fruitful audibility to the audiences and variants of the singers or vocalists as well nevertheless numerous notes will always be intact to intone by which note or set of notes exact raga or its corresponding Thhats have been categorized. The previous history of Indian music said the explicit explanations about the raga characteristics and the actual timing of playing the ragas.

The Neural networks are self-possessed of trouble-free elements working in analogous systems or essentials. These elements are habitually motivated by biological nervous systems and as designs and operations perspectives, they are similar to the operations of human beings. As in nature, the network function is defined principally by the associations among elements. A neural network can be trained to perform a particular function by amending the ideals of the connections namely weights between elements. Frequently neural networks are familiar or trained, as if a particular input escorts to a precise target output. Such a situation has been shown in to this contribution below. In this contribution the network is adjusted, depending upon a comparison of the production and the target, until the network output is equivalent to the target.

Here in this contribution, the time-based raga recommendation and modeling on the actual playing time of raga are analyzed. The ragas are classified with the help of neural networks which divides the set of raga samples into two classes of times or sessions of performances namely, 'Purvango' (from 12 pm to 12 am) and 'Uttarango' (from 12 am to 12 pm). The information processing neurons of the neural network are trained by the dataset and then tested by a number of samples. The training procedure has been continued till the optimum accuracy occurred of the execution.

Due to several disparities in notes structures usually denoted in Indian Classical Music for defining the thhats the unique characteristics of ragas also must be fluctuated. By this discussion, the time-based raga recommendation and modeling on the actual playing time of raga can be analyzed.

2. HISTORICAL BACKGROUNDS

Numerous works have been approached on the generation of music recommendation system. The automated music classification, modeling and personalized music library creation is one of the hardest problem areas. This is because of constraints and satisfying those constraints to get the feasible and optimized solution as computational music pattern research involve a lot of musical parameters. Computer-assist music analysis on the rhythmic structures based on Indian music has also been relatively infrequent, and up to this viewpoint rare attempts have been prepared and proposed to categorize the rhythmic structures repeatedly. On the contrary, the classification of the properties in Indian Classical Ragas has been an innermost focus where quite a few attempts have been made to detect some divergence among the raga patterns. In a paper, the authors have nicely explained the Western music by object-oriented programming and methods. In this paper, the modern analysis has been explained through simple harmonic analysis to clustering or grouping analysis with the simple melody. Various types of structural analysis are also available in their works (Lande & Vollsnes, 1995). In another research work, the values of pitch variations with same scale of music has been proposed with different performances by the vocalists because of changing the positions of 'shruti' in the notes used in music based on Indian Classical Ragas (Datta et al., 1990; 1995; 1997; 1998; 2000). In a work of statistical pattern recognition approach (Ellis, 2003), the statistical pattern recognition using neural networks has been elaborated with the music signals. It has been proposed the spectrogram analysis based on Fourier Transform too. The Bayes' classifier has also used upon training data and test data for classification. Further in the addition in raga notes identification, Tansen: a system for automatic raga identification proposed using Hidden Markov Models (Pandey, Mishra & Ipe, 2003). How the music patterns are documented based on actual rhythmic structures of music and explained several thoughts about the rhythm complexity cycles are to be erased and also introduced the brief innovative interaction between rhythm structures and music (Shmulevich et al., 1997; 1998; 2001). In Time in Indian Music: Rhythm, Metre, and Form in North Indian Raga Performance explained rhythm, musical forms are used for flowing influential strategies in the Indian Classical Ragas (Clayton, 2000). Computational Ethnomusicology, has been prejudiced with the various types of musical instruments in world music and procedural sense on the musical instruments are used in music making (Tzanetakis, Kapur, Schloss & Wright, 2007). In several papers, there has been adequately decorated on the Indian music ornaments like, rhythm, raga, raga identifications in different schemas, numerous musical instruments used in making music melodious and their unique patterns and so on so forth (Chordia, 2004; 2006; 2008). The contribution on the platform of pattern recognition in the domain of object-oriented analysis (Chakraborty & De, 2011; 2012), a modern practical approach has been specified on Raga Identification and musical pattern recognition based on object-oriented modeling and pitch extraction using Error-minimizing algorithm. The effort consists an addition is an innovative addition to the aforesaid research works to explore in an innovative way of representation of musical features and pattern harmonizing paradigms based on some of the nonspecific properties of object-oriented methodologies.

Computer-assist modeling on fundamental musical appearances, their corresponding rhythmic structures and attributes of musical information has been reasonably infrequent, and up to this point of view several remarkable attempts have been made to categorize the vocal and rhythmic formations by design and their implementations. On this contrary, the recognition of the patterns in Hindustani Classical Ragas would has been a close region where several challenges have been prepared to perceive a quantity of distinction among the raga design and equivalent rhythmic features imposed over the vocal data. In a work, the researchers demonstrated a survey on computationally supported musical composition by hub on Petri Nets and gave several major ways of their applications. On this basis in terms of Petri nets this involvement provided innovative steps for generating these labors operational in concrete computerized backgrounds, not just at the level of prescribed abstraction (Trček & Trcek, 2013). The researchers have elaborated the alternative approaches for exploring and involving to the design and function of the software project "Nodal". This particular job aims to construct a graphical environment which enables the user to configure a spatial, directed graph that generates music in real-time systems. Such graphs as composition or nodal networks have been referred. The discussion in this work has been related to the elementary design constraints that have been imposed within these limitations that give augment to different musical behaviors (Mcilwain & McCormack, 2005). In another piece of works an evaluation methodology has been clarified to authenticate the presentation of a UML-based demonstration, in lieu of structural designing of software. The proposed advancement is entirely depended upon unwrapped and well-known principles: OMG Profile for Performance, Time Specification and Scalability, for the recital clarification into software-based UML modeling paradigms. This has also been cited more expressly to the planning to the performance from the PCM. To validate the proposed technique, an in-depth analysis has been provided of a web application for music streaming (Distefano, Scarpa & Puliafito, 2011). In another application, the researchers have given the analysis the performance of musical bits concerning chronological prototypes and isolated interactive proceedings. Allen relations to constrain these structures are partially defined a temporal order on these. A replica on Petri nets for this phase has been used. It has also been endowed here with elucidation to set down global restraints in addition to local temporal restraints stimulated by the NTCC formation. (Allombert, Assayag & Desainte-Catherine, 2007). The analysis on original orchestral score, music object recognition has been made within a score, mapping the musical objects, testing and hypothesis of the music modeling architecture and so on have been elaborated successfully by the authors (Goffredo & Rodriguez, 1993). In complicated synthetic systems, such as manufacturing systems, the systems' specific properties, such as conflicts, deadlocks, limited buffer sizes, and finite resource constraints have easily been represented in the Petri net model (Music et al. 2012). Iteration, concurrency, ordering, hierarchy, causality, timing, synchrony, non-determinism have evidently been represented based on the modeling concepts of Petri nets. (Barate, 2008). In another paper the approaches to be synthesized music scores by executing formal models have been displayed. The kind of models an "ad hoc" arrangement of Petri Nets and the music algebra have been exercised (Goffredo & Alberto, 1991). The adoption of Petri Nets (PNs) has been addressed by the researchers in order to describe music processes (Baratè, Haus, Ludovico & Luca, 2007). Several such formalisms can be exploited to represent the consequences coming from the analysis of previously existing musical contributions. Additionally, string rewriting grammars based on L-Systems have been adopted into a harmonization for music masterpieces. Illustration of pitch periods, interval and timbre are arranged as grammar cryptogram, upon which sequence of re-writing rules are applied (McCormack, 1996). Researchers have introduced a system for recognition of the patterns of music by using key sequences with Recursive Median Filter (Coyle & Shmulevich, 1998). This has supportively been explicated in this framework to the abovementioned procedural mechanisms to explore a pioneering mode of implementation of musical features and pattern matching trials based on Petri Net and its modeling concepts.

In the recent years, Computational Musicology is a new and emerging area for multimedia and pattern recognition research which sketches heavily from Computer Science and information technology. Indian Classical Music is relatively unexplored owing to its intricate grammar structures and it is so difficult that the rendition of the intact raga by the different singers is not similar. A linguistic model of Tabla, an instrument, improvisation and evaluation derived from pattern languages and formal grammars has been put into practice in the Bol-Processor, a software modeling system designed in interactive fieldwork (Conklin & Witten, 1995). A valuable approach for classification and recognition of automatic musical genre had been developed and evaluated patterns for any type of content-based analysis of musical signals (Tzanetakis & Cook, 2002). Automatic transformations of Hindustani Music into the acoustic signal from Hindustani vocal song have also been explained. A Latent Dirichlet Allocation (LDA) model was used to identify the Raga of South Indian Carnatic music where LDA is an unsupervised statistical approach that is being specified to determine the underlying topics in a given document (Chordia, Sastry & Albin, 2010). Hidden Markov Models (HMM) was used to identify the melakartha ragas (Walton 2010). Nearest Neighbor classification focused a mechanism for finding distance between neighbors using Cosine Distance (CD), Earth Movers Distance (EMD) and formulas are used to identify nearest neighbors, algorithm for classification in training and testing for identifying ragas (Sridhar, Karthiga & Geeta, 2010). Further some others deal with the implementation of pattern recognition by mathematical expressions. A new method for arranging different melodious audio stream had been suggested into some specific type of classes based on object-oriented paradigm (Tarakeswara et al., 2011). The segmentation method of phrases has been introduced through identification of any as or long note and computes similarity with the reference characteristic phrase (Reddy, Tarakeswara, Sudha and Hari, 2011). Nearest Neighbor classification has been focused a mechanism for finding distance between neighbors using algorithm for classification in training and testing for identifying ragas (Vasudha, Iyshwarya, Selvi, Iniyaa & Jeyakumar, 2011). GA was applied for the automatic versatile music rhythm generation using the calculation of fitness value by the help of Roulette Wheel Selection Method (Ross & Rao, 2012).

There are some previous research works that inspired to be performed to the object oriented UML based paradigms to model musical raga features and applications to the music e-learning. In last few years many scientists and engineers explore their interest on research related to musical automation. These efforts contribute a lot in automated musical research. Some works have been done on the use of pervasive computing in teaching and learning environment. In a Paper (Rothermel, Schnitzer, Lange, Dürr & Farrell, 2012), two approaches were presented for the scalable tracking of mobile object trajectories and the efficient processing of continuous spatial range queries and also displayed in detail how both approaches were utilized the basic concepts of accuracy relaxation and utilization of context information. At Central Washington University, music students utilized PDAs to write music whenever inspiration hit them (Bonwell & Eison, 1991). Another paper has deployed (Avanzato, 2001) where the students learn French III by using their keyboarded PalmIIIx handhelds to download and contact class notes and quizzes and obtain maintained materials beamed to them via an infrared point within their classrooms. Few researchers developed a system for test taking using handheld devices (Chen, Meyers & Yaron, 2000). In an Interactive Classroom (Abut & Ozturk, 1997), the students usually share a virtual whiteboard, electronic textbook, and access the World Wide Web over a networked environment to actively partake in class discussions and learning. At ASU, a Smart classroom (Yau, Gupta, Karim, Ahamed, Wang & Wang, 2003) has assembled that used pervasive computing technology to enhance collaborative learning among college and university students. Pervasive computing devices facilitate the children to exploit a pen reader to store texts from a book into their PDA's Users like to utilize the predefined device in diverse fields. As these devices are portable, they become a part and parcel of everyday life. In the education field, these devices can engage in recreation. Both instructors and students can be greatly benefited by the utility of these smart devices. Some works have been done on the usability of pervasive computing in teaching and learning environment (palmOne). Smart Kindergarten uses sensor data have been collected from children or toys to make a record for the instructor to review activities of children and track their learning progress. Classroom 2000 captures classroom context to automatically produce Web-accessible multimedia class files for the instructor and students. Paper (Jones and Copley 2003) describes the study of usefulness of Genetic Algorithm for music composition. This paper also guided us to be understood that Genetic Algorithm is one important tool that can be functionally applied in Musicology and create complete and fruitful music composition. Another paper again established that the Genetic Algorithm is one of the most important mechanisms for composing music. This paper produces a new rhythm from a pre-defined rhythm applied to initial population using modified Genetic Algorithm operator (Matic, 2010). A work introduces a new concept of automated generating of realistic drum-set rhythm using Genetic Algorithm in the year 2005 (Dostal, 2005). Additionally, in an involvement has been described the use of Genetic Algorithm for the automatic music generation using the calculation of Fitness value by the help of Normalized Compression Distance (Alfonceca, Cebrian & Ortega, 2006).

On the contrary, the recognition of the patterns in Hindustani Classical Ragas is being gone to a close area where several challenges have been arranged to recognize a quantity of distinction among the raga blueprints and analogous rhythmic features. The alternative approaches have been achieved for exploring and relating to the design and function of the software estimation titled "Nodal". This particular work aims to create a graphical and functional environment that enables the user to configure a spatial, directed graph to generate music in real-time systems. They referred to such graphs as composition or nodal networks. The talk in this work has been related to the elementary design constraints that have been obligatory within these constraints which give rise to different musical behaviors (Mcilwain & McCormack, 2005). In another piece of works the author has described and researched on the computational music theory that has been recognized by John Clough. According to the thought of Computational Music, this has been definite that the research of John Clough was not only restricted to the mathematical theory but also encircled in sciences and humanities too. The specific and generic intermission has also been illustrated which is known as the Myhill's property (Clampitt, 2007). The researchers have afforded the performance of music can improve the behavioral performances like the human intelligence systems in both structural and functional altitudes. A particular music can lead to think a listener to improve some behavioral mechanisms of music like the vocal performance namely the language that might be more fruitful and ornamental. The future trend has also been explored about the interrelationships among music and the languages (Moreno, 2009). The authors in their contribution (Montiel & Gomez, 2014) have mentioned the music in the pedagogy of mathematics which has been calculated by Mathematical Music Theory. The fundamental intension of the authors is elaborated to popularize the musical project broadly Mathematics and Music form the regional culture to world level. They also view to create the didactic materials by which everybody can gather the novel thoughts and sketches about Mathematical Music theory. Additionally, the researchers exercised the method of time series analysis to compare the expertise groups and individuals in dynamic unremitting discernment of arousal in music. For testing the validity, they have thought the general linear autoregressive moving average (Dean, Bailes & Dunsmuir 2014). The authors have evidently represented the explication and discussion of methodologies in computational, mathematical and statistical music approach (Volk & Honingh, 2012). The inter-association of music has also been discussed with science, cognitive science and humanities. In a dissertation the raga has been approached and identified to recognize from a regional music performance like Carnatic music signal. The method has been deployed to separate the vocal data and instrumental performances from a polyphonic music signal through signal separation or clustering algorithm. According to only the vocal data retrieval, the notes have been predictable by their initial frequencies (Sridhar and Geetha, 2009). In a contribution the musical emotion recognition system has been present developed by the one-class-in-one phenomena of neural networks (Nicholson, Takahashi & Nakatsu, 2000). Here the system is entirely speaker and context-independent. Additionally, string rewriting grammars based on L-Systems have been adopted into a harmonization for music masterpieces. Illustration of pitch periods, interval and timbre are prearranged as grammar cryptogram, upon which sequence of re-writing rules are applied (McCormack, 1996). Additionally, in several efforts by the authors have been described the musical pattern recognition and rhythmic features exposures by object-oriented manner (De & Roy, 2012, 2012). A lot of discussions are available about the features classification using UML-oriented class diagrams and the way of implementations of musical rhythmic cycles for the percussion-based instruments (Chakraborty & De, 2012; 2012). The automated rhythm generation is one of the hardest problem areas. This is because of constraints and satisfying those constraints to get the feasible and optimized rhythm. In an effort by the authors have been modeled (Quality Measure model) an optimized algorithm on rhythmic cycles used in Indian Classical Music using the Roulette-Wheel Selection of Genetic Algorithm Concept (Chakraborty & De, 2012). Several papers have been considered those are based on the creativity of music using Genetic Algorithm technique. Further some other papers deal with the implementation of Musical pattern recognition by mathematical expressions. They suggested a new method for arranging different melodious audio stream into some specific type of classes based on object oriented paradigm. In a paper, the authors have explained elaborately the notes and the notes structures as well as the ten thhats or raga origin in Indian classical music which is imposed to be constructed the songs in Indian or Hindustani musical patterns. The algorithm has been defined here which can determine the thhat or raga origin in which a song in Indian music belongs (Bhattacharyya & De, 2012). Several contributions have been depicted upon audio or speech recognition systems which are content based, featured-based parameterization for music information retrieval using Neural Networks approach as well (Dalibor, Zeppelzauer, & Breiteneder, 2010; Emmanuel et al., 2010; Stavros, Potamitis, & Fakotakis, 2008; 2009). In an effort the audio characteristics also modeled those are emanated from the hearing aids using Neural Networks with user input (Freeman, Dony, & Areibi, 2007). The works of the researchers have elucidated also the entire music composition and classification by neural approaches (Scott, 2001; Douglas & Schmidhuber, 2002) as well as their semantic, episodic (Platel et al., 2003) and music-emotion behavior (Roddy, Douglas-Cowie, and Cox., 2005; Todd, Peter, and Loy, 1991). The supporting themes upon music i.e., instrumental performances which has also been classified productively (Herrera et al., 2000) using their performing features (Antti & Anssi, 2000; Brown, 1999). The classical music orientations have been done in several contributions using some modeling concept like Petri net (Roy et al., 2014; Roy, Chakrabarty, & De, 2014). The context-aware pervasive diary for music computing has been discussed by Linear Rank Selection mechanism of Genetic Algorithm (Roy, Chakrabarty, & De, 2014). Numerous approaches are based on musical features extraction from the Indian Classical Raga or instrumental rhythms (Roy, Chakrabarty, & De, 2014; Kippen & Bel, 1992; Clayton, 2000). The authors have explicated the formations of musical pieces by fuzzy logic (Lopez-Ortega & Lopez-Popa, 2012) and constraints by integration of DSP algorithms (Mani and Hamid Nawab, 1998). The contributions of the researchers have also been highlighted to the novel approaches for music recommendation (Song, Dixon & Pearce, 2012; Lu & Tseng 20,09). This has been supportively explained in this framework to the aforesaid procedural mechanism to explore a pioneering mode of depiction of musical features and pattern matching trials based on Neural Networks concepts.

There are some previous research works that inspire us to perform our experiment. In last few years many scientists and engineers explore their interest on research related to musical automation. These works contribute a lot in automated musical research. Unified modeling language contribute a lot to represent any automation system with real life entity (i.e. Object). It elaborates a precise and practical method for specifying pattern solutions articulated in the unified modeling language (France & Ghosh 2004). The specification method paves the mode for the improvement of tools that support rigorous purpose of design patterns to UML models and it has been taken to form stipulation of solutions for a number of admired design patterns (Schmidt, Stal, Rohnert & Buschmann, 2000).

Another paper discusses the alteration from platform independent replica, received from calculation independent model, to the one, ready for production of platform specific replica. To execute this alteration, "two-hemisphere" model motivated design to system modelling is chosen. The class diagram in UML notation is defined as transformation result. The paper discusses the alteration into class diagram, and the option of automation of such alteration. With the intention of research mechanization potential, custom device is planned and implemented. This device allows creating elements of class diagram founded on provided transformations. It is applied on examples triplet of original model, represented in diverse notations and different areas. These research proof that examined changes are independent of problem field and details which expresses unique knowledge (Nikiforova & Pavlova, 2008).

An innovative dimension as valuable as object oriented of modeling namely aspect-oriented modeling. Aspect-orientation has given a new structure of modularization by undoubtedly sorting out overlapping concerns from non-overlapping objects. While aspect-orientation initially has at the programming perspective, it now extended also over other expansion chapters. For example, already a number of proposed features for aspect-oriented modeling, pursuing eminent objective, on condition that dissimilar concepts with notations, and viewing various intensity of development. Active surveys and thoughts around here focus more on clarity respecting expansion phases or evaluated alternatives more eagerly than on comparability based on an evaluation framework and modeling. A requirement for a profound evaluation, an abstract orientation shape has been offered as the article's first contribution, centrally catching the vital design concepts of AOM and its relationships in terms of a UML class diagram. Based on this model, an assessment framework has been planned. This approach of evaluation is complemented with a wide-ranging report, shortening the models" strengths and shortcomings (Wimmer et al., 2011).

An assessment has shown that steady pitch disseminations give rise to mental schemas that structure expectations and facilitate the processing of musical information (Castellano, Bharucha & Krumhansl, 1984). Using the prominent probe-tone method, that displayed auditor ratings of the suitability of a test tone in the relation to a tonal context are directly related to the relative prevalence of that pitch-class in a provided key. Sensitive adjectives have been proposed (Huron, 2006) has shown that used to describe a tone are highly correlated with the frequency of a tone in an applicable corpus of music. The PCDs are relatively secure in large corporation of tonal Western music escorted to the development of key- and mode-finding algorithms based on correlating PCDs of a given selection, with empirical PCDs considered on a large sample of related music (Churan & Chew, 2005).

Raga classification and recognition has been a central topic in Indian music theory for centuries, motivating prosperous challenge on the crucial features of ragas and the features that make two ragas similar or dissimilar. Developed a system to habitually recognize ragas Yaman and Bhupali using a Markov model a success rate of 77% has been estimated on thirty-one samples in a two-target test, although the system was not well documented. An additional stage that searched for definite pitch progression enhanced performance to 87% (Vatkande, 1934).

Another research dissertation focuses principally on music similarity. While treating music similarity from diverse perspective, copious advancements for generating playlists have been anticipated. For example, several approaches for generation of playlists are untainted audio-based (Pohle, Pampalk, Widmer, 2005), other utilize a hybrid arrangement of audio-content and unrestricted music similarity (Knees, Pohle, Schedl & Widmer, 2006). The formation of playlists that get together provided constraints has been concentrate on (Alghoniemy & Tewfik, 2001; Aucouturier & Pachet, 2002), and advance that incorporate user responses have also been measured (Pampalk, Pohle & Widmer, 2005; Pauws & Eggen, 2002). Several works have been equipped on data and query paradigms for music and playlist manipulation (Deliege, Pedersen & Jensen et. al., 2007). However, the existing efforts either disregards similarity queries and playlists (Rubenstein 2004), or addresses specific scenarios of playlist management (Deliege, Pedersen & Jensen et. al., 2007).

3. MOBILE CLOUD COMPUTING

The term Cloud refers to a network or internet which is present at remote location. Cloud provides services over public networks or private networks like Local Area Network (LAN), Wide Area Network (WAN), and Virtual Private Network (VPN). Cloud Computing refers to a pay-per-use model for enabling available, convenient, network access to computing resources like, networks, servers, applications, storage, services, etc. It offers online data storage, infrastructure for applications, servers, storage, network, management software, and deployment software and platform virtualization. Several cloud deployment models are Public Cloud Model, Private Cloud Model, Hybrid Cloud Model, and Community Cloud Model. The Public Cloud Model allows systems and services to be easily accessible to general public. The Private Cloud allows systems and services to be accessible within an organization. The Private Cloud is operated only within a single organization. However, it may be managed internally or by third-party. Hybrid cloud is the mixture of the public cloud and private cloud. The Community Cloud allows system and services to be accessible by group of organizations. It shares the infrastructure between several organizations from a specific community. It may be managed internally or by the third-party.

Cloud Management involves a number of tasks to be performed by the cloud provider to ensure efficient use of cloud resources. Cloud Storage is a service that allows saving data on offsite storage rather onsite storage system and it is managed by a third party and is made accessible by a web services API. Security in cloud computing is one of the major issue. Data in cloud should be stored in encrypted form. To restrict client from direct accessing the shared data, proxy and brokerage services should be employed. Today various Cloud Computing platforms are available like, Salesforce.com, Appistry, AppScale, AT&T, Engine Yard, Enomaly, FlexiScale, GCloud3, Gizmox, GoGrid, Google, LongJump, Microsoft, OrangeScape, RackSpace, Amazon EC2, etc. Cloud Computing offers smart phones that have rich internet media experience and require less processing, less power. The primary concept of Mobile Cloud Computing (MCC) is that the data is processing is in cloud and data is also storing in cloud using some devices like mobile devices serve as a media for display the data. Today smart phones are engaged with rich cloud services by interacting applications with the help of web services and those services are deployed in cloud. Several Smartphone operating systems are Windows Mobile Phone, Google's Android, RIM BlackBerry, Apple's iOS, Symbian, etc. Each of these platforms support third party applications and are deployed in cloud. The Figure 1 depicts the architecture of mobile cloud computing.

Cloud Computing Providers use third-party computer resources, or cloud services to execute different computing functions. On smart phones, we can find cloud computing with certain applications like Dropbox, which automatically syncs all the phone's pictures with our laptop or computer. One very important use of cloud computing is to make a backup copy of files automatically. Cloud computing uses third-party resources to store files for big data storage. That means all the files are stored in a data center that a company rents for cloud computing services. In Figure1, the control node will need to provide on-demand dynamic application scalability. This means integration with the virtualization and the ability to be ornamented into a process that manages provisioning opportunity.

Cloud storage is the storage of data online in the cloud where a company's data is stored in and accessible from multiple distributed and connected resources that comprise a cloud. Cloud storage provides the greater accessibility, reliability, rapid deployment, protection for data-backup, archival and disaster recovery purposes and overall storage costs as a result of not having to purchase, manage and maintain expensive hardware. However, cloud storage has the potential for security and compliance concerns. In Figure 1, mobile devices are connected to the mobile networks via three base stations - Base Trans-

Figure 1. Architecture of mobile cloud computing

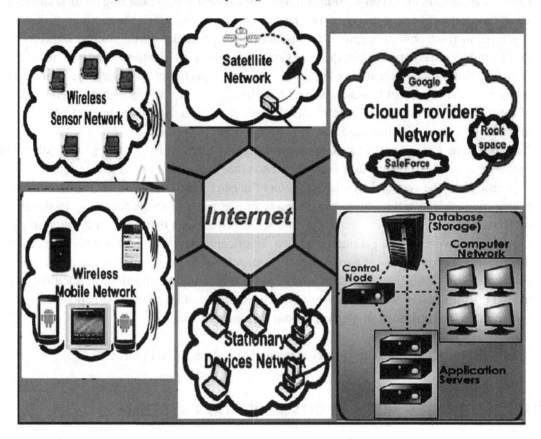

ceiver Station (BTS), Access Point, and Satellite that establish and control the air links connections and functional interfaces between the networks and mobile devices. Mobile users' requests and information are transmitted to the central processors that are connected to servers providing mobile network services. This information are ID and location. Mobile network operators can provide different services like, authentication, authorization, and accounting. These services are fully based on the home agent and subscribers' data stored in databases. The subscribers' requests are delivered to a cloud through the Internet. In Cloud Computing, cloud controller processes the requests to provide mobile users with the corresponding cloud services.

4. MUSIC RECOMMENDATION SYSTEM

Recommendation Systems are software tools and techniques providing suggestions for items to be of use to a user. A Music Recommendation System estimates the user's music preference from a localized music collection and then generates a set of songs based on these estimates from a wider music collection. There are two very common approaches to implement a Music Recommendation System are: Content-Based Learning and Collaborative Filtering.

1. **Content Based Music Recommendation System:** Content-Based Learning method analyses music in the music collection and then matches songs which have musically similar attributes, such as tempo, instrumentation or genre. If a listener likes a particular music, usually indicated by the user listening to the entire music, then the Content-Based System will recommend music that are similar to that music. Content-based systems examine properties of the items to recommend items that are similar in content to items the user has already liked in the past, or matched to attributes of the user. Some examples of content based music recommendation systems are - Music recommendation systems with the same singer, music director, genres, etc.

2. **Collaborative Filtering Based Recommendation:** Collaborative-Filtering is a collaboration process that employs a multi-user utility approach that uses explicit preference to match music to a specific user. The system then relates this set of music by identifying another user with a similar choice in music. Then the system recommends similar types of songs according to similar types of users. This is achieved by creating a rule set which defines the music order in a playlist. To summaries, environmental parameters have a significant effect on mood and therefore influence the music selection process. Environmental features have great potential as big data to allow the listener greater flexibility when searching or accessing a music collection. In addition, environmental features may provide a valuable source of information for an automatic playlist generation algorithm in the generation of playlists to suit a listener's mood.

The different parameter based music recommendation is depicted in Figure 2.

5. TIME SLOT BASED MUSIC RECOMMENDATION SYSTEM

Today mobile is one of the most useful devices for human being. According to eMarketer near about 4.55 billion people use mobile phones in worldwide. According to eMarketer, mobile phone penetration will rise from 61.1% to 69.4% of the global population. With the increasing access of mobile, it is now possible to offer personalized, context relevant music recommendations to the music listeners on mobile. According to music listeners' perspective, some music is well suited for morning, some other music is well suited for evening, and some music is attracted for night, and so on. Therefore, time slot based music recommender is very effective for mobile music listeners. The primary objective of this work is to find out the playing time of any song from listener's music library and create time slot based different music libraries from generating Raga name of that particular song and then matching with the raga time playing database.

To find the raga name of music, it requires that the music run through Wave Surfer software which is used in this experiment to get the pitch value of that song. WaveSurfer is an open source tool for sound visualization and manipulation. WaveSurfer is a free audio editing software widely used for studies of acoustic phonetics. It is not only very simple but also very powerful tool for interactive display of sound waveforms, spectral sections, spectrograms, pitch contour, and pitch transcriptions. WaveSurfer can read and write a number of pitch transcription file formats used in speech processing research. '.wav' music file is appropriate to create the pitch file of the music. Keeping sample encoding at line 16 and sample rate at 22050 the pitch contour of the music is generated. This will give all the pitches that are used in

Figure 2. Different types of intelligent music recommendation system

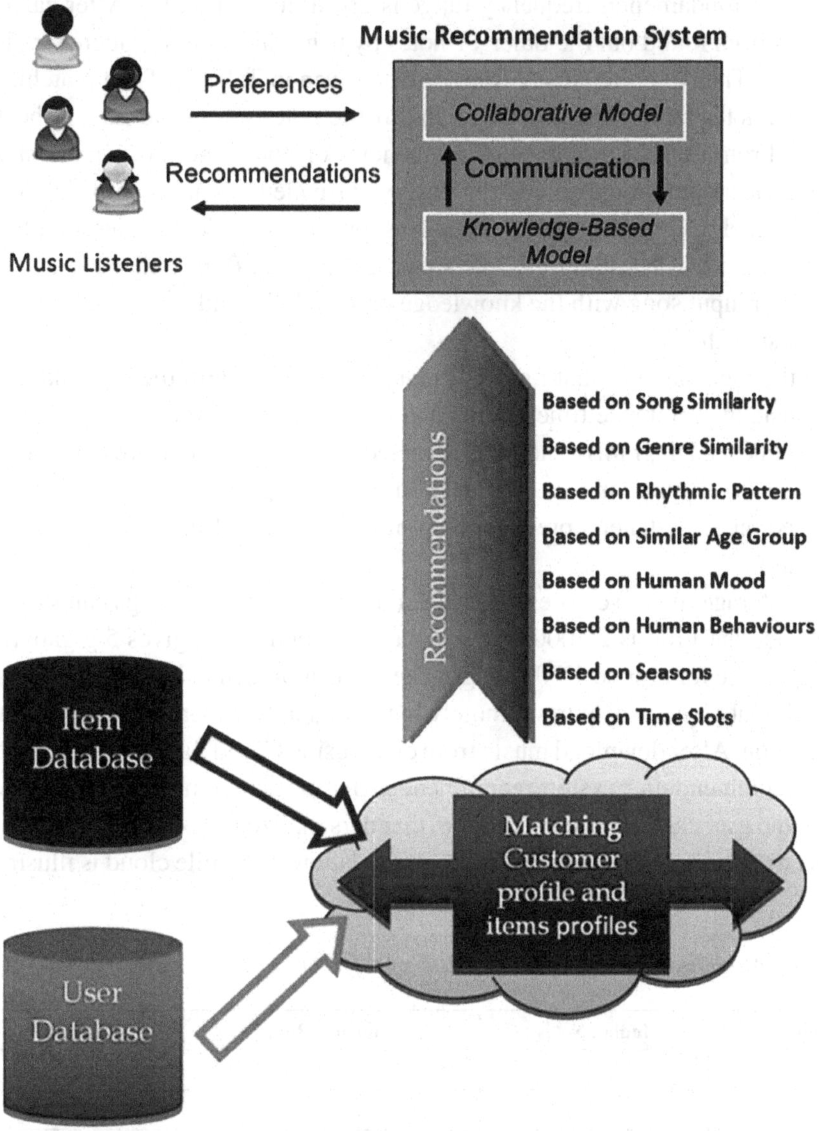

the song and the pitch data are saved in the .f0 format. Some other types of files may also use the .f0 file extension. It consists of huge number of frequencies of monotonic song and we convert this .f0 into .xls format. Then analyse the FFT (Fast Fourier Transform) of the fo file values. An FFT of a time domain signal takes the samples and gives the frequencies, amplitudes, and phases of the sine waves that make up the sound wave analyzed. In this case, the sample rate is 44.1 kHz and the FFT size is 1024, so the bin width is the Nyquist frequency (44,100/2 = 22,050) divided by the FFT size or near about 22 Hz.

Accepted only those frequency values within 50 to 500. Then the number of occurrences has been calculated of each frequency ranging from 50 to 500. The frequency that contains highest occurrences is the most important note and got the name of the most important note by matching with their fundamental frequency range. The fundamental frequency range is given in the Table 1. After calculating the most important Note has been found out the other 11 notes by using the Note Frequency ratio table and also finds out the Octave. The Note Frequency Ratio is also given in Table 1. Then matching the frequency values of all the 12 notes from the Excel Sheet and if the notes are in the Excel Sheet then takes the value as one note. From each of the range of frequencies of notes, the most frequently occurring frequencies with significant amplitude among the observed frequencies are identified. 1n all there will be 12 such frequencies and from among these 12 the most prominent 7 frequencies are identified. We have a Raga Knowledge base that consists of 7 note structures of each Raga and we match that particular 7 note structures of our input song with the knowledge base and if found then print the name of the Raga, otherwise print Mismatch.

After finding the raga name of that music, it requires to match with the raga playing time database and saving the music in preference time folders and create personalized time slot based music recommendation. The Sequence Diagram of the work depicted in Figure 3. There are two major types of music cloud services. The first is similar to a radio station. Create a profile with the service and build up a music library based on the listener's preferences. With this model of music cloud service, we will still encounter new music.

With the cloud storage music services, there are a limited number of songs can save to users mobile. With Google Music, that limit is 20,000 songs; Amazon Cloud Drive gives 5 gigabytes of storage for free that is enough space for around 1,000 songs. The main approach behind this work is that the ability to leverage storage that physically exists remotely but is logically a local storage for that music recommendation application. After download music from cloud using Cloud SaaS (Storage-as-a-Service), time slot based music recommendation system recommended that particular music to upload the particular raga playing database and user can play the music from that personalized music libraries. The overall process work flow of this work time slot based music recommendation on mobile cloud is illustrated in Figure 4.

Table 1. Frequency range and note frequency ratio of different notes

Western Notes	Indian Notes	Frequency Range	Note Frequency Ratio
A	(Dha)	215.5 – 226.5	1.000
A#	(ni)	226.6 – 239.9	1.054
B	(Ni)	240.0 – 252.5	1.125
C	(Sa)	252.6 – 269.5	1.186
C#	(re)	269.6 – 285.3	1.253
D	(Re)	285.4 – 302.3	1.333
D#	(ga)	302.4 – 320.3	1.415
E	(Ga)	320.4 – 339.3	1.500
F	(ma)	339.4 – 359.4	1.580
F#	(MA)	359.5 – 380.9	1.691
G	(Pa)	381.0 – 403.5	1.777
G#	(dha)	403.6 – 427.5	1.893

Figure 3. Sequence diagram of time slot based music recommendation system

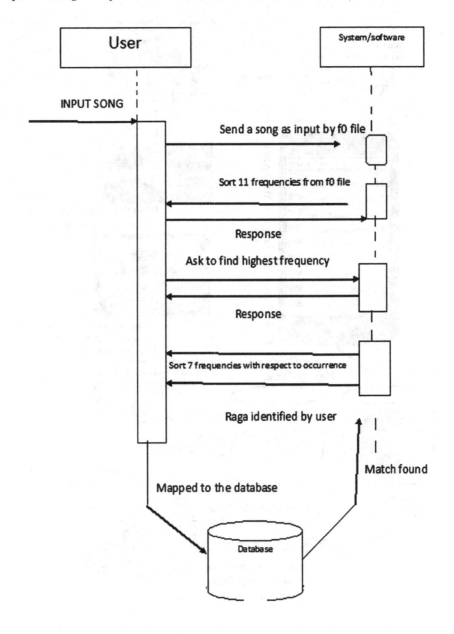

6. ANALYSIS AND DISCUSSION

The Ragas are based on a time theory. Each raga is allotted a special time slot of the day. It is believed that every note has a different emotional value and depends on each note structures raga playing time differs and its proper use can intensify or pacify emotions. So, the allotment of time depends on the notes included in the Raga and their melodic value. Rules of the melodic structure vary for each Raga. Some notes of a raga are strong and some notes are weak, some used only in specific cases, some are avoided, etc.

Figure 4. Workflow model of time slot based music recommendation system

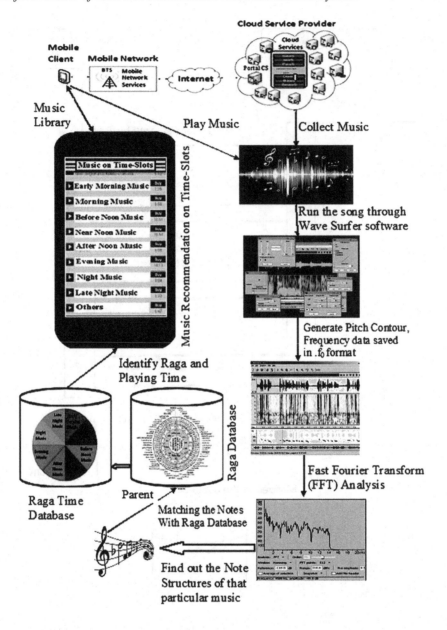

The primary aim of this chapter is to find out the song playing time automatically by determining the Raga name of that particular song by finding out the notation structure of that song and then matching this notation Patterns with the Raga music knowledge base. Then find out the playing time of that song by matching with the Raga time database. To find the playing time of a particular song, the steps are required:

Step 1: Take a song.
Step 2: Determine .f0 file that contains all the pitch values of that song using WaveSurfer Software.
Step 3: Calculate the number of occurrences of each frequency ranging from 50 to 500.

Step 4: Then calculate Most important note which frequency value contains highest occurrences and calculate Second most important note which frequency value contains second highest occurrences and also calculate other ten frequency values by using the Note Frequency Ratio.

Step 5: Among these twelve frequencies the most prominent 7 frequencies are identified and this is the note structure of that particular song.

Step 6: Matching this note structure with the Ragabase and find the raga name of that song.

Step 7: Then find the playing time of that raga from the raga timebase and generate the personalized time slot based intelligent music library. This is an intelligent recommender as it clusters groups of songs from a huge number of songs according to playing time of that song like other cognitive tools.

To illustrates the concept of this chapter, a practical example is described below:

Take a hindi song title as "Aji rooth kar" of Arzoo film (1965) and the playback singer is Lata Mangeshkar. Play this song through waveSurfer and generate .f0 file and find the most important note as "D/Re" as it has highest occurrences of 4646 and the second most important note as "G/Pa' as it has second highest occurrences 4512. Then finding out all the other notes using note-frequency ratio and mapping with the values of .f0 file and got the other notes as Sa/C, ma/F, Pa/G, Ni/B, ni/A#, Dha/A, Pa/G, ma/F, Ga/E, Re/D, Sa/C. After that matching these note structure with the Ragabase, determine the raga name is Desh and the thhat name is Khammaj. Then determine the playing time of that raga from raga timebase and find out the play time of the given song. The playing time of that song is "Late Night" as because the playing time of Desh Raga is "Late Night".

Some other hindi songs of raga Desh of same playing time are:

- Hindi song title as "Aap Ko Pyar Chupane Ki Buri Adat Hai" of film Neela Akash (1965) and the playback singers are Mohd. Rafi, Asha Bhosle.
- Hindi song title as "Beqasi Had Se Jab Guzar Jaye" of film Kalpana (1960) and the playback singer is Asha Bhosle.
- Hindi song title as "Dukh Ke Ab Din Bitat Nahi" of film Devdas (1936) and the playback singer is K. L. Saigal.
- Hindi song title as "Gori Tore Naina, Nainava Kajar Bin Kare Kare" of film Main Suhagan Hun (1964) and the playback singers are Mohd. Rafi, Asha Bhosle.
- Hindi song title as "Kadam Chale Age" of film Bhakta Surdas (1942) and the playback singer is K. L. Saigal.

If all of the above five songs run through the waveSurfer software and generate the .fo file and from this .f0 file if we follow our algorithmic steps then we observe the following outcomes-

1. **Thaat Name:** Khammaj.
2. **Raga Name:** Desh.
3. **Most Important Note:** D/Re.
4. **Second Important Note:** G/Pa.
5. **Notes:** Sa/C, Re/D, ma/F, Pa/G, Ni/B, ni/A#, Dha/A, Pa/G, ma/F, Ga/E, Re/D, Sa/C.
6. **Ascent:** Sa/C, Re/D, ma/F, Pa/G, Ni/B.

7.   **Decent:** ni/A#, Dha/A, Pa/G, ma/F, Ga/E, Re/D, Sa/C.
8.   **Species or Jati:** Pentatonic – Heptatonic (5 – 7).
9.   **Playing Time:** Late Night.

7. FUTURE CHALLENGES

In this Section of the chapter, it has been highlighted some of the most important challenges in deploying and utilizing Music Recommendation System using different time slots of a day on Mobile Cloud approaches as the future research directions. Future open challenges are presented in Figure 5. Some of the future challenging issues are:

1.   Mobile Cloud Computing poses challenges due to the intrinsic nature and constraints of wireless networks and devices.
2.   Limited processing power and storage capacities stimulate MCC.
3.   MCC moves processing and data storage away from the device, delivered via web technologies.
4.   Cloud applications require permanent Internet connection.
5.   Indian Music is a vast area. There are a lot of raga system presents like South Indian and North Indian music ragas. Some of ragas are parent ragas and some of the ragas are child raga. So concerning raga database and the raga playing database is one of the most challenging issues.

Figure 5. Open challenges of time slot based music recommendation system

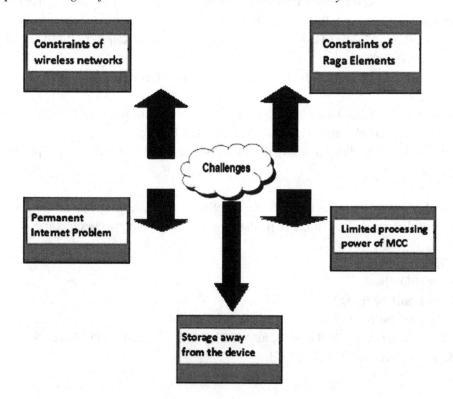

8. CONCLUSION

In this contribution, an innovation on analysis musical patterns is represented using several salient features, like polymorphism, Inheritance, generalization, specialization as on of the object-oriented programming methodologies and modeling. Although, the musical signal processing and pattern recognition is really a sturdy task especially in Indian Classical Music, this tiny effort is certainly be very supportive in the Musical Pattern Recognition perspective in the domain of object-oriented modeling and analysis approach.

Several imperative ragas can be considered and obtaining the songs of that particular raga to institute the work. The primary aspire of this work is to generate the behavioral model of any particular song using different elements of musical presentation with the help of UML. In future, all the different types of raga UML patterns may be intended to merge into the Raga Knowledge base and evaluate each of the solutions all over again.

Raga is an arrangement of notes that are played in a certain progression in ascending order and certain sequence in descending order. The ascending and descending notes sequence generate melody and no two different ragas are identical; that is, they do not have the same group of notes in the ascending and descending scales in order while playing. So behavioral modeling of any Indian Classical Music is very crucial and complex job. In this tiny endeavor, one very simple and intelligent method has implemented for automatically modeling for generating time-slot based music recommendation. For this, all the note patterns have been extracted from an input monotonic song signals and then make the necessary UML diagrams, principally Class diagram, Sequence diagrams and Object diagrams.

Raga identification by their nomenclatures of any Indian Classical Music is very important and in this tiny endeavor one very simple method is elaborated for automatically raga identification from the provided input vocal performances. For this, all the note patterns can be extracted from an input signals and then matches that notation with Raga Knowledgebase and generate the Raga name and also essential raga ingredients. The input patterns with Raga Knowledge base patterns matched for identification of raga name using feature extraction. This contribution might be implemented as a step towards developing a method to assist and evaluate the Raga recognition of Indian Classical Music. This Raga Pattern optimization is entirely based on the monotonic music. This approach will escort in future to extract the musical note-structures from the polyphonic musical patterns.

An intelligent archetype has also been introduced of Web-based rhythm structures learning system. In the analysis using a set of hardware and software tools the implemented system, all music rhythms have been evaluated exist with the same meter and then evaluate. The evaluation is appropriate for any musical performance. On the technical region, the developments were originated to be robust, and allowed for quick prototyping of versatile music rhythm generation for pervasive music rhythm teaching and learning process. A single user was able to install and operate the entire system with no trouble.

The proposed analysis performs sound for the monophonic vocal performances of classical ragas which resources for only vocal patterns of the song or raga in Indian Classical Music. Although in this tiny speculation the emotional features of musical performances in Indian Music are not explainable, in the prolific music viewpoint the musical pieces are explicated by the plentiful sessions of performances of Raga habitually play by the vocalists. This method can be further enhanced to classify the raga performed with instruments and rhythms. This classification also based on two broad classes of performing time of a raga. This can be improved by dividing the given samples into more specific performing session of a precise time like morning, noon, afternoon, dawn etc.

This chapter describes time slot based music recommendation system; a technique that allows listeners to personalized music depends on the appropriate raga playing time using raga time knowledgebase. This article has been implemented as a step towards developing a method to assist and evaluate the Raga recognition of Indian Music and also identify the playing time of that raga and generates the music recommender for mobile users using mobile cloud services. In this contribution, there are eighty Indian song music have been tested and find out the raga name and raga playing time and create appropriate mobile music recommendation system using different time slots of a day on mobile cloud.

ACKNOWLEDGMENT

Authors are grateful to Department of Science and Technology (DST) for sanctioning a research Project entitled "Dynamic Optimization of Green Mobile Networks: Algorithm, Architecture and Applications" under Fast Track Young Scientist scheme reference no.: SERB/F/5044/2012-2013 and No.DST/INSPIRE Fellowship/2013/327 under which this article has been completed.

REFERENCES

Abburu, S. (2012). Knowledge based Semantic Annotation Generation of Music. *International Journal of Computers and Applications*, *47*(8), 8–12. doi:10.5120/7206-9990

Abut, H., & Öztürk, Y. (1997, April). Interactive Classroom for DSP/Communications Courses.*Proc. of ICASSP 1997*.

Alfonceca, M., Cebrian, M., &Ortega, A. (2006). A Fitness Function for Computer-Generated Music using Genetic Algorithms. *WSEAS Trans. On Information Science & Applications*, *3*(3), 518-525.

Alghoniemy, M., & Tewfik, A. H. (2001). A network flow model for playlist generation.*Proc IEEE Intl Conf Multimedia and Expo*.

Allombert, G. A., & Desainte-Catherine, D. (2007). A system of interactive scores based on Petri nets. *Proceedings of the4th Sound and Music Computing Conference* (pp. 158-165).

Antti, E., & Anssi, K. (2000). Musical instrument recognition using cepstral coefficients and temporal features. *Proceedings of the2000 IEEE International Conference*Acoustics, Speech, and Signal Processing ICASSP'00.

Aucouturier, J. J., & Pachet, F. (2002). Scaling up music playlist generation. *Proceedings of the 2002 IEEE International Conference on Multimedia and Expo ICME'02* (Vol. 1, pp. 105-108). IEEE. doi:doi:10.1109/ICME.2002.1035729 doi:10.1109/ICME.2002.1035729

Avanzato, R. (2001). Student Use of Personal Digital Assistants in a Computer Engineering Course. *Proc. of 31st ASEE/IEEE Frontiers in Education Conference*. doi:10.1109/FIE.2001.963668

Baratè, A. (2008). *Music Description and Processing: An Approach Based on Petri Nets and XML*. INTECH Open Access Publisher.

Barate, A., Haus, G., & Ludovico, L. A. (2007). Petri nets applicability to music analysis and composition.*Proceedings of the 2007 International Computer Music Conference, International Computer Music Association, International Computer Music Conference* (pp. 97-100).

Bellini, P., Barthelemy, J., Bruno, I., Nesi, P., & Spinu, M. B. (2003). Multimedia music sharing among mediateques: Archives and distribution to their attendees. *Applied Artificial Intelligence*, *17*(8-9), 773–795. doi:10.1080/713827259

Bernard, W. E., & Jacobson, P. A. (1999). *U.S. Patent No. 5,918,213*. Washington, DC: U.S. Patent and Trademark Office.

Bhatkande, V. N. (1934). *Hindusthani Sangeet Paddhati*. Sangeet Karyalaya.

Bhattacharyya, M., & De, D. (2012). An Approach to identify Thhat of Indian Classical Music. *Proceedings of International Conference on Communications, Devices and Intelligent Systems (CODIS)* (pp. 592-595). IEEE. doi:10.1109/CODIS.2012.6422267

Bonwell, C., & Eison, G. (1991). ASHE-ERIC Higher Education Report: Vol. 1. *Active learning: Creating excitement in the classroom*. Washington, DC: George Washington University.

Bresin, R. (1998). Artificial neural networks based models for automatic performance of musical scores. *Journal of New Music Research. Taylor and Francis*, *27*(3), 239–270. doi:10.1080/09298219808570748

Brown, J. C. (1999). Computer identification of musical instruments using pattern recognition with cepstral coefficients as features. *The Journal of the Acoustical Society of America*, *105*(3), 1933–1941. doi:10.1121/1.426728 PMID:10089614

Castellano, M. A., Bharucha, J. J., & Krumhansl, C. L. (1984). Tonal hierarchies in the music of north India. *Journal of Experimental Psychology. General*, *113*(3), 394–412. doi:10.1037/0096-3445.113.3.394 PMID:6237169

Chakrabarty, S., & De, D. (2012). Quality Measure Model of Music Rhythm using Genetic Algorithm. *Proceedings of International Conference on Radar, Communication and Computing (ICRCC)* (pp. 125-130). IEEE. doi:10.1109/ICRCC.2012.6450561

Chakrabarty, S., Roy, S., & De, D. (2014). Pervasive Diary in Music Rhythm Education: A Context-Aware Learning Tool Using Genetic Algorithm. In Advanced Computing, Networking and Informatics (Vol. 1, pp. 669-677). Springer International Publishing. doi:doi:10.1007/978-3-319-07353-8_77 doi:10.1007/978-3-319-07353-8_77

Chakraborty, S., & De, D. (2012). Object Oriented Classification and Pattern Recognition of Indian Classical Ragas. *Proceedings of the 1st International Conference on Recent Advances in Information Technology (RAIT)*. IEEE. doi:10.1109/RAIT.2012.6194630

Chakraborty, S., & De, D. (2012). Object Oriented Classification and Pattern Recognition of Indian Classical Ragas. *Proceedings of the 1st International Conference on Recent Advances in Information Technology (RAIT)*. IEEE. doi:10.1109/RAIT.2012.6194630

Chakraborty, S., & De, D. (2012). Pattern Classification of Indian Classical Ragas based on Object Oriented Concepts. *International Journal of Advanced Computer engineering & Architecture*, *2*, 285-294.

Chakraborty, S., De, D., & Roy, K. (2011). A Knowledge Sharing Virtual Community for identification of different Indian Classical Ragas. NCICT, Allied Publishers.

Chemillier, M. (2004). Synchronization of musical words. *Theoretical Computer Science, 310*(1-3), 35–60. doi:10.1016/S0304-3975(03)00309-8

Chen, F., Meyers, B., & Yaron, D. (2000, July). *Using Handhelds Devices for Tests in Classes.* Carnegie Mellon University School of Computer Science Technical Report, No. CMUCS-00-152, and Human Computer Interaction Institute Technical Report CMU-HCII-00-101.

Chordia, P. (2004). Automatic raga classification using spectrally derived tone profiles. In *Proceedings of the International Computer Music Conference.*

Chordia, P. (2006). Automatic raag classification of pitch tracked performances using pitch-class and pitch-class dyad distributions. *Proceedings of International Computer Music Conference.*

Chordia, P. (2006). *Automatic Transcription of Solo TablaMusic* [Ph.D. diss.]. Stanford University.

Chordia, P., & Rae, A. (2008).TablaGyan: A System for RealtimeTabla Recognition and Resynthesis. In *Proceedings of the International Computer Music Conference.*

Chordia, P., Sastry, A., & Albin, A. (2010). Evaluating Multiple Viewpoint Models of Tabla Sequences. *Proceedings of 3rd International workshop on Machine learning and music* (pp. 21-24). ACM.

Chuan, C. H., & Chew, E. (2005, July). Polyphonic audio key finding using the spiral array CEG algorithm. *Proceedings of the IEEE International Conference on Multimedia and Expo ICME '05* (pp. 21-24). IEEE.

Clampitt, D. (2007). The legacy of John Clough in mathematical music theory. *Journal of Mathematics and Music, Taylor and Francis, 1*(2), 73–78. doi:10.1080/17459730701494710

Clayton, M. (2000). *Time in Indian Music: Rhythm, Metre, and Form in North Indian RâgPerformance.* Oxford, UK: Oxford University Press.

Conklin, D., & Witten, I. H. (1995). Multiple viewpoint systems for music prediction. *Journal of New Music Research, 24*(1), 51–73. doi:10.1080/09298219508570672

Coyle, E. J., & Shmulevich, I. (1998). A System for machine recognition of music patterns. *Proceedings of the Acoustic, Speech and Signal Processing* (pp. 3597-3600).

Crombie, D., Diikstra, S., Lenoir, R., McKenzie, N., & Schut, E. (2002). Towards accessible multimedia music. *Proceedings of the Second International Conference on Web Delivering of Music WEDELMUSIC '02* (pp. 192-199). IEEE. doi:doi:10.1109/WDM.2002.1176211 doi:10.1109/WDM.2002.1176211

Crombie, D., Lenoir, R., & McKenzie, N. (2003, September). Producing accessible multimedia music. *Proceedings of the Third International Conference on Web Delivering of Music WEDELMUSIC '03* (pp. 45-48). IEEE. doi:doi:10.1109/WDM.2003.1233872 doi:10.1109/WDM.2003.1233872

Dalibor, M., Zeppelzauer, M., & Breiteneder, C. (2010). Features for content-based audio retrieval. *Advances in Computers, 78,* 71-150.

Datta, A. K., et al. (1995). Relevance of Consonance in Indian Musical Scale: Theory and Practice. *J. Acoust. Soc. Ind., 23*.

Datta, A. K., et al. (1997). Pitch Analysis of Recorded Vocal Performances in Hindustani Music: Evidence of a Personal Scale. *J. Acoust. Soc. Ind., 25*.

Datta, A. K., et al. (1998). Multiple States in a Note in Hindustani Music and their Relevance to Consonance. *J. Acoust. Soc. Ind., 26*.

Datta, A. K., Sengupta, R., Dey, N., & Nag, D. (2000, December). On Scientific Approaches to the Study of Vaditya in Indian Music. *Proc. Fifth Int. Workshop on Recent Trends in Speech,Music and Allied Signal Processing*.

De, D., & Roy, S. (2012, December). Polymorphism in Indian Classical Music: A Pattern Recognition Approach. *Proceedings of International Conference on Communications, Devices and Intelligent Systems (CODIS)* (pp. 612-615). IEEE. doi:10.1109/CODIS.2012.6422277

De, D., & Roy, S. (2012, December). Inheritance in Indian Classical Music: An Object-Oriented Analysis and Pattern Recognition Approach. *Proceedings of International Conference on Radar, Communication and Computing (ICRCC)*, (pp. 193-198). IEEE. doi:10.1109/ICRCC.2012.6450575

Dean, R. T., Bailes, F., & Dunsmuir, W. T. M. (2014). Time series analysis of real-time music perception: Approaches to the assessment of individual and expertise differences in perception of expressed affect. *Journal of Mathematics and Music, 8*(3), 183–205. doi:10.1080/17459737.2014.928752

Deliège, F., & Pedersen, T. B. (2008). Using fuzzy lists for playlist management. In *Advances in Multimedia Modeling* (pp. 198–209). Springer Berlin Heidelberg. doi:10.1007/978-3-540-77409-9_19

Deliège, F., & Pedersen, T. B. (2009). Using fuzzy song sets in music warehouses. *Scalable Fuzzy Algorithms for Data Management and Analysis: Methods and Design: Methods and Design, 54*.

Distefano, S., Scarpa, M., & Puliafito, A. (2011). From UML to Petri Nets: The PCM-Based Methodology. *IEEE Transactions on Software Engineering, 37*(1), 65–79. doi:10.1109/TSE.2010.10

Dostal, M. (2005). Genetic Algorithms as a model of musical creativity – on generating of a human-like rhythmic accompaniment. *Computing and Informatics, 22*, 321–340.

Douglas, E., & Schmidhuber, J. (2002). *A first look at music composition using lstm recurrent neural networks*. Istituto Dalle Molle Di Studi Sull Intelligenza Artificiale.

El-Maleh, K., Klein, M., Petrucci, G., & Kabal, P. (2000). Speech/music discrimination for multimedia applications. *Proceedings of the 2000 IEEE International Conference on Acoustics, Speech, and Signal Processing ICASSP'00* (Vol. 6, pp. 2445-2448). IEEE.

Ellis, D. (2003). *Pattern Recognition Applied to Music Signals*. New York: JHU CLSP Summer School, Laboratory for Recognition and Organization of Speech and Audio, Columbia University.

Emmanuel, D. (2010). A wavelet-based parameterization for speech/music discrimination. *Computer Speech & Language, 24*(2), 341–357. doi:10.1016/j.csl.2009.05.003

Essid, S., Richard, G., & David, B. (2004). Musical instrument recognition based on class pair-wise feature selection. *Proceedings of International Conference on Music Information Retrieval*. 2004.

Foote, J., & Cooper, M. (2001). Visualizing Musical Structure and Rhythm via Self-Similarity. *Proceedings of the International Computer Music Conference* (pp. 419-422).

France, R. B., Kim, D. K., Ghosh, S., & Song, E. (2004). A UML-based pattern specification technique. *IEEE Transactions on* Software Engineering, *30*(3), 193–206.

Freeman, G., Dony, R., & Areibi, S. (2007). Audio environment classification for hearing aids using artificial neural networks with windowed input. *Proceedings of IEEE Symposium on Computational Intelligence in Image and Signal Processing*. doi:10.1109/CIISP.2007.369314

Gartland-Jones, A., & Copley, P. (2003). The Suitability of Genetic Algorithms for Musical Composition. *Contemporary Music Review*, *22*(3), 43–55. doi:10.1080/0749446032000150870

Gillet, O., & Richard, G. (2003). Automatic Labeling of TablaSignals. *Proceedings of the International Conference on Music Information Retrieval* (pp. 117-124).

Haus, G., & Rodriguez, A. (1993). Formal music representation; a case study: the model of Ravel's Bolero by Petri nets. *Music Processing. Computer Music and Digital Audio Series*, 165-232.

Haus, G., & Sametti, A. (1991). Scoresynth: A system for the synthesis of music scores based on petri nets and a music algebra. *Computer*, *24*(7), 56–60. doi:10.1109/2.84837

Herrera, P. (2000). Towards instrument segmentation for music content description: a critical review of instrument classification techniques. *Proceedings of theInternational symposium on music information retrieval, ISMIR*.

Heykin, S. (2005). Neural Networks: A Comprehensive Foundation (2nd ed.). Pearson Prentice Hall, Pearson Education.

Hopfgartner, F., & Jose, J. M. (2010). Semantic user profiling techniques for personalised multimedia recommendation. *Multimedia Systems*, *16*(4-5), 255–274. doi:10.1007/s00530-010-0189-6

Huron, D. B. (2006). *Sweet anticipation: Music and the psychology of expectation*. MIT press.

Iordache, M., & Antsaklis, P. J. (2007). *Supervisory control of concurrent systems: a Petri net structural approach*. Springer Science & Business Media.

Iordache, V. M., & Antsaklis, P. J. (n. d.). Supervisory Control of Concurrent Systems. In *A Petri Net Structural Approach*. Birkhauser Boston.

Java3D Object Controlling over PDA-Server Connection. (n. d.). Retrieved from http://aspen.ucs.indiana.edu/collabtools/extras/Java3d_waba_files/frame.html

Jensen, C. A., Mungure, E. M., Pedersen, T. B., & Sorensen, K. (2007, April). A data and query model for dynamic playlist generation. *Proceedings of the2007 IEEE 23rd International Conference onData Engineering Workshop* (pp. 65-74). IEEE. doi:doi:10.1109/ICDEW.2007.4400975 doi:10.1109/ICDEW.2007.4400975

Khan, M., Wasfi, G. A. K., & Moinuddin, M. (2004). Automatic classification of speech and music using neural networks. *Proceedings of the 2nd ACM international workshop on Multimedia databases*. ACM. doi:10.1145/1032604.1032620

Kippen, J., & Bel, B. (1992). Modelling music with grammars: formal language representation in the BolProcessor. In A. Marsden & A. Pople (Eds.), *Computer Representations andModels in Music*. London: Academic Press.

Knees, P., Pohle, T., Schedl, M., & Widmer, G. (2006, October). Combining audio-based similarity with web-based data to accelerate automatic music playlist generation.*Proceedings of the 8th ACM international workshop on Multimedia information retrieval* (pp. 147-154). ACM. doi:10.1145/1178677.1178699

Lande, T. S., & Vollsnes, A. O. (1995). Object Oriented Music Analysis. *Computers and the Humanities*, *28*(4-5), 253–257. doi:10.1007/BF01830272

Lee, S. K., Cho, Y. H., & Kim, S. H. (2010). Collaborative filtering with ordinal scale-based implicit ratings for mobile music recommendations. *Information Sciences*, *180*(11), 2142–2155. doi:10.1016/j.ins.2010.02.004

Lee, S. K., Cho, Y. H., & Kim, S. H. (2010). Collaborative filtering with ordinal scale-based implicit ratings for mobile music recommendations. *Information Sciences*, *180*(11), 2142–2155. doi:10.1016/j.ins.2010.02.004

Lehtiniemi, A. (2008, December). Evaluating SuperMusic: streaming context-aware mobile music service. *Proceedings of the 2008 International Conference on Advances in Computer Entertainment Technology* (pp. 314-321). ACM. doi:10.1145/1501750.1501826

Lidy, T., Silla, C. N. Jr, Cornelis, O., Gouyon, F., Rauber, A., Kaestner, C. A., & Koerich, A. L. (2010). On the suitability of state-of-the-art music information retrieval methods for analyzing, categorizing and accessing non-Western and ethnic music collections. *Signal Processing*, *90*(4), 1032–1048. doi:10.1016/j.sigpro.2009.09.014

Lopez-Ortega, O., & Lopez-Popa, S. I. (2012). Fractals, Fuzzy Logic and expert Systems to assist in the construction of musical pieces. Expert Systems with Applications, 39, 11911-11923.

Lu, C., & Tseng, V. S. (2009). A novel method for personalized music recommendation. Expert Systems with Applications, 36, 10035-10044.

Mani, R., & Nawab, S. H. (1998). Integration Of DSP Algorithms And Musical Constraints For The Separation Of Partials In Polyphonic Music. IEEE.

Matic, D. (2010). A Genetic Algorithm for composing Music.*In proceedings of the Yugoslav Journal of Operations Research*, *20*(1), 157-177.

McCormack, J. (1996). Grammar Based Music Composition. In R. Stocker et al. (Eds.), *Complex Systems. From local Interactions to Global Phenomena* (pp. 320–336). Amsterdam: ISO Press.

Mcilwain, P., & McCormack, J. (2005). Design Issues in Musical Composition Networks, Generate and Test. *Proceedings of the Australasian Computer Music Conference*, (pp. 96 – 101).

Mcilwain, P., & McCormack, J. (2005). Design Issues in Musical Composition Networks, Generate and Test.*Proceedings of the Australasian Computer Music Conference* (pp. 96 – 101).

Montiel, M., & Gómez, F. (2014). Music in the pedagogy of mathematics. *Journal of Mathematics and Music. Taylor and Francis*, 8(2), 151–156. doi:10.1080/17459737.2014.936109

Moreno, S. (2009). Can Music Influence Language and Cognition? *Journal of Mathematics and Music. Contemporary Music Review. Taylor and Francis*, 28(3), 329–345. doi:10.1080/07494460903404410

Mozer, M. C. (1994). Neural Network Music Composition by Prediction: Exploring the Benefits of Psychoacoustic Constraints and Multi-scale Processing. *Journal of Connection Science. Taylor and Francis*, 6(2-3), 247–280. doi:10.1080/09540099408915726

Mušic, G., Hafner, I., Winkler, S., & Škrjanc, I. (2012). A Matlab based Petri net Tool for E-learning: Examples for timed simulation and scheduling. Proceedings of MATHMOD, Vienna (pp. 15-17).

Nicholson, T. J. K., & Nakatsu, R. (2000). Emotion Recognition in Speech Using Neural Networks. *Neural Computing and Applications, 9*, 290–296.

Nikiforova, O., & Pavlova, N. (2008, October). Development of the tool for generation of UML class diagram from two-hemisphere model. *Proceedings of the Third International Conference on Software Engineering Advances ICSEA'08* (pp. 105-112). IEEE. doi:doi:10.1109/ICSEA.2008.37 doi:10.1109/ICSEA.2008.37

palmOne: Education Solutions Success Stories. Various colleges utilizing PDA's in Education. (n. d.). Retrieved from http://www.palmone.com/us/education/studies/study61.html

Pampalk, E., Pohle, T., & Widmer, G. (2005, September). *Dynamic Playlist Generation Based on Skipping Behavior* (Vol. 5). ISMIR.

Pandey, G., Mishra, C., & Ipe, P. (2003). Tansen: A system for automatic raga identification. In *Proceedings of the 1st Indian International Conference on Artificial Intelligence* (pp. 1350–1363).

Pauws, S., & Eggen, B. (2002, October). PATS: Realization and user evaluation of an automatic playlist generator. In ISMIR.

PDA Resources. (n. d.). Retrieved from http://www.marietta.edu/ ~littlea/PDAindex.html

Platel, H., Baron, J.-C., Desgranges, B., Bernard, F., & Eustache, F. (2003). Semantic and episodic memory of music are subserved by distinct neural networks. *NeuroImage*, 20(1), 244–256. doi:10.1016/S1053-8119(03)00287-8 PMID:14527585

Platt, J. (1991). A resource-allocating network for function interpolation. *Neural Computation*, 3(2), 213–225. doi:10.1162/neco.1991.3.2.213

Pohle, T., Pampalk, E., & Widmer, G. (2005, September). Generating similarity-based playlists using traveling salesman algorithms.*Proceedings of the 8th International Conference on Digital Audio Effects (DAFx-05)* (pp. 220-225).

Priya, K., Ramani, G. R., & Jacob, G. S. (2012). Data Mining Techniques for Automatic recognition of Carnatic Raga Swaram notes. *International Journal of Computers and Applications, 52*(10), 4–10. doi:10.5120/8236-1444

Rao, B., Tarakeswara, Chinnam, S., Kunth, L. P., &Gargi, M. (2012). Automatic Melakartha Raaga Identification System: Carnatic Music. *International Journal of Advanced Research in Artificial Intelligence, 1*(4), 43–44.

Reddy, P., Tarakeswara, B. R., & Sudha, K. R., & Hari. (2011). K-Nearest Neighbour and Earth Mover Distance for Raaga Recognition. *International Journal of Computers and Applications, 33*(5), 30–38.

Roddy, C., Douglas, C. E., & Cox, C. (2005). Beyond emotion archetypes: Databases for emotion modelling using neural networks. *Neural Networks, 18*(4), 371–388. doi:10.1016/j.neunet.2005.03.002 PMID:15961273

Ross, C. J., & Rao, P. (2012). Detection of Raga-Characteristics Phrases From Hindustani Classical Music Audio. *Proceedings of the 2nd CompMusic Workshop* (pp. 133-138).

Rothermel, K., Schnitzer, S., Lange, R., Dürr, F., & Farrell, T. (2012). *Context-aware and quality-aware algorithms for efficient mobile object management. In Proceedings of Elsevier Journal of Pervasive and Mobile Computing* (pp. 131–146). Elsevier.

Roy, S., Chakrabarty, S., Bhakta, P., & De, D. (2013). Modelling High Performing Music Computing using Petri Nets.*Proceedings of International Conference on Control, Instrumentation, Energy and Communication* (pp. 757-761).

Roy, S., Chakrabarty, S., & De, D. (2014). A Framework of Musical Pattern Recognition Using Petri Nets. In *Emerging Trends in Computing and Communication* (pp. 245–252). Springer India. doi:10.1007/978-81-322-1817-3_26

Roy, S., Chakrabarty, S., & De, D. (2014). Automatic Raga Recognition using fundamental Frequency Range of Extracted Musical notes. *Proceedings of theInternational Conference on Image and Signal Processing (ICISP-2014)*, (pp. 337-345). Elsevier.

Rubenstein, W. B. (1987, December). A database design for musical information. *SIGMOD Record, 16*(3), 479–490. doi:10.1145/38714.38762

Schildt, H. (2011). Java: The Complete Reference (7th ed.). New Delhi, India: Tata Mcgraw Hill Education Private Limited.

Schmidt, D. C., Stal, M., Rohnert, H., & Buschmann, F. (2013). *Pattern-Oriented Software Architecture, Patterns for Concurrent and Networked Objects* (Vol. 2). John Wiley & Sons.

Scott, P. (2001). Music classification using neural networks. Manuscript Class ee373a, Stanford.

Secrest, B. G., & Doddington, G. R. (1983). An integrated pitch tracking algorithm for speech systems. *Proc. IEEE ICASSP* (pp.1352-1355). IEEE. doi:10.1109/ICASSP.1983.1172016

Sengupta, R. (1990). Study on some Aspects of the Singer's Formant in North Indian Classical Singing. *Journal of Voice, Raven Press, New York, 4*(2), 129.

Shmulevich, I., & Coyle, E. J. (1997). Establishing the Tonal Context for Musical Pattern Recognition. *Proceedings of the 1997 IEEE Workshop on Applications of Signal Processing to Audio and Acoustics.* doi:10.1109/ASPAA.1997.625608

Shmulevich, I., & Povel, D. (1998). Rhythm Complexity Measures for Music Pattern Recognition. *Proceedings of IEEE Workshop on Multimedia Signal Processing.* doi:10.1109/MMSP.1998.738930

Shmulevich, I., Yli-Harja, O., Coyle, E. J., Povel, D., & Lemstrm, K. (2001). *Perceptual Issues in Music Pattern Recognition Complexity of Rhythm and Key Finding. Computers and the Humanities.* Kluwer Academic Publishers.

Sinha, P. (2008). Artificial Composition: An Experiment on Indian Music. *Journal of New Music Research. Taylor and Francis, 37*(3), 221–232. doi:10.1080/09298210802535010

Song, Y., Dixon, S., & Pearce, M. (2012). A Survey of Music Recommendation Systems and Future Perspectives. *Proceedings of theInternational Symposium on Computer Music Modelling and Retrieval* (pp. 395-410). IEEE.

Sridhar, R., & Geetha, T. V. (2009). Raga identification of carnatic music for music information retrieval. *International Journal of Recent Trends in Engineering, 1*(1), 571–574.

Sridhar, R., Karthiga, S., & Geetha, T. V. (2010). Fundamental Frequency Estimation of Carnatic Music Songs Based on the Principle of Mutation. *IJCSI, 7*(4).

Sridhar, R., & Subramanian, M. (2011). Latent Dirichlet Allocation Model for Raga Identification of Caenatic Music. *Journal of Computer Science*, 1711-1716.

Srimani, P. K., & Parimala, Y. G. (2012). Artificial Neural Network (ANN) Approach for an Intelligent System: A Case Study in Carnatic Classical Music (CCM). *Proceedings of International Conference on Intelligent Computational Systems* (pp. 101-105).

Stavros, N., & Fakotakis, N. (2008). *Speech/music discrimination based on discrete wavelet transform. In Artificial Intelligence: Theories, Models and Applications* (pp. 205–211). Berlin: Springer.

Stavros, N., Potamitis, I., & Fakotakis, N. (2009). Exploiting temporal feature integration for generalized sound recognition. *EURASIP Journal on Advances in Signal Processing, 1*, 807162.

Su, J. H., Yeh, H. H., Yu, P. S., & Tseng, V. S. (2010). Music recommendation using content and context information mining. *IEEE Intelligent Systems, 25*(1), 16–26. doi:10.1109/MIS.2010.23

Sun, X. (2000). A pitch determination algorithm based on sub-harmonic to harmonic ratio. *Proceedings of International Conference of Speech and Language Processing.*

Tarakeswara, B. R., & Reddy, P. (2011). A Novel Process for Melakartha Raaga Recognition using Hidden Marcov Models (HMM). *International Journal of Research and Reviews in Computer Science, 2*(2), 508–513.

Todd, P. M., & Loy, G. D. (Eds.). (1991). *Music and connectionism.* MIT Press.

Trček, D., & Trček, G. (2013). *Computationally Supported Musical Composition Using Petri Nets.* Latest Trends in Applied Computational Science.

Tzanetakis, G., & Cook, P. (2002). Musical Genre Classification of Audio Signals. *IEEE Transactions on Speech and Audio Processing, 10*(5), 293–302. doi:10.1109/TSA.2002.800560

Tzanetakis, G., Kapur, A., Schloss, W. A., & Wright, M. (2007). Computational Ethnomusicology. *Journal of Interdisciplinary Music Studies, 1*(2), 1-24.

Vasudha, J., Iyshwarya, G., Selvi, T. A., Iniyaa, S., & Jeyakumar, G. (2011). Application of Computer-Aided Music Composition in Music Therapy. *International Journal of Innovation. Management & Technology, 2*(1), 55–57.

Volk, A., & Honingh, A. (2012). Mathematical and computational approaches to music: challenges in an interdisciplinary enterprise. *Journal of Mathematics and Music. Taylor and Francis, 6*(2), 73–81. doi:10.1080/17459737.2012.704154

Walton. A. (2010). A graph theoretic approach to tonal modulation. *Journal of Mathematics and Music,* 45-56.

Wang, X., Rosenblum, D., & Wang, Y. (2012, October). Context-aware mobile music recommendation for daily activities. In *Proceedings of the 20th ACM international conference on Multimedia* (pp. 99-108). ACM.

Wang, X., Rosenblum, D., & Wang, Y. (2012, October). Context-aware mobile music recommendation for daily activities.*Proceedings of the 20th ACM international conference on Multimedia* (pp. 99-108). ACM. doi:10.1145/2393347.2393368

Williams, D. B., & Webster, P. R. (1996). *Music Technology.* Academic Press.

Williams, R. J., & David, Z. (1989). A learning algorithm for continually running fully recurrent neural networks. *Neural Computation, 1*(2), 270–280. doi:10.1162/neco.1989.1.2.270

Wimmer, M., Schauerhuber, A., Kappel, G., Retschitzegger, W., Schwinger, W., & Kapsammer, E. (2011). A survey on UML-based aspect-oriented design modeling. *ACM Computing Surveys, 43*(4), 28. doi:10.1145/1978802.1978807

Xia, F., Asabere, N. Y., Ahmed, A. M., Li, J., & Kong, X. (2013). Mobile multimedia recommendation in smart communities: A survey. *Access, 1,* 606–624. doi:10.1109/ACCESS.2013.2281156

Yau, S. S., Gupta, S. K. S., Karim, F., Ahamed, S. I., Wang, Y., & Wang, B. (2003, June). Smart Classroom: Enhancing Collaborative Learning Using Pervasive Computing Technology. *Proc. of American Society of Engineering Education 2003 Annual Conference.*

Zhu, J. (2011, July). Multimedia Music Teaching System Application. *Key Engineering Materials, 474,* 1903–1908. doi:10.4028/www.scientific.net/KEM.474-476.1903

Chapter 13
Content Coverage and Redundancy Removal in Video Summarization

Hrishikesh Bhaumik
RCC Institute of Information Technology, India

Siddhartha Bhattacharyya
RCC Institute of Information Technology, India

Susanta Chakraborty
Indian Institute of Engineering Science and Technology, India

ABSTRACT

Over the past decade, research in the field of Content-Based Video Retrieval Systems (CBVRS) has attracted much attention as it encompasses processing of all the other media types i.e. text, image and audio. Video summarization is one of the most important applications as it potentially enables efficient and faster browsing of large video collections. A concise version of the video is often required due to constraints in viewing time, storage, communication bandwidth as well as power. Thus, the task of video summarization is to effectively extract the most important portions of the video, without sacrificing the semantic information in it. The results of video summarization can be used in many CBVRS applications like semantic indexing, video surveillance copied video detection etc. However, the quality of the summarization task depends on two basic aspects: content coverage and redundancy removal. These two aspects are both important and contradictory to each other. This chapter aims to provide an insight into the state-of-the-art approaches used for this booming field of research.

1. INTRODUCTION

With the ever decreasing cost of digital storage devices and advancement of technology in recent years, video recorders have gained immense popularity. A large number of videos are produced and uploaded at an ever increasing rate. Digital libraries and video repositories like YouTube, DailyMotion, MyVideo etc. enable users to upload, retrieve, view and share videos over the internet. This has also been facilitated

DOI: 10.4018/978-1-5225-0498-6.ch013

by a many fold increase in communication bandwidth provided by Internet Service Providers (ISPs). Due to its inherent structure, a video encompasses the other three media types as well, i.e. text, image and audio, combining them into a single data stream. As a consequence, the analysis and retrieval of videos has attracted much attention from researchers and application developers. The research issues include feature extraction, similarity/dissimilarity measures, segmentation (temporal and semantic), key-frame extraction, indexing, annotation, classification and retrieval of videos. Video summarization is an application which lies on the crossroads of these research issues. The objective of video summarization is to reproduce and represent a video to the user in a concise manner such that its overall semantic meaning is preserved. The time and bandwidth constraints besetting the user are balanced to a great extent by such summarization task. Real-time video summarization helps in immediate indexing of videos for facilitating retrieval from the repository. Also it facilitates the user in assessing whether watching the entire video would be useful or not. Video summarization and representation through key frames have been frequently adopted as an efficient method to preserve the overall contents of the video with a minimum amount of time. The types of video summarization include static (also known as storyboard representation) and dynamic (also called video skimming). Storyboard or static representation is produced by means of selecting key-frames from a set of video frames, obtained after decomposing a video. Audio clips have temporal characteristics and are therefore not an integral part of static summaries. However, some keywords in the form of meta-data may be tagged with the static video frames to assist in keyword based indexing and retrieval. The set of key-frames serve as features of the video and these key-frames help in indexing task. During the process of retrieval, the key-frames corresponding to a video may be matched with the key-frames extracted from the query video. As such, the task of video mining is facilitated through this process.

On the contrary, video skimming techniques aim at selecting shots or scenes from the entire video and collating it together to produce a meaningful summary. Due to the intrinsic nature of dynamic summaries, the other three media types may feature in it. This enables the user to assimilate the contents of the video in a short time, so as to ascertain if the same is of interest to him/her. Video summarization is one of the key application areas of video indexing and content based video retrieval. Video summarization and representation through key frames have been frequently adopted as an efficient method to preserve the overall contents of the video with a minimum amount of time. The results of video summarization can be reused in many areas such as content-based video retrieval (Patel & Meshram, 2012), semantic indexing (Papadimitriou et al., 1998; Marcus & Maletic, 2003; Smith et al., 2003), Copied Video Detection (CVD) (Kim et al., 2008) etc. A video summary can be categorized as a static summary (storyboard), which is a set of selected key-frames (Chang et al., 1999; DeMenthon et al., 1998; Hanjalic & Zhang, 1999; Yeung & Yeo, 1997), or a dynamic video representation (Lienhart, 2000; Nam & Tewfik, 1999; Gon & Liu, 2000a; Smith & Kanade, 1997) formed by concatenating short video segments. Dynamic video summarization methods include semantic analysis (Nam & Tewfik, 1999; Ma et al., 2002), motion model (Ma & Zhang, 2002; Vasconcelos & Lippman, 1998), expectation maximization (Orriols & Binefa, 2001) and singular value decomposition (Gong & Liu, 2000a). As there are plentiful redundancies in the frames of a shot, the frames which appropriately portray the contents in the best possible way are selected (Sze et al., 2005; Truong & Venkatesh, 2007; Besiris, 2007; Mukherjee et al., 2007). These frames are termed as key-frames. The various features taken into consideration for key-frame extraction include edges of objects in the frames, optical flow, RGB histograms, shapes of objects, spatial distribution of MPEG-7 (Narasimha et al., 2003) discrete cosine coefficient of MPEG (Moving Picture Experts Group) motion vectors (Wang et al., 2007), and derived features due to camera movement (Guironnet et al., 2007; Fauvet et al., 2004). The state of the art methods in key-frame extraction techniques have been classified (Truong & Venkatesh, 2007) as sequential contrast, simplification of the curve, global comparison, reference frame, clustering and event/object-based methods. The goal of video summarization is to provide semantically rich visual content, eliminate redundancies and have good performance which can work effectively in large databases. Furthermore, it would perform better in real time as well as in limited bandwidth.

The rest of the chapter is organized as follows. Section 1.2 describes the basic concepts. A review of the video summarization techniques is presented in section 1.3. Section 1.4 elucidates the objectives of video summarization. The steps of video summarization, indexing and retrieval are detailed in section 1.5. The aspects of video summarization with respect to content coverage and redundancy elimination are presented in section 1.6. Section 1.6 also includes a sub-section on the evaluation metrics in video summarization. Finally, conclusion is drawn in section 1.7.

2. BASIC CONCEPTS

2.1. Hierarchy of Video Decomposition

Video decomposition is the process of detecting and identifying meaningful segments of a video. A video is a collection of image frames arranged in a time-sequenced manner. Hierarchically, the frames composing a video exist at the lowest level of granularity. Initially, the given video can be disintegrated into its constituent frames by using a codec corresponding to the file type/compression used. A given video, may thus be represented as a set of frames, $V = \{f_1, f_2, f_3, ..., f_{n-1}, f_n\}$, where f_i represents the ith frame. Again, each shot is a subset of consecutive frames taken from set V. Thus, $V = \{s_1, s_2, s_3, ..., s_{k-1}, s_k\}$ represents the set of shots composing the video arranged in a time-sequenced manner. The jth shot may be represented as a set of consecutive frames such that $s_j = \{f_p, f_{p+1}, f_{p+2}, ..., f_{q-1}, f_q\}$. The following postulates hold for the mentioned sets:

P1: $V = s_1 \cup s_2 \cup s_3 \cup ...... \cup s_{k-1} \cup s_k$

P2: $s_i \neq \varphi, \ \forall i = 1, 2, 3...k$

P3: $s_i \cap s_j = \varphi, i \neq j$

P4: $(\forall m) f_m \in s_i, p \leq m \leq q, q - p > 0, s_i \in V$

P1 depicts that the whole video is a conglomeration of a number of shots. Each of the shots contains a certain number of frames. Thus, P2 portrays that each of the shots has a definite duration and none of the shots has zero length. According to P3, each frame of the video belongs to only one shot and there is no frame belonging to multiple shots. This is true when there are clear boundaries (hard cuts) between the shots. In case of dissolve sequences, a definite boundary does not exist between the shots and in such cases it is rather difficult to classify a dissolve frame into a set of frames representing a shot. In other words, the concept of crisp sets may not be applicable for dissolve sequences. As a dissolve sequence frame may belong to multiple sets, it is imperative to note that such frames may belong to multiple shots, having different degrees of membership to the concerned shots. In such cases a membership function may be used to denote the fuzzy membership values of a frame to a set of shots. Postulate P4 ensures that a set of consecutive time-sequenced frames form a shot and there are no missing frames in the shot sequence.

Feature extraction is necessary step for analysis of the video frames. This leads to the automatic determination of shot boundaries by devising algorithms. The features extracted from the video frames may be low-level, mid-level or high level features. The low-level features are based on characteristics of the image that does not take into consideration the visual or semantic content portrayed in an image. The low-level features consist of RGB values/histograms, intensity values, mean, variance, skewness, entropy of the pixel values etc. The mid-level features are intermediate between the low-level features and high level semantics. The mid-level features consist of feature point detectors and descriptors. Many feature point detectors and descriptors have been devised such as SIFT (Lowe, 1999), SURF (Bay et al., 2008), DAISY (Tola et al., 2010), BRIEF (Calonder et al., 2010) etc. Salient points in the image are identified by these detectors which serve as features of the image. The salient points detected by the algorithm are represented by means of a feature vector. Although, the feature points may be used for object identification in an image, these are not appropriate for high level semantic description of the content depicted in an image. High-level features of an image include the shapes of objects, trajectory of paths followed by objects, motion vectors etc. These may be used for high level description of the content in an image.

The identification of shot boundaries is an important step towards analysis and indexing of videos. The shot boundaries are an outfall of the editing process in the studio where different shots are combined together to form the final video sequence. In the literature, a shot has been defined as a sequence of frames captured by a single camera in a definite period of time. The shot boundaries encountered in real life are either abrupt transitions or gradual changes. After the process of shot boundary analysis, the shots so obtained have specific features which can be used to determine the similarity between the shots. This is useful for clustering shots and determining the scenes composing the video. Thus, a scene consists of a set of shots having similar background. In other words, similar shots having temporal adjacency are grouped together as scenes. Hence, a scene may be described as a collection of shots sharing a semantic relationship. A scene thus portrays and imparts a high-level story. A group of scenes comprises of a sequence/story. In the literature, semantic decomposition of a video has been referred to as scene detection. This has been illustrated in Figure 1.

2.2. Video Segmentation

The process of video segmentation consists of decomposing a video into its constituent units. These units may be scenes or shots. A semantic disintegration of the video in the temporal domain leads to scenes, while a temporal decomposition based on camera breaks, leads to shots. A video sequence is analogous to a document or an article. The logical units can be viewed as described below.

An analogy between a video and a document reveals that the video scenes are analogous to the paragraphs of an article. At the next level of granularity, since the scenes are composed of video shots, these are analogous to sentences constituting the paragraph. Again, the shots can be broken down into frames, much like the sentences can be defragmented into the composing words. The smallest unit of a video sequence is a frame. A video can also be fragmented in the spatial domain leading to the extraction of objects. Spatial segmentation is a vital step for object tracking, applied mainly in video surveillance and event detection. Figure 2 depicts the shot boundary between two shots of the NASA 25th Anniversary Seg03 video available at www.open-video.org. Figure 3 shows a few shot boundary frames of the same video.

Figure 1. Hierarchy of video decomposition

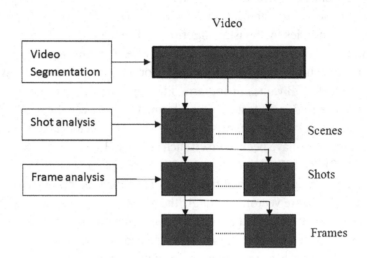

Figure 2. Few decomposed frames from NASA 25th Anniversary

Figure 3. A few shot boundary frames from NASA

3. REVIEW OF VIDEO SUMMARIZATION TECHNIQUES

Video summarization is the process of presenting a concise and meaningful representation of a video. Video abstraction and summarization techniques are required to harness the rich visual content of a video. The summarized video has a length which is far lesser than the original one. Thereby, it enables the user to browse through the contents in much lesser time. Moreover, it contains non-redundant video data in a short and structured format. Usually, a subset of the video data, such as key frames or highlights (such as shots, scenes, or stories) is extracted for a compact representation and fast browsing of the video content. A shot is a sequence of frames captured through a single click of the camera. It serves as the basic building block of a video. A scene on the other hand is a collection of a set of continuous semantically related shots. A video is thus a conglomeration of several scenes. Given the significance of shots in videos, detection of shots or shot boundary analysis is a key step towards video summarization. Shot boundary analysis has also been referred to as temporal video segmentation in the literature. In video summarization (Truong & Venkatesh, 2007; Otsuka et al., 2005; Wan et al., 2005; Li et al., 2006), the redundant information from videos are eliminated and the relevant segments are retained in order to generate a concise and meaningful representation of the same. There are two types of video summarization.

1. **Static Summary (Storyboard Representation):** It is a set of selected frames from the original video. The selection process is dictated by means of an algorithm to form a representative set of the frames. The representative set is also known as the key-frames set. This set of representative frames serves as the feature set of a video and can be used for indexing purposes.
2. **Dynamic Summary (Video Skimming):** It is a set of shots taken from the original video, collated together to form a summary. The chosen shots of the video form the synopsis of the whole video, thereby portraying the content in it. As the dynamic representation contains audio, it is a challenge to stitch together shots which are temporally distant to each other. The algorithms designed for this purpose focus on ways to choose a subset of shots from the set of shots constituting a video in order to maximize user satisfaction and understanding.

Any video summary (static or dynamic), must possess three qualities, viz. conciseness, complete coverage and visual coherence (Lu et al., 2004b) so that it provides a better understandability to the user.

Static video summarization (storyboard representation) involves primarily three steps i.e. extraction of features, selection of key-frames and redundancy removal which have been detailed below.

3.1. Extraction of Features

This is the first step towards video summarization. Feature extraction is the building block for efficient video retrieval and indexing. The features which have high discrimination power are considered. Extraction of unnecessary features leads to more processing time and poor results. As content-based video retrieval systems rely on analyzing the semantic content in videos, extraction of visual features is of utmost importance.

1. **Key Frames as Features:** Features of the video are best reflected using the key-frames of the video. Certain conventional techniques were implemented to get the key-frames for video retrieval and indexing applications. The selection of key-frames as features is based on color, shape and texture.
    a. **Features Based on Color:** Color based feature extraction is dependent on the color spaces like HSV, RGB, YC_BC_R, HVC, normalized R-G and YUV. The choice of color space depends mainly on the applications. Color features can be extracted from an image or a set of images. It is considered to be the most effective feature in case of video retrieval and indexing task. (Amir *et al.*, 2003) computed the color histogram and color moments for concept detection and retrieval of the videos. (Yan and Hauptmann, 2007) segmented images into 5 x 5 chunks.

Subsequently, the color histogram, color moments and blocks were extracted from each of the chunks for performing video retrieval. Color corral grams have been used in (Adcock *et al.*, 2004) for implementing a video search engine. Although, the color based features are simple, it is ineffective in applications where shape and texture are essential. In Kumthekar and Patil, (2013) a method was developed for video key frame extraction based on color histogram and edge detection. It allowed removal of redundant frames and reduction of computational complexity with significant improvement in recognition efficiency.

i.   **Texture Based Features:** Co-occurrence matrices, simultaneous autoregressive models, Tamura features, wavelet transformation-based texture features and orientation features are the commonly used texture features. Tamura features using contrast, coarseness and co-occurrence texture were used in (Amir et al., 2003) for video recovery in TRECVID 2003. In (Hauptmann et al., 2004a; Hauptmann et al., 2004b) Gabor wavelet filters were used for the video search engine by capturing texture information. Twelve oriented energy filters were designed for the purpose. The approach involved segmentation of the image into 5 X 5 blocks. Gabor wavelet filters were used to compute the texture features in each block.

ii. **Shape Based Features:** Features based on shapes, actually mean the shapes of an object, whether it is a region or any contour in an image. These shapes are extracted by using edge detection techniques. Edge Histogram Descriptor (EHD) was used in (Hauptmann et al., 2004a) for capturing the spatial edges distribution in the video search task of TRECVID 2005. (Foley et al., 2005) divided images into 4 x 4 blocks to capture features of local shape following which edge histogram is extracted for every block.

b.   **Object Based Features:** Objects in an image include texture, size and the dominant color. In the video retrieval task, similar objects can be used as features (Visser et al., 2002). Video retrieval has been performed by (Sivic et al., 2005) using the face of a specific person as query. In case of broadcast news videos, integration of temporal information with intensity has been used for the retrieval task by (Le et al., 2006). Li and Doermann, (2002) extracted the texts in the video as single object types. This was used to assist and realize content of the video.

c.   **Motion Based Feature:** Motion is a key feature in videos and forms an integral part of it. The visual content in a video is greatly characterized by motion information. The motion based attributes can be categorized into object-based and camera-based features. The background motion in a scene is due to camera, while movement of the objects characterizes the movement in the foreground. The camera based features founded on camera motions are zoom-in, zoom-out, left and right panning, up or down tilting etc. These are widely used for video indexing applications. A shortcoming of video retrieval is that the key object motions are not easily describable.

i.   **Statistics Based Features:** Without prior motion segmentation or the use of dense optic flow fields, (Fablet et al., 2002) provide a global interpretation for the dynamic content of video shots. The spatio-temporal distribution of intensity information in a shot is used for the measurement of local motion. These distributions are further represented by causal Gibbs models. For immunity to camera movement, the motion-related measurements are computed in the image sequence by compensating the estimated dominant image motion in the original sequence. The similarity measure used in this work is inspired from Kullback-Leibler divergence. The retrieval with query-by-example is performed by using a binary tree constructed from the hierarchical structure of the processed video database according to motion content similarity using the maximum a posteriori (MAP) criterion. A general framework statistics was utilized for video indexing and retrieval in (Ma and Zhang, 2002), where the motion vector field was converted into the directional amount of a slice with respect to the motion's energy. The slices gave rise to the set of moments to create a multidimensional vector known as texture of the motion which was used for the motion based retrieval of the shot.

ii. **Trajectory Based Features:** (Quack et al., 2006) extracted trajectory features in videos by modeling the motion trajectories of objects. An online video retrieval system was proposed by (Chang et al., 1998) which supported spatio-temporal queries and object based automatic indexing. (Bashir et al., 2007) presented a trajectory based motion indexing system for a compact and proficient retrieval mechanism for sequences of a video. Segmentation of the trajectory and creation of index based wavelet decomposition based on velocity features was experimented on by (Chen and Chang, 1999). A curve fitting method for polynomial motion model was proposed by (Jung et al., 2001). The model for motion is used as key indexing in case of individual access. However, to generate information for trajectory, motion flow was embedded in MPEG bit streams by (Su et al., 2007). (Hsieh et al., 2006) embarked on a different approach by dividing the trajectories into many small segments and every segment was defined with a semantic symbol.

iii. **Relationships among Objects:** (Bimbo et al., 1995) described the link among objects by using the symbolic representation scheme for video retrieval. By the expression of every object, (Yajima et al., 2002) demonstrated the arrangements of several moving objects and the specifications for the spatio-temporal relationships.

As described earlier, a set of selected key-frames constitute a static video summary, whereas a dynamic video summary is generally created by joining short video segments. Static summaries constitute video frames, with some keywords, but do not include the audio track. On the other hand, all media types can be present in a dynamic video summary. The process of dynamic video summarization involves two basic steps:

1. Calculating weight of shots and
2. Selecting k number of most significant shots.

A static video summary consists of two major steps i.e. a) Extraction/Selection of key-frames and b) Redundancy reduction/elimination as described in further sub-sections.

3.2. Extraction of Key Frames

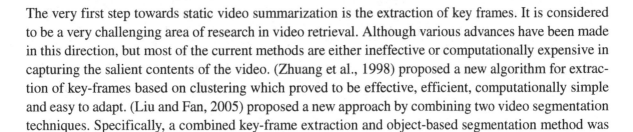

The very first step towards static video summarization is the extraction of key frames. It is considered to be a very challenging area of research in video retrieval. Although various advances have been made in this direction, but most of the current methods are either ineffective or computationally expensive in capturing the salient contents of the video. (Zhuang et al., 1998) proposed a new algorithm for extraction of key-frames based on clustering which proved to be effective, efficient, computationally simple and easy to adapt. (Liu and Fan, 2005) proposed a new approach by combining two video segmentation techniques. Specifically, a combined key-frame extraction and object-based segmentation method was developed which was based on state-of-the-art video segmentation algorithms and statistical clustering approaches. The proposed approach was effective and flexible due to the integration of the two segmentation methods. (Calic and Izuierdo, 2002) pinned the analysis on the compressed video features and introduced a real-time algorithm for scene change detection and key-frame extraction. (Song and Fan, 2005) proposed a technique for extracting a small number of key-frames within a shot which was helpful to build a unified framework for content-based analysis and structured video representation.

In the feature extraction phase, (Liu et al., 2010) used a key-frame extraction method based on clustering. This effectively reduced redundant frames in videos. (Chatzigiorgaki and Skodras, 2009) used a sequential search algorithm for key-frame extraction in MPEG videos. It was an efficient, real-time and fully automatic way of extracting key-frames in videos. The laborious task of offline video database indexing was avoided and at the same time query video processing was performed in the same manner as the reference video database. (Geetha et al., 2012) suggested a quantifying visual attention method to extract key-frames in order to generate a meaningful video summary.

(Zhang et al., 2003) carried out segmentation of a video sequence into a number of video shots. Thereafter, several key-frames were selected in each shot using a dynamic selection technique. Consequently, a motion-based clustering algorithm was applied on those key-frames so that key-frames in the same cluster were same in sense for motion compensation error. Key-frames from different clusters were quite dissimilar. Thereafter, a cluster-based coding scheme was developed for efficient representation of the key-frames. (Jinda-Apiraksa et al., 2012) introduced visual life logging which was a new concept for recording the daily life of a person by using wearable cameras to automatically capture images from one's surroundings. Contrary to videos, two consecutive frames were not necessarily similar in life log sequences. Thus, video processing techniques are not directly applicable in such cases. Hence a key-frame selection technique was proposed based on measuring image quality and distance to the middle frame. (Cooper and Foote, 2005) used methods for key-frame selection based on two criteria: capturing the similarity to the represented segment and preserving the differences from other segment key-frames. This allowed different segments to have visually distinct representations. (Gautam, 2014) used Minkowski distance to measure the similarity between two images and compare them with a threshold value to find the key-frames. (Panagiotakis et al., 2009) used a key-frames selection algorithm based on Iso-Content Distance, Iso-Content Error and Iso-Content Distortion principles. In addition, two automatic approaches for defining the most appropriate number of key-frames were proposed by exploiting supervised and unsupervised content criteria. (Kim et al., 2014) proposed and demonstrated the use of geo-tagged, crowd-sourced mobile videos by automatically generating panoramic images from UGVs for web-based geographic information systems. The proposed algorithms saved time and retained image quality when generating panoramas. A key-point based framework to address the key-frame selection problem was proposed by (Guan et al., 2013) so that local features could be employed in selecting key-frames. The method achieved a good content coverage while minimizing redundancy. (Girgensohn and Boreczky, 1999) proposed a technique for determining key-frames by clustering the frames in a video and then selecting a representative frame from each cluster. Temporal constraints were used to filter out some clusters and to determine the representative frame for a cluster. (Farag and Abdel-Wahab, 2002) used two sets of algorithms to effectively select key-frames from segmented video shots. The algorithms in both sets applied a two-level adaptation mechanism. The first level is done based on the size of the input MPEG file while the second level is performed on a shot by shot basis to account for the fact that different shots have different levels of activity inside them. The algorithms were shown to be efficient and robust in selecting the near optimal set of key-frames required to represent each shot in the video stream. (Hasebe et al., 2004) presented a new method for selecting key-frames from a given video sequence. It is characterized by the fact that the entire process worked in a wavelet transform domain. At first, shot boundaries were detected to define initial key-frames. A specified number of key-frames were then selected by clustering feature vectors. Its effectiveness is evaluated in terms of precision rates and processing speeds. (Zhao and Elgammal, 2008) presented an approach for human action recognition by finding the discriminative key-frames from a video sequences.

3.3. Redundancy Reduction

Redundancy reduction refers to the elimination of those key-frames in the key-frame set which have similar visual content. After redundancy elimination, the final generated summary of the video contains key-frames which have dissimilar visual content. This ensures that the user is able to browse through the contents quickly even in low-bandwidth scenarios. The identification of key-frames also ensures that only those frames are chosen which can be used for indexing video databases. At the same time, the target is to ensure that appropriate coverage of the contents has been done. Several methods have been applied on a diverse set of video data to minimize the redundancies as enumerated in section 1.6.2.

The various approaches to video summarization are depicted in Figure 4. A classification of the features extracted for the different approaches are also listed.

Figure 4. Classification of features for different video summarization techniques

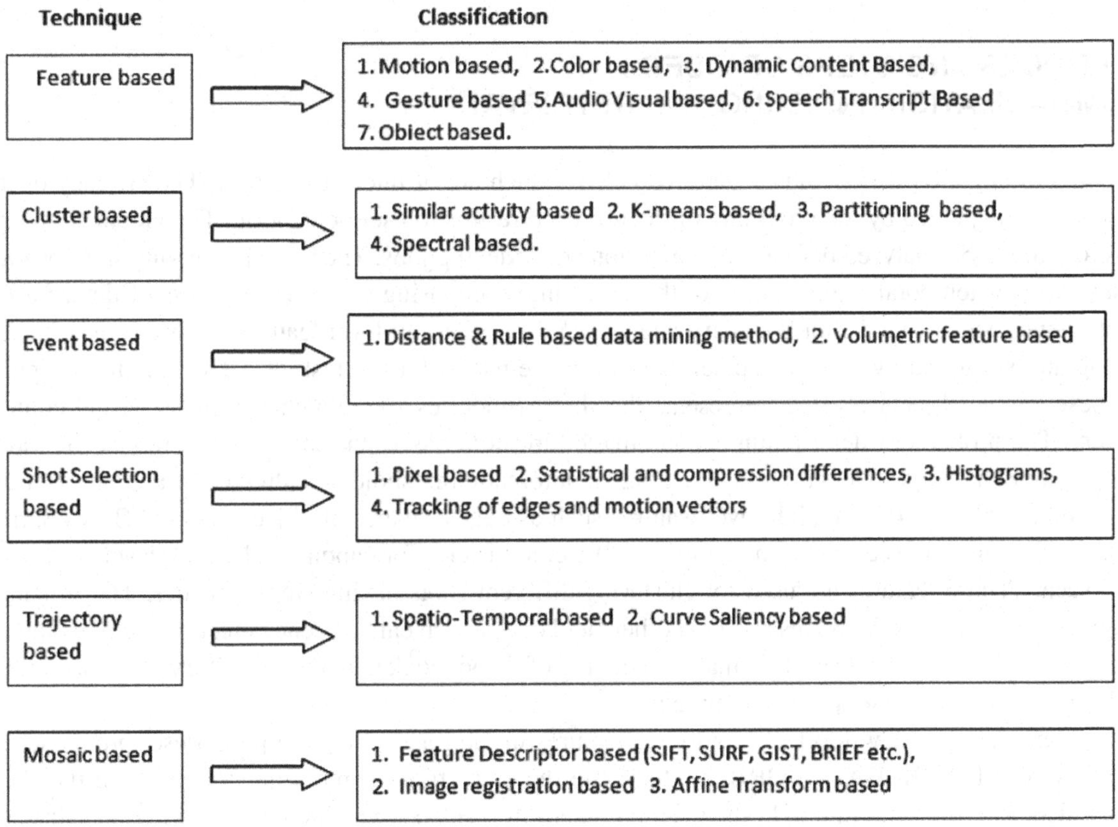

Technique		Classification
Feature based	⟹	1. Motion based, 2. Color based, 3. Dynamic Content Based, 4. Gesture based 5. Audio Visual based, 6. Speech Transcript Based 7. Object based.
Cluster based	⟹	1. Similar activity based 2. K-means based, 3. Partitioning based, 4. Spectral based.
Event based	⟹	1. Distance & Rule based data mining method, 2. Volumetric feature based
Shot Selection based	⟹	1. Pixel based 2. Statistical and compression differences, 3. Histograms, 4. Tracking of edges and motion vectors
Trajectory based	⟹	1. Spatio-Temporal based 2. Curve Saliency based
Mosaic based	⟹	1. Feature Descriptor based (SIFT, SURF, GIST, BRIEF etc.), 2. Image registration based 3. Affine Transform based

4. OBJECTIVES OF VIDEO SUMMARIZATION

It is common knowledge that huge volumes of video data are distributed over the web. The video data is unstructured and contains duplicate data. The task of browsing, managing and retrieval of such video data from the database is often a time consuming and laborious task. Thus, video summarization helps the user to quickly grasp the contents of the video with ease and eliminates the time constraint besetting the user. An ideal video summarization system aims to provide a good coverage of the video content. It also aims at developing a method which can work effectively in real time and produces a summary which is free from redundant information. Video summarization is also useful in bandwidth constrained scenarios where the user is able to view only a concise summary of the video in the form of representative frames or certain clips extracted from the original sequence. This is relevant in remote locations where the internet connectivity and bandwidth are a challenge. Moreover, video summarization is widely used for indexing videos in digital libraries and online repositories.

From the user's point of view, video summaries with good quality should maintain three important attributes, i.e. conciseness, comprehensive content coverage, and visual consistency. Conciseness necessitates that the dynamic summary should not exceed a given duration limit and the static summary should not have images which convey very less information. In addition, an informative video summary should comprehensively cover the visual diversity and temporal distribution of the original video. It is obvious from these facts that conciseness and content coverage are contradictory attributes which pose major challenges to the researchers. Finally, for a dynamic video summary, too frequent scene change may not be acceptable to the user. A coherent video skim is consequently more preferable.

5. PROCESSING STEPS OF VIDEO FOR SUMMARIZATION, INDEXING AND RETRIEVAL

The aim of any CBVR system is to retrieve videos which are of interest to a user. The efficacy of the system can be judged by the proximity of the retrieved results to user perception. The videos in the repository are to be analyzed before summarization and indexing jobs. The basic processing step for such tasks involves temporal segmentation of the video into composing shots. The process of determining shot boundaries is called shot boundary analysis (SBA). The low-level features such as color model, histogram, statistical measures on pixel values etc. are useful for the task of SBA. The discontinuity in these low-level feature values represents the shot boundaries where a change in the visual content occurs. The problem of determining an automatic threshold based on the characteristics of the video is the major challenge. The problem of setting an automatic threshold is addressed to a great extent in (Bhaumik et al., 2014). The high-level features such as edges, shapes of objects, optical flow (Barron et al., 1994), motion vectors (Wang et al., 2007) etc. are useful for capturing the high level semantics of a scene. These features are used for clustering different shots having similar scenes. The semantic fragmentation of the video gives rise to another field of research called scene detection. Understanding the semantic content also leads to semantic indexing of the video data in the repository and is useful for video classification, annotation and mining.

The extraction of low-level and mid-level features in the form of feature point descriptors such as SIFT, SURF, BRISK, DAISY, ORB etc. facilitate the extraction of important frames from the shots in a video. These frames highlight the overall content in a video stream and are known as key-frames.

However, it is useful to note that the set of key-frames extracted from the shots may contain redundant information in the form of similar scenes or objects. Due to the redundant content, the size of the summary is increased. Thus, it affects the conciseness of the video synopsis. Redundancy reduction plays an important role here by enhancing the conciseness, without affecting the coverage of the summary. The final set of key-frames selected obtained after redundancy reduction is known as a static summary. A dynamic summary may be obtained by selecting significant shots from the set of shots composing the video. This is done by assigning weights to the different shots based on high level semantic features.

Retrieval of similar videos forms an integral part of the CBVR system. The query to such a system may be in the form of an input video from the user which is used for retrieving other videos from the database similar to it. In such case, the feature extraction process employed on the query video is similar to the feature extraction mechanism used for the indexing of videos in the repository. A similarity matching function on the extracted features is then employed to obtain a numerical value representing the amount of match. A ranking algorithm is used to present the best matches to the user in a graded order. The various steps involved in summarization of videos, indexing and retrieval is depicted in Figure 5.

6. ASPECTS OF VIDEO SUMMARIZATION

Conciseness, content coverage and redundancy removal are the key aspects of a good quality video summarization system. For a given video, conciseness refers to the compact representation of its visual contents. A succinct representation ensures that the contents of a video are well represented without any unnecessary details being included. Conciseness ensures that the user will be able to browse through the summary in least possible time and grasp the essence of the video. A decision whether the summary is useful or not can also be made quickly. On the other hand, content coverage refers to the aspect of representing the salient contents of a video such that no important portions are left out. As content coverage increases the understandability of the video also increases.

6.1. Content Coverage

(Ngo et al., 2003; Ngo et al., 2005) applied normalized cut technique and temporal graph analysis to maximize content coverage and reduce the duplicate video data. Similarly, for automatic generation of video summaries, (Mundur et al., 2006) utilized Delaunay Triangulation mechanism. This was quite fruitful as human interaction was not required and meaningful visual content was achieved in less number of frames. (Lu et al., 2004a) modeled each scene of a video as a spatial-temporal relation graph to determine the extent to which each scene is favorable for skimming. This was done after the determination of the scene boundaries. The summary length of each video scene was also obtained. This yielded a significant coverage of the video content. (He et al., 1999) carried out three evaluation mechanisms to determine the extent of automatic summaries with audio, slides and video presentations. Results showed that the use of key points in the skimming was quite effective. Three steps were applied in (Lu et al., 2004b) to obtain the video summary. Initially, the video was segmented for selection of candidate shots. Then a dissimilarity function was given to denote the spatio-temporal relation. Thereafter the candidate shot was formulated into a directional graph and the longest path was obtained. This provided a good content coverage in the summary.

Figure 5. Steps for video summarization, indexing and retrieval

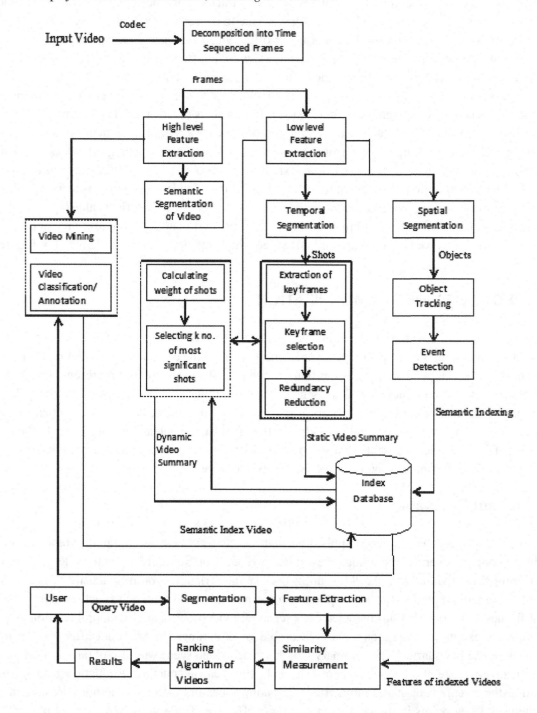

(Gong and Liu, 2000a) applied the Singular Value Decomposition to generate the video summary. Redundancy was removed and significant content retained. (Uchihashi et al., 1999) depicted techniques for automatic generation of pictorial video summaries which had large content coverage. In (Bhaumik et al., 2015), a Minimal Spanning Tree (MST) is constructed from the frames of a shot. An adaptive threshold is calculated separately for each shot based on the mean and standard deviation of the edge weights of the MST. The density of a node is the number of frames lying within a disc, the radius of which is equal to the computed threshold. A greedy method is used to choose frames from the list with maximum density. Frames represented by the chosen key-frame are eliminated from the list. This ensures that the most appropriate representatives are chosen as key-frames. It can easily be seen that the chosen key-frames provide a full coverage of the shot. In (Chang et al., 1999) the coverage has been defined as the number of visually similar frames represented by a chosen key-frame. Hence, coverage may be computed by the following formula:

$$\text{cov}\,erage = \frac{number\_of\_frames\_represented}{total\_number\_of\_frames}$$

In (Guan et al., 2013), the coverage is based on the number of feature points covered by a frame from the unique pool of feature points created from the composing frames of a shot. Initially all the feature points are part of the set $K_{un\,cov\,ered}$. The coverage of a frame is computed using the formula:

$$C = \eta(K_{un\,cov\,ered} \cap FP_i)$$

The redundancy of a frame is given by:

$$R = \eta(K_{cov\,ered} \cap FP_i)$$

where, $\eta(X)$ is the cardinality of set X and FP_i is the set of feature points in a which contain at least one frame which is similar to the candidate frame. Coverage is thus another metric which reveals the quality of a video summary.

6.2. Redundancy Removal

(Dumont and Merialdo, 2008) adapted the sequence alignment approach termed as Smith-Waterman algorithm, to remove the visual redundancies. This was done by detecting similar occurrence of video segments. (Quenot et al., 2008) used two different mechanisms to reduce the redundancy. In the first approach, a semantic clustering based on shots was used to remove the redundant video sequences. The second technique was based on a different clustering algorithm termed as hierarchical agglomerative (HA) mechanism. Both the techniques worked well in eliminating the redundancies. (Gao et al., 2008) used the HA mechanism for detecting two-level redundancy. Initially at the shot level, this removed the duplicate video content and portions of shots were selected for generation of summaries. Later a repetitive frame segment detection process was introduced to further eliminate the duplicate video content. (Gong and Liu, 2001) used a redundancy metric to determine as to how much redundancy was present in a summarized video content. Moreover, summarization based on the Singular Value Decomposition (SVD) was presented in (Gong and Liu, 2000b) to determine the extent of visual changes. Redundancy removal using SURF and GIST (Oliva and Torralba, 2001) descriptors have also been applied in (Bhaumik et al., 2014; Bhaumik et al., 2015).

6.3. Evaluation Metrics for Video Summarization

6.3.1. Recall, Precision, and F1 Score

Evaluation of a video summarization system is an important task as it allows different summarizers to be compared. The evaluation mechanism also indicates the efficacy of the summarization system. Initially, the output received from a video summarizer is called a System Generated Summary (SGS). In order to evaluate the quality of this summary, the SGS is compared with the ground truth. It is obvious that the ground truth must be as close to human perception as possible. Hence, the ground truth is generated by a set of users and is called the User Summary (Bhaumik et al., 2014; Cahuina & Camara Chavez, 2013) in the literature. The summary generated by the users are amalgamated together to form the Final User Summary (FUS). The User Summary (US) is generated by a group of users. The extent of overlap between the FUS and SGS depicts the efficacy of the summary. The recall and precision are computed as follows:

$$recall = \frac{\eta(FUS \cap SGS)}{\eta(FUS)}$$

$$precision = \frac{\eta(FUS \cap SGS)}{\eta(SGS)},$$

where,

FUS : Set of frames in user summary

SGS : Set of frames in system generated summary

$\eta(X)$: Cardinal no. of set X

The precision and recall associated with a system are contradictory measures for the reason that, one tends to decrease when the other increases. The design of a system should be such that it maximizes both. The F1 score is a culmination of both recall and precision and is computed as the harmonic mean of the two scores. It provides a consistent measure for determining the overall efficiency of an information retrieval system. The following expression is used to compute the F1 score:

$$F_1 = 2\frac{precision * recall}{precision + recall},$$

The F1 score varies in the range [0, 1] where a score of 1 indicates the best efficacy of a system.

6.3.2. Significance, Overlap, and Compression Factors

Three new metrics was proposed by (Mundur et al., 2006) for ascertaining the quality of a summary. The *Significance Factor* denotes the importance of the content represented a cluster of frames. The significance of the i_{th} cluster is given as:

$$Significance\_Factor(i) = \frac{C_i}{\sum_{j=1}^{k} C_j}$$

where C_i is the total number of frames in the i_{th} cluster and *k* is the total number of clusters.

The *Overlap Factor* determines the total significance of the overlapped clusters found in two summaries. In other words, we compute the cumulative significance of those clusters which have a common key-frame set with the ground-truth summary. This is an important metric for comparing two summaries. This factor is computed as:

$$Overlap\_Factor = \frac{\sum_{p \in Common\_keyframe\_clusters} C_p}{\sum_{j=1}^{k} C_j}$$

A higher value of the *Overlap Factor* denotes a better representative summary with respect to the ground-truth.

The *Compression Factor* for a video denotes the size of the summary with respect to the original size of the video. It is defined as:

$$Compression\_Factor = \frac{Number\_of\_keyframes\_in\_summary}{Total\_number\_of\_keyframes}$$

7. CONCLUSION

Researchers have proposed various methods for real-time video summarization on a diverse video dataset. It has been found that there is a minimal drop in performance when compared to the non-real-time methods, possessing a low summarization time. Techniques like Temporal Graph Analysis, Delaunay triangulation method and Singular value decomposition worked well for content coverage in the summarization process. Clustering method, SVD and adaptive threshold has been used for redundancy reduction which is dependent on the video and does not demand any human intervention. The promising results help us to conclude that the salient contents of a video and reduction of redundant data can be represented on the fly and in a concise manner, thereby saving the browsing and retrieval time in content based video retrieval systems. A complete and a good quality summarization system would encompass both the static and dynamic video summarization systems.

Though several works and applications have been carried out to preserve the maximum content, eliminate the duplicate video data from the original video, performance in a lengthy video data remains an open area of research.

REFERENCES

Adcock, J., Girgensohn, A., Cooper, M., Liu, T., Wilcox, L., & Rieffel, E. (2004). Fxpal experiments for TRECVID 2004.*Proceedings of the TREC Video Retrieval Evaluation (TRECVID)*, (pp. 70-81).

Amir, A., Berg, M., Chang, S. F., Hsu, W., Iyengar, G., Lin, C. Y., & Smith, J. R. (2003). IBM research TRECVID-2003 video retrieval system. *NIST TRECVID-2003*.

Barron, J. L., Fleet, D. J., & Beauchemin, S. S. (1994). Performance of optical flow techniques. *International Journal of Computer Vision*, *12*(1), 43–77. doi:10.1007/BF01420984

Bashir, F. I., Khokhar, A. A., & Schonfeld, D. (2007). Real-time motion trajectory-based indexing and retrieval of video sequences. *IEEE Transactions on* Multimedia, *9*(1), 58–65.

Bay, H., Ess, A., Tuytelaars, T., & Van Gool, L. (2008). Speeded-up robust features (SURF). *Computer Vision and Image Understanding*, *110*(3), 346–359. doi:10.1016/j.cviu.2007.09.014

Besiris, D., Laskaris, N., Fotopoulou, F., & Economou, G. (2007, October). Key frame extraction in video sequences: a vantage points approach. *Proceedings of the IEEE 9th Workshop on Multimedia Signal Processing MMSP '07* (pp. 434-437). IEEE. doi:10.1109/MMSP.2007.4412909

Bhaumik, H., Bhattacharyya, S., & Chakraborty, S. (2014, April). Video Shot Segmentation Using Spatio-Temporal Fuzzy Hostility Index and Automatic Threshold. *Proceedings of the 2014 Fourth International Conference on Communication Systems and Network Technologies (CSNT)* (pp. 501-506). IEEE. doi:10.1109/CSNT.2014.106

Bhaumik, H., Bhattacharyya, S., Das, M., & Chakraborty, S. (2015, February). Enhancement of perceptual quality in static video summarization using minimal spanning tree approach. *Proceedings of the 2015 IEEE International Conference on Signal Processing, Informatics, Communication and Energy Systems (SPICES)* (pp. 1-7). IEEE. doi:10.1109/SPICES.2015.7091401

Bhaumik, H., Bhattacharyya, S., Dutta, S., & Chakraborty, S. (2014, September). Towards redundancy reduction in storyboard representation for static video summarization. *Proceedings of the 2014 International Conference on Advances in Computing, Communications and Informatics (ICACCI)* (pp. 344-350). IEEE. doi:10.1109/ICACCI.2014.6968601

Bimbo, A. D., Vicario, E., & Zingoni, D. (1995). Symbolic description and visual querying of image sequences using spatio-temporal logic. *IEEE Transactions on* Knowledge and Data Engineering, *7*(4), 609–622.

Cahuina, E. J., & Camara Chavez, G. (2013, August). A new method for static video summarization using local descriptors and video temporal segmentation. *Proceedings of the 2013 26th SIBGRAPI-Conference on Graphics, Patterns and Images (SIBGRAPI)* (pp. 226-233). IEEE. doi:10.1109/SIBGRAPI.2013.39

Calic, J., & Izuierdo, E. (2002, April). Efficient key-frame extraction and video analysis. *Proceedings of the International Conference on Information Technology: Coding and Computing '02* (pp. 28-33). IEEE. doi:10.1109/ITCC.2002.1000355

Calonder, M., Lepetit, V., Strecha, C., & Fua, P. (2010). Brief: Binary robust independent elementary features. *Computer Vision–ECCV, 2010*, 778–792.

Chang, H. S., Sull, S., & Lee, S. U. (1999). Efficient video indexing scheme for content-based retrieval. *IEEE Transactions on* Circuits and Systems for Video Technology, *9*(8), 1269–1279.

Chang, S. F., Chen, W., Meng, H. J., Sundaram, H., & Zhong, D. (1998). A fully automated content-based video search engine supporting spatiotemporal queries. *IEEE Transactions on* Circuits and Systems for Video Technology, *8*(5), 602–615.

Chatzigiorgaki, M., & Skodras, A. N. (2009, July). Real-time keyframe extraction towards video content identification. *Proceedings of the 2009 16th International Conference on Digital Signal Processing* (pp. 1-6). IEEE. doi:10.1109/ICDSP.2009.5201141

Chen, W., & Chang, S. F. (1999, December). Motion trajectory matching of video objects. In *Electronic Imaging* (pp. 544–553). International Society for Optics and Photonics.

Cooper, M., & Foote, J. (2005, July). Discriminative techniques for keyframe selection. *Proceedings of the IEEE International Conference on Multimedia and Expo ICME '05* (pp. 4-pp). IEEE. doi:10.1109/ICME.2005.1521470

DeMenthon, D., Kobla, V., & Doermann, D. (1998, September). Video summarization by curve simplification.*Proceedings of the Sixth ACM International Conference on Multimedia* (pp. 211-218). ACM. doi:10.1145/290747.290773

Dumont, E., & Mérialdo, B. (2008, October). Sequence alignment for redundancy removal in video rushes summarization.*Proceedings of the 2nd ACM TRECVid video summarization workshop* (pp. 55-59). ACM. doi:10.1145/1463563.1463572

Fablet, R., Bouthemy, P., & Pérez, P. (2002). Nonparametric motion characterization using causal probabilistic models for video indexing and retrieval. *IEEE Transactions on* Image Processing, *11*(4), 393–407.

Farag, W. E., & Abdel-Wahab, H. M. (2002, March). *Adaptive Key Frames Selection Algorithms for Summarizing Video Data* (pp. 1017–1020). JCIS.

Fauvet, B., Bouthemy, P., Gros, P., & Spindler, F. (2004). A geometrical key-frame selection method exploiting dominant motion estimation in video. In *Image and Video Retrieval* (pp. 419–427). Springer Berlin Heidelberg. doi:10.1007/978-3-540-27814-6_50

Foley, C., Gurrin, C., Jones, G. J., Lee, H., McGivney, S., O'Connor, N. E., ... & Wilkins, P. (2005). *TRECVid 2005 experiments at Dublin City University*. Academic Press.

Gao, Y., Wang, W. B., & Yong, J. H. (2008). A video summarization tool using two-level redundancy detection for personal video recorders. *Consumer Electronics. IEEE Transactions on, 54*(2), 521–526.

Gautam, Arun, & Kumar. (2014). Key Frame Selection From Video Based on Weighted Minkowski Distance. *International Journal of Advanced Computational Engineering and Networking, 2*(8), 83-86.

Geetha, P., & Pandeeswari, S., Thiruchadai, & MohananSony. (2012). Visual Attention Based Keyframes Extraction and Video Summarization. *Proceedingsof theComputer Science Conference* (pp. 179-190).

Girgensohn, A., & Boreczky, J. (1999, July). Time-constrained keyframe selection technique. *Proceedings of the IEEE International Conference on Multimedia Computing and Systems '99* (Vol. 1, pp. 756-761). IEEE. doi:10.1109/MMCS.1999.779294

Gong, Y., & Liu, X. (2000a). Video summarization using singular value decomposition. *Proceedings of the IEEE Conference on Computer Vision and Pattern Recognition '00* (Vol. 2, pp. 174-180). IEEE. doi:10.1007/s00530-003-0086-3

Gong, Y., & Liu, X. (2000b). Generating optimal video summaries. *Proceedings of the 2000 IEEE International Conference on Multimedia and Expo ICME '00* (Vol. 3, pp. 1559-1562). IEEE.

Gong, Y., & Liu, X. (2001). Video summarization with minimal visual content redundancies. In *Proceedings of the 2001 International Conference on Image Processing '01* (Vol. 3, pp. 362-365). IEEE. doi:10.1109/ICIP.2001.958126

Guan, G., Wang, Z., Lu, S., Deng, J. D., & Feng, D. D. (2013). Keypoint-based keyframe selection. *IEEE Transactions on* Circuits and Systems for Video Technology, *23*(4), 729–734.

Guironnet, M., Pellerin, D., Guyader, N., & Ladret, P. (2007). Video summarization based on camera motion and a subjective evaluation method. *EURASIP Journal on Image and Video Processing, 2007*(1), 060245. doi:10.1186/1687-5281-2007-060245

Hanjalic, A., & Zhang, H. (1999). An integrated scheme for automated video abstraction based on unsupervised cluster-validity analysis. *IEEE Transactions on* Circuits and Systems for Video Technology, *9*(8), 1280–1289.

Hasebe, S., Nagumo, M., Muramatsu, S., & Kikuchi, H. (2004, September). Video key frame selection by clustering wavelet coefficients. *Proceedings of the2004 12th EuropeanSignal Processing Conference* (pp. 2303-2306). IEEE.

Hauptmann, A., Baron, R. V., Chen, M. Y., Christel, M., Duygulu, P., Huang, C., & Moraveji, N. (2004a). *Informedia at TRECVID 2003: Analyzing and searching broadcast news video.* Carnegie-Mellon Univ Pittsburgh PA School of Computer Science.

Hauptmann, A., Chen, M. Y., Christel, M., Huang, C., Lin, W. H., Ng, T., & Yang, H. et al. (2004b, November). Confounded expectations: Informedia at TRECVID 2004.*Proc. of TRECVID.*

He, L., Sanocki, E., Gupta, A., & Grudin, J. (1999, October). Auto-summarization of audio-video presentations. *Proceedings of the seventh ACM international conference on Multimedia* (Part 1) (pp. 489-498). ACM. doi:10.1145/319463.319691

Hsieh, J. W., Yu, S. L., & Chen, Y. S. (2006). Motion-based video retrieval by trajectory matching. *Circuits and Systems for Video Technology. IEEE Transactions on, 16*(3), 396–409.

Jinda-Apiraksa, A., Machajdik, J., & Sablatnig, R. (2012). A keyframe selection of lifelog image sequences. *IEEE Transactions on Intelligent Transportation Systems, 2*(3), 151–163.

Kim, H. S., Lee, J., Liu, H., & Lee, D. (2008, July). Video linkage: group based copied video detection. *Proceedings of the 2008 international conference on Content-based image and video retrieval* (pp. 397-406). ACM. doi:10.1145/1386352.1386404

Kim, S. H., Lu, Y., Shi, J., Alfarrarjeh, A., Shahabi, C., Wang, G., & Zimmermann, R. (2014). Key Frame Selection Algorithms for Automatic Generation of Panoramic Images from Crowdsourced Geo-tagged Videos. In *Web and Wireless Geographical Information Systems* (pp. 67–84). Springer Berlin Heidelberg.

Kumthekar, V. A., & Patil, K. J. (2013, July). Key frame extraction using color histogram method. *International Journal of Scientific Research Engineering & Technology, 2*(4), 207–214.

Le, D. D., Satoh, S. I., & Houle, M. E. (2006). Face retrieval in broadcasting news video by fusing temporal and intensity information. In *Image and Video Retrieval* (pp. 391–400). Springer Berlin Heidelberg. doi:10.1007/11788034_40

Li, H., & Doermann, D. (2002, December). Video indexing and retrieval based on recognized text. *Proceedings of the 2002 IEEE Workshop on Multimedia Signal Processing* (pp. 245-248). IEEE.

Li, Y., Lee, S. H., Yeh, C. H., & Kuo, C. J. (2006). Techniques for movie content analysis and skimming: Tutorial and overview on video abstraction techniques. *Signal Processing Magazine, 23*(2), 79–89. doi:10.1109/MSP.2006.1621451

Lienhart, R. (2000, June). *Dynamic Video Summarization of Home Video*. SPIE: Storage and Retrieval for Media Database, Vol. 3972.

Liu, D., Shyu, M. L., Chen, C., & Chen, S. C. (2010, August). *Integration of global and local information in videos for key frame extraction*. IRI. doi:10.1109/IRI.2010.5558944

Liu, L., & Fan, G. (2005). Combined key-frame extraction and object-based video segmentation. *IEEE Transactions on* Circuits and Systems for Video Technology, *15*(7), 869–884.

Lowe, D. G. (1999). Object recognition from local scale-invariant features. In *The proceedings of the seventh IEEE International Conference on Computer vision '99* (Vol. 2, pp. 1150-1157). IEEE. doi:10.1109/ICCV.1999.790410

Lu, S., King, I., & Lyu, M. R. (2004a, June). Video summarization by video structure analysis and graph optimization. *Proceedings of the 2004 IEEE International Conference on Multimedia and Expo ICME'04* (Vol. 3, pp. 1959-1962). IEEE.

Lu, S., Lyu, M. R., & King, I. (2004b, May). Video summarization by spatial-temporal graph optimization. *Proceedings of the 2004 International Symposium onCircuits and Systems ISCAS'04* (Vol. 2, pp. II-197). IEEE.

Ma, Y. F., Lu, L., Zhang, H. J., & Li, M. (2002, December). A user attention model for video summarization.*Proceedings of the tenth ACM international conference on Multimedia* (pp. 533-542). ACM. doi:10.1145/641007.641116

Ma, Y. F., & Zhang, H. J. (2002). A model of motion attention for video skimming. I *Proceedings. 2002 International Conference on Image Processing '02* (Vol. 1, pp. I-129). IEEE.

Ma, Y. F., & Zhang, H. J. (2002). Motion texture: a new motion based video representation. *Proceedings of the 16th International Conference on Pattern Recognition '02* (Vol. 2, pp. 548-551). IEEE.

Marcus, A., & Maletic, J. I. (2003, May). Recovering documentation-to-source-code traceability links using latent semantic indexing. *Proceedings of the 25th International Conference on Software Engineering '03* (pp. 125-135). IEEE. doi:10.1109/ICSE.2003.1201194

Mukherjee, D. P., Das, S. K., & Saha, S. (2007). Key frame estimation in video using randomness measure of feature point pattern. *IEEE Transactions on* Circuits and Systems for Video Technology, *17*(5), 612–620.

Mundur, P., Rao, Y., & Yesha, Y. (2006). Keyframe-based video summarization using Delaunay clustering. *International Journal on Digital Libraries, 6*(2), 219–232. doi:10.1007/s00799-005-0129-9

Nam, J., & Tewfik, A. H. (1999, October). Dynamic video summarization and visualization. *Proceedings of the seventh ACM international conference on Multimedia (Part 2)* (pp. 53-56). ACM. doi:10.1145/319878.319892

Narasimha, R., Savakis, A., Rao, R. M., & De Queiroz, R. (2003, November). Key frame extraction using MPEG-7 motion descriptors. *Conference Record of the Thirty-Seventh Asilomar Conference onSignals, Systems and Computers '04* (Vol. 2, pp. 1575-1579). IEEE. doi:10.1109/ACSSC.2003.1292250

Ngo, C., Ma, Y., & Zhang, H. (2003, October). Automatic video summarization by graph modeling. In *Proceedings of Ninth IEEE International Conference on Computer Vision* (pp. 104-109). IEEE.

Ngo, C. W., Ma, Y. F., & Zhang, H. J. (2005). Video summarization and scene detection by graph modeling. *IEEE Transactions on* Circuits and Systems for Video Technology, *15*(2), 296–305.

Oliva, A., & Torralba, A. (2001). Modeling the shape of the scene: A holistic representation of the spatial envelope. *International Journal of Computer Vision, 42*(3), 145–175. doi:10.1023/A:1011139631724

Orriols, X., & Binefa, X. (2001). An EM algorithm for video summarization, generative model approach. *Proceedings of the Eighth IEEE International Conference on Computer Vision. ICCV '01* (Vol. 2, pp. 335-342). IEEE. doi:10.1109/ICCV.2001.937645

Otsuka, I., Nakane, K., Divakaran, A., Hatanaka, K., & Ogawa, M. (2005). A highlight scene detection and video summarization system using audio feature for a personal video recorder. *IEEE Transactions on* Consumer Electronics, *51*(1), 112–116.

Panagiotakis, C., Doulamis, A., & Tziritas, G. (2009). Equivalent key frames selection based on iso-content principles. *IEEE Transactions on* Circuits and Systems for Video Technology, *19*(3), 447–451.

Papadimitriou, C. H., Tamaki, H., Raghavan, P., & Vempala, S. (1998, May). Latent semantic indexing: A probabilistic analysis.*Proceedings of the seventeenth ACM SIGACT-SIGMOD-SIGART symposium on Principles of database systems* (pp. 159-168). ACM. doi:10.1145/275487.275505

Patel, B. V., & Meshram, B. B. (2012). *Content based video retrieval systems.* arXiv preprint arXiv:1205.1641

Quack, T., Ferrari, V., & Van Gool, L. (2006). Video mining with frequent itemset configurations. In *Image and Video Retrieval* (pp. 360–369). Springer Berlin Heidelberg. doi:10.1007/11788034_37

Quenot, G., Benois-Pineau, J., Mansencal, B., Rossi, E., Cord, M., Precioso, F., & Pellerin, D. et al. (2008, October). Rushes summarization by IRIM consortium: redundancy removal and multi-feature fusion.*Proceedings of the 2nd ACM TRECVID video summarization workshop* (pp. 80-84). ACM. doi:10.1145/1463563.1463577

Sivic, J., Everingham, M., & Zisserman, A. (2005). Person spotting: video shot retrieval for face sets. In *Image and Video Retrieval* (pp. 226–236). Springer Berlin Heidelberg. doi:10.1007/11526346_26

Smith, J. R., Naphade, M., & Natsev, A. (2003, July). Multimedia semantic indexing using model vectors. *Proceedings of the 2003 International Conference on Multimedia and Expo ICME'03* (Vol. 2, pp. II-445). IEEE. doi:10.1109/ICME.2003.1221649

Smith, M. A., & Kanade, T. (1997, June). Video skimming and characterization through the combination of image and language understanding techniques. *Proceedings of the 1997 IEEE Computer Society Conference on Computer Vision and Pattern Recognition '97* (pp. 775-781). IEEE. doi:10.1109/CVPR.1997.609414

Song, X., & Fan, G. (2005, January). Joint key-frame extraction and object-based video segmentation. Proceedings of the Seventh IEEE Workshops on Application of Computer Vision (Vol. 2, pp. 126-131). IEEE. doi:10.1109/ACVMOT.2005.66

Su, C.-W., Liao, H.-Y., Tyan, H.-R., Lin, C.-W., Chen, D.-Y., & Fan, K.-C. (2007). Motion flow-based video retrieval. *IEEE Transactions on* Multimedia, *9*(6), 1193–1201.

Sze, K. W., Lam, K. M., & Qiu, G. (2005). A new key frame representation for video segment retrieval. *IEEE Transactions on* Circuits and Systems for Video Technology, *15*(9), 1148–1155.

Tola, E., Lepetit, V., & Fua, P. (2010). Daisy: An efficient dense descriptor applied to wide-baseline stereo. *IEEE Transactions on* Pattern Analysis and Machine Intelligence, *32*(5), 815–830.

Truong, B. T., & Venkatesh, S. (2007). Video abstraction: A systematic review and classification. *ACM Transactions on Multimedia Computing, Communications, and Applications, 3*(1), 3, es. doi:10.1145/1198302.1198305

Uchihashi, S., Foote, J., Girgensohn, A., & Boreczky, J. (1999, October). Video manga: generating semantically meaningful video summaries. *Proceedings of the seventh ACM international conference on Multimedia (Part 1)* (pp. 383-392). ACM. doi:10.1145/319463.319654

Vasconcelos, N., & Lippman, A. (1998, June). A spatiotemporal motion model for video summarization. *Proceedings of the 1998 IEEE Computer Society Conference on Computer Vision and Pattern Recognition* (pp. 361-366). IEEE. doi:10.1109/CVPR.1998.698631

Visser, R., Sebe, N., & Bakker, E. (2002). Object recognition for video retrieval. In *Image and Video Retrieval* (pp. 262–270). Springer Berlin Heidelberg. doi:10.1007/3-540-45479-9_28

Wan, K., Yan, X., & Xu, C. (2005, July). Automatic mobile sports highlights. *Proceedings of the IEEE International Conference on Multimedia and Expo ICME 05* (pp. 4-pp). IEEE.

Wang, T., Wu, Y., & Chen, L. (2007, April). An approach to video key-frame extraction based on rough set. *Proceedings of the International Conference on Multimedia and Ubiquitous Engineering MUE'07* (pp. 590-596). IEEE. doi:10.1109/MUE.2007.65

Yajima, C., Nakanishi, Y., & Tanaka, K. (2002). Querying video data by spatio-temporal relationships of moving object traces. In Visual and Multimedia Information Management (pp. 357-371). Springer US. doi:10.1007/978-0-387-35592-4_25

Yan, R., & Hauptmann, A. G. (2007). A review of text and image retrieval approaches for broadcast news video. *Information Retrieval, 10*(4-5), 445–484. doi:10.1007/s10791-007-9031-y

Yeung, M. M., & Yeo, B. L. (1997). Video visualization for compact presentation and fast browsing of pictorial content. *IEEE Transactions on* Circuits and Systems for Video Technology., *7*(5), 771–785.

Zhang, X. D., Liu, T. Y., Lo, K. T., & Feng, J. (2003). Dynamic selection and effective compression of key frames for video abstraction. *Pattern Recognition Letters, 24*(9), 1523–1532. doi:10.1016/S0167-8655(02)00391-4

Zhao, Z., & Elgammal, A. M. (2008, September). *Information Theoretic Key Frame Selection for Action Recognition*. BMVC. doi:10.5244/C.22.109

Zhuang, Y., Rui, Y., Huang, T. S., & Mehrotra, S. (1998, October). Adaptive key frame extraction using unsupervised clustering. *Proceedings of the 1998 International Conference on Image Processing ICIP 98* (Vol. 1, pp. 866-870). IEEE.

Chapter 14
Compressive Sensing for Biometric System

Rohit M. Thanki
C. U. Shah University, India

Komal R. Borisagar
Atmiya Institute of Technology and Science, India

ABSTRACT

Biometric system is used by many institution, organization and industry for automatic recognition of person. One of the main reason for popularity of used for biometric system is that the ability of the system to identify between an authorized person and unauthorized person. There are many challenges associated with the biometric system such as designing of human recognition algorithm, compression of biometric templates, privacy and security of biometric templates in biometric systems. This chapter gives an application of Compressive Sensing (CS) theory for solutions of the above mentioned challenges in biometric systems. Recent research and trends in a biometric system indicated that many challenging of biometric system problems are being solved using Compressive Sensing (CS) theory and sparse representation algorithms. This chapter gives an overview of sparsity property of various image transforms and application of compressive sensing and sparse representation with regards to biometric image compression, biometric image recognition and biometric image protection.

1. INTRODUCTION

The term "biometrics" is coming from the two Greek words "bio" means life and "metrics" means to measure (National Science & Technology Council, 2007). Biometrics are a generally used to describe physiological and behavioral characteristics of the individual. A biometric is measured physiological and behavioral characteristics of a person which can be used for recognition and authentication of person (National Science & Technology Council, 2007; ITU-T Technology Watch Report, 2009). Popularly biometric modalities such as fingerprint, face, iris, voice, signature and hand geometry is used for research and implementation of any biometric system. Nowadays, new biometric modality such as gait, retina, ear structure, odor and palm prints are existed and research is going on these biometrics modalities.

DOI: 10.4018/978-1-5225-0498-6.ch014

Figure 1. Various biometric traits (a) Fingerprint (b) Face (c) Iris (d) Palm print (e) DNA (f) Signature (g) Ear (h) Voice

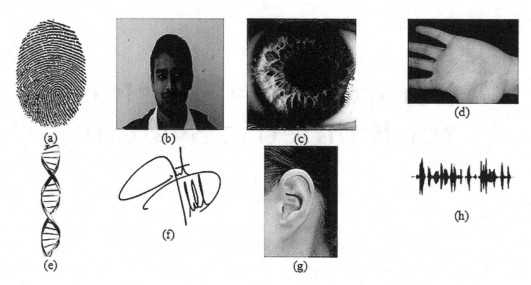

The Biometric is divided into two parts such as physiological trait and behavioral traits. Physiological traits are also known as passive traits. These traits are stable and invariant with time. The fingerprints, shape of face, hands, fingers or ears of the person, irises, teeth and samples of DNA are lying into physiological traits. The physiological traits of person are distinctive and permanent unless destroyed due to accident, illness (Jain & Kumar, 2012; ITU-T Technology Watch Report, 2009). Behavioral traits are also known as active traits. These traits are dynamics and vary with time. The gait, voice, keystroke and signature are lying into behavioral traits (Jain & Kumar, 2012; ITU-T Technology Watch Report, 2009). The various biometric traits are shown in Figure 1. Any biometric traits were following properties such as universality, distinctiveness, permanence and collectability.

- **Universality:** Every person should have own biometric traits.
- **Distinctiveness:** Any two people should not have same biometric traits.
- **Permanence:** The biometric should be invariant with time.
- **Collectability:** The biometric should collect easily.

A biometric system is a computerized system that uses physiological or behavioral characteristics information about person to identify that person. The automated biometric system is developed around 2000s due to significant research in the field of pattern recognition and computer processing (National Science & Technology Council, 2007). Many of automated biometric techniques are based on ideas that were originally conceived thousands of years ago. The most popular older technique is the recognition of individual by face. Persons are used faces to identify authenticated and unauthenticated individuals. Face recognition of person became more challenging task with increasing populations. So that person recognition has taken place by using other characteristics such as fingerprint, voice, iris and palm prints. There are various techniques used for person recognition throughout the history of civilization is available in the literature (National Science & Technology Council, 2007, pp. 55 – 56).

Nowadays, many organizations, institutes and companies are implementing a biometric system for security and person authentication. The basic biometric system is shown in Figure 2. A typical biometric system has different modules such as sensor, Feature extractor, Data storage, Matcher and Decision (Jain, Kumar & Pankanti, 2006; Jain, Ross & Prabhakar, 2004). The first step of biometric systems is the acquisition of biometric characteristics of a person using an appropriate sensor. The second step is extract salient characteristics of the biometric template using feature extractor modules which is based on software algorithm. The third step is store extracted features at system database. Then matcher module performs matching between query features and stored features at system database and gives a similarity score. Finally, the decision module gives decision about authentication or person based on similarity score.

Any biometric system is performed two fundamental operations such as verification operation and authentication operation. In both operations, the first process is the enrollment of biometric features of an authorized person is required. The enrollment process is shown in Figure 3 (a). In verification operation, an authorized person is verified or rejected by the biometric system by comparing query biometric features with stored biometric features of the authorized person. The verification process is shown in Figure 3 (b). In authentication operation, the biometric system recognizes an authorized person from the entire enrolled person of the organization. It searches all stored features in a system database for authenticity of person which is shown in Figure 3 (c).

The biometric is used in various applications which are summarized below (Jain, Ross & Prabhakar, 2004).

- **Forensic Application:** In criminal investigations.
- **Government Application:** Personal documents such as passports, Individual Detection (ID) cards, driver license, immigration and E-governance.
- **Commercial Application:** Physical access control, network logins, ATMs, credit card.

Figure 2. Biometric system

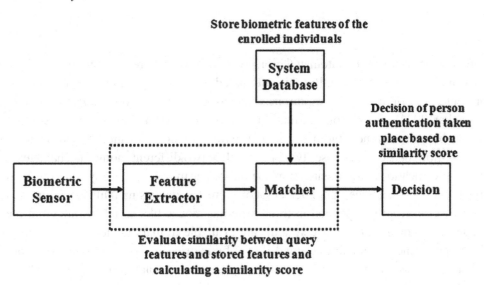

377

Figure 3. Various operation of biometric system (a) Enrollment process (b) Verification operation (c) Authentication operation

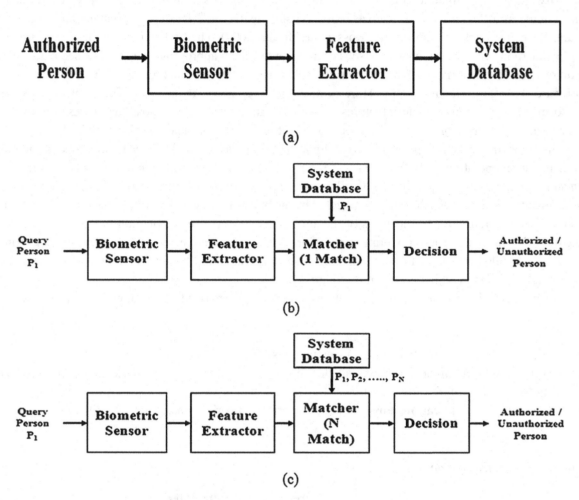

There are many advantages of automated biometric system compared to older biometric recognition techniques available in the literature. But this automated biometric system has several limitations such as noise present in sensor, intra-class variations, distinctiveness, nonuniversality and spoof attack (Jain, Ross & Prabhakar, 2004). To overcome limitations of biometric systems, Jain and its research team (Jain & Ross, 2004) introduced a new biometric system which is known as multimodal or multibiometric system. The multibiometric system uses two or more than two different biometric characteristics of the same person for verification and authentication operation. The multibiometric system is reduced problem related large population coverage, spoof detection of biometric data using multiple biometric traits. The multibiometric system can be operated in three different modes like serial, parallel and hierarchical. They are many types of multibiometric systems are available in marker such as a multiple sensor (as example is taking biometric templates using different biometric sensors); multiple biometric templates (ax example is takes two or more than two different biometric templates of same individual); multiple units (as example is acquired two or more fingerprint of different fingers of individual); multiple matching (as example is matches individual biometric templates using different matching algorithms) (Jain, Ross & Prabhakar, 2004; Jain & Ross, 2004; Jain, Ross & Pankanti, 2006). The various multibiometric system scenarios are shown in Figure 4.

Recently, many researches have taken place in the area of biometrics. There are many challenges associated with the biometric system such as designing of human recognition algorithm, compression of biometric templates, privacy and security of biometric templates in biometric systems. In this chapter, we have given an application of compressive sensing (CS) theory for solutions of the above mentioned challenges in biometric systems. The introduction of compressive sensing (CS) theory in signal and image processing arena, many applications in biometric system has been looking at different ways. Recent research and trends in a biometric system indicated that many challenging of biometric system problems are being solved using compressive sensing (CS) theory and sparse representation algorithms.

The compressive sensing (CS) theory is a new image acquisition theory where images can be reconstructed accurately from some projection of transform coefficients of an image. The compressive sensing (CS) theory is nonlinear sampling theory. Compressive sensing (CS) theory is break limitation of the conventional sampling theory which is given by Shannon – Nyquist. The compressive sensing theory is divided into two parts such as acquisition of sparse measurements and recovery of image forms its sparse measurements. Compressive sensing (CS) theory obeys properties of sparsity, incoherent sampling and restricted Isometric hypothesis. In this chapter, we have demonstrated sparsity property of various image transforms like Discrete Cosine Transform (DCT), Discrete Wavelet Transform (DWT) and Singular Value Decomposition (SVD) is used for compressive sensing theory. This chapter also

Figure 4. Various scenarios in a multibiometric system
(Taken form Jain & Ross, 2004)

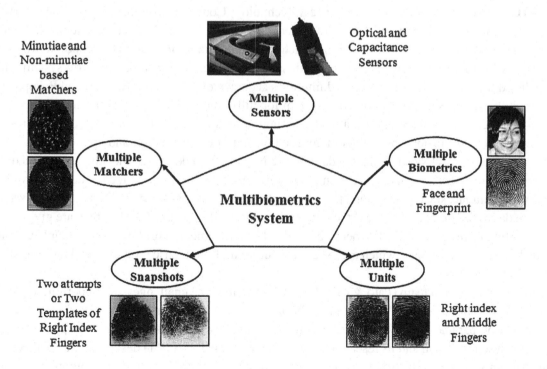

gives some application of compressive sensing and sparse representation with regards to biometric image compression, biometric image recognition and biometric image protection. The rest of chapter is organized such as: a literature review of biometric system and compressive sensing (CS) theory; a brief concept of compressive sensing (CS) theory; application of compressive sensing (CS) theory in biometric systems, conclusion and future work.

2. LITERATURE REVIEW

The brief literature review of research works carried out in the area of biometric system and compressive sensing (CS) theory is given below.

2.1 Literature Review of Biometric System

N. Ratha, J. Connell and R. Bolle (Ratha, Connell & Bolle, 2001) described the strengths of a biometric based authentication system, identify the weak links in biometric systems and give solutions for some of these weak links. M. Thieme (Thieme, 2003) described operation, designing approaches and application of multibiometric systems which included various applications like physical access, civil ID and criminal ID. Jain and its research team (Jain, Ross & Prabhakar, 2004; Jain & Ross, 2004; Jain, Ross & Pankanti, 2006) described the limitations of the unimodal biometric authentication system and suggested new biometric system to overcome the limitation of the unimodal biometric authentication system. K. Teddy (Teddy, 2005) described limitation of biometric systems, various scenarios for multibiometric system using fingerprint, and face and iris recognition at levels of fusion that can be adopted by fusing information and improved overall system accuracy.

NSTC research members (National Science & Technology Council, 2007) are described characteristics of various biometrics, working of biometric system and applications of biometric system. M. Agrawal (Agrawal, 2007) described various design approaches for multibiometric system. He proposed two design approaches for multistage verification and multistage identification for multibiometric system which has reduced the time for identification and improves accuracy of the system. E. Lupu and P. Pop (Lupu & Pop, 2008) described a multibiometric system for fulfilling some limitation and increase security level of biometric systems. They are also discussing various features of multibiometric systems like architecture, level of fusion, the methodology used for multiple verification and applications. A. Jain, K. Nandakumar and A. Nagar (Jain, Nandakumar & Nagar, 2008) described the advantages and disadvantages of biometrics template protection approaches likes the bio hashing technique, non-invertible transform technique, key binding biometric crypto system and key generating biometric crypto systems. They are described limitation of these techniques for large scale application. Also, they are giving some new direction of research in the biometric area like developing new hybrid biometric template protection technique and techniques which are used for securing multibiometric templates and multibiometric authentication systems.

Pato and its research team (Pato & Millett, 2010) described the challenges and opportunities of biometric systems. In this report, they are given basic concepts of biometric systems, various operations and evaluation parameters for biometric system. They are also given future research opportunities of biometric systems. Kolan and its research team (Kolan & Thapaliya, 2011) described the application of biometrics in security of electronic passport. They are given an application of cryptography technique and biometrics to make electronic passport more secure. A. Jain and A. Kumar (Jain & Kumar, 2012) described various biometric traits of a person. They are also described various issues in biometric system such as biometric template protection, spoof detection, biometric system security and need to design a new biometric authentication system which covers a large scale population. They also point out need of a new biometric recognition system which is used for soft biometrics like scars, marks, tattoos, color of eye and hair color.

Sui and its research team (Sui, Zou & Du, 2013) described the concept of cancellable biometrics to provide security and privacy to a biometric template in biometric systems. Ashboum (Ashboum, 2014) described various biometric characteristics, various issues such as application, usage and social related to a biometric system. He is also described application of biometrics in could computing, mobile phones, multimodal biometric system design and issues related to biometric technology design for any application. Harinda and its research team (Harinda & Natgwirumugara, 2015) described designing of biometric based ID card for Rwanda universities. They are described challenges, parameters and issues required for design biometric based ID card.

2.2 Literature Review of Compressive Sensing (CS) Theory

D. Donoho (Donoho, 2006) introduced the new signal acquisition theory which is named as compressive sensing or sampling, where data is acquired in a compressed manner. He says that it is possible to reconstruct signal or image accurately from few numbers of samples which is very smaller than the desired resolution of the signal or image. E. Candès (Candès, 2006) gives mathematically models, properties and theorems of compressive sensing (CS) theory. E. Candès and J. Romberg (Candès & Romberg, 2005) described convex optimization programming and L_1 minimization technique for recovery of signal from corrupted and inaccurate measurements. R. Baraniuk (Baraniuk, 2007) gives an overview of compressive sensing (CS) theory and compressive sensing recovery procedure using L_1 minimization technique. A. Gilbert and its research team (Gilbert, 2007) described properties, rules and requirement for various CS theory recovery algorithms. They are also proposing new CS recovery algorithm like Heavy Hitters on Steroids (HHS) pursuit and compared this algorithm with other recovery algorithms. J. Tropp and A. Gilbert (Tropp & Gilbert, 2007) demonstrates the greedy algorithm such as orthogonal matching pursuit (OMP) for recovery of signal or image from nonzero measurements. This algorithm is easy to implement compared to the other CS recovery algorithm.

J. Laska and its research team (Laska, Davenport & Baraniuk, 2009) described signal or image recovery procedure for sparsely corrupted measurements using the pursuit of justice and basis pursuit Denoising algorithm. W. Dai and Om Milenkovic (Dai & Milenkovic, 2009) proposed subspace pursuit (SP) algorithm for recovery of sparse signal or image with and without noise. This algorithm has two important characteristics like low computational complexity, applied to very sparse signal compared to other CS theory recovery algorithms. D. Needell (Needell, 2009) give a mathematically derivation and implementation of different CS theory recovery algorithms in Matlab. R. Lopez and N. Boulgouris (Lopez & Boulgouris, 2010) described image compression using CS theory framework and compared the proposed compression procedure with the existing image compression procedure. M. Duarte and Y. Eldar (Duarte & Eldar, 2011) gives a complete summary about the properties of CS theory, a basic requirement of CS theory, various CS recovery algorithm such as L norm minimization, greedy algorithms for signal or image recovery from its sparse measurements. A. Ahmed and J. Romberg (Ahmed & Romberg, 2012) proposed two compressive multiplexers for sampling of correlated signals. This compressive multiplexer is design using simple modulation and filtering architectures. These correlated signals are recorded from micro sensor arrays which are used in several applications in biology and robotics, for example, in MRI. These compressive multiplexers used for reconstructing of these types of correlated signal without error.

C. Turnes and its research team (Turnes, Balcan & Romberg, 2012) described a CS recovery process for reconstruction of images that have been modified or corrupted by a certain class of image filters. The image can degrade by using a linear system of equations involved two-level Toeplitz matrix with a triangular structure on either the block or sub block level of image. They are described two-level super-fast recovery algorithm for calculation of Toeplitz matrix inversion based on Fast Fourier Transform. A. Salman and J. Romberg (Salman & Romberg, 2013) described two homotopy-based CS recovery algorithms for solving re-weighted L_1 problems. In the first CS recovery algorithm, replaces the old weights with the new ones by a small number of computational inexpensive steps. The second CS recovery algorithm solves a weighted L_1 problem by adaptively selecting the weights while recovering the signal. These two algorithms are overcome limitation of weighted L_1 norm minimization such as update the weights at every iteration using the solution of a weighted L_1 problem from the previous iteration. They are also comparison of these proposed algorithms with existing CS recovery algorithms. A. Aghasi and J. Romberg (Aghasi & Romberg, 2013) described a new image reconstruction technique using various shapes for application to various imaging problems. In this technique, using a collection of various shapes dictionaries and chooses right shapes and geometric for dictionary form desired regions in the image. This technique can be used for standard imaging problems such as image segmentation, X-ray and diffusive tomography.

A. Ahmed and its research team (Ahmed, Recht & Romberg, 2014) described a CS recovery procedure for two unknown same size sparse measurement vectors from their circular convolution. In this technique, sparse measurement is generated by the convolution of two individual sparse measurements of signal. This technique is used; security of message on a multipath channel where the message is first encoded by encoding matrix and then multiplied response of unknown channel. The decoder is separate the encoded message and channel response from convolution. Then apply this technique on an encoded message to the actual message. M. Asif and J. Romberg (Asif & Romberg, 2014) described a CS recovery algorithm for streaming system where the unknown signal changes over time. The authors described a CS recovery algorithm for two steaming systems such as overlapping measurements of a signal and lapped orthogonal transform (LOT) based representation of a signal. The authors described a homotopy-based CS recovery algorithm for quickly solving the associated weighted L_1 norm minimization programs for steam signals and digital video reconstruction. A. Aghasi and J. Romberg (Aghasi & Romberg, 2015) described a shape-based modeling technique for imaging applications in industry. In this technique, a collection of shape dictionary, based on application as choosing the right shape elements and geometrically composing them through basic set operations to generate a desired portion of an image. This technique can be used for shape-based characterization, object tracking and optical character recognition.

3. OVERVIEW ON COMPRESSIV SENSING (CS) THEORY

Using Image acquisition is a basic part of any image processing technique. The digital image is taken sampling and quantization process. The first sampling theory is introduced by Shannon – Nyquist sampling theory. The limitation of the Shannon – Nyquist sampling theory is that it is required twice sampling rate for signal reconstructions from its samples. The limitation of the Shannon – Nyquist sampling theory is overcome by introducing the new signal sampling theory which is known as compressive sensing or sampling theory. This theory is described by D. Donoho and E. Candès (Donoho, 2006; Candès, 2006) around 2006. They are proving that original signal or image can be exactly reconstructed from its few transform coefficients. Compressive sensing theory is basic on mathematic of linear algebra and sparsity properties of various transform. Compressive sensing theory is acquired signal or image in a compressed format and reconstructed image using solving an optimization problem. Compressive sensing theory is divided into two parts such as CS theory acquisition process and CS theory recovery process.

In CS theory acquisition process, image or signal is converted in its sparse measurements using sparsity properties of various transform and measurement matrix. The sparse measurements of image or signal can be generated using compressing sensing theory acquisition process is given by formula 1 and 2. The size of measurement matrix is decided compression ratio for image or signal.

$$y = A \times x \tag{1}$$

$$x = \psi \times f \tag{2}$$

In formula 1 and 2, y = sparse measurements of image or signal, A = measurement matrix, x = sparse coefficients of image or signal, Ψ = image transform, f = image or signal.

Compressive Sensing (CS) theory lies on some important properties such as sparsity and incoherent sampling. The signal or image can be successfully reconstructed from its sparse measurements when it is fulfilled condition of these two properties. The sparsity property is related to CS theory acquisition process and signal or image representation. The incoherent sampling property is related to CS theory recovery process and sparse measurements of signal or image. The brief concept of these two properties is given below:

3.1 Sparsity

The signal or image can be defined, sparse if and only if the signal or image has fewer number of non – zero elements (Donoho, 2006; Baraniuk, 2007). Many images are sparse when it converts into its transform domain using various image transforms. Any signal or image which is represented into the orthonormal basis is described by below formula 3.

$$x(t) = \sum_{i=1}^{N} \psi_i(t) f_i(t) \tag{3}$$

It is a function of $x = \Psi \times f$, where Ψ is the basis matrix with size of N × N and f is the signal or image with size of N × N. It is a necessary condition that signal or image must be sparse into its own transform domain when compressive sensing (CS) theory is applied to it (Donoho, 2006; Candès, 2006; Baraniuk, 2007). The transform such as discrete cosine transform (DCT), discrete wavelet transform (DWT) and singular value decomposition (SVD) is used for generation of sparse coefficients of any signal or image.

3.2 Incoherent Sampling

When a signal or image is sampled using compressive sensing (CS) theory, the coherence of sampled signal or image with respect to its transform matrix is described by below formula 4.

$$\mu(A, \psi) = \sqrt{N} \cdot \max_{1 \leq j \leq m, 1 \leq i \leq n} \left| \langle A_j, \psi_i \rangle \right| \tag{4}$$

where Ψ and A is the transform basis and measurement matrix respectively. It follows the condition of linear algebra such as $\mu(A, \psi) \in \left| 1, \sqrt{N} \right|$. The transform basis and measurement matrix are more coherent than signal or image cannot reconstruct from its sparse measurement. It is a necessary condition for signal or image reconstruction using the compressive sensing theory is that transform basis and measurement matrix must be incoherent.

In CS theory recovery process, image or signal is recovered from its sparse measurements using various CS theory recovery techniques. The CS theory recovery technique is based on optimization and properties of linear algebra. Let A be measurement matrix, f is an image to be sampled and y is sparse measurements of sensing image. Then the image can be recovered by solving using convex optimization algorithm such L norm minimization (Donoho, 2006; Candès, 2006; Baraniuk, 2007). The sparse coefficients of the image or signal in transform domain Φ and hence the image recovered by solving below constrained minimization problem.

$$\min \|f\|_l, \; such \; that \; y = Ax \tag{5}$$

There is a necessary condition for a signal or image reconstruction from its sparse measurements is satisfied Restricted Isometric Property (RIP) for any sparse measurements y. The matrix A of size M × N obeys the RIP of order S (S<=m) if measurement matrix A approximately preserves the squared magnitude of any S sparse measurements y using below formula:

$$\forall y \; for \; which \; \|y\|_0 \leq S, (1 - \delta_s) \|y\|^2 \leq \|Ay\|^2 \leq (1 + \delta_s) \|y\|^2, \; where \; 0 < \delta_s < 1 \tag{6}$$

There are various CS theory recovery techniques available in the literature. The CS theory recovery techniques are divided into two types such as linear optimization based techniques and greedy techniques. L norm minimization technique (Baraniuk, 2007) is based on linear optimization and provides good stability for signal or image reconstruction. But this technique is taken more computation time for image or signal reconstruction. When greedy techniques (Gilbert, 2007; Tropp & Gilbert, 2007; Laska, Davenport & Baraniuk, 2009; Dai & Milenkovic, 2009; Duarte & Eldar, 2011) such as orthogonal matching pursuit (OMP), compressive sampling matching pursuit (COSAMP), basis pursuit (BP), subspace pursuit (SP) and Iterative Hard Thresholding (IHT) are based on iteration calculation for approximation coefficients of image until a convergence criterion is fulfilled. These CS theory recovery techniques are faster than L norm minimization technique, but not provide good stability.

4. APPLICATION OF CS THEORY FOR BIOMETRIC SYSTEM

The CS theory is mostly used for image acquisition in compressed format. This theory also provides more computational security compared to tradition image acquisition process. The application of compressive sensing (CS) theory regards to biometric image compression, biometric image recognition and biometric image protection are described here. Iris biometric image (CASIA Iris Database, 2002) is taken for testing of the application of compressive sensing (CS) theory for biometric system. Iris image is chosen because of iris image of the individual is easy to available and different for every individual.

The first application deals with biometric image compression, which is based on compressive sensing (CS) theory acquisition process and compressive sensing (CS) theory recovery process. Here sparsity properties of various image transform are explored and described various approaches for generation of sparse measurements of biometric image. The results of various approaches of biometric image compression are examined and compared. The second application deals with a biometric image recognition system based on sparse representation of the image. In this technique, using sparse features of biometric image, human can be identified. Finally, third application deals with biometric image protection using watermarking against imposter manipulation. In this technique, generate sparse measurements of watermark biometric image and inserted into standard image to provide security of biometric image when it is transferred in open source network. The brief description of all applications of compressive sensing (CS) theory in a biometric system described below.

4.1 Biometric Image Compression Using CS Theory

In this application, generate sparse measurements of biometric image using compressive sensing (CS) theory acquisition process where the size of sparse measurements is less than actual size of biometric image. Then the biometric image is reconstructed using compressive sensing (CS) theory recovery process using these sparse measurements and result of this process is compressed biometric image. There are various approaches available for generation of sparse measurements of biometric image is given in Table 1.

The steps of biometric image compression using compressive sensing (CS) theory are given below:

- Take a biometric image with size of N × N and compute the size of the image. Then convert biometric image into vector with size of $N^2 \times 1$.
- Then convert biometric image vector into its sparse coefficients using various image transform. These sparse coefficients are denoted as x.
- Generate measurement matrix A with size of $M \times N^2$ using a random seed. Here M is the size the compression factor for biometric image.
- Then generate sparse measurements y of biometric image using compressive sensing acquisition process which is described in equation 1.
- After getting sparse measurements y of biometric image, applied compressive sensing (CS) recovery process on sparse measurements for biometric image reconstruction.
- Finally, compared reconstructed biometric image with original biometric image using various quality measures.

Table 1. Various approaches of generation of sparse measurements of biometric image

Sr. No.	Image Transform Used	Description
1	Discrete Cosine Transform (DCT)	Apply DCT directly on biometric image and convert into DCT coefficients. These DCT coefficients are taken as sparse coefficients of biometric image.
2	Discrete Wavelet Transform (DWT)	Apply single level DWT directly on biometric image and convert into approximation and detail wavelet coefficients. Then details wavelet coefficients are taken as sparse coefficients of biometric image.
3	Discrete Wavelet Transform (DWT)	Generate sparse wavelet matrix using a wavelet matrix generation procedure with the size of biometric image using DWT. Then multiply sparse wavelet matrix with the biometric image to generate sparse coefficients of biometric image.
4	Singular Value Decomposition (SVD)	Applied SVD on biometric image and decomposed into three matrices such as diagonal matrix which is known as singular value and two orthogonal matrices. Then the singular value of biometric image has chosen as sparse coefficients of biometric image.
5	Discrete Wavelet Transform (DWT) + Singular Value Decomposition (SVD)	Apply single level DWT directly on biometric image and convert into approximation and detail wavelet coefficients. Then apply SVD on detail wavelet coefficients of biometric image. Then the singular values of wavelet coefficients are taken as sparse coefficients of biometric image.

For testing of this application, Iris biometric image (CASIA Iris Database, 2002) with size of 256 × 256 pixels is taken which is shown in Figure 5. The compressive sensing (CS) theory recovery technique such as orthogonal matching pursuit (Tropp & Gilbert, 2007) is used for biometric image reconstruction. The quality measures such as PSNR and SSIM (Wang & Bovik, 2004) is used comparison of compressed biometric image and original biometric image. Figure 6 shows the results of biometric image compression using the Sparsity Property of Discrete Cosine Transform (DCT) and CS theory. Figure 7 shows the results of biometric image compression using the Sparsity Property of Discrete Wavelet Transform (DWT) and CS theory. Table 2 shows quality measures for biometric image compression using compressive sensing (CS) theory process. The Compression Ratio (CR) between reconstructed image and the original image can be calculated using the equation below.

$$CR = \frac{Size\_of\_Sparse\_Measuremets\_of\_Biometric\_Image}{Size\_of\_Biometric\_Image} * 100 \qquad (7)$$

Figure 6 and 7 shows that using a CS theory process, biometric image can be reconstructed from its sparse measurements successfully when the compression ratio is greater than 40%. This is a limitation of CS theory based biometric image compression. The reconstructed image using discrete cosine transform (DCT) is better than reconstructed image using discrete wavelet transform (DWT). These results indicated that the discrete cosine transform (DCT) is the best choice when CS theory is used for biometric image compression. This approach such as Compressive Sensing (CS) theory process for compression of biometric image can be applied on various biometric images like fingerprint, face, signature and palm print.

4.2 Biometric Image Recognition Using CS Theory

In the biometric image recognition process, feature extraction is one of important process. In this application, biometric image features are extracted using compressive sensing (CS) theory process. The

Figure 5. Test iris image
(Taken from CASIA Iris Database, 2002)

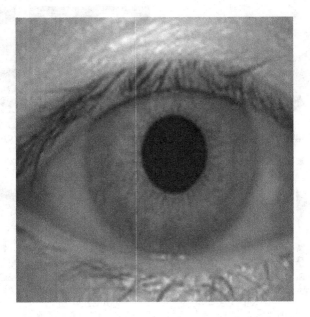

Figure 6. Biometric image compression using sparsity property of DCT and CS theory

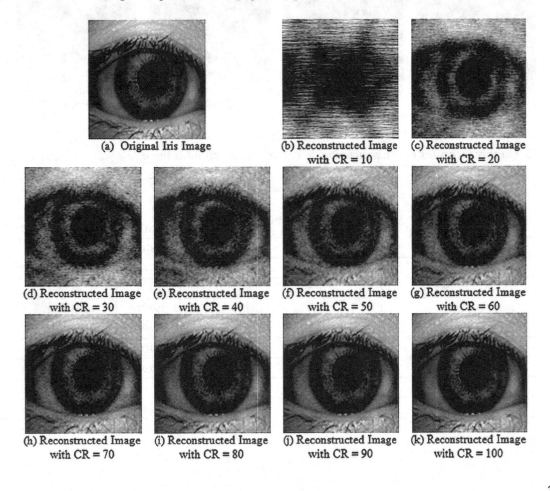

Figure 7. Biometric image compression using sparsity property of DWT and CS theory

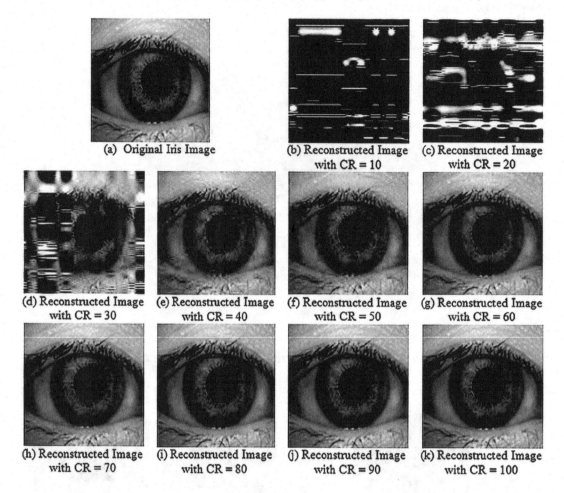

Table 2. Quality measures for biometric image compression using CS theory

Test Iris Biometric Image = 256 × 256 Pixels						
Size of Sparse Measurements, $y = Ax$	Compression Ratio (CR)	Using DCT		Using DWT		
		PSNR (dB)	SSIM (%)	PSNR (dB)	SSIM (%)	
6400 {25 × 256}	0.1	19.14	98.45	1.28	8.07	
13,056 {51 × 256}	0.2	25.58	99.65	3.90	47.28	
19,456 {76 × 256}	0.3	27.89	99.79	11.66	91.20	
26,112 {102 × 256}	0.4	29.93	99.87	32.81	99.93	
32,768 {128 × 256}	0.5	32.36	99.93	35.60	99.96	
39,168 {153 × 256}	0.6	35.25	99.96	37.85	99.97	
45,824 {179 × 256}	0.7	37.93	99.98	40.01	99.98	
52,224 {204 × 256}	0.8	40.37	99.98	41.85	99.99	
58,880 {230 × 256}	0.9	42.76	99.99	43.64	99.99	
65,536 {256 × 256}	1.0	45.23	99.99	45.40	99.99	

biometric image features are converted into sparse representation using compressive sensing (CS) theory acquisition process. Then this sparse biometric feature is compared with enrolled sparse biometric features for human identification. The block diagram of biometric image recognition using compressive sensing (CS) theory acquisition process is shown in Figure 8.

There are two processes are associated such as enrollment and verification with biometric image recognition using CS theory acquisition process is given below.

4.2.1 Enrollment Process

- Take a biometric image with size of N × N and compute the size of the image. Then convert biometric image into vector with size of $N^2 \times 1$.
- Apply Discrete Cosine Transform (DCT) on biometric image vector into its sparse domain vector. This sparse domain vector is denoted as x.
- Generate measurement matrix A with size of $M \times N^2$ using the normal distribution. Here M is deciding the size of extracting biometric features.
- Then generate sparse measurements y with size of M × 1of biometric image using CS theory acquisition process.
- These sparse measurements are reshaping and stored in the system database.

Figure 8. Block diagram of biometric image recognition using CS theory acquisition process

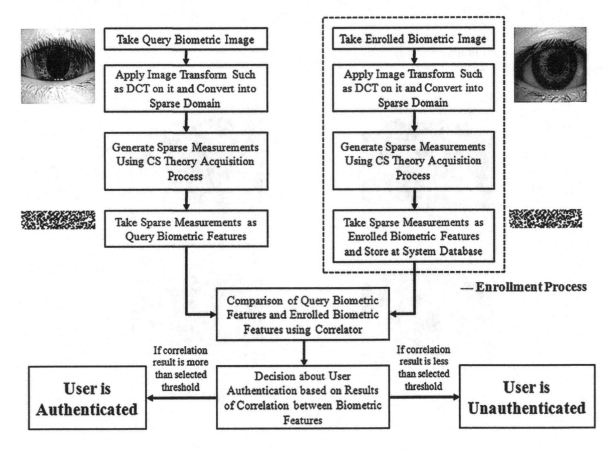

4.2.2 Verification Process

- Take a biometric image with size of N × N as query image and convert into sparse measurements *y* using the enrollment process.
- These sparse measurements are taken as query biometric features.
- Then compared query biometric features with enrolled biometric features using Correlator.
- Then two conditions are described below for user authentication based on results of correlation between query biometric features and enrolled biometric features.
  Condition 1: User is authenticated if correlation result is greater than the threshold value.
  Condition 2: User is not authenticated if the correlation result is less than the threshold value.

For testing of this application, Iris biometric image (CASIA Iris Database, 2002) of 50 different users with size of 150 × 150 pixels is taken. There are few sample iris biometric images are shown in Figure 9. The iris feature can be extracted using Compressive Sensing (CS) theory acquisition process is described below. First convert iris biometric image into vector with size of 22500 × 1. Then applied Discrete Cosine transform (DCT) on it and convert into sparse domain with size of 22500 × 1. Generate the measurement matrix with size of 1024 × 22500 using a random seed. Sparse measurements of iris biometric image with size of 1024 × 1 are generated by multiplication of DCT coefficients of iris biometric image and measurement matrix. These sparse measurements of iris biometric image are reshaping with size of 64 × 16 and taken as biometric features which is stored in the system database. The extracted biometric features of sample iris biometric images are shown in Figure 10.

Figure 9. Sample iris biometric images
(Taken from CASIA Iris Database, 2002)

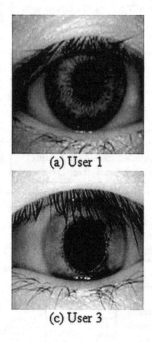

(a) User 1

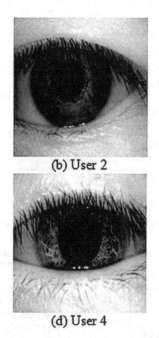

(b) User 2

(c) User 3

(d) User 4

Figure 10. Extracted iris biometric features using CS theory acquisition process

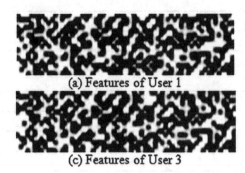

(a) Features of User 1

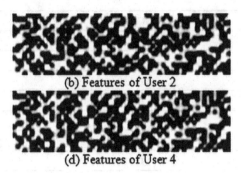

(b) Features of User 2

(c) Features of User 3

(d) Features of User 4

When any iris biometric image is coming for recognition at biometric sensor, then first generate sparse measurements of query iris biometric image using compressive sensing (CS) theory acquisition process. These sparse measurements are taken as query biometric features. Then query biometric features are compared with enrolled biometric features using Correlator. If the results of correlation are greater than the selected threshold, then the user is authenticated otherwise it is unauthenticated. The value of the selected threshold for suggestively recognition of user is 0.80 (80%). Here, take enrolled biometric features 1 as query biometric features and comparison with entire enrolled biometric features of 50 users using Correlator. The results of correlation between query biometric features and enrolled biometric features are shown in Table 3. The results shows are shown in Table 3 indicated that correlation between query biometric features 1 and enrolled biometric features 1 is 1.00 (100%). Otherwise the correlation result with other enrolled biometric features is less than selected threshold. This situation indicated that compressive sensing (CS) theory acquisition process can be used for user recognition.

There are two major operations such as verification accuracy and the authentication accuracy of proposed biometric recognition when it is used for user recognition in biometric systems. The verification accuracy of biometric systems is calculated using below equation 8. The verification accuracy of iris biometric recognition using CS theory based results getting using equation 8 is shown in Table 4. Based on results put in Table 4, the graph of verification accuracy of iris biometric recognition using

Table 3. Correlation results between query biometric features and enrolled biometric features

Enrolled Biometric Features	Correlation Between Query Biometric Features and Enrolled Biometric Features	Matching Percentage
1	1.00	100
7	0.76	76
15	0.61	61
20	0.76	76
28	0.65	65
33	0.49	49
34	0.40	40
42	0.56	56
46	0.76	76
49	0.69	69

Table 4. Verification accuracy of iris biometric recognition using CS theory

Selected Threshold	Verification Accuracy
0.0	0.00
0.1	0.00
0.2	0.00
0.3	0.00
0.4	0.00
0.5	10.00
0.6	28.00
0.7	56.00
0.8	88.00
0.9	98.00

the CS theory is shown in Figure 11. The verification accuracy of iris biometric recognition using the CS theory is greater than 88% when selected threshold value is 0.8.

$$Verification\_Accuracy = \frac{No.\_of\_Correlation\_\text{Re} sults < Selected\_Threshold}{Total\_No.\_of\_Correlation\_\text{Re} sults} \tag{8}$$

Figure 11. Verification accuracy of iris biometric recognition using CS theory

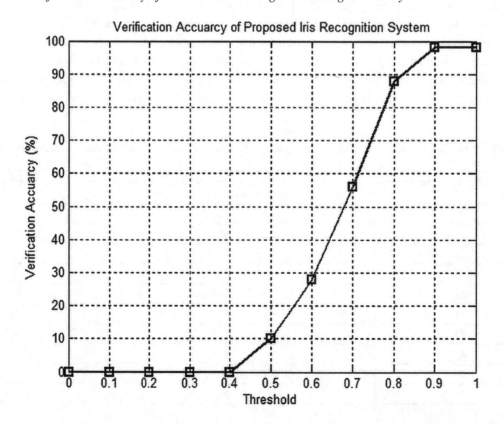

When calculation for authentication accuracy of proposed biometric recognition, two quality measures such as False Acceptance Rate (FAR) (Giot, El-Abed & Rosenberger, 2012) and False Rejection Rate (FRR) (Giot, El-Abed & Rosenberger, 2012) is calculated using below equation 9 and 10. For calculation of FAR, 50 fake user biometric features are extracted and stored in the system database. The results of FRR and FAR for iris biometric recognition using CS theory are shown in Table 5. Based on the results of FAR and FRR, the graph of the authentication performance of iris biometric recognition using the CS theory is shown in Figure 12.

Table 5. FRR and FAR values of iris biometric recognition using CS theory

Selected Threshold	False Rejection Rate (FRR)	False Acceptance Rate (FAR)
0.0	1.00	0.00
0.1	1.00	0.00
0.2	1.00	0.00
0.3	1.00	0.00
0.4	0.98	0.02
0.5	0.90	0.18
0.6	0.72	0.44
0.7	0.40	0.78
0.8	0.10	0.98
0.9	0.02	1.00

Figure 12. Authentication performance of iris biometric recognition using CS theory

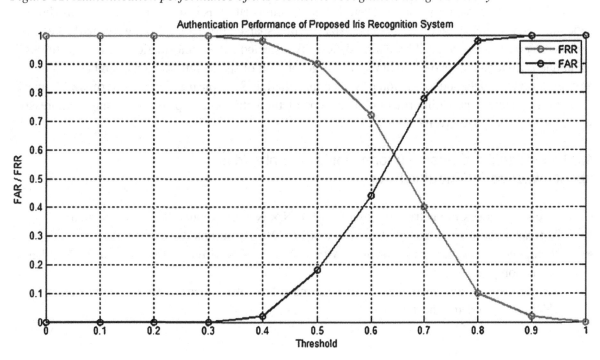

$$FRR = \frac{No.\_of\_Correlation\_\mathrm{Re}\,sults > Selected\_Threshold}{Total\_No.\_of\_Correlation\_\mathrm{Re}\,sults} \tag{9}$$

$$FAR = \frac{No.\_of\_Correlation\_\mathrm{Re}\,sults \leq Selected\_Threshold}{Total\_No.\_of\_Correlation\_\mathrm{Re}\,sults} \tag{10}$$

This application is represented a combination of sparse representation and pattern recognition. This iris biometric recognition has provided security against spoofing attack of biometric system because of it is difficult to unauthenticated person to generate biometric features without proper knowledge of measurement matrix, applied image transform and size of biometric features.

4.3 Biometric Image Protection Using CS Theory

Today's world, many users are using biometric data for security and privacy of their important data for various applications such as ATM, banking, copyright protection and copyright authentication. But when these biometric data are transferred in open source network, there are vulnerable against various attacks at the open source network. So security of biometric data is required when it is transferring at the open source network. The one of solution of security of biometric data over an open source network is a digital watermarking technology. Here digital watermarking technique is combined with compressive sensing (CS) theory to provide security to biometric data.

In this watermarking technique, the biometric data is used as watermark and embedded into standard multimedia such as images. The compressive sensing (CS) theory is used to provide additional security to biometric data before embedding into host medium. The compressive sensing (CS) theory is converting biometric data in sparse information. Then the sparse information is inserted into the host medium to generate watermarked content. At decoding size, extract sparse information from watermarked content and then reconstructed original biometric data from extracted sparse information. This watermarking technique is divided into two procedures such as generation of sparse information & embedding of watermark biometric data and extraction of sparse information & reconstruction of watermark biometric data from extracted sparse information. The steps of biometric image protection using compressive sensing (CS) theory are given below.

4.3.1 Generation of Sparse Information and Embedding about Watermark Biometric Data

- Take a watermark biometric image with size of N × N and compute the size of the image.
- Generate measurement matrix A with size of M × N uses normal distribution matrix.
- Then generate sparse measurements *y* with size of M × N of biometric image using CS theory acquisition process.
- Now this sparse information *y* of the watermark biometric image is taken secure information, which is embedded in host medium.

- Take standard multimedia image with size of M × N as host image and compute the size of image in term of raw and column.
- Apply Discrete Cosine Transform (DCT) on host image and get DCT coefficients of host image.
- Then DCT coefficients of host image are modified according to the sparse information of the watermark biometric image and gain factor. Here sparse information is inserted into host image using COX watermarking equation (Cox et al., 1997) is given below.

$$I_W(x,y) = I(x,y) * (1 + K \times W(x,y)) \tag{11}$$

where, $I_w(x, y)$ = Watermarked Image; $I(x, y)$ = Host Image; K = Gain Factor; $W(x, y)$ = Sparse Information of Watermark Biometric Data.

- Apply Inverse Discrete Cosine Transform (IDCT) on modified DCT coefficients of the host image to get watermarked image.

4.3.2 Extraction of Sparse Information and Reconstruction of Watermark Biometric Data Forms Extracted Sparse Information

- Take a watermarked image and compute the size of image in term of raw and column.
- Apply Discrete Cosine Transform (DCT) on watermarked image and get DCT coefficients of watermarked image.
- Take an original host image. Apply Discrete Cosine Transform (DCT) on host image and get DCT coefficients of host image.
- Extracted sparse information of watermark biometric data using the reverse process of embedding.
- After extracting sparse information, reconstruction of original watermark biometric data from its extracted sparse information using compressive sensing (CS) theory recovery process is performed.
- For reconstruction of biometric data, first generate a DCT basis matrix with size of original watermark biometric image.
- Then apply Orthogonal Matching Pursuit (OMP) (Tropp & Gilbert, 2007) with a DCT basis matrix and measurement matrix which is generated at embedder side on extracted sparse information of watermark biometric data.
- The output of OMP is sparse coefficients of watermark biometric data. By multiplying these sparse coefficients with DCT basis matrix to get reconstructed watermark biometric data at the decoder side.

For testing of this application, Iris biometric image (CASIA Iris Database, 2002) with size of 128 × 128 pixels is taken as watermark information. The standard Lena image with size of 128 × 128 pixels is taken as host image. The sparse information of iris biometric image can be generated using compressive sensing (CS) theory is described below. First generate a measurement matrix with size of 128 × 128 using a random seed. Then multiply this measurement matrix with the watermark iris image to generate sparse information of the watermark iris image. Then the sparse information of the watermark iris image is embedded into DCT coefficients of a standard Lena image to generate watermarked Lena image. The Figure 13 show original Lena Image, original watermark iris image, sparse information of the watermark iris image, watermarked Lena Image, extracted sparse information of watermark iris image and reconstructed watermark iris image.

This biometric watermarking approach is tested against various watermarking attacks such as compression, addition of external noise, applying image filtering on watermarked image and geometric attacks such as cropping, histogram Equalization. The quality measures such as PSNR, MSE, NCC and SSIM is used for evaluation of this biometric watermarking approach. Table 6 shows the results of this biometric watermarking approach against various watermarking attacks.

Figure 13. Results of iris biometric protection using CS theory based watermarking technique

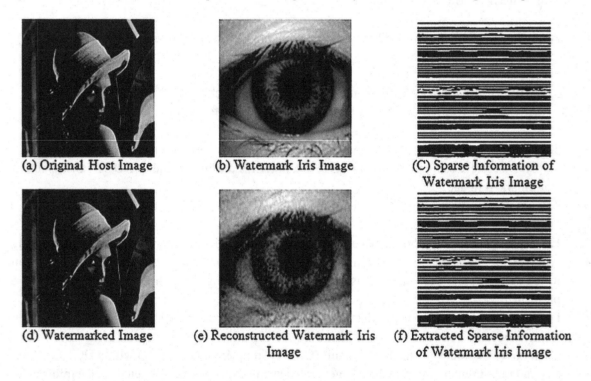

Table 6. Quality measures for biometric image protection using CS theory

Results	No Attack	JPEG Compression Attack	Gaussian Noise Attack	Salt & Pepper Noise Attack	Median Filter Attack	Mean Filter Attack	Histogram Equalization	Cropping Attack
NCC	0.99	1.00	0.99	0.98	1.00	1.00	0.99	0.83
MSE	2.17	30.67	69.86	113.72	46.72	21.28	1520.60	1034.30
PSNR (dB)	44.76	33.26	29.69	27.57	26.06	34.85	16.31	17.98
SSIM	0.999	0.04	0.14	0.10	1.47	0.10	0.03	0.57

The result of the biometric watermarking approach is indicated that when an attack is applied on watermarked image, then watermark biometric data is not reconstructed successfully at the decoder side. This situation is indicated that this watermarking technique is fragile against watermarking attacks. This technique can be used for protection of biometric data when transfer over open source network. This application is represented a combination of compressive sensing (CS) theory and biometric watermarking technique. This technique also provides security to biometric data against modification attack at communication channel between two modules of any biometric system.

5. CONCLUSION AND FUTURE WORK

An application of new signal processing theory known as compressive sensing for biometrics is described in a chapter. The application of compressive sensing (CS) theory in various applications related to biometric system such as biometric image compression, biometric image recognition and biometric image protection is also described in a chapter. The compressive sensing theory provides computation security and data reduction to image at acquisition time. The results show that the various applications related to biometric system using CS theory are overcome few limitations of existing techniques such as pattern recognition and image protection in the biometric system. The compressive sensing (CS) theory can be applied various image processing area such as image compression, image recognition and image protection with improving in image acquisition procedure.

In future, this theory can be applied to various signal and image processing area such as video compression, video watermarking and speech recognition. This theory can be also applied to area of image fusion, image registration, EEG signal processing and ECG signal processing because much of this information is easy to convert into its sparse domain when any image or signal transform applied to it.

REFERENCES

Aghasi, A., & Romberg, J. (2013). Sparse Shape Reconstruction. *SIAM Journal on Imaging Sciences*, *6*(4), 2075–2108. doi:10.1137/130911573

Aghasi, A., & Romberg, J. (2015). *Convex Cardinal Shape Composition.* ArXiv preprint arXiv: 1501.01347

Agrawal, M. (2007, August). *Design Approaches for Multimodal Biometric System.* (M. Tech). Thesis, Department of Computer Science and Engineering, IIT, Kanpur.

Ahmed, A., Recht, B., & Romberg, J. (2014). Blind Deconvolution using Convex Programming. *IEEE Transactions on Information Theory*, *60*(3), 1711–1732. doi:10.1109/TIT.2013.2294644

Ahmed, A., & Romberg, J. (2012). Compressive Multiplexers for Correlated Signals. *2012 IEEE Conference Record of the Forty Sixth Asilomar Conference on Signals, Systems and Computers (ASILOMAR).* doi:10.1109/ACSSC.2012.6489159

Ashboum, J. (2014). *Biometrics in the World - The Cloud, Mobile Technology and Pervasive Identity.* Berlin: Springer International Publishing.

Asif, M., & Romberg, J. (2014). Sparse Recovery of Streaming Signals Using L1 Homotopy. *IEEE Transactions on Signal Processing*, *62*(16), 4209–4223. doi:10.1109/TSP.2014.2328981

Baraniuk, R. (2007, July). Compressive Sensing. *IEEE Signal Processing Magazine*, *24*(4), 118–124. doi:10.1109/MSP.2007.4286571

Candès, E. (2006). Compressive Sampling. In *Proceedings of the International Congress of Mathematicians*.

Candès, E., & Romberg, J., (2005, October). *L1-Magic: Recovery of Sparse Signals via Convex Programming*. Academic Press.

Cox, I., Kilian, J., Shamoon, T., & Leighton, F. (1997, December). Secure Spread Spectrum Watermarking for Multimedia. *IEEE Transactions on Image Processing*, *6*(12), 1673–1687. doi:10.1109/83.650120 PMID:18285237

Dai, W., & Milenkovic, O., (2009). *Subspace Pursuit for Compressive Sensing Signal Reconstruction*. Academic Press.

Donoho, D. (2006, April). Compressed Sensing. *IEEE Transactions on Information Theory*, *52*(4), 1289–1306. doi:10.1109/TIT.2006.871582

Duarte, M., & Eldar, Y. (2011, September). Structured Compressed Sensing: From Theory to Applications. *IEEE Transactions on Signal Processing*, *59*(9), 4053–4085. doi:10.1109/TSP.2011.2161982

For Iris Database. (n.d.). Retrieved from http://www.sinobiometrics.com/caisairis.html

Gilbert, A., Strauss, M., Tropp, J., & Vershynin, R. (2007, June). One Sketch for all: Fast Algorithms for Compressed Sensing. *39th ACM Symposium on Theory of Computing (STOC)*. doi:10.1145/1250790.1250824

Giot, R., El-Abed, M., & Rosenberger, C. (2012, February). Fast Computation of the Performance Evaluation of Biometric Systems: Application to Multibiometrics. *Future Generation Computer Systems*, *1*, 1–30.

Harinda, E., & Natgwirumugara, E. (2015). Security & Privacy Implications in the Placement of Biometric-Based ID Card for Rwanda Universities. *Journal of Information Security*, *6*(02), 93–100. doi:10.4236/jis.2015.62010

Jain, A., & Kumar, A. (2012). Biometric Recognition: An Overview. In E. Mordini & D. Tzovaras (Eds.), *Second Generation Biometrics: The Ethical, Legal and Social Context* (pp. 49–79). Springer. doi:10.1007/978-94-007-3892-8_3

Jain, A., Nandakumar, K., & Nagar, A., (2008, January). Biometric Template Security. *EURASIP Journal on Advances in Signal Processing*, 1 – 17.

Jain, A., & Ross, A. (2004, January). Multibiometric Systems. *Communications of the ACM*, *47*(1), 34–40. doi:10.1145/962081.962102

Jain, A., Ross, A., & Pankanti, S. (2006, June). Biometrics: A Tool for Information Security. *IEEE Transactions on Information Forensics and Security*, *1*(2), 125–143. doi:10.1109/TIFS.2006.873653

Jain, A., Ross, A., & Prabhakar, S. (2004, January). An Introduction to Biometric Recognition. *IEEE Transactions on Circuits and Systems for Video Technology, 14*(1), 4–20.

Kolan, H., & Thapaliya, T. (2011). *Biometric Passport: Security and Privacy Aspects of Machine Readable Travel Document.* Retrieved from https://diuf.unifr.ch/main/is/sites/diuf.unifr.ch.main.is/files/documents/student-projects/eGov_2011_Hesam_Kolahan_&_Tejendra_Thapaliya.pdf

Laska, J., Davenport, M., & Baraniuk, R. (2009, November). Exact Signal Recovery from Sparsely Corrupted Measurements through the Pursuit of Justice. *Asilomar Conference on Signals, Systems and Computers.* doi:10.1109/ACSSC.2009.5470141

Lopez, R., & Boulgouris, N., (2010, August). *Compressive Sensing and Combinatorial Algorithms for Image Compression.* A Project Report, King's College, London, UK.

Lupu, E., & Pop, P. (2008). Multimodal Biometric Systems Overview. *ACTA Technica Napocensis, 49*(3), 39–44.

National Science & Technology Council. (2007). *Introduction to Biometrics.* Retrieved from http://www.biometrics.gov/documents/biofoundationdocs.pdf

Needell, D. (2009). *Topics in Compressed Sensing.* (Ph.D. Thesis). University of California.

Pato, J., & Millett, L. (2010). Biometric Recognition: Challenges and Opportunities. *Whither Biometric Board.* Retrieved from http://dataprivacylab.org/TIP/2011sept/Biometric.pdf

Ratha, N., Connell, J., & Bolle, R. (2001). Enhancing Security and Privacy in Biometric Based Authentication Systems. *IBM Systems Journal, 40*(3), 614–634. doi:10.1147/sj.403.0614

Salman, A., & Romberg, J. (2013). Fast and Accurate Algorithms for Re-weighted-norm Minimization. *IEEE Transactions on Signal Processing, 61*(23), 5905–5916. doi:10.1109/TSP.2013.2279362

Shih, F. (2008). Digital Watermarking and Steganography – Fundamentals and Techniques. CRC Press.

Sui, Y., Zou, X., & Du, Y. (2013). Cancellable Biometrics. In Biometrics: from Fiction to Practice. Pan Stanford Publishing Pte. Ltd.

Technology Watch Report, I. T. U.-T. (December, 2009). *Biometrics and Standards.* Retrieved from http://www.itu.int/dms_pub/itu-t/oth/23/01/T230100000D0002MSWE.doc

Teddy, K. O. (2005). Multimodal Biometric Identification for Large User Population Using Fingerprint, Face and Iris Recognition. *Proceeding of the IEEE 34th Applied Imagery and Pattern Recognition Workshop (AIPR05).* doi:10.1109/AIPR.2005.35

Thieme, M. (2003). Multimodal Biometric Systems: Applications and Usage Scenarios. *Biometric Consortium Conference.*

Tropp, J., & Gilbert, A. (2007, December). Signal Recovery from Random Measurements via Orthogonal Matching Pursuit. *IEEE Transactions on Information Theory, 53*(12), 4655–4666. doi:10.1109/TIT.2007.909108

Turnes, C., Balcan, D., & Romberg, J. (2012). Image Deconvolution via Superfast Inversion of a Class of two-level Toeplitz Matrices. *2012 19th IEEE International Conference on Image Processing (ICIP),* (pp. 3073 – 3076).

Wang, Z., & Bovik, A. (2004). A Universal Image Quality Index. *Journal of IEEE Signal Processing Letters, 9*(3), 84–88.

Chapter 15
Integration of Different Analytical Concepts on Multimedia Contents in Service of Intelligent Knowledge Extraction

Goran Klepac
University College for Applied Computer Engineering Algebra, Croatia & Raiffeisenbank Austria, Croatia

ABSTRACT

This chapter will introduce methodology how to use analytical potential of multimedia contents like YouTube, Bing Videos or Vimeo for discovering behavioral consumer characteristics. Chapter will also show how to consolidate unstructured text data sources from blogs and Twitter with revealed knowledge from multimedia contents for better understanding consumer habits and needs. For this purposes Social Network Analysis will be used as well as text mining techniques on different internet data sources. Presented methodology has practical value where information about customer behavior, preferences and changes in preferences during different time periods is valuable information for campaign planning, campaign management and new product development. Presented methodology also captures different techniques for data crawling from different internet resources, as well as analytical consolidation of revealed results which aim is better understanding of client behavior.

INTRODUCTION

Sites with video content like YouTube, Bing Videos or Vimeo, could be wealth source of information for discovering behavioral characteristics of their consumers. Behavioral characteristics, preferences, profiles, segments, clusters can be discovered by analyzing crawled data from mentioned sites.

Consumer behavior and preferences could be discovered regarding watching preferences.

DOI: 10.4018/978-1-5225-0498-6.ch015

Initial watcher population can be extracted by snowball sampling where root node is some specific user which has published some specific video material, or based on some specific keyword.

Initial population is base for deeper investigation regarding consumer segmentation, consumer behavior recognition and pattern recognition process.

For that purpose, key role has social network analysis (SNA) which helps us find interesting patterns and segments among specific watcher population. SNA gives us opportunity for discovering hidden influencer and leaders among network of watched videos. That leads us on giving answers on questions like: "Which type of videos, consumers like to watch after watching some aimed video? ", "Is there any hidden connections between different video segments regarding consumer preferences?", "Which video/videos within population acts key role for consumer motivation for watching videos from another segment (genre) ? ".

Another valuable source of information is consumer comments associated with video content. That fact leads us on natural language processing area. Recognized patterns and segments via SNA can be additionally analyzed through text mining.

Chapter gives framework and solution for analyzing video consumer behavior using social network analysis and text mining with technical details how to realize proposed solution.

Integral part of the chapter is complete case study from Croatian market. Case study will show proposed framework in action in situation before premiere of film "Fifty shades of gray".

Analysis based on previously explained methodology has been used. Central point of analysis was keyword *"Pedeset nijansi sive"* (Croatian translation of "Fifty shades of gray") on YouTube for data crawling.

As a result, analysis showed interesting patterns and preferences based on consumer behavior, which shows what average consumer interested in forthcoming movie also prefers to watch, and which is focus of his interest beside aimed content.

Same analysis has been performed on YouTube content after mentioned movie started to play in cinema and analysis shows new patterns and changes in consumer behavior.

Text mining analysis has been performed in parallel on text content associated with videos, and those types of analyzed data also shows interesting patterns valuable for market planning.

Same analysis also used Twitter data with the same keyword *"Pedeset nijansi sive"* (Croatian translation of "Fifty shades of gray").

Captured data from Twitter was used for conducting SNA and text mining. At the end, different results were integrated and used for marketing strategy.

Chapter also shows usage of different open source platforms, programming languages, program libraries in service of realization proposed framework and methodology.

Scientific contribution of proposed methodology is in integration of different analytical concepts on multimedia contents in service of intelligent knowledge extraction, which can be used in marketing strategy development.

Background

Understanding of customer behaviour is a key factor of market success, especially in competitive market conditions (Berry, 2000; Giudici, 2003; Giudici, 2009).

Extracting important behavioural information from transactional customer data, and enabling better decision-making throughout an organization is one of the aims when a company wants to understand their customers (Hemalatha, 2012). By increasing usage of social networks, blogs, forums, and Internet as communication channel beside traditional data sources like transactional databases and data warehouses, analytics of unstructured data became important topics. (Klepac, 2015c).

Multimedia data sources can contain patterns usable for customer behaviour recognition. Video content and images beside unstructured text can be used for segmentation purposes (De, 2013; De, 2014). In that case image content uploaded buy users can be treated as extended information for campaign strategy. In combination with textual information as a big data concept (Klepac, 2015b) it opens new perspective in area of data analytics.

Integration of text mining techniques (Miner,2012; Mirchev, 2014; Debole, 2003; Engel, 2009), social network analysis (Papadopulos, 2010), image analysis (De, 2013; De,2014) like other disciplines are crucial for qualitative analytical strategies in big data environment.

Video content also begins to play significant role in data analysis, not only on tag level, but with deeper understanding video content, which is base for advanced video content analysis (Raikwar, 2015).

Video content can be clustered thanks to mentioned advanced analytical techniques, as well as image content (Gebara, 2009).

All that leads to fact that multimedia content in combination with advanced analytical techniques can provide qualitative input for customer and consumer behavioural analysis and understanding of their habits. We assume that consumers and customers as users of some service like YouTube, Flickr, Twitter, provides some multimedia content along their comments and posts.

Recognition of customer segments based on their activities regarding provided multimedia content is a challenge (Katzenbeitsser, 2009; Garotte, 2013) especially in big data environment.

Additional problem in multimedia data collection and analysis is in their dynamic in big data environment where it is hard to determine optimal snapshot with which we will cover adequate data sample representative for our analysis. Sites like YouTube, Twitter and blogs on daily bases receive a much of new materials, and it has an influence on analytical results due to data capturing periods (Cointet, 2009).

From the other hand services like Twitter contains wisdom of the crowd (Reips, 2011), and multimedia content along with textual data with help of analytical techniques can discover hidden patterns important for campaign planning, product planning etc.

Textual data is important factor, which is additional part of multimedia content analysis. It should be combined with multimedia content for analytical purposes. Reason for that is more than obvious, and that is fact that services like Flickr, You Tube, Twitter and others contains textual contents within most of the posts along with images, video content and sounds.

Regarding that fact, textual data also should be sampled to cover area and period for which we are making analysis on multimedia data, and should be in relation with them (Webb, 2014).

Text mining techniques (Feldman, 2007) also can be introduction to mining multimedia content, in way they can provide us important information after analysis for what we should looking for within multimedia content. Also, textual data is important factor in opinion analysing, and multimedia content gives additional value to data and analysis when we are talking about market analysis. Techniques for multimedia content mining (Bhattacharyya, 2013) plays important role in market research because algorithms are able to recognise patterns within image content, not only based on predefined indices.

Analysis of unstructured data and multimedia content depends on new innovative methods (Chisholm, 1999), but as well on experienced analyst, which knows how to prepare data and to use adequate data mining method, which will extract hidden piece of information.

Big data environment with huge amount of unstructured data demands new concepts of analytical approaches. It should not be neglected role of collective intelligence which is barred deeper under surface of that content (Garrido, 2008). Taking in consideration that fact, methods and techniques associated with collective intelligence and evolutionary computing takes place along with multimedia content analysis (Klepac, 2015).

Social Network Analysis (Easley, 2010; Hansen, 2010) can be solid starting point for analytical activities, if we take in consideration most of the disposable data sources on Internet where we can find multimedia content, user comments, posts are organised in networks. Social networks can be good starting point for advanced analysis, which multimedia content puts into new dimension which can be observed thought network metrics. That approach determines importance of some user within network, as well as content, which he has provided.

New era of big data and social networks contributes in complexity of data sources for analytical purposes, and offers new challenges and also additional useful information for understanding customer behaviour (Scot, 2012; Raine, 2012). That leads us to taking in account social network analysis as an important factor for understanding hidden relations within a portfolio.

POTENTIAL OF MULTIMEDIA DATA IN MARKETING

Traditional approach on market research is mainly focused on data collected through questioners, structured data from structured data sources like databases or data warehouses, or on combination of all mentioned sources as base for marketing analysis.

Main criticism regarding questioners stems from fact that it is not easy to create representative sample for interviewing. In practice it is always danger that significant part of targeted population from the sample will not cooperate with interviewers. That can cause problem of sample distortion, which means that collected answers are not representative for targeted population. Market researchers use specific techniques, like pondering for solving that kind of problem or they simply extend research on specific population for achieving representative sample.

Another important problem which is highlighted during telephone surveys or some other way of interviewing is sincerity. It is hard to achieve reliable answers on questions at some specific moment where interviewed person is often interrupted from some activity and it is practically forced to think and to give answers on some subject on which they are not prepared. Often on that situation, an interviewed person gives the answers mechanically without deeper thinking.

Regarding fact that examiner has limited time for conducting interview per person on phone, and that answers should be structured for further analysis it has limited set of disposable answers on each question. Sometimes offered answers does not cover all potential answers and interviewed person should choose one of the answer, even it is not fully in line with his or her opinion.

Questions and offered answers are product of evaluation that those set of questions and offered answers will be sufficient for finding analytical solution for specific problem. It is always dangerous in questions which is not answered and could be crucial factor for understanding nature of the observed problem.

Last mentioned problem is the mutual problem with market research, product planning, product analysis based on databases and transactional data. Transactional information systems are designed for transactions, and their designers often did not have in mind future needs on market research. That leads us to conclusion that market research are based on limited data sets, which are transactional oriented and there is no guarantee that it contains sufficient data sets crucial for market research and understanding customer needs.

It does not mean that mentioned approaches are useless; contrary it can be very efficient. Main intention is to emphasize problems as an introduction for seeking solutions for it.

Alternative approach or approach which supplements traditional ways of market research can be focused as well on unstructured data on Internet which includes also multimedia data.

Motivations for leaving traces in virtual spaces regarding some product or service are often emotionally supported, like bad experience with buying used car from car dealer. Those messages can be serious milestones for future customers for not buying cars from this car dealer.

It is extreme example. More often people leave videos or texts on blogs or social networks if they are excited, satisfied or have some comments on some specific product or services. That content can contain some minor complaints on existing products, wishes on functionality on future version of some products, or some other comments which can be interesting for potential buyers.

Multimedia content and way of consuming multimedia content gives the answers about customer profiles, behavior, and preferences. If we a talking about video content, it is not the same if the watcher starts to look on specific video content as a result of aimed search, or it start to look on specific video content as a result of recommendation. Important factor is path how watcher has reached specific content as well as frequency of using recognized path for reaching specific video content. That information gives us insight of customer behavior, preferences, and it can be used as milestones for campaign management.

Contrary to mentioned market research approach which includes questioners or databases as data source for analysis from perspective of sampling, multimedia content in data sources like YouTube, Vimeo provides data sources with predefined data sample (real watchers of specific content).

Another advantage is dynamic – real time data source which is continuously updated and reflects market conditions and market trends.

That means, contrary to data from questioners which represents snapshot on specific date, data from Internet sources with video content are dynamic, because of continuous usage. It means that based on that, it is possible to make trend analysis and to recognize changes on market trends.

Speaking about multimedia data, video content is often followed by user comments and their attitudes, recommendation, which is wealth source of information which can be analyzed along with video or image content.

Another strategy for discovering knowledge could be consolidation of information and content from different data sources like Twitter, Vimeo and YouTube.

Data crawling can be done based on keywords or specific theme. Collected data from different sources can give holistic analytical picture for making better decisions and for better understanding of customer needs and habits.

Such collected data and data types give new perspectives in analytics. Traditionally approach in market research especially questioner oriented, presupposes finite number of answers for the given question. Presented approach based on multimedia data analytics searching for the answers without previously determined limited set of the possible answers.

Social Network Analysis in combination with text mining and tag analysis can reveal some hidden patterns and hidden knowledge which analyst at beginning of the analysis cannot assume. From the other hand, those patterns can be / are changeable at different time periods, and it reflects real market situation, as well as customer satisfaction, customer interest on some product or service, willingness to continue or to stop buying some product or service. It is also alternative approach to segmentation based on Social Network Analysis which can show clusters regarding similar behavior, or propensity to additional contents. That is the real power from analyzing multimedia data, stored on sites like Twitter, Vimeo, Youtube and similar sites.

It is line with big data concept, but most important thing is methodological frame based on advanced analytics which will be introduced through this chapter. Firstly, as a concept, and lately as a real case study which illustrate presented analytical concept.

MARKET RESEARCH MODEL BASED ON MULTIMEDIAL DATA

General Discussion

Common approaches in situation where companies do market research, as it was previously mentioned are leaned on transactional or data based on questioners. Market research model based on multimedia data demands different approach, because data sources are generally Internet oriented.

In other worlds, we are talking about big data approach, which demands adequate planning regarding analytical techniques usage as well as data source exploitation and usage.

The most important component in each analytically oriented project is clear aim definition. Precisely defined aim is crucial for other analytical stages and for solution finding. It is a common task in all situations relating to analytical modeling and is not specific only in the big data environment.

The analytical process, from the perspective of needed steps for achieving aims, is not much different in a big data environment with multimedia content or in a situation where a company leans on traditional data sources. A fundamental difference is in strategic analytical thinking, which demands consideration regarding possible directions and integration of external data sources as well as techniques, which can be applied on such data integrated with internal data sources. Regarding that, in a situation where a company takes into account external data sources, and other disposable data sources like unstructured data, videos, images which can be declared as big data, analytical process are much more complex and holistic.

Business aims should be defined, taking into consideration additional benefits from integration of data sources, like social networks, Twitter, forums and similar data sources, on which companies did not put focus, if we are talking about analytics in big data environment. Contrary to traditional analytical approach, big data strategic thinking, implies knowledge extracting from additional data sources, which does not have to be relationally connected through existing databases or data warehouses. It implies using disposable knowledge from other sources, and its integration into analytical process, having in mind achieving greater efficiency for decision support.

For example, let's assume that an insurance company would like to develop a predictive model, which will calculate churn probability on the customer level. Traditional model development would be concentrated on local databases, capturing client behavior characteristics within the local database framework. This approach is a result of an adopted way of thinking, caused by the common methodology where big data and its potential are not used for building solutions. Traditional solutions offer answers about the churner's patterns (if we are observing the previous example). Other activities where clients exchange opinions about the company and share some attitudes, which at the end leads to churn, could stay unrevealed if the company does not change strategic way of analytical thinking.

Unstructured data could exist as well in internal sources, like memo fields within call center databases, which stays out of the analytical process. Analytical thinking from the perspective of big data also includes facts, that data does not have to be connected through relational keys within databases. In the described churn example, it indicates that data for predictive modeling should be consolidated from data sources such as databases, blogs, forums and other unstructured data sources like videos and images.

Richness of data sources does not guarantee a successful analytical process if it is not well and objectively planned, with clear aims and understanding of business problems. Often, it is hard to make clear analytical objectives for big data environment, where data volume and complexity is bigger than in traditional local data environment. Even in such conditions, unclear vision and methodology on how to achieve analytical aim based on business needs could be crucial for project failure or success.

In the big data area, requirements for clear analytical aims are crucial for setting the right analytical strategy. More choices and sources gives an opportunity for better and precise results, but also hides the potential danger of missing the point, if these kind of projects are not adequately and not strategically planned from perspective of business decision needs. Business decision needs also require strategic analytical planning, and the big data concept enters some new standards and requirements into this process.

There is no guarantee that external data or internal data will deliver additional information about problems, which would be of great value for finding business solutions. The basic idea from the perspective of a big data analytical strategy is to cover all disposable and usable data sources and techniques, which potentially could be useful for additional knowledge extraction. For such purposes, during the project planning stage, it is important to have in mind all possibilities, which big data concepts could offer. This stage in the big data approach, has a powerful influence on the following steps in analytical process:

- Disposable data recognition.
- Solution design.
- Solution building.
- Knowledge extraction.

Disposable data recognition is concentrated on external data sources. A few problems existing within this step are that the company:

- Often does not know the data potential of external, useful data sources, and
- Potential problems with data sampling (Snijders, 2012).

After the business aim definition, which includes strategy based on the big data paradigm, disposable data has the potential to have a strong influence on solution design and solution building. It can consolidate traditional model development along with analytical solutions, based on the big data paradigm. It is important to stress that in such situations, knowledge extraction demands much more human expert involvement. Especially in situations where results and knowledge from different kinds of models exist, and it demands expert judgment and evaluation. During the business decision process, expert explanations and conclusions play a crucial role in the understanding and interpretation of given results. This is due to the fact that results are derived from different data sources, which provide different perspectives of the problem and desire experts for their explanation.

A big data environment leads to unknown territory, where a company is often unsure what it could dig from those data sources, which are mostly unstructured, big in volume and complex, sometimes without clear vision. Along to these problems, it offers rich sources of new data.

Basic Concept

With Internet as a data source for analytical purposes, which contains unstructured data with multimedia content, it is challenge to find analytical way, which will extract useful information from this amount of data, as well as unconnected data sources.

As on traditional data mining projects which are mainly based on structured data from databases, most important thing is to set the aim of analytical project. This is the first step, which determines other steps in the project.

Aim definition can direct to disposable data sources, time spans for which we should collect data, as well as what we should analyze.

Let assume situation, in which we would like to determine customer profiles preferences and other characteristics in situation where new album of some singer will arrive.

Firstly, it is important to determine multimedia content on the Internet where content in connection with observed singer exists. It can be YouTube, Twitter, some Blogs, and other sources in connection with this singer. From the other hand it is not unimportant when, and for which period of time we will collect the data from different sources.

It is important to include relevant period (periods), because if we are capturing data before new album will arrive, it is questionable would those data reflect real customer attitudes and behavioral characteristic in relation with expected album.

From the other hand, analytics on data set before new album will arrive is good benchmark for trend evaluation in customer perception and acceptance of the new album.

Recommendation is to capture data set before and after new album of singer will arrive, because in that case analyst can compare results from two different time periods, and it can be helpful for trend observing. Also, good strategy can be data capturing for analytical purposes in history, when we had same situation (new album arrival).

In that case we are talking about four data samples:

- Sample of period in history before old album has arrived.
- Sample of period in history when old album has arrived.
- Sample of period in near history before new album arrived.
- Sample of period when new album has arrived.

Another important question is which time period should be included for each sample? For example, if we are talking about sample of period in near history before new album arrived it is inappropriate to define this period in time units. Much more appropriate is to define events which define beginning period and end period of data capturing.

In this example appropriate period for data capturing should be beginning of campaigns on services like YouTube, Twitter, blogs, and other multimedia sources, and end of data capturing should be date when new album has arrived. In that case we do not define specific timelines, because some campaigns last few weeks, some few months, depending on product or service, which is subject of campaign.

Another important step is data source selection for analysis purpose. That include observation and taking in consider all relevant data sources like social networks, and other data sources which contains multimedia data, and can be used for campaign purposes.

It includes sources (already mentioned) like YouTube, Twitter, blogs, Facebook, LinkedIn. As it is visible on first sight, enumerated data sources contain different type of usable unstructured data like movies, pictures, text, and they contain information about structural connectivity between objects. All those different unstructured data sources demand different analytical approaches, which include usage of Social Network Analysis techniques, text mining, and standard data mining techniques.

Prerequisite for applying mentioned techniques is collected and prepared data from different data sources, captured at different time spans, like it is already explained.

Social Network Analysis, after data capturing can be applied on YouTube data, Twitter data, Facebook data in parallel, because it is no guarantee that connection between those data will be recognized. Also, in case that analyst can make direct connection between those data sources by ID's, there is no guarantee that recognized data sample of connected data are statistically relevant.

Making direct connectivity for analytical purposes between different data sources like YouTube data, Twitter data, Facebook is recommended, but as an additional analytical task, not main and only analytical task.

Main idea is to make snowball sampling on aimed data source (YouTube, Twitter, Facebook) by selected keyword. It can be in presented example name of the singer, and name of his new and old album.

In that case, used keyword is starting point for snowball sampling, which associates multimedia content. Snowball sampling is common sampling technique used for Social Network Analysis purpose, which can be used primary for Social Network Analysis but it also can be adopted to contain multimedia content, like images, movies, sounds and text as an objects.

Let assume that we are making snowball sampling on YouTube with keyword, which contain name of singer, which new album we are expecting soon.

After data capturing for determined period of time, based on selected keyword, we will get social network around that "keyword" with other content as an objects associated with captured nodes.

It is good starting point for conducting classical Social Network Analysis to find out hidden patterns, influencer in the captured social network, as well as behavioral models of main influencer, and their preferences with strong reference on multimedia content (movies if we are talking about YouTube).

Also, YouTube contains comments and other multimedia content like pictures, which also can be used as an object of analysis. For recognized influencer in social network we can make analysis based on their comments.

Basic idea is to apply text mining only on text patterns associated with recognized influencers within social network. Reason for that is consumption (colloquially speaking) "It is not important what do they said, important is who said".

Generally, if influencer in the social network told something, it has significant importance for whole network or part of the network. Influencer can be opinion maker with great influence on social network members.

From the other side, comment or recommendation from the node, which does not have great influence into the network, is not important in general, and it is generally unimportant to analyze textual patterns from those nodes.

Social Network Analysis can also be used for multimedia content analysis because it can give us information about preferences and behavior of social network members conjoint by snowball sampling abut other preferences regarding other singers and content they watch. It is important for user profiling, new product development, finding patterns regarding other preferable video content. Wealth source of information in combination with adequate analytical techniques can provide detailed picture about user behavior, preferences, mood, will they accept new product/did they accept new product.

Additional usage of other data sources and additional analysis can give better picture and explanation regarding customer behavior, mood, and acceptance of the product. That means in presented case that we can apply described analysis on Twitter, Facebook data and we can compare results with intention to make hypothesis and prove of hypothesis important for campaign development.

Data Collection Strategies

Presented model takes data from different data sources. As it was previously explained, it is important to estimate right time span in which data should be collected. Along that, other important topic is strategy of linking different data sources for analytical purposes.

It is important to keep in mind that data preparation process takes almost 80% of time in modeling. It is commonly evident on traditional data mining projects. Proposed model is not exceptions in that, especially in situation like this when we are dealing with data sources from the Internet. Those data sources demand special treatment in collection, linking, data cleansing and processing.

Data preparation should also keep prerequisites to reflect business logic, and should reflect all the requirements connected with the scope of the analytical project.

It means that sampling process and data preparation process follows business needs.

If we are talking about multimedia data and Internet as a data source, where we are dealing with unstructured data and additionally unstructured data from different sources which has different scope and often could not be directly connected on data level, it is necessary to take different strategies on data collection and preparation in comparison with structured data sources.

It means that connectivity should be done based on analytical results. For that purpose, first step is selection of data sources on Internet, which can provide some sort of relevant data, which analytical results can be chained. Chaining process should give additional hidden information and holistic picture of the observed problem.

Much simpler in lower level of abstraction it means that if we are talking about new album in arrival of famous singer, for analytical purposes we should carefully chose aimed data sources for analytical purposes.

First step is observation of main actions regarding his campaign strategies and Internet sources. If campaign is significantly YouTube oriented, then it is for sure one of the main data sources for further analysis. Also if there is significant activity on Twitter, Flickr or other services, it is also potential data sources for conducting analysis on that data. It is same for the social networks like Facebook, Google+ and similar services.

Each data source contains variety data types like structural connectivity between users, pictures, movies, text, sounds, and analytical process should be concentrated on single data source not on all sources as a unified data source for analytical purposes. It means that data should be collected e.g. from YouTube as an independent data source on which we will apply analytical techniques, and after that same will be done with other data sources which will be collected independently, and analyzed independently.

Reason for that is in fact that it is very hard or practically impossible to make direct connections between different data sources from variety of different sites. One reason is in technical aspect of the data, and another reason is that different users can have different user names in different services. Also fact that member which use one service, it does not does not mean that he/she uses another service.

Regarding that, connectivity can be achieved on analytical level. It means that analytical results can be compared for seeking additional patterns and that can result on additional solutions, which will physically connect different data sources after finishing this step.

Example for that can be in hypothetically revealed pattern which shows that part of the users which watch video contents related to specific singer like to watch some specific video content related to some writer of bestsellers. It can be the glue for searching patterns on services like Twitter for finding some hidden connections and patterns, which can lead analyst to some another glue.

From the other hand, that approach gives opportunity for active seeking patterns between user populations, as well as for segmentation. Recognized patterns and segments can be additionally analyzed, not only from perspective of general characteristics and profiling, but also through temporal dimension, which gives us an opportunity for additional knowledge extraction which is time dependent.

Presented example shows importance of good data collection strategy, because it is starting point for potential good direction in exploration of hidden patterns relevant for the understanding nature of observed trends.

Regarding fact, that subject of analysis is not structured data sources with connections between tables with primary and secondary keys, and regarding fact that we are talking about multimedia data which contain images, movies, sound, text, links between objects, and it is hard to make unified solution purely mathematically oriented.

In here, expert knowledge and expert judgment along with exact models comes gives on his importance. Also, we should emphasize spiral approach in analytical process, which means that all the process can be/should be conducted in several iterations in seeking optimal solution.

Each solution should be validated and compared, using common statistical tests, as well as expert knowledge and logical conclusion, because nature of this kind of projects is seeking of hidden patterns. As we are talking about multimedia data and unstructured data, where combinatory explosion of data as well as solutions are present, expert knowledge plays important role in reducing data processing, as well as in determination of potential analytical solutions.

Role of Analytical Waves and Analytical Techniques

Main advantage of data sources from Internet is their reliability, and accuracy regarding current market opinion. It is worth to mention that those data we can declare as big data, because of their characteristics. This data is also volatile, regarding new inputs, which can be intensive and less intensive depending on campaigns, market opinion, or some other factors in relation with consumer awareness. Different data types within unstructured data sources like images, movies, text, and sound can vary as input and analytical strategies should cover and have analytical strategies for different scenarios regarding structures of new data sources, and their combination.

Analytical waves planning takes in consideration campaigns, market opinion, and other factors in relation with consumer awareness. It is event driven, not time driven. It means that time for data collection and length of captured sample depends on market conditions and it can be in strong correlation with camping stages. As it was previously mentioned, several analytical waves assure diversification in consumer moods, opinions, and trend observation depending on market activities.

In that way it is possible to measure effects of some actions on market, customer satisfaction on new functionality of the product or service, or simply customer opinion, after product is offered for sale.

For achieving analytical purposes on described data sets which are unstructured and which contains variety unstructured data types it is necessary to use different analytical areas and to combine results from them.

Different algorithms can be used for finding matching patterns among images, and files, which contain sounds. Social Network Analysis can be useful in finding structural patterns, connectivity and influencers between members of observed social network.

Also, natural language processing is important for lexical analysis and for analysis of consumer opinions especially between members with highest influence in the network. Degree of influence can be measured by Social Network Analysis usage, and it can be introduction for deeper investigation based on natural language processing.

Also it is interesting which multimedia content provide members with highest influence in the network. Sometimes that content is indexed, and can be analyzed on that level, and sometimes we should spend additional effort for finding patterns within contents like images, movies, sound files.

It is important which multimedia content is assigned to influencer in network, and which message it spreads.

Multimedia content also has power to transfer message, ideas and opinions, as well as text. Sometimes preferences for consuming multimedia content can be transferred from influencer within social network to followers. It is important to recognize those trends and to find potential future preferences of the followers based on influencer recommendation.

That is the reason, why pure analytics on multimedia data often is not sufficient, and it should be combined with other analytics based on Social Network Analysis, text mining and traditional data mining techniques.

There is no cookbook for spending these analytical activities, and it depends on analytical aims.

Sometimes, starting point can be image content clustering based on images from Twitter, Facebook, and Flickr. Image content can determine social network segmentation by specific interest. Image content can discover some general characteristics of social network user profile.

Let suppose that we are searching for segments in Twitter based on images, which Twitter users have tweeted. Let suppose that we found variety of profiles based upon that analysis, and we are especially interested on users, which mostly like to tweet old vintage muscle cars, as a part dealers for vintage cars.

Another step can be segmentation based on textual data (tweets), which contains sentence patterns in connection with old vintage muscle cars and their parts.

Those two segments, found by images and tweets, should be consolidated. In that step it should be taken in consideration that tweets could contain images and textual contents, which are in relation with the same subject. That leads us to fact that we should prepare data sample taking in consider that fact.

Final step can be creation of Social Network based on Twitter users interested in old vintage muscle cars, where users, which satisfied those condition gives, attribute as member of that segment. Social Network Analysis can provide additional information about influencers in population, who is opinion maker, which of the other segments are also interesting to this population, and is it significant part of that population. Social Network Analysis also can give information about gatekeepers within network if they do exist.

Given results can be used for future strategies in campaign planning. For the influencer company can give some benefits or discounts on car parts. If it is any other recognized interest within population of old vintage muscle cars fans, it can be space for cobranding, or developing new product based on discovered new sub segments.

Whole twitter population, as well as observed segment can change their characteristics and attitudes during different periods of time, as well their preferences on other products.

Recognition of those trends should be committing same analytical procedures at different time periods. It will assure trend recognition and opportunity recognition for efficient marketing strategies.

Important factor is aimed population. For example, old vintage muscle cars fans can be declared as relatively stable population regarding their attitudes and values. Expected variation can be expected in preferences of other product usage which is not directly associated with this subject. Contrary if we are observing population of video game players for some specific video game, that population is much more unstable and have minor lifetime.

Depending on analytical aims, target group, disposable data sources it is recommended to choose analytical strategies and analytical tools depending on mentioned factors. Whole process cannot be automatically, it demands taking in consideration business and technical factors for extracting useful patterns and knowledge about consumers of some product or service.

CASE STUDY

Short Description

Main aim of presented case study is to investigate market trends within population of potential Fifty shades of gray film watchers in area of south-eastern Europe, precisely Croatia, Bosnia and Herzegovina, Serbia, Monte Negro. Reason, why enumerated countries enter into sample is fact of language similarity. Fifty shades of gray in translation on Croatian language is: *Pedeset nijansi sive*, which is the same translation for mentioned countries.

Main idea was data collection strategy based on keyword, which is translation of film title in English. Data collection will follow period before film was broadcasted, and period after film was broadcasted after some period of time.

Target data sources for analytical purposes are YouTube and Twitter. YouTube, because movie distributor in Croatia as well as distributors for other mentioned regions, published film trailers few months before projections in cinema. Consumption was that people interested in that film or just curious people will watch it, and regarding behavior after watching or searching those content will leave comments, and will watch other multimedia content.

That can be valuable source of information, because, it is clustered and localized by mutual translation, and that imply territorial determination of potential watchers.

Idea is potential watchers' main characteristics determination upon multimedia content which they are watching and which is concentrated on movie trailer Fifty shades of gray, with translation and tags in Croatian language. Analysis should be conducted in two or more waves, for finding out trends in watchers population, as well as opinions among them.

Even, YouTube has comments as additional content potentially associated to each movie; it is not sufficient for holistic analysis. Reason for that is that comments can be valuable source of additional information regarding subject of the movie, but not main source of information. Users do not visit YouTube with intention for giving general opinions regarding some subject. They are mostly motivated to give comments regarding specific content, which they are watching.

YouTube is most important as a data source which contains specific multimedia content, and which can give us answers regarding user watching preferences along aimed content.

For that purposes data from YouTube has been captured for Social Network Analysis taking in consideration:

- Tags, in way when a pair of videos is tagged with the same keyword.
- Comments made by same user. An edge between a pair of videos will be created when the same user comments them on.
- Video response. Videos are linked by response videos.

Data source which is much more adequate for general opinion investigation is Twitter. Twitter contains text as well other multimedia content. Micro blogging is much suitable data source for opinion investigation. Motivation for posting tweets is much opinion expression oriented than comments on YouTube.

Data crawling for text collection and social network construction was conducted by collecting tweets with mentioning *Pedeset nijansi sive* in their tweets, and all of the follows, replies-to, and Mentions relationships between them.

Textual data has been stored with respect of the tweeters, regarding fact that tweets of the most influenced Twitter members within constructed network will be analyzed with natural language processing techniques.

Whole process was repeated for two analytical waves before film was broadcasted, and period after film was broadcasted.

On captured YouTube data, Social Network Analysis has been conducted with intention for finding patterns regarding preferences in watching videos which are connected with aimed keywords: *Pedeset nijansi sive*.

Comments from YouTube in relation with this keyword have also been stored with user identification number. Reason for that is the same as for Twitter data. Comments of the most influenced YouTube members within constructed network will be analyzed with natural language processing techniques.

For diversification purposes, additionally for both data sources, natural language processing will be used on non-influencers just to check if there is any significant pattern between them.

That is important if we would like to hear *vox populi* within some population, which is common by itself, and it does not have a significant influence on other members of the network.

We can call it as spontaneous *collective attitude*, because there is no influencer, which affected on that attitude. Exception could only be, if that "collective attitude" matches with opinion makers (influencers) within network.

Multimedia content from Twitter like images, and videos, could also be investigated for seeking additional knowledge, especially if it is tagged.

As it is previously mentioned, there are no possibilities to make direct connection between data set collected from YouTube, and data set collected from Twitter. Connections can only be made in analytical way by comparison of discovered patterns between these two data sets.

Also, discovered pattern within one data set can be base for additional analysis on another data set, as well as inspiration for additional analysis based on discovered hypotheses.

Data collection data preparation and social networks metrics calculation

For data collection purposes NodeXL tool (Hansen, 2010) was used. It was used for data capturing from Twitter as well as from YouTube. Data has been captured in two waves. First wave was at 10th February 2015, and second wave was at 20th February 2015.

In first wave data was captured from Twitter and YouTube based on phrase *Pedeset nijansi sive* which is Croatian translation for *Fifty Shades of Gray*.

Captured Twitter data on 10th February 2015 did not show any interesting patterns, because of small sample.

YouTube data was collected on 10th February 2015 by following criteria:

- Tags, in way when a pair of videos is tagged with the same keyword.
- Comments made by same user. An edge between a pair of videos will be created when the same user comments them on.
- Video response. Videos are linked by response videos.

YouTube data showed potential, because of sample size. Main reason for better activities on YouTube was film trailer published on YouTube by film distributor.

Data collected with NodeXL from Twitter and YouTube was exported to .net (Pajek) network format. This is one of the formats supported by NetworkX library. NetworkX is a Python package for the creation, manipulation, and study of the structure, dynamics, and functions of complex networks.

Following program in Python processed exported data in .net (Pajek) format.

```
import networkx as nx
from operator import itemgetter
G=nx.Graph()
G=nx.read_pajek("Tube.net")
print "Info:"
print nx.info(G)
print "Degree histogram:"
print nx.degree_histogram(G)
print "Density:"
print nx.density(G)
print "Number of nodes:"
print G.number_of_nodes()
print "Number of edges:"
print G.number_of_edges()
dc= nx.degree_centrality(G)
Sorted_degree = sorted(dc.items(), key=itemgetter(1), reverse=True)
print "Sorted degree:"
print Sorted_degree [0:5]
bc= nx.betweenness_centrality(G)
Sorted_betweenness = sorted(bc.items(), key=itemgetter(1), reverse=True)
print "Sorted betweenness:"
print Sorted_betweenness [0:5]
cc= nx.closeness_centrality(G)
```

```
Sorted_closeness = sorted(cc.items(), key=itemgetter(1), reverse=True)
print "Sorted closeness:"
print Sorted_closeness [0:5]
```

Program opens network, calculate main characteristic of the whole observed network like density, number of nodes, number of edges. Second part of the program calculates social network metrics: degree centrality, betweenness centrality, closeness centrality. Taking in consider fact, regarding expected number of nodes, program gives for each social network metrics top five nodes. It can be parameterized and can vary, but for these purpose initially top five nodes is listed.

Results from First Analytical Wave

At first analytical wave data from Twitter had few tweets regarding *Fifty shades of gray* in Croatian translation. Reason for that is awaiting screening of the film in theatres.

YouTube data had much richer data sample, 320 nodes, with graph density of 0,2204.

Analysis shows that most appropriate and reliable metrics in the network is betweenness. It shows some interesting relations within network. Betweenness measure extent to which a node lies between other nodes in the network, this measure takes into account the connectivity of the node's neighbors, giving a higher value for nodes which bridge clusters, the measure reflects the number of people who a person is connecting indirectly through their direct links.

As it is visible from Figure 1, node A (*Fifty Shades Of Grey - Unofficial Trailer [Jamie Dornan & Dakota Johnson]*) and node B (*Mistakes and illogical staffs from the film*) is the bridges for contents in cluster C which is dedicated to themes like: fifty things which you should know about Fifty shades of gray. Also node A and node B is bridges for the video spots of regional reaper, which has new hit dedicated to film *Fifty shades of gray.* It is obvious that watchers, which are seeking for the content regarding trailers of *Fifty shades of gray,* are interested to watch this hit, and also they watch other songs from the same singer. It is the cluster united about unofficial trailer. Also, these watchers are interested in topics regarding illogical scenes and mistakes in film, during network investigation it is visible that part of that cluster are seeking for that content.

Node D represents official trailer, and it is visible that watcher of that trailer are much more "formal" in way that watchers which has crossed this bridge are seeking more formal official content for this film.

Node E (From The "Fifty Shades Of Grey" Soundtrack) and node F (Fifty Shades of Grey - Crazy in Love Original Sound Track) are bridges for watching soundtracks from other films.

Other social metrics did not sow significant results. There is no recognized influencer within network recognized by social network measures like degree centrality, closeness centrality.

Results from Second Analytical Wave

At second analytical wave data from Twitter had much more tweets regarding *Fifty shades of gray* in Croatian translation, 1726 nodes, with graph density of 0,00005.

Data from YouTube had, 2383 nodes, with graph density of 0,1236.

As it is visible from F*igure 2*, cluster A (clips from *Fifty shades of gray*) are bridge for trailers of the new films (cluster B). Node C (new trailer *Fifty shades of gray*) is key driven factor for that clusters.

Figure 1. Betweenness centrality measure on YouTube network at 10th February 2015

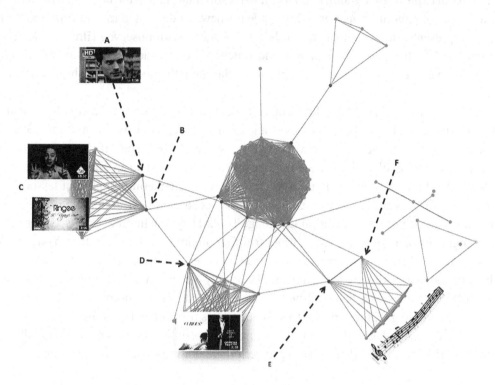

Figure 2. Betweenness centrality measure on YouTube network at 20th February 2015

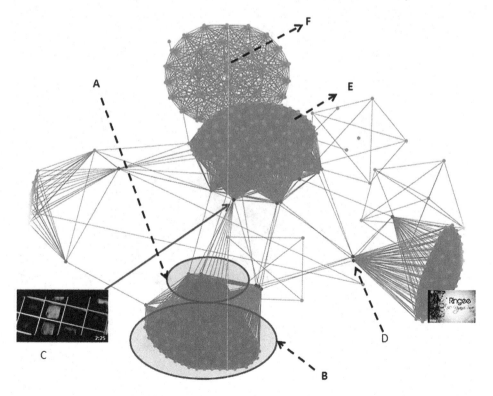

Node D (*Mistakes and illogical staffs from the film*) is still important in the network and it is still bridge for the video spots of regional reaper, which include his new, hit dedicated to film *Fifty shades of gray.*

Cluster E represents video content, which has connections with observed film. Cluster F is video content related to Croatian show *Book or life*, and watchers were attracted with one episode dedicated to book of *Fifty shades of gray*. In the same episode of the show theme was Malcolm Lowry and Greek literature.

Twitter network are not so coherent like YouTube data, which witnesses density coefficient. All the metrics are relatively weak, except two nodes A and B from which is visible from Figure 3.

Node A caused many flowers and re-tweets with message "Fifty shades of gray learnt us if you are rich pervert than you are cool, and if you are not rich and pervert, than you are maniac." Node B contains tweet "What Fifty shades of gray learnt us from perspective of marketing, important lessons". Node B also caused many flowers and re-tweets. Author of that tweet are blogger in domain of marketing.

For natural language processing Natural Language Toolkit (Python library) was used (Perkins, 2010).

Natural language processing gave much more fruitful outcome from Twitter, than YouTube data. As it was presumed, YouTube is concentrated on specific content, and comments regarding that content are mostly in connection with watched materials. Twitter by its character covers wider scope, and opens much more different topics with name of the film as mutual common denominator.

Main finding regarding text mining are that Twitter users recommend reading book before watching movie. Also, there is mutual attitude that movie scenario is partially based on book. Generally observed population in approximately ten days of film projection are not impressed with the movie.

Figure 3. Betweenness centrality measure on Twitter network at 20th February 2015

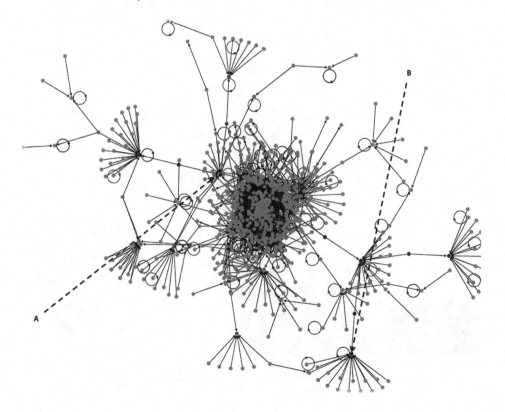

CONCLUSION

Analysis was done in two waves. It is observed significant change of sample structure and analysis results between two observation periods. First wave shows activates in YouTube subpopulation users united through trailers, official and unofficial. Official trailer has attracted more formal sub population interested in more formal content, and unofficial trailer together with movie clips regarding observed illogicality and errors attracted subpopulation attracted watcher of local reaper, which has hit dedicated to Fifty shades of gray. Watching of this hit is also trigger for watching his other songs. Also, same subpopulation, like to watch topics like fifty facts which you should know about Fifty shades of gray.

New wave brings, after projection changes in structure of YouTube watchers, which has been attracted with newest official trailers, and we have almost same situation regarding local reaper, which has hit dedicated to *Fifty Shades of Gray*. Also, it is evident that soundtracks from *Fifty Shades of Gray* attracts some sub population of watchers to watch soundtracks from other movies.

It is also evident that, after movie projection, new cluster of movie trailer watcher is noticed. It is cluster, which unites literature-oriented watchers of Croatian show, dedicated to culture. One episode has subject dedicated to movie and book *Fifty Shades of Gray*. It was trigger to watch other episodes of that show.

It is evident that YouTube network from first wave was smaller but with highest density, and YouTube network from second wave was bigger with lowest density. It can be explained as an increasing interest of watchers, triggered by commercials after beginning of movie projections. Density shows that network became less coherent and unconnected, which is expectable regarding increasing number of nodes.

YouTube analysis shows marketing potentials in area of music industry, and discovers some new potential market segments like watchers interested in content like illogicality and errors in movies.

Text mining findings from YouTube are practically unusable for marketing campaigns, because it is mostly oriented on specific watched content, without deeper expertise and attitudes regarding observed subject.

Contrary to YouTube, Twitter data from second wave gives some new horizons based on textual content. Twitter data analysis shows, that Twitter users recommend reading book before watching movie. Also, there is mutual attitude that movie scenario is partially based on book. Captured Twitter populations in approximately ten days of film projection are not impressed with the movie.

Twitter showed two influencers, one, which has generally sarcastic-funny comments, and has been rewetted and followed by significant number of Twitter users.

Other influencer, blogger in domain of marketing gave link what can we learn from the movie *Fifty Shades of Gray* –marketing perspective.

Those two clusters show different preferences united through same subject.

Generally speaking, there is a lot of room for marketing strategies. Main role here plays cross selling strategies, which can be focused on discovered clusters and their bridges with highest betweenness measure. Root term and subject of interest is movie Fifty shades of gray, which shows diversification of interest for music, new movie soundtracks, local reap music, philosophical themes in connection with subject of the movie, educational themes in domain of marketing and literature view on movie subject. There is lot of new areas, which can be fruitful for marketing strategies and future marketing strategies planning.

One of the benefits can be targeted advertisement for watchers of specific content, close to some of the observed bridges to motivate watchers to watch new material, or for buying something in connection with subject of his potential interest. In that case we can talk about recommendation systems.

Another benefit can be in profile recognition based on watched material, as an additional base for recommendation system. User profiles prone to watch reap music, or to watch illogicality and errors in movies, or to watch new movie soundtracks has potentials for cross selling, which can be revealed by multimedia content mining.

FUTURE RESEARCH DIRECTIONS

Presented methodology shows analysis of multimedia content by using potential of Social Networks. There is more room for advancement presented methodology. One direction can be mining image and video content as additional feature to presented methodology. In that case, recommendation systems will not take in consideration only textual patterns or network patterns, it would also take in account patterns from media like images and video materials.

Another direction can be aimed on profile extraction based on importance within social network and watched materials from social networks like Facebook, Twitter or from YouTube.

In that case main stress is on customer profiling, which is wider concept than customer behavioral characteristics, because customer profile can be determined also by customer behavioral characteristics.

Big data analytics and its doctrine have great influence on analytical projects like this. Customer behavior, preferences, and acting are volatile through period of time, especially if it is caused on some factors. Those factors can be campaigns, influencer's opinion, and position in lifecycle. All that can be, if we are talking about big data decoded from social network activities, if we are talking about persons active on social network, or more social networks. All that data demands special treatment, from perspective of data collection, analytical wave planning and elaboration of analytical strategies for achieving aims.

Those entire topics can be subjects of future research. Also, there is great potential for using traditional data mining techniques like Bayesian networks, neural networks, clustering methods, fuzzy logic, decision trees for profiling and segmentation purposes based on multimedia data collected from social networks.

Synergy of presented methodology along with inclusion of pattern recognition as active elements into analysis with usage of traditional data mining methods as additional feature in analytical process can contribute too much more complex and efficient analytical solutions.

DISCUSSION

Data mining solutions for profiling are always complex in way of chaining and usage of more than one data mining method. Presented project in is no exception in complexity.

Usage of numerous data mining methods is not guarantee of project success. More than that it is cooperation between analyst, business insider within company, which initiate project, and creativity of all project members.

Traditional assurance, that profiling modeling is developing predictive model, which calculates probabilities, is not correct. It is more than that. We should understand customer profiles, their behavior, interaction, power to disintegrate network if we are talking about social networks.

Unfortunately, there is no cookbook for profiling, each business case is a unique story, and each step forward in analysis can change initial analysis direction.

Most important of all things is to derive useful information for decision support, because main aim of business modeling with data mining methods is knowledge recognition, understanding of customer behavior which can be applied in decision-making.

Understanding of Customer Behaviour Is Key Factor of Market Success, Especially in Competitive Market Conditions

Extracting information from social networks is one of the aims when a company wants to understand their customers. New era of big data and social networks contributes in complexity of data sources for analytical purposes, and offers new challenges and also additional useful information for understanding customer behavior. That leads us to taking in account social network analysis as an important factor for understanding hidden relations.

Traditional data mining approach, which is commonly used, offers well known methods typically used on internal data sources. External data sources along with traditional data mining methods offer solutions for the use of text mining methods, social network analysis and expert systems which can be centrally placed for the integration of differing aspects of analysis depending upon the strategic business or/and analytical aims. Looking in that direction, answers for churn detection and mitigation of contract breaking by clients could be extracted in combination from predictive models, developed on local data sources and text patterns from forums or blogs, as well as from social networks like Facebook, twitter or other, by using appropriate analytical techniques.

Richness of data sources does not guarantee a successful analytical process if it is not well and objectively planned, with clear aims and understanding of business problems. Often, it is hard to make clear analytical objectives for big data environment, where data volume and complexity is bigger than in traditional local data environment. Even in such conditions, unclear vision and methodology on how to achieve analytical aim based on business needs could be crucial for project failure or success.

In the big data area, requirements for clear analytical aims are crucial for setting the right analytical strategy. More choices and sources gives an opportunity for better and precise results, but also hides the potential danger of missing the point, if these kind of projects are not adequately and not strategically planned from perspective of business decision needs. Business decision needs also require strategic analytical planning, and the big data concept enters some new standards and requirements into this process. Basic ideas from perspective of business suggest the use of the most efficient disposable data sources which are reachable thought big data concept, along with new type of methodological framework for achieving better market position, by using such infrastructure.

Traditional approach in data mining analytics, which are concentrated mostly on internal data sources, should not be neglected, as advantages are present. While, it does has some limitations, because it covers limited information, contained within predefined database structures. This kind of data source, even limited by its scope, offers opportunity for making the analytical process on more or less known data with the expected type of output due to defined analytical aims.

A big data environment leads to unknown territory, where a company is often unsure what it could dig from those data sources, which are mostly unstructured, big in volume and complex, sometimes without clear vision. Along to these problems, it offers rich sources of new data, which can be combined, with internal data sources. That synergy can result with much more appropriate models and findings, which can be used for better business decisions. All of that needs proposal of the new approach, which will give a direction how to integrate those two concepts. Approach, which integrates best practice from both concepts and introduce new one concept, which should result with a more efficient tool for business decision support.

Traditional approaches in business analytics and usage of data mining methods are mostly concentrated on solving single problems like segmentation, fraud detection and churn detection on data disposable within local databases. Those data could be huge by volume, collected through transactional databases and consolidated through data warehouses.

Even if it seems complex and sufficient, it often represents a narrow set of data for specific purposes like segmentation, fraud detection and churn detection. The reason for that lies in the fact that transactional databases are not constructed, or have been rarely constructed with the intention to fulfill analytical needs. Specifically, it is evident for some exact needs like fraud detection or churn detection. Transactional databases are constructed with a general scope, and transactional business needs. This does not mean that such databases are useless for analytical purposes; it simply means that it provides a narrow set of information with which some predictive analytical data mining model or other model or reporting for specific business needs could be constructed.

Value of the existing data, dislocated within different transactional systems could be increased by integration into a data warehouse system. It still does not mean that a company does not have limited information about some problem space. Other problems in relation with the traditional analytical approach is often avoidance of unstructured data source usage for business modeling purposes, even unstructured data exists within systems like call centers data or similar sources.

Unstructured data usage is mainly focused on pure text mining analytics in connection with specific problems based on textual data sources, or in web mining analytics. Integration of structured and unstructured data sources as well as internal or external data sources (from web, blogs, social networks) is not the case when we are speaking about traditional business analytics.

All of that leads to the question regarding potential business strategy based on analytical models.

Data mining is defined as a discipline, which reveals hidden unexpected patterns from the data. From the perspective of business planning, it should serve to as an efficient business strategy. The traditional approach reveals hidden unexpected patterns from the internal, mostly structured, relational data sets, and results from those models could be plausible and usable for decision-making. Internal data, collected within a company data warehouse has (could have) limited scope on some problems such as fraud, because it does not contain enough relevant information for efficient fraud detection modeling and analytic. The developed model (in this case fraud detection model based on an internal data warehouse) could show plausible performance, but relevant patterns could stay undetected, because other data sources like blogs, social networks and web sources are not used for analytical purposes.

Contrary to traditional analytical approach, big data strategic thinking, implies knowledge extracting from additional data sources, which does not have to be relationally connected through existing databases or data warehouses. It implies using disposable knowledge from other sources, and its integration into analytical process, having in mind achieving greater efficiency for decision support.

For example, let's assume that an insurance company would like to develop a predictive model, which will calculate churn probability on the customer level. Traditional model development would be concentrated on local databases, capturing client behavior characteristics within the local database framework. This approach is a result of an adopted way of thinking, caused by the common methodology where big data and its potential are not used for building solutions. Traditional solutions offer answers about the churner's patterns (if we are observing the previous example). Other activities where clients exchange opinions about the company and share some attitudes, which at the end leads to churn, could stay unrevealed if the company does not change strategic way of analytical thinking.

Unstructured data could exist as well in internal sources, like memo fields within call center databases, which stays out of the analytical process. Analytical thinking from the perspective of big data also includes facts, that data does not have to be connected through relational keys within databases. In the described churn example it indicates that data for predictive modeling should be consolidated from data sources such as databases, blogs, forums and other unstructured data sources.

There is no guarantee that external data or internal data will deliver additional information about problems, which would be of great value for finding business solutions. The basic idea from the perspective of a big data analytical strategy is to cover all disposable and usable data sources and techniques, which potentially could be useful for additional knowledge extraction. For such purposes, during the project planning stage, it is important to have in mind all possibilities, which big data concepts could offer.

After the business aim definition, which includes strategy based on the big data paradigm, disposable data has the potential to have a strong influence on solution design and solution building. It can consolidate traditional model development along with analytical solutions, based on the big data paradigm. It is important to stress that in such situations, knowledge extraction demands much more human expert involvement. Especially in situations where results and knowledge from different kinds of models exist, and it demands expert judgment and evaluation. During the business decision process, expert explanations and conclusions play a crucial role in the understanding and interpretation of given results. This is due to the fact that results are derived from different data sources, which provide different perspectives of the problem and desire experts for their explanation.

CONCLUSION

Multimedia content gives new dimension on customer analytics. In last decade multimedia content in area of customer analytics gets on its importance by social networks. Huge amounts of data have been posted each day, that data contains textual content, video clips, images, soundtracks and similar content.

Each emitter of that content contributes to holistic picture which can be discovered by usage of advanced analytic methods. Those methods unite big data area, social network analysis, multimedia analysis as well as many different doctrines.

Presented methodology gives one of possible solution, how to use disposable multimedia data if we observe it as a part of social networks, and how it can be used for analytical purposes.

Result of analysis, is valuable information usable for campaign management, campaign planning, strategic planning, market trend observation, new product development, customer profiling, and customer behavioral habits recognition.

Presented case study shows importance of some multimedia content as a bride or attractor for watching additional content. Social network analysis in that case helps us to locate and to recognize such content (nodes). Those nodes are important as bridges to new opportunities for cross-selling activities and recommendation systems.

Recognized clusters can also be the base for watcher profiling upon watched materials. Recommendation is not to limit exploration only on one data source like YouTube. Case study illustrates this on usage Twitter data on same subject, which supplement analysis and expected output.

Data source selection for analytical purposes depends on subject, which we investigate. In presented case study it was YouTube, as a logical choice because film distributor started campaign with movie trailers, and same source contained unofficial trailers and other materials in connection with observed subject.

Twitter was selected, because it was noticed increasing activities in connection with observed subject, and sub-population of Twitter users write comments regarding film.

For some other situation it is possible that Facebook in combination with YouTube and Flickr would be better choice for data collection and analysis. As it was already stated it depends on subject and nature of analysis, as well on character of marketing campaign.

Presented methodology applied in practice with case study showed one new perspective how to extract new knowledge and patterns from multimedia data, if we observe it in social network structure.

Network metrics gives new meaning, usable for decision and planning support. By combination of analytical results from different sources, based on variety data types it is possible to construct holistic picture valuable for customer behavior understanding.

REFERENCES

Bhattacharyya, S., & Maulik, U. (2013). *Soft Computing for Image and Multimedia Data Processing*. Springer. doi:10.1007/978-3-642-40255-5

Chisholm, E., & Kolda, T. G. (1999). *New term weighting formulas for the vector space method in information retrieval*. Technical Report ORNL-TM-13756. Oak Ridge National Laboratory.

Cointet, J. P., & Roth, C. (2009). Socio-semantic dynamics in a blog network. *Proceedings of theInternational Conference onComputational Science and Engineering*. doi:10.1109/CSE.2009.105

Conte, R., Gilbert, N., Bonelli, G., & Helbing, D. (2011). FuturICT and social sciences: Big Data, big thinking. *Zeitschrift für Soziologie*, *40*, 412–413.

De, S., Bhattacharyya, S., & Chakraborty, S. (2013). Multilevel Image Segmentation by a Multiobjective Genetic Algorithm Based OptiMUSIG Activation Function. In S. Bhattacharyya & P. Dutta (Eds.), *Handbook of Research on Computational Intelligence for Engineering, Science, and Business* (pp. 122–162). Hershey, PA, USA: IGI Global. doi:10.4018/978-1-4666-2518-1.ch005

De, S., Bhattacharyya, S., & Chakraborty, S. (2014). Efficient Color Image Segmentation by a Parallel Optimized (ParaOptiMUSIG) Activation Function. In B. Tripathy & D. Acharjya (Eds.), *Global Trends in Intelligent Computing Research and Development* (pp. 19–50). Hershey, PA, USA: IGI Global. Doi:

Debole, F., & Sebastiani, F. (2003). Supervised Term Weighting for Automated Text Categorization. *Proceedings of SAC-03,18th ACM Symposium on Applied Computing*, Melbourne, FL. ACM Press. doi:doi:10.1145/952532.952688 doi:10.1145/952532.952688

Easley, D., & Kleinberg, J. (2010). *Networks, crowds, and markets: Reasoning about a highly connected world*. New York: Cambridge University Press. doi:10.1017/CBO9780511761942

Engel, D., Whitney, P., Calapristi, A., & Brockman, F. (2009). Mining for emerging technologies within text streams and documents.*Proceedings of the Ninth SIAM International Conference on Data Mining*. Society for Industrial and Applied Mathematics.

Feldman, R., & Sagner, J. (2007). *The Text Mining Handbook*. Cambridge, UK: Cambridge University Press.

Garrido, P., & Lemahieu, W. (2008). Collective Intelligence. In G. Putnik & M. Cruz-Cunha (Eds.), *Encyclopedia of Networked and Virtual Organizations* (pp. 280–287). Hershey, PA, USA: IGI Global. doi:10.4018/978-1-59904-885-7.ch037

Garrote, A., & García, M. N. (2013). News Trends Processing Using Open Linked Data. In P. Ordóñez de Pablos, M. Lytras, R. Tennyson, & J. Gayo (Eds.), *Cases on Open-Linked Data and Semantic Web Applications* (pp. 192–198). Hershey, PA, USA: IGI Global. doi:10.4018/978-1-4666-2827-4.ch010

Gebara, D., & Alhajj, R. (2009). Improving Image Retrieval by Clustering. In Z. Ma (Ed.), *Artificial Intelligence for Maximizing Content Based Image Retrieval* (pp. 20–43). Hershey, PA, USA: IGI Global. doi:10.4018/978-1-60566-174-2.ch002

Giudici, P. (2003). *Applied Data Mining: Statistical Methods for Business and Industry*. NY: John Wiley &Sons Inc.

Giudici, P., & Figini, S. (2009). *Applied Data Mining for Business and Industry (Statistics in Practice)*. NY: Wiley. doi:10.1002/9780470745830

Hansen, D. L., Schneiderman, B., & Smith, M. A. (2010). *Analyzing social media networks with NodeXL: insights from a connected world*. Amsterdam: M. Kaufmann.

Hemalatha, M. (2012). A Predictive Modeling of Retail Satisfaction: A Data Mining Approach to Retail Service Industry. In P. Ordóñez de Pablos & M. Lytras (Eds.), *Knowledge Management and Drivers of Innovation in Services Industries* (pp. 175–189). Hershey, PA, USA: IGI Global. doi:10.4018/978-1-4666-0948-8.ch014

Katzenbeisser, S., Liu, H., & Steinebach, M. (2010). Challenges and Solutions in Multimedia Document Authentication. In C. Li (Ed.), *Handbook of Research on Computational Forensics, Digital Crime, and Investigation: Methods and Solutions* (pp. 155–175). Hershey, PA, USA: IGI Global. doi:10.4018/978-1-60566-836-9.ch007

Klepac, G. (2015). Particle Swarm Optimization Algorithm as a Tool for Profiling from Predictive Data Mining Models. In S. Bhattacharyya & P. Dutta (Eds.), *Handbook of Research on Swarm Intelligence in Engineering* (pp. 406–434). Hershey, PA, USA: IGI Global. Doi:

Klepac, G., & Berg, K. L. (2015b). Proposal of Analytical Model for Business Problems Solving in Big Data Environment. In J. Girard, D. Klein, & K. Berg (Eds.), *Strategic Data-Based Wisdom in the Big Data Era* (pp. 209–228). Hershey, PA, USA: IGI Global. doi:10.4018/978-1-4666-8122-4.ch012

Klepac, G., & Velić, M. (2015c). Natural Language Processing as Feature Extraction Method for Building Better Predictive Models. In J. Žižka & F. Dařena (Eds.), *Modern Computational Models of Semantic Discovery in Natural Language* (pp. 141–166). Hershey, PA, USA: IGI Global. doi:10.4018/978-1-4666-8690-8.ch006

Matsuo, Y., & Ishizuka, M. (2004). Keyword extraction from a single document using word co-occurrence statistical information. *International Journal of Artificial Intelligence Tools*, *13*(1), 157–169. doi:10.1142/S0218213004001466

Michaell, B. J. A., & Gordon, L. (2000). *Mastering data mining*. John Wiley &Sons Inc.

Michaell, B. J. A., & Gordon, L. (2003). *Mining the web*. John Wiley &Sons Inc.

Miner, G. (2012). *Practical Text Mining and Statistical Analysis for Non-structured Text Data Applications*. Oxford: Academic Press.

Mirchev, U., & Last, M. (2014). Multi-Document Summarization by Extended Graph Text Representation and Importance Refinement. In A. Fiori (Ed.), *Innovative Document Summarization Techniques: Revolutionizing Knowledge Understanding* (pp. 28–53). Hershey, PA, USA: IGI Global. doi:10.4018/978-1-4666-5019-0.ch002

Papadopoulos, S., Vakali, A., & Kompatsiaris, I. (2010). The Dynamics of Content Popularity in Social Media. *International Journal of Data Warehousing and Mining*, *6*(1), 20–37. doi:10.4018/jdwm.2010090802

Perkins, J. (2010). *Python text processing with NLTK 2.0 cookbook over 80 practical recipes for using Python's NLTK suite of libraries to maximize your natural language processing capabilities*. Cambridge, MA: MIT Press.

Raikwar, S. C., Bhatnagar, C., & Jalal, A. S. (2015). A Novel Framework for Efficient Extraction of Meaningful Key Frames from Surveillance Video. *International Journal of System Dynamics Applications*, *4*(2), 56–73. doi:10.4018/ijsda.2015040104

Reips, U.-D., & Garaizar, P. (2011). Mining Twitter: Microblogging as a source for psychological wisdom of the crowds. *Behavior Research Methods*, *43*(3), 635–642. doi:10.3758/s13428-011-0116-6 PMID:21701948

Scott, J. (2012). *Social Network Analysis*. London: SAGE Publications.

Smith, M., Milic-Frayling, N., Shneiderman, B., Mendes Rodrigues, E., Leskovec, J., & Dunne, C. (2010). *NodeXL: a free and open network overview, discovery and exploration add-in for Excel 2007/2010*. Retrieved from http://www.smrfoundation.org

Snijders, C., Matzat, U., & Reips, U.-D. (2012). 'Big Data': Big gaps of knowledge in the field of Internet. *International Journal of Internet Science*, *7*, 1–5. Retrieved from http://www.ijis.net/ijis7_1/ijis7_1_editorial.html

Webb, L. M., & Wang, Y. (2014). Techniques for Sampling Online Text-Based Data Sets. In W. Hu & N. Kaabouch (Eds.), *Big Data Management, Technologies, and Applications* (pp. 95–114). Hershey, PA, USA: IGI Global. doi:10.4018/978-1-4666-4699-5.ch005

ADDITIONAL READING

Almeida, F., & Santos, M. (2014). A Conceptual Framework for Big Data Analysis. In I. Portela & F. Almeida (Eds.), *Organizational, Legal, and Technological Dimensions of Information System Administration* (pp. 199–223). Hershey, PA, USA: IGI Global. doi:10.4018/978-1-4666-4526-4.ch011

Bakshi, K. (2014). Technologies for Big Data. In W. Hu & N. Kaabouch (Eds.), *Big Data Management, Technologies, and Applications* (pp. 1–22). Hershey, PA, USA: IGI Global. doi:10.4018/978-1-4666-4699-5.ch001

Bhattacharyya, S., & Dutta, P. (2012). Fuzzy Logic: Concepts, System Design, and Applications to Industrial Informatics. In M. Khan & A. Ansari (Eds.), *Handbook of Research on Industrial Informatics and Manufacturing Intelligence: Innovations and Solutions* (pp. 33–71). Hershey, PA, USA: IGI Global. doi:10.4018/978-1-4666-0294-6.ch003

Bird, S., Klein, E., & Loper, E. (2009). *Natural Language Processing with Python*. Sebastopol: O'Reilly.

Casabayó, M., & Agell, N. (2012). A Fuzzy Segmentation Approach to Guide Marketing Decisions. In A. Meier & L. Donzé (Eds.), *Fuzzy Methods for Customer Relationship Management and Marketing: Applications and Classifications* (pp. 291–311). Hershey, PA, USA: IGI Global. doi:10.4018/978-1-4666-0095-9.ch013

Chen, G., & Hoon Joo, Y. (2009). Fuzzy Control Systems: An Introduction. In J. Rabuñal Dopico, J. Dorado, & A. Pazos (Eds.), *Encyclopedia of Artificial Intelligence* (pp. 688–695). Hershey, PA, USA: IGI Global. doi:10.4018/978-1-59904-849-9.ch103

Dagiasis, A. P. (2013). Logistics Modeling and Forecasting with Regression. In D. Folinas (Ed.), *Outsourcing Management for Supply Chain Operations and Logistics Service* (pp. 223–237). Hershey, PA, USA: IGI Global. doi:10.4018/978-1-4666-2008-7.ch013

Donzé, L., & Meier, A. (2013). Applying Fuzzy Logic and Fuzzy Methods to Marketing. In IRMA International (Ed.), Supply Chain Management: Concepts, Methodologies, Tools, and Applications (pp. 1056-1068). Hershey, PA, USA: IGI Global. doi:doi:10.4018/978-1-4666-2625-6.ch062 doi:10.4018/978-1-4666-2625-6.ch062

Feng, J., Xu, L., & Ramamurthy, B. (2009). Overlay Construction in Mobile Peer-to-Peer Networks. In B. Seet (Ed.), *Mobile Peer-to-Peer Computing for Next Generation Distributed Environments: Advancing Conceptual and Algorithmic Applications* (pp. 51–67). Hershey, PA, USA: IGI Global. doi:10.4018/978-1-60566-715-7.ch003

Han, J., & Kamber, M. (2000). *Data Mining: Concepts and Techniques*. San Francisco: Morgan Kaufmann.

Hemalatha, M. (2012). A Predictive Modeling of Retail Satisfaction: A Data Mining Approach to Retail Service Industry. In P. Ordóñez de Pablos & M. Lytras (Eds.), *Knowledge Management and Drivers of Innovation in Services Industries* (pp. 175–189). Hershey, PA, USA: IGI Global. doi:10.4018/978-1-4666-0948-8.ch014

Hu, W., & Kaabouch, N. (2014). *Big Data Management, Technologies, and Applications* (pp. 1–342). Hershey, PA, USA: IGI Global. doi:10.4018/978-1-4666-4699-5

Kantardžić, M. (2003). *Data Mining: Concepts, Models, Methods and Algorithms*. New York, USA: John Wiley & Sons.

Klepac, G. (2010). Preparing for New Competition in the Retail Industry. In A. Syvajarvi & J. Stenvall (Eds.), *Data Mining in Public and Private Sectors: Organizational and Government Applications* (pp. 245–266). Hershey, PA, USA: IGI Global. Doi:

Klepac, G. (2013). Risk Evaluation in the Insurance Company Using REFII Model. In S. Dehuri, M. Patra, B. Misra, & A. Jagadev (Eds.), *Intelligent Techniques in Recommendation Systems: Contextual Advancements and New Methods* (pp. 84–104). Hershey, PA, USA: IGI Global. doi:10.4018/978-1-4666-2542-6.ch005

Klepac, G. (2014). Data Mining Models as a Tool for Churn Reduction and Custom Product Development in Telecommunication Industries. In P. Vasant (Ed.), *Handbook of Research on Novel Soft Computing Intelligent Algorithms: Theory and Practical Applications* (pp. 511–537). Hershey, PA, USA: IGI Global. doi:10.4018/978-1-4666-4450-2.ch017

Kolomvatsos, K., & Hadjiefthymiades, S. (2012). On the Use of Fuzzy Logic in Electronic Marketplaces. In V. Mago & N. Bhatia (Eds.), *Cross-Disciplinary Applications of Artificial Intelligence and Pattern Recognition: Advancing Technologies* (pp. 609–632). Hershey, PA, USA: IGI Global. doi:10.4018/978-1-61350-429-1.ch030

Landow, K. C., Fandre, M., Nambiath, R., Shringarpure, N., Gates, H., Lugmayr, A., & Barker, S. (2008). Internet Protocol Television. In Y. Dwivedi, A. Papazafeiropoulou, & J. Choudrie (Eds.), *Handbook of Research on Global Diffusion of Broadband Data Transmission* (pp. 538–562). Hershey, PA, USA: IGI Global. doi:10.4018/978-1-59904-851-2.ch034

Marvuglia, A., Cellura, M., & Pucci, M. (2012). A Generalization of the Orthogonal Regression Technique for Life Cycle Inventory. *International Journal of Agricultural and Environmental Information Systems*, *3*(1), 51–71. doi:10.4018/jaeis.2012010105

Mehran, K., Zahawi, B., & Giaouris, D. (2011). Fuzzy Logic for Non-smooth Dynamical Systems. In Y. Dai, B. Chakraborty, & M. Shi (Eds.), *Kansei Engineering and Soft Computing: Theory and Practice* (pp. 147–168). Hershey, PA, USA: IGI Global. doi:10.4018/978-1-61692-797-4.ch008

Merlin, B., & Raynal, M. (2012). Soft Keyboard Evaluations: Integrating User's Background in Predictive Models. In E. Alkhalifa & K. Gaid (Eds.), *Cognitively Informed Intelligent Interfaces: Systems Design and Development* (pp. 21–40). Hershey, PA, USA: IGI Global. doi:10.4018/978-1-4666-1628-8.ch002

Pomazalová, N. (2013). Public Sector Transformation Processes and Internet Public Procurement: Decision Support Systems. Hershey, PA, USA: IGI Global. doi:10.4018/978-1-4666-2665-2

Prilop, M., Tonisson, L., & Maicher, L. (2013). Designing Analytical Approaches for Interactive Competitive Intelligence. *International Journal of Service Science, Management, Engineering, and Technology*, *4*(2), 34–45. doi:10.4018/jssmet.2013040103

Qi, J., Li, Y., Li, C., & Zhang, Y. (2009). Telecommunication Customer Detainment Management. In I. Lee (Ed.), *Handbook of Research on Telecommunications Planning and Management for Business* (pp. 379–399). Hershey, PA, USA: IGI Global. doi:10.4018/978-1-60566-194-0.ch024

Raine, L., & Wellman, B. (2012). *Networked. The new social operating system.* Cambridge: MIT Press.

Rokach, L. (2009). Incorporating Fuzzy Logic in Data Mining Tasks. In J. Rabuñal Dopico, J. Dorado, & A. Pazos (Eds.), *Encyclopedia of Artificial Intelligence* (pp. 884–891). Hershey, PA, USA: IGI Global. doi:10.4018/978-1-59904-849-9.ch131

Ruta, D., Adl, C., & Nauck, D. (2009). New Churn Prediction Strategies in the Telecom Industry. In H. Wang (Ed.), *Intelligent Data Analysis: Developing New Methodologies Through Pattern Discovery and Recovery* (pp. 218–235). Hershey, PA, USA: IGI Global. doi:10.4018/978-1-59904-982-3.ch013

Scott, J. (2012). *Social Network Analysis.* London: SAGE Publications.

Sirkeci, I., & Mannix, R. (2010). Segmentation Challenges Posed by 'Transnationals' in Mobile Marketing. In K. Pousttchi & D. Wiedemann (Eds.), *Handbook of Research on Mobile Marketing Management* (pp. 94–114). Hershey, PA, USA: IGI Global.; doi:10.4018/978-1-60566-074-5.ch006

Varnali, K. (2013). Mobile Social Networks: Communication and Marketing Perspectives. In I. Lee (Ed.), *Strategy, Adoption, and Competitive Advantage of Mobile Services in the Global Economy* (pp. 248–258). Hershey, PA, USA: IGI Global. doi:10.4018/978-1-4666-1939-5.ch014

Vasant, P., Barsoum, N., Kahraman, C., & Dimirovski, G. (2008). Application of Fuzzy Optimization in Forecasting and Planning of Construction Industry. In I. Vlahavas & D. Vrakas (Eds.), *Artificial Intelligence for Advanced Problem Solving Techniques* (pp. 254–265). Hershey, PA, USA: IGI Global. doi:10.4018/978-1-59904-705-8.ch010

Vasant, P., Ganesan, T., & Elamvazuthi, I. (2012). Hybrid Tabu Search Hopfield Recurrent ANN Fuzzy Technique to the Production Planning Problems: A Case Study of Crude Oil in Refinery Industry. *International Journal of Manufacturing, Materials, and Mechanical Engineering*, 2(1), 47–65. doi:10.4018/ijmmme.2012010104

Venkateswaran, P., Kundu, M., Shaw, S., Orea, K., & Nandi, R. (2013). Fuzzy Logic-based Mobility Metric Clustering Algorithm for MANETs. In V. Sridhar & D. Saha (Eds.), *Web-Based Multimedia Advancements in Data Communications and Networking Technologies* (pp. 207–219). Hershey, PA, USA: IGI Global. doi:10.4018/978-1-4666-2026-1.ch011

Vose, D. (2000). *Quantitative Risk Analysis.* New York, USA: John Wiley & Sons.

Watson, H. J. (2013). All About Analytics. *International Journal of Business Intelligence Research*, 4(1), 13–28. doi:10.4018/jbir.2013010102

Watts, D. J. (1999). *Small Worlds: The Dynamics of Networks between Order and Randomness.* Princeton, NJ: Princeton University Press.

Watts, D. J., & Strogatz, S. H. (1998). Collective dynamics of 'small-world' networks. *Nature*, 393(6684), 440–442. doi:10.1038/30918 PMID:9623998

Webb, L. M., & Wang, Y. (2014). Techniques for Sampling Online Text-Based Data Sets. In W. Hu & N. Kaabouch (Eds.), *Big Data Management, Technologies, and Applications* (pp. 95–114). Hershey, PA, USA: IGI Global. doi:10.4018/978-1-4666-4699-5.ch005

Weiss, G. (2009). Data Mining in the Telecommunications Industry. In J. Wang (Ed.), *Encyclopedia of Data Warehousing and Mining* (2nd ed., pp. 486–491). Hershey, PA, USA: IGI Global. doi:10.4018/978-1-60566-010-3.ch076

Werro, N., & Stormer, H. (2012). A Fuzzy Logic Approach for the Assessment of Online Customers. In A. Meier & L. Donzé (Eds.), *Fuzzy Methods for Customer Relationship Management and Marketing: Applications and Classifications* (pp. 252–270). Hershey, PA, USA: IGI Global. doi:10.4018/978-1-4666-0095-9.ch011

Willis, R., Serenko, A., & Turel, O. (2007). Contractual Obligations between Mobile Service Providers and Users. In D. Taniar (Ed.), *Encyclopedia of Mobile Computing and Commerce* (pp. 143–148). Hershey, PA, USA: IGI Global. doi:10.4018/978-1-59904-002-8.ch025

Willis, R., Serenko, A., & Turel, O. (2009). Contractual Obligations Between Mobile Service Providers and Users. In D. Taniar (Ed.), *Mobile Computing: Concepts, Methodologies, Tools, and Applications* (pp. 1929–1936). Hershey, PA, USA: IGI Global. doi:10.4018/978-1-60566-054-7.ch155

Yang, Y. (2009). Behavioral Pattern-Based Customer Segmentation. In J. Wang (Ed.), *Encyclopedia of Data Warehousing and Mining* (2nd ed., pp. 140–145). Hershey, PA, USA: IGI Global. doi:10.4018/978-1-60566-010-3.ch023

Yıldırım, A. A., Özdoğan, C., & Watson, D. (2014). Parallel Data Reduction Techniques for Big Datasets. In W. Hu & N. Kaabouch (Eds.), *Big Data Management, Technologies, and Applications* (pp. 72–93). Hershey, PA, USA: IGI Global. doi:10.4018/978-1-4666-4699-5.ch004

KEY TERMS AND DEFINITIONS

Betweenness: The extent to which a node lies between other nodes in the network, this measure takes into account the connectivity of the node's neighbors, giving a higher value for nodes which bridge clusters, the measure reflects the number of people who a person is connecting indirectly through their direct links.

Centrality: This measure gives a rough indication of the social power of a node based on how well they "connect" the network. "Betweenness," "Closeness," and "Degree" are all measures of centrality.

Closeness: The degree an individual is near all other individuals in a network (directly or indirectly). It reflects the ability to access information through the "grapevine" of network members. Thus, closeness is the inverse of the sum of the shortest distances between each individual and every other person in the network, the shortest path may also be known as the "geodesic distance".

Data Mining: Discipline, which reveals useful, patterns from huge amount of data.

Predictive Model: Model, mostly based on data mining methodology and historical data which has purpose to predict some event.

Chapter 16
Digital Watermarking:
Technical Art of Hiding a Message

Rohit M. Thanki
C. U. Shah University, India

Ashish M. Kothari
Atmiya Institute of Technology and Science, India

ABSTRACT

Nowadays, Multimedia contents such as images, videos, e-books and texts are easy to available for download through internet in worldwide. Duplication of multimedia contents is to create using different software. This type of operation some time created problem of copyright and ownership authentication. Digital watermarking techniques are one of the solutions for providing protection to multimedia contents. This chapter gives various watermarking techniques in transform domain and sparse domain for protection of multimedia contents. This chapter has demonstrated various watermarking techniques such as Discrete Cosine Transform (DCT), Discrete Wavelet Transform (DWT), Singular Value Decomposition (SVD), Fast Discrete Curvelet Transform (FDCT), and CS theory based technique. All watermarking techniques can be applicable to every type of multimedia contents such as grayscale images or videos and color image or videos.

1. INTRODUCTION

In the 21st century, the multimedia contents such as images, videos and texts are easy to share using the internet. The easy transfer facilitates of internet to transfer multimedia contents with one user to another user with modification, distribution, subscription and trading of various digital contents such as databases, e-books, images and videos without the owner's consent. Sometimes, owners are unwilling to distribute digital contents on the internet because of lack of security of digital contents on public networks. The availability of advance software on the internet and the market provides duplication of these digital contents is easy without owner acknowledgement. This prevents issues of copyright protection and copyright authentication of digital contents. Digital watermarking techniques are providing

DOI: 10.4018/978-1-5225-0498-6.ch016

security against these issues. The digital signature contents could reduce copyright violation and help to determine ownership of contents.

The best possible way, in which the multimedia contents are protected against illegal duplication, is to put some identity information behind the multimedia content for the authentication of the owner. This identifying information is called as "watermark". The technique is known as Digital Watermarking (Wolfgang & Podilchuk, 1999; Langelaar, Setyawan & Lagendijk, 2000) which is a state of art technique to insert a identity information behind the multimedia content in such a manner that the authorized or public can't visualize the identity information with common human visualization system (HVS). The identity information may be name of the owner, company logo or any important information which can be getting after application of specific algorithm and in this way the proof of ownership can be got. The prevent security to proof of ownership and avoid unauthorized tampering of important multimedia contents, the industry and researchers are developing various digital watermarking techniques. These techniques are proposed for various application areas such as copyright protection and authentication, source tracking, broadcast monitoring, video authentication, access control and biometric template protection.

The term "watermark" was coming from the German word "watermarke". The name is probably given because of the identity information resembles the effects of water on paper. Paper watermarks are used in the art of papermaking in Fabriano, Italy nearly 700 years ago (Kim & Ro, 2004; Hartung & Kutter, 1999). Watermarks are initially used for indicating brand of paper and mill information which produced the paper. The first example of a technology which is similar to the digital watermarking technique is a patented by Emil Hembrooke for identifying music works in 1954 (Bender et al., 1996). In 1988, Komatsu and Tominaga first time used term of "digital watermarking" (Cox, Shamoon & Leighton, 1997). The interest in digital watermarking techniques began to mushroom after 1995.

Digital Watermarking technique is the process of inserting digital information into host digital content. The digital information can be identified by the owner of the work, authentication content. The host digital content could be a still image, an audio clip, a video clip, a text document or digital data which owner would like to protect (Langelaar, Setyawan & Lagendijk, 2000). A watermarking system can be treated as a simple digital communication system. This system has three main components such as an embedder or encoder; transmission medium which is optional; a detector or decoder. The general watermarking system is shown in figure 1. The embedder or encoder is inserted or encoded the water-

Figure 1. General digital watermarking system

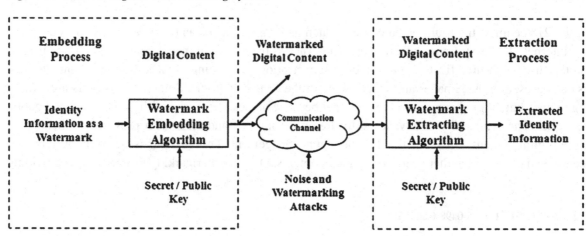

mark into the host digital content. The input of embedder is host digital content, watermark and output of embedder is watermark digital content. The detector or decoder is extracted original watermark from watermarked digital content. The input of the detector or decoder is watermarked digital content and output of the detector is extracted original watermark.

1.1. Requirements of Watermarking Techniques

When designing any watermarking techniques, then these techniques should be followed some requirements (Wolfgang & Podilchuk, 1999; Langelaar, Setyawan & Lagendijk, 2000; Chandramouli, Memon & Rabbani, 2002; Huang & Wu, 2004) which are described below:

- **Robustness:** The watermarking technique is able to protect identity information against various operations such as compression, rotation, scaling or noise addition, then that technique is said to be robust.
- **Imperceptibility:** After identity information is inserted into host digital content, if the visual quality of host digital content is such that the modification can't be recognized by HVS, then the technique is said to be imperceptible.
- **Payload Capacity:** It is the size of the identity information than can be inserted into a host digital content.

1.2. Types of Watermarking Techniques

With multimedia data widely available on the web, a watermark could be used to provide authentication in terms of a secondary data which is overlaid on the primary data to provide protection to primary data (Gayyar, 2006). Watermarking techniques can be divided into four categories according to the type of digital to be watermarked as follows as text watermarking, image watermarking, audio watermarking and video watermarking. The digital watermark can be divided into noise and image according to inserted watermark type. The digital watermark can be divided into visible watermark and invisible watermark according to the perceptibility. The watermarking techniques can be classified in various ways according to its requirement (Wolfgang & Podilchuk, 1999; Langelaar, Setyawan & Lagendijk, 2000). Each of the different types of watermarking techniques mentioned below has different applications.

- **Robust and Fragile Watermarking:** Robust watermarking is a technique does not affect the watermark data if watermarked data is tampered. Fragile watermarking is techniques destroy the watermark data if watermarked data is tampered.
- **Visible and Invisible Watermarking:** Visible watermarking is a technique which embeds watermark data, such a way that watermark data is visible in watermarked data. Invisible watermarking is a technique which embeds watermark data, such a way that watermark data is invisible in watermarked data.
- **Public and Private Watermarking:** In public watermarking, the public users are authorized to detect the watermark. In private watermarking, the public users are not authorized to detect the watermark.
- **Asymmetric and Symmetric Watermarking:** Asymmetric watermarking (also called asymmetric key watermarking) is a technique where different secret keys are used for embedding and

detecting the watermark data. In symmetric watermarking (also called symmetric key watermarking), the same secret key is used for embedding and detecting the watermark data.

- **Steganographic and Non-Steganographic Watermarking:** Steganographic watermarking is a technique where the user is unaware of the presence of a watermark data. In non-steganographic watermarking, the user is aware of the presence of a watermark data.

Digital watermarking is a state of art technique to put secret information behind a host medium in such a manner that the imposter can't be visualized the secret information with a naked eye and he/she perceives it as a normal host medium. There are two major domains where the multimedia data are watermarked namely spatial domain and transform domain. Spatial domain watermarking provides high perceptible such that the quality of the original and watermarked multimedia data is almost same. However, the problem of spatial domain watermarking is that the robustness achieved is far less comparatively. Transform domain watermarking is far better than spatial domain watermarking so far as robustness is concerned and that is the reason why transform domain watermarking techniques are used to preferred for multimedia data protection. When watermark data embed into host data, watermark embedding techniques are modifying the host data according to watermark information in a perceptually invisible manner (Wolfgang & Podilchuk, 1999; Langelaar, Setyawan & Lagendijk, 2000). There is various way of host data modification in any domain can be used for watermarking purpose. For watermark embedding or extraction, the host data can be modified in spatial domain; for converting into frequency domain using properties of various image transforms such as the discrete Fourier transform, discrete cosine transform, discrete wavelet transform or fractal domain. In spatial domain watermarking technique, the host digital data can be modified by least significant bit changing or add different noise sequence. In transform domain watermarking technique, the host data can be modified by coefficient modification, coefficient removal, coefficients reordering and coefficients block similarities (Wolfgang & Podilchuk, 1999; Langelaar, Setyawan & Lagendijk, 2000). The robustness of watermarking techniques is depending on watermark embedding approaches and size of watermark data.

The chapter is organized as follows. First discuss a brief literature review of watermarking. Then discuss the comparison of watermarking technique with the other data hiding techniques and data used for implementation of watermarking techniques. Then discuss basic digital watermarking techniques based on LSB modification and correlation of different noise sequences in spatial domain. And then discuss various digital watermarking techniques in the transform domain. Then discuss advance digital watermarking techniques for multimedia protection. The last section presents conclusion of the chapter, including a brief discussion on recent applications of digital watermarking area.

2. BRIEF LITERATURE REVIEW OF WATERMARKING

Inventions in the watermarking started with embedding watermark data in the spatial domain. Inventions further carried out in the transform domain with a single transform used for embedding purpose. Further, some of the inventors embedded watermark data with the help of combinations of two transform and achieved more robustness. Nowadays, some of the inventors embedded watermark data with the help of various encryption algorithms and combinations of various transforms. Following is the brief summary of the works carried out in watermarking area.

C. Podilchuk and R. Wolfgang (Wolfgang & Podilchuk, 1999) described the invisible watermarking scheme for image as well as video. They explained the concepts of image and video watermarking using DCT and modification of the frequency coefficients. G. Langelaar, I. Setyawan and R. Lagendijk (Langelaar, Setyawan & Lagendijk, 2000) beautifully reviewed the current watermarking techniques, need of watermarking, application of watermarking and requirement of watermarking techniques. The authors lightened a lamp on techniques that has already been implied in spatial and frequency domain. Y. Lee and L. Chen (Lee & Chen, 2000) proposed a spatial domain image watermarking technique where they used equal size of grayscale images as host digital data and watermark data. They embedded most significant one to five bits of the watermark data in the least significant one to five bits of the host digital data. C. Podilchuk and E. Delp (Podilchuk & Delp, 2001) given the idea of what has already been done in the field of watermarking. They lighten the lamp on how various multimedia can be watermarked using concepts of digital watermarking. Chandramouli, Memon and Rabbani (Chandramouli, Memon & Rabbani, 2002) explained various concepts of digital watermarking, requirement of watermarking and differences between the steganography and watermarking. C. Chan and L. Cheng (Chan & Cheng, 2004) proposed a spatial domain image watermarking technique based on LSB substitution and explained that if the number of bits to be embedded is increased, a perceptible of the original host image is reduced and vice-versa. C. Huang and J. Wu (Huang & Wu, 2004) highlighted the current visible watermarking schemes specially used for intellectual property rights (IPR) protection. They mentioned that visible watermarking techniques can be very useful for distributing multimedia data with copyrights over the internet. R. Paul (Paul, 2011) explained important aspects of video watermarking and common attacks that can degrade the quality of both video and the watermark data, applications of video watermarking and watermarking techniques using DCT and PCA in the frequency domain. M. Ramalingam (Ramalingam, 2011) has given the idea of spatial domain video watermarking with a beautiful GUI where one can select the video file to be watermarked along with the key for the embedding purpose.

I. Cox and its research team (Cox et al. 1997) described a robust watermarking technique based on DCT and Spread Spectrum technique which can be used for any type of multimedia data. S. Arena, M. Caramma and R. Lancini (Arena, Caramma & Lancini, 2000) explained the technique for MPEG video watermarking where they used the bit stream domain so that the process of watermark data embedding became easy. J. Hernandez and its research team (Hernandez et al. 2000) suggested a transform domain watermarking technique for the purposed of copyright protection of digital images wherein they made use of a DCT. They made use of likelihood estimation function in the proposed technique. C. Lu and H. Liao (Lu & Liao, 2001) claimed a proposed technique to be the first one that is robust towards the geometric attacks such as blurring, filtering, scaling etc. They explained that in video the problem of synchronization caused by rotation and flipping is solved by making use of eigenvectors. R. Bangaleea and H. Rughooputh (Bangaleea & Rughooputh, 2002) presented a technique for copyright protection which made use of spatial domain and the attack characterization approach. The authors described that imperceptibility of the host digital data and robustness of the watermark data is analyzed using the perceptual analysis wherein the robustness should be increased with perceptibly a very small loss in the host digital data. H. Dajun, S. Qibin and Q. Tian (Dajun, Qibin & Tian, 2003) proposed a semi-fragile watermarking technique for video wherein they made use of DFT to convert the video from the spatial domain to the transform domain. They embedded the watermark data bits in the selected angular, radial transform coefficients. R. Preda and D. Vizireanu (Prada & Vizireanu, 2007) explained a blind video watermarking technique using DCT. They tested watermarked video with various bit rates and hamming and reed-Solomon codes. A. Koz and A. Alatan (Koz & Alatan, 2008) suggests a video watermarking technique where maximum energy of watermark data embedded and also taken care of the perceptibility of the video. They explained the concepts of temporal redundancy and given the importance in context to the HVS. Sridevi and its research team (Sridevi et al. 2010) described a DCT based watermarking technique for MPEG video where watermark data to be embedded is a grayscale image. Watermark data is preprocessed using DCT and frequency masking. They claimed that because of this preprocessing the capacity of the video watermarking is greatly increased. Y. Ding and its research team (Ding et al. 2010) described one of the unique techniques to embed a watermark data behind the video. They made use of the video features to embed the watermark data where they found the distance between adjacent key frames and made them as watermark data. They proved that this technique is robust, especially since the copy attack. R. Thanki and its research team (Thanki et al. 2011) presented a spatial domain watermarking technique using correlation properties of WGN for copyright protection of digital images.

M. Ejima and A. Miyazaki (Ejima & Miyazaki, 2000) proposed watermarking technique whose heart is sub band coding and specifically discrete wavelet transform (DWT). C. Serdean and its research team (Serdean et al. 2002) described the use of one the most powerful transform called DWT in the video watermarking wherein they also combined log-log and log-polar transform. The authors made use of speeded PN sequence for the purpose of the watermark embedding. M. Raval and P. Rege (Raval & Rege, 2003) proposed wavelets based adaptive watermarking technique for multiple watermark data embedding. The author claims that if the watermark data is embedded into low frequency coefficients, then robust against LPF, compression and geometric attacks. If a watermark data is embedded into higher frequency coefficients, then robust against contrast, histogram equalization and cropping attacks. L. Fan and F. Yanmei (Fan & Yanmei, 2006) suggested the watermarking technique using DWT and gold sequences. They achieved good visual quality and robust against compression, noise and geometric attacks. E. Elbasi (Elbasi, 2007) proposed a semi blind watermarking technique wherein a pseudo random sequence based on the watermark data is embedded in all frequency coefficients higher that a threshold. A. Essaouabi and E. Ibnelhaj (Essaouabi & Ibnelhaj, 2009) proposed a blind watermarking technique which based on video scene segmentation and 3-D wavelet transform. In this authors fist applied the DWT to the grayscale image and decomposed it into four bands. Similarly, they decomposed the host video frames into four bands and modified the host bands according to the respective four bands of the watermark data. They proved the technique robust against frame dropping, averaging and lossy compression. K. Raghavendra and K. Chetan (Raghavendra & Chetan, 2009) proposed a blind watermarking technique based on DWT for digital video. In this author divided the binary watermark data into four different parts and then embedded into each part into the sub bands of the host video frames. J. Hussein and A. Mohammed (Hussein & Mohammed, 2009) proposed a robust watermarking technique using DWT and motion estimation algorithm. S. Mostafa and its research team (Mostafa et al. 2009) combined the DWT and PCA for the purpose of video watermarking. In the embedding side first the original host video frame is decomposed into four sub-bands and the block based PCA is applied to one of the band. The result is added with the watermark frame and inverse DWT would give the watermarked frame.

E. Ganic and M. Eskicioglu (Ganic & Eskicioglu, 2004) proposed an image authentication technique where quantization values of singular values of host digital data block are modified according to bit of watermark data in the spatial domain. F. Huang and Z. Guan (Huang & Guan, 2004) combined DCT and SVD so as to embed the watermark data into the host digital data. They used a technique called PSNR wherein they set the value of the PSNR and accordingly they embedded the gray scale watermark data into the host digital data by modifying singular values of DCT coefficients of host digital data. R. Dili and E. Mwangi (Dili & Mwangi, 2007) proposed watermarking technique where the monochrome watermark image is embedded into singular values of selected DWT blocks of horizontal and vertical sub-bands of host digital data. The embedded blocks are selected by a secret key to enhance imperceptibility. T. Khatib, A. Haj and L. Rajab (Haj & Rajab, 2008) beautifully made use of one of the most important linear algebra tool i.e. singular value decomposition. They explained the embedding of a watermark data in all three matrices namely U, V and one singular matrix S. A. Mansouri and its research team (Mansouri et al. 2009) described the watermarking technique where they first applied complex wavelet transform to both the host digital data and watermark. Then they changed the singular values of the sub-band of the host digital data according to the singular values of the sub-band of the watermark data. V. Santhi and A. Thangavelu (Santhi & Thangavelu, 2009) explained that embedding the watermark into the RGB color space is not suggestible because information on R, G and B color space are highly correlated and therefore they suggested YUV color space for putting the watermark data behind the host digital data. They also explained the concept of combining the SVD and DWT for the purpose of watermarking. M. Kamlakar, C. Gosavi and A. Patankar (Kamlakar, Gosavi & Patankar, 2012) explained a watermarking technique based on block based SVD for video. They first divided the frames in the blocks and selected one of the blocks for the embedding purpose. They explained this method to be robust against the compression, rotation, noise and scaling attack. A. Gupta and M. Raval (Gupta & Raval, 2012) proposed a robust watermarking technique based on pure SVD and DWT+SVD for copyright protection.

In 2007, inventors are introducing a new watermarking approach based on sparsity properties of the image transform and compressive sensing (CS) theory (Donoho, 2006; Candès, 2006; Baraniuk, 2007) for copyright authentication of digital images. M. Sheikh and R. Baraniuk (Sheikh & Baraniuk, 2007) described DCT domain image watermarking technique using a compressive sensing framework. This is a first watermarking technique proposed by inventor using CS theory framework. M. Tagliasacchi and its research team (Tagliasacchi et al. 2009) described a CS theory based watermarking scheme for image tamper identification which is fragile watermarking technique. X. Zhang and its research team (Zhang et al. 2011) described fragile watermarking technique based on compressive sensing and discrete cosine transform. Then extracted watermark data for checking sparseness in DCT domain without any modification. This scheme is used for image tampering identification. M. Raval and its research team (Raval et al. 2011) described the CS theory and wavelets transform based image watermarking technique for detection of image tamper. In CS theory based techniques, CS theory is used for reducing dimensions and improved security of watermark data. M. Walled Fakhr (Fakhr, 2012) described a robust watermarking technique using CS Theory framework for audio signals and give a comparison against different attacks liked MP3 audio compression and additive noise. F. Tiesheng and its research team (Tiesheng et al. 2013) described watermarking techniques based on CS theory which includes compressed sensing acquisition process and compressed sensing recovery process.

M. Kutter and F. Petitcolas (Kutter & Petitcolas, 1999) gave mathematical expressions of visual quality metrics. They gave the expressions for the purpose of comparison and evaluation of robust and invisible watermarking techniques. The authors explained various attacks that degrade the multimedia data. F. Petitcolas (Petitcolas, 2000) explained the importance to the common platform for the evaluation of the watermarking scheme for the comparison purpose. Author divided the evaluation criteria into two groups where first group is a functionality where evaluation is performed using an agreed series of tests. The second group is an assurance which includes a set of levels to check the first group. S. Voloshynovskly, S. Pereira and T. Pun (Voloshynovskly, Pereira & Pun, 2001) said that after watermarking is completed and it transmits in the channel there are operations that may degrade the quality of the host digital data. They explained the properties of various watermarking attacks. The authors also highlighted that most watermarking techniques are evaluated using PSNR and NCC quality metrics.

3. COMPARISON OF WATERMARKING TECHNIQUE WITH THE OTHER DATA HIDING TECHNIQUES

Data hiding techniques can be divided many sub-disciplines. The important sub-disciplines are Cryptography, Steganography and Watermarking. Cryptography can be defined as encryption of information for secure transmission. Through the use of a secret "key" the receiver can decode the encrypted information to recover the original information. This technique is used as a science of secret writing and provides security to text information over an insecure channel. A limitation of cryptography is that it is does not always provide safe communication. This technique mostly used for security of text data and can be not applicable for image and video data security.

Cryptography technique is used for data encoding. Cryptography technique is for using data unreadable for unauthentic party, while steganography technique is used for hiding data for unauthentic party (Katzenbeisser & Petitcolas, 2000). Steganography is used for hiding information which can only the sender and the receiver know it. Steganography technique is used for data hiding rather than data encoding. Watermarking techniques are described as same technique as steganography, but there are difference between these two techniques (Podilchuk & Delp, 2001; Chandramouli, Memon & Rabbani, 2002; Paul, 2011). Steganography can be used for line of sight communication while watermarking can be used for multipoint communication. Steganography techniques are very sensitive against attacks while watermarking techniques are very regard against attacks. In steganography, if the digital content is a change, then the identity information completely vanishes. But in the case of watermarking, there are techniques protecting identity information if the digital content is changing.

4. DATA USED FOR IMPLEMENTATION OF WATERMARKING TECHNIQUES

For implementation of watermarking techniques in this chapter, color girl image with various sizes such as 512×512 pixels, 256×256 pixels taken as host image and standard cameraman image with various sizes such as 256×256 pixels, 64×64 pixels and riya name image with size of 64×64 pixels taken as the watermark image. All watermarking techniques are implemented using an image processing toolbox and a wavelet toolbox of MATLAB 2013a.

The performance of watermarking techniques can be evaluated on the bases of various visual quality measures (Kutter & Petitcolas, 1999; Petitcolas, 2000). These measures give the idea of visual degradations of the host medium because of the embedding of the watermark. These values also give the idea of strength of both watermark and watermarking techniques. In this chapter, Peak Signal to Noise Ratio (PSNR) quality measure used for quality check between watermarked data and original host data which is described by equation 1 and 2. At the detector side, quality of watermark measure using correlation. A watermark is extracted at detector side and finds a correlation between the original watermark data and extracted watermark data for decision about the robustness of watermarking technique.

$$MSE = \frac{1}{M \times N} \sum_{x=1}^{M} \sum_{y=1}^{N} \{(I(x,y) - IW(x,y))^{\wedge}2\} \tag{1}$$

$$PSNR = 10 \times \log \frac{255^2}{MSE} \tag{2}$$

where MSE = Mean Square Error, PSNR = Peak Signal to Noise Ratio, I (x, y) = Original Host Data, IW (x, y) = Watermarked Data.

As per the equations it is observed that measurement of PSNR includes the measurement of MSE which actually finds the difference between the image and modified version of the same. PSNR is measured in the logarithmic scale and MSE is measured in the general scale.

5. DIGITAL WATERMARKING TECHNIQUES IN SPATIAL DOMAIN

The basically two watermarking techniques, namely as LSB modification and correlation of different noise sequences are available in spatial domain. These techniques are easy to implement without prior knowledge of digital watermarking technique concept. The more details of these techniques are given below.

5.1. LSB Modification Based Watermarking Technique

In Least significant bit (LSB) modification technique (Lee & Chan, 2000; Chan & Cheng, 2004; Ramalingam, 2011), most significant bits of the watermark are replaced with the least significant bits of the host digital data. The visual degradation of host digital data is very less in this technique because of the important information of the host digital data are less affected due to modification.

In any 8-bit image, the most significant bit plane (i.e. Bit plane 7) contains most important and visual information while the last or the least significant bit plane (i.e. Bit plane 0) contains no visual information. All other bit planes contribute various information of the image. The bit plane of any 8 bit image can be visually elaborated in Figure 2. It can be shown that the most visual information lies in the MSB of the Image and visual information start to degrade when going from MSB plane to the LSB plane of the image. It can be seen that LSB does not contain any important information. There LSB plane of the image is chosen for watermarking purpose.

In LSB substitution technique, watermark data can be inserted into host digital data using the following steps. Take original host digital data and original watermark digital data. The image divided into R, G and B planes. Then LSB of each pixel of the R plane of host digital data is replaced with the MSB of the watermark data and the result is a watermarked digital data with watermark data embedded into it. Then combine all these R, G and B planes to generate watermarked digital data. Figure 3 shows a bit plane representation of watermarked digital data. The implementation of the LSB modification technique of watermark embedding in a digital image is depicted in Figure 4. The color host data and monochrome watermark data with size of 512×512 pixels is taken for implementation of this technique.

Figure 2. Original host image and its bit plane representation

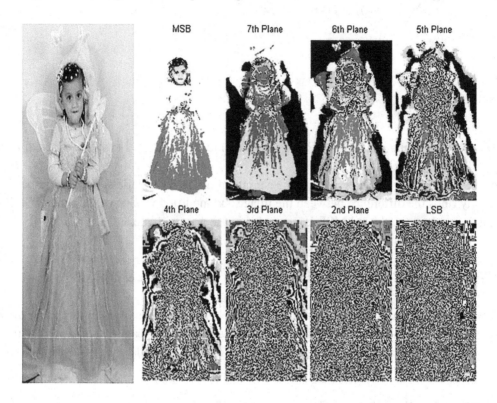

Figure 3. Bit plane representation of r plane of watermarked digital image

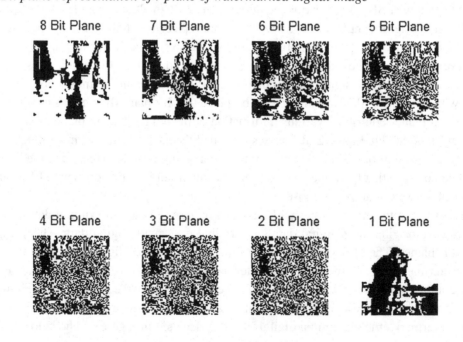

Figure 4. Results of watermark embedding procedure of LSB modification technique

(a) Host Image

(b) Watermarked Image

Since the watermark data is inserted into the LSB of R plane the host digital data, the extraction procedure involves extracting LSB from each pixel of R plane. The extraction of watermark data from watermarked digital data using the following steps. Take Watermarked digital data and the data is divided into R, G and B planes. Then take an R plane of watermarked digital data because of this plane is used for the watermark embedding purpose. LSB of each pixel of R plane is taken and copied into other 7 planes. These steps are performed for the entire R plane to extract watermark data from it. The implementation of the LSB modification technique of watermark extraction from watermarked image is depicted in Figure 5. The quality measures such as PSNR between watermarked data and host digital data is around 65 dB and correlation between watermark data and extracted watermark data is 1.

The main advantage of the LSB modification technique is that after embedding procedure, quality of host digital data is not affected by watermark data. Hence, under the normal circumstances, an average person can't observe changing in host digital data where watermark data are embedding and hence the transfer of watermark data remains unnoticed form average person. The limitation of this technique is that watermark data can't be extracted when various watermarking attacks are applied on watermarked digital data which is generated by using this technique. The technique is also used for protection of black and white watermark data or binary data. The payload capacity of this technique is 100 percentages.

Figure 5. Results of watermark extraction procedure of LSB modification technique

(a) Watermark Data

(b) Extracted Watermark Data

5.2. Correlation-Based Watermarking Technique

The other watermarking technique in the spatial domain is to exploit the correlation properties (Lange-laar, Setyawan & Lagendijk, 2000; Arena, Caramma & Lancini, 2000; Bangaleea & Rughooputh, 2002; Thanki, Trivedi, Kher & Vyas, 2011) of the pseudo-random noise patterns and white Gaussian noise patterns which are additive in nature. These patterns are utilized for the purpose of watermarking because of they have low amplitude like noise, great correlation property and less affect by interference. These noise sequences are utilized for the purpose of watermarking due to the following reasons.

1. These noise sequences are random in nature. An initial seed is required for generation of sequences.
2. It becomes very difficult to predict these sequences by imposter until and unless there is a prior knowledge of the seed as well as the knowledge of technique.

In correlation-based watermarking technique, two noise sequences are generated using the same private key. One will be used when the watermark data is bit 1 and the other is used when it is bit 0. Figure 6 shows the basic idea of correlation-based watermarking technique in spatial domain. The watermark data are embedded into host digital data using following sequential procedure.

1. Take host digital data and broken into the block. The block size is decided based on size of host digital data.
2. Then two high uncorrelated noise sequences are generated using the private key.

Figure 6. Basic idea of correlation based watermarking technique

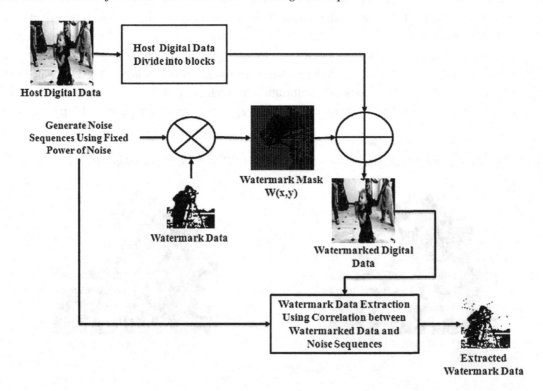

3. Then create the watermark mask based on noise sequences and size of host digital data.
   a. If the watermark data bit is zero, add noise sequence zero at that portion of the mask.
   b. Otherwise mask is filled with noise sequence one.
   c. This process is repeated for all the block of host digital data.
4. Add a watermark mask to host digital data using gain factor using formula shown below:

$$I_W(x,y) = I(x,y) + k \times W(x,y) \tag{3}$$

In formula (3), $I_w(x, y)$ represents Watermarked data; $I(x, y)$ represents host digital data; k represents Gain Factor; $W(x, y)$ represents Watermark mask.

The watermark data are extracted from watermarked digital data using following sequential procedure.

1. Watermarked digital data are broken into blocks. The block size is the same which is selected at watermark embedding procedure.
2. Then two high uncorrelated noise sequences are generated using the private key.
3. The correlation of each block of watermarked digital data with each noise sequence is calculated.
4. If correlation with noise sequence one is higher than that with the correlation with noise sequence zero than make the watermark bit 1. Otherwise, make it bit 0. Perform this operation for all blocks of watermarked digital data and get the watermark data.

Here, two noise sequences such as PN sequence and WGN sequence based correlation watermarking technique is implemented for multimedia data such as digital color images and digital videos. The implementation of the correlation based technique in digital image using PN and WGN sequence is depicted in Figure 7. The implementation of the correlation based technique in digital video using a PN sequence is depicted in Figure 8. The color host data with size of 256×256 pixels and monochrome watermark data with size of 64×64 pixels for implementation of these watermarking techniques. When this technique is applied to digital video, then video is divided into various frames and watermark data is inserted into every individual frame to generate watermarked video. The quality measures such as PSNR between watermarked data and host digital data is around 40 dB and correlation between watermark data and extracted watermark data is 0.92.

Following are some of the observations made after implementing watermarking techniques for multimedia data. The quality of watermarked digital data is decreased when the increase in gain factor. When the gain factor and noise power increases, the visibility of the extracted watermark also increases. The host digital data may be degraded when increases noise power. These two spatial domain watermarking techniques have more advantages and easy to implement for protection of multimedia data, but there is limitation of these techniques that they can't be embedded grayscale and color watermark data into host digital data. The payload capacity of this technique around is 25 percentages.

6. DIGITAL WATERMARKING TECHNIQUES IN TRANSFORM DOMAIN

In transform domain watermarking techniques (Langelaar, Setyawan & Lagendijk, 2000; Dajun, Qibin & Tian, 2003), frequency domain version of the image is used for watermark information embedding. The

Figure 7. Results of correlation based watermarking technique for image using gain factor = 10 and blocksize = 4 (a) Original host digital image & watermark data (b) Watermarked digital image & extracted watermark data using correlation based watermarking technique using PN sequences (c) Watermarked digital data & extracted watermark data using correlation based watermarking technique using WGN sequences

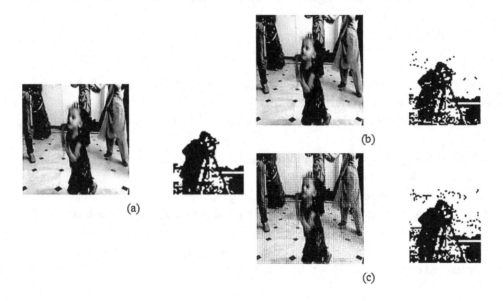

Figure 8. Results of correlation based watermarking technique for video using gain factor = 100 and blocksize = 4 (a) First five frames of original video (b) Watermarked frames of video (c) Extracted watermark data

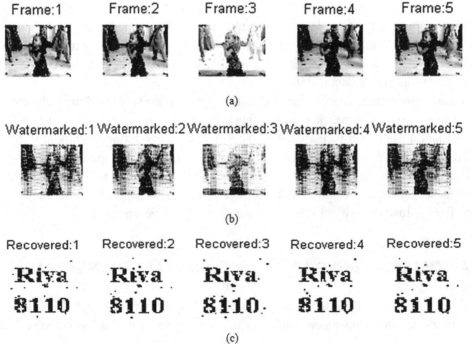

Discrete Cosine Transform (DCT) and Discrete Wavelet Transform (DWT) are two of most frequently image transform used for transform watermarking techniques. In this technique, an image is transformed from the spatial to frequency domain. Then, according to the human visual system, transform coefficients are arranged into various priorities. Then the magnitudes of transform coefficients are changes according to watermark data bits. The watermarking technique in transform domain is performed mainly in three steps. The first step is to perform forward transform which converts the spatial domain data into the frequency domain and get the transform coefficients. The second step is to modify the transform coefficients according to the watermark data. The last step is performing the inverse transform to get watermarked data. There are basically two watermarking techniques such as Discrete Cosine Transform (DCT) based technique and Discrete Wavelet Transform (DWT) based technique is available in transform domain which are explained below.

6.1. Discrete Cosine Transform (DCT) Based Watermarking Technique

Discrete Cosine Transform (Langelaar, Setyawan & Lagendijk, 2000; Arena, Caramma & Lancini, 2000; Hernandez, Amado & Perez-Gonzalez, 2000; Lu & Liao, 2001; Huang & Guan, 2004; Preda & Vizireanu, 2007; Koz & Alatan, 2008; Sridevi et al. 2010; Ding et al. 2010) converts host digital data from the spatial domain into the frequency domain. DCT converts a spatial domain 2-D representation into its frequency domain equivalent. The output of DCT is that the size of the transformed frequency domain data is exactly equal to that in the spatial domain. The DC coefficient of the DCT transformed data is situated at the upper left side and contains very important of information of data because of it is low frequency coefficients. All coefficients other than DC coefficients are called as AC coefficients. The DC DCT coefficients are always an integer and the range of coefficients would be in between -1024 to 1023 while AC DCT coefficients may be integer or non-integer. Figure 9 shows the idea of frequency discrimination by Discrete Cosine Transform (DCT). Here F_L denote low frequency coefficients, F_M denote mid frequency coefficients and F_H denote the high frequency coefficients. Figure 10 shows the example application of DCT on an Image. The most important information lies in the low frequency DCT coefficients and when the data undergoes compression it is the high frequency DCT coefficients that are very easily removed and therefore mid frequency DCT coefficients are used in watermarking technique.

Figure 9. (a) Frequency discrimination by DCT (b) Quantization values used in JPEG compression scheme

(a)

16	11	10	26	24	40	51	61
12	12	14	19	26	58	60	55
14	13	16	24	40	57	69	56
14	17	22	29	51	87	80	62
18	22	37	56	68	109	103	77
24	35	55	64	81	104	113	92
49	64	78	87	103	121	120	101
72	92	95	98	112	100	103	99

(b)

Figure 10. Energy concentration of DCT (a) Original image (b) DCT of the Image (c) Block wise DCT of the image

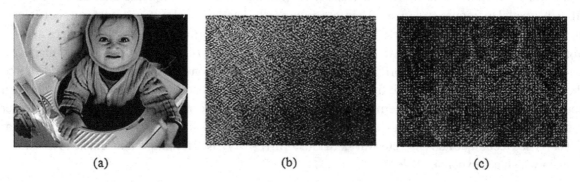

(a)   (b)   (c)

There are two approaches, namely mid band frequency DCT coefficient comparison (Langelaar, Setyawan & Lagendijk, 2000) and the addition of PN noise sequences in mid band frequency DCT coefficients (Shoemaker, 2002) is available in the literature. The more details of these two techniques are given below.

6.1.1. Mid Band Frequency DCT Coefficients Comparison Based Watermarking Technique

In this technique, two nearby locations having same values are chosen from mid frequency DCT coefficients for comparison. From the JPEG quantization table shown in Figure 9 (b), one can take two locations (5, 2) and (4, 3) of mid frequency DCT coefficients which are having same quantization values. The advantage of taking these two coefficients is that if any of the coefficients is scaled by factor than the other is also scaled by the same factor. Following is the sequence used for embedding watermark data into host digital data.

- Take host digital data and divided into non overlapping blocks. Then DCT is applied to each and every block.
- Then chose two locations (5, 2) and (4, 3) from the mid frequency DCT band for watermark data embedding.
- If watermark data is bit 0, it is taken care that DCT_block (5, 2) value is greater than DCT_block (4, 3) value and if it is not they are swapped.
- If watermark data is bit 1, it is taken care that DCT_block (5, 2) value is less than DCT_block (4, 3) value and if it is not they are swapped.
- Step 3 and 4 taken care that the difference between the two mid frequency DCT coefficients is kept more than the gain factor and if it is not found to be greater, than gain factor is added and subtracted so as to maintain the difference between DCT coefficients greater than gain factor.
- Inverse DCT is applied to each modified block to generate watermarked digital data.

The steps described below show the extraction of watermark data from the watermarked digital data.

- Take watermarked digital data and divided into non overlapping blocks. Then applied DCT on each and every block.
- Two mid band DCT coefficients block (5, 2) and (4, 3) are checked and compared because of this block is used for watermark data embedding.
- If DCT_block (5, 2) value is found to be greater than DCT_block (4, 3) value, then assigned watermark data is bit 0 and if DCT_block (5, 2) value is less than DCT_block (4, 3) value then assigned watermark data is bit 1. Repeat this step for all blocks of watermarked digital data to extract watermark data.

The implementation of this technique in digital image and digital video is depicted in Figure 11 and 12. The color host data with size of 512×512 pixels and monochrome watermark data with size of 64×64 pixels for implementation of this watermarking technique. When this technique is applied to digital video, then video is divided into various frames and watermark data is inserted into every individual frame to generate watermarked video. The quality measures such as PSNR between watermarked data and host digital data is around 75 dB and correlation between watermark data and extracted watermark data is 0.95. There is limitation of this technique that it can't be embedded grayscale and color watermark data into host digital data. The payload capacity of this technique around is 25 percentages.

6.1.2. Addition of PN Noise Sequences in Mid Band Frequency DCT Coefficients Based Watermarking Technique

In this technique, two PN noise sequences are added to mid band frequency DCT coefficients of host digital data according to watermark data bits. Following is the sequence used for embedding watermark data into host digital data using this technique.

- Take host digital data and divided into non overlapping blocks. Then DCT is applied to each and every block. Then find mid band DCT coefficients in each block of host digital data.
- Then two high uncorrelated noise sequences are generated using the private key.

Figure 11. Results of mid band frequency DCT coefficients based watermarking technique for image using gain factor = 10 and blocksize = 8 (a) Original host digital image & watermark data (b) Watermarked digital data & Extracted watermark data

(a)   (b)

Figure 12. Results of mid band frequency DCT coefficients based watermarking technique for image using gain factor = 100 and blocksize = 8 (a) First five frames of original video (b) Watermarked frames of video (c) Extracted watermark data

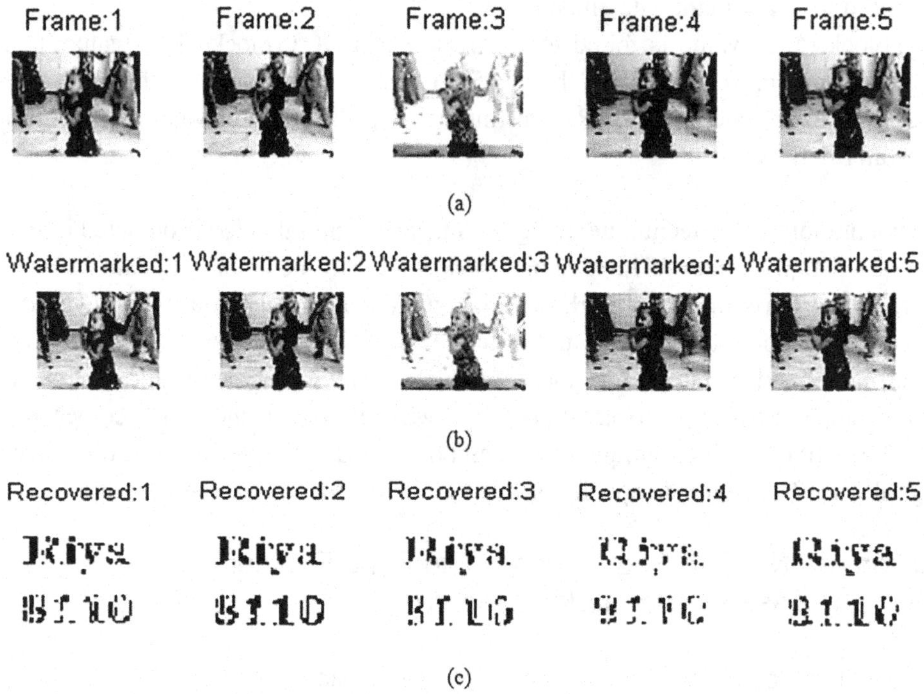

- If watermark data bit contains zero, then embed a PN sequence zero added into the mid band DCT coefficients of the DCT block of host digital data. Otherwise, embed PN sequence one into the mid band DCT coefficients of host digital data. Then applied inverse DCT on a modified block of host digital data.
- Repeat procedure of step 3 for all DCT blocks of host digital data to get watermarked digital data.

The steps described below show the extraction of watermark data from the watermarked digital data.

- Take watermarked digital data and divided into non overlapping blocks. Then DCT is applied to each and every block. Then find mid band DCT coefficients in each block of watermarked digital data.
- Then two high uncorrelated noise sequences are generated using the private key.
- The correlation of mid band DCT coefficients of each block with each noise sequence is calculated.
- If correlation with noise sequence one is higher than that with the correlation with noise sequence zero than make the watermark bit 1. Otherwise, make it bit 0.
- Perform this operation for all blocks of watermarked digital data and get the watermark data.

The implementation of this technique in digital image is depicted in Figure 13. The color host data with size of 512×512 pixels and monochrome watermark data with size of 64×64 pixels for implementa-

Figure 13. Results of addition of PN sequences in mid band frequency DCT coefficients based watermarking technique for image using gain factor = 10 and blocksize = 8 (a) Original host digital image & watermark data (b) Watermarked digital image & extracted watermark data

(a)   (b)

tion of this watermarking technique. The quality measures such as PSNR between watermarked data and host digital data is around 75 dB and correlation between watermark data and extracted watermark data is 0.95. There is limitation of this technique that it can't be embedded grayscale and color watermark data into host digital data. The payload capacity of this technique around is 25 percentages.

6.2 Discrete Wavelet Transform (DWT) Based Watermarking Technique

In most of applications such as compression, digital watermarking, image fusion of the field of image processing, the wavelet transform has very important contributions to make the application smooth and fruitful. Waves are periodic in nature and are oscillating with respect to time or space. Actually the DWT performed convolution operation between 1-D or 2-D signals with particular instances of wavelets at various time scales and positions. The Discrete Wavelet Transform (Ejima & Miyazaki, 2000; Serdean et al. 2002; Raval & Rege, 2003; Fan & Yanmei, 2006; Elbasi, 2007; Essaouabi & Ibnelhaj, 2009; Raghavendra & Chetan, 2009; Hussein & Mohammed, 2009; Mostafa et al. 2009) is based on sub band coding, is easy to implement, does require limited time and resources and yield fast computations of wavelet transform. In wavelet analysis two words such as approximations and details are frequently used. The approximations wavelets are the high-scale, low frequency coefficients of the signal. The details wavelets are the low-scale, high frequency coefficients of the signal. For a 2-D image I (x, y), the forward and reverse decomposition can be done by discrete wavelet transform (DWT) and inverse discrete wavelet transform (IDWT) first on dimension x and then the same procedure can be performed for the other dimension y. The image can be converted into four sub bands, namely, approximation sub band, horizontal sub band, vertical sub band and diagonal sub band using DWT decomposition. Figure 14 describes the basic wavelet decomposition steps for image. An example of 1st level and 2nd level Wavelet decomposition of the image is demonstrated in Figure 15.

Here the concepts of DWT and the correlation of noise sequence are combined to embed the watermark data into the host digital data. Following is the sequence used for embedding watermark data into host digital data using this technique.

Figure 14. Basic wavelet decomposition steps of image

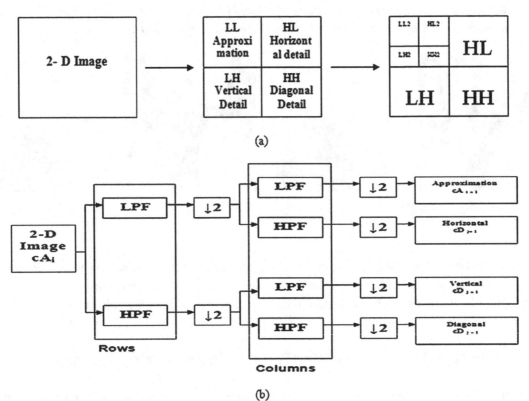

(a)

(b)

Figure 15. Decomposition of an image using DWT (a) Original image (b) 1ˢᵗ level wavelet decomposition (c) 2ⁿᵈ level wavelet decomposition

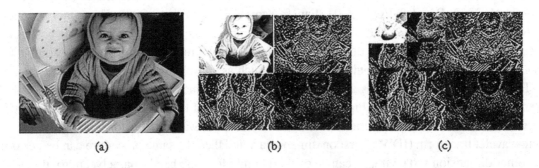

(a)　　　　　　　　(b)　　　　　　　　(c)

- Take host digital data and perform color space conversion from RGB to YCbCr. Here are some of the reasons for choosing an YCbCr color space. When JPEG compression is performed on the frame in RGB color space is affected more as compared to the YCbCr color space. It requires less disk space and less bandwidth.
- Two random noise sequences are generated using a secret key and named give as sequence_one and sequence_zero.

- Discrete wavelet transform is applied to Y plane and horizontal wavelet coefficients HL is chosen for the watermark data embedding purpose. Then HL coefficients are divided into non overlapping blocks.
- If the watermark bit is zero, watermark block is filled with sequence_zero; otherwise it is filled with sequence_one. The same thing is repeated for all blocks.
- Then original HL coefficients are added to the weighted watermark block wherein the weight is called the gain factor.
- Inverse DWT is applied to get a watermarked Y plane. Inverse color space conversion is applied so as to get watermarked digital data.

The steps described below show the extraction of watermark data from the watermarked digital data.

- Take watermarked digital data and perform color space conversion from RGB to YCbCr.
- Two random noise sequences are generated using a secret key and named give as sequence_one and sequence_zero. These sequences must be same as that at the embedding side.
- Discrete wavelet transform is applied to Y plane and horizontal wavelet coefficients HL is chosen for the watermark data embedding purpose. Then HL coefficients are divided into non overlapping blocks.
- The correlation of a block with both the sequences is calculated. If correlation is found more in case of sequence_zero than watermark bit is assigned to 0; otherwise it is assigned 1. The same procedure is performed for all blocks to extract watermark data.

The implementation of this technique in digital image and digital video is depicted in Figure 16 and Figure 17. The color host data with size of 512×512 pixels and monochrome watermark data with size of 64×64 pixels for implementation of this watermarking technique. The quality measures such as PSNR between watermarked data and host digital data is around 48 dB and correlation between watermark data and extracted watermark data is 0.81. There is limitation of this technique that it can't be embedded grayscale and color watermark data into host digital data. The payload capacity of this technique around is 25 percentages.

Figure 16. Results of DWT coefficients based watermarking technique for image using gain factor = 10 and blocksize = 8 (a) Original host digital image & watermark data (b) watermarked digital image & extracted watermark data

(a)　　　　　　　　　　　　　　　　　　(b)

Figure 17. Results of DWT coefficients based watermarking technique for video using gain factor = 100 and blocksize = 8 (a) First five frames of original video (b) Watermarked frames of video (c) Extracted watermark data

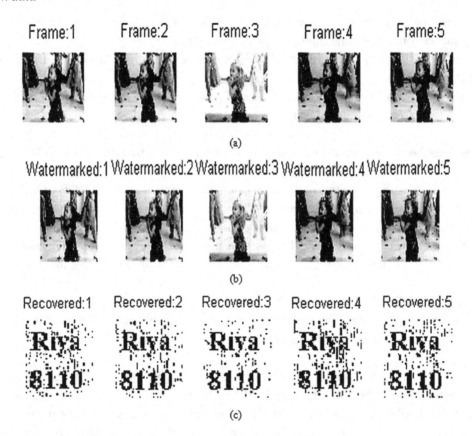

7. ADVANCE DIGITAL WATERMARKING TECHNIQUES

There are various limitations of above all watermarking techniques in term of less computational security and less payload capacity, less ability to embed grayscale and color watermark data. To overcome these limitations of watermarking techniques, inventors are proposed new watermarking techniques for protection of multimedia data. The inventors described watermarking techniques such as Singular Value Decomposition (SVD) based watermarking technique for hiding grayscale watermark data; hybrid watermarking technique using various images transform such as DCT, DWT, SVD for protection of digital video data; DWT based watermarking technique for hiding color watermark data; compressive sensing (CS) theory and curvelet based watermarking technique for protection of digital image. The more details on these watermarking techniques are given below.

7.1. Singular Value Decomposition (SVD) Based Watermarking Technique for Hiding Grayscale Watermark Data

Singular value decomposition (Ganic & Eskicioglu, 2004; Huang & Guan, 2004; Dili & Mwangi, 2007; Khatib, Haj & Rajab, 2008; Mansouri et al. 2009; Santhi & Thangavelu, 2009; Kamlakar, Gosavi &

Patankar, 2012; Gupta & Raval, 2012) is a numerical technique based on the linear algebra and it is used to diagonalize matrices in numerical analysis. There are lots of areas where SVD finds its application. When SVD is applied to an image with size of M×N, three matrices are found, namely U, V and S. The U and V matrices are called unitary matrices having size of M×M and N×N respectively. S matrix is called diagonal matrix having size of M×N. The singular matrix is very important for watermarking purpose and entries in this matrix are arranged diagonally and in ascending order. One of the most important properties of the singular values is that they are very much stable and hence if a small change is made in the value of host digital data its singular values do not have any significant change. One example of the SVD procedure is explained in Figure 18.

The following steps are performed when the grayscale watermark data are embedded behind the host digital data.

- Take original host digital data and perform color space conversion from RGB to YCbCr. The Y plane is chosen for the watermark embedding purpose.
- The singular value decomposition (SVD) is applied to the selected Y plane.
- A watermark is rescaled to the size of the singular matrix S. Singular matrix value is modified as S = S + k*W where W is the watermark data and k is the gain factor.
- Again SVD is applied to the modified singular matrix. The selected sub band is modified as New_value = U*Modified_S*V^T.
- Inverse color space conversion is applied to get watermarked digital data.

The steps described below show the extraction of watermark data from the watermarked digital data.

- Take watermarked digital data and perform color space conversion from RGB to YCbCr. The Y plane is selected for the watermark extraction purpose. The SVD is applied to the selected Y plane.
- Singular matrix is resized to have the size same as the watermark so as to have D = U*S*V^T. The watermark data is generated by applying (D – S)/k.

Figure 18. Example of SVD on matrix

Original Matrix		
1	2	3
4	5	6
7	8	9
10	11	12

U Matrix			
0.140877	-0.82471	-0.54556	0.048576
0.343946	-0.42626	0.691212	-0.47141
0.547016	-0.02781	0.254268	0.797087
0.750086	0.370637	-0.39992	-0.37426

V Matrix		
0.504533	0.760776	0.408248
0.574516	0.057141	-0.8165
0.644498	-0.64649	0.408248

S Matrix		
25.46241	0	0
0	1.290662	0
0	0	1.46E-15
0	0	0

The implementation of this technique in digital image and digital video is depicted in Figure 19 and Figure 20. The color host data with size of 512×512 pixels and gray scale watermark data with size of 256×256 pixels for implementation of this watermarking technique. The quality measures such as PSNR between watermarked data and host digital data is around 95 dB and correlation between watermark data and extracted watermark data is 0.99. The payload capacity of this technique around is 50 percentages.

Figure 19. Results of SVD based watermarking technique for image using gain factor = 10 (a) Original host digital image & watermark data (b) Watermarked digital image & extracted watermark data

Figure 20. Results of SVD based watermarking technique for video using gain factor = 100 (a) First five frames of original video (b) Watermarked frames of video (c) Extracted watermark data

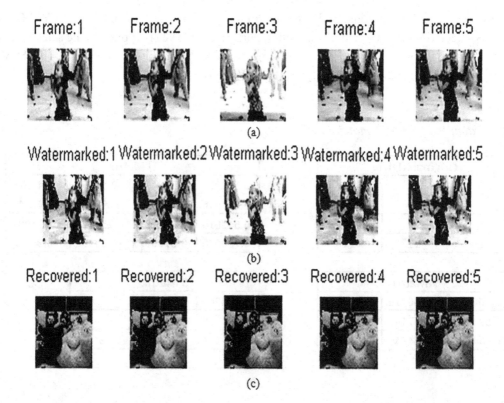

7.2. Hybrid Watermarking Technique Using Various Image Transform Such as DCT, DWT, SVD for Protection of Digital Video Data

Up to this point it had been seen that individual DCT and DWT based watermarking technique is better in perceptibility as compare to correlation based watermarking technique while SVD based watermarking technique is better than correlation, DCT or DWT based watermarking technique because it is able to embed grayscale watermark data into the digital data. So in this technique, hybridization of the two transforms namely DCT and DWT and one linear algebra named SVD is used for achieving high perceptible watermarked video data. The following steps are performed when the grayscale watermark data are embedded behind the host digital video.

- Take original video and broken into a number of frames. Then first frame is taken and perform color space conversion from RGB to YCbCr. The Y plane of the frame is selected for the embedding purpose of the watermark.
- A 2-D DCT is applied to the Y plane of the frame. Then 3rd level DWT is applied on the DCT transformed frame.
- Then SVD is applied to both DWT transformed frame and the watermark data.
- The singular value of the frame is modified according to the singular values of watermark.
- Inverse SVD is applied to get the watermarked DWT frame. Then inverse 3rd level DWT is performed to get a watermarked DCT frame. Inverse DCT is applied to get the watermarked Y plane.
- Then inverse color space conversion is performed to get a watermarked frame.
- Steps 2 to 6 are executed for the next frame and the process continues until the last frame to get watermarked video.

The steps described below show the extraction of watermark data from the watermarked digital video.

- Take watermarked video and broken into a number of frames. Then first frame is taken and perform color space conversion from RGB to YCbCr. The Y plane of the frame is selected for the extraction of watermark data.
- A 2-D DCT is applied to the Y plane of the frame. Then 3rd level DWT is applied on the DCT transformed Y plane of the frame. Singular value decomposition is applied to DWT transformed Y plane of the frame.
- Singular values are modified to get the watermark data back.

The implementation of this technique in digital video is depicted in Figure 21. The color host data with size of 512×512 pixels and monochrome watermark data with size of 64×64 pixels for implementation of this watermarking technique. The quality measures such as PSNR between watermarked data and host digital data is around 43 dB and correlation between watermark data and extracted watermark data is 0.96.

7.3. DWT Based Watermarking Technique for Hiding Color Watermark Data

Up to this point it had been seen that all above watermarking techniques are used for embedding monochrome and grayscale watermark data into the host digital data. So in this technique, DWT is used for

Figure 21. Results of hybrid watermarking technique for video using gain factor = 100 (a) First five frames of original video (b) Watermarked frames of video (c) Extracted watermark data

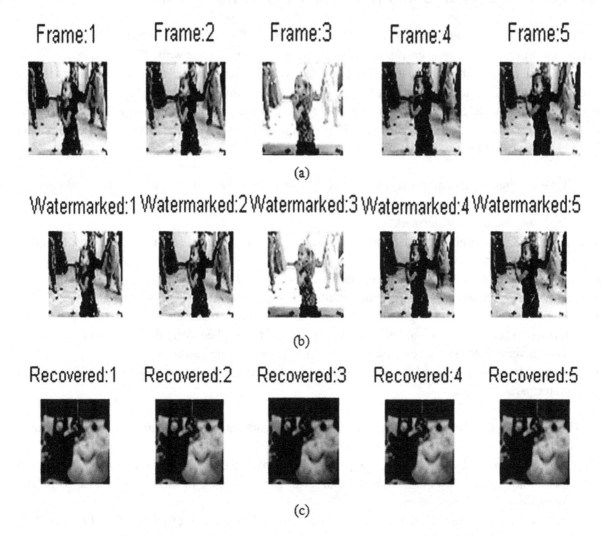

embedding color watermark data into color host digital image. This technique is visible watermarking technique and used for owner identification. The following steps are performed when the color watermark data are embedded behind the host color digital image.

- Set gain factor for watermark embedding.
- Take a color host image and compute the size of host image. Take color watermark data and compute the size of watermark data.
- Apply single level 2D wavelet decomposition on host image and watermark image.
- Take lowest frequency coefficients such as LL, HL, LH of host image and weighted high frequency coefficients HH of watermark image where weight is gain factor.
- Apply inverse 2D wavelet reconstruction on low frequency coefficients of host image and high frequency coefficients of watermark image to get a color watermarked image.

The steps described below show the extraction of color watermark data from the watermarked digital image.

- Take a color watermarked image and compute the size of watermarked image. Take color watermark data and compute the size of watermark data.
- Apply single level 2D wavelet decomposition on watermarked image and watermark image.
- Take highest frequency coefficients such as HL, LH, HH of watermarked image and lowest frequency coefficients LL of watermark image.
- Apply inverse 2D wavelet reconstruction on high frequency coefficients of watermarked image and low frequency coefficients of watermark image to extract color watermark data.

The implementation of this technique in color digital image is depicted in Figure 22. The color host data with size of 512×512 pixels and color watermark data with size of 512×512 pixels for implementation of this watermarking technique. The quality measures such as PSNR between watermarked data and host digital data is around 70 dB and correlation between watermark data and extracted watermark data is 0.90.

7.4. Compressive Sensing (CS) Theory and Curvelet Based Watermarking Technique for Protection of Digital Image

Up to this point it had been seen that all watermarking techniques are embedded direct watermark data into the host digital data. Then imposter or unauthorized people can easily get watermark data by applying various manipulations on watermarked data. So in this technique, compressive sensing (CS) theory (Donoho, 2006; Candès, 2006; Baraniuk, 2007) has provided protection for watermark data before embedding into the host digital data. This technique adds two procedures such as CS theory acquisition procedure and CS theory recovery procedure in traditional watermarking technique. The compressive sensing (CS) theory based watermarking technique is depicted in Figure 23.

In this technique, watermark data are first converted into its sparse measurement using CS theory acquisition procedure at embedder side and at detector side, watermark data are reconstructed from

Figure 22. Results of DWT based watermarking technique for hiding color watermark data (a) Original host color digital image & color watermark data (b) Watermarked color digital image & extracted color watermark data

(a)   (b)

Figure 23. Compressive sensing (CS) Theory based watermarking technique (a) Watermark embedding procedure (b) Watermark extraction procedure

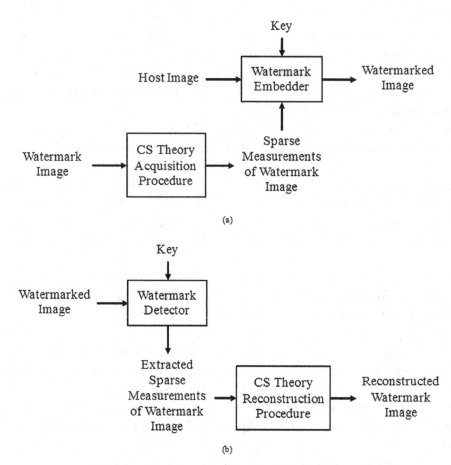

extracted sparse measurements using the CS theory recovery procedure. There is necessary condition is application of CS theory on image is that the image must be sparse in its own domain. In this technique, sparse measurements of watermark data are embedded into transform coefficients of host digital data to generate watermarked digital data. In this technique, fast discrete curvelet transform (FDCT) coefficients of host digital data is used for watermark data embedding.

In 2005, Candès, Demanet and Donoho described new image transform, namely curvelet transform based on sparsity theory. Curvelet transform is calculated the inner relationship between the image and its curvelet function to realize sparse representation of the image. There are two types of curvelet transform such as continuous curvelet transform and discrete curvelet transform available in the literature. Discrete fast curvelet transform is used most of image processing applications such as compression, watermarking, sparse representation and edge detection (Candès, Demanet & Donoho, 2005). There are two types of fast discrete curvelet transform, namely unequispaced fast Fourier transform (USFFT) and frequency wrapping. The frequency wrapping based discrete curvelet transform technique is easy to implement, less computation time and easy to understand compared to the USFFT technique (Candès, Demanet & Donoho, 2005). Therefore, frequency wrapping based curvelet transform technique is used in many im-

Figure 24. Curvelet Decomposition of the image (a) Curvelet decomposition (b) High frequency curvelet coefficients

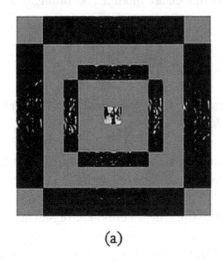

(a)   (b)

age processing applications. When the frequency wrapping based curvelet transform (Candès, Demanet & Donoho, 2005) applied to an image, then the image is converted into low frequency coefficients and high frequency coefficients. The curvelet decomposition of image by frequency wrapping based curvelet transform with 4 scales and 16 orientation parameter are given as C {1, 1}; C {1, 2}; C {1, 3}; C {1, 4}. Given the decomposition scale 4, the curvelet coefficients C {1, 1} is the low frequency coefficients and the other coefficients C {1, 2}; C {1, 3}; C {1, 4} is the high frequency coefficients. The curvelet decomposition of the image is shown in Figure 24.

The following steps are performed when the watermark data are embedded behind the host color digital image using this technique.

- Take a watermark data with size of N×N and compute the size of the image.
- Then generate the DCT basis matrix. This basis matrix is multiplied with watermark data to get sparse coefficients of a watermark data.
- Generate measurement matrix A with size of N×N using normal distribution with mean =0 and variance = 1. This measurement matrix A is same for embedder and decoder side.
- Generate sparse measurements of a watermark data by multiplication of the measurement matrix with sparse coefficients of a watermark data.
- Then multiply sampling factor with sparse measurements of the watermark data which is denoted as W_{sparse}. This sampling factor range should be 0.01 to 0.001. This sampling factor must be same for embedder and decoder side.
- Take an original color image and perform color space conversion from RGB to YCbCr. The Y plane is selected for the embedding purpose of the watermark.
- Then the frequency wrapping based fast discrete curvelet transform (FDCT) with 4 scales and 16 orientation parameter is applied to Y plane of the host image convert into various curvelet coef-

ficients such as C {1, 1}; C {1, 2}; C {1, 3}; C {1, 4}. The high frequency curvelet coefficients C {1, 4} is chosen for embedding because of size of W_{sparse} is same as size of C {1, 4}.

- Then high frequency curvelet coefficients of the host digital image are modified according to values of W_{sparse} and gain factor.

$$C_W\{1,4\} = C\{1,4\} * (1 + k * W_{sprase}) \tag{4}$$

where C_w *{1, 4}* = Modified high frequency curvelet coefficients; C *{1, 4}* = original high frequency curvelet coefficients; K = gain factor which is varying from 0.2 to 0.5.

- Applied inverse frequency wrapping based fast discrete curvelet transform on modified curvelet coefficients with another unmodified curvelet coefficient to get watermarked digital image.

The steps described below show the extraction of watermark data from the watermarked digital image.

- Take a color watermarked image and compute the size of watermarked image. Then first frame is taken and perform color space conversion from RGB to YCbCr. The Y plane of the frame is selected for the extraction of watermark data.
- Then the frequency wrapping based fast discrete curvelet transform (FDCT) with 4 scales and 16 orientation parameter is applied to Y plane of watermarked image convert into various curvelet coefficients such as C_w {1, 1}; C_w {1, 2}; C_w {1, 3}; C_w {1, 4}. The high frequency curvelet coefficients C {1, 4} is chosen for embedding because of size of W_{sparse} is same as size of C {1, 4}.
- Take an original color image and perform color space conversion from RGB to YCbCr. The Y plane is selected for the embedding purpose of the watermark.
- Then the frequency wrapping based fast discrete curvelet transform (FDCT) with 4 scales and 16 orientation parameter is applied to Y plane of the host image convert into various curvelet coefficients such as C {1, 1}; C {1, 2}; C {1, 3}; C {1, 4}.
- Extracted sparse measurements of a watermark data using the reverse procedure of embedding.

$$W_{Extracted} = \frac{\left(\dfrac{C_W\{1,4\}}{C\{1,4\}} - 1\right)}{k} \tag{5}$$

where C_w *{1, 4}* = Watermarked high frequency curvelet coefficients; C *{1, 4}* = original high frequency curvelet coefficients; K = gain factor which is varying from 0.2 to 0.5.

- Then extracted sparse measurements of the watermark data are divided sampling factor which is used at embedder side to get actual sparse measurements of the watermark data. After getting actual sparse measurements of the watermark data, then reconstructed actual watermark data from its sparse measurements using CS theory recovery process.
- For reconstruction of watermark data, first generate DCT basis with size of N×N and then this DCT basis, multiply by measurement matrix A to generate a Theta matrix.

- Then apply orthogonal matching pursuit (OMP) (Tropp & Gilbert, 2007) algorithm on actual sparse measurements of the watermark data along with Theta matrix. The output of OMP algorithm is sparse coefficients of a watermark data.
- Ultimately, the DCT basis matrix is multiplied with sparse coefficients of a watermark data to get reconstructed watermark data at detector side.

The implementation of this technique in color digital image is depicted in Figure 25. The color host data with size of 256×256 pixels and gray scale watermark data with size of 256×256 pixels for implementation of this watermarking technique. The quality measures such as PSNR between watermarked data and host digital data is around 65 dB and correlation between watermark data and extracted watermark data is 0.99. The payload capacity of this technique around is 100 percentages.

8. CONCLUSION AND FUTURE WORK

The conclusion of the work that the LSB based watermarking technique is not a good technique because of limited robustness against various watermarking attacks. In addition to that this work concluded that

Figure 25. Results of compressive sensing (CS) theory and curvelet based watermarking technique (a) Original host digital image (b) Original watermark data (C) Sparse measurements of watermark data (d) Watermarked digital image (e) Reconstructed watermark data (f) Extracted sparse measurements of watermark data

(a)   (b)   (c)

(d)   (e)   (f)

in correlation based watermarking techniques, when the noise power is increased, then the perception of recovered watermark data is increasing. The spatial domain watermarking techniques are easy to be applied on any multimedia data and provide high payload capacity. But the limitation of spatial domain watermarking techniques is that there are not robust against watermarking attacks. The transform domain watermarking techniques based on DCT and DWT provide more robustness against watermarking attacks. But the limitation of transform domain watermarking techniques can't be applied for larger size watermark data. The limitation of spatial and transform domain watermarking techniques can be overcome by using a hybrid approach of watermarking. The perceptibility and robustness of multimedia data using the hybrid watermarking techniques are higher than spatial and transform domain watermarking techniques. The SVD based watermarking technique is used for embedding grayscale watermark data into host digital data. This chapter has also given watermarking technique for color watermark data embedding. Also new watermarking technique for grayscale watermark data embedding into host digital data is described using new signal processing theory namely CS theory and curvelet transform.

The PSNR and correlation values are the major quality measures determining the quality of the watermarked data and recovered watermark data. By analyzing the results, it is observed that these two values are above 40dB and 0.8 respectively. In future, these all watermarking techniques are applied to other multimedia data such as audio and text. Also CS theory based watermarking technique is implemented for multimedia data such as video and audio.

REFERENCES

Arena, S., Caramma, M., & Lancini, R. (2000). Digital Watermarking Applied to MPEG-2 Coded Video Sequences Exploiting Space and Frequency Masking. *Proceedings of International Conference on Image Processing*. doi:10.1109/ICIP.2000.900989

Bangaleea, R., & Rughooputh, H. (2002). Performance Improvement of Spread Spectrum Spatial Domain Watermarking Scheme Through Diversity and Attack Characterization. *IEEE Conference Africon* (pp. 293 – 298).

Baraniuk, R. (2007, July). Lecture notes on Compressive Sensing. *IEEE Signal Processing Magazine*, 24, 118–124. doi:10.1109/MSP.2007.4286571

Bender, W., Gruhl, D., Morimoto, N., & Lu, A. (1996). Techniques for Data Hiding. *IBM Systems Journal*, 35(3&4), 313–336. doi:10.1147/sj.353.0313

Candès, E. (2006). Compressive Sampling. *Proceedings of the International Congress of Mathematicians*.

Candès, E., Demanet, L., & Donoho, D., (2005). Fast Discrete Curvelet Transforms. *Applied and Computational Mathematics*, 1 – 44.

Chan, C., & Cheng, L. (2004). Hiding Data in Images by Simple LSB Substitution. *Pattern Recognition*, 37(3), 469–474. doi:10.1016/j.patcog.2003.08.007

Chandramouli, R., Memon, N., & Rabbani, M. (2002). Digital Watermarking. Encyclopedia of Imaging Science and Technology.

Cox, I., Kilian, J., Shamoon, T., & Leighton, F. (1997, December). Secure Spread Spectrum Watermarking for Multimedia. *IEEE Transactions on Image Processing*, *6*(12), 1673–1687. doi:10.1109/83.650120 PMID:18285237

Dajun, H., Qibin, S., & Tian, Q. (2003). A Semi-fragile Object based Video Authentication System. *Proceedings of the International Symposium on Circuits and Systems*, (pp. 814 – 817). doi:10.1109/ISCAS.2003.1205144

Dili, R., & Mwangi, E. (2007). An Image Watermarking Method Based on the Singular Value Transformation and the Wavelet Transformation.*Proceedings of IEEE AFRICON*.

Ding, Y., Zheng, X., Zhao, Y., & Liu, G. (2010, July). A Video Watermarking Algorithm Resistant to Copy Attack.*Proceedings of 3rd International Symposium on Electronic Commerce and Security*. doi:10.1109/ISECS.2010.70

Donoho, D. (2006, April). Compressed Sensing. *IEEE Transactions on Information Theory*, *52*(4), 1289–1306. doi:10.1109/TIT.2006.871582

Ejima, M., & Miyazaki, A. (2000, August). A Wavelet Based Watermarking for Digital Images and Videos. *IEEE International Conference on Image Processing*, (pp. 678 – 681). doi:10.1109/ICIP.2000.899545

El-Gayyar (2006, May). *Watermarking Techniques – Spatial Domain Digital Rights Seminar*. Media Informatics, University of Bonn, Germany.

Elbasi, E. (2007). Robust MPEG Video Watermarking in Wavelet Domain. *Trakya University Journal of Science*, *8*(2), 87–93.

Essaouabi, A., & Ibnelhaj, E. (2009, July). A 3D Wavelet based Method for Digital Video Watermarking.*Proceedings of the 4th IEEE Intelligent Information Hiding and Multimedia Signal Processing*. doi:10.1109/NDT.2009.5272116

Fakhr, M. (2012, December). Robust Watermarking Using Compressed Sensing Framework with Application to MP3 Audio. *The International Journal of Multimedia & Its Applications*, *4*(6), 27–43. doi:10.5121/ijma.2012.4603

Fan, L., & Yanmei, F., (2006, November). A DWT based Video Watermarking Algorithm Applying DS-CAMA. *IEEE Region 10 Conference TENCON 2006*.

Ganic, E., & Eskicioglu, A. (2004). Secure DWT-SVD Domain Image Watermarking Embedding Data in All Frequencies.*ACM Multimedia and Security Workshop 2004*.

Gupta, A., & Raval, M. (2012, August). A Robust and Secure Watermarking Scheme Based on Singular Value Replacement. *Sadhana*, *37*(4), 425–440. doi:10.1007/s12046-012-0089-x

Hartung, F., & Kutter, M. (1999, July). Multimedia Watermarking Techniques. *Proceedings of the IEEE*, *87*(7), 1085–1103. doi:10.1109/5.771066

Hernandez, J., Amado, M., & Perez-Gonzalez, F. (2000, January). DCT domain Watermarking Techniques for Still Image: Detector Performance Analysis and a New Structure. *IEEE Transactions on Image Processing*, *9*(1), 55–68. doi:10.1109/83.817598 PMID:18255372

Huang, C., & Wu, J. (2004, February). Attacking Visible Watermarking Schemes. *IEEE Transactions on Multimedia, 6*(1), 16–30. doi:10.1109/TMM.2003.819579

Huang, F., & Guan, Z. (2004). A Hybrid SVD-DCT Watermarking Method Based on LPSNR. *Pattern Recognition Letters, 25*(15), 1769–1775. doi:10.1016/j.patrec.2004.07.003

Hussein, J., & Mohammed, A. (2009). Robust Video Watermarking using Multiband Wavelet Transform. *IJCSI International Journal of Computer Science Issues, 6*(1), 44–49.

Kamlakar, M., Gosavi, C., & Patankar, A. (2012, April). Single Channel Watermarking for Video Using Block based SVD. *International Journal of Advances in Computing and Information Researches, 1*(2).

Katzenbeisser, S., & Petitcolas, F. (2000). *Information Hiding Techniques for Steganography and Digital Watermarking*. Norwood, MA: Artech House, Inc.

Kim, K., & Ro, Y. (2004, November). Enhancement Methods of Image Quality in Screen Mark Attack. IWDW 2003, LNCS 2939, 474 – 482.

Koz, A., & Alatan, A. (2008, March). Oblivious Spatio-Temporal Watermarking of Digital Video by Exploiting the Human Visual System. *IEEE Transactions on Circuits and Systems for Video Technology, 18*(3), 326–337. doi:10.1109/TCSVT.2008.918446

Kutter, M., & Petitcolas, F. (1999, January). A Fair Benchmark for Image Watermarking Systems. *Electronic Imaging Security and Watermarking of Multimedia Contents, 3657*, 25–27.

Langelaar, G., Setyawan, I., & Lagendijk, R. (2000, September). Watermarking of Digital Image and Video Data – A State of Art Review. *IEEE Signal Processing Magazine, 17*(5), 20–46. doi:10.1109/79.879337

Lee, Y., & Chen, L. (2000, June). High Capacity Image Steganographic Model. *IEEE Proceedings of Vision Image and Signal Processing*, (pp. 288 – 294).

Lu, C., & Liao, H. (2001). Video Object based Watermarking: A Rotation and Flipping Resilient Scheme. *Proceedings of International Conference on Image Processing*.

Mansouri, A., & Mahmoudi, A. (2009, June). SVD based Digital Image Watermarking using Complex Wavelet Transform. *Sadhana, 34*(3), 393–406. doi:10.1007/s12046-009-0016-y

Mostafa, S., Tolba, A., Abdelkader, F., & Elhindy, H. (2009, August). Video Watermarking Scheme Based on Principal Component Analysis and Wavelet Transform. *IJCSNS International Journal of Computer Science and Network Security, 9*(8), 45–52.

Paul, R. (2011). Review of Robust Video Watermarking Techniques. *NCCSE, 3*, 90–95.

Petitcolas, F. (2000, September). Watermarking Schemes Evaluation. *IEEE Signal Processing Magazine, 17*(5), 58–64. doi:10.1109/79.879339

Podilchuk, C., & Delp, E. (2001). Digital Watermarking: Algorithms and Applications. *IEEE Signal Processing Magazine, 18*(4), 33–46. doi:10.1109/79.939835

Preda, R., & Vizireanu, D. (2007, September). Blind Watermarking Capacity Analysis of MPEG2 Coded Video.*Proceedings of Conference of Telecommunications in Modern Satellite, Cable and Broadcasting Services, Serbia*, 465 – 468. doi:10.1109/TELSKS.2007.4376042

Raghavendra, K., & Chetan, K. (2009, December). A Blind and Robust Watermarking Scheme with Scrambled Watermark for Video Authentication.*Proceedings of IEEE International Conference on Internet Multimedia Services Architecture and Applications*. doi:10.1109/IMSAA.2009.5439475

Rajab, L., Al-Khatib, T., & Ai-Haj, A. (2008, December). Hybrid DWT-SVD Video Watermarking. *Proceedings of International Conference on Innovations in Information Technology*.

Ramalingam, M. (2011). Stego Machine – Video Steganography using Modified LSB Algorithm. *World Academy of Science. Engineering and Technology*, *74*, 502–505.

Raval, M., Joshi, M., Rege, P., & Parulkar, S. (2011, December). Image Tampering Detection Using Compressive Sensing Based Watermarking Scheme. In *Proceedings of MVIP 2011*.

Raval, M., & Rege, P. (2003). Discrete Wavelet Transform Based Multiple Watermarking Scheme. *Proceedings of the Convergent Technologies for the Asia-Pacific Region*, *3*, 935–938.

Santhi, V., & Thangavelu, A. (2009, October). DWT SVD Combined Full Band Robust Watermarking Technique for Color Images in YUV Color Space. *International Journal of Computer Theory and Engineering*, *1*(4).

Serdean, C., Ambroze, M., Tomlinson, M., & Wade, G. (2002, June). Combating Geometrical Attacks in a DWT based Blind Video Watermarking System. *IEEE Region 8 International Symposium on Video/Image Processing and Multimedia Communications, Zadar*.

Sheikh, M., & Baraniuk, R. (2007, September). Blind Error Free Detection of Transform Domain Watermarks.*IEEE International Conference on Image Processing*.

Shoemaker, C. (2002). *Hidden bits: A Survey of Techniques for Digital Watermarking. Independent Study, EER 290, Prof.* Rudko.

Sridevi, T., Krishnaveni, B., Vijayakumar, V., & Ramadevi, Y., (2010, September). A Video Watermarking Algorithm for MPEG Videos. *A2CWiC 2010 – Amrita ACM-W Celebration of Women in Computing*.

Tagliasacchi, M., Valenzise, G., Tubaro, S., Cancelli, G., & Barni, M. (2009). A Compressive Sensing Based Watermarking Scheme for Sparse Image Tampering Identification.*Proc. ICIP 2009*, (pp. 1265 – 1268).

Thanki, R., Trivedi, R., Kher, R., & Vyas, D. (2011). Digital Watermarking Using White Gaussian Noise (WGN) in Spatial Domain. *Proceedings of International Conference on Innovative Science & Engineering Technology (ICISET)*, (pp. 38 – 42).

Tiesheng, F., Guiqiang, L., Chunyi, D., & Danhua, W. (2013, May). A Digital Image Watermarking Method Based on the Theory of Compressed Sensing. *International Journal Automation and Control Engineering*, *2*(2), 56–61.

Tirkel, A., Rankin, G., Schyndel, R., Ho, W., Mee, N., & Osborne, C. (1993). Electronics Watermark. *DICTA 93*. Macquarie University.

Tropp, J., & Gilbert, A. (2007, December). Signal Recovery from Random Measurements via Orthogonal Matching Pursuit. *IEEE Transactions on Information Theory*, *53*(12), 4655–4666. doi:10.1109/TIT.2007.909108

Voloshynovskiy, S., Pereira, S., Pun, T., Eggers, J. J., & Su, J. K. (2001, August). Attacks on Digital Watermarks: Classification, Estimation based Attacks and Benchmarks. *IEEE Communications Magazine*, *39*(8), 118–126. doi:10.1109/35.940053

Wolfgang, R., Podilchuk, C., & Delp, E. J. (1999, July). Perceptual Watermarks for Digital Images and Video. *Proceedings of the IEEE*, *87*(7), 1277–1281. doi:10.1109/5.771067

Zhang, X., Qian, Z., Ren, Y., & Feng, G. (2011). Watermarking with Flexible Self-recovery Quality based on Compressive Sensing and Compositive Reconstruction. *IEEE Transactions on Information Forensics and Security*, *6*(4), 1123–1132. doi:10.1109/TIFS.2011.2159208

Compilation of References

Abburu, S. (2012). Knowledge based Semantic Annotation Generation of Music. *International Journal of Computers and Applications*, *47*(8), 8–12. doi:10.5120/7206-9990

Abdelali, A. B., Nidhal Krifa, M., Touil, L., Mtibaa, A., & Bourennane, E. (2009). A study of the color-structure descriptor for shot boundary detection. *International Journal of Sciences and Techniques of Automatic control and computer engineering*, 956-971.

Abdeljaoued, Y., Ebrahimi, T., Christopoulos, C., & Ivars, I. M. (2000, September). A new algorithm for shot boundary detection.*Proceedings of the 10th European Signal Processing Conference* (pp. 151-154). SPIE.

Abido, A. (2002). Optimal power flow using particle swarm optimization. *International Journal of Electrical Power & Energy Systems*, *24*(7), 563–571. doi:10.1016/S0142-0615(01)00067-9

Abut, H., & Öztürk, Y. (1997, April). Interactive Classroom for DSP/Communications Courses.*Proc. of ICASSP 1997*.

Adamatzky, A. (1994). *Identification of Cellular Automata*. London: Taylor & Francis Ltd.

Adcock, J., Girgensohn, A., Cooper, M., Liu, T., Wilcox, L., & Rieffel, E. (2004). Fxpal experiments for TRECVID 2004.*Proceedings of the TREC Video Retrieval Evaluation (TRECVID)*, (pp. 70-81).

Aghasi, A., & Romberg, J. (2015). *Convex Cardinal Shape Composition*. ArXiv preprint arXiv: 1501.01347

Aghasi, A., & Romberg, J. (2013). Sparse Shape Reconstruction. *SIAM Journal on Imaging Sciences*, *6*(4), 2075–2108. doi:10.1137/130911573

Agrawal, M. (2007, August). *Design Approaches for Multimodal Biometric System*. (M. Tech). Thesis, Department of Computer Science and Engineering, IIT, Kanpur.

Ahmed, A., Recht, B., & Romberg, J. (2014). Blind Deconvolution using Convex Programming. *IEEE Transactions on Information Theory*, *60*(3), 1711–1732. doi:10.1109/TIT.2013.2294644

Ahmed, A., & Romberg, J. (2012). Compressive Multiplexers for Correlated Signals.*2012 IEEE Conference Record of the Forty Sixth Asilomar Conference on Signals, Systems and Computers (ASILOMAR)*. doi:10.1109/ACSSC.2012.6489159

Alexandrov, A. D., Ma, W. Y., El Abbadi, A., & Manjunath, B. S. (1995, March). Adaptive filtering and indexing for image databases. In *IS&T/SPIE's Symposium on Electronic Imaging: Science & Technology* (pp. 12-23). International Society for Optics and Photonics.

Alfonceca, M., Cebrian, M., &Ortega, A. (2006). A Fitness Function for Computer-Generated Music using Genetic Algorithms. *WSEAS Trans. On Information Science & Applications*, *3*(3), 518-525.

Alghoniemy, M., & Tewfik, A. H. (2001). A network flow model for playlist generation.*Proc IEEE Intl Conf Multimedia and Expo.*

Allombert, G. A., & Desainte-Catherine, D. (2007). A system of interactive scores based on Petri nets. *Proceedings of the4th Sound and Music Computing Conference* (pp. 158-165).

Amir, A., Berg, M., Chang, S. F., Hsu, W., Iyengar, G., Lin, C. Y., & Smith, J. R. (2003). IBM research TRECVID-2003 video retrieval system. *NIST TRECVID-2003.*

Anger, H. O. (1958). Scintillation camera. *The Review of Scientific Instruments, 29*(1), 27–33. doi:10.1063/1.1715998

Antti, E., & Anssi, K. (2000). Musical instrument recognition using cepstral coefficients and temporal features. *Proceedings of the2000 IEEE International Conference*Acoustics, Speech, and Signal Processing ICASSP'00.

Apostolidis, E., & Mezaris, V. (2014, May). Fast shot segmentation combining global and local visual descriptors. *Proceedings of 2014 IEEE International Conference on Acoustics, Speech and Signal Processing (ICASSP)* (pp. 6583-6587). IEEE. doi:10.1109/ICASSP.2014.6854873

Ardakany, A. R., & Joula, A. M. (2012). Gender recognition based on edge histogram. *International Journal of Computer Theory and Engineering, 4*(2), 127–130. doi:10.7763/IJCTE.2012.V4.436

Arena, S., Caramma, M., & Lancini, R. (2000). Digital Watermarking Applied to MPEG-2 Coded Video Sequences Exploiting Space and Frequency Masking.*Proceedings of International Conference on Image Processing.* doi:10.1109/ICIP.2000.900989

Ashboum, J. (2014). *Biometrics in the World - The Cloud, Mobile Technology and Pervasive Identity.* Berlin: Springer International Publishing.

Asif, M., & Romberg, J. (2014). Sparse Recovery of Streaming Signals Using L1 Homotopy. *IEEE Transactions on Signal Processing, 62*(16), 4209–4223. doi:10.1109/TSP.2014.2328981

Aucouturier, J. J., & Pachet, F. (2002). Scaling up music playlist generation. *Proceedings of the 2002 IEEE International Conference on Multimedia and Expo ICME'02* (Vol. 1, pp. 105-108). IEEE. doi:doi:10.1109/ICME.2002.1035729 doi:10.1109/ICME.2002.1035729

Avanzato, R. (2001). Student Use of Personal Digital Assistants in a Computer Engineering Course. *Proc. of 31st ASEE/IEEE Frontiers in Education Conference.* doi:10.1109/FIE.2001.963668

Baber, J., Afzulpurkar, N., Dailey, M. N., & Bakhtyar, M. (2011, July). Shot boundary detection from videos using entropy and local descriptor. *Proceedings of the 2011 17th International Conference on Digital Signal Processing (DSP)* (pp. 1-6). IEEE. doi:10.1109/ICDSP.2011.6004918

Bach, J. R., Fuller, C., Gupta, A., Hampapur, A., Horowitz, B., Humphrey, R., . . . Shu, C. F. (1996, March). Virage image search engine: an open framework for image management. In Electronic Imaging: Science & Technology (pp. 76-87). International Society for Optics and Photonics.

Bai, L., Lao, S. Y., Liu, H. T., & Bu, J. (2008, July). Video shot boundary detection using petri-net. *Proceedings of the 2008 International Conference on Machine Learning and Cybernetics* (Vol. 5, pp. 3047-3051). IEEE.

Bandyopadhyay, S. (2005). Satellite image classification using genetically guided fuzzy clustering with spatial information. *International Journal of Remote Sensing, 26*(3), 579–593. doi:10.1080/01431160512331316432

Banerjee, S., Saha, D., & Jana, N. D. (2015). Color image segmentation using cauchy-mutated PSO. *Advances in Intelligent Systems and Computing, 343,* 239–250. doi:10.1007/978-81-322-2268-2_26

Bangaleea, R., & Rughooputh, H. (2002). Performance Improvement of Spread Spectrum Spatial Domain Watermarking Scheme Through Diversity and Attack Characterization.*IEEE Conference Africon* (pp. 293 – 298).

Bao, Z., Han, B., & Wu, S. (2006). A novel clustering algorithm based on variable precision rough-fuzzy sets. In *Computational Intelligence* (pp. 284–289). Springer Berlin Heidelberg. doi:10.1007/978-3-540-37275-2_36

Baraniuk, R. (2007, July). Compressive Sensing. *IEEE Signal Processing Magazine, 24*(4), 118–124. doi:10.1109/MSP.2007.4286571

Baratè, A. (2008). *Music Description and Processing: An Approach Based on Petri Nets and XML.* INTECH Open Access Publisher.

Barate, A., Haus, G., & Ludovico, L. A. (2007). Petri nets applicability to music analysis and composition.*Proceedings of the 2007 International Computer Music Conference, International Computer Music Association, International Computer Music Conference* (pp. 97-100).

Barber, D. C. (2000). Electrical impedance tomography. In J. D. Bronzino (Ed.), *Biomedical Engineering Handbook* (2nd ed.; Vol. 1). Boca Raton, FL: CRC Press/IEEE Press.

Barbosa, D., Dietenbeck, T., Schaerer, J., D'hooge, J., Friboulet, D., & Bernard, O. (2012). B-spline explicit active surfaces: An efficient framework for real-time 3-D region-based segmentation. *Image Processing. IEEE Transactions on, 21*(1), 241–251.

Barbu, Ciobanu, & Costin. (2002). *Unsupervised Color - Based Image Recognition Using A Lab Feature Extraction Technique.* Academic Press.

Barbu, T. (2009). Novel automatic video cut detection technique using Gabor filtering. *Computers & Electrical Engineering, 35*(5), 712–721. doi:10.1016/j.compeleceng.2009.02.003

Barron, J. L., Fleet, D. J., & Beauchemin, S. S. (1994). Performance of optical flow techniques. *International Journal of Computer Vision, 12*(1), 43–77. doi:10.1007/BF01420984

Bashir, F. I., Khokhar, A. A., & Schonfeld, D. (2007). Real-time motion trajectory-based indexing and retrieval of video sequences. *IEEE Transactions on* Multimedia, *9*(1), 58–65.

Bay, H., Ess, A., Tuytelaars, T., & Van Gool, L. (2008). Speeded-up robust features (SURF). *Computer Vision and Image Understanding, 110*(3), 346–359. doi:10.1016/j.cviu.2007.09.014

Bebis, G., Boyle, R., Parvin, B., Koracin, D., Paragios, N., Tanveer, S.-M., & Malzbender, T. et al. (Eds.). (2007). *ISVC, Part II, LNCS 4842. Springer-Verlag Berlin Heidelberg.*

Beckmann, N., Kriegel, H. P., Schneider, R., & Seeger, B. (1990). The R*-tree: an efficient and robust access method for points and rectangles: Vol. 19. *No. 2.* ACM.

Bellini, P., Barthelemy, J., Bruno, I., Nesi, P., & Spinu, M. B. (2003). Multimedia music sharing among mediateques: Archives and distribution to their attendees. *Applied Artificial Intelligence, 17*(8-9), 773–795. doi:10.1080/713827259

Belongie, S., Carson, C., Greenspan, H., & Malik, J. (1998, January). Color-and texture-based image segmentation using EM and its application to content-based image retrieval. In *Computer Vision, 1998. Sixth International Conference on* (pp. 675-682). IEEE. doi:10.1109/ICCV.1998.710790

Bender, W., Gruhl, D., Morimoto, N., & Lu, A. (1996). Techniques for Data Hiding. *IBM Systems Journal, 35*(3&4), 313–336. doi:10.1147/sj.353.0313

Bentley, J. L. (1980). Multidimensional divide-and-conquer. *Communications of the ACM, 23*(4), 214–229. doi:10.1145/358841.358850

Bernard, W. E., & Jacobson, P. A. (1999). *U.S. Patent No. 5,918,213*. Washington, DC: U.S. Patent and Trademark Office.

Bescós, J., Cisneros, G., Martínez, J. M., Menéndez, J. M., & Cabrera, J. (2005). A unified model for techniques on video-shot transition detection. *IEEE Transactions on* Multimedia, *7*(2), 293–307.

Besiris, D., Laskaris, N., Fotopoulou, F., & Economou, G. (2007, October). Key frame extraction in video sequences: a vantage points approach. *Proceedings of the IEEE 9th Workshop on Multimedia Signal Processing MMSP '07* (pp. 434-437). IEEE. doi:10.1109/MMSP.2007.4412909

Bezdek, J. C. (1980). A Convergence theorem for fuzzy ISODATA clustering algorithm. *IEEE Transactions on Pattern Analysis and Machine Intelligence, 2*(1), 1–8. doi:10.1109/TPAMI.1980.4766964 PMID:22499617

Bhatkande, V. N. (1934). *Hindusthani Sangeet Paddhati*. Sangeet Karyalaya.

Bhattacharyya, M., & De, D. (2012). An Approach to identify Thhat of Indian Classical Music. *Proceedings of International Conference on Communications, Devices and Intelligent Systems (CODIS)* (pp. 592-595). IEEE. doi:10.1109/CODIS.2012.6422267

Bhattacharyya, S., Dutta, P., & Maulik, U. (2008). Self organizing neural network (SONN) based gray scale object extractor with a multilevel sigmoidal (MUSIG) activation function. *Foundations of Computing and Decision Sciences, 33*(2), 131–165.

Bhattacharyya, S., & Maulik, U. (2013). *Soft Computing - Image and Multimedia Data Processing*. Heidelberg, Germany: Springer. doi:10.1007/978-3-642-40255-5

Bhattacharyya, S., Maulik, U., & Dutta, P. (2009). High-speed target tracking by fuzzy hostility-induced segmentation of optical flow field. *Applied Soft Computing, 9*(1), 126–134. doi:10.1016/j.asoc.2008.03.012

Bhaumik, H., Bhattacharyya, S., & Chakraborty, S. (2014, April). Video Shot Segmentation Using Spatio-Temporal Fuzzy Hostility Index and Automatic Threshold. *Proceedings of the 2014 Fourth International Conference on Communication Systems and Network Technologies (CSNT)* (pp. 501-506). IEEE. doi:10.1109/CSNT.2014.106

Bhaumik, H., Bhattacharyya, S., Das, M., & Chakraborty, S. (2015, February). Enhancement of perceptual quality in static video summarization using minimal spanning tree approach. *Proceedings of the 2015 IEEE International Conference on Signal Processing, Informatics, Communication and Energy Systems (SPICES)* (pp. 1-7). IEEE. doi:10.1109/SPICES.2015.7091401

Bhaumik, H., Bhattacharyya, S., Dutta, S., & Chakraborty, S. (2014, September). Towards redundancy reduction in storyboard representation for static video summarization. *Proceedings of the 2014 International Conference on Advances in Computing, Communications and Informatics (ICACCI)* (pp. 344-350). IEEE. doi:10.1109/ICACCI.2014.6968601

Bijnens, B. (1997). *Exploiting Radiofrequency Information in Echocardiography*. (Ph.D. dissertation). Catholic University of Leuven, Belgium.

Bimbo, A. D., Vicario, E., & Zingoni, D. (1995). Symbolic description and visual querying of image sequences using spatio-temporal logic. *IEEE Transactions on* Knowledge and Data Engineering, *7*(4), 609–622.

Bloch, F. (1946). Nuclear induction. *Physical Review, 70*(7-8), 460–474. doi:10.1103/PhysRev.70.460

Boccignone, G., Chianese, A., Moscato, V., & Picariello, A. (2005). Foveated shot detection for video segmentation. *IEEE Transactions on* Circuits and Systems for Video Technology, *15*(3), 365–377.

Bonwell, C., & Eison, G. (1991). ASHE-ERIC Higher Education Report: Vol. 1. *Active learning: Creating excitement in the classroom*. Washington, DC: George Washington University.

Boone, J. M. (2000). X-ray production, interaction and detection in diagnostic imaging. In J. Beutel, H. L. Kundel, & R. L. Van Metter (Eds.), *Handbook of Medical Imaging* (Vol. I). Washington, DC: SPIE Press. doi:10.1117/3.832716.ch1

Boreczky, J. S., & Wilcox, L. D. (1998, May). A hidden Markov model framework for video segmentation using audio and image features. *Proceedings of the 1998 IEEE International Conference onAcoustics, Speech and Signal Processing* (*Vol. 6*, pp. 3741-3744). IEEE. doi:10.1109/ICASSP.1998.679697

Bresin, R. (1998). Artificial neural networks based models for automatic performance of musical scores. *Journal of New Music Research. Taylor and Francis*, *27*(3), 239–270. doi:10.1080/09298219808570748

Bronzino, J. D. (1995). *Biomedical Engineering Handbook*. Boca Raton, FL: CRC Press/IEEE Press.

Brown, J. C. (1999). Computer identification of musical instruments using pattern recognition with cepstral coefficients as features. *The Journal of the Acoustical Society of America*, *105*(3), 1933–1941. doi:10.1121/1.426728 PMID:10089614

Brusilovsky. (n.d.). *Methods and Techniques of Adaptive Hypermedia*. Academic Press.

Budinger, T. F., & VanBrocklin, H. F. (1995). Positron emission tomography. In J. D. Bronzino (Ed.), *Biomedical Engineering Handbook*. Boca Raton, FL: CRC Press.

Burrus, C. S., Gopinath, R. A., & Guo, H. (1998). *Introduction to Wavelets and Wavelet Transforms*. Prentice Hall.

Bushberg, J. T., Seibert, J. A., Leidholdt, E. M., & Boone, J. M. (2002). *The Essential Physics of Medical Imaging*. Baltimore, MD: Lippincott Williams & Wilkins.

Cahuina, E. J., & Camara Chavez, G. (2013, August). A new method for static video summarization using local descriptors and video temporal segmentation. *Proceedings of the 2013 26th SIBGRAPI-Conference on Graphics, Patterns and Images (SIBGRAPI)* (pp. 226-233). IEEE. doi:10.1109/SIBGRAPI.2013.39

Calic, J., & Izuierdo, E. (2002, April). Efficient key-frame extraction and video analysis. *Proceedings of the International Conference on Information Technology: Coding and Computing '02* (pp. 28-33). IEEE. doi:10.1109/ITCC.2002.1000355

Callan, C. G. Jr, Coleman, S., & Jackiw, R. (1970). A new improved energy-momentum tensor. *Annals of Physics*, *59*(1), 42–73. doi:10.1016/0003-4916(70)90394-5

Calonder, M., Lepetit, V., Strecha, C., & Fua, P. (2010). Brief: Binary robust independent elementary features. *Computer Vision–ECCV*, *2010*, 778–792.

Candès, E., & Romberg, J., (2005, October). *L1-Magic: Recovery of Sparse Signals via Convex Programming*. Academic Press.

Candès, E., Demanet, L., & Donoho, D., (2005). Fast Discrete Curvelet Transforms. *Applied and Computational Mathematics*, 1 – 44.

Candès, E. (2006). Compressive Sampling. In *Proceedings of the International Congress of Mathematicians*.

Canny, J. (1986). A computational approach to edge detection. *IEEE Transactions on Pattern Analysis and Machine Intelligence*, (6), 679-698.

Canny, J. (1986). A computational approach to edge detection. *IEEE Transactions on Pattern Analysis and Machine Intelligence*, *8*(, 6), 679–698. doi:10.1109/TPAMI.1986.4767851 PMID:21869365

Carson, C., Belongie, S., Greenspan, H., & Malik, J. (2002). Blobworld: Image segmentation using expectation-maximization and its application to image querying. *Pattern Analysis and Machine Intelligence. IEEE Transactions on, 24*(8), 1026–1038.

Castellano, M. A., Bharucha, J. J., & Krumhansl, C. L. (1984). Tonal hierarchies in the music of north India. *Journal of Experimental Psychology. General, 113*(3), 394–412. doi:10.1037/0096-3445.113.3.394 PMID:6237169

Černeková, Z., Pitas, I., & Nikou, C. (2006). Information theory-based shot cut/fade detection and video summarization. *IEEE Transactions on* Circuits and Systems for Video Technology, *16*(1), 82–91.

Chakrabarty, S., Roy, S., & De, D. (2014). Pervasive Diary in Music Rhythm Education: A Context-Aware Learning Tool Using Genetic Algorithm. In Advanced Computing, Networking and Informatics (Vol. 1, pp. 669-677). Springer International Publishing. doi:doi:10.1007/978-3-319-07353-8_77 doi:10.1007/978-3-319-07353-8_77

Chakrabarty, S., & De, D. (2012). Quality Measure Model of Music Rhythm using Genetic Algorithm. *Proceedings of International Conference on Radar, Communication and Computing (ICRCC)* (pp. 125-130). IEEE. doi:10.1109/ICRCC.2012.6450561

Chakraborty & Chakraborty. (2008). Fuzzy linear and polynomial regression modelling of IF-THEN fuzzy rulebase. *IJUFKBS, 16*(2), 219-232.

Chakraborty, S., & De, D. (2012). Pattern Classification of Indian Classical Ragas based on Object Oriented Concepts. *International Journal of Advanced Computer engineering & Architecture, 2*, 285-294.

Chakraborty, S., De, D., & Roy, K. (2011). A Knowledge Sharing Virtual Community for identification of different Indian Classical Ragas. NCICT, Allied Publishers.

Chakraborty, S., & De, D. (2012). Object Oriented Classification and Pattern Recognition of Indian Classical Ragas. *Proceedings of the 1st International Conference on Recent Advances in Information Technology (RAIT)*. IEEE. doi:10.1109/RAIT.2012.6194630

Chan, C., & Alexander, W. (2011). Shot boundary detection using genetic algorithm optimization. *Proceedings of the 2011 IEEE International Symposium on Multimedia (ISM)* (pp. 327-332). IEEE. doi:10.1109/ISM.2011.58

Chan, C., & Cheng, L. (2004). Hiding Data in Images by Simple LSB Substitution. *Pattern Recognition, 37*(3), 469–474. doi:10.1016/j.patcog.2003.08.007

Chanda, B., Majumder, D.D. (n.d.). *Digital Image Processing and Analysis.* PHI Publication.

Chandler, D. M., & Hemami, S. S. (2005). Dynamic contrast-based quantization for lossy wavelet image compression. *IEEE Transactions on Image Processing, 14*(4), 397–410. doi:10.1109/TIP.2004.841196 PMID:15825476

Chandramouli, R., Memon, N., & Rabbani, M. (2002). Digital Watermarking. Encyclopedia of Imaging Science and Technology.

Chang, L. Y., & Hsu, W. H. (2009, June). Foreground segmentation for static video via multi-core and multi-modal graph cut. In *Multimedia and Expo, 2009. ICME 2009. IEEE International Conference on* (pp. 1362-1365). IEEE. doi:10.1109/ICME.2009.5202756

Chang, S. F. (1995, October). Compressed-domain techniques for image/video indexing and manipulation. In *Image Processing, 1995. Proceedings., International Conference on* (Vol. 1, pp. 314-317). IEEE.

Chang, S. F. (1996). Compressed-domain content-based image and video retrieval. In Multimedia Communications and Video Coding (pp. 375-382). Springer US. doi:10.1007/978-1-4613-0403-6_46

Chang, S. F., & Smith, J. R. (1995, October). Single color extraction and image query. In *Image processing, 1995. Proceedings., International conference on* (Vol. 3, pp. 528-531). IEEE.

Chang, S., Smith, J. R., Meng, H. J., Wang, H., & Zhong, D. (1997). *Finding Images/Video in Large Archives: Columbia's Content-Based VisualQuery Project.* Academic Press.

Chang, H. S., Sull, S., & Lee, S. U. (1999). Efficient video indexing scheme for content-based retrieval. *IEEE Transactions on* Circuits and Systems for Video Technology, *9*(8), 1269–1279.

Chang, S. F., Chen, W., Meng, H. J., Sundaram, H., & Zhong, D. (1998). A fully automated content-based video search engine supporting spatiotemporal queries. *Circuits and Systems for Video Technology. IEEE Transactions on, 8*(5), 602–615.

Chang, S. F., Chen, W., Meng, H. J., Sundaram, H., & Zhong, D. (1998). A fully automated content-based video search engine supporting spatiotemporal queries. *IEEE Transactions on* Circuits and Systems for Video Technology, *8*(5), 602–615.

Chang, S. F., & Smith, J. R. (1995, April). Extracting multidimensional signal features for content-based visual query. In *Visual Communications and Image Processing'95* (pp. 995–1006). International Society for Optics and Photonics. doi:10.1117/12.206632

Chasanis, V., Likas, A., & Galatsanos, N. (2009). Simultaneous detection of abrupt cuts and dissolves in videos using support vector machines. *Pattern Recognition Letters, 30*(1), 55–65. doi:10.1016/j.patrec.2008.08.015

Chatzigiorgaki, M., & Skodras, A. N. (2009, July). Real-time keyframe extraction towards video content identification. *Proceedings of the 2009 16th International Conference on Digital Signal Processing* (pp. 1-6). IEEE. doi:10.1109/ICDSP.2009.5201141

Chavez, G. C., Precioso, F., Cord, M., Philipp-Foliguet, S., & Araujo, A. D. A. (2006). Shot boundary detection at TRECVID 2006.*Proc. TREC Video Retrieval Evaluation.*

Chemillier, M. (2004). Synchronization of musical words. *Theoretical Computer Science, 310*(1-3), 35–60. doi:10.1016/S0304-3975(03)00309-8

Chen, F., Meyers, B., & Yaron, D. (2000, July). *Using Handhelds Devices for Tests in Classes.* Carnegie Mellon University School of Computer Science Technical Report, No. CMUCS-00-152, and Human Computer Interaction Institute Technical Report CMU-HCII-00-101.

Chen, G., Hu, T., Guo, X., & Meng, X. (2009, October). A fast region-based image segmentation based on least square method. In *Systems, Man and Cybernetics, 2009. SMC 2009. IEEE International Conference on* (pp. 972-977). IEEE. doi:10.1109/ICSMC.2009.5346073

Chen, W., & Chang, S. F. (1999, December). Motion trajectory matching of video objects. In *Electronic Imaging* (pp. 544–553). International Society for Optics and Photonics.

Chen, X., Udupa, J. K., Bagci, U., Zhuge, Y., & Yao, J. (2012). Medical image segmentation by combining graph cuts and oriented active appearance models. *Image Processing. IEEE Transactions on, 21*(4), 2035–2046.

Chen, Y., & Wang, J. Z. (2002). A region-based fuzzy feature matching approach to content-based image retrieval. *Pattern Analysis and Machine Intelligence. IEEE Transactions on, 24*(9), 1252–1267.

Chisholm, E., & Kolda, T. G. (1999). *New term weighting formulas for the vector space method in information retrieval.* Technical Report ORNL-TM-13756. Oak Ridge National Laboratory.

Chiu, P., Girgensohn, A., Polak, W., Rieffel, E., & Wilcox, L. (2000). A genetic algorithm for video segmentation and summarization. *Proceedings of the 2000 IEEE International Conference on Multimedia and Expo ICME '00* (Vol. 3, pp. 1329-1332). IEEE. doi:10.1109/ICME.2000.871011

Choras, R. S. (2007). Image feature extraction techniques and their applications for CBIR and biometrics systems. *International Journal of Biology and Biomedical Engineering, 1*(1), 6-16.

Chordia, P. (2006). *Automatic Transcription of Solo TablaMusic* [Ph.D. diss.]. Stanford University.

Chordia, P., Sastry, A., & Albin, A. (2010). Evaluating Multiple Viewpoint Models of Tabla Sequences. *Proceedings of 3rd International workshop on Machine learning and music* (pp. 21-24). ACM.

Chordia, P. (2004). Automatic raga classification using spectrally derived tone profiles. In *Proceedings of the International Computer Music Conference.*

Chordia, P. (2006). Automatic raag classification of pitch tracked performances using pitch-class and pitch-class dyad distributions. *Proceedings of International Computer Music Conference.*

Chordia, P., & Rae, A. (2008).TablaGyan: A System for RealtimeTabla Recognition and Resynthesis. In *Proceedings of the International Computer Music Conference.*

Cho, S. B., & Lee, J. Y. (2002). A human-oriented image retrieval system using interactive genetic algorithm. *Systems, Man and Cybernetics, Part A: Systems and humans. IEEE Transactions on, 32*(3), 452–458.

Cho, Z. H., Jones, J. P., & Singh, M. (1993). *Foundations of Medical Imaging.* New York: John Wiley & Sons.

Chuan, C. H., & Chew, E. (2005, July). Polyphonic audio key finding using the spiral array CEG algorithm. *Proceedings of the IEEE International Conference on Multimedia and Expo ICME '05* (pp. 21-24). IEEE.

Clampitt, D. (2007). The legacy of John Clough in mathematical music theory. *Journal of Mathematics and Music, Taylor and Francis, 1*(2), 73–78. doi:10.1080/17459730701494710

Clayton, M. (2000). *Time in Indian Music: Rhythm, Metre, and Form in North Indian RâgPerformance.* Oxford, UK: Oxford University Press.

Coden & Brown. (2001). *Speech Transcript Analysis for Automatic Search.* Academic Press.

Cointet, J. P., & Roth, C. (2009). Socio-semantic dynamics in a blog network. *Proceedings of theInternational Conference onComputational Science and Engineering.* doi:10.1109/CSE.2009.105

Conklin, D., & Witten, I. H. (1995). Multiple viewpoint systems for music prediction. *Journal of New Music Research, 24*(1), 51–73. doi:10.1080/09298219508570672

Conte, R., Gilbert, N., Bonelli, G., & Helbing, D. (2011). FuturICT and social sciences: Big Data, big thinking. *Zeitschrift für Soziologie, 40*, 412–413.

Cooper, M., & Foote, J. (2005, July). Discriminative techniques for keyframe selection. *Proceedings of the IEEE International Conference on Multimedia and Expo ICME '05* (pp. 4-pp). IEEE. doi:10.1109/ICME.2005.1521470

Cordasco, G., Scara, V., & Rosenberg, A. L. (2007). Bounded-collision memory-mapping schemes for data structures with applications to parallel memories. *IEEE Transactions on Parallel and Distributed Systems, 18*(7), 973–982. doi:10.1109/TPDS.2007.1024

Cox, I., Kilian, J., Shamoon, T., & Leighton, F. (1997, December). Secure Spread Spectrum Watermarking for Multimedia. *IEEE Transactions on Image Processing, 6*(12), 1673–1687. doi:10.1109/83.650120 PMID:18285237

Coyle, E. J., & Shmulevich, I. (1998). A System for machine recognition of music patterns. *Proceedings of the Acoustic, Speech and Signal Processing* (pp. 3597-3600).

Croft, B. Y., & Tsui, B. M. W. (1995). Nuclear medicine. In J. D. Bronzino (Ed.), *Biomedical Engineering Handbook.* Boca Raton, FL: CRC Press.

Crombie, D., Diikstra, S., Lenoir, R., McKenzie, N., & Schut, E. (2002). Towards accessible multimedia music. *Proceedings of the Second International Conference on Web Delivering of Music WEDELMUSIC '02* (pp. 192-199). IEEE. doi:doi:10.1109/WDM.2002.1176211 doi:10.1109/WDM.2002.1176211

Crombie, D., Lenoir, R., & McKenzie, N. (2003, September). Producing accessible multimedia music. *Proceedings of the Third International Conference on Web Delivering of Music WEDELMUSIC '03* (pp. 45-48). IEEE. doi:doi:10.1109/WDM.2003.1233872 doi:10.1109/WDM.2003.1233872

Cui, W., & Zhang, Y. (2010, October). Graph based multispectral high resolution image segmentation. In *Multimedia Technology (ICMT), 2010 International Conference on* (pp. 1-5). IEEE. doi:10.1109/ICMULT.2010.5631004

da Silva Torres, R., & Falcao, A. X. (2006). Content-Based Image Retrieval: Theory and Applications. *Research Initiative, Treatment Action, 13*(2), 161–185.

Dai, W., & Milenkovic, O., (2009). *Subspace Pursuit for Compressive Sensing Signal Reconstruction.* Academic Press.

Dajun, H., Qibin, S., & Tian, Q. (2003). A Semi-fragile Object based Video Authentication System.*Proceedings of the International Symposium on Circuits and Systems*, (pp. 814 – 817). doi:10.1109/ISCAS.2003.1205144

Dalibor, M., Zeppelzauer, M., & Breiteneder, C. (2010). Features for content-based audio retrieval. *Advances in Computers, 78,* 71-150.

Daneels, D., Van Campenhout, D., Niblack, C. W., Equitz, W., Barber, R., & Fierens, F. (1993, April). Interactive outlining: An improved approach using active contours. In *IS&T/SPIE's Symposium on Electronic Imaging: Science and Technology* (pp. 226-233). International Society for Optics and Photonics.

Dang, Kumar, & Radha. (n.d.). *Key frame extraction from consumer videos using epitome.* Michigan State University.

Datta, A. K., et al. (1995). Relevance of Consonance in Indian Musical Scale: Theory and Practice. *J. Acoust. Soc. Ind., 23.*

Datta, A. K., et al. (1997). Pitch Analysis of Recorded Vocal Performances in Hindustani Music: Evidence of a Personal Scale. *J. Acoust. Soc. Ind., 25.*

Datta, A. K., et al. (1998). Multiple States in a Note in Hindustani Music and their Relevance to Consonance. *J. Acoust. Soc. Ind., 26.*

Datta, A. K., Sengupta, R., Dey, N., & Nag, D. (2000, December). On Scientific Approaches to the Study of Vaditya in Indian Music. *Proc. Fifth Int. Workshop on Recent Trends in Speech,Music and Allied Signal Processing.*

Daubechies, I. (1992). *Ten Lectures on Wavelets.* Rutgers University and AT&T Bell Labaratories. doi:10.1137/1.9781611970104

Davies, D. L., & Bouldin, D. W. (1979). A Cluster Separation Measure, *IEEE Transactions on Pattern Analysis and Machine Intelligence. PAMI, 1*(2), 224–227. doi:10.1109/TPAMI.1979.4766909

Dawant, B. M., & Zijdenbos, A. P. (2000). Image segmentation. In Handbook of Medical Imaging, Vol. 2, Medical Image Processing and Analysis. SPIE, International Society for Optical Engineering. doi:10.1117/3.831079.ch2 de Hoon, M. J. L., Imoto, S., Nolan, J., & Miyano, S. (2004). Open source clustering software. *Bioinformatics (Oxford, England)*, *20*(9), 1453–1454. doi:10.1093/bioinformatics/bth078 PMID:14871861

de Souto, M. C. P., Soares, R.G.F., de Araujo, D.S.A., Costa, I.G., Ludermir, T.B., & Schliep, A. (2008) Ranking and Selecting Clustering Algorithms Using a Meta-Learning Approach. In *Proc. of IEEE International Joint Conference on Neural Networks*. IEEE Computer Society. doi:doi:10.1109/IJCNN.2008.4634333 doi:10.1109/IJCNN.2008.4634333

De, S., Bhattacharyya, S., & Chakraborty, S. (2012). Multilevel Image Segmentation by a Multiobjective Genetic Algorithm Based OptiMUSIG Activation Function. In Handbook of Research on Computational Intelligence for Engineering, Science and Business. IGI Global.

De, S., Bhattacharyya, S., & Chakraborty, S. (2013). Efficient Color Image Segmentation by a Parallel Optimized (ParaOptiMUSIG) activation Function. In Global Trends in Intelligent Computing Research and Development. IGI Global.

De, S., Bhattacharyya, S., & Datta, P. (2008). OptiMUSIG: An Optimized Gray Level Image Segmentor. In *Proceedings of 16th International Conference on Advanced Computing and Communications*.

De, S., Bhattacharyya, S., & Dutta, P. (2009) Multilevel Image Segmentation using OptiMUSIG Activation Function with Fixed and Variable Thresholding: A Comparative Study. In Applications of Soft Computing: From Theory to Praxis, Advances in Intelligent and Soft Computing. Springer.

Dean, R. T., Bailes, F., & Dunsmuir, W. T. M. (2014). Time series analysis of real-time music perception: Approaches to the assessment of individual and expertise differences in perception of expressed affect. *Journal of Mathematics and Music, 8*(3), 183–205. doi:10.1080/17459737.2014.928752

Debnath, L. (2002). *Wavelet Transforms and Their Applications*. Boston: Birkhauser. doi:10.1007/978-1-4612-0097-0

Debole, F., & Sebastiani, F. (2003). Supervised Term Weighting for Automated Text Categorization. *Proceedings of SAC-03,18th ACM Symposium on Applied Computing*, Melbourne, FL. ACM Press. doi:doi:10.1145/952532.952688 doi:10.1145/952532.952688

De, D., & Roy, S. (2012, December). Inheritance in Indian Classical Music: An Object-Oriented Analysis and Pattern Recognition Approach. *Proceedings of International Conference on Radar, Communication and Computing (ICRCC)*, (pp. 193-198). IEEE. doi:10.1109/ICRCC.2012.6450575

De, D., & Roy, S. (2012, December). Polymorphism in Indian Classical Music: A Pattern Recognition Approach. *Proceedings of International Conference on Communications, Devices and Intelligent Systems (CODIS)* (pp. 612-615). IEEE. doi:10.1109/CODIS.2012.6422277

Deliège, F., & Pedersen, T. B. (2009). Using fuzzy song sets in music warehouses. *Scalable Fuzzy Algorithms for Data Management and Analysis: Methods and Design: Methods and Design*, 54.

Deliège, F., & Pedersen, T. B. (2008). Using fuzzy lists for playlist management. In *Advances in Multimedia Modeling* (pp. 198–209). Springer Berlin Heidelberg. doi:10.1007/978-3-540-77409-9_19

Dembele, D., & Kastner, P. (2003). Fuzzy c-means method for clustering microarray data. *Bioinformatics (Oxford, England)*, *19*(8), 973–980. doi:10.1093/bioinformatics/btg119 PMID:12761060

DeMenthon, D., Kobla, V., & Doermann, D. (1998, September). Video summarization by curve simplification. *Proceedings of the Sixth ACM International Conference on Multimedia* (pp. 211-218). ACM. doi:10.1145/290747.290773

Dereniak, E. L., & Boreman, G. D. (1996). *Infrared Detectors and Systems*. New York: John Wiley & Sons.

De, S., Bhattacharyya, S., & Chakraborty, S. (2013). Multilevel Image Segmentation by a Multiobjective Genetic Algorithm Based OptiMUSIG Activation Function. In S. Bhattacharyya & P. Dutta (Eds.), *Handbook of Research on Computational Intelligence for Engineering, Science, and Business* (pp. 122–162). Hershey, PA, USA: IGI Global. doi:10.4018/978-1-4666-2518-1.ch005

De, S., Bhattacharyya, S., & Chakraborty, S. (2014). Application of Pixel Intensity Based Medical Image Segmentation Using NSGA II Based OptiMUSIG Activation Function. *2014 Sixth International Conference on Computational Intelligence and Communication Networks.*

De, S., Bhattacharyya, S., & Chakraborty, S. (2014). Efficient Color Image Segmentation by a Parallel Optimized (ParaOptiMUSIG) Activation Function. In B. Tripathy & D. Acharjya (Eds.), *Global Trends in Intelligent Computing Research and Development* (pp. 19–50). Hershey, PA, USA: IGI Global. Doi:

De, S., Bhattacharyya, S., & Dutta, P. (2010). Efficient grey-level image segmentation using an optimised MUSIG (OptiMUSIG) activation function. *International Journal of Parallel, Emergent and Distributed Systems, 26*(1), 1–39. doi:10.1080/17445760903546618

Deserno, T. M. (Ed.). (2011). *Fundamentals of Biomedical Image Processing.* Springer. doi:10.1007/978-3-642-15816-2

Destrempes, F., Angers, J. F., & Mignote, M. (2006). Fusion of hidden Markov random field models and its Bayesian estimation. *IEEE Transactions on Image Processing, 15*(10), 2920–2935. doi:10.1109/TIP.2006.877522 PMID:17022259

Devijver, P. A., & Dekesel, M. M. (1987). Learning the parameters of a hidden Markov random field image model: A simple example. In *Pattern Recognition Theory and Applications* (pp. 141–163). Springer Berlin Heidelberg. doi:10.1007/978-3-642-83069-3_13

Dhillon, P. K. (2012). A Novel framework to Image Edge Detection using Cellular Automata. *IJCA.*

Dili, R., & Mwangi, E. (2007). An Image Watermarking Method Based on the Singular Value Transformation and the Wavelet Transformation. *Proceedings of IEEE AFRICON.*

Dimitrova, N., & Abdel-Mottaleb, M. (1997, January). Content-based video retrieval by example video clip. In *Electronic Imaging'97* (pp. 59–70). International Society for Optics and Photonics.

Ding, Y., Zheng, X., Zhao, Y., & Liu, G. (2010, July). A Video Watermarking Algorithm Resistant to Copy Attack. *Proceedings of 3rd International Symposium on Electronic Commerce and Security.* doi:10.1109/ISECS.2010.70

Distefano, S., Scarpa, M., & Puliafito, A. (2011). From UML to Petri Nets: The PCM-Based Methodology. *IEEE Transactions on Software Engineering, 37*(1), 65–79. doi:10.1109/TSE.2010.10

Donate, A., & Liu, X. (2010, June). Shot boundary detection in videos using robust three-dimensional tracking. *Proceedings of the 2010 IEEE Computer Society Conference on Computer Vision and Pattern Recognition Workshops (CVPRW)* (pp. 64-69). IEEE. doi:10.1109/CVPRW.2010.5543811

Donoho, D. (2006, April). Compressed Sensing. *IEEE Transactions on Information Theory, 52*(4), 1289–1306. doi:10.1109/TIT.2006.871582

Dostal, M. (2005). Genetic Algorithms as a model of musical creativity – on generating of a human-like rhythmic accompaniment. *Computing and Informatics, 22*, 321–340.

Douglas, E., & Schmidhuber, J. (2002). *A first look at music composition using lstm recurrent neural networks.* Istituto Dalle Molle Di Studi Sull Intelligenza Artificiale.

Drew, M. S., Li, Z. N., & Zhong, X. (2000). Video dissolve and wipe detection via spatio-temporal images of chromatic histogram differences. *Proceedings of the 2000 International Conference on Image Processing* (Vol. 3, pp. 929-932). IEEE. doi:10.1109/ICIP.2000.899609

Duan & Wang. (2008). *Shot-Level Camera Motion Estimation Based on a Parametric Model.* Academic Press.

Duarte, M., & Eldar, Y. (2011, September). Structured Compressed Sensing: From Theory to Applications. *IEEE Transactions on Signal Processing*, *59*(9), 4053–4085. doi:10.1109/TSP.2011.2161982

Dugelay, J.-L., Fintzel, K., & Valente, S. (1999). Synthetic Natural Hybrid Video Processing for Virtual Teleconferencing Systems. *IEEE Picture Coding Symposium.*

Dumont, E., & Mérialdo, B. (2008, October). Sequence alignment for redundancy removal in video rushes summarization. *Proceedings of the 2nd ACM TRECVid video summarization workshop* (pp. 55-59). ACM. doi:10.1145/1463563.1463572

Dunn, J. C. (1973). A Fuzzy Relative of the ISODATA Process and Its Use in Detecting Compact Well-Separated Clusters. *Journal of Cybernetics*, *3*(3), 32–57. doi:10.1080/01969727308546046

Eakins, J. P., & Graham, M. E. (1999). *Content-based image retrieval, a report to the JISC Technology Applications programme.* Academic Press.

Easley, D., & Kleinberg, J. (2010). *Networks, crowds, and markets: Reasoning about a highly connected world.* New York: Cambridge University Press. doi:10.1017/CBO9780511761942

Eberhart, R., Shi, Y., & Kennedy, J. (2001). *Particle swarm optimization: Developments, applications and resources.* San Mateo, CA: Morgan Kaufmann.

Eisen, M., Spellman, P., Brown, P., & Botstein, D. (1998). Cluster analysis and display of genome-wide expression patterns. *Proceedings of the National Academy of Sciences of the United States of America*, *95*(25), 14863–14868. doi:10.1073/pnas.95.25.14863 PMID:9843981

Ejima, M., & Miyazaki, A. (2000, August). A Wavelet Based Watermarking for Digital Images and Videos.*IEEE International Conference on Image Processing*, (pp. 678 – 681). doi:10.1109/ICIP.2000.899545

Elbasi, E. (2007). Robust MPEG Video Watermarking in Wavelet Domain. *Trakya University Journal of Science*, *8*(2), 87–93.

El-Gayyar (2006, May). *Watermarking Techniques – Spatial Domain Digital Rights Seminar.* Media Informatics, University of Bonn, Germany.

Ellis, D. (2003). *Pattern Recognition Applied to Music Signals.* New York: JHU CLSP Summer School, Laboratory for Recognition and Organization of Speech and Audio, Columbia University.

El-Maleh, K., Klein, M., Petrucci, G., & Kabal, P. (2000). Speech/music discrimination for multimedia applications. *Proceedings of the 2000 IEEE International Conference on Acoustics, Speech, and Signal Processing ICASSP'00* (Vol. 6, pp. 2445-2448). IEEE.

Emmanuel, D. (2010). A wavelet-based parameterization for speech/music discrimination. *Computer Speech & Language*, *24*(2), 341–357. doi:10.1016/j.csl.2009.05.003

Engel, D., Whitney, P., Calapristi, A., & Brockman, F. (2009). Mining for emerging technologies within text streams and documents.*Proceedings of the Ninth SIAM International Conference on Data Mining.* Society for Industrial and Applied Mathematics.

Equitz, W., & Niblack, W. (1994). *Retrieving images from a database: using texture algorithms from the QBIC system, IBM Research Division*. Research Report 9805.

Essaouabi, A., & Ibnelhaj, E. (2009, July). A 3D Wavelet based Method for Digital Video Watermarking.*Proceedings of the 4th IEEE Intelligent Information Hiding and Multimedia Signal Processing*. doi:10.1109/NDT.2009.5272116

Essid, S., Richard, G., & David, B. (2004). Musical instrument recognition based on class pair-wise feature selection. *Proceedings of International Conference on Music Information Retrieval*. 2004.

Fabijanska, A. (2011). Variance filter for edge detection and edge-based image segmentation. In Perspective Technologies and Methods in MEMS Design.

Fablet, R., Bouthemy, P., & Pérez, P. (2002). Nonparametric motion characterization using causal probabilistic models for video indexing and retrieval. *IEEE Transactions on* Image Processing, *11*(4), 393–407.

Fakhr, M. (2012, December). Robust Watermarking Using Compressed Sensing Framework with Application to MP3 Audio. *The International Journal of Multimedia & Its Applications*, *4*(6), 27–43. doi:10.5121/ijma.2012.4603

Faloutsos, C., Barber, R., Flickner, M., Hafner, J., Niblack, W., Petkovic, D., & Equitz, W. (1994). Efficient and effective querying by image content. *Journal of Intelligent Information Systems*, *3*(3-4), 231–262. doi:10.1007/BF00962238

Fan, L., & Yanmei, F., (2006, November). A DWT based Video Watermarking Algorithm Applying DS-CAMA. *IEEE Region 10 Conference TENCON 2006.*

Fang, H., Jiang, J., & Feng, Y. (2006). A fuzzy logic approach for detection of video shot boundaries. *Pattern Recognition*, *39*(11), 2092–2100. doi:10.1016/j.patcog.2006.04.044

Fan, J., & Xie, W. (1999). Distance measure and induced fuzzy entropy. *Fuzzy Sets and Systems*, *104*(2), 305–314. doi:10.1016/S0165-0114(99)80011-6

Farag, W. E., & Abdel-Wahab, H. M. (2002, March). *Adaptive Key Frames Selection Algorithms for Summarizing Video Data* (pp. 1017–1020). JCIS.

Fasel, Q., & Khan, K. A. (2012). Investigations of Cellular Automata Linear Rules for Edge Detection. *International Journal Computer Network and Information Security*, 47-53.

Fauvet, B., Bouthemy, P., Gros, P., & Spindler, F. (2004). A geometrical key-frame selection method exploiting dominant motion estimation in video. In *Image and Video Retrieval* (pp. 419–427). Springer Berlin Heidelberg. doi:10.1007/978-3-540-27814-6_50

Feldman, R., & Sagner, J. (2007). *The Text Mining Handbook*. Cambridge, UK: Cambridge University Press.

Felzenszwalb, P. F., & Huttenlocher, D. P. (2004). Efficient graph-based image segmentation. *International Journal of Computer Vision*, *59*(2), 167–181. doi:10.1023/B:VISI.0000022288.19776.77

Fenster, A., & Downey, D. B. (2000). Three-dimensional ultrasound imaging. In J. Beutel, H. L. Kundel, & R. L. van Metter (Eds.), *Handbook of Medical Imaging* (Vol. I). Washington, DC: SPIE Press.

Flickner, M., Sawhney, H., Niblack, W., Ashley, J., Huang, Q., Dom, B., & Steele, D. et al. (1995). Query by image and video content: The QBIC system. *Computer*, *28*(9), 23–32. doi:10.1109/2.410146

Foley, C., Gurrin, C., Jones, G. J., Lee, H., McGivney, S., O'Connor, N. E., ... & Wilkins, P. (2005). *TRECVid 2005 experiments at Dublin City University*. Academic Press.

Foote, J., & Cooper, M. (2001). Visualizing Musical Structure and Rhythm via Self-Similarity. *Proceedings of the International Computer Music Conference* (pp. 419-422).

For Iris Database. (n.d.). Retrieved from http://www.sinobiometrics.com/caisairis.html

France, R. B., Kim, D. K., Ghosh, S., & Song, E. (2004). A UML-based pattern specification technique. *IEEE Transactions on* Software Engineering, *30*(3), 193–206.

Freedman, D., & Zhang, T. (2005, June). Interactive graph cut based segmentation with shape priors. In *Computer Vision and Pattern Recognition, 2005. CVPR 2005. IEEE Computer Society Conference on* (Vol. 1, pp. 755-762). IEEE. doi:10.1109/CVPR.2005.191

Freeman, G., Dony, R., & Areibi, S. (2007). Audio environment classification for hearing aids using artificial neural networks with windowed input. *Proceedings of IEEE Symposium on Computational Intelligence in Image and Signal Processing*. doi:10.1109/CIISP.2007.369314

Furini, M., & Ghini, V. (2006). *An Audio-Video Summarization Scheme Based on Audio and Video Analysis*. IEEE. doi:10.1109/CCNC.2006.1593230

Ganic, E., & Eskicioglu, A. (2004). Secure DWT-SVD Domain Image Watermarking Embedding Data in All Frequencies.*ACM Multimedia and Security Workshop 2004*.

Gao, Y., Chan, K. L., & Yau, W. Y. (2007, December). Learning in content-based image retrieval-a brief review. In *Information, Communications & Signal Processing, 2007 6th International Conference on* (pp. 1-5). IEEE.

Gao, X. B., Han, B., & Ji, H. B. (2005). A shot boundary detection method for news video based on rough sets and fuzzy clustering. In *Image Analysis and Recognition* (pp. 231–238). Springer Berlin Heidelberg.

Gao, X., & Tang, X. (2002). Unsupervised video-shot segmentation and model-free anchorperson detection for news video story parsing. *IEEE Transactions on* Circuits and Systems for Video Technology, *12*(9), 765–776.

Gao, Y., Wang, W. B., & Yong, J. H. (2008). A video summarization tool using two-level redundancy detection for personal video recorders. *Consumer Electronics. IEEE Transactions on*, *54*(2), 521–526.

Gargi, U., Kasturi, R., & Strayer, S. H. (2000). Performance characterization of video-shot-change detection methods. *IEEE Transactions on* Circuits and Systems for Video Technology, *10*(1), 1–13.

Garrido, P., & Lemahieu, W. (2008). Collective Intelligence. In G. Putnik & M. Cruz-Cunha (Eds.), *Encyclopedia of Networked and Virtual Organizations* (pp. 280–287). Hershey, PA, USA: IGI Global. doi:10.4018/978-1-59904-885-7.ch037

Garrote, A., & García, M. N. (2013). News Trends Processing Using Open Linked Data. In P. Ordóñez de Pablos, M. Lytras, R. Tennyson, & J. Gayo (Eds.), *Cases on Open-Linked Data and Semantic Web Applications* (pp. 192–198). Hershey, PA, USA: IGI Global. doi:10.4018/978-1-4666-2827-4.ch010

Gartland-Jones, A., & Copley, P. (2003). The Suitability of Genetic Algorithms for Musical Composition. *Contemporary Music Review*, *22*(3), 43–55. doi:10.1080/0749446032000150870

Gautam, Arun, & Kumar. (2014). Key Frame Selection From Video Based on Weighted Minkowski Distance. *International Journal of Advanced Computational Engineering and Networking*, *2*(8), 83-86.

Gawrys, M., & Sienkiewicz, J. (1994). Rsl–the rough set library version 2.0. ICS Research Report 27/94. Institute of Computer Science.

Gebara, D., & Alhajj, R. (2009). Improving Image Retrieval by Clustering. In Z. Ma (Ed.), *Artificial Intelligence for Maximizing Content Based Image Retrieval* (pp. 20–43). Hershey, PA, USA: IGI Global. doi:10.4018/978-1-60566-174-2.ch002

Geetha, P., & Pandeeswari, S., Thiruchadai, & MohananSony. (2012). Visual Attention Based Keyframes Extraction and Video Summarization. *Proceedingsof theComputer Science Conference* (pp. 179-190).

Geetha, M. K., & Palanivel, S. (2012). Unsupervised Approach for Retrieving Shots from Video. *International Journal of Computers and Applications, 60*(6).

Gharehchopogh, F. S., & Ebrahimi, S. (2012). A Novel Approach for Edge Detection in Images Based on Cellular Learning Automata. *International Journal of Computer Vision and Image Processing, 2*(4), 51–61. doi:10.4018/ijcvip.2012100105

Ghodeswar, S., & Meshram, B. B. (2010). Content-based video retrieval. *Proceedings of ISCET*, 135.

Gilbert, A., Strauss, M., Tropp, J., & Vershynin, R. (2007, June). One Sketch for all: Fast Algorithms for Compressed Sensing. *39th ACM Symposium on Theory of Computing (STOC)*. doi:10.1145/1250790.1250824

Gilles, S. (1998). *Robust Description and Matching of Images*. (PhD thesis). University of Oxford.

Gillet, O., & Richard, G. (2003). Automatic Labeling of TablaSignals. *Proceedings of the International Conference on Music Information Retrieval* (pp. 117-124).

Giot, R., El-Abed, M., & Rosenberger, C. (2012, February). Fast Computation of the Performance Evaluation of Biometric Systems: Application to Multibiometrics. *Future Generation Computer Systems, 1*, 1–30.

Girarda & Cohna. (2014). *Automated Audiovisual Depression Analysis*. Academic Press.

Girgensohn, A., & Boreczky, J. (1999, July). Time-constrained keyframe selection technique. *Proceedings of the IEEE International Conference on Multimedia Computing and Systems '99* (Vol. 1, pp. 756-761). IEEE. doi:10.1109/MMCS.1999.779294

Girgensohn, A., Boreczky, J., & Wilcox, L. (2001). Keyframe-based user interfaces for digital video. *Computer, 34*(9), 61–67. doi:10.1109/2.947093

Gitte, M., Bawaskar, H., Sethi, S., & Shinde, A. (2014). Content-based video retrieval system. *Int J Res Eng Technol, 3*(6).

Giudici, P. (2003). *Applied Data Mining: Statistical Methods for Business and Industry*. NY: John Wiley &Sons Inc.

Giudici, P., & Figini, S. (2009). *Applied Data Mining for Business and Industry (Statistics in Practice)*. NY: Wiley. doi:10.1002/9780470745830

Glowinski, Camurri, & Volpe. (2008). *Body gesture analysis: Technique for automatic emotion recognition*. Academic Press.

Gong, Y., & Liu, X. (2000a). Video summarization using singular value decomposition. *Proceedings of the IEEE Conference on Computer Vision and Pattern Recognition '00* (Vol. 2, pp. 174-180). IEEE. doi:10.1007/s00530-003-0086-3

Gong, Y., & Liu, X. (2000b). Generating optimal video summaries. *Proceedings of the 2000 IEEE International Conference on Multimedia and Expo ICME '00* (Vol. 3, pp. 1559-1562). IEEE.

Gong, Y., & Liu, X. (2001). Video summarization with minimal visual content redundancies. In *Proceedings of the 2001 International Conference on Image Processing '01* (Vol. 3, pp. 362-365). IEEE. doi:10.1109/ICIP.2001.958126

Gonzalez, R. C., Woods, R. E., & Eddins, S. L. U. (2004). Digital Image Processing Using MATLAB. Pearson Prentice Hall.

Gonzalez, R. C., & Woods, R. E. (1992). *Digital image processing*. Addison-Wesley.

Grana, C., & Cucchiara, R. (2007). Linear transition detection as a unified shot detection approach. *IEEE Transactions on Circuits and Systems for Video Technology, 17*(4), 483–489. doi:10.1109/TCSVT.2006.888818

Guan, G., Wang, Z., Lu, S., Deng, J. D., & Feng, D. D. (2013). Keypoint-based keyframe selection. *IEEE Transactions on* Circuits and Systems for Video Technology, *23*(4), 729–734.

Gudivada, V. N., & Raghavan, V. V. (1995). Content-based image retrieval systems. *Computer, 28*(9), 18–22. doi:10.1109/2.410145

Guironnet, M., Pellerin, D., Guyader, N., & Ladret, P. (2007). Video summarization based on camera motion and a subjective evaluation method. *EURASIP Journal on Image and Video Processing, 2007*(1), 060245. doi:10.1186/1687-5281-2007-060245

Gupta, A., & Jain, R. (1997). Visual information retrieval. *Communications of the ACM, 40*(5), 70–79. doi:10.1145/253769.253798

Gupta, A., & Raval, M. (2012, August). A Robust and Secure Watermarking Scheme Based on Singular Value Replacement. *Sadhana, 37*(4), 425–440. doi:10.1007/s12046-012-0089-x

Hahn. (1950). E. Spin echoes. *Phys. Rev., 20*(4), 580–594.

Halder, A., & Dasgupta, A. (2012). Image segmentation using rough set based *k*-means algorithm. *Proceedings of the CUBE International Information Technology Conference*. doi:10.1145/2381716.2381728

Hamdaoui, F., Sakly, A., & Mtibaa, A. (2015). An efficient multi level thresholding method for image segmentation based on the hybridization of modified PSO and otsus method. *Studies in Computational Intelligence, 575*, 343–367. doi:10.1007/978-3-319-11017-2_14

Hammouche, K., Diaf, M., & Siarry, P. (2008). A multilevel automatic thresholding method based on a genetic algorithm for a fast image segmentation. *Computer Vision and Image Understanding, 109*(2), 163–175. doi:10.1016/j.cviu.2007.09.001

Hanjalic, A. (2002). Shot-boundary detection: Unraveled and resolved? *IEEE Transactions on* Circuits and Systems for Video Technology, *12*(2), 90–105.

Hanjalic, A., & Zhang, H. (1999). An integrated scheme for automated video abstraction based on unsupervised cluster-validity analysis. *IEEE Transactions on* Circuits and Systems for Video Technology, *9*(8), 1280–1289.

Hansen, D. L., Schneiderman, B., & Smith, M. A. (2010). *Analyzing social media networks with NodeXL: insights from a connected world*. Amsterdam: M. Kaufmann.

Haridas, K., & Thanamani, A. S. (2014). Well-Organized Content-based Image Retrieval System in RGB Color Histogram, Tamura Texture and Gabor Feature. *International Journal of Advanced Research in Computer and Communication Engineering, 3*(10).

Harinda, E., & Natgwirumugara, E. (2015). Security & Privacy Implications in the Placement of Biometric-Based ID Card for Rwanda Universities. *Journal of Information Security, 6*(02), 93–100. doi:10.4236/jis.2015.62010

Hartung, F., & Kutter, M. (1999, July). Multimedia Watermarking Techniques. *Proceedings of the IEEE, 87*(7), 1085–1103. doi:10.1109/5.771066

Hasebe, S., Nagumo, M., Muramatsu, S., & Kikuchi, H. (2004, September). Video key frame selection by clustering wavelet coefficients. *Proceedings of the 2004 12th European Signal Processing Conference* (pp. 2303-2306). IEEE.

Hauptmann, A., Baron, R. V., Chen, M. Y., Christel, M., Duygulu, P., Huang, C., & Moraveji, N. (2004a). *Informedia at TRECVID 2003: Analyzing and searching broadcast news video.* Carnegie-Mellon Univ Pittsburgh PA School of Computer Science.

Hauptmann, A., Chen, M. Y., Christel, M., Huang, C., Lin, W. H., Ng, T., & Yang, H. et al. (2004b, November). Confounded expectations: Informedia at TRECVID 2004. *Proc. of TRECVID.*

Haus, G., & Rodriguez, A. (1993). Formal music representation; a case study: the model of Ravel's Bolero by Petri nets. *Music Processing. Computer Music and Digital Audio Series*, 165-232.

Hauschild, M., Bhatia, S., & Pelikan, M. (2012). Image segmentation using a genetic algorithm and hierarchical local search. *Proceedings of the 14th International Conference on Genetic and Evolutionary Computation.* doi:10.1145/2330163.2330253

Haus, G., & Sametti, A. (1991). Scoresynth: A system for the synthesis of music scores based on petri nets and a music algebra. *Computer*, *24*(7), 56–60. doi:10.1109/2.84837

Hawkes, P. (Ed.). (1985). The beginnings of electron microscopy. Academic Press.

He, L., Sanocki, E., Gupta, A., & Grudin, J. (1999, October). Auto-summarization of audio-video presentations. *Proceedings of the seventh ACM international conference on Multimedia* (Part 1) (pp. 489-498). ACM. doi:10.1145/319463.319691

Hemalatha, M. (2012). A Predictive Modeling of Retail Satisfaction: A Data Mining Approach to Retail Service Industry. In P. Ordóñez de Pablos & M. Lytras (Eds.), *Knowledge Management and Drivers of Innovation in Services Industries* (pp. 175–189). Hershey, PA, USA: IGI Global. doi:10.4018/978-1-4666-0948-8.ch014

Hemaltha, M. (2012). Similar Image Retrieval using DWT and LIM based Image Matching Technique. *International Journal of Advanced Research in Computer Science*, *3*(2).

Hermes, T., Klauck, C., Kreyss, J., & Zhang, J. (1995, March). Image retrieval for information systems. In *IS&T/SPIE's Symposium on Electronic Imaging: Science & Technology* (pp. 394-405). International Society for Optics and Photonics.

Hernandez, J., Amado, M., & Perez-Gonzalez, F. (2000, January). DCT domain Watermarking Techniques for Still Image: Detector Performance Analysis and a New Structure. *IEEE Transactions on Image Processing*, *9*(1), 55–68. doi:10.1109/83.817598 PMID:18255372

Herrera, P. (2000). Towards instrument segmentation for music content description: a critical review of instrument classification techniques. *Proceedings of the International symposium on music information retrieval, ISMIR.*

Heykin, S. (2005). Neural Networks: A Comprehensive Foundation (2nd ed.). Pearson Prentice Hall, Pearson Education.

Hiremath, P. S., & Pujari, J. (2007, December). Content-based image retrieval using color, texture and shape features. In *Advanced Computing and Communications, 2007. ADCOM 2007. International Conference on* (pp. 780-784). IEEE. doi:10.1109/ADCOM.2007.21

Hollander, M., & Wolfe, D. (1999). *Nonparametric statistical methods* (2nd ed.). Weily.

Hong, J. S., Chen, H. Y., & Hsiang, J. (2000, June). A digital museum of Taiwanese butterflies. In *Proceedings of the fifth ACM conference on Digital libraries* (pp. 260-261). ACM. doi:10.1145/336597.336694

Hopfgartner, F., & Jose, J. M. (2010). Semantic user profiling techniques for personalised multimedia recommendation. *Multimedia Systems*, *16*(4-5), 255–274. doi:10.1007/s00530-010-0189-6

Hounsfield, G. N. (1973). Computerized transverse axial scanning (tomography): Part I. *The British Journal of Radiology*, *46*, 1016–1022. doi:10.1259/0007-1285-46-552-1016 PMID:4757352

Hrivnák, I. (1986). *Electron Microscopy of Steels*. Bratislava, Slovakia: Veda.

Hsieh, J. W., Yu, S. L., & Chen, Y. S. (2006). Motion-based video retrieval by trajectory matching. *Circuits and Systems for Video Technology. IEEE Transactions on, 16*(3), 396–409.

Hsu, C. F., Ku, M. K., & Liu, L. Y. (2009, September). Support vector machine FPGA implementation for video shot boundary detection application. *Proceedings of theIEEE InternationalSOC Conference SOCC '09* (pp. 239-242). IEEE. doi:10.1109/SOCCON.2009.5398049

Huang, C., & Wu, J. (2004, February). Attacking Visible Watermarking Schemes. *IEEE Transactions on Multimedia, 6*(1), 16–30. doi:10.1109/TMM.2003.819579

Huang, F., & Guan, Z. (2004). A Hybrid SVD-DCT Watermarking Method Based on LPSNR. *Pattern Recognition Letters, 25*(15), 1769–1775. doi:10.1016/j.patrec.2004.07.003

Huang, L. K., & Wang, M. J. (1995). Image Thresholding by minimizing the measure of fuzzyness. *Pattern Recognition, 28*(1), 41–51. doi:10.1016/0031-3203(94)E0043-K

Huang, P. W., & Dai, S. K. (2003). Image retrieval by texture similarity. *Pattern Recognition, 36*(3), 665–679. doi:10.1016/S0031-3203(02)00083-3

Huron, D. B. (2006). *Sweet anticipation: Music and the psychology of expectation*. MIT press.

Hussein, J., & Mohammed, A. (2009). Robust Video Watermarking using Multiband Wavelet Transform. *IJCSI International Journal of Computer Science Issues, 6*(1), 44–49.

Hu, W., Xie, N., Li, L., Zeng, X., & Maybank, S. (2011). A survey on visual content-based video indexing and retrieval. *IEEE Transactions on* Systems, Man, and Cybernetics, Part C: Applications and Reviews, *41*(6), 797–819.

Idrissi, N., Martinez, J., & Aboutajdine, D. (2009). Bridging the semantic gap for texture-based image retrieval and navigation. *Journal of Multimedia, 4*(5), 277–283. doi:10.4304/jmm.4.5.277-283

Ilachinski, A. (2001). Cellular Automata – A Discrete Universe. World Scientific Publishing Co. Pte. Ltd.

Ionescu, B., & Vertan, C. (2011). Dissolve Detection In Abstract Video Contents. IEEE.

Ionescu, B., Vertan, C., & Lambert, P. (2011, May). Dissolve detection in abstract video contents. *Proceedings of the 2011 IEEE International Conference on Acoustics, Speech and Signal Processing (ICASSP)* (pp. 917-920). IEEE. doi:10.1109/ICASSP.2011.5946554

Iordache, M., & Antsaklis, P. J. (2007). *Supervisory control of concurrent systems: a Petri net structural approach.* Springer Science & Business Media.

Iordache, V. M., & Antsaklis, P. J. (n. d.). Supervisory Control of Concurrent Systems. In *A Petri Net Structural Approach.* Birkhauser Boston.

Ishibuchi, H., & Nakashimaa, T. (1999). Performance evaluation of fuzzy classifier systems for multi-dimensional pattern classification problems. *IEEE Transactions on Systems, Man, and Cybernetics. Part B, Cybernetics, 29*(5), 601–618. doi:10.1109/3477.790443 PMID:18252338

ITU-R BT.500-13(2012) recommendation, 18.

Jadon, R. S., Chaudhury, S., & Biswas, K. K. (2001). A fuzzy theoretic approach for video segmentation using syntactic features. *Pattern Recognition Letters, 22*(13), 1359–1369. doi:10.1016/S0167-8655(01)00041-1

Jaffard, S., Meyer, Y., & Ryan, R. D. (2001). *Wavelets – Tools for Science & Technology*. Philadelphia: SIAM. doi:10.1137/1.9780898718119

Jagiwala, D. D., & Sah. (2012). Analysis of Block Matching Algorithm for Motion Estimation in H.264 Video CODEC. *International Journal of Engineering Research and Applications, 2*.

Jahne, B., Haussecker, H., & Geissler, P. (Eds.). (1999). *Handbook of Computer Vision and Applications* (Vol. 1). New York: Academic Press.

Jain, A., Nandakumar, K., & Nagar, A., (2008, January). Biometric Template Security. *EURASIP Journal on Advances in Signal Processing*, 1 – 17.

Jain, A. K., Murty, M. N., & Flynn, P. J. (1999). Data Clustering: A Review. *ACM Computing Surveys, 31*(3), 264–323. doi:10.1145/331499.331504

Jain, A., & Kumar, A. (2012). Biometric Recognition: An Overview. In E. Mordini & D. Tzovaras (Eds.), *Second Generation Biometrics: The Ethical, Legal and Social Context* (pp. 49–79). Springer. doi:10.1007/978-94-007-3892-8_3

Jain, A., & Ross, A. (2004, January). Multibiometric Systems. *Communications of the ACM, 47*(1), 34–40. doi:10.1145/962081.962102

Jain, A., Ross, A., & Pankanti, S. (2006, June). Biometrics: A Tool for Information Security. *IEEE Transactions on Information Forensics and Security, 1*(2), 125–143. doi:10.1109/TIFS.2006.873653

Jain, A., Ross, A., & Prabhakar, S. (2004, January). An Introduction to Biometric Recognition. *IEEE Transactions on Circuits and Systems for Video Technology, 14*(1), 4–20.

Janc, K., Tarasiuk, J., Bonnet, A. S., & Lipinski, P. (2013). Genetic algorithms as a useful tool for trabecular and cortical bone segmentation. *Computer Methods and Programs in Biomedicine, 111*(1), 72–83. doi:10.1016/j.cmpb.2013.03.012 PMID:23602574

Jan, J. (2006). *Medical Image Processing Reconstruction and Restoration: Concepts and Methods*. Taylor and Francis.

Jaswal, G., & Kaul, A. (2009). Content-Based Image Retrieval-A literature Review. In *National Conference on Computing Communication and Control*.

Java3D Object Controlling over PDA-Server Connection. (n. d.). Retrieved from http://aspen.ucs.indiana.edu/collabtools/extras/Java3d_waba_files/frame.html

Jensen, C. A., Mungure, E. M., Pedersen, T. B., & Sorensen, K. (2007, April). A data and query model for dynamic playlist generation. *Proceedings of the2007 IEEE 23rd International Conference onData Engineering Workshop* (pp. 65-74). IEEE. doi:doi:10.1109/ICDEW.2007.4400975 doi:10.1109/ICDEW.2007.4400975

Jhanwar, N., Chaudhuri, S., Seetharaman, G., & Zavidovique, B. (2004). Content-based image retrieval using motif cooccurrence matrix. *Image and Vision Computing, 22*(14), 1211–1220. doi:10.1016/j.imavis.2004.03.026

Ji, Q. G., Feng, J. W., Zhao, J., & Lu, Z. M. (2010, September). Effective dissolve detection based on accumulating histogram difference and the support point. *Proceedings of the 2010 First International Conference on Pervasive Computing Signal Processing and Applications (PCSPA)* (pp. 273-276). IEEE. doi:10.1109/PCSPA.2010.73

Jiang, M., Yi, X., & Ling, N. (2005) On enhancing H.264 rate control by PSNR-based frame complexity estimation. *Proceedings of ICCE 2005 International Conference on Consumer Electronics* (pp. 231-238).

Jinda-Apiraksa, A., Machajdik, J., & Sablatnig, R. (2012). A keyframe selection of lifelog image sequences. *IEEE Transactions on Intelligent Transportation Systems, 2*(3), 151–163.

Jin, Y., Khan, L., Wang, L., & Awad, M. (2005, November). Image annotations by combining multiple evidence & wordnet. In *Proceedings of the 13th annual ACM international conference on Multimedia* (pp. 706-715). ACM. doi:10.1145/1101149.1101305

Joyce, R. A., & Liu, B. (2006). Temporal segmentation of video using frame and histogram space. *IEEE Transactions on* Multimedia, *8*(1), 130–140.

Kaihua, W., & Tao, B. (2011, January). Optimal threshold image segmentation method based on genetic algorithm in wheel set online measurement. In *Measuring Technology and Mechatronics Automation (ICMTMA), 2011 Third International Conference on* (Vol. 2, pp. 799-802). IEEE. doi:10.1109/ICMTMA.2011.483

Kak, A. C., & Slaney, M. (2001). *Principles of Computerized Tomographic Imaging*. Paper presented at SIAM Society for Industrial and Applied Mathematics, Philadelphia, PA.

Kamlakar, M., Gosavi, C., & Patankar, A. (2012, April). Single Channel Watermarking for Video Using Block based SVD. *International Journal of Advances in Computing and Information Researches, 1*(2).

Kang, C. C., Wang, W. J., & Kang, C. H. (2012). Image segmentation with complicated background by using seeded region growing. *AEÜ. International Journal of Electronics and Communications, 66*(9), 767–771. doi:10.1016/j.aeue.2012.01.011

Kannan, A., Mohan, V., & Anbazhagan, N. (2010, December). Image clustering and retrieval using image mining techniques. In *IEEE International Conference on Computational Intelligence and Computing Research* (Vol. 2).

Kanungo, T., Mount, D. M., Netanyahu, N. S., Piatko, C. D., Silverman, R., & Wu, A. Y. (2002). An efficient *k*-means clustering algorithm: Analysis and implementation. *IEEE Transactions on Pattern Analysis and Machine Intelligence, 24*(7), 881–892. doi:10.1109/TPAMI.2002.1017616

Karpagachelvi, Arthanari, & Shivakumar. (2010). *ECG feature extraction technique- A survey approach*. Academic Press.

Katayama, N., & Satoh, S. I. (1997, June). The SR-tree: An index structure for high-dimensional nearest neighbor queries. *SIGMOD Record, 26*(2), 369–380. doi:10.1145/253262.253347

Kato, T. (1992, April). Database architecture for content-based image retrieval. In *SPIE/IS&T 1992 Symposium on Electronic Imaging: Science and Technology* (pp. 112-123). International Society for Optics and Photonics.

Katzenbeisser, S., Liu, H., & Steinebach, M. (2010). Challenges and Solutions in Multimedia Document Authentication. In C. Li (Ed.), *Handbook of Research on Computational Forensics, Digital Crime, and Investigation: Methods and Solutions* (pp. 155–175). Hershey, PA, USA: IGI Global. doi:10.4018/978-1-60566-836-9.ch007

Katzenbeisser, S., & Petitcolas, F. (2000). *Information Hiding Techniques for Steganography and Digital Watermarking*. Norwood, MA: Artech House, Inc.

Kaur, Singh, & Kundra. (2013). Algorithm for object recognition. *American International Journal of Research in Science, Technology, Engineering & Mathematics*.

Kawai, Y., Sumiyoshi, H., & Yagi, N. (2007, November). Shot Boundary Detection at TRECVID 2007. Proceedings of TRECVID '07.

Kawashima, T., Tateyama, K., Iijima, T., & Aoki, Y. (1998, October). Indexing of baseball telecast for content-based video retrieval. In *Image Processing, 1998. ICIP 98. Proceedings. 1998 International Conference on* (Vol. 1, pp. 871-874). IEEE. doi:10.1109/ICIP.1998.723657

Keen, N. (2005). *Color moments*. School Of Informatics, University Of Edinburgh.

Keller, J. M., Gray, M. R., & Givens, J. A. (1985). A fuzzy k-nearest neighbour algorithm. *IEEE Transactions on Systems, Man, and Cybernetics, 15*(4), 580–585. doi:10.1109/TSMC.1985.6313426

Kennedy, J., & Eberhart, R. C. (1995). Particle swarm optimization. *Proc. of the 1995 IEEE International Conference on Neural Networks.*

Kennedy, J., & Eberhart, R. C. (1997). A discrete binary version of the particle swarm algorithm, *Proceedings of the 1997 Conference on Systems, Man, and Cybernetics.* doi:10.1109/ICSMC.1997.637339

Khalifa, A. R. (2010). Evaluating The Effectiveness of Region Growing And Edge Detection Segmentation Algorithms. *Journal of American Science.*

Khan, M., Wasfi, G. A. K., & Moinuddin, M. (2004). Automatic classification of speech and music using neural networks. *Proceedings of the 2nd ACM international workshop on Multimedia databases.* ACM. doi:10.1145/1032604.1032620

Khan, S. S., & Ahamed, A. (2004). Cluster center initialization algorithm for *K*-means clustering. *Pattern Recognition Letters, 25*(11), 1293–1302. doi:10.1016/j.patrec.2004.04.007

Kherfi, M. L., Ziou, D., & Bernardi, A. (2004). Image retrieval from the world wide web: Issues, techniques, and systems. *ACM Computing Surveys, 36*(1), 35–67. doi:10.1145/1013208.1013210

Khokher, M. R., Ghafoor, A., & Siddiqui, A. M. (2012, December). Multilevel Graph Cuts Based Image Segmentation. In *Digital Image Computing Techniques and Applications (DICTA), 2012 International Conference on* (pp. 1-8). IEEE. doi:10.1109/DICTA.2012.6411726

Kilian, P., Jan, J., & Bijnens, B. (2000). Dynamic filtering of ultrasonic responses to compensate for attenuation and frequency shift in tissues. *Proceedings of the 15th EURASIP Conference BIOSIGNAL* (pp. 261–263).

Kim, K., & Ro, Y. (2004, November). Enhancement Methods of Image Quality in Screen Mark Attack. IWDW 2003, LNCS 2939, 474 – 482.

Kim, H. S., Lee, J., Liu, H., & Lee, D. (2008, July). Video linkage: group based copied video detection. *Proceedings of the 2008 international conference on Content-based image and video retrieval* (pp. 397-406). ACM. doi:10.1145/1386352.1386404

Kim, S. D., Jang, S. K., Kim, M. J., & Ra, J. B. (1999). Efficient block-based coding of noise images by combining prefiltering and DCT. *Proc. IEEE Int. Symp. Circuits Syst.*

Kim, S. H., Lu, Y., Shi, J., Alfarrarjeh, A., Shahabi, C., Wang, G., & Zimmermann, R. (2014). Key Frame Selection Algorithms for Automatic Generation of Panoramic Images from Crowdsourced Geo-tagged Videos. In *Web and Wireless Geographical Information Systems* (pp. 67–84). Springer Berlin Heidelberg.

Kippen, J., & Bel, B. (1992). Modelling music with grammars: formal language representation in the BolProcessor. In A. Marsden & A. Pople (Eds.), *Computer Representations and Models in Music.* London: Academic Press.

Kirsch, R. (1971). Computer determination of the constituent structure of biological images. *Computers and Biomedical Research, an International Journal, 4*(3), 315–328. doi:10.1016/0010-4809(71)90034-6 PMID:5562571

Klepac, G. (2015). Particle Swarm Optimization Algorithm as a Tool for Profiling from Predictive Data Mining Models. In S. Bhattacharyya & P. Dutta (Eds.), *Handbook of Research on Swarm Intelligence in Engineering* (pp. 406–434). Hershey, PA, USA: IGI Global. Doi:

Klepac, G., & Berg, K. L. (2015b). Proposal of Analytical Model for Business Problems Solving in Big Data Environment. In J. Girard, D. Klein, & K. Berg (Eds.), *Strategic Data-Based Wisdom in the Big Data Era* (pp. 209–228). Hershey, PA, USA: IGI Global. doi:10.4018/978-1-4666-8122-4.ch012

Klepac, G., & Velić, M. (2015c). Natural Language Processing as Feature Extraction Method for Building Better Predictive Models. In J. Žižka & F. Dařena (Eds.), *Modern Computational Models of Semantic Discovery in Natural Language* (pp. 141–166). Hershey, PA, USA: IGI Global. doi:10.4018/978-1-4666-8690-8.ch006

Knees, P., Pohle, T., Schedl, M., & Widmer, G. (2006, October). Combining audio-based similarity with web-based data to accelerate automatic music playlist generation.*Proceedings of the 8th ACM international workshop on Multimedia information retrieval* (pp. 147-154). ACM. doi:10.1145/1178677.1178699

Knezović, J., Kovač, M., Žagar, M., Mlinarić, H., & Hofman, D. (2011). Novel Based Prediction Technique for Efficient Compression of Medical Imaging Data. In G. Graschew (Ed.), *Telemedicine Techniques and Applications* (pp. 169–184). Rijeka, Croatia: INTECH. doi:10.5772/18126

Kolan, H., & Thapaliya, T. (2011). *Biometric Passport: Security and Privacy Aspects of Machine Readable Travel Document*. Retrieved from https://diuf.unifr.ch/main/is/sites/diuf.unifr.ch.main.is/files/documents/student-projects/eGov_2011_Hesam_Kolahan_&_Tejendra_Thapaliya.pdf

Koprinska, I., & Carrato, S. (2001). Temporal video segmentation: A survey. *Signal Processing Image Communication, 16*(5), 477–500. doi:10.1016/S0923-5965(00)00011-4

Koumousis, K. I., Fotopoulos, V., & Skodras, A. N. (2012, October). A new approach to gradual video transition detection. *Proceedings of the 2012 16th Panhellenic Conference on Informatics* (pp. 245-249). IEEE. doi:10.1109/PCi.2012.85

Kovač, M. (2014). E-Health Demystified: An E-Government Showcase. IEEE Computer, 47(20), 34-42.

Koz, A., & Alatan, A. (2008, March). Oblivious Spatio-Temporal Watermarking of Digital Video by Exploiting the Human Visual System. *IEEE Transactions on Circuits and Systems for Video Technology, 18*(3), 326–337. doi:10.1109/TCSVT.2008.918446

Krestel, E. (Ed.). (1990). *Imaging Systems for Medical Diagnostics*. Berlin, Germany: Siemens Aktiengesellschaft.

Küçüktunç, O., Güdükbay, U., & Ulusoy, Ö. (2010). Fuzzy color histogram-based video segmentation. *Computer Vision and Image Understanding, 114*(1), 125–134. doi:10.1016/j.cviu.2009.09.008

Kumar & Chauhan. (2014). *A survey on feature extraction techniques for color images*. Academic Press.

Kumar & Chauhan. (2014). A Survey On Feature Extraction Techniques For Color Images. *International Journal of Scientific and Engineering Research, 5*(9).

Kumar, & Chauhan. (2014). A Survey On Feature Extraction Techniques For Color Images. *International Journal of Scientific and Engineering Research, 5*(9).

Kumthekar, V. A., & Patil, K. J. (2013, July). Key frame extraction using color histogram method. *International Journal of Scientific Research Engineering & Technology, 2*(4), 207–214.

Kuncheva, L. I. (2005). *Combining Pattern Classifiers, Methods and Algorithms*. New York, NY: Wiley Interscience.

Kundu, M. K., & Mondal, J. (2012, December). A novel technique for automatic abrupt shot transition detection. *Proceedings of the 2012 International Conference on Communications, Devices and Intelligent Systems (CODIS)* (pp. 628-631). IEEE. doi:10.1109/CODIS.2012.6422281

Kutter, M., & Petitcolas, F. (1999, January). A Fair Benchmark for Image Watermarking Systems. *Electronic Imaging Security and Watermarking of Multimedia Contents, 3657*, 25–27.

Lai, C. C., & Chen, Y. C. (2011). A user-oriented image retrieval system based on interactive genetic algorithm. *Instrumentation and Measurement. IEEE Transactions on, 60*(10), 3318–3325.

Lande, T. S., & Vollsnes, A. O. (1995). Object Oriented Music Analysis. *Computers and the Humanities*, *28*(4-5), 253–257. doi:10.1007/BF01830272

Langelaar, G., Setyawan, I., & Lagendijk, R. (2000, September). Watermarking of Digital Image and Video Data – A State of Art Review. *IEEE Signal Processing Magazine*, *17*(5), 20–46. doi:10.1109/79.879337

Laska, J., Davenport, M., & Baraniuk, R. (2009, November). Exact Signal Recovery from Sparsely Corrupted Measurements through the Pursuit of Justice. *Asilomar Conference on Signals, Systems and Computers*. doi:10.1109/ACSSC.2009.5470141

Lauterbur, P. (1973). Image formation by induced local interactions: Examples employing nuclear magnetic resonance. *Nature*, *242*, 190–191.

Le Saux & Amato. (n.d.). *Image classifiers for scene analysis*. Academic Press.

Le, D. D., Satoh, S. I., & Houle, M. E. (2006). Face retrieval in broadcasting news video by fusing temporal and intensity information. In *Image and Video Retrieval* (pp. 391–400). Springer Berlin Heidelberg. doi:10.1007/11788034_40

Lee, D., Barber, R., Niblack, W., Flickner, M., Hafner, J., & Petkovic, D. (1994, October). Indexing for complex queries on a query-by-content image database. In *Pattern Recognition, 1994. Vol. 1-Conference A: Computer Vision & Image Processing.,Proceedings of the 12th IAPR International Conference on* (Vol. 1, pp. 142-146). IEEE. doi:10.1109/ICPR.1994.576246

Lee, K.Y. & Park, J.B. (2010). Application of Particle Swarm Optimization to Economic Dispatch Problem: Advantages and Disadvantages. *Power Systems Conference and Exposition*, 188–192.

Lee, Y., & Chen, L. (2000, June). High Capacity Image Steganographic Model. *IEEE Proceedings of Vision Image and Signal Processing*, (pp. 288 – 294).

Lee, I., Muneesawang, P., & Guan, L. (1996). Automatic Relevance Feedback for Distributed Content-based Image Retrieval. *International Congress for Global Science*.

Lee, S. K., Cho, Y. H., & Kim, S. H. (2010). Collaborative filtering with ordinal scale-based implicit ratings for mobile music recommendations. *Information Sciences*, *180*(11), 2142–2155. doi:10.1016/j.ins.2010.02.004

Lefèvre, S., Holler, J., & Vincent, N. (2003). A review of real-time segmentation of uncompressed video sequences for content-based search and retrieval. *Real-Time Imaging*, *9*(1), 73–98. doi:10.1016/S1077-2014(02)00115-8

Lehtiniemi, A. (2008, December). Evaluating SuperMusic: streaming context-aware mobile music service.*Proceedings of the 2008 International Conference on Advances in Computer Entertainment Technology* (pp. 314-321). ACM. doi:10.1145/1501750.1501826

Lempitsky, V., Kohli, P., Rother, C., & Sharp, T. (2009, September). Image segmentation with a bounding box prior. In *Computer Vision, 2009 IEEE 12th International Conference on* (pp. 277-284). IEEE. doi:10.1109/ICCV.2009.5459262

Lew, M. S., Sebe, N., Djeraba, C., & Jain, R. (2006). Content-based multimedia information retrieval: State of the art and challenges. *ACM Transactions on Multimedia Computing, Communications, and Applications*, *2*(1), 1–19. doi:10.1145/1126004.1126005

Li, B., & Sezan, M. I. (2001). Event detection and summarization in sports video. *Proceedings of the IEEE Workshop on Content-Based Access of Image and Video Libraries (CBAIVL '01)* (pp. 132-138). IEEE. doi:10.1109/IVL.2001.990867

Li, H., & Doermann, D. (2002, December). Video indexing and retrieval based on recognized text. *Proceedings of the 2002 IEEE Workshop on Multimedia Signal Processing* (pp. 245-248). IEEE.

Li, J., Ding, Y., Shi, Y., & Zeng, Q. (2009, August). DWT-based shot boundary detection using support vector machine. *Proceedings of the Fifth International Conference on Information Assurance and Security IAS'09* (Vol. 1, pp. 435-438). IEEE. doi:10.1109/IAS.2009.16

Lidy, T., Silla, C. N. Jr, Cornelis, O., Gouyon, F., Rauber, A., Kaestner, C. A., & Koerich, A. L. (2010). On the suitability of state-of-the-art music information retrieval methods for analyzing, categorizing and accessing non-Western and ethnic music collections. *Signal Processing, 90*(4), 1032–1048. doi:10.1016/j.sigpro.2009.09.014

Lienhart, R. (2000, June). *Dynamic Video Summarization of Home Video.* SPIE: Storage and Retrieval for Media Database, Vol. 3972.

Lienhart, R. W. (2001, January). Reliable dissolve detection. In Photonics West 2001-Electronic Imaging (pp. 219-230). International Society for Optics and Photonics.

Lienhart. (n.d.). *Comparison of Automatic Shot Boundary Detection Algorithms.* Microcomputer Research Labs, Intel Corporation.

Lienhart, R. W. (1999). Comparison of automatic shot boundary detection algorithms. *Proc. of SPIE Conf. Image and Video Processing VII,* (pp. 290-301).

Li, F., Kim, T., Humayun, A., Tsai, D., & Rehg, J. (2013). Video segmentation by tracking many figure-ground segments. *Proceedings of the IEEE International Conference on Computer Vision* (pp. 2192-2199). doi:10.1109/ICCV.2013.273

Lin, C. H., Chen, R. T., & Chan, Y. K. (2009). A smart content-based image retrieval system based on color and texture feature. *Image and Vision Computing, 27*(6), 658–665.

Ling, X., Yuanxin, O., Huan, L., & Zhang, X. (2008, May). A method for fast shot boundary detection based on SVM. Proceedings of the Congress on Image and Signal Processing CISP'08 (Vol. 2, pp. 445-449). IEEE. doi:10.1109/CISP.2008.605

Li, P., & Li, Z. (2014). Color image segmentation using PSO-based histogram thresholding. *WIT Transactions on Information and Communication Technologies, 52,* 1601–1607. doi:10.2495/SSSIT132142

Liping, C. H. E. N., & Tat-Seng, C. H. U. A. (2001, August). A match and tiling approach to content-based video retrieval. In null (p. 77). IEEE. doi:10.1109/ICME.2001.1237716

Li, S., & Lee, M.-C. (2007). *Effective Detection of Various Wipe Transitions. IEEE Transactions on Circuits and Systems for Video Technology, 17(6).*

Liu & Zhao. (2009). Key Frame Extraction from MPEG Video Stream. *International Computer Science and Computational Technology.*

Liu, C., & Song, G. (2011, October). A method of measuring the semantic gap in image retrieval: Using the information theory. In *Image Analysis and Signal Processing (IASP), 2011 International Conference on* (pp. 287-291). IEEE.

Liu, S., Zhu, M., & Zheng, Q. (2008, October). Video shot boundary detection with local feature post refinement. *Proceedings of the 9th International Conference on Signal Processing ICSP '08* (pp. 1548-1551). IEEE.

Liu, X., & Chen, T. (2002, May). Shot boundary detection using temporal statistics modeling. *Proceedings of the 2002 IEEE International Conference on Acoustics, Speech, and Signal Processing (ICASSP)* (Vol. 4, pp. IV-3389). IEEE. doi:10.1109/ICASSP.2002.5745381

Liu, D., Shyu, M. L., Chen, C., & Chen, S. C. (2010, August). *Integration of global and local information in videos for key frame extraction.* IRI. doi:10.1109/IRI.2010.5558944

Liu, J., & Yang, Y. H. (1994). Multi-resolution color image segmentation. *IEEE Transactions on Pattern Analysis and Machine Intelligence, 16*(7), 689–700. doi:10.1109/34.297949

Liu, L., & Fan, G. (2005). Combined key-frame extraction and object-based video segmentation. *IEEE Transactions on Circuits and Systems for Video Technology, 15*(7), 869–884.

Liu, T. Y., Lo, K. T., Zhang, X. D., & Feng, J. (2004). A new cut detection algorithm with constant false-alarm ratio for video segmentation. *Journal of Visual Communication and Image Representation, 15*(2), 132–144. doi:10.1016/j. jvcir.2003.10.001

Liu, Y., Mu, C., Kou, W., & Liu, J. (2015). Modified particle swarm optimization-based multilevel thresholding for image segmentation. *Soft Computing, 19*(5), 1311–1327. doi:10.1007/s00500-014-1345-2

Liu, Y., Zhang, D., Lu, G., & Ma, W. Y. (2007). A survey of content-based image retrieval with high-level semantics. *Pattern Recognition, 40*(1), 262–282. doi:10.1016/j.patcog.2006.04.045

Li, Y., Lee, S. H., Yeh, C. H., & Kuo, C. J. (2006). Techniques for movie content analysis and skimming: Tutorial and overview on video abstraction techniques. *Signal Processing Magazine, 23*(2), 79–89. doi:10.1109/MSP.2006.1621451

Long, F., Zhang, H., & Feng, D. D. (2003). Fundamentals of content-based image retrieval. In *Multimedia Information Retrieval and Management* (pp. 1–26). Springer Berlin Heidelberg.

Lopez, R., & Boulgouris, N., (2010, August). *Compressive Sensing and Combinatorial Algorithms for Image Compression.* A Project Report, King's College, London, UK.

Lopez-Ortega, O., & Lopez-Popa, S. I. (2012). Fractals, Fuzzy Logic and expert Systems to assist in the construction of musical pieces. Expert Systems with Applications, 39, 11911-11923.

Lowe, D. G. (1999). Object recognition from local scale-invariant features. *Proceedings of the seventh IEEE international conference on Computer vision* (Vol. 2, pp. 1150-1157). IEEE. doi:10.1109/ICCV.1999.790410

Lowe, D. G. (2004). Distinctive image features from scale-invariant keypoints. *International Journal of Computer Vision, 60*(2), 91–110. doi:10.1023/B:VISI.0000029664.99615.94

Lu, C., & Tseng, V. S. (2009). A novel method for personalized music recommendation. Expert Systems with Applications, 36, 10035-10044.

Lu, S., King, I., & Lyu, M. R. (2004a, June). Video summarization by video structure analysis and graph optimization. *Proceedings of the 2004 IEEE International Conference on Multimedia and Expo ICME'04* (Vol. 3, pp. 1959-1962). IEEE.

Lu, S., Lyu, M. R., & King, I. (2004b, May). Video summarization by spatial-temporal graph optimization. *Proceedings of the 2004 International Symposium onCircuits and Systems ISCAS'04* (Vol. 2, pp. II-197). IEEE.

Lu, C., & Liao, H. (2001). Video Object based Watermarking: A Rotation and Flipping Resilient Scheme.*Proceedings of International Conference on Image Processing.*

Lukashin, A., & Futchs, R. (1999). Analysis of temporal gene expression profiles, clustering by simulated annealing and determining optimal number of clusters. *Nature Genetics, 22*(3), 281–285. doi:10.1038/10343 PMID:10391217

Łukasiewicz, J., & Tarski, A. (1930). Untersuchungen über den Aussagenkalkül [Investigations into the sentential calculus]. Comptes Rendus des séances de la Société des Sciences et des Lettres de Varsovie, 23, 31–32.

Lupu, E., & Pop, P. (2008). Multimodal Biometric Systems Overview. *ACTA Technica Napocensis, 49*(3), 39–44.

Lu, Z. M., & Shi, Y. (2013). Fast video shot boundary detection based on SVD and pattern matching. *IEEE Transactions on* Image Processing, *22*(12), 5136–5145.

Ma, C., Yu, J., & Huang, B. (2012). A rapid and robust method for shot boundary detection and classification in uncompressed MPEG video sequences. *Int. J. Comput. Sci. Issues, 5*, 368-374.

Ma, W. Y., & Manjunath, B. S. (1996). A pattern thesaurus for browsing large aerial photographs. *Department of Electrical and Computer Engineering, University of Califórnia, ECE Technical Report 96, 10.*

Ma, W. Y., & Manjunath, B. S. (1996, June). Texture features and learning similarity. In *Computer Vision and Pattern Recognition, 1996. Proceedings CVPR'96, 1996 IEEE Computer Society Conference on* (pp. 425-430). IEEE. doi:10.1109/CVPR.1996.517107

Ma, W. Y., & Manjunath, B. S. (1997, June). Edge flow: a framework of boundary detection and image segmentation. In *Computer Vision and Pattern Recognition, 1997. Proceedings., 1997 IEEE Computer Society Conference on* (pp. 744-749). IEEE. doi:10.1109/CVPR.1997.609409

Ma, Y. F., & Zhang, H. J. (2002). A model of motion attention for video skimming. I *Proceedings. 2002 International Conference on Image Processing '02* (Vol. 1, pp. I-129). IEEE.

Ma, Y. F., & Zhang, H. J. (2002). Motion texture: a new motion based video representation. *Proceedings of the 16th International Conference on Pattern Recognition '02* (Vol. 2, pp. 548-551). IEEE.

MacQueen, J. (1967). Some Methods for classification and Analysis of Multivariate Observations. *Proceedings of 5th Berkeley Symposium on Mathematical Statistics and Probability.* University of California Press. Retrieved from http://projecteuclid.org/euclid.bsmsp/1200512992

Madugunki, M., Bormane, D. S., Bhadoria, S., & Dethe, C. G. (2011, April). Comparison of different CBIR techniques. In *Electronics Computer Technology (ICECT), 2011 3rd International Conference on* (Vol. 4, pp. 372-375). IEEE. doi:10.1109/ICECTECH.2011.5941923

Mahesh, K., & Kuppusamy, K. (2012). A New Hybrid Algorithm for Video Segmentation. In *Advances in Computer Science, Engineering & Applications* (pp. 587–595). Springer Berlin Heidelberg. doi:10.1007/978-3-642-30157-5_59

Mallat, S. (1999). *A Wavelet Tour of Signal Processing.* London: Academic Press.

Mani, R., & Nawab, S. H. (1998). Integration Of DSP Algorithms And Musical Constraints For The Separation Of Partials In Polyphonic Music. IEEE.

Manjunath, B. S., & Ma, W. Y. (1996). Texture features for browsing and retrieval of image data. *Pattern Analysis and Machine Intelligence. IEEE Transactions on, 18*(8), 837–842.

Manjunath, S., Guru, D. S., Suraj, M. G., & Harish, B. S. (2011, March). A non parametric shot boundary detection: an eigen gap based approach.*Proceedings of the Fourth Annual ACM Bangalore Conference* (p. 14). ACM. doi:10.1145/1980422.1980436

Mansfield, P. (1977). Multi-planar image formation using NMR spin echoes. *Journal of Physical Chemistry, 10,* L55–L58.

Mansouri, A., & Mahmoudi, A. (2009, June). SVD based Digital Image Watermarking using Complex Wavelet Transform. *Sadhana, 34*(3), 393–406. doi:10.1007/s12046-009-0016-y

Marcus, A., & Maletic, J. I. (2003, May). Recovering documentation-to-source-code traceability links using latent semantic indexing. *Proceedings of the 25th International Conference on Software Engineering '03* (pp. 125-135). IEEE. doi:10.1109/ICSE.2003.1201194

Martinkauppi, J. B., Soriano, M. N., & Laaksonen, M. H. (2001). Behavior of skin color under varying illumination seen by different cameras at different color spaces.*Proc. SPIE, Machine Vision Applications in Industrial Inspection IX*. doi:10.1117/12.420902

Matic, D. (2010). A Genetic Algorithm for composing Music.*In proceedings of the Yugoslav Journal of Operations Research, 20*(1), 157-177.

Matsuo, Y., & Ishizuka, M. (2004). Keyword extraction from a single document using word co-occurrence statistical information. *International Journal of Artificial Intelligence Tools, 13*(1), 157–169. doi:10.1142/S0218213004001466

Maulik, U., Mukhopadhyay, A., & Bandyopadhyay, S. (2009). Combining Pareto-Optimal Clusters using Supervised Learning for Identifying Co-expressed Genes. *BMC Bioinformatics, 10*(1), 27. doi:10.1186/1471-2105-10-27 PMID:19154590

Maulik, U., & Sarkar, A. (2012). Efficient parallel algorithm for pixel classification in remote sensing imagery. *GeoInformatica, 16*(2), 391–407. doi:10.1007/s10707-011-0136-5

Ma, W. Y., & Manjunath, B. S. (1995, November). Image indexing using a texture dictionary. In *Photonics East'95* (pp. 288–298). International Society for Optics and Photonics; doi:10.1007/978-3-662-05300-3_1

Ma, W. Y., & Manjunath, B. S. (1999). Netra: A toolbox for navigating large image databases. *Multimedia Systems, 7*(3), 184–198. doi:10.1007/s005300050121

Ma, Y. F., Lu, L., Zhang, H. J., & Li, M. (2002, December). A user attention model for video summarization.*Proceedings of the tenth ACM international conference on Multimedia* (pp. 533-542). ACM. doi:10.1145/641007.641116

McCormack, J. (1996). Grammar Based Music Composition. In R. Stocker et al. (Eds.), *Complex Systems. From local Interactions to Global Phenomena* (pp. 320–336). Amsterdam: ISO Press.

Mcilwain, P., & McCormack, J. (2005). Design Issues in Musical Composition Networks, Generate and Test. *Proceedings of the Australasian Computer Music Conference*, (pp. 96 – 101).

Mcilwain, P., & McCormack, J. (2005). Design Issues in Musical Composition Networks, Generate and Test.*Proceedings of the Australasian Computer Music Conference* (pp. 96 – 101).

Meguro, M., Taguchi, A., & Hamada, N. (2001). Data-dependent weighted median filtering with robust motion information for image sequence restoration. IEICE Trans. Fundamentals, 2, 424–428.

Mehrotra, S., Rui, Y., Ortega-Binderberger, M., & Huang, T. S. (1997, June). Supporting content-based queries over images in MARS. In *Multimedia Computing and Systems' 97. Proceedings., IEEE International Conference on* (pp. 632-633). IEEE. doi:10.1109/MMCS.1997.609791

Memar, Ksantini, & Boufama. (2014). *Multiple Object Detection With Occlusion using Active Contour Model and Fuzzy C Means*. Academic Press.

Meng, Y., Wang, L. G., & Mao, L. Z. (2009, July). A shot boundary detection algorithm based on particle swarm optimization classifier. *Proceedings of the 2009 International Conference on Machine Learning and Cybernetics,* (Vol. 3, pp. 1671-1676). IEEE. doi:10.1109/ICMLC.2009.5212297

Michaell, B. J. A., & Gordon, L. (2000). *Mastering data mining*. John Wiley &Sons Inc.

Michaell, B. J. A., & Gordon, L. (2003). *Mining the web*. John Wiley &Sons Inc.

Mich, O., Brunelli, R., & Modena, C. M. (1999). A survey on the automatic indexing of video data. *Journal of Visual Communication and Image Representation, 10*(2), 78–112. doi:10.1006/jvci.1997.0404

Miene, A., Hermes, T., Ioannidis, G. T., & Herzog, O. (2003, November). Automatic shot boundary detection using adaptive thresholds.*Proc. TRECVID Workshop* (pp. 1-7).

Miner, G. (2012). *Practical Text Mining and Statistical Analysis for Non-structured Text Data Applications.* Oxford: Academic Press.

Minka, T. P., & Picard, R. W. (1996, June). Interactive learning with a "society of models". In *Computer Vision and Pattern Recognition, 1996. Proceedings CVPR'96, 1996 IEEE Computer Society Conference on* (pp. 447-452). IEEE.

Mirchev, U., & Last, M. (2014). Multi-Document Summarization by Extended Graph Text Representation and Importance Refinement. In A. Fiori (Ed.), *Innovative Document Summarization Techniques: Revolutionizing Knowledge Understanding* (pp. 28–53). Hershey, PA, USA: IGI Global. doi:10.4018/978-1-4666-5019-0.ch002

Mishra, D., Bose, I., Chandra De, U., & Pradhan, B. (2014). A multilevel image thresholding using particle swarm optimization. *IACSIT International Journal of Engineering and Technology, 6*(2), 1204–1211.

Mishra, D., Bose, I., De, U. C., & Das, M. (2015). Medical Image Thresholding Using Particle Swarm Optimization. *Advances in Intelligent Systems and Computing, 308*(1), 379–383. doi:10.1007/978-81-322-2012-1_39

Mitra, S., & Acharya, T. (2005). *Data mining: multimedia, soft computing, and bioinformatics.* John Wiley & Sons.

Mittalkod, S. P., & Srinivasan, G. N. (2011). Shot Boundary Detection Algorithms and Techniques: A Review. *International Journal of Computer System Engineering.*

Mohammed, J., & Nayak, D. R. (2013). *An Efficient Edge Detection Technique by Two Dimensional Rectangular Cellular Automata.* Retrieved from http://arxiv.org/ftp/arxiv/papers/1312/1312.6370.pdf

Montiel, M., & Gómez, F. (2014). Music in the pedagogy of mathematics. *Journal of Mathematics and Music. Taylor and Francis, 8*(2), 151–156. doi:10.1080/17459737.2014.936109

Moreno, S. (2009). Can Music Influence Language and Cognition? *Journal of Mathematics and Music. Contemporary Music Review. Taylor and Francis, 28*(3), 329–345. doi:10.1080/07494460903404410

Mostafa, S., Tolba, A., Abdelkader, F., & Elhindy, H. (2009, August). Video Watermarking Scheme Based on Principal Component Analysis and Wavelet Transform. *IJCSNS International Journal of Computer Science and Network Security, 9*(8), 45–52.

Motlicek, Duffner, Korchagin, Bourlard, Scheffler, Odobez, … Thiergart. (2013). *Real-Time Audio-Visual Analysis for Multiperson Videoconferencing.* Academic Press.

Mozer, M. C. (1994). Neural Network Music Composition by Prediction: Exploring the Benefits of Psychoacoustic Constraints and Multi-scale Processing. *Journal of Connection Science. Taylor and Francis, 6*(2-3), 247–280. doi:10.1080/09540099408915726

Mukherjee, A., & Kundu, D. Motion analysis in video surveillance using edge detection techniques. *IOSR Journal of Computer Engineering.*

Mukherjee, D. P., Das, S. K., & Saha, S. (2007). Key frame estimation in video using randomness measure of feature point pattern. *IEEE Transactions on Circuits and Systems for Video Technology, 17*(5), 612–620.

Müller, H., Michoux, N., Bandon, D., & Geissbuhler, A. (2004). A review of content-based image retrieval systems in medical applications—clinical benefits and future directions. *International Journal of Medical Informatics, 73*(1), 1–23. doi:10.1016/j.ijmedinf.2003.11.024 PMID:15036075

Mundur, P., Rao, Y., & Yesha, Y. (2006). Keyframe-based video summarization using Delaunay clustering. *International Journal on Digital Libraries, 6*(2), 219–232. doi:10.1007/s00799-005-0129-9

Mušic, G., Hafner, I., Winkler, S., & Škrjanc, I. (2012). A Matlab based Petri net Tool for E-learning: Examples for timed simulation and scheduling. Proceedings of MATHMOD, Vienna (pp. 15-17).

Nakashimaa, T., Schaefer, G., Yokota, Y., & Ishibuchi, H. (2007). A weighted fuzzy classifier and its application to image processing tasks. *Fuzzy Sets and Systems, 158*(3), 284–294. doi:10.1016/j.fss.2006.10.011

Nam, J., & Tewfik, A. H. (1999, October). Dynamic video summarization and visualization. *Proceedings of the seventh ACM international conference on Multimedia (Part 2)* (pp. 53-56). ACM. doi:10.1145/319878.319892

Namekava, K., Kasai, C., Tsukamoto, M., & Koyano, A. (1982). Real time blood flow imaging system utilizing autocorrelation techniques. In R. A. Lerski & P. Morley (Eds.), *Ultrasound '82* (pp. 203–208). New York: Pergamon.

Nam, J., & Tewfik, A. H. (2005). Detection of gradual transitions in video sequences using b-spline interpolation. *Multimedia. IEEE Transactions on, 7*(4), 667–679.

Naranjo, V., Angulo, J., Albiol, A., Mossi, J. M., Albiol, A., & Gomez, S. (2007). Gradual transition detection for video partitioning using morphological operators. *Image Analysis & Stereology, 26*(2), 51–61. doi:10.5566/ias.v26.p51-61

Narasimha, R., Savakis, A., Rao, R. M., & De Queiroz, R. (2003, November). Key frame extraction using MPEG-7 motion descriptors. *Conference Record of the Thirty-Seventh Asilomar Conference onSignals, Systems and Computers '04 (Vol. 2,* pp. 1575-1579). IEEE. doi:10.1109/ACSSC.2003.1292250

National Science & Technology Council. (2007). *Introduction to Biometrics.* Retrieved from http://www.biometrics.gov/documents/biofoundationdocs.pdf

Nayak, D. R., Sumit, K. S., & Jahangir, M. (2013). A Cellular Automata based Optimal Edge Detection Technique using Twenty-Five Neighborhood Model. *International Journal of Computer Applications, 84*(10).

Needell, D. (2009). *Topics in Compressed Sensing.* (Ph.D. Thesis). University of California.

Ngo, C. W., Ma, Y. F., & Zhang, H. J. (2005). Video summarization and scene detection by graph modeling. *IEEE Transactions on* Circuits and Systems for Video Technology, *15*(2), 296–305.

Ngo, C., Ma, Y., & Zhang, H. (2003, October). Automatic video summarization by graph modeling. In *Proceedings of Ninth IEEE International Conference on Computer Vision* (pp. 104-109). IEEE.

Ngo, C.-W. (2003). A robust dissolve detector by support vector machine.*Proceedings of the eleventh ACM international conference on Multimedia.* ACM. doi:10.1145/957013.957072

Nicholson, T. J. K., & Nakatsu, R. (2000). Emotion Recognition in Speech Using Neural Networks. *Neural Computing and Applications, 9,* 290–296.

Nikiforova, O., & Pavlova, N. (2008, October). Development of the tool for generation of UML class diagram from two-hemisphere model. *Proceedings of the Third International Conference on Software Engineering Advances ICSEA'08* (pp. 105-112). IEEE. doi:doi:10.1109/ICSEA.2008.37 doi:10.1109/ICSEA.2008.37

Ojo, O., & Kwaaitaal-Spassova, T. G. (2000). An algorithm for integrated noise reduction and sharpness enhancement. *IEEE Transactions on Consumer Electronics, 46*(3), 474–480. doi:10.1109/30.883396

Oliva, A., & Torralba, A. (2001). Modeling the shape of the scene: A holistic representation of the spatial envelope. *International Journal of Computer Vision, 42*(3), 145–175. doi:10.1023/A:1011139631724

Omran, M., Engelbrecht, A., & Salman, A. (2005). Particle swarm optimization method for image clustering. *International Journal of Pattern Recognition and Artificial Intelligence*, *19*(3), 297–322. doi:10.1142/S0218001405004083

Orban, R., Faheem, M.T., & Sarhan, A. (2008). *Comparison between Discrete Wavelet Transform and Dual-Tree Complex wavelet Transform in Video Sequences Using Wavelet-Domain*. Faculty of Computers & Information-Cairo University.

Orriols, X., & Binefa, X. (2001). An EM algorithm for video summarization, generative model approach. *Proceedings of the Eighth IEEE International Conference on Computer Vision. ICCV '01* (Vol. 2, pp. 335-342). IEEE. doi:10.1109/ICCV.2001.937645

Ortega, M., Rui, Y., Chakrabarti, K., Mehrotra, S., & Huang, T. S. (1997, November). Supporting similarity queries in MARS. In *Proceedings of the fifth ACM international conference on Multimedia* (pp. 403-413). ACM. doi:10.1145/266180.266394

Otsuka, I., Nakane, K., Divakaran, A., Hatanaka, K., & Ogawa, M. (2005). A highlight scene detection and video summarization system using audio feature for a personal video recorder. *IEEE Transactions on* Consumer Electronics, *51*(1), 112–116.

Otsu, N. (1979). A Threshold Selection Method from Gray-Level Histograms. *IEEE Transactions on Systems, Man, and Cybernetics*, *9*(1), 62–66. doi:10.1109/TSMC.1979.4310076

Pachouri. (2015). *A Comparative Analysis & Survey of various Feature Extraction Techniques*. Academic Press.

palmOne: Education Solutions Success Stories. Various colleges utilizing PDA's in Education. (n. d.). Retrieved from http://www.palmone.com/us/education/studies/study61.html

Pal, S. K., & Dasgupta, A. (1992). Special fuzzy sets and soft thresholding. *Information Sciences*, *65*(1-2), 65–97. doi:10.1016/0020-0255(92)90078-M

Pampalk, E., Pohle, T., & Widmer, G. (2005, September). *Dynamic Playlist Generation Based on Skipping Behavior* (Vol. 5). ISMIR.

Panagiotakis, C., Doulamis, A., & Tziritas, G. (2009). Equivalent key frames selection based on iso-content principles. *IEEE Transactions on* Circuits and Systems for Video Technology, *19*(3), 447–451.

Pandey, G., Mishra, C., & Ipe, P. (2003). Tansen: A system for automatic raga identification. In *Proceedings of the 1st Indian International Conference on Artificial Intelligence* (pp. 1350–1363).

Papadimitriou, C. H., Tamaki, H., Raghavan, P., & Vempala, S. (1998, May). Latent semantic indexing: A probabilistic analysis.*Proceedings of the seventeenth ACM SIGACT-SIGMOD-SIGART symposium on Principles of database systems* (pp. 159-168). ACM. doi:10.1145/275487.275505

Papadopoulos, S., Vakali, A., & Kompatsiaris, I. (2010). The Dynamics of Content Popularity in Social Media. *International Journal of Data Warehousing and Mining*, *6*(1), 20–37. doi:10.4018/jdwm.2010090802

Pardo, A. (2005). *Simple and Robust Hard Cut Detection using Interframe Differences*. DIE, Facultad de Ingeniera y Tecnologas, Universidad Catolica del Uruguay IIE, Facultad de Ingeniera, Universidad de la Republica. doi:10.1007/11578079_43

Pass, G., & Zabih, R. (1996, December). Histogram refinement for content-based image retrieval. In *Applications of Computer Vision, 1996. WACV'96.,Proceedings 3rd IEEE Workshop on* (pp. 96-102). IEEE.

Patel, B. V., & Meshram, B. B. (2012). *Content based video retrieval systems*. arXiv preprint arXiv:1205.1641

Patel, Shah, & Panchal. (2013). Shot Detection using Pixel wise Difference with Adaptive Threshold and color Histogram Method in Compressed and Uncompressed Video. *International Journal of Computer Application, 64*(4).

Patel, Shah, & Panchal. (2013). Threshold and Color Histogram Method in Compressed and Uncompressed Video. *International Journal of Computer Applications*.

Patel, U., Shah, P., & Panchal, P. (2013). Shot Detection Using Pixel wise Difference with Adaptive Threshold and Color Histogram Method in Compressed and Uncompressed Video. *International Journal of Computers and Applications, 64*(4).

Pato, J., & Millett, L. (2010). Biometric Recognition: Challenges and Opportunities. *Whither Biometric Board.* Retrieved from http://dataprivacylab.org/TIP/2011sept/Biometric.pdf

Paul, R. (2011). Review of Robust Video Watermarking Techniques. *NCCSE, 3*, 90–95.

Pauws, S., & Eggen, B. (2002, October). PATS: Realization and user evaluation of an automatic playlist generator. In ISMIR.

Pawlak, Z. (1982). Rough sets. *International Journal of Computer and Information., 11*(5), 341–356. doi:10.1007/BF01001956

Pawlak, Z. (1991). *Rough sets, Theoretical aspects of reasoning about data.* Kluwer Academic Publishers.

PDA Resources. (n. d.). Retrieved from http://www.marietta.edu/ ~littlea/PDAindex.html

Pearson, K. (1901). On Lines and Planes of Closest Fit to Systems of Points in Space. *Philosophical Magazine, 2*(11), 559–572. doi:10.1080/14786440109462720

Pentland, A., Picard, R. W., & Sclaroff, S. (1996). Photobook: Content-based manipulation of image databases. *International Journal of Computer Vision, 18*(3), 233–254. doi:10.1007/BF00123143

Perez, P., Hue, C., Vermaak, J., & Gangnet, M. (2002). Color-based probabilistic tracking. *Proc. Eur. Conf. Computer Vision.*

Perkins, J. (2010). *Python text processing with NLTK 2.0 cookbook over 80 practical recipes for using Python's NLTK suite of libraries to maximize your natural language processing capabilities.* Cambridge, MA: MIT Press.

Petitcolas, F. (2000, September). Watermarking Schemes Evaluation. *IEEE Signal Processing Magazine, 17*(5), 58–64. doi:10.1109/79.879339

Petkovic, M. (2000). *Content-based video retrieval.* Academic Press.

Petrán, M., Hadravsky, M., Egger, M. D., & Galambos, R. (1968). Tandem scanning reflected-light microscope. *Journal of the Optical Society of America, 58*(5), 661–664. doi:10.1364/JOSA.58.000661

Picard, R. W. (1996). A society of models for video and image libraries. *IBM Systems Journal, 35*(3-4), 292-312.

Picard, R. W., Minka, T. P., & Szummer, M. (1996, September). Modeling user subjectivity in image libraries. In *Image Processing, 1996. Proceedings., International Conference on* (Vol. 1, pp. 777-780). IEEE. doi:10.1109/ICIP.1996.561018

Picard, R. W. (1995). *Digital libraries: Meeting place for high-level and low-level vision.* Springer Berlin Heidelberg.

Platel, H., Baron, J.-C., Desgranges, B., Bernard, F., & Eustache, F. (2003). Semantic and episodic memory of music are subserved by distinct neural networks. *NeuroImage, 20*(1), 244–256. doi:10.1016/S1053-8119(03)00287-8 PMID:14527585

Platt, J. (1991). A resource-allocating network for function interpolation. *Neural Computation, 3*(2), 213–225. doi:10.1162/neco.1991.3.2.213

Podilchuk, C., & Delp, E. (2001). Digital Watermarking: Algorithms and Applications. *IEEE Signal Processing Magazine, 18*(4), 33–46. doi:10.1109/79.939835

Pohle, T., Pampalk, E., & Widmer, G. (2005, September). Generating similarity-based playlists using traveling salesman algorithms.*Proceedings of the 8th International Conference on Digital Audio Effects (DAFx-05)* (pp. 220-225).

Poleg, Y., Arora, C., & Peleg, S. (2014). Temporal segmentation of egocentric videos.*Proceedings of the IEEE Conference on Computer Vision and Pattern Recognition* (pp. 2537-2544).

Ponomarenko, N., Jin, L., Lukin, V. V., & Egiazarian, K. (2011). *Self-Similarity Measure for Assessment of Image Visual Quality*. Advanced Concepts for Intelligent Vision Systems (ACIVS).

Ponomarenko, N., Lukin, V., Zelensky, A., Egiazarian, K., Carli, M., Battisti, F. (2009). TID2008 - A Database for Evaluation of Full-Reference Visual Quality Assessment Metrics. *Advances of Modern Radio electronics, 10*, 30-45.

Popovici, A., & Popovici, D. (2014). *Cellular Automata in Image Processing*. Retrieved from http://www-ics.acs.i.kyoto-u.ac.jp/mtns2002/papers/17761_4.pdf

Porter, S. V., Mirmehdi, M., & Thomas, B. T. (2001, September). *Detection and Classification of Shot Transitions*. BMVC.

Preda, R., & Vizireanu, D. (2007, September). Blind Watermarking Capacity Analysis of MPEG2 Coded Video.*Proceedings of Conference of Telecommunications in Modern Satellite, Cable and Broadcasting Services, Serbia*, 465 – 468. doi:10.1109/TELSKS.2007.4376042

Prewitt, J. M. S. (1970). Object enhancement and extraction. In Picture Analysis and Psychopictorics. Academic Press.

Priya, G., & Domnic, S. (2012). Transition detection using Hilbert transform and texture features. *American J. of Signal Proc., 10*, 35–40. doi:10.5923/j.ajsp.20120202.06

Priya, K., Ramani, G. R., & Jacob, G. S. (2012). Data Mining Techniques for Automatic recognition of Carnatic Raga Swaram notes. *International Journal of Computers and Applications, 52*(10), 4–10. doi:10.5120/8236-1444

Purcell, E. M., Torrey, H. C., & Pound, R. V. (1946). Resonance absorption by nuclear magnetic resonance in a solid. *Physical Review, 69*(1-2), 37–38. doi:10.1103/PhysRev.69.37

Qi, Y., Hauptmann, A., & Liu, T. (2003, July). Supervised classification for video shot segmentation. *Proceedings of the 2003 International Conference on Multimedia and Expo ICME'03* (Vol. 2, pp. II-689). IEEE.

Qin, T., Gu, J., Chen, H., & Tang, Z. (2010, September). A fast shot-boundary detection based on k-step slipped window. *Proceedings of the 2010 2nd IEEE International Conference on Network Infrastructure and Digital Content* (pp. 190-195). IEEE. doi:10.1109/ICNIDC.2010.5657841

Qin, J., Lewis, D., & Noble, W. (2003). Kernel hierarchical gene clustering from microarray gene expression data. *Bioinformatics (Oxford, England), 19*(16), 2097–2104. doi:10.1093/bioinformatics/btg288 PMID:14594715

Quack, T., Ferrari, V., & Van Gool, L. (2006). Video mining with frequent itemset configurations. In *Image and Video Retrieval* (pp. 360–369). Springer Berlin Heidelberg. doi:10.1007/11788034_37

Quenot, G., Benois-Pineau, J., Mansencal, B., Rossi, E., Cord, M., Precioso, F., & Pellerin, D. et al. (2008, October). Rushes summarization by IRIM consortium: redundancy removal and multi-feature fusion.*Proceedings of the 2nd ACM TRECVID video summarization workshop* (pp. 80-84). ACM. doi:10.1145/1463563.1463577

Raghavendra, K., & Chetan, K. (2009, December). A Blind and Robust Watermarking Scheme with Scrambled Watermark for Video Authentication.*Proceedings of IEEE International Conference on Internet Multimedia Services Architecture and Applications*. doi:10.1109/IMSAA.2009.5439475

Raikwar, S. C., Bhatnagar, C., & Jalal, A. S. (2015). A Novel Framework for Efficient Extraction of Meaningful Key Frames from Surveillance Video. *International Journal of System Dynamics Applications, 4*(2), 56–73. doi:10.4018/ijsda.2015040104

Rajab, L., Al-Khatib, T., & Ai-Haj, A. (2008, December). Hybrid DWT-SVD Video Watermarking.*Proceedings of International Conference on Innovations in Information Technology.*

Ramalingam, M. (2011). Stego Machine – Video Steganography using Modified LSB Algorithm. *World Academy of Science. Engineering and Technology, 74*, 502–505.

Rao.Singiresu, S. (2009). *Engineering Optimization Theory and Practice* (4th ed.). JohnWiley and Sons.

Rao, B., Tarakeswara, Chinnam, S., Kunth, L. P., &Gargi, M. (2012). Automatic Melakartha Raaga Identification System: Carnatic Music. *International Journal of Advanced Research in Artificial Intelligence, 1*(4), 43–44.

Rao, P. C., & Patnaik, M. R. (2014). Contourlet Transform Based Shot Boundary Detection. *International Journal of Signal Processing. Image Processing and Pattern Recognition, 7*(4), 381–388. doi:10.14257/ijsip.2014.7.4.36

Ratha, N., Connell, J., & Bolle, R. (2001). Enhancing Security and Privacy in Biometric Based Authentication Systems. *IBM Systems Journal, 40*(3), 614–634. doi:10.1147/sj.403.0614

Raval, M., Joshi, M., Rege, P., & Parulkar, S. (2011, December). Image Tampering Detection Using Compressive Sensing Based Watermarking Scheme. In *Proceedings of MVIP 2011.*

Raval, M., & Rege, P. (2003). Discrete Wavelet Transform Based Multiple Watermarking Scheme. *Proceedings of the Convergent Technologies for the Asia-Pacific Region, 3*, 935–938.

Rawat & Singhai. (2013). *Review of Motion Estimation and Video Stabilization techniques for hand held mobile video.* Academic Press.

Reddy, P., Tarakeswara, B. R., & Sudha, K. R., & Hari. (2011). K-Nearest Neighbour and Earth Mover Distance for Raaga Recognition. *International Journal of Computers and Applications, 33*(5), 30–38.

Reiber, J. H. C. (2000). Angiography and intravascular ultrasound. In Handbook of Medical Imaging, Vol. 2, Medical Image Processing and Analysis. SPIE, International Society for Optical Engineering. doi:10.1117/3.831079.ch13

Reips, U.-D., & Garaizar, P. (2011). Mining Twitter: Microblogging as a source for psychological wisdom of the crowds. *Behavior Research Methods, 43*(3), 635–642. doi:10.3758/s13428-011-0116-6 PMID:21701948

Rieder, P., & Scheffler, G. (2001). New concepts on denoising and sharpening of video signals. *IEEE Transactions on Consumer Electronics, 47*(8), 666–671. doi:10.1109/30.964161

Roddy, C., Douglas, C. E., & Cox, C. (2005). Beyond emotion archetypes: Databases for emotion modelling using neural networks. *Neural Networks, 18*(4), 371–388. doi:10.1016/j.neunet.2005.03.002 PMID:15961273

Rong, J., Ma, Y. F., & Wu, L. (2005, January). Gradual transition detection using em curve fitting.*Proceedings of the 11th InternationalMultimedia Modelling Conference MMM '05*(pp. 364-369). IEEE.

Ross, C. J., & Rao, P. (2012). Detection of Raga-Characteristics Phrases From Hindustani Classical Music Audio. *Proceedings of the 2nd CompMusic Workshop* (pp. 133-138).

Rothermel, K., Schnitzer, S., Lange, R., Dürr, F., & Farrell, T. (2012). *Context-aware and quality-aware algorithms for efficient mobile object management. In Proceedings of Elsevier Journal of Pervasive and Mobile Computing* (pp. 131–146). Elsevier.

Rousseeuw, P. J. (1987). Silhouettes: A Graphical Aid to the Interpretation and Validation of Cluster Analysis. *Computational & Applied Mathematics, 20*, 53–65. doi:10.1016/0377-0427(87)90125-7

Rowlands, J. A., & Yorkston, J. (2000). Flat panel detectors for digital radiography. In J. Beutel, H. L. Kundel, & R. L. Van Metter (Eds.), *Handbook of Medical Imaging* (Vol. I). Washington, DC: SPIE Press.

Roy, S., Chakrabarty, S., & De, D. (2014). Automatic Raga Recognition using fundamental Frequency Range of Extracted Musical notes. *Proceedings of theInternational Conference on Image and Signal Processing (ICISP-2014)*, (pp. 337-345). Elsevier.

Roy, S., Chakrabarty, S., Bhakta, P., & De, D. (2013). Modelling High Performing Music Computing using Petri Nets. *Proceedings of International Conference on Control, Instrumentation, Energy and Communication* (pp. 757-761).

Roy, S., Chakrabarty, S., & De, D. (2014). A Framework of Musical Pattern Recognition Using Petri Nets. In *Emerging Trends in Computing and Communication* (pp. 245–252). Springer India. doi:10.1007/978-81-322-1817-3_26

Rubenstein, W. B. (1987, December). A database design for musical information. *SIGMOD Record, 16*(3), 479–490. doi:10.1145/38714.38762

Rui, Y., Huang, T. S., & Mehrotra, S. (1997, October). Content-based image retrieval with relevance feedback in MARS. In *Image Processing, 1997. Proceedings., International Conference on* (Vol. 2, pp. 815-818). IEEE. doi:10.1109/ICIP.1997.638621

Rui, Y., Huang, T. S., & Chang, S. F. (1999). Image retrieval: Current techniques, promising directions, and open issues. *Journal of Visual Communication and Image Representation, 10*(1), 39–62. doi:10.1006/jvci.1999.0413

Saini, S., & Gupta, P. (2015). Video Shot Boundary Detection Using Various Techniques. *International Journal of Emerging Technologies and Innovative Research, 2*(4), 1109–1115.

Salman, A., & Romberg, J. (2013). Fast and Accurate Algorithms for Re-weighted-norm Minimization. *IEEE Transactions on Signal Processing, 61*(23), 5905–5916. doi:10.1109/TSP.2013.2279362

Santhi, V., & Thangavelu, A. (2009, October). DWT SVD Combined Full Band Robust Watermarking Technique for Color Images in YUV Color Space. *International Journal of Computer Theory and Engineering, 1*(4).

Sao, N., & Mishra, R. (2014). A survey based on video shot boundary detection techniques. *International Journal of Advanced Research in Computer and Communication Engineering, 3*(4).

Šarić, M., Dujmić, H., & Baričević, D. (2008). Shot boundary detection in soccer video using twin-comparison algorithm and dominant color region. *Journal of Information and Organizational Sciences, 32*(1), 67–73.

Sarkar, A., & Maulik, U. (2009) Parallel Point symmetry Based Clustering for Gene Microarray Data, In *Proceedings of Seventh International Conference on Advances in Pattern Recognition-2009 (ICAPR, 2009)*. IEEE Computer Society. doi:doi:10.1109/ICAPR.2009.40 doi:10.1109/ICAPR.2009.40

Sarkar, A., & Maulik, U. (2009). Parallel Clustering Technique Using Modified Symmetry Based Distance. In *Proceedings of 1st International Conference on Computer, Communication, Control and Information Technology (C3IT 2009)*. MacMillan Publishers India Ltd.

Scassellati, B. M., Alexopoulos, S., & Flickner, M. D. (1994, April). Retrieving images by 2D shape: a comparison of computation methods with human perceptual judgments. In *IS&T/SPIE 1994 International Symposium on Electronic Imaging: Science and Technology* (pp. 2-14). International Society for Optics and Photonics.

Schade, O. H. (1956). Optical and photoelectric analog of the eye. *Journal of the Optical Society of America, 46*(9), 721–739. doi:10.1364/JOSA.46.000721 PMID:13358013

Schildt, H. (2011). Java: The Complete Reference (7th ed.). New Delhi, India: Tata Mcgraw Hill Education Private Limited.

Schmidt, D. C., Stal, M., Rohnert, H., & Buschmann, F. (2013). *Pattern-Oriented Software Architecture, Patterns for Concurrent and Networked Objects* (Vol. 2). John Wiley & Sons.

Schneiderman, H., & Kanade, T. (n.d.). *CMU/VASC Image database*. Retrieved from http://vasc.ri.cmu.edu/idb/html/face/profile_images/

Scott, P. (2001). Music classification using neural networks. Manuscript Class ee373a, Stanford.

Scott, C. (1998). *Introduction to Optics and Optical Imaging*. Washington, DC: IEEE Press.

Scott, J. (2012). *Social Network Analysis*. London: SAGE Publications.

Secrest, B. G., & Doddington, G. R. (1983). An integrated pitch tracking algorithm for speech systems. *Proc. IEEE ICASSP* (pp.1352-1355). IEEE. doi:10.1109/ICASSP.1983.1172016

Sengupta, R. (1990). Study on some Aspects of the Singer's Formant in North Indian Classical Singing. *Journal of Voice, Raven Press, New York, 4*(2), 129.

Serdean, C., Ambroze, M., Tomlinson, M., & Wade, G. (2002, June). Combating Geometrical Attacks in a DWT based Blind Video Watermarking System. *IEEE Region 8 International Symposium on Video/Image Processing and Multimedia Communications, Zadar.*

Setnes, M., & Babuska, R. (1999). Fuzzy relational classifier trained by fuzzy clustering. *IEEE Transactions on Systems, Man, and Cybernetics. Part B, Cybernetics, 29*(5), 619–625. doi:10.1109/3477.790444 PMID:18252339

Sezgin, M., & Sankur, B. (2004). Survey over image thresholding techniques and quantitative performance evaluation. *Journal of Electronic Imaging, 13*(1), 146–165. doi:10.1117/1.1631315

Shannon, C. E. (1948). A Mathematical Theory of Communication. *The Bell System Technical Journal, 27*(3), 379–423. doi:10.1002/j.1538-7305.1948.tb01338.x

Sharma, O., Mioc, D., & Anton, F. (2008). Polygon feature extraction from satellite imagery based on colour image segmentation and medial axis. The International Archives of the Photogrammetry, Remote Sensing and Spatial Information Sciences.

Sharmay, O. (2009). Polygon Feature Extraction From Satellite Imagery Based On Colour Image Segmentation And Medial Axis. Academic Press.

Sheehan, F., Wilson, D. C., Shavelle, D., & Geiser, E. A. (2000). Echocardiography. In Sonka, M. & Fitzpatrick, J.M. (Eds.), Handbook of Medical Imaging, Vol. 2, Medical Image Processing and Analysis. SPIE, International Society for Optical Engineering.

Sheikh, M., & Baraniuk, R. (2007, September). Blind Error Free Detection of Transform Domain Watermarks. *IEEE International Conference on Image Processing.*

Shen, S., & Cao, J. (2011, March). Abrupt shot boundary detection algorithm based on fuzzy clustering neural network. *Proceedings of the 2011 3rd International Conference on Computer Research and Development.*

Sherlock, G. (2000). Analysis of large-scale gene-expression data. *Current Opinion in Immunology, 12*(1), 201–205. doi:10.1016/S0952-7915(99)00074-6 PMID:10712947

Shih, F. (2008). Digital Watermarking and Steganography – Fundamentals and Techniques. CRC Press.

Shi, J., & Malik, J. (2000). Normalized cuts and image segmentation. *Pattern Analysis and Machine Intelligence. IEEE Transactions on, 22*(8), 888–905.

Shirahama, K., Matsuoka, Y., & Uehara, K. (2012). Event retrieval in video archives using rough set theory and partially supervised learning. *Multimedia Tools and Applications, 57*(1), 145–173. doi:10.1007/s11042-011-0727-z

Shmulevich, I., & Coyle, E. J. (1997). Establishing the Tonal Context for Musical Pattern Recognition. *Proceedings of the 1997 IEEE Workshop on Applications of Signal Processing to Audio and Acoustics.* doi:10.1109/ASPAA.1997.625608

Shmulevich, I., & Povel, D. (1998). Rhythm Complexity Measures for Music Pattern Recognition. *Proceedings of IEEE Workshop on Multimedia Signal Processing.* doi:10.1109/MMSP.1998.738930

Shmulevich, I., Yli-Harja, O., Coyle, E. J., Povel, D., & Lemstrm, K. (2001). *Perceptual Issues in Music Pattern Recognition Complexity of Rhythm and Key Finding. Computers and the Humanities.* Kluwer Academic Publishers.

Shoemaker, C. (2002). *Hidden bits: A Survey of Techniques for Digital Watermarking. Independent Study, EER 290, Prof.* Rudko.

Shyu, C. R., Brodley, C. E., Kak, A. C., Kosaka, A., Aisen, A. M., & Broderick, L. S. (1999). ASSERT: A physician-in-the-loop content-based retrieval system for HRCT image databases. *Computer Vision and Image Understanding, 75*(1), 111–132. doi:10.1006/cviu.1999.0768

Singh & Budhiraja. (2011). *Feature extraction and classification techniques in O.C.R systems for handwritten Gurumukhi script.* Academic Press.

Singha, M., & Hemachandran, K. (2012). Content-based image retrieval using color and texture. *Signal & Image Processing: An International Journal, 3*(1), 39–57.

Sinha, P. (2008). Artificial Composition: An Experiment on Indian Music. *Journal of New Music Research. Taylor and Francis, 37*(3), 221–232. doi:10.1080/09298210802535010

Sivic, J., Everingham, M., & Zisserman, A. (2005). Person spotting: video shot retrieval for face sets. In *Image and Video Retrieval* (pp. 226–236). Springer Berlin Heidelberg. doi:10.1007/11526346_26

Smeulders, A. W., Worring, M., Santini, S., Gupta, A., & Jain, R. (2000). Content-based image retrieval at the end of the early years. *Pattern Analysis and Machine Intelligence. IEEE Transactions on, 22*(12), 1349–1380.

Smith, J. R., & Chang, S. F. (1994, November). Transform features for texture classification and discrimination in large image databases. In *Image Processing, 1994. Proceedings. ICIP-94.,IEEE International Conference* (*Vol. 3*, pp. 407-411). IEEE. doi:10.1109/ICIP.1994.413817

Smith, J. R., & Chang, S. F. (1996, May). Automated binary texture feature sets for image retrieval. In *Acoustics, Speech, and Signal Processing, 1996. ICASSP-96. Conference Proceedings., 1996 IEEE International Conference on* (Vol. 4, pp. 2239-2242). IEEE. doi:10.1109/ICASSP.1996.545867

Smith, J. R., Naphade, M., & Natsev, A. (2003, July). Multimedia semantic indexing using model vectors. *Proceedings of the 2003 International Conference on Multimedia and Expo ICME'03* (Vol. 2, pp. II-445). IEEE. doi:10.1109/ICME.2003.1221649

Smith, M. A., & Kanade, T. (1997, June). Video skimming and characterization through the combination of image and language understanding techniques. *Proceedings of the 1997 IEEE Computer Society Conference on Computer Vision and Pattern Recognition '97* (pp. 775-781). IEEE. doi:10.1109/CVPR.1997.609414

Smith, M., Milic-Frayling, N., Shneiderman, B., Mendes Rodrigues, E., Leskovec, J., & Dunne, C. (2010). *NodeXL: a free and open network overview, discovery and exploration add-in for Excel 2007/2010.* Retrieved from http://www.smrfoundation.org

Smith, A. R. III. (1971). Two-dimensional Formal Languages and Pattern Recognition by Cellular Automata. In *IEEE Conference Record of 12th Annual Symposium on Switchinh and Automata Theory.* doi:10.1109/SWAT.1971.29

Smith, J. R., & Chang, S. F. (1996). *Searching for images and videos on the world-wide web.* IEEE Multimedia Magazine.

Smith, J. R., & Chang, S. F. (1997). Visually searching the web for content. *IEEE MultiMedia, 4*(3), 12–20. doi:10.1109/93.621578

Smith, J. R., & Chang, S. F. (1997, February). VisualSEEk: a fully automated content-based image query system. In *Proceedings of the fourth ACM international conference on Multimedia* (pp. 87-98). ACM.

Snijders, C., Matzat, U., & Reips, U.-D. (2012). 'Big Data': Big gaps of knowledge in the field of Internet. *International Journal of Internet Science, 7,* 1–5. Retrieved from http://www.ijis.net/ijis7_1/ijis7_1_editorial.html

Sobel, I. (1970). *Camera Models and Perception.* (Ph.D. Thesis). Stanford University, Stanford, CA.

Song, S. M., Kwon, T. H., Kim, W. M., Kim, H., & Rhee, B. D. (1997, December). Detection of gradual scene changes for parsing of video data. In Photonics West'98 Electronic Imaging (pp. 404-413). International Society for Optics and Photonics.

Song, X., & Fan, G. (2005, January). Joint key-frame extraction and object-based video segmentation. Proceedings of the Seventh IEEE Workshops on Application of Computer Vision (Vol. 2, pp. 126-131). IEEE. doi:10.1109/ACVMOT.2005.66

Song, Y., Dixon, S., & Pearce, M. (2012). A Survey of Music Recommendation Systems and Future Perspectives. *Proceedings of theInternational Symposium on Computer Music Modelling and Retrieval* (pp. 395-410). IEEE.

Sowmya, R., & Shettar, R. (2013). Analysis and verification of video summarization using shot boundary detection. *Am Int J Res Sci Technol Eng Math, 3*(1), 82–86.

Spang, R. (2003). Diagnostic signatures from microarrays, a bioinformatics concept for personalized medicine. *BIO-SILICO, 1*(2), 64–68. doi:10.1016/S1478-5382(03)02329-1

Spearman, C. (1904). The proof and measurement of association between two things. *The American Journal of Psychology, 15*(1), 72–101. doi:10.2307/1412159 PMID:3322052

Sridevi, T., Krishnaveni, B., Vijayakumar, V., & Ramadevi, Y., (2010, September). A Video Watermarking Algorithm for MPEG Videos. *A2CWiC 2010 – Amrita ACM-W Celebration of Women in Computing.*

Sridhar, R., & Subramanian, M. (2011). Latent Dirichlet Allocation Model for Raga Identification of Caenatic Music. *Journal of Computer Science,* 1711-1716.

Sridhar, R., Karthiga, S., & Geetha, T. V. (2010). Fundamental Frequency Estimation of Carnatic Music Songs Based on the Principle of Mutation. *IJCSI, 7*(4).

Sridhar, R., & Geetha, T. V. (2009). Raga identification of carnatic music for music information retrieval. *International Journal of Recent Trends in Engineering, 1*(1), 571–574.

Srimani, P. K., & Parimala, Y. G. (2012). Artificial Neural Network (ANN) Approach for an Intelligent System: A Case Study in Carnatic Classical Music (CCM). *Proceedings of International Conference on Intelligent Computational Systems* (pp. 101-105).

Stavros, N., & Fakotakis, N. (2008). *Speech/music discrimination based on discrete wavelet transform. In Artificial Intelligence: Theories, Models and Applications* (pp. 205–211). Berlin: Springer.

Stavros, N., Potamitis, I., & Fakotakis, N. (2009). Exploiting temporal feature integration for generalized sound recognition. *EURASIP Journal on Advances in Signal Processing*, *1*, 807162.

Stegmann, H., Wepf, R., & Schroder, R. R. (1999). Electron microscopic image acquisition. In B. Jahne, H. Haussecker, & P. Geissler (Eds.), *Handbook of Computer Vision and Applications* (Vol. 1). New York: Academic Press.

Stelzer, E. H. K. (1999). Three-dimensional light microscopy. In B. Jahne, H. Haussecker, & P. Geissler (Eds.), *Handbook of Computer Vision and Applications* (Vol. 1). New York: Academic Press.

Stollnitz, E. J., Derose, T. D., & Salesin, D. H. (1996). *Wavelets for Computer Graphics, Theory and applications*. San Francisco: Morgan Kaufmann Publishers.

Stricker, O., M. (1995). Similarity of color images.*Proceedings of SPIE Storage and Retrieval for Image and Video Databases III*. doi:10.1117/12.205308

Su, C. W., Liao, H. Y. M., Tyan, H. R., Fan, K. C., & Chen, L. H. (2005). A motion-tolerant dissolve detection algorithm. *IEEE Transactions on* Multimedia, *7*(6), 1106–1113.

Su, C.-W., Liao, H.-Y., Tyan, H.-R., Lin, C.-W., Chen, D.-Y., & Fan, K.-C. (2007). Motion flow-based video retrieval. *IEEE Transactions on* Multimedia, *9*(6), 1193–1201.

Sui, Y., Zou, X., & Du, Y. (2013). Cancellable Biometrics. In Biometrics: from Fiction to Practice. Pan Stanford Publishing Pte. Ltd.

Su, J. H., Huang, W. J., Yu, P. S., & Tseng, V. S. (2011). Efficient relevance feedback for content-based image retrieval by mining user navigation patterns. *Knowledge and Data Engineering. IEEE Transactions on*, *23*(3), 360–372.

Su, J. H., Yeh, H. H., Yu, P. S., & Tseng, V. S. (2010). Music recommendation using content and context information mining. *IEEE Intelligent Systems*, *25*(1), 16–26. doi:10.1109/MIS.2010.23

Sulaiman, S. N., & Isa, N. A. M. (2010). Adaptive fuzzy-K-means clustering algorithm for image segmentation. *Consumer Electronics. IEEE Transactions on*, *56*(4), 2661–2668.

Sun, X., Zhao, L., & Zhang, M. (2011, August). A Novel Shot Boundary Detection Method Based on Genetic Algorithm-Support Vector Machine. *Proceedings of the 2011 International Conference on Intelligent Human-Machine Systems and Cybernetics (IHMSC)* (Vol. 1, pp. 144-147). IEEE. doi:10.1109/IHMSC.2011.41

Sun, X. (2000). A pitch determination algorithm based on sub-harmonic to harmonic ratio. *Proceedings of International Conference of Speech and Language Processing*.

Sun, X., Zhang, Y., Hao, X., & Min, W. (2014). Shot Boundary Detection Based on SVM Optimization Model. *Open Automation and Control Systems Journal*, *6*(1), 393–397. doi:10.2174/1874444301406010393

Swain, M. J., & Ballard, D. H. (1991). Color indexing. *International Journal of Computer Vision*, *7*(1), 11–32. doi:10.1007/BF00130487

Sze, K. W., Lam, K. M., & Qiu, G. (2005). A new key frame representation for video segment retrieval. *IEEE Transactions on* Circuits and Systems for Video Technology, *15*(9), 1148–1155.

Tagliasacchi, M., Valenzise, G., Tubaro, S., Cancelli, G., & Barni, M. (2009). A Compressive Sensing Based Watermarking Scheme for Sparse Image Tampering Identification.*Proc. ICIP 2009*, (pp. 1265 – 1268).

Takagi, T., & Sugeno, M. (1985). Fuzzy Identification of Systems and Its Applications to Modelling and Control. *IEEE Transactions on Systems, Man, and Cybernetics, 15*(1), 116–132. doi:10.1109/TSMC.1985.6313399

Tamura, H., Mori, S., & Yamawaki, T. (1978). Textural features corresponding to visual perception. *Systems, Man and Cybernetics. IEEE Transactions on, 8*(6), 460–473.

Tangelder, J. W., & Veltkamp, R. C. (2008). A survey of content-based 3D shape retrieval methods. *Multimedia Tools and Applications, 39*(3), 441–471. doi:10.1007/s11042-007-0181-0

Tang, Y. Y., Wickerhauser, V., Yuen, P. C., & Li, G. H. (2001). *Wavelet Analysis and Its Applications.* Berlin: Springer-Verlag. doi:10.1007/3-540-45333-4

Tao, W. B., Tian, J. W., & Liu, J. (2003). Image segmentation by three-level thresholding based on maximum fuzzy entropy and genetic algorithm. *Pattern Recognition Letters, 24*(16), 3069–3078. doi:10.1016/S0167-8655(03)00166-1

Tarakeswara, B. R., & Reddy, P. (2011). A Novel Process for Melakartha Raaga Recognition using Hidden Marcov Models (HMM). *International Journal of Research and Reviews in Computer Science, 2*(2), 508–513.

Tariq, A., Flail, N., & Ghazi, A. (2014). Using Daub achy Wavelet for Shot Boundary Detection. *IOSR Journals, 1*(16), 66–70.

Taskiran, Amir, Ponceleon, & Delp. (2002). *Automated Video Summarization Using Speech Transcripts.* IBM Almaden Research Center and Video and Image Processing Laboratory.

Taskirany, Amirz, Ponceleonz, & Delp. (2001). *Automated Video Summarization Using Speech Transcripts.* Academic Press.

Tavazoie, S., Hughes, J., Campbell, M., Cho, R., & Church, G. (2001). Systematic determination of genetic network architecture. *Bioinformatics (Oxford, England), 17*, 405–414. PMID:11331234

Technology Watch Report, I. T. U.-T. (December, 2009). *Biometrics and Standards.* Retrieved from http://www.itu.int/dms_pub/itu-t/oth/23/01/T230100000D0002MSWE.doc

Teddy, K. O. (2005). Multimodal Biometric Identification for Large User Population Using Fingerprint, Face and Iris Recognition. *Proceeding of the IEEE 34th Applied Imagery and Pattern Recognition Workshop (AIPR05).* doi:10.1109/AIPR.2005.35

Thakare, S. (2012). Intelligent processing and analysis of image for shot boundary detection. *International Journal of Emerging Technology and Advanced Engineering, 2*(2), 208–212.

Thakre, K. S. (2014). Analysis and Review of Formal Approaches to Automatic Video Shot Boundary Detection. *Analysis, 3*(1).

Thanki, R., Trivedi, R., Kher, R., & Vyas, D. (2011). Digital Watermarking Using White Gaussian Noise (WGN) in Spatial Domain. *Proceedings of International Conference on Innovative Science & Engineering Technology (ICISET),* (pp. 38 – 42).

Thieme, M. (2003). Multimodal Biometric Systems: Applications and Usage Scenarios. *Biometric Consortium Conference.*

Tiesheng, F., Guiqiang, L., Chunyi, D., & Danhua, W. (2013, May). A Digital Image Watermarking Method Based on the Theory of Compressed Sensing. *International Journal Automation and Control Engineering, 2*(2), 56–61.

Tirkel, A., Rankin, G., Schyndel, R., Ho, W., Mee, N., & Osborne, C. (1993). Electronics Watermark. *DICTA 93.* Macquarie University.

Todd, P. M., & Loy, G. D. (Eds.). (1991). *Music and connectionism.* MIT Press.

Tola, E., Lepetit, V., & Fua, P. (2010). Daisy: An efficient dense descriptor applied to wide-baseline stereo. *IEEE Transactions on* Pattern Analysis and Machine Intelligence, *32*(5), 815–830.

Trček, D., & Trček, G. (2013). *Computationally Supported Musical Composition Using Petri Nets.* Latest Trends in Applied Computational Science.

Tropp, J., & Gilbert, A. (2007, December). Signal Recovery from Random Measurements via Orthogonal Matching Pursuit. *IEEE Transactions on Information Theory, 53*(12), 4655–4666. doi:10.1109/TIT.2007.909108

Truong, B. T., Dorai, C., & Venkatesh, S. (2000, October). New enhancements to cut, fade, and dissolve detection processes in video segmentation.*Proceedings of the eighth ACM international conference on Multimedia* (pp. 219-227). ACM. doi:10.1145/354384.354481

Truong, B. T., & Venkatesh, S. (2007). Video abstraction: A systematic review and classification. *ACM Transactions on Multimedia Computing, Communications, and Applications, 3*(1), 3, es. doi:10.1145/1198302.1198305

Tsamoura, E., Mezaris, V., & Kompatsiaris, I. (2008a, October). Gradual transition detection using color coherence and other criteria in a video shot meta-segmentation framework. *Proceedings of the 15th IEEE International Conference on Image Processing ICIP '08* (pp. 45-48). IEEE. doi:10.1109/ICIP.2008.4711687

Tsamoura, E., Mezaris, V., & Kompatsiaris, I. (2008b, June). Video shot meta-segmentation based on multiple criteria for gradual transition detection. *Proceedings of the International Workshop on Content-Based Multimedia Indexing CBMI '08* (pp. 51-57). IEEE. doi:10.1109/CBMI.2008.4564927

Turk. (2014). *Gesture Recognition.* Academic Press.

Turnes, C., Balcan, D., & Romberg, J. (2012). Image Deconvolution via Superfast Inversion of a Class of two-level Toeplitz Matrices. *2012 19th IEEE International Conference on Image Processing (ICIP),* (pp. 3073 – 3076).

Tzanetakis, G., Kapur, A., Schloss, W. A., & Wright, M. (2007). Computational Ethnomusicology. *Journal of Interdisciplinary Music Studies, 1*(2), 1-24.

Tzanetakis, G., & Cook, P. (2002). Musical Genre Classification of Audio Signals. *IEEE Transactions on Speech and Audio Processing, 10*(5), 293–302. doi:10.1109/TSA.2002.800560

Uchihashi, S., Foote, J., Girgensohn, A., & Boreczky, J. (1999, October). Video manga: generating semantically meaningful video summaries. *Proceedings of the seventh ACM international conference on Multimedia (Part 1)* (pp. 383-392). ACM. doi:10.1145/319463.319654

Ullman. (1996). *High Level Vision: Object Recognition and Visual Cognition.* Academic Press.

Urquhart, R. (1982). Graph theoretical clustering based on limited neighbourhood sets. *Pattern Recognition, 15*(3), 173–187. doi:10.1016/0031-3203(82)90069-3

Vasconcelos, N., & Lippman, A. (1998, June). A spatiotemporal motion model for video summarization. *Proceedings of the 1998 IEEE Computer Society Conference on Computer Vision and Pattern Recognition* (pp. 361-366). IEEE. doi:10.1109/CVPR.1998.698631

Vasudha, J., Iyshwarya, G., Selvi, T. A., Iniyaa, S., & Jeyakumar, G. (2011). Application of Computer-Aided Music Composition in Music Therapy. *International Journal of Innovation. Management & Technology, 2*(1), 55–57.

Verma, P., Mahajan, M., & Mohali, P. (2012). *Retrieval of better results by using shape techniques for content-based retrieval.* Academic Press.

Vineet, V., & Narayanan, P. J. (2008, June). CUDA cuts: Fast graph cuts on the GPU. In *Computer Vision and Pattern Recognition Workshops, 2008. CVPRW'08. IEEE Computer Society Conference on* (pp. 1-8). IEEE.

Visser, R., Sebe, N., & Bakker, E. (2002). Object recognition for video retrieval. In *Image and Video Retrieval* (pp. 262–270). Springer Berlin Heidelberg. doi:10.1007/3-540-45479-9_28

Voges, M. argnera, & Martin. (2006). *Algorithms for Audiovisual Speaker Localisation in Reverberant Acoustic Environments.* Academic Press.

Volk, A., & Honingh, A. (2012). Mathematical and computational approaches to music: challenges in an interdisciplinary enterprise. *Journal of Mathematics and Music. Taylor and Francis, 6*(2), 73–81. doi:10.1080/17459737.2012.704154

Volkmer, T., Tahaghoghi, S. M., & Williams, H. E. (2004, June). Gradual transition detection using average frame similarity. *Proceedings of theConference onComputer Vision and Pattern Recognition Workshop CVPRW'04* (pp. 139-139). IEEE. doi:10.1109/CVPR.2004.357

Voloshynovskiy, S., Pereira, S., Pun, T., Eggers, J. J., & Su, J. K. (2001, August). Attacks on Digital Watermarks: Classification, Estimation based Attacks and Benchmarks. *IEEE Communications Magazine, 39*(8), 118–126. doi:10.1109/35.940053

von Neumann, J. (1966). *Theory of Self-Reproducing Automata.* Univ. of Illinois Press.

Wahl, R. L. (Ed.). (2002). *Principles and Practice of Positron Emission Tomography.* Baltimore, MD: Lippincott Williams & Wilkins.

Walton. A. (2010). A graph theoretic approach to tonal modulation. *Journal of Mathematics and Music,* 45-56.

Wan, K., Yan, X., & Xu, C. (2005, July). Automatic mobile sports highlights. *Proceedings of the IEEE International Conference on Multimedia and Expo ICME 05* (pp. 4-pp). IEEE.

Wang, T., Wu, Y., & Chen, L. (2007, April). An approach to video key-frame extraction based on rough set. *Proceedings of the International Conference on Multimedia and Ubiquitous Engineering MUE'07* (pp. 590-596). IEEE. doi:10.1109/MUE.2007.65

Wang, Thiesson, Xu, & Cohen. (n.d.). *Image and Video Segmentation by Anisotropic Kernel Mean Shift.* Microsoft Research.

Wang, H., Zhang, H., & Ray, N. (2013). Adaptive shape prior in graph cut image segmentation. *Pattern Recognition, 46*(5), 1409–1414. doi:10.1016/j.patcog.2012.11.002

Wang, J. Z., Li, J., & Wiederhold, G. (2001). SIMPLIcity: Semantics-sensitive integrated matching for picture libraries. *Pattern Analysis and Machine Intelligence. IEEE Transactions on, 23*(9), 947–963.

Wang, J., Wiederhold, G., Firschein, O., & We, S. (1998). Content-based Image Indexing and Searching Using Daubechies' Wavelets. *International Journal on Digital Libraries, 1*(4), 311–328. doi:10.1007/s007990050026

Wang, X., Rosenblum, D., & Wang, Y. (2012, October). Context-aware mobile music recommendation for daily activities. In *Proceedings of the 20th ACM international conference on Multimedia* (pp. 99-108). ACM.

Wang, Z., & Bovik, A. (2004). A Universal Image Quality Index. *Journal of IEEE Signal Processing Letters, 9*(3), 84–88.

Webb, L. M., & Wang, Y. (2014). Techniques for Sampling Online Text-Based Data Sets. In W. Hu & N. Kaabouch (Eds.), *Big Data Management, Technologies, and Applications* (pp. 95–114). Hershey, PA, USA: IGI Global. doi:10.4018/978-1-4666-4699-5.ch005

White, D. A., & Jain, R. (1996, February). Similarity indexing with the SS-tree. In *Data Engineering, 1996.Proceedings of the Twelfth International Conference on* (pp. 516-523). IEEE. doi:10.1109/ICDE.1996.492202

Wickerhauser, M. V. (1994). *Adapted Wavelet Analysis from Theory to Software*. IEEE Press.

Williams, D. B., & Webster, P. R. (1996). *Music Technology*. Academic Press.

Williams, R. J., & David, Z. (1989). A learning algorithm for continually running fully recurrent neural networks. *Neural Computation*, *1*(2), 270–280. doi:10.1162/neco.1989.1.2.270

Wimmer, M., Schauerhuber, A., Kappel, G., Retschitzegger, W., Schwinger, W., & Kapsammer, E. (2011). A survey on UML-based aspect-oriented design modeling. *ACM Computing Surveys*, *43*(4), 28. doi:10.1145/1978802.1978807

Wojtczuk, Armitage, Binnie, & Chamberlain. (2012). *Simple Gesture Recognition using a PIR Sensor Array*. Research Gate.

Wolfgang, R., Podilchuk, C., & Delp, E. J. (1999, July). Perceptual Watermarks for Digital Images and Video. *Proceedings of the IEEE*, *87*(7), 1277–1281. doi:10.1109/5.771067

Wolfram, S. (1983). A Universal Computation Class of Cellular Automata. *Los Alamos Science*.

Wolfram, S. (1983). Statistical mechanics of cellular automata. *Reviews of Modern Physics*, *55*(3), 601–644. doi:10.1103/RevModPhys.55.601

Wolfram, S. (1986). Cryptography with cellular automata. *Lecture Notes in Computer Science*, *218*, 429–432. doi:10.1007/3-540-39799-X_32

Wolfram, S. (2002). *A new kind of science*. Champaign, IL: Wolfram Media Inc.

Wongthanavasu, S. (2011). Cellular Automata for Medical Image Processing. *Cellular Automata - Innovative Modelling for Science and Engineering*. InTech. Retrieved from: http://www.intechopen.com/books/cellular-automata-innovative-modelling-for-science-and-engineering/cellular-automata-for-medical-image-processing

Woodward, P. (Ed.). (1995). *MRI for Technologists* (2nd ed.). New York: McGraw-Hill.

Wu, X., Xu, W., Li, L., Shao, G., & Zhang, J. (2011, May). An interactive segmentation method using graph cuts for mammographic masses. In *Bioinformatics and Biomedical Engineering,(iCBBE) 2011 5th International Conference on* (pp. 1-4). IEEE. doi:10.1109/icbbe.2011.5780190

Xia, F., Asabere, N. Y., Ahmed, A. M., Li, J., & Kong, X. (2013). Mobile multimedia recommendation in smart communities: A survey. *Access, 1*, 606–624. doi:10.1109/ACCESS.2013.2281156

Xie, X. L., & Beni, G. (1991). A Validity Measure for Fuzzy Clustering. *IEEE Transactions on Pattern Analysis and Machine Intelligence*, *13*(8), 841–847. doi:10.1109/34.85677

Xiong, W., Lee, C. M., & Ma, R. H. (1997). Automatic video data structuring through shot partitioning and key-frame computing. *Machine Vision and Applications*, *10*(2), 51–65. doi:10.1007/s001380050059

Xu, A., Wang, L., Feng, S., & Qu, Y. (2010, November). Threshold-based level set method of image segmentation. In *Intelligent Networks and Intelligent Systems (ICINIS), 2010 3rd International Conference on* (pp. 703-706). IEEE. doi:10.1109/ICINIS.2010.181

Xu, C., Pham, D. L., & Prince, J. L. (2002). Image Segmentation Using Deformable Models. In Handbook of Medical Imaging, Vol. 2, Medical Image Processing and Analysis. SPIE, International Society for Optical Engineering.

Xu, Y., Olman, V., & Xu, D. (2002). Clustering gene expression data using a graph theoretic approach, an application of minimum spanning trees. *Bioinformatics (Oxford, England)*, *18*, 536–545. PMID:12016051

Xu, Z. B., Chen, P. J., Yan, S. L., & Wang, T. H. (2014). Study on Otsu threshold method for image segmentation based on genetic algorithm. *2014 International Conference on Applied Sciences, Engineering and Technology*. doi:10.4028/www.scientific.net/AMR.998-999.925

Yaffe, M. J. (2000). Digital mammography. In J. Beutel, H. L. Kundel, & R. L. Van Metter (Eds.), *Handbook of Medical Imaging* (Vol. I). Washington, DC: SPIE Press.

Yajima, C., Nakanishi, Y., & Tanaka, K. (2002). Querying video data by spatio-temporal relationships of moving object traces. In Visual and Multimedia Information Management (pp. 357-371). Springer US. doi:10.1007/978-0-387-35592-4_25

Yang, A. Y., Wright, J., Sastry, S., & Ma, Y. (2006). Unsupervised segmentation of natural images via lossy data compression. Berkeley, CA: Elect. Eng. Comput. Sci. Dept. Univ. Available from http://www.eecs.berkeley.edu/Pubs/TechRpts/2006/EECS-2006-195.html

Yang. (2002). *Object Recognition*. Academic Press.

Yang. (2007). *Object Recognition*. University of California at Merced.

Yang, Liu, & Shah. (n.d.). Video Scene Understanding Using Multi-scale Analysis. *Computer Vision Lab University of Central Florida*.

Yang, M., Kpalma, K., & Ronsin, J. (2008). A survey of shape feature extraction techniques. *Pattern Recognition*, 43–90.

Yan, R., & Hauptmann, A. G. (2007). A review of text and image retrieval approaches for broadcast news video. *Information Retrieval*, *10*(4-5), 445–484. doi:10.1007/s10791-007-9031-y

Yasira Beevi, C. P., & Natarajan, S. (2009). *An efficient video segmentation algorithm with real time adaptive threshold technique*. Citeseer.

Yasmin, M., Sharif, M., Masood, S., Raza, M., & Mohsin, S. (2012). Brain image enhancement-A survey. *World Applied Sciences Journal*, *17*(9), 1192–1204.

Yau, S. S., Gupta, S. K. S., Karim, F., Ahamed, S. I., Wang, Y., & Wang, B. (2003, June). Smart Classroom: Enhancing Collaborative Learning Using Pervasive Computing Technology. *Proc. of American Society of Engineering Education 2003 Annual Conference*.

Yeung, M. M., & Yeo, B. L. (1997). Video visualization for compact presentation and fast browsing of pictorial content. *IEEE Transactions on* Circuits and Systems for Video Technology., *7*(5), 771–785.

Yi, F., & Moon, I. (2012, May). Image segmentation: A survey of graph-cut methods. In *Systems and Informatics (ICSAI), 2012 International Conference on* (pp. 1936-1941). IEEE. doi:10.1109/ICSAI.2012.6223428

Yoo, H. W., Ryoo, H. J., & Jang, D. S. (2006). Gradual shot boundary detection using localized edge blocks. *Multimedia Tools and Applications*, *28*(3), 283–300. doi:10.1007/s11042-006-7715-8

Yu, Z., Xu, M., & Gao, Z. (2011, August). Biomedical image segmentation via constrained graph cuts and pre-segmentation. In *Engineering in Medicine and Biology Society, EMBC, 2011 Annual International Conference of the IEEE* (pp. 5714-5717). IEEE.

Yu. (2011). Dissolve Detection Based On Twin-Comparison With Curve Fitting. *International Journal of Innovative Computing, Information, & Control*, *7*(5).

Yuan, J., Li, J., & Zhang, B. (2007, September). Gradual transition detection with conditional random fields. *Proceedings of the 15th international conference on Multimedia* (pp. 277-280). ACM. doi:10.1145/1291233.1291291

Yuan, J., Wang, H., Xiao, L., Zheng, W., Li, J., Lin, F., & Zhang, B. (2007). A formal study of shot boundary detection. *IEEE Transactions on* Circuits and Systems for Video Technology, *17*(2), 168–186.

Yu, F., Lu, Z., & Li, Y. (2011). Dissolve detection based on twin-comparison with curve fitting. *International Journal of Innovative Computing, Information, & Control, 7,* 2417–2426.

Zabih, R., Miller, J., & Mai, K. (1995). A Feature-Based Algorithm for Detecting and Classifying Scene Breaks. *ACM Multimedia, 95,* 189–200.

Zabih, R., Miller, J., & Mai, K. (1999). A feature-based algorithm for detecting and classifying production effects. *Multimedia Systems, 7*(2), 119–128. doi:10.1007/s005300050115

Zadeh, L. A. (1965). Fuzzy Sets. *Information and Control, 8*(3), 338–353. doi:10.1016/S0019-9958(65)90241-X

Zadeh, L. A. (1973). Outline of a New Approach to the Analysis of Complex Systems and Decision Processes. *IEEE Transactions on Systems, Man, and Cybernetics, 3*(1), 28–44. doi:10.1109/TSMC.1973.5408575

Žagar, M., Kovač, M., & Hofman, D. (2012). Framework for 4D Medical Data Compression. *Technical Gazette, 1*(19), 99-106.

Žagar, M. (2011). *4D Medical Data Compression Architecture.* Saarbrucken: LAP Lambert Academic Publishing GmbH.

Zahn, C. T. (1971). Graph-theoretical methods for detecting and describing gestalt clusters. *Computers. IEEE Transactions on, 100*(1), 68–86.

Zajić, G. J., Reljin, I. S., & Reljin, B. D. (2011). Video shot boundary detection based on multifractal analysis. *Telfor Journal, 3*(2), 105–110.

Zalik, K. R. (2008). An efficient *k*-means clustering algorithm. *Pattern Recognition Letters, 29*(9), 1385–1391. doi:10.1016/j.patrec.2008.02.014

Zayed, H. H. (2005). A High Hiding Capacity Technique for Hiding data in Image based on K-bit LSB substitution. *The 30th International Conference on Artificial Intelligence Applications* (ICAIA- 2005).

Zhang, H., & Zhong, D. (1995, March). Scheme for visual feature-based image indexing. In *IS&T/SPIE's Symposium on Electronic Imaging: Science & Technology* (pp. 36-46). International Society for Optics and Photonics. doi:10.1016/B978-155860651-7/50110-8

Zhang, L., & Deng, X. (2010, November). The research of image segmentation based on improved neural network algorithm. In *Semantics Knowledge and Grid (SKG), 2010 Sixth International Conference on* (pp. 395-397). IEEE. doi:10.1109/SKG.2010.68

Zhang, H. J., Wu, J., Zhong, D., & Smoliar, S. W. (1997). An integrated system for content-based video retrieval and browsing. *Pattern Recognition, 30*(4), 643–658. doi:10.1016/S0031-3203(96)00109-4

Zhang, X. D., Liu, T. Y., Lo, K. T., & Feng, J. (2003). Dynamic selection and effective compression of key frames for video abstraction. *Pattern Recognition Letters, 24*(9), 1523–1532. doi:10.1016/S0167-8655(02)00391-4

Zhang, X., Qian, Z., Ren, Y., & Feng, G. (2011). Watermarking with Flexible Self-recovery Quality based on Compressive Sensing and Compositive Reconstruction. *IEEE Transactions on Information Forensics and Security, 6*(4), 1123–1132. doi:10.1109/TIFS.2011.2159208

Zhang, Y. (1996). A survey on evaluation methods for image segmentation. *Pattern Recognition, 29*(8), 1335–1346. doi:10.1016/0031-3203(95)00169-7

Zhang, Y.-J. (2006). *An Overview of Image and Video Segmentation in the Last 40 Years*. Beijing, China: Tsinghua University. doi:10.4018/978-1-59140-753-9

Zhao, Z., & Elgammal, A. M. (2008, September). *Information Theoretic Key Frame Selection for Action Recognition*. BMVC. doi:10.5244/C.22.109

Zheng, L., Li, G., & Bao, Y. (2010). Improvement of grayscale image 2D maximum entropy threshold segmentation method. *2010 International Conference on Logistics Systems and Intelligent Management*. doi:10.1109/ICLSIM.2010.5461410

Zheng, L., Pan, Q., Li, G., & Liang, J. (2009). Improvement of Grayscale Image Segmentation Based on PSO Algorithm. *Fourth International Conference on Computer Sciences and Convergence Information Technology*. doi:10.1109/ICCIT.2009.68

Zhou, S., Yang, P., & Xie, W. (2011). Infrared image segmentation based on Otsu and genetic algorithm. *2011 International Conference on Multimedia Technology*. doi:10.1109/ICMT.2011.6003109

Zhuang, Y., Rui, Y., Huang, T. S., & Mehrotra, S. (1998, October). Adaptive key frame extraction using unsupervised clustering. *Proceedings of the 1998 International Conference on Image Processing ICIP 98* (Vol. 1, pp. 866-870). IEEE.

Zhu, B., Ramsey, M., & Chen, H. (2000). Creating a large-scale content-based airphoto image digital library. *Image Processing. IEEE Transactions on, 9*(1), 163–167.

Zhu, J. (2011, July). Multimedia Music Teaching System Application. *Key Engineering Materials, 474*, 1903–1908. doi:10.4028/www.scientific.net/KEM.474-476.1903

Zuzana, Pitas, & Nikou. (2004). *Information Theory-Based Shot Cut/Fade Detection and Video Summarization*. Methods for Unified Multimedia Information Retrieval (MOUMIR) project - RTN-1999-00177 MOUMIR.

About the Contributors

Siddhartha Bhattacharyya did his Bachelors in Physics, Bachelors in Optics and Optoelectronics and Masters in Optics and Optoelectronics from University of Calcutta, India in 1995, 1998 and 2000 respectively. He completed PhD in Computer Science and Engineering from Jadavpur University, India in 2008. He is the recipient of the University Gold Medal from the University of Calcutta for his Masters. He is currently the Professor and Head of Information Technology of RCC Institute of Information Technology, Kolkata, India. In addition, he is serving as the Dean of Research and Development of the institute from November 2013. Prior to this, he was an Associate Professor of Information Technology of RCC Institute of Information Technology, Kolkata, India from 2011-2014. Before that, he served as an Assistant Professor in Computer Science and Information Technology of University Institute of Technology, The University of Burdwan, India from 2005-2011. He was a Lecturer in Information Technology of Kalyani Government Engineering College, India during 2001-2005. He is a co-author of 3 books and the co-editor of 4 books and has more than 145 research publications in international journals and conference proceedings to his credit. He has got a patent on intelligent colorimeter technology. He was the convener of the AICTE-IEEE National Conference on Computing and Communication Systems (CoCoSys-09) in 2009. He was the member of the Young Researchers' Committee of the WSC 2008 Online World Conference on Soft Computing in Industrial Applications. He has been the member of the organizing and technical program committees of several national and international conferences. He served as the Editor-In-Chief of International Journal of Ambient Computing and Intelligence (IJACI) published by IGI Global, Hershey, PA, USA from 17th July 2014 to 06th November 2014. He was the General Chair of the IEEE International Conference on Computational Intelligence and Communication Networks (ICCICN 2014) organized by the Department of Information Technology, RCC Institute of Information Technology, Kolkata in association with Machine Intelligence Research Labs, Gwalior and IEEE Young Professionals, Kolkata Section and held at Kolkata, India in 2014. He is the Associate Editor of International Journal of Pattern Recognition Research. He is the member of the editorial board of International Journal of Engineering, Science and Technology and ACCENTS Transactions on Information Security (ATIS). He is also the member of the editorial advisory board of HETC Journal of Computer Engineering and Applications. He is the Associate Editor of the International Journal of BioInfo Soft Computing since 2013. He is the Lead Guest Editor of the Special Issue on Hybrid Intelligent Techniques for Image Analysis and Understanding of Applied Soft Computing, Elsevier, B. V. He is the Lead Guest Editor of the Special Issue on Computational Intelligence and Communications in International Journal of Computers and Applications (IJCA); Publisher: Taylor & Francis, UK in 2016. He is the Issue Editor of International Journal of Pattern Recognition Research since January 2016. He is the General Chair of the 2016 International Conference on Wireless Communications, Network

Security and Signal Processing (WCNSSP2016) to be held during June 26-27, 2016 at Chiang Mai, Thailand. His research interests include soft computing, pattern recognition, multimedia data processing, hybrid intelligence and quantum computing. Dr. Bhattacharyya is a senior member of Institute of Electrical and Electronics Engineers (IEEE), USA and Association for Computing Machinery (ACM), USA. He is a member of International Rough Set Society and International Association for Engineers (IAENG), Hong Kong. He is a life member of Computer Society of India, Optical Society of India and Indian Society for Technical Education.

Hrishikesh Bhaumik is currently serving as an Associate Professor in the Department of Information Technology at RCCIIT. Hrishikesh did his BSc. from Calcutta University in 1997, AMIE in Electronics and Comm. Engg in 2000 and M.Tech in Information Technology from BE College, Shibpur in 2004. He is with RCCIIT for more than thirteen years. Prior to joining RCCIIT he has worked with the Instrumentation Division of Lawrence & Mayo at Mumbai and Nasan Medical Instruments at Pune. In 2008, Hrishikesh received appreciation from Mr. Srikantan Moorty (Sr. Vice President & Head of Education and Research) at Infosys Technologies Ltd. for his contribution to the American Express sponsored project "XML Data Collection Component of Business Process Sniffer Tool" undertaken at Infosys Development Centre in Bhubneswar. He received several sponsorships from ICTP, Italy and acted as a major contributor to the EUIndia Grid project during 2010 to 2012. Hrishikesh has acted as a coordinator and resource person in several AICTE /ISTE sponsored workshops held in different parts of the India. He was previously the Head of Dept. of IT and acted as the Nodal Officer (Academic) of TEQIP II at RCCIIT. He was also the Convenor IIIC at RCCIIT. His research interests include Content Based Video Retrieval Systems, Text Mining and High Performance Computing.

Sourav De did his Bachelors in Information Technology from The University of Burdwan, Burdwan, India in 2002. He did his Masters in Information Technology from West Bengal University of Technology, Kolkata, India in 2005. He completed PhD in Computer Science and Technology from Indian Institute of Engineering & Technology, Shibpur, Howrah, India in 2015. He is an Assistant Professor in the Department of Computer Science and Information Technology of University Institute of Technology, The University of Burdwan, Burdwan, India since 2006. He served as a Junior Programmer in Apices Consultancy Private Limited, Kolkata, India in 2005. He has more than about 20 research publications in internationally reputed journals, international edited books and international IEEE conferences. He served as reviewer in several International IEEE conferences and also in several international editorial books. He has been the member of the organizing and technical program committees of several national and international conferences. He has been invited in different seminars as an expert speaker. He is a co-author of a proposed book on soft computing. His research interests include soft computing, pattern recognition, image processing and data mining. Dr. De is a member of IEEE, ACM, Computer Science Teachers Association (CSTA) and IAENG, Hong Kong. He is a life member of ISTE, India.

Goran Klepac, PhD, University College Professor, works as a head of Strategic unit in Sector of credit risk in Raiffeisenbank Austria d.d., Croatia, Europe. In several universities in Croatia, he lectures subjects in domain of data mining, predictive analytics, decision support system, banking risk, risk evaluation models, expert system, database marketing and business intelligence. As a team leader, he successfully finished many data mining projects in different domains like retail, finance, insurance, hospitality, telecommunications, and productions. He is an author/coauthor of several books published in Croatian and English in domain of data mining.

* * *

Petre Anghelescu received the B.E. degree in applied electronics from the University of Pitesti, Romania, in 2002, the M.Tech. in intelligent communication systems and Ph.D. degrees in electrical engineering and telecommunication from the University of Pitesti, Romania, in 2004 and 2008, respectively. In 2002, he joined the Department of Electronics, Communication and Computers, University of Pitesti, as Assistant, then PhD. Lecturer, and in 2013 became an Associate Professor. His current research interests focus on complex systems and methods of computational and artificial intelligence, mainly on bio-inspired systems – cellular automata & genetic algorithms, self-adaptation and self-organizational systems and reconfigurable computing.

Anindita Das Bhattacharjee started her career in industry as a Trainee Software Developer for a year. She had to quit industry carrier as she wanted to pursue higher studies. She has done M-Tech in Computer Science from National Institute of Technology (NIT), Durgapur. She secured a position of First class Second in M-Tech. She has done many projects on Data clustering, Fuzzy logic, Multi-Objective Genetic Algorithm on Time table problem, which are basically a part of Artificial Intelligence & Soft Computing. She has been teaching for more than 7.5 years in Computer Science as an Asst. Prof. Her area of interest includes Genetic Algorithm, Data Clustering, Computer Graphics Design, Design and Analysis of algorithm and Distributed Operating System. She started her teaching carrier in Bengal College of Engineering & Technology (BCET) Durgapur, as an Asst. Prof. Currently she is working in Swami Vivekananda Institute of Science & Technology (SVIST) Kolkata, as an Asst. Prof. in computer science department. She is the author of the book "Artificial Intelligence and Soft computing for beginner" published in 2013 and the 2nd edition of the book with modern soft computing techniques was published in 2014, which has gained good popularity and has received positive feedbacks.

Komal R. Borisagar received B.E. degree in Electronics and Communication from C. U. Shah Engineering College, Saurashtra University, Rajkot, Gujarat, India in 2002 and M.E. degree in Communication System Engineering from Changa Institute of Technology, Gujarat University, and Ahmedabad in 2008. In 2012, she received her doctoral degree from the Department of Electronics and Communication Engineering, JJT University, Rajasthan. She has teaching experience of over 10 years. She is working as Assistant Professor at Electronics & Communication Department, Atmiya Institute of Technology and Science, Rajkot. Her areas of interest are wireless communication, speech processing and signal & image processing.

Sudipta Chakrabarty obtained his M.Tech degree in Information Technology from Bengal Engineering and Science University, presently known as IIEST. Presently he is working as an Assistant Professor in Techno India, Salt Lake in the Department of Master of Computer Application affiliated by West Bengal University of Technology. His research interest is on the field of Pattern Recognition using Soft Computing Optimizing techniques. He has more than four book publications and some research papers in his credit.

Manideepa Chakraborty is a student of M.Tech in the Department of Information Technology at RCC Institute of Information Technology. She completed her B.Tech in Computer Science from RCCIIT in 2013.

Susanta Chakraborty received the Bachelors (B. Tech) and Masters (M.Tech) degree in Technology from the University of Calcutta in 1983 and 1985 respectively. and Ph.D(Tech) degree in computer science in 1999 from University of Calcutta and Research work done at Advance computing and Microelectronic Unit, Indian Statistical Institute, Kolkata. He is currently a Professor in the department. Computer Science and Technology of the Bengal Engineering Science and University, West Bengal, India. Prior to this he has served University of Kalyani as a Dean of Engineering, Technology and Management faculty. He has published around 31 research papers, appeared in very reputed International Journals including IEEE Transactions on CAD and refereed international conference proceedings of IEEE Computer Science Press. Dr. Chakraborty awarded INSA-JSPS Fellowship of Indian National Science Academy (INSA) in the session 2003-2004 and works have been done in collaboration with Professor H. Fujiwara of Nara Institute of Science and Technology, Japan, in the area of Test Generation of Sequential Circuits and Low Power Design. He has been invited from Institute of Information Technology, University of Potsdam, Germany with German Gov. Fellowship, to do research work as a guest scientist with Prof. M. Gossel in the area of VLSI testing and fault diagnosis from September 2000. He has been also invited from University of Michigan, Advanced Computer Architecture Lab,USA deptt of Electrical Engineering and Computer Science and works have been done in collaboration with Professor John P.Hays, Shannon Professor of Engineering Science in the area of Quantum circuit" and Testable Design of Nano-Circuit in the year 2007. He also invited to Nara Institute of Science and Technology Nara, Japan to deliver a Lecture on Quantum Circuit in 2013. 25 years research experience of Dr. Chakraborty has been primarily focused on Logic Synthesis and Testing of VLSI Circuits, DFT, BIST design Test-Pattern Generation, Fault-Tolerant Computing, Image Processing, Fault Diagnosis, Low Power Design and Synthesis and Testing of Quantum Circuit and Micro Fluidic Bio-chips. He has served as a Publicity Co-Chair, 18th International Conference on VLSI Design, January, 2005 and Fifteenth Asian test Symposium, December, India, 2005, Publicity Chair & Program Committee member of 1st and 2nd IEEE International workshop on Reliability Aware system Design and Test (RASDAT), January, India, 2010 and 2011 Advisory Committee member of International Conference on computing and systems, November 19 – 20,2010, 2011, 2012 and 2013. Publication Chair, IEEE WRTLT-2011 International workshop. Publicity Chair & Program Committee member of 3rd IEEE International workshop on Reliability Aware system Design and Test (RASDAT), January, India, 2013.

Subhasish Das was awarded his Ph.D. thesis in School of Water Resources Engineering, Jadavpur University, India in 2014. He has completed his Bachelor's degree in Mechanical Engineering in 2003 and Master's degree in Water Resources & Hydraulic Engineering (Recipient of University Gold Medal Award for securing the First position) from the same University in 2006. He is working as an Assistant Professor in School of Water Resources Engineering, Jadavpur University since 2006. He has experience in hydraulic transients and open channel flow. He has guided 32 PG scholars until now. He has 24 international and eight national journals and 18 conference publications to his credit.

Debashis De obtained his M.Tech degree in Radio physics & Electronics, University of Calcutta(2002). He obtained his Ph.D. (Engineering) from Jadavpur University in 2005. He worked in the field of Nano Technology and Communication. He worked as R&D Engineer at Telektronics and Programmer, CTS. His research interest is on nano-structure semiconductor devices. He has more than 30 publications in International Journals and Conferences to his credit. His current research interest is in nanotechnology, QCA and Mobile Computing.He received young Scientist Award by URSI (Belgium) and Received the award from president of India Dr. A.P.J. Kalam at rashtrapati Bhavan, India on 2005. was awarded the prestigious Boyscast Fellowship 2008 by department of Science and Technology, Govt. of India to work in the nanofabrication Group of Kevin Prior at Heriot-Watt University, Scotland, UK. He is also awarded Endeavour Fellowship Award during 2008 - 2009 by DEST Australia to work in the University of Western Australia, Perth, Australia.

Indrajit De has research experience of over 7 years in fuzzy image processing and soft computing. He has over eleven publications, several sponsored projects to his credit. He is also an acclaimed reviewer of journals like applied Soft Computing, Elsevier, Infrared Physics and Technology, Elsevier, etc.

Firoj Haque is currently pursuing Master degree in Computer Science and Engineering from The University of Kalyani, Kalyani, India. He received Bachelor of Engineering degree in Computer Science and Engineering from University Institute of Technology, The University of Burdwan, Burdwan, India in 2013. His research interests include Soft Computing, Image Processing, Steganography, Data Mining etc. He possesses interest in playing card, listening to music.

Josip Knezović received his B.Sc., M.Sc. and Ph.D. degree in Computer Science from the Faculty of Electrical Engineering and Computing, University of Zagreb in 2001, 2005 and 2009, respectively. Since 2001 he has been affiliated with Faculty of Electrical Engineering and Computing. He is assistant professor at the Department of Control and Computer Engineering. His research interests include programming models for parallel systems in multimedia, image and signal processing. He is a member of IEEE and ACM.

Ashish M. Kothari has completed his bachelor and masters degree in the Electronics & Communication Engineering from Saurashtra University, Gujarat, India and completed his Ph. D. in the same discipline from Shree Jagdishprasad Jhambarmal Tibrewal University, Rajsthan, India. His Area of research is to design a robust method for the video watermarking. He is currently working as an Assistant Professor in the department of electronics & communication engineering at Atmiya Institute of Technology & Science, Rajkot, India. His area of interest is Image and video processing, microcontrollers and embedded systems.

Smita Majumder completed her PhD in 2014 from Tripura University, Agartala Tripura.

Swanirbhar Majumder completed his BTech in ECE from NEHU, Shillong in 2004 followed by his MTech in 2006 from Dept of Applied Physics University of Calcutta. Since then he has been working on Biomedical and Image Processing research area as well as a faculty in the Dept of ECE NERIST, a CFTI and a Deemed University in Arunachal Pradesh since 2006. He recently completed his PhD from Dept of ETCE Jadavpur University in 2015.

Anupam Mukherjee has obtained B.Tech. and M.Tech. in Computer Science from West Bengal University of Technology. Presently he is working as an Assistant Professor in the department of Computer Science & Engineering in Siliguri Institute of Technology. His research interest is in Digital Image Processing, Multimedia Technology, Computer Networking, Cryptography and Network Security.

Samarjit Roy is working as an Assistant Professor in Techno India Silli in the Department of Computer Science and Engineering. His research interest is on the field of Pattern Recognition using different Optimizing techniques. He has a few research publications in his credit.

Rohit M. Thanki was born in Porbandar, Gujarat, India on 26th September, 1987. His received B.E. degree in Electronics and Communication from Atmiya Institute of Technology & Science, Saurashtra University, Rajkot, Gujarat, India in 2008 and M.E. degree in Communication Engineering from G H Patel College of Engineering and Technology, Sardar Patel University, Vallabh Vidyanagar, Gujarat, India in 2010. He is currently pursuing his PhD in Electronics and Communication Engineering from C U Shah University, Wadhwan, Gujarat, India. He has guided more than 15 UG students in their project work. He has published and presented more than 25 research papers in various high impact factor international journals and various international as well as national conferences. He has published books entitled Comparative analysis of digital watermarking techniques and Design of Operational Transconductance Amplifier with Lambert Publishing House, Germany. He is life member of ISTE and Student member of IEEE. His areas of interests are Digital Signal Processing, Digital Image Processing, Digital VLSI Design, Digital Watermarking, Compressive Sensing, Pattern Recognition.

Martin Žagar is a Lecturer at the University of Applied Sciences Velika Gorica. His research interests include multimedia algorithms systems, e-Health and e-Government applications. Martin Žagar received a PhD in Computer Engineering from the University of Zagreb, Faculty of Electrical Engineering and Computing. He is a member of Croatian Academy of Engineering, IEEE Computer Society, HiPEAC Society and AASCIT society.

Index

S

scene 1, 3-5, 16, 52, 54, 56-57, 59, 64, 68, 78, 80-81, 84-85, 103, 145, 149, 161, 193, 198, 200, 285-287, 292, 296, 304, 355, 357, 360, 362-363, 436

segmentation 1-4, 14-16, 24-30, 32-45, 49-50, 56-58, 63, 68, 70, 72, 89, 91, 100, 106-112, 116-118, 137, 140, 142, 148-149, 159, 164, 170-171, 179, 200, 207, 212, 232-233, 242, 283-291, 328, 353, 355, 357, 359-360, 362, 382, 402-403, 405, 411-412, 420, 422, 436

SEM 181, 204-205, 211

semantic gap 152, 161-162, 171, 179

Sensory gap 161, 171, 180

sparse representation 375, 379-380, 385, 389, 394, 458

static 26, 73-74, 88, 90, 100, 286, 353, 357, 359, 362-363, 367

super pixels 32, 37

T

TEM 181, 204-205, 211

temporal video segmentation 283-284, 286-287, 290-291, 357

thresholding 7, 25-26, 38-39, 61, 107, 109, 180, 217, 231, 384

tomography 184-185, 187, 190, 192-193, 206, 211, 382

U

Ultrasonography 181, 193, 195, 197-198, 211

V

Validity Index 246

video segmentation 26-27, 57-58, 170-171, 283-287, 290-291, 355, 357, 359-360

video summarization 14, 88-90, 283, 352-354, 356-357, 359, 361-364, 366-367

volumetric neuroimage 268-269, 279

W

watermarking 385, 394, 396-397, 431-439, 441-449, 451-458, 461-462

wavelet analysis 268-269, 281, 449

wavelet bases 268-270, 279, 281

waveSurfer 334, 339

X

x-ray 109, 147, 181-187, 189, 200, 206, 211, 229, 382

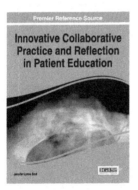

Printed in the United States
By Bookmasters